with MyManagementLab®

- **Dynamic Study Modules**—Helps students study effectively on their own by continuously assessing their activity and performance in real time. Here's how it works: students complete a set of questions with a unique answer format that also asks them to indicate their confidence level. Questions repeat until the student can answer them all correctly and confidently. Once completed, Dynamic Study Modules explain the concept using materials from the text. These are available as graded assignments prior to class, and accessible on smartphones, tablets, and computers.

- **Learning Catalytics™**—Is an interactive, student response tool that uses students' smartphones, tablets, or laptops to engage them in more sophisticated tasks and thinking. Now included with MyLab with eText, Learning Catalytics enables you to generate classroom discussion, guide your lecture, and promote peer-to-peer learning with real-time analytics.

- **Reporting Dashboard**—View, analyze, and report learning outcomes clearly and easily, and get the information you need to keep your students on track throughout the course with the new Reporting Dashboard. Available via the MyLab Gradebook and fully mobile-ready, the Reporting Dashboard presents student performance data at the class, section, and program levels in an accessible, visual manner.

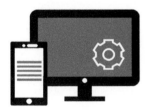

- **Accessibility (ADA)**—Pearson works continuously to ensure our products are as accessible as possible to all students. The platform team for our Business MyLab products is working toward achieving WCAG 2.0 Level AA and Section 508 standards, as expressed in the **Pearson Guidelines for Accessible Educational Web Media**. Moreover, our products support customers in meeting their obligation to comply with the Americans with Disabilities Act (ADA) by providing access to learning technology programs for users with disabilities.
  The following information provides tips and answers to frequently asked questions for those using assistive technologies to access the Business MyLab products. As product accessibility evolves continuously, please email our Accessibility Team at **disability.support@pearson.com** for the most up-to-date information.

D0126867

- **LMS Integration**—You can now link from Blackboard Learn, Brightspace by D2L, Canvas, or Moodle to MyManagementLab. Access assignments, rosters, and resources, and synchronize grades with your LMS gradebook.
  For students, single sign-on provides access to all the personalized learning resources that make studying more efficient and effective.

Fourteenth Edition

ESSENTIALS OF ORGANIZATIONAL BEHAVIOR

Stephen P. Robbins
San Diego State University

Timothy A. Judge
The Ohio State University

 Pearson

New York, NY

Vice President, Business Publishing: Donna Battista
Director of Portfolio Management: Stephanie Wall
Portfolio Manager: Kris Ellis-Levy
Editorial Assistant: Hannah Lamarre
Vice President, Product Marketing: Roxanne McCarley
Director of Strategic Marketing: Brad Parkins
Strategic Marketing Manager: Deborah Strickland
Product Marketer: Becky Brown
Field Marketing Manager: Lenny Ann Kucenski
Product Marketing Assistant: Jessica Quazza
Vice President, Production and Digital Studio, Arts and Business: Etain O'Dea
Director of Production, Business: Jeff Holcomb
Managing Producer, Business: Ashley Santora
Content Producer: Claudia Fernandes

Operations Specialist: Carol Melville
Creative Director: Blair Brown
Manager, Learning Tools: Brian Surette
Content Developer, Learning Tools: Lindsey Sloan
Managing Producer, Digital Studio, Arts and Business: Diane Lombardo
Digital Studio Producer: Monique Lawrence
Digital Studio Producer: Alana Coles
Full-Service Project Management and Composition: Cenveo Publisher Services
Interior and Cover Designer: Cenveo Publisher Services
Cover Art: LeitnerR/Fotolia
Printer/Binder: LSC Communications/Crawfordsville
Cover Printer: Phoenix Color/Hagerstown

Library of Congress Cataloging-in-Publication Data
Names: Robbins, Stephen P., author. | Judge, Tim, author.
Title: Essentials of organizational behavior / Stephen P. Robbins, San Diego
    State University, Timothy A. Judge, University of Notre Dame.
Description: Fourteen edition. | Boston : Pearson Education, [2016] |
    Includes index.
Identifiers: LCCN 2016022886 (print) | LCCN 2016034760 (ebook) | ISBN
    9780134523859 (pbk. : alk. paper) | ISBN 9780134527314
Subjects: LCSH: Organizational behavior.
Classification: LCC HD58.7 .R6 2017 (print) | LCC HD58.7 (ebook) | DDC
    658.3—dc23
LC record available at https://lccn.loc.gov/2016022886

3 2019

ISBN 10: 0-13-452385-7
ISBN 13: 978-0-13-452385-9

*This book is dedicated to our friends and colleagues in
The Organizational Behavior Teaching Society
who, through their teaching, research and commitment
to the leading process, have significantly
improved the ability of students
to understand and apply OB concepts.*

BRIEF CONTENTS

CONTENTS

PREFACE

This book was created as an alternative to the 600- or 700-page comprehensive text in organizational behavior (OB). It attempts to provide balanced coverage of all the key elements comprising the discipline of OB in a style that readers will find both informative and interesting. We're pleased to say that this text has achieved a wide following in short courses and executive programs as well as in traditional courses as a companion volume to experiential, skill development, case, and readings books. It is currently used at more than 500 colleges and universities in the United States, Canada, Latin America, Europe, Australia, and Asia. It's also been translated into Spanish, Portuguese, Japanese, Chinese, Dutch, Polish, Turkish, Danish, and Bahasa Indonesian.

KEY CHANGES FOR THE FOURTEENTH EDITION

- Increased content coverage was added to include updated research, relevant discussion, and new exhibits on current issues of all aspects of organizational behavior.
- Increased integration of contemporary global issues was added into topic discussions.
- Extensive reorganization of all chapters with new headings and subsections to make navigating the print and digital versions of the text easier and bring important content to the fore.
- Increased cross-references between chapters to link themes and concepts for the student's quick access and to provide a more in-depth understanding of topics.
- New assisted and auto-graded questions that students can complete and submit via MyManagementLab are provided for each chapter.
- A new feature, *Try It*, has been added to 14 chapters to direct the student's attention to MyManagementLab simulations specific to the content in the text.

RETAINED FROM THE PREVIOUS EDITION

What do people like about this book? Surveys of users have found general agreement about the following features. Needless to say, they've all been retained in this edition.

- *Length.* Since its inception in 1984, we've tried diligently to keep this book in the range of 325 to 400 pages. Users tell us this length allows them considerable flexibility in assigning supporting materials and projects.
- *Balanced topic coverage.* Although short in length, this book continues to provide balanced coverage of all the key concepts in OB. This includes not only traditional topics such as personality, motivation, and leadership but also cutting-edge issues such as emotions, diversity, negotiation, and teamwork.
- *Writing style.* This book is frequently singled out for its fluid writing style and extensive use of examples. Users regularly tell us that they find this book "conversational," "interesting," "student friendly," and "very clear and understandable."

- *Practicality.* This book has never been solely about theory. It's about *using* theory to better explain and predict the behavior of people in organizations. In each edition of this book, we have focused on making sure that readers see the link between OB theories, research, and implications for practice.
- *Absence of pedagogy.* Part of the reason we've been able to keep this book short in length is that it doesn't include review questions, cases, exercises, or similar teaching/learning aids. It continues to provide only the basic core of OB knowledge, allowing instructors the maximum flexibility in designing and shaping their courses.
- *Integration of globalization, diversity, and ethics.* The topics of globalization and cross-cultural differences, diversity, and ethics are discussed throughout this book. Rather than being presented only in separate chapters, these topics have been woven into the context of relevant issues. Users tell us they find that this integrative approach makes these topics more fully part of OB and reinforces their importance.
- *Comprehensive supplements.* Although this book may be short in length, it's not short on supplements. It comes with a complete, high-tech support package for both faculty and students. Instructors are provided with a comprehensive Instructor's Manual and Test Bank, TestGenerator, and PowerPoint slides. The MyManagementLab course provides both instructors and students with various types of assessments, video exercises, decision-making simulations, and Personal Inventory Assessments.

CHAPTER-BY-CHAPTER CHANGES

Chapter 1: What Is Organizational Behavior?

- **New content:** Effective versus Successful Managerial Activities; Current Usage of, New Trends in, and Limitations of Big Data; Workforce Demographics; Social Media; and Inputs, Processes, and Outcomes of our General Model of Organizational Behavior
- **Newly revised sections:** Management and Organizational Behavior
- **New research incorporated in the following areas:** Introduction to Organizational Behavior, Big Data, Adapting to Differing Cultural and Regulatory Norms, Positive Work Environments, and Ethical Behavior
- **New features:** *Watch It (*Herman Miller: Organizational Behavior*)* and *Personal Inventory Assessments* (Multicultural Awareness Scale)

Chapter 2: Diversity in Organizations

- **New content:** Stereotype Threat and Hidden Disabilities
- **Newly revised sections:** *Learning Objectives*, Demographic Characteristics, Discrimination, Implementing Diversity Management Strategies, and *Implications for Managers*
- **New research incorporated in the following areas:** Discrimination in the Workplace; Biographical Characteristics, including Age, Sex, Race, and Ethnicity; Disabilities; the Wonderlic Intellectual Ability Test; Diversity in Groups; and International Research on Religion, Sexual Orientation, Gender Identity, and Physical Abilities

- **New features:** *Personal Inventory Assessments* (Intercultural Sensitivity Scale), *Watch It* (Verizon: Diversity), and *Try It* (Simulation: Human Resources)

Chapter 3: Attitudes and Job Satisfaction

- **New content:** The Causes of Job Satisfaction, including Job Conditions, Personality, Pay, and Corporate Social Responsibility; Life Satisfaction as an Outcome of Job Satisfaction; and Counterproductive Work Behavior (CWB) as an Outcome of Job Dissatisfaction
- **Newly revised sections:** *Learning Objectives* and *Implications for Managers*
- **New research incorporated in the following areas:** Attitudes and Behavior, Employee Engagement, Measured Job Satisfaction Levels, How Satisfied Are People in Their Jobs, and Organizational Citizenship Behavior (OCB) as an Outcome of Job Satisfaction
- **New features:** *Watch It* (Gawker Media: Attitudes and Job Satisfaction), *Personal Inventory Assessments* [Core Self-Evaluation (CSE) Scale], and *Try It* (Simulation: Attitudes & Job Satisfaction)

Chapter 4: Emotions and Moods

- **New content:** Moral Emotions; the Functions of Emotions, including Whether or Not Emotions Make Us Ethical; Emotion Regulation Influences, Outcomes, and Techniques; and the Ethics of Emotion Regulation
- **Newly revised sections:** *Learning Objectives*, Time of the Day as a Source of Emotions and Moods, *Implications for Managers*
- **New research incorporated in the following areas:** Stress, Sleep, Age, and Sex as Sources of Emotions and Moods; Controlling Emotional Displays; Emotional Intelligence; Safety and Injury at Work as Outcomes of Emotions and Moods; and International Research on the Basic Emotions, Experiencing Moods, and Emotions, as well as on the Day of the Week and Weather as Sources of Emotions and Moods
- **New features:** *Personal Inventory Assessments* (Emotional Intelligence Assessment) and *Try It* (Simulation: Emotions & Moods)

Chapter 5: Personality and Values

- **New content:** Whether or Not the Big Five Personality Traits Predict Behavior at Work, Other Dark-Side Traits, and Other Dimensions of Fit
- **Newly revised sections:** *Learning Objectives*, Personality Frameworks, the Myers-Briggs Type Indicator, Cultural Values, *Summary*, and *Implications for Managers*
- **New research incorporated in the following areas:** Describing Personality; the Big Five Personality Model; the Dark Triad, Proactive Personality; Organizational Situations, Generational Values; Person–Organization Fit; and International Research on Measuring Personality, Narcissism, and Person–Job Fit
- **New features:** *Watch It* (Honest Tea: Ethics—Company Mission and Values), and *Personality Inventory Assessment* (Personality Style Indicator)

Chapter 6: Perception and Individual Decision Making

- **New content:** The Perceiver, Target, and Context as Factors That Influence Perception, Randomness Error; Nudging as an Influence on Decision Making; Choosing between the Three Ethical Decision Criteria; Lying and Ethical Decision Making; and Ethics and Creativity
- **Newly revised sections:** *Learning Objectives*, the Halo Effect, Escalation of Commitment, Creative Potential, and *Implications for Managers*
- **New research incorporated in the following areas:** Person Perception: Making Judgments about Others; Attribution Theory; the Link between Perception and Individual Decision Making; Gender as an Influence on Decision Making; Creative Behavior; Intelligence, Personality, and Expertise as Causes of Creative Behavior; the Creative Environment; and International Research on the Three Ethical Decision Criteria
- **New features:** *Watch It* (Orpheus Group Casting: Social Perception and Attribution), *Try It* (Simulation: Perception & Individual Decision Making), and *Personal Inventory Assessments* (How Creative Are You?)

Chapter 7: Motivation Concepts

- **New content:** Goal-Setting and Ethics, Reinforcement Theory, Influencing Self-Efficacy in Others, Ensuring Justice, and Culture and Justice
- **Newly revised sections:** *Learning Objectives*, Goal-Setting Theory, and Equity Theory/Organizational Justice
- **New research incorporated in the following areas:** Hierarchy of Needs Theory as well as International Research on McClelland's Theory of Needs, Goal-Setting Theory, Self-Determination Theory, Self-Efficacy Theory, and Equity Theory/Organizational Justice
- **New features:** *Watch It* [Motivation (TWZ Role Play)], *Try It* (Simulation: Motivation), and *Personal Inventory Assessments* (Work Motivation Indicator)

Chapter 8: Motivation: From Concepts to Applications

- **Newly revised sections:** The Job Characteristics Model, Job Rotation, Rewarding Individual Employees through Variable-Pay Programs, and Using Benefits to Motivate Employees
- **New research incorporated in the following areas:** Job Rotation; Relational Job Design; Flextime; Job Sharing; Participative Management; Establishing a Pay Structure; Merit-Based Pay; Employee Stock Ownership Plans; Using Intrinsic Rewards; and International Research on the Job Characteristics Model, Telecommuting, Cultural Employee Involvement Programs, Representative Participation, Rewarding Individual Employees through Variable-Pay Programs, Piece-Rate Pay, Bonuses, and Profit-Sharing Plans
- **New features:** *Personal Inventory Assessments* (Diagnosing the Need for Team Building), *Watch It* (Zappos: Motivating Employees through Company Culture), and *Try It* (Simulation: Extrinsic & Intrinsic Motivation)

Chapter 9: Foundations of Group Behavior

- **New content:** Social Identity, Ingroups and Outgroups, Norms and Emotions, Positive and Negative Norms and Group Outcomes, Norms and Culture, Group Status Inequity, and Group Status and Stigmatization
- **Newly revised sections:** *Learning Objectives*; Role Expectations; Role Conflict; Group Status, Group Size, and Dynamics, Group Cohesiveness; Group Diversity; and *Implications for Managers*
- **New research incorporated in the following areas:** Group Norms, Group Status and Norms, Group Status and Group Interaction, Group Size and Dynamics, Challenges of Group Diversity, Group Effectiveness and Efficiency, and International Research in Group Diversity
- **New features:** *Watch It* (Witness.org: Managing Groups & Teams), *Personal Inventory Assessments* (Communicating Supportively), and *Try It* (Simulation: Group Behavior)

Chapter 10: Understanding Work Teams

- **New content:** Cultural Differences in Work Teams, Team Identity, Team Cohesion, and Shared Mental Models
- **Newly revised sections:** Problem-Solving Teams, *Summary*, and *Implications for Managers*
- **New research incorporated in the following areas:** The Popularity of Teams, Cross-Functional Teams, Virtual Teams, Multiteam Systems, Creating Effective Teams, Team Composition, Personality of Team Members, Size of Teams, and International Research on Climate of Trust
- **New features:** *Watch It* [Teams (TWZ Role Play)], *Personal Inventory Assessments* (Team Development Behaviors), and *Try It* (Simulation: Teams)

Chapter 11: Communication

- **New content:** Managing Behavior, Feedback, Emotional Feedback, Emotional Sharing, Persuasion, and Information Exchange
- **Newly revised sections:** Downward and Upward Communication, The Grapevine, Oral Communication, and Telephone
- **New research incorporated in the following areas:** Functions of Communication and Information Overload
- **New features:** *Watch It* [Communication (TWZ Role Play)], *Personal Inventory Assessments* (Communication Styles), and *Try It* (Simulation: Communication)

Chapter 12: Leadership

- **New content:** Dark Side Traits, Leader–Member Exchange Theory, How Transformational Leadership Works, Transformational versus Charismatic Leadership, Emotional Intelligence and Leadership, Leader-Participation Model, and Trust and Culture
- **Newly revised sections:** *Learning Objectives*, Trait Theories of Leadership, Contemporary Theories of Leadership, Behavioral Theories, Responsible Leadership, and Authentic Leadership

- **New research incorporated in the following areas:** Big Five Traits, Transactional and Transformational Leadership, Path–Goal Theory, Servant Leadership, and International Research on Charismatic Leadership and the Evaluation of Transformational Leadership
- **New features:** *Watch It* [Leadership (TWZ Role Play)], *Personal Inventory Assessments* (Ethical Leadership Assessment), and *Try It* (Simulation: Leadership)

Chapter 13: Power and Politics

- **New content:** The General Dependence Postulate, Social Network Analysis, Sexual Harassment, Inter-Organizational Factors Contributing to Political Behavior, Interviews and Impression Management, Scarcity, and Nonsubstitutability
- **Newly revised sections:** *Learning Objectives* and Individual Factors Contributing to Political Behavior
- **New research incorporated in the following areas:** Impression Management, Performance Evaluations and Impression Management, Organizational Factors, and Contributing to Political Behavior
- **New features:** *Watch It* (Power and Political Behavior), *Personal Inventory Assessments* (Gaining Power and Influence), and *Try It* (Simulation: Power & Politics)

Chapter 14: Conflict and Negotiation

- **New content:** Negotiating in a Social Context, Reputation and Relationships in Negotiations, and Third-Party Negotiations
- **Newly revised sections:** *Learning Objectives*, A Definition of Conflict, Loci of Conflict, and Stage IV of the Conflict Process: Behavior, Personality Traits, and Gender Differences in Negotiations
- **New research incorporated in the following areas:** Functional Outcomes, Preparation and Planning for Negotiation, and International Research on Personal Variables as Sources of Conflict and Cultural Influences on Negotiation
- **New features:** *Watch It* (Gordon Law Group: Conflict and Negotiation) and *Personal Inventory Assessments* (Strategies for Handling Conflict)

Chapter 15: Foundations of Organization Structure

- **New content:** Implications of Organizational Structure for OB; Boundary Spanning; Types of Organizational Structures, including Functional, Divisional, Team, and Circular Structures; and Institutions and Strategy
- Newly revised sections: *Learning Objectives* and Description of Organizational Structure
- **New research incorporated in the following areas:** The Leaner Organization: Downsizing, Organizational Strategies and Structure, and International Research on Technology and Strategy
- **New features:** *Personal Inventory Assessments* (Organizational Structure Assessment), *Try It* (Simulation: Organizational Structure), and *Watch It* (ZipCar: Organizational Structure)

Chapter 16: Organizational Culture

- **New content:** The Ethical Dimensions of Culture, Culture and Sustainability, Culture and Innovation, Culture as an Asset, Strengthening Dysfunctions, Rivals, and Influencing an Organizational Culture
- **Newly revised sections:** Description of Organizational Culture, Barriers to Acquisitions and Mergers, Ethical Culture, Positive Culture, Rewarding More Than Punishing, and Building on Employee Strengths
- **New research incorporated in the following areas:** Organizational Socialization
- **New features:** *Try It* (Simulation: Organizational Culture) and *Personal Inventory Assessments* (Organizational Structure Assessment)

Chapter 17: Organizational Change and Stress Management

- **New content:** Reactionary versus Planned Change; The Politics of Change; Action Research; Sensitivity Training, Managing the Change Paradox; Describing and Creating a Learning Organization; Organizational Change and Stress; Allostasis; Potential Sources of Stress at Work; Environmental, Personal, and Organizational Factors Leading to Stress; Stress Additivity; Perception and Stress; Job Experience and Stress; Personality Traits and Stress; Cultural Differences and Stress; and Wellness Programs
- **Newly revised sections:** Description of Change, Forces for Change, Coercion as a Tactic to Overcome Resistance to Change, Demands and Resources, Social Support and Stress, *Summary*, and *Implications for Managers*
- **New research incorporated in the following areas:** Resistance to Change, Developing Positive Relationships to Overcome Resistance to Change, Context and Innovation, Behavioral Symptoms of Stress, and International Research on Communication to Overcome Resistance to Change and on Idea Champions
- **New features:** *Try It* (Simulation: Change), *Watch It* (East Haven Fire Department: Managing Stress), and *Personal Inventory Assessments* (Tolerance of Ambiguity Scale)

INSTRUCTOR RESOURCES

At Pearson's Higher Ed catalog, https://www.pearsonhighered.com/sign-in.html, instructors can easily register to gain access to a variety of instructor resources available with this text in downloadable format. If assistance is needed, our dedicated technical support team is ready to help with the media supplements that accompany this text. Visit https://support.pearson.com/getsupport for answers to frequently asked questions and toll-free user support phone numbers.

The following supplements are available with this text:

- Instructor's Resource Manual
- Test Bank
- TestGen® Computerized Test Bank
- PowerPoint Presentation

This title is available as an eBook and can be purchased at most eBook retailers.

ACKNOWLEDGMENTS

We owe a debt of gratitude to all those at Pearson who have supported this text over the past 25 years and who have worked so hard on the development of this latest edition. On the editorial side, we want to thank Director of Portfolio Management Stephanie Wall, Portfolio Manager Kris Ellis-Levy, Managing Producer Ashley Santora, Content Producer Claudia Fernandes, and Editorial Assistant Hannah Lamarre. On the production side, we want to thank Moumita Majumdar and Revathi Viswanathan, Project Managers at Cenveo Publisher Services. The authors are grateful for Lori Ehrman Tinkey of the University of Notre Dame for her invaluable assistance in manuscript editing and preparation. Thank you also to David Glerum, Ph.D., for his input. Last but not least, we would like to thank the marketing team for promoting the book to the market, and the sales staff who have been selling this book over its many editions. We appreciate the attention you've given this book.

ABOUT THE AUTHORS

Stephen P. Robbins,
Ph.D. University of Arizona

Stephen P. Robbins is Professor Emeritus of Management at San Diego State University and the world's best-selling textbook author in the areas of both management and organizational behavior. His books are used at more than a thousand U.S. colleges and universities, have been translated into 19 languages, and have adapted editions for Canada, Australia, South Africa, and India. Dr. Robbins is also the author of the best-selling books *The Truth About Managing People*, 2nd ed. (Financial Times/Prentice Hall, 2008) and *Decide & Conquer* (Financial Times/Prentice Hall, 2004).

In his "other life," Dr. Robbins actively participates in masters' track competitions. Since turning 50 in 1993, he's won 18 national championships and 12 world titles, and set numerous U.S. and world age-group records at 60, 100, 200, and 400 meters. In 2005, Dr. Robbins was elected into the USA Masters' Track & Field Hall of Fame.

Timothy A. Judge,
Ph.D. University of Illinois at Urbana-Champaign

Timothy A. Judge is currently the Alutto Professor of Leadership at The Ohio State University and Visiting Professor, Division of Psychology & Language Sciences, University College London. He has held academic positions at the University of Notre Dame, University of Florida, University of Iowa, Cornell University, Charles University in the Czech Republic, Comenius University in Slovakia, and University of Illinois at Urbana-Champaign. Dr. Judge's primary research interests are in (1) personality, moods, and emotions; (2) job attitudes; (3) leadership and influence behaviors; and (4) careers (person–organization fit, career success). Dr. Judge has published more than 154 articles in these and other major topics in journals such as the *Academy of Management Journal* and the *Journal of Applied Psychology*. He is a fellow of several organizations, including the American Psychological Association and the Academy of Management. Among the many professional acknowledgments of his work, most recently Dr. Judge was awarded the Academy of Management Human Resources Division's Scholarly Achievement Award for 2014. Dr. Judge is a co-author of *Organizational Behavior*, 17th ed., with Stephen P. Robbins, and *Staffing Organizations*, 8th ed., with Herbert G. Heneman III. He is married and has three children—a daughter who is a health care social worker, a daughter who is studying for a master's degree, and a son in middle school.

1

What Is Organizational Behavior?

MyManagementLab®

⭐ Improve Your Grade!

When you see this icon ⭐, visit **mymanagementlab.com** for activities that are applied, personalized, and offer immediate feedback.

LEARNING OBJECTIVES

After studying this chapter, you should be able to:

1. Define **organizational behavior** (referred to as **OB** throughout the text).
2. Show the value of systematic study to OB.
3. Identify the major behavioral science disciplines that contribute to OB.
4. Demonstrate why few absolutes apply to OB.
5. Identify managers' challenges and opportunities in applying OB concepts.
6. Compare the three levels of analysis in this text's OB model.

⭐ Chapter Warm-up

If your professor has chosen to assign this, go to the Assignments section of **mymanagementlab.com** to complete the chapter warm-up.

As you begin your study of this text, you might be wondering, "What is organizational behavior and why does it matter to me?" We get to the definition of organizational behavior, or OB, in a moment, but let's begin with the end in mind—why OB matters, and what the study of OB offers you.

First, a bit of history. Until the late 1980s, business school curricula emphasized the technical aspects of management, focusing on economics, accounting, finance, and quantitative techniques. Course work in human behavior and people skills received relatively less attention. Since then, however, business schools have realized the significant role interpersonal skills play in determining a manager's effectiveness. In fact, a survey of over 2,100 CFOs across 20 industries indicated that a lack of interpersonal skills is the top reason why some employees fail to advance.[1]

One of the principal applications of OB is toward an improvement in interpersonal skills. Developing managers' interpersonal skills helps organizations attract and keep high-performing employees, which is important since outstanding employees are always in short supply and are costly to replace. But the development of interpersonal skills is not the only reason OB matters. Secondly, from the organizational standpoint, incorporating OB principles can help transform a workplace from good to great, with a positive impact on the bottom line. Companies known as good places to work—such as Genentech, the Boston Consulting Group, Qualcomm, McKinsey & Company, Procter & Gamble, Facebook, and Southwest Airlines[2]—have been found to generate superior financial performance.[3] Third, there are strong associations between the quality of workplace relationships and employee job satisfaction, stress, and turnover. For example, one very large survey of hundreds of workplaces and more than 200,000 respondents showed that social relationships among coworkers and supervisors were strongly related to overall job satisfaction. Positive social relationships also were associated with lower stress at work and lower intentions to quit.[4] Further research indicates that employees who relate to their managers with supportive dialogue and proactivity find that their ideas are endorsed more often, which improves workplace satisfaction.[5] Fourth, increasing the OB element in organizations can foster social responsibility awareness. Accordingly, universities have begun to incorporate social entrepreneurship education into their curriculum in order to train future leaders to address social issues within their organizations.[6] This is especially important because there is a growing need for understanding the means and outcomes of corporate social responsibility, known as CSR.[7] We discuss CSR more fully in Chapter 3.

We understand that in today's competitive and demanding workplace, managers can't succeed on their technical skills alone. They also have to exhibit good people skills. This text has been written to help both managers and potential managers develop those people skills with the knowledge that understanding human behavior provides. In so doing, we believe you'll also obtain lasting skills and insight about yourself and others.

MANAGEMENT AND ORGANIZATIONAL BEHAVIOR

The roles of a manager—and the necessary skills needed to perform as one—are constantly evolving. More than ever, individuals are placed into management positions without management training or informed experience. According to a large-scale survey, more than 58 percent of managers reported they had not received any training and 25 percent admitted they were not ready to lead others when they were given the role.[8] Added to that challenge, the demands of the job have increased: the average manager has seven direct reports (five was once the norm), and has less management time to spend with them than before.[9] Considering that a Gallup poll found organizations chose the wrong candidate for management positions 82 percent of the time,[10] we conclude that the more you can learn about people and how to manage them, the better prepared you will be to *be* that right candidate. OB will help you get there.

Organizational Behavior (OB) Defined

Organizational behavior (OB) is a field of study that investigates the impact individuals, groups, and structure have on behavior within organizations, for the purpose of applying such knowledge toward improving an organization's effectiveness. That's a mouthful, so let's break it down.

OB is a field of study, meaning that it is a distinct area of expertise with a common body of knowledge. What does it study? It studies three determinants of behavior within organizations: individuals, groups, and structure. In addition, OB applies the knowledge gained about individuals, groups, and the effect of structure on behavior in order to make organizations work more effectively.

To sum up our definition, OB is the study of what people do in an organization and the way their behavior affects the organization's performance. Because OB is concerned specifically with employment-related situations, it examines behavior in the context of job satisfaction, absenteeism, employment turnover, productivity, human performance, and management. Although debate exists about the relative importance of each, OB includes these core topics:[11]

Organizational behavior
A field of study that investigates the impact individuals, groups, and structure have on behavior within organizations, for the purpose of applying such knowledge toward improving an organization's effectiveness.

- Motivation
- Leader behavior and power
- Interpersonal communication
- Group structure and processes
- Attitude development and perception
- Change processes
- Conflict and negotiation
- Work design

Effective versus Successful Managerial Activities

Now that we understand what OB is, we may begin to apply some concepts. Consider the important issue of effective management. What makes one manager more effective than another? To answer the question, Fred Luthans, a prominent OB researcher, and his associates looked at what managers do from a unique perspective.[12] They asked, "Do managers who move up most quickly in an organization do the same activities and with the same emphasis as managers who do the best job?" You might think the answer is yes, but that's not always the case.

Luthans and his associates studied more than 450 managers. All engaged in four managerial activities:

1. **Traditional management.** Decision making, planning, and controlling.
2. **Communication.** Exchanging routine information and processing paperwork.
3. **Human resources (HR) management.** Motivating, disciplining, managing conflict, staffing, and training.
4. **Networking.** Socializing, politicking, and interacting with outsiders.

The "average" manager spent 32 percent of his or her time in traditional management activities, 29 percent communicating, 20 percent in HR management activities, and 19 percent networking. However, the time and effort different *individual* managers spent

When you see this icon, Global OB issues are being discussed in the paragraph.

on those activities varied a great deal. Among managers who were *successful* (defined in terms of speed of promotion within their organizations), networking made the largest relative contribution to success and HR management activities made the least relative contribution, which is the opposite of the average manager. Indeed, other studies in Australia, Israel, Italy, Japan, and the United States confirm the link between networking, social relationships, and success within an organization.[13] However, Luthans and associates found that among *effective* managers (defined in terms of quantity and quality of their performance and the satisfaction and commitment of their employees), communication made the largest relative contribution and networking the least. This finding is more in line with the average manager, with the important exception of increased emphasis on communication. The connection between communication and effective managers is clear. Managers who explain their decisions and seek information from colleagues and employees—even if the information turns out to be negative—are the most effective.[14]

⭐ WATCH IT

If your professor has assigned this, go to the Assignments section of **mymanagementlab .com** to complete the video exercise titled **Herman Miller: Organizational Behavior**.

COMPLEMENTING INTUITION WITH SYSTEMATIC STUDY

Whether you've explicitly thought about it before or not, you've been "reading" people almost all your life by watching their actions and interpreting what you see, or by trying to predict what people might do under different conditions. The casual approach to reading others can often lead to erroneous predictions, but using a systematic approach can improve your accuracy.

Underlying the systematic approach is the belief that behavior is not random. Rather, we can identify fundamental consistencies underlying the behavior of all individuals and modify them to reflect individual differences. These fundamental consistencies are very important. Why? Because they allow for predictability. Behavior is generally predictable, and the *systematic study* of behavior is a means to making reasonably accurate predictions. When we use the term **systematic study**, we mean looking at relationships, attempting to attribute causes and effects, and basing our conclusions on scientific evidence—that is, on data gathered under controlled conditions and measured, and interpreted, in a rigorous manner.

Systematic study
Looking at relationships, attempting to attribute causes and effects, and drawing conclusions based on scientific evidence.

Evidence-based management (EBM)
The basing of managerial decisions on the best available scientific evidence.

Evidence-based management (EBM) complements systematic study by basing managerial decisions on the best available scientific evidence. For example, we want doctors to make decisions about patient care based on the latest available evidence, and EBM argues that managers should do the same, thinking more scientifically about management problems. A manager might pose a question, search for the best available evidence, and apply the relevant information to the question or case at hand. You might wonder what manager would not base decisions on evidence, but the vast majority of management decisions are still made "on the fly," with little to no systematic study of available evidence.[15]

Intuition
An instinctive feeling not necessarily supported by research.

Systematic study and EBM add to **intuition**, or those "gut feelings" about what makes others (and ourselves) "tick." Of course, the things you have come to believe in an unsystematic way are not necessarily incorrect. Jack Welch (former CEO of General

Electric) noted, "The trick, of course, is to know when to go with your gut."[16] But if we make *all* decisions with intuition or gut instinct, we're likely working with incomplete information—like making an investment decision with only half the data about the potential for risk and reward.

Big Data

Data, the foundation of EBM, have been used to evaluate behavior since at least 1749, when the word "statistic" was coined to mean a "description of the state."[17] Statistics back then were used for purposes of governance, but since the data collection methods were clumsy and simplistic, so were the conclusions. "Big data"—the extensive use of statistical compilation and analysis—didn't become possible until computers were sophisticated enough to both store and manipulate large amounts of information. The use of big data began with online retailers but has since permeated virtually every business.

CURRENT USAGE No matter how many terabytes of data firms collect or from how many sources, the reasons for data analytics include: *predicting* events, from a book purchase to a spacesuit malfunction; detecting how much *risk* is incurred at any time, from the risk of a fire to that of a loan default; and *preventing* catastrophes large and small, from a plane crash to the overstocking of a product.[18] With big data, U.S. defense contractor BAE Systems protects itself from cyber-attacks, San Francisco's Bank of the West uses customer data to create tiered pricing systems, and London's Graze.com analyzes customers' preferences to select snack samples to send with their orders.[19]

NEW TRENDS The use of big data for understanding, helping, and managing people is relatively new but holds promise. In fact, research on 10,000 workers in China, Germany, India, the United Kingdom, and the United States indicated that employees expect the next transformation in the way people work will rely more on technological advancements than on any other factor, such as demographic changes.[20]

It is good news for the future of business that researchers, the media, and company leaders have identified the potential of data-driven management and decision making. A manager who uses data to define objectives, develop theories of causality, and test those theories can determine which employee activities are relevant to the objectives.[21] Big data has implications for correcting management assumptions and increasing positive performance outcomes. Increasingly, it is applied toward making effective decisions (Chapter 6) and managing organizational change (Chapter 17). It is quite possible that the best use of big data in managing people will come from OB and psychology research where it might, for instance, even help employees with mental illnesses monitor and change their behavior.[22]

LIMITATIONS As technological capabilities for handling big data have increased, so have issues of privacy and appropriate application. This is particularly true when data collection includes surveillance instruments. For instance, an experiment in Brooklyn, New York, has been designed to improve the quality of life for residents, but the researchers will collect potentially intrusive data from infrared cameras, sensors, and smartphone Wi-Fi signals.[23] Through similar methods of surveillance monitoring, a bank call center and a pharmaceutical company found that employees were more productive with more social interaction, so they changed their break time policies so more people took breaks together. They then saw sales increase and turnover decrease. Bread Winners Café in Dallas, Texas, constantly monitors all employees in the restaurant through surveillance and uses that data to promote or discipline its servers.[24] Privacy and application issues abound with these techniques, but abandoning them is not necessarily the fix.

An understanding of deeper OB issues can help find the productive balance. These big data tactics and others might yield results—and research indicates that, in fact, electronic performance monitoring does increase task performance and citizenship behavior (helping behaviors towards others), at least in the short term. But critics point out that after Frederick Taylor introduced surveillance analytics in 1911 to increase productivity through monitoring and feedback controls, his management control techniques were surpassed by Alfred Sloan's greater success with management outcomes, achieved by providing meaningful work to employees.[25]

We are not advising you to throw intuition out the window. In dealing with people, leaders often rely on hunches, and sometimes the outcomes are excellent. At other times, human tendencies get in the way. What we are advising is to use evidence as much as possible to inform your intuition and experience. The prudent use of big data, along with an understanding of human behavioral tendencies, can contribute to sound decision making and ease natural biases. That is the promise of OB.

DISCIPLINES THAT CONTRIBUTE TO THE OB FIELD

OB is an applied behavioral science built on contributions from a number of behavioral disciplines, mainly psychology and social psychology, sociology, and anthropology. Psychology's contributions have been principally at the individual or micro-level of analysis, while the other disciplines have contributed to our understanding of macro concepts such as group processes and organization. Exhibit 1-1 is an overview of the major contributions to the study of OB.

Psychology

Psychology
The science that seeks to measure, explain, and sometimes change the behavior of humans and other animals.

Psychology seeks to measure, explain, and sometimes change the behavior of humans and other animals. Contributors to the knowledge of OB are learning theorists, personality theorists, counseling psychologists, and, most important, industrial and organizational psychologists.

Early industrial and organizational psychologists studied the problems of fatigue, boredom, and other working conditions that could impede efficient work performance. More recently, their contributions have expanded to include learning, perception, personality, emotions, training, leadership effectiveness, needs and motivational forces, job satisfaction, decision-making processes, performance appraisals, attitude measurement, employee-selection techniques, work design, and job stress.

Social Psychology

Social psychology
An area of psychology that blends concepts from psychology and sociology to focus on the influence of people on one another.

Social psychology, generally considered a branch of psychology, blends concepts from both psychology and sociology to focus on people's influence on one another. One major study area is *change*—how to implement it and how to reduce barriers to its acceptance. Social psychologists also contribute to measuring, understanding, and changing attitudes; identifying communication patterns; and building trust. Finally, they have made important contributions to our study of group behavior, power, and conflict.

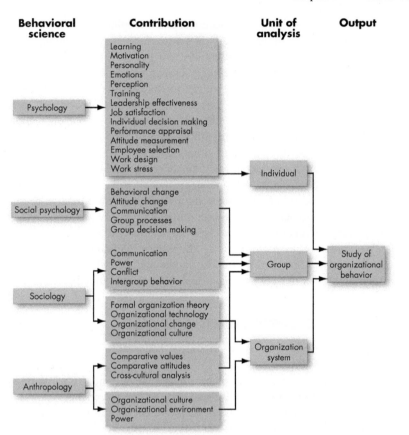

EXHIBIT 1-1
Toward an OB Discipline

Sociology

While psychology focuses on the individual, **sociology** studies people in relation to their social environment or culture. Sociologists have contributed to OB through their study of group behaviors in organizations, particularly formal and complex organizations. Perhaps most importantly, sociologists have studied organizational culture, formal organization theory and structure, organizational technology, communications, power, and conflict.

Sociology
The study of people in relation to their social environment or culture.

Anthropology

Anthropology is the study of societies in order to learn about human beings and their activities. Anthropologists' work on cultures and environments has helped us understand differences in fundamental values, attitudes, and behavior among people in different countries and within different organizations. Much of our current understanding of organizational culture, organizational climate, and differences among national cultures is a result of the work of anthropologists or those using their methods.

Anthropology
The study of societies to learn about human beings and their activities.

THERE ARE FEW ABSOLUTES IN OB

Laws in the physical sciences—chemistry, astronomy, physics—are consistent and apply in a wide range of situations. They allow scientists to generalize about the pull of gravity or to be confident about sending astronauts into space to repair satellites. Human beings are complex, and few, if any, simple and universal principles explain human behavior. Because we are not alike, our ability to make simple, accurate, and sweeping generalizations about ourselves is limited. Two people often act very differently in the same situation, and the same person's behavior changes in different situations. For instance, not everyone is motivated by money, and people may behave differently at a religious service than they do at a party.

This doesn't mean, of course, that we can't offer reasonably accurate explanations of human behavior or make valid predictions. It does mean that OB concepts must reflect situational, or contingency, conditions. We can say *x* leads to *y,* but only under conditions specified in *z*—the **contingency variables**. The science of OB was developed by applying general concepts to a particular situation, person, or group. For example, OB scholars would avoid stating that everyone likes complex and challenging work (a general concept). Why? Because not everyone wants a challenging job. Some people prefer routine over varied work, or simple over complex tasks. A job attractive to one person may be unattractive to another; its appeal is contingent on the person who holds it. Often, we find both general effects (money does have some ability to motivate most of us) and contingencies (some of us are more motivated by money than others, and some situations are more about money than others). We best understand OB when we realize how both (general effects and the contingencies that affect them) often guide behavior.

Contingency variables
Situational factors or variables that moderate the relationship between two or more variables.

CHALLENGES AND OPPORTUNITIES FOR OB

Understanding organizational behavior has never been more important for managers. Take a quick look at the dramatic changes in organizations. The typical employee is getting older; the workforce is becoming increasingly diverse; and global competition requires employees to become more flexible and cope with rapid change.

As a result of these changes and others, employment options have adapted to include new opportunities for workers. Exhibit 1-2 details some of the types of options individuals may find offered to them by organizations or for which they would like to negotiate. Under each heading in the exhibit, you will find a grouping of options from which to choose—or combine. For instance, at one point in your career you may find yourself employed full time in an office in a localized, nonunion setting with a salary and bonus compensation package, while at another point you may wish to negotiate for a flextime, virtual position and choose to work from overseas for a combination of salary and extra paid time off.

In short, today's challenges bring opportunities for managers to use OB concepts. In this section, we review some—but not nearly all—of the critical developing issues confronting managers for which OB offers solutions or, at least, meaningful insights toward solutions.

Continuing Globalization

Organizations are no longer constrained by national borders. Samsung, the largest South Korean business conglomerate, sells most of its products to organizations in other countries; Burger King is owned by a Brazilian firm; and McDonald's sells hamburgers in 118 countries on 6 continents. Even Apple—arguably the U.S. company with the strongest U.S. identity—employs twice as many workers outside the United States as it does inside the country. And all major automobile makers now manufacture cars outside their borders; Honda builds cars in Ohio, Ford in Brazil, Volkswagen in Mexico, and both Mercedes and BMW in the United States and South Africa. The world has become a global village. In the process, the manager's job has changed. Effective managers anticipate and adapt their approaches to the global issues we discuss next.

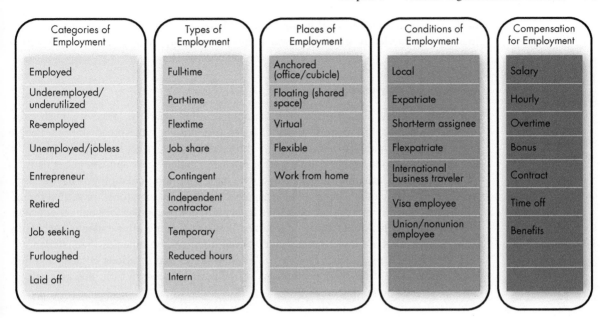

Categories of Employment	Types of Employment	Places of Employment	Conditions of Employment	Compensation for Employment
Employed	Full-time	Anchored (office/cubicle)	Local	Salary
Underemployed/ underutilized	Part-time	Floating (shared space)	Expatriate	Hourly
Re-employed	Flextime	Virtual	Short-term assignee	Overtime
Unemployed/jobless	Job share	Flexible	Flexpatriate	Bonus
Entrepreneur	Contingent	Work from home	International business traveler	Contract
Retired	Independent contractor		Visa employee	Time off
Job seeking	Temporary		Union/nonunion employee	Benefits
Furloughed	Reduced hours			
Laid off	Intern			

EXHIBIT 1-2
Employment Options

Sources: J.R. Anderson Jr., et al., "Action Items: 42 Trends Affecting Benefits, Compensation, Training, Staffing and Technology," *HR Magazine* (January 2013) p. 33; M. Dewhurst, B. Hancock, and D. Ellsworth, "Redesigning Knowledge Work," *Harvard Business Review* (January-February 2013), 58–64; E. Frauenheim, "Creating a New Contingent Culture," *Workforce Management* (August 2012), 34–39; N. Koeppen, "State Job Aid Takes Pressure off Germany," *The Wall Street Journal* (February 1, 2013), p. A8; and M. A. Shaffer, M. L. Kraimer, Y,-P. Chen, and M.C. Bolino, "Choices, Challenges, and Career Consequences of Global Work Experiences: A Review and Future Agenda," *Journal of Management* (July 2012), 1282–1327.

WORKING WITH PEOPLE FROM DIFFERENT CULTURES In your own country or on foreign assignment, you'll find yourself working with bosses, peers, and other employees born and raised in different cultures. What motivates you may not motivate them. Or your communication style may be straightforward and open, which others may find uncomfortable and threatening. To work effectively with people from different cultures, you need to understand how their culture and background have shaped them and how to adapt your management style to fit any differences.

ADAPTING TO DIFFERING CULTURAL AND REGULATORY NORMS To be effective, managers need to know the cultural norms of the workforce in each country where they do business. For instance, in some countries a large percentage of the workforce enjoys long holidays. There are national and local regulations to consider, too. Managers of subsidiaries abroad need to be aware of the unique financial and legal regulations applying to "guest companies" or else risk violating them. Violations can have implications for their operations in that country and also for political relations between countries. Managers also need to be cognizant of differences in regulations for competitors in that country; many times, understanding the laws can lead to success or failure. For example, knowing local banking laws allowed one multinational firm—the Bank of China—to seize control of a storied (and very valuable) London building, Grosvenor House, from under the nose of the owner, the Indian hotel group Sahara. Management at Sahara contended that the loan default that led to the seizure was a misunderstanding regarding one of their other properties in New York.[26] Globalization can get complicated.

Workforce Demographics

The workforce has always adapted to variations in the economy, longevity, birth rates, socioeconomic conditions, and other changes that have a widespread impact. People adapt to survive, and OB studies the way those adaptations affect individuals' behavior. For instance, even though the 2008 global recession ended years ago, some trends from those years are continuing: many people who have been long unemployed have left the workforce,[27] while others have cobbled together several part-time jobs[28] or settled for on-demand work.[29] Further options that have been particularly popular for younger educated workers have included obtaining specialized industry training after college,[30] accepting full-time jobs that are lower-level,[31] and starting their own companies.[32] As students of OB, we can investigate what factors lead employees to make various choices and how their experiences affect their perceptions of their workplaces. In turn, this can help us predict organizational outcomes.

 Longevity and birth rates have also changed the dynamics in organizations. Global longevity rates have increased by six years in a very short time (since 1990),[33] while birth rates are decreasing for many developed countries; trends that together indicate a lasting shift toward an older workforce. OB research can help explain what this means for employee attitudes, organizational culture, leadership, structure, and communication. Finally, socioeconomic shifts have a profound effect on workforce demographics. For example, the days when women stayed home because it was expected are just a memory in some cultures, while in others, women face significant barriers to entry into the workforce. We are interested in how these women fare in the workplace, and how their conditions can be improved. This is just one illustration of how cultural and socioeconomic changes affect the workplace, but it is one of many. We discuss how OB can provide understanding and insight on workforce issues throughout this text.

Workforce Diversity

Workforce diversity
The concept that organizations are becoming more heterogeneous in terms of gender, age, race, ethnicity, sexual orientation, and other characteristics.

One of the most important challenges for organizations is **workforce diversity**, a trend by which organizations are becoming more heterogeneous in terms of employees' gender, age, race, ethnicity, sexual orientation, and other characteristics. Managing this diversity is a global concern. Though we have more to say about it in the next chapter, suffice it to say here that diversity presents great opportunities and poses challenging questions for managers and employees. How can we leverage differences within groups for competitive advantage? Should we treat all employees alike? Should we recognize individual and cultural differences? What are the legal requirements in each country? Does increasing diversity even matter? It is important to address the spoken and unspoken concerns of organizations today.

Social Media

As we discuss in Chapter 11, social media in the business world is here to stay. Despite its pervasiveness, many organizations continue to struggle with employees' use of social media in the workplace. For instance, in February 2015, a Texas pizzeria fired an employee before her first day of work because she tweeted unflattering comments about her future job. In December 2014, Nordstrom fired an Oregon employee who had posted a personal Facebook comment seeming to advocate violence against white police officers.[34] These examples show that social media is a difficult issue for today's managers, presenting both a challenge and an opportunity for OB. For instance, how much should HR look into a candidate's social media presence? Should a hiring manager read the candidate's Twitter feeds, or just do a quick perusal of his or her Facebook profile? Managers need to adopt policies designed to protect employees and their organizations with balance and understanding.

Once employees are on the job, many organizations have policies about accessing social media at work—when, where, and for what purposes. But what about the impact of social media on employee well-being? One recent study found that subjects who woke up in a positive mood and then accessed Facebook frequently found their mood worsened during the day. Moreover, subjects who checked Facebook frequently over a two-week period reported a decreased level of satisfaction with their lives.[35] Managers—and OB— are trying to increase employee satisfaction, and therefore improve and enhance positive organizational outcomes. We discuss these issues further in Chapters 3 and 4.

Employee Well-Being at Work

One of the biggest challenges to maintaining employee well-being is the reality that many workers never get away from the virtual workplace. While communication technology allows many technical and professional employees to do their work at home, in their cars, or on the beach in Tahiti, it also means many feel like they're not part of a team. "The sense of belonging is very challenging for virtual workers, who seem to be all alone out in cyberland," said Ellen Raineri of Kaplan University, and many can relate to this feeling.[36] Another challenge is that organizations are asking employees to put in longer hours. According to one recent study, one in four employees shows signs of burnout, and two in three report high stress levels and fatigue.[37] This may actually be an underestimate because workers report maintaining "always on" access for their managers through e-mail and texting. Finally, employee well-being is challenged by heavy outside commitments. Millions of single-parent employees and employees with dependent parents face significant challenges in balancing work and family responsibilities, for instance.

As you'll see in later chapters, the field of OB offers a number of suggestions to guide managers in designing workplaces and jobs that can help employees deal with work–life conflicts.

Positive Work Environment

A growing area in OB research is **positive organizational scholarship** (POS; also called *positive organizational behavior*), which studies how organizations develop human strengths, foster vitality and resilience, and unlock potential. Researchers in this area say too much of OB research and management practice has been targeted toward identifying what's wrong with organizations and their employees. In response, they try to study what's *good* about them.[38] Some key subjects in positive OB research are engagement, hope, optimism, and resilience in the face of strain. Researchers hope to help practitioners create positive work environments for employees.

Positive organizational scholarship An area of OB research that concerns how organizations develop human strengths, foster vitality and resilience, and unlock potential.

Although positive organizational scholarship does not deny the value of the negative (such as critical feedback), it does challenge researchers to look at OB through a new lens and pushes organizations to make use of employees' strengths rather than dwell on their limitations. One aspect of a positive work environment is the organization's culture, the topic of Chapter 16. Organizational culture influences employee behavior so strongly that organizations have employed "culture officers" to shape and preserve the company's personality.[39]

Ethical Behavior

In an organizational world characterized by cutbacks, expectations of increasing productivity, and tough competition; it's not surprising many employees feel pressured to cut corners, break rules, and engage in other questionable practices. Increasingly they face **ethical dilemmas and ethical choices** in which they are required to identify right and wrong conduct. Should they "blow the whistle" if they uncover illegal activities in their companies? Do they follow orders with which they don't personally agree? Should they "play politics" to advance their careers?

Ethical dilemmas and ethical choices Situations in which individuals are required to define right and wrong conduct.

What constitutes good ethical behavior has never been clearly defined and, in recent years, the line differentiating right from wrong has blurred. We see people all around us engaging in unethical practices—elected officials pad expense accounts or take bribes; corporate executives inflate profits to cash in lucrative stock options; and university administrators look the other way when winning coaches encourage scholarship athletes to take easy courses or even, in the recent case at the University of North Carolina–Chapel Hill, sham courses with fake grades.[40] When caught, we see people give excuses such as "Everyone does it" or "You have to seize every advantage."

Today's manager must create an ethically healthy climate for employees in which they can do their work productively with minimal ambiguity about right and wrong behaviors. Companies that promote a strong ethical mission, encourage employees to behave with integrity, and provide strong leadership can influence employee decisions to behave ethically.[41] Classroom training sessions in ethics have also proven helpful in maintaining a higher level of awareness of the implications of employee choices as long as the training sessions are given on an ongoing basis.[42] In upcoming chapters, we discuss the actions managers can take to create an ethically healthy climate and help employees sort through ambiguous situations.

COMING ATTRACTIONS: DEVELOPING AN OB MODEL

We conclude this chapter by presenting a general model that defines the field of OB and stakes out its parameters, concepts, and relationships. By studying the model, you will have a good picture of how the topics in this text can inform your approach to management issues and opportunities.

Overview

Model An abstraction of reality, a simplified representation of some real-world phenomenon.

A **model** is an abstraction of reality, a simplified representation of some real-world phenomenon. Exhibit 1-3 presents the skeleton of our OB model. It proposes three types of variables (inputs, processes, and outcomes) at three levels of analysis (individual, group, and organizational). In the chapters to follow, we proceed from the individual level

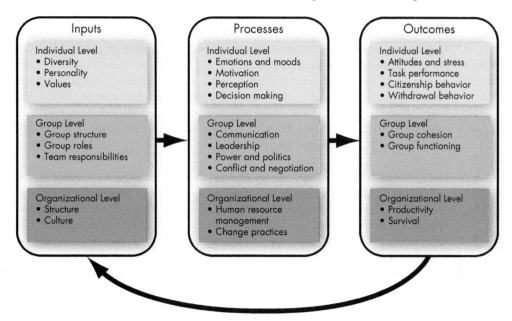

EXHIBIT 1-3
A Basic OB Model

(Chapters 2 through 8) to group behavior (Chapters 9 through 14) to the organizational system (Chapters 15 through 17). The model illustrates that inputs lead to processes, which lead to outcomes; we discuss interrelationships at each level of analysis. Notice that the model also shows that outcomes can influence inputs in the future, which highlights the broad-reaching effect OB initiatives can have on an organization's future.

Inputs

Inputs are the variables like personality, group structure, and organizational culture that lead to processes. These variables set the stage for what will occur in an organization later. Many are determined in advance of the employment relationship. For example, individual diversity characteristics, personality, and values are shaped by a combination of an individual's genetic inheritance and childhood environment. Group structure, roles, and team responsibilities are typically assigned immediately before or after a group is formed. Finally, organizational structure and culture are usually the result of years of development and change as the organization adapts to its environment and builds up customs and norms.

Inputs
Variables like personality, group structure, and organizational culture that lead to processes.

Processes

If inputs are like the nouns in OB, processes are like verbs. **Processes** are actions that individuals, groups, and organizations engage in as a result of inputs and that lead to certain outcomes. At the individual level, processes include emotions and moods, motivation, perception, and decision making. At the group level, they include communication, leadership, power and politics, and conflict and negotiation. Finally, at the organizational level, processes include HR management and change practices.

Processes
Actions that individuals, groups, and organizations engage in as a result of inputs and that lead to certain outcomes.

Outcomes

Outcomes
Key factors that are affected by some other variables.

Outcomes are the key variables that you want to explain or predict, and that are affected by some other variables. What are the primary outcomes in OB? Scholars have emphasized individual-level outcomes, such as attitudes and stress, task performance, citizenship behavior, and withdrawal. At the group level, cohesion and functioning are the dependent variables. Finally, at the organizational level, we look at overall productivity and survival. Because these outcomes are covered in all the chapters, we briefly discuss each so you can understand the goal of OB.

Attitudes
Evaluative statements or judgments concerning objects, people, or events.

Stress
An unpleasant psychological process that occurs in response to environmental pressures.

ATTITUDES AND STRESS   As we discuss in depth in Chapter 3, employee **attitudes** are the evaluations employees make, ranging from positive to negative, about objects, people, or events. For example, the statement "I really think my job is great" is a positive job attitude, while "My job is boring and tedious" is a negative job attitude. **Stress** is an unpleasant psychological condition that occurs in response to environmental pressures.

Some people might think influencing employee attitudes and stress is purely soft stuff and not the business of serious managers, but as you will learn, attitudes often have behavioral consequences that directly relate to organizational effectiveness. Ample evidence shows that employees who are more satisfied and treated fairly are more willing to engage in the above-and-beyond citizenship behavior that is so vital in the contemporary business environment.

Task performance
The combination of effectiveness and efficiency at doing core job tasks.

TASK PERFORMANCE   The combination of effectiveness and efficiency at doing your core job tasks is a reflection of your level of **task performance**. If we think about the job of a factory worker, task performance could be measured by the number and quality of products produced in an hour. The task performance measurement of a teacher would be the level of education that students obtain. The task performance measurement of consultants might be the timeliness and quality of the presentations they offer to the client. All these types of performance relate to the core duties and responsibilities of a job and are often directly related to the functions listed on a formal job description.

Organizational citizenship behavior (OCB)
Discretionary behavior that contributes to the psychological and social environment of the workplace.

ORGANIZATIONAL CITIZENSHIP BEHAVIOR (OCB)   The discretionary behavior that is not part of an employee's formal job requirements, and that contributes to the psychological and social environment of the workplace, is called **organizational citizenship behavior (OCB)**, or simply citizenship behavior. Successful organizations have employees who do more than their usual job duties—who provide performance *beyond* expectations. Organizations want and need employees who make positive contributions that aren't in any job description, and evidence indicates organizations that have such employees outperform those that don't. As a result, OB is concerned with citizenship behavior as an outcome variable.

Withdrawal behavior
The set of actions employees take to separate themselves from the organization.

WITHDRAWAL BEHAVIOR   We've already mentioned behavior that goes above and beyond task requirements, but what about behavior that in some way is below task requirements? **Withdrawal behavior** is the set of actions that employees take to separate themselves from the organization. There are many forms of withdrawal, ranging from showing up late or failing to attend meetings to absenteeism and turnover. Employee withdrawal can have a very negative effect on an organization.

GROUP COHESION   Although many outcomes in our model can be conceptualized as individual-level phenomena, some relate to the way groups operate. **Group cohesion** is the extent to which members of a group support and validate one another at work. In other words, a cohesive group is one that sticks together. When employees trust one another, seek common goals, and work together to achieve these common ends, the group is cohesive; when employees are divided among themselves in terms of what they want to achieve and have little loyalty to one another, the group is not cohesive. We can apply OB concepts toward group cohesion.

Group cohesion
The extent to which members of a group support and validate one another while at work.

GROUP FUNCTIONING   In the same way that positive job attitudes can be associated with higher levels of task performance, group cohesion should lead to positive group functioning. **Group functioning** refers to the quantity and quality of a group's work output. In the same way that the performance of a sports team is more than the sum of each individual player's performance, group functioning in work organizations is more than the sum of individual task performances.

Group functioning
The quantity and quality of a group's work output.

PRODUCTIVITY   The highest level of analysis in OB is the organization as a whole. An organization is productive if it achieves its goals by transforming inputs into outputs at the lowest cost. Thus **productivity** requires both **effectiveness** and **efficiency**.

A business firm is *effective* when it attains its sales or market share goals, but its productivity also depends on achieving those goals *efficiently*. Popular measures of organizational efficiency include return on investment, profit per dollar of sales, and output per hour of labor.

Service organizations must include customer needs and requirements in assessing their effectiveness. Why? Because a clear chain of cause and effect runs from employee attitudes and behavior to customer attitudes and profitability. For example, a recent study of six hotels in China indicated that negative employee attitudes decreased customer satisfaction and ultimately harmed the organization's profitability.[43]

Productivity
The combination of the effectiveness and efficiency of an organization.

Effectiveness
The degree to which an organization meets the needs of its clientele or customers.

Efficiency
The degree to which an organization can achieve its ends at a low cost.

SURVIVAL   The final outcome we consider is **organizational survival**, which is simply evidence that the organization is able to exist and grow over the long term. The survival of an organization depends not just on how productive the organization is, but also on how well it fits with its environment. A company that is very productively making goods and services of little value to the market is unlikely to survive for long, so survival also relies on perceiving the market successfully, making good decisions about how and when to pursue opportunities, and successfully managing change to adapt to new business conditions.

Organizational survival
The degree to which an organization is able to exist and grow over the long term.

SUMMARY

Managers need to develop their interpersonal, or people, skills to be effective in their jobs. OB investigates the impact that individuals, groups, and structure have on behavior within an organization, and then applies that knowledge to make organizations work more effectively.

IMPLICATIONS FOR MANAGERS

- Resist the inclination to rely on generalizations; some provide valid insights into human behavior, but many are erroneous. Get to know the person, and understand the context.

- Use metrics rather than hunches to explain cause-and-effect relationships.
- Work on your interpersonal skills to increase your leadership potential.
- Improve your technical skills and conceptual skills through training and staying current with OB trends like big data.
- OB can improve your employees' work quality and productivity by showing you how to empower your employees, design and implement change programs, improve customer service, and help your employees balance work–life conflicts.

PERSONAL INVENTORY ASSESSMENTS

✪ PERSONAL INVENTORY ASSESSMENTS

Multicultural Awareness Scale

Any study of organizational behavior (OB) starts with knowledge of yourself. As one step, take this PIA to determine your multicultural awareness.

1-1. How do you think an understanding of organizational behavior (OB) might contribute to your ability to manage others effectively?

2

Diversity in Organizations

MyManagementLab®

⭐ Improve Your Grade!

When you see this icon ⭐, visit **mymanagementlab.com** for activities that are applied, personalized, and offer immediate feedback.

LEARNING OBJECTIVES

After studying this chapter, you should be able to:

1. Demonstrate how workplace discrimination undermines organizational effectiveness.
2. Explain how stereotypes function in organizational settings.
3. Describe how key biographical characteristics are relevant to OB.
4. Explain how other differentiating characteristics factor into OB.
5. Demonstrate the relevance of intellectual and physical abilities to OB.
6. Describe how organizations manage diversity effectively.

⭐ Chapter Warm-up

If your professor has chosen to assign this, go to the Assignments section of **mymanagementlab.com** to complete the chapter warm-up.

DIVERSITY

We are, each of us, unique. This is obvious enough, but managers sometimes forget they need to recognize and capitalize on individual differences to get the most from their employees. In this chapter, you'll learn how individual characteristics like age, gender, race, ethnicity, and abilities can influence employee performance. You'll also see how managers can develop awareness about these characteristics and manage a diverse workforce effectively. But first, let's take an overview perspective of the changing workforce.

Demographic Characteristics

Worldwide, workplace demographics have undergone rapid and lasting change toward equality in the past 50–60 years. Perhaps most noticeably, the predominantly White, male managerial workforce of the past has given way to a gender-balanced, multi-ethnic workforce. For instance, in 1950 only 29.6 percent of the U.S. workforce was female,[1] but by 2014, women comprised 47 percent.[2] Both in the United States and internationally, women today are much more likely than before to be employed full time, have an advanced education, and earn wages comparable to those of men.[3] In addition, the earnings gap between Whites and other racial and ethnic groups in the United States has decreased significantly, partially due to the rising number of minorities in the workforce. Hispanics will grow from 13 percent of the workforce back in 2014 to 25.1 percent in 2044; Blacks will increase from 12 to 12.7 percent, and Asians from 5 to 7.9 percent.[4] Workers over the age of 55 are an increasingly large portion of the workforce as well, both in the United States and globally. In the United States, the 55-and-older age group will increase from 19.5 percent of the labor force back in 2010 to 25.2 percent by 2020.[5] Currently, in Australia there are more workers over age 55 than there are under age 25, and that shift is set to continue.[6] These changes are increasingly reflected in the makeup of managerial and professional jobs. They also indicate organizations must make diversity management a central component of their policies and practices.

Levels of Diversity

Although much has been said about diversity in age, race, gender, ethnicity, religion, and disability status, experts now recognize that these demographic characteristics are just the tip of the diversity iceberg.[7] Demographics mostly reflect **surface-level diversity**, not thoughts and feelings, and can lead employees to perceive one another through stereotypes and assumptions. However, evidence has shown that people are less concerned about demographic differences if they see themselves as sharing more important characteristics, such as personality and values, that represent **deep-level diversity**.[8]

Surface-level diversity Differences in easily perceived characteristics such as gender, race, ethnicity, age, or disability, that do not necessarily reflect the ways people think or feel but that may activate certain stereotypes.

Deep-level diversity Differences in values, personality, and work preferences that become progressively more important for determining similarity as people get to know one another better.

To understand the difference between surface- and deep-level diversity, consider an example. Luis and Carol are managers who seem to have little in common. Luis is a young, recently hired male from a Spanish-speaking neighborhood in Miami with a business degree. Carol is an older woman from rural Kansas who started as a customer service trainee after high school and worked her way up the hierarchy. At first, these coworkers may notice their surface-level differences in education, ethnicity, regional background, and gender. However, as they get to know one another, they may find they are both deeply committed to their families, share a common way of thinking about work problems, like to work collaboratively, and are interested in international assignments. These deep-level similarities can overshadow the more superficial differences between them, and research suggests they will work well together.

Throughout this text, you will encounter differences between deep- and surface-level diversity in various contexts. Diversity is an important concept in OB since individual differences shape preferences for rewards, communication styles, reactions to leaders, negotiation styles, and many other aspects of behavior in organizations. Unfortunately, increased diversity may give way to discriminatory practices, which we discuss next.

DISCRIMINATION

Although diversity presents many opportunities for organizations, diversity management includes working to eliminate unfair **discrimination**. To discriminate is to note a difference between things, which in itself isn't necessarily bad. Noticing one employee is more qualified is necessary for making good hiring decisions; noticing another is taking on leadership responsibilities exceptionally well is necessary for making strong promotion decisions. Usually when we talk about discrimination, though, we mean allowing our behavior to be influenced by stereotypes about *groups* of people. **Stereotyping** is judging someone on the basis of our perception of the group to which that person belongs. To use a machine metaphor, you might think of stereotypes as the fuel that powers the discrimination engine. Stereotypes can be insidious not only because they may affect the fairness of the organization, but because they can affect how potential targets of discrimination see themselves.

Stereotype Threat

Let's say you are sitting in a restaurant, waiting for the blind date your coworker arranged to find you in the crowded room. How do you think your coworker described you to this person? Now consider how you would describe yourself to this new person if you'd talked on the phone before the date. What identifiable characteristics would you mention as a shorthand way for your date to know a bit about you so he or she could recognize you in the restaurant?

Chances are good that you'd mention your race, something about how you express your gender (such as the way you dress), how old you are, and maybe what you do for a living. You might also mention how tall you are if you are remarkably tall or short, and—if you're candid—you might mention something about your build (heavyset, petite, in between). Overall, you'd give cues to your blind date about characteristics that are *distinctive*, or stand out, about you. Interestingly, what you tell someone about yourself says a lot about what you think about yourself. Just as we stereotype others, we also stereotype ourselves.

Stereotype threat describes the degree to which we internally agree with the generally negative stereotyped perceptions of our groups. Along with that comes a fear of being judged when we are identified with the negative connotations of that group. This can happen when we are a minority in a situation. For instance, an older worker applying for a job in a predominately millennial-age workforce may assume the interviewer thinks he is out of touch with current trends. What creates a stereotype threat is not whether this worker is or is not up to date with trends, but whether he internally agrees that older workers (the group he identifies with) are out of date (the stereotype).

Stereotype threat has serious implications for the workplace. Employees who feel it may have lower performance, lower satisfaction, negative job attitudes, decreased engagement, decreased motivation, higher absenteeism, more health issues, and higher turnover intentions.[9] Thankfully, this is something we can combat in the workplace by treating employees as individuals, and not highlighting group differences. The following organizational changes can be successful in reducing stereotype threat: increasing awareness of how stereotypes may be perpetuated; reducing differential and preferential treatment through objective assessments; banning stereotyped practices and messages; confronting even small, seemingly innocuous aggressions against minority groups and adopting transparent practices that signal the value of all employees.[10]

Discrimination
Noting of a difference between things; often we refer to unfair discrimination, which means making judgments about individuals based on stereotypes regarding their demographic group.

Stereotyping
Judging someone on the basis of one's perception of the group to which that person belongs.

Stereotype threat
The degree to which we internally agree with the generally negative stereotyped perceptions of our groups.

Discrimination in the Workplace

To review, rather than looking at individual characteristics, unfair discrimination assumes everyone in a group is the same. This discrimination is often very harmful for employees, as we've just discussed, and for organizations.

Exhibit 2-1 provides definitions and examples of some forms of discrimination in organizations. Although many are prohibited by law and therefore are not a part of organizations' official policies, the practices persist. Tens of thousands of cases of employment discrimination are documented every year, and many more go unreported. Since discrimination has increasingly come under both legal scrutiny and social disapproval, most overt forms have faded, which may have resulted in an increase in more covert forms like incivility or exclusion, especially when leaders look the other way.[11]

As you can see, discrimination can occur in many ways, and its effects can vary depending on organizational context and the personal biases of employees. Some forms

Type of Discrimination	Definition	Examples from Organizations
Discriminatory policies or practices	Actions taken by representatives of the organization that deny equal opportunity to perform or unequal rewards for performance.	Older workers may be targeted for layoffs because they are highly paid and have lucrative benefits.
Sexual harassment	Unwanted sexual advances and other verbal or physical conduct of a sexual nature that create a hostile or offensive work environment.	Salespeople at one company went on company-paid visits to strip clubs, brought strippers into the office to celebrate promotions, and fostered pervasive sexual rumors.
Intimidation	Overt threats or bullying directed at members of specific groups of employees.	African American employees at some companies have found nooses hanging over their workstations.
Mockery and insults	Jokes or negative stereotypes; sometimes the result of jokes taken too far.	Arab Americans have been asked at work whether they were carrying bombs or were members of terrorist organizations.
Exclusion	Exclusion of certain people from job opportunities, social events, discussions, or informal mentoring; can occur unintentionally.	Many women in finance claim they are assigned to marginal job roles or are given light workloads that don't lead to promotion.
Incivility	Disrespectful treatment, including behaving in an aggressive manner, interrupting the person, or ignoring varying opinions.	Female lawyers note that male attorneys frequently cut them off or do not adequately address their comments.

EXHIBIT 2-1

Forms of Discrimination in Organizations

Sources: J. Levitz and P. Shishkin, "More Workers Cite Age Bias after Layoffs," *The Wall Street Journal,* March 11, 2009, D1–D2; W. M. Bulkeley, "A Data-storage Titan Confronts Bias Claims," *The Wall Street Journal*, September 12, 2007, A1, A16; D. Walker, "Incident with Noose Stirs Old Memories," *McClatchy-Tribune Business News*, June 29, 2008; D. Solis, "Racial Horror Stories Keep EEOC Busy," *Knight-Ridder Tribune Business News*, July 30, 2005, 1; H. Ibish and A. Stewart, *Report on Hate Crimes and Discrimination against Arab Americans: The Post-September 11 Backlash, September 11, 2001-October 11, 2001* (Washington, DC: American-Arab Anti-Discrimination Committee, 2003); A. Raghavan, "Wall Street's Disappearing Women," *Forbes*, March 16, 2009, 72–78; and L. M. Cortina, "Unseen Injustice: Incivility as Modern Discrimination in Organizations," *Academy of Management Review* 33, no. 1 (2008): 55–75.

of discrimination like exclusion or incivility are especially hard to root out since they may occur simply because the actor isn't aware of the effects of his or her actions. Like stereotype threat, actual discrimination can lead to increased negative consequences for employers, including reduced productivity and organizational citizenship behavior (OCB; see Chapter 1), more conflict, increased turnover, and even increased risk-taking behavior.[12] Unfair discrimination also leaves qualified job candidates out of initial hiring and promotions. Thus, even if an employment discrimination lawsuit is never filed, a strong business case can be made for aggressively working to eliminate unfair discrimination.

Whether it is overt or covert, intentional or unintentional, discrimination is one of the primary factors that prevents diversity. On the other hand, recognizing diversity opportunities can lead to an effective diversity management program and ultimately to a more successful organization. *Diversity* is a broad term, and the phrase *workplace diversity* can refer to any characteristic that makes people different from one another. The following section covers some important surface-level characteristics that differentiate members of the workforce.

BIOGRAPHICAL CHARACTERISTICS

Biographical characteristics such as age, gender, race, ethnicity, and disability are some of the most obvious ways employees differ. Let's begin by looking at factors that are easily definable and readily available—data that can be obtained, for the most part, from an employee's human resources (HR) file. Variations in surface-level characteristics may be the basis for discrimination against classes of employees, so it is worth knowing how related they actually are to work outcomes. As a general rule, many biographical differences are not important to actual work outcomes, and far more variation occurs *within* groups sharing biographical characteristics than between them.

Biographical characteristics
Personal characteristics—such as age, gender, race, and length of tenure—that are objective and easily obtained from personnel records. These characteristics are representative of surface-level diversity.

Age

Age in the workforce is likely to be an issue of increasing importance during the next decade for many reasons. For one, the workforce is aging worldwide in most developed countries;[13] by estimates, 93 percent of the growth in the labor force from 2006 to 2016 came from workers over age 54.[14] In the United States, the proportion of the workforce age 55 and older is 22 percent and increasing.[15] Legislation has, for all intents and purposes, outlawed mandatory retirement. Moreover, the United States and Australia, among other countries, have laws directly against age discrimination.[16] Most workers today no longer have to retire at age 70, and 62 percent of workers age 45 to 60 plan to delay retirement.[17]

Stereotypes of older workers as being behind the times, grumpy, and inflexible are changing. Managers often see a number of positive qualities that older workers bring to their jobs, such as experience, judgment, a strong work ethic, and a commitment to quality. For example, the Public Utilities Board, the water agency of Singapore, reports that 27 percent of its workforce is over age 55 and the older workers provide workforce stability.[18] Industries like health care, education, government, and nonprofit service often welcome older workers.[19] However, older workers are still perceived as less adaptable and less motivated to learn new technology.[20] When organizations seek individuals who are open to change and training, the perceived negatives associated with age clearly hinder the initial hiring of older workers and increase the likelihood they will be let go during cutbacks.

Now let's take a look at the evidence. What effect does age actually have on two of our most important outcomes, job performance and job satisfaction?

AGE AND JOB PERFORMANCE   Despite misperceptions, the majority of studies show "virtually no relationship between age and job performance," according to Director Harvey Sterns of the Institute for Life-Span Development and Gerontology.[21] Indeed, some studies indicate that older adults perform better than their younger counterparts. For example, in Munich a four-year study of 3,800 Mercedes-Benz workers found that "the older workers seemed to know better how to avoid severe errors," said Matthias Weiss, the academic coordinator of the study.[22] Related to performance, there is a conception that creativity diminishes as people age. Researcher David Galenson, who studied the ages of peak creativity, found that people who create through experimentation do "their greatest work in their 40s, 50s, and 60s. These artists rely on wisdom, which increases with age."[23]

AGE AND JOB SATISFACTION   Regarding job satisfaction, an important topic in Chapter 3, a review of more than 800 studies found that older workers tend to be more satisfied with their work, report better relationships with coworkers, and are more committed to their organizations.[24] Other studies, however, have found that job satisfaction increases up to middle age, at which point it begins to drop off. When we separate the results by job type, we find that satisfaction tends to increase among professionals as they age, whereas among nonprofessionals it falls during middle age and then rises again in the later years.

Sex

Few issues initiate more debates, misconceptions, and unsupported opinions than whether women perform as well on jobs as men do. In reality, few—if any—differences between men and women affect job performance.[25] Though in general men may have slightly higher math ability and women slightly higher verbal ability, the differences are fairly small, and there are no consistent male–female differences in problem-solving ability, analytical skills, or learning ability.[26] In the workplace, one meta-analysis of job performance studies found that women scored slightly higher than men did on performance measures.[27] A separate meta-analysis of 95 leadership studies indicated that women and men are rated equally effective as leaders.[28]

Yet biases and stereotypes persist. In the hiring realm, managers are influenced by gender bias when selecting candidates for certain positions.[29] For instance, men are preferred in hiring decisions for male-dominated occupations, particularly when men are doing the hiring.[30] Once on the job, men and women may be offered a similar number of developmental experiences, but females are less likely to be assigned challenging positions by men, assignments that could help them achieve higher organizational positions.[31] Moreover, men are more likely to be chosen for leadership roles even though men and women are equally effective leaders. A study of 20 organizations in Spain, for example, suggested that men are generally selected for leadership roles that require handling organizational crises.[32] According to Naomi Sutherland, senior partner in diversity at recruiter Korn Ferry, "Consciously or subconsciously, companies are still hesitant to take the risk on someone who looks different from their standard leadership profile."[33]

Worldwide, there are many misconceptions and contradictions about male and female workers. Thankfully, many countries have laws against sex discrimination, including Australia, the United Kingdom, and the United States. Other countries, such as Belgium, France, Norway, and Spain, are seeking gender diversity through laws to increase the percentage of women on boards of directors. Gender biases and gender discrimination are still serious issues, but there are indications that the situation is improving.

Race and Ethnicity

Race is a controversial issue in society and in organizations. We define *race* as the heritage people use to identify themselves; *ethnicity* is the additional set of cultural characteristics that often overlaps with race. Typically, we associate race with biology and ethnicity with culture, but there is a history of self-identifying for both classifications. Laws against race and ethnic discrimination are in effect in many countries, including Australia, the United Kingdom, and the United States.[35]

Race and ethnicity have been studied as they relate to employment outcomes such as hiring decisions, performance evaluations, pay, and workplace discrimination. Individuals may slightly favor colleagues of their own race in performance evaluations, promotion decisions, and pay raises, although such differences are not found consistently, especially when highly structured methods of decision making are employed.[36] Also, some industries have remained less racially diverse than others. For instance, U.S. advertising and media organizations suffer from a lack of racial diversity in their management ranks, even though their client base is increasingly ethnically diverse.[37]

Finally, members of racial and ethnic minorities report higher levels of discrimination in the workplace.[38] African Americans generally fare worse than Whites in employment decisions (a finding that may not apply outside the United States). They receive lower ratings in employment interviews, lower job performance ratings, less pay, and fewer promotions.[39] Lastly, while this does not necessarily prove overt racial discrimination, African Americans are often discriminated against even in controlled experiments. For example, one study of low-wage jobs found that African American applicants with no criminal history received fewer job offers than did White applicants with criminal records.[40]

Disabilities

Workplace policies, both official and circumstantial, regarding individuals with physical or mental disabilities vary from country to country. Countries such as Australia, the United States, the United Kingdom, and Japan have specific laws to protect individuals with disabilities.[41] These laws have resulted in greater acceptance and accommodation of people with physical or mental impairments. In the United States, for instance, the representation of individuals with disabilities in the workforce rapidly increased with the passage of the Americans with Disabilities Act (ADA, 1990).[42] According to the ADA, employers are required to make reasonable accommodations so their workplaces will be accessible to individuals with physical or mental disabilities.

SCOPE OF DISABILITIES   The U.S. Equal Employment Opportunity Commission (EEOC), the federal agency responsible for enforcing employment discrimination laws, classifies a person as *disabled* who has any physical or mental impairment that substantially limits one or more major life activities. One of the most controversial aspects of the ADA is the provision that requires employers to make reasonable accommodations for people with psychiatric disabilities.[43] Examples of recognized disabilities include missing limbs, seizure disorder, Down syndrome, deafness, schizophrenia, alcoholism, diabetes, depression, and chronic back pain. These conditions share almost no common features, so there's no specific definition about how each condition is related to employment.

DISABILITIES AND OUTCOMES   The impact of disabilities on employment outcomes has been explored from a variety of perspectives. On the one hand, when disability status was randomly manipulated among hypothetical candidates in a study, disabled individuals were rated as having superior personal qualities like dependability.[44] Another review suggested that workers with disabilities receive higher performance evaluations. However, according to research, individuals with disabilities tend to encounter lower performance expectations and are less likely to be hired.[45] Mental disabilities may impair performance more than physical disabilities: Individuals with such common mental health issues as depression and anxiety are significantly more likely to be absent from work.[46]

The elimination of discrimination against the disabled workforce has long been problematic. In Europe, for instance, policies to motivate employers have failed to boost the workforce participation rate for workers with disabilities, and outright quota systems in Germany, France, and Poland have backfired.[47] However, the recognition of the talents and abilities of individuals with disabilities has made a positive impact. In addition, technology and workplace advancements have greatly increased the scope of available jobs for those with all types of disabilities. Managers need to be attuned to the true requirements of each job and match the skills of the individual to them, providing accommodations when needed. But what happens when employees do not disclose their disabilities? Let's discuss this next.

Hidden Disabilities

As we mentioned earlier, disabilities include observable characteristics like missing limbs, illnesses that require a person to use a wheelchair, and blindness. Other disabilities may not be obvious, at least at first. Unless an individual decides to disclose a disability that isn't easily observable, it can remain hidden at the discretion of the employee. These are called *hidden disabilities* (or invisible disabilities). Hidden disabilities generally fall under the categories of sensory disabilities (for example, impaired hearing), autoimmune disorders (like rheumatoid arthritis), chronic illness or pain (like carpal tunnel syndrome), cognitive or learning impairments (like ADHD), sleep disorders (like insomnia), and psychological challenges (like PTSD).[48]

As a result of recent changes to the Americans with Disabilities Act Amendments Act of 2008, U.S. organizations must accommodate employees with a very broad range of impairments. However, employees must disclose their conditions to their employers in order to be eligible for workplace accommodations and employment protection. Since many employees do not want to disclose their invisible disabilities, they are prevented from getting the workplace accommodations they need in order to thrive in their jobs. Research indicates that individuals with hidden disabilities are afraid of being stigmatized or ostracized if they disclose their disabilities to others in the workplace, and they believe their managers will think they are less capable of strong job performance.[49]

In some ways, a hidden disability is not truly invisible. For example, a person with undisclosed autism will still exhibit the behaviors characteristic of the condition, such as difficulties with verbal communication and adaptability.[50] You may observe behaviors that lead you to suspect an individual has a hidden disability. Unfortunately, you may attribute the behavior to other causes—for instance, you may incorrectly ascribe the slow, slurred speech of a coworker to an alcohol problem rather than to the long-term effects of a stroke.

As for the employee, research suggests that disclosure helps all—the individual, others, and organizations. Disclosure may increase the job satisfaction and well-being of the individual, help others understand and assist the individual to succeed in the workplace, and allow the organization to accommodate the situation to achieve top performance.[51]

OTHER DIFFERENTIATING CHARACTERISTICS

The last set of characteristics we'll look at includes religion, sexual orientation, gender identity, and cultural identity. These characteristics illustrate deep-level differences that provide opportunities for workplace diversity, as long as discrimination can be overcome.

Religion

Not only do religious and nonreligious people question each other's belief systems, often people of different religious faiths conflict with one another. There are few—if any—countries in which religion is a nonissue in the workplace. For this reason, employers are prohibited by law from discriminating against employees based on religion in many countries, including Australia, the United Kingdom, and the United States.[52] Islam is one of the most popular religions in the world, and it is the majority religion in many countries. However, in the United States, Muslims are a minority group that is growing. There are nearly three million Muslims in the United States, and the number is predicted to double by 2030, when they will represent 1.7 percent of the population, according to the Pew Research Center. At that point, there will be as many Muslims in the United States as there are Jews and Episcopalians.[53] Despite these numbers, there is evidence in studies that people are discriminated against for their Islamic faith. For instance, U.S. job applicants in Muslim-identified religious attire who applied for hypothetical retail jobs had shorter, more interpersonally negative interviews than applicants who did not wear Muslim-identified attire.[54]

Religious discrimination has been a growing source of discrimination claims in the United States, partially because the issues are complex. Recently, Samantha Elauf, who was turned down for employment because she wears a hijab—a black head scarf—sued for religious discrimination. "I learned I was not hired by Abercrombie because I wear a head scarf, which is a symbol of modesty in my Muslim faith," she said. When she interviewed, she was not aware of the organization's rule against head coverings and did not mention her reason for the scarf. Should employers be required to deduce why applicants dress as they do and then protect them? Even the Supreme Court is not certain.[55]

Sexual Orientation and Gender Identity

While much has changed, the full acceptance and accommodation of lesbian, gay, bisexual, and transgender (LGBT) employees remains a work in progress. In the United States, a Harvard University study sent fictitious but realistic resumés to 1,700 actual entry-level job openings. The applications were identical with one exception: Half mentioned involvement in gay organizations during college, and the other half did not. The applications without the mention received 60 percent more callbacks than the ones with it.[56]

Perhaps as a result of perceived discrimination, many LGBT employees do not disclose their status. For example, John Browne, former CEO of British Petroleum (BP), hid his sexual orientation until he was 59 years old, when the press threatened to disclose that he was gay. Fearing the story would result in turmoil for the company, he resigned. Browne wrote, "Since my outing in 2007, many societies around the world have done more to embrace people who are lesbian, gay, bisexual, or transgender. But the business world has a long way to go."[57]

SEXUAL ORIENTATION LAWS U.S. federal law does not prohibit discrimination against employees based on sexual orientation, although 29 states and more than 160 municipalities do. In those states and municipalities that do protect against discrimination based on sexual orientation, roughly as many claims are filed for sexual orientation discrimination as for sex and race discrimination.[58] Some other countries are more progressive: for instance, Australia has laws against discriminating on the basis of sexual preference, and the United Kingdom has similar laws regarding sexual orientation.[59] However, the distinctions in these laws may not be broad enough—researchers have acknowledged a new acronym, QUILTBAG, to describe individuals who are queer/questioning, undecided, intersex, lesbian, transgender, bisexual, asexual, or gay.[60]

As a first step in the United States, the federal government has prohibited discrimination based on sexual orientation against *government* employees. The Equal Employment Opportunity Commission (EEOC) held that sex-stereotyping against lesbian, gay, and bisexual individuals represents gender discrimination enforceable under the Civil Rights Act of 1964.[61] Also, pending federal legislation against discrimination based on sexual orientation—the Employment Non-Discrimination Act (ENDA)—passed the Senate but is not yet law.[62]

ORGANIZATIONAL POLICIES ON SEXUAL ORIENTATION Even in the absence of federal legislation, many organizations have implemented policies and procedures that cover sexual orientation. For example, IBM, once famous for requiring all employees to wear white shirts and ties, has changed its ultra-conservative environment. Former vice-president Ted Childs said, "IBM ensures that people who are gay, lesbian, bisexual, or transgender feel safe, welcomed, and valued within the global walls of our business. . . . The contributions that are made by [gay and transgender] IBMers accrue directly to our bottom line and ensure the success of our business."[63]

IBM is not alone. Surveys indicate that more than 90 percent of the *Fortune* 500 have policies that cover sexual orientation. As for gender identity, companies are increasingly adopting policies to govern the way their organizations treat transgender employees. In 2001, only eight companies in the *Fortune* 500 had policies on gender identity. That number is now more than 250.

However, among the *Fortune* 1,000, some noteworthy companies do not currently have domestic-partner benefits or nondiscrimination clauses for LGBT employees, including ExxonMobil, currently second in the *Fortune* rankings of the largest U.S. companies.[64] Some companies claim they do not need to provide LGBT benefits for religious reasons. Moreover, some organizations that claim to be inclusive don't live up to the claim. For example, a recent study of five social cooperatives in Italy indicated that these so-called inclusive organizations actually expect individuals to remain quiet about their status.[65]

Cultural Identity

We have seen that people sometimes define themselves in terms of race and ethnicity. Many people carry a strong *cultural identity* as well, a link with the culture of family ancestry that lasts a lifetime, no matter where the individual may live in the world. People choose their cultural identity, and they also choose how closely they observe the norms of that culture. Cultural norms influence the workplace, sometimes resulting in clashes. Organizations must adapt. Workplace practices that coincided with the norms of a person's cultural identity were commonplace years ago, when societies were less mobile. People looked for work near familial homes, and organizations established holidays, observances, practices, and customs that suited the majority. Organizations were generally not expected to accommodate each individual's preferences.

Thanks to global integration and changing labor markets, today's organizations do well to understand and respect the cultural identities of their employees, both as groups and as individuals. A U.S. company looking to do business in, say, Latin America, needs to understand that employees in those cultures expect long summer holidays. A company that requires employees to work during this culturally established break will meet strong resistance.

An organization seeking to be sensitive to the cultural identities of its employees should look beyond accommodating its majority groups and instead create as much of an individualized approach to practices and norms as possible. Often, managers can provide the bridge of workplace flexibility to meet both organizational goals and individual needs.

⭐ WATCH IT

If your professor has assigned this, go to the Assignments section of **mymanagementlab .com** to complete the video exercise titled **Verizon: Diversity.**

ABILITY

Contrary to what we were taught in grade school, we weren't all created equal in our abilities. For example, regardless of how motivated you are, you may not be able to act as well as Jennifer Lawrence, play basketball as well as LeBron James, or write as well as Stephen King. Of course, all of us have strengths and weaknesses that make us relatively superior or inferior to others in performing certain tasks or activities. From management's standpoint, the challenge is to understand the differences to increase the likelihood that a given employee will perform their job well.

What does *ability* mean? As we use the term, **ability** is an individual's current capacity to perform the various tasks of a job. Overall abilities are essentially made up of two sets of factors: intellectual and physical.

Ability An individual's capacity to perform the various tasks in a job.

Intellectual Abilities

Intellectual abilities are abilities needed to perform mental activities—thinking, reasoning, and problem solving. Most societies place a high value on intelligence, and for good reason. Smart people generally earn more money and attain higher levels of education. They are also more likely to emerge as leaders of groups. However, assessing and measuring intellectual ability are not always simple, partially because people aren't consistently

Intellectual abilities The capacity to do mental activities— thinking, reasoning, and problem solving.

capable of correctly assessing their own cognitive ability.[66] IQ tests are designed to ascertain a person's general intellectual abilities, but the origins, influence factors, and testing of intelligence quotient (IQ) are controversial.[67] So, too, are popular college admission tests, such as the SAT and ACT, and graduate admission tests in business (GMAT), law (LSAT), and medicine (MCAT). The firms that produce these tests don't claim they assess intelligence, but experts know they do.[68]

DIMENSIONS OF INTELLECTUAL ABILITY   The seven most frequently cited dimensions making up intellectual abilities are number aptitude, verbal comprehension, perceptual speed, inductive reasoning, deductive reasoning, spatial visualization, and memory.[69] Exhibit 2-2 describes these dimensions.

 Intelligence dimensions are positively correlated, so if you score high on verbal comprehension, for example, you're more likely to also score high on spatial visualization. The correlations aren't perfect, meaning people do have specific abilities that predict important work-related outcomes when considered individually.[70] However, they are high

General mental ability (GMA)
An overall factor of intelligence, as suggested by the positive correlations among specific intellectual ability dimensions.

enough that researchers also recognize a general factor of intelligence, **general mental ability (GMA)**. Evidence supports the idea that the structures and measures of intellectual abilities can be generalized across cultures. Someone in Venezuela or Sudan, for instance, does not have a different set of mental abilities than an American or Czech individual. There is some evidence that IQ scores vary to some degree across cultures, but those differences become much smaller when we take into account educational and economic differences.[71]

THE WONDERLIC INTELLECTUAL ABILITY TEST   It might surprise you that the intelligence test most widely used in hiring decisions takes only 12 minutes to complete.

Dimension	Description	Job Example
Number aptitude	Ability to do speedy and accurate arithmetic.	Accountant: Computing the sales tax on a set of items.
Verbal comprehension	Ability to understand what is read or heard and the relationship of words to each other.	Plant manager: Following corporate policies on hiring.
Perceptual speed	Ability to identify visual similarities and differences quickly and accurately.	Fire investigator: Identifying clues to support a charge of arson.
Inductive reasoning	Ability to identify a logical sequence in a problem and then solve the problem.	Market researcher: Forecasting demand for a product in the next time period.
Deductive reasoning	Ability to use logic and assess the implications of an argument.	Supervisor: Choosing between two different suggestions offered by employees.
Spatial visualization	Ability to imagine how an object would look if its position in space were changed.	Interior decorator: Redecorating an office.
Memory	Ability to retain and recall past experiences.	Salesperson: Remembering the names of customers.

EXHIBIT 2-2
Dimensions of Intellectual Ability

It's the Wonderlic Cognitive Ability Test. There are different forms of the test, but each has 50 questions and the same general construct. Here are two questions to try:

- When rope is selling at $0.10 a foot, how many feet can you buy for $0.60?
- Assume the first two statements are true. Is the final one:
  1. True.
  2. False.
  3. Not certain.
     a. The boy plays baseball.
     b. All baseball players wear hats.
     c. The boy wears a hat.

The Wonderlic measures both speed (almost nobody has time to answer every question) and power (the questions get harder as you go along), so the average score is quite low—about 21 of 50. Because the Wonderlic is able to provide valid information cheaply (for $5 to $10 per applicant), many organizations use it in hiring decisions including Publix supermarkets, Manpower staffing systems, BP, and Dish satellite systems.[72] Most of these companies don't give up other hiring tools, such as application forms or interviews. Rather, they add the Wonderlic for its ability to provide valid data on applicants' intelligence levels.

INTELLECTUAL ABILITY AND JOB SATISFACTION   While intelligence is a big help in performing a job well, it doesn't make people happier or more satisfied with their jobs. Why not? Although intelligent people perform better and tend to have more interesting jobs, they are also more critical when evaluating their job conditions. Thus, smart people have it better, but they also expect more.[73]

Physical Abilities

Though the changing nature of work suggests intellectual abilities are increasingly important for many jobs, **physical abilities** have been and will remain valuable. Research on hundreds of jobs has identified nine basic abilities needed in the performance of physical tasks.[74] These are described in Exhibit 2-3. High employee performance is likely to be achieved when the extent to which a job requires each of the nine abilities matches the abilities of employees in that job.

Physical abilities
The capacity to do tasks that demand stamina, dexterity, strength, and similar characteristics.

Organizations are increasingly aware that an optimally productive workforce includes all types of people and does not automatically exclude anyone on the basis of broad categories of abilities. For example, a pilot program of software company SAP in Germany, India, and Ireland has found that employees with autism perform excellently in precision-oriented tasks like debugging software.[75] The potential benefits of diversity are enormous for forward-thinking managers. Of course, integrating diverse people into an optimally productive workforce takes skill. We discuss how to bring the talents of a diverse workforce together in the next section.

IMPLEMENTING DIVERSITY MANAGEMENT STRATEGIES

As we mentioned before, discrimination—for any reason—leads to increased turnover, which is detrimental to organizational performance. While a better representation of all racial groups in organizations remains a goal, an individual of minority status is much

EXHIBIT 2-3
Types of Physical Abilities

Strength Factors	
1. Dynamic strength	Ability to exert muscular force repeatedly or continuously over time.
2. Trunk strength	Ability to exert muscular strength using the trunk (particularly abdominal) muscles.
3. Static strength	Ability to exert force against external objects.
4. Explosive strength	Ability to expend a maximum of energy in one or a series of explosive acts.
Flexibility Factors	
5. Extent flexibility	Ability to move the trunk and back muscles as far as possible.
6. Dynamic flexibility	Ability to make rapid, repeated flexing movements.
Other Factors	
7. Body coordination	Ability to coordinate the simultaneous actions of different parts of the body.
8. Balance	Ability to maintain equilibrium despite forces pulling off balance.
9. Stamina	Ability to continue maximum effort requiring prolonged effort over time.

Positive diversity climate
In an organization, an environment of inclusiveness and an acceptance of diversity.

less likely to leave the organization if there is a feeling of inclusiveness, known as a **positive diversity climate**.[76] Although the reasons aren't completely understood, a positive climate for diversity can also lead to increased sales, suggesting there are organizational performance gains associated with reducing racial and ethnic discrimination.[77]

How do we move beyond the destructiveness of discrimination? The answer is in understanding one another's viewpoints. Evidence suggests that some people find interacting with other racial groups uncomfortable unless there are clear behavioral scripts to guide their behavior,[78] so creating diverse work groups focused on mutual goals could be helpful, along with developing a positive diversity climate.

We have discussed the facts surrounding stereotypes and discrimination, the effect of employee differences and how they influence important employment outcome variables, explained some of the laws countries use to curtail discrimination, explored some of the policies organizations employ to mandate inclusiveness, and suggested ways organizations can address certain specific employee conditions. We now look at how a manager can and should manage employee differences. Active **diversity management** makes everyone more aware of and sensitive to the needs and differences of others. This definition highlights the fact that diversity programs include and are meant for everyone, regardless of characteristics and in light of varying specific abilities. Diversity is much more likely to be successful when we see it as everyone's business than when we believe it helps only certain groups of employees.

Diversity management
The process and programs by which managers make everyone more aware of and sensitive to the needs and differences of others.

Attracting, Selecting, Developing, and Retaining Diverse Employees

One method of enhancing workforce diversity is to target recruitment messages to specific demographic groups that are underrepresented in the workforce. This means placing advertisements in publications geared toward those groups; pairing with colleges, universities, and other institutions with significant numbers of underrepresented minorities, such as what Microsoft is doing to encourage women to pursue technology studies;[79] and forming partnerships with associations like the Society of Women Engineers or the National Minority Supplier Development Council.

Research has shown that women and minorities have greater interest in employers that make special efforts to highlight a commitment to diversity in their recruiting materials. Diversity advertisements that fail to show women and minorities in positions of organizational leadership send a negative message about the diversity climate at an organization.[80] Of course, to show the pictures, organizations must actually have diversity in their management ranks.

Some companies have been actively working toward recruiting less-represented groups. Etsy, an online retailer, hosts engineering classes and provides grants for aspiring women coders, and then hires the best.[81] McKinsey & Co., Bain & Co., Boston Consulting Group, and Goldman Sachs have similarly been actively recruiting women who left the workforce to start families by offering phase-in programs and other benefits.[82]

The selection process is one of the most important places to apply diversity efforts. Hiring managers need to value fairness and objectivity in selecting employees and focus on the productive potential of new recruits. When managers use a well-defined protocol for assessing applicant talent and the organization clearly prioritizes nondiscrimination policies, qualifications become far more important factors than demographic characteristics in determining who gets hired.[83]

Individuals who are demographically different from their coworkers may be more likely to feel lower commitment and to leave, but a positive diversity climate can aid retention. Many diversity training programs are available to employers, and research efforts are focusing on identifying the most effective initiatives. It seems that the best programs are inclusive in both their design and implementation.[84] A positive diversity climate should be the goal since all workers appear to prefer an organization that values diversity.

Diversity in Groups

Most contemporary workplaces require extensive work in group settings. When people work in groups, they need to establish a common way of looking at and accomplishing the major tasks, and they need to communicate with one another often. If they feel little sense of membership and cohesion in their groups, all group attributes are likely to suffer.

In some cases, diversity in various traits can hurt team performance, whereas in other cases it can facilitate performance.[85] Whether diverse or homogeneous teams are more effective depends on the characteristic of interest. Demographic diversity (in gender, race, and ethnicity) does not appear to help or hurt team performance in general, although racial diversity in management groups may increase organizational performance in the right conditions.[86]

Teams of individuals who are highly intelligent, conscientious, and interested in working in team settings are more effective. Thus, diversity in these variables is likely to be a bad thing—it makes little sense to try to form teams that mix in members who are lower in intelligence or conscientiousness, or who are uninterested in teamwork. In other cases, diversity can be a strength. Groups of individuals with different types of expertise and education are more effective than homogeneous groups. Similarly, a group made entirely of assertive people who want to be in charge, or a group whose members all prefer to follow the lead of others, will be less effective than a group that mixes leaders and followers.

Regardless of the composition of the group, differences can be leveraged to achieve superior performance. The most important factor is to emphasize the similarities among members.[87] Managers who emphasize higher-order goals and values in their leadership style are more effective in managing diverse teams.[88]

Diversity Programs

Organizations use a variety of diversity programs in recruiting and selection policies, as well as in training and development practices. Effective, comprehensive workforce programs encouraging diversity have three distinct components. First, they teach managers about the legal framework for equal employment opportunity and encourage fair treatment of all people regardless of their demographic characteristics. Second, they teach managers how a diverse workforce will be better able to serve a diverse market of customers and clients. Third, they foster personal development practices that bring out the skills and abilities of all workers, acknowledging how differences in perspective can be a valuable way to improve performance for everyone.[89]

Most negative reactions to employment discrimination are based on the idea that discriminatory treatment is unfair. Regardless of race or gender, people are generally in favor of diversity-oriented programs, including affirmative action programs (AAP), to increase the representation of minority groups and ensure everyone a fair opportunity to show their skills and abilities.

Organizational leaders should examine their workforces to determine whether target groups have been underutilized. If groups of employees are not proportionally represented in top management, managers should look for any hidden barriers to advancement. Managers can often improve recruiting practices, make selection systems more transparent, and provide training for those employees who have not had adequate exposure to diversity material in the past. The organization should also clearly communicate its policies to employees so they can understand how and why certain practices are followed. Communications should focus as much as possible on qualifications and job performance; emphasizing certain groups as needing more assistance could backfire.

 Finally, research indicates a tailored approach will be needed for international organizations. For instance, a case study of the multinational Finnish company TRANSCO found it was possible to develop a consistent global philosophy for diversity management. However, differences in legal and cultural factors across nations forced the company to develop unique policies to match the cultural and legal frameworks of each country in which it operated.[90]

SUMMARY

This chapter looked at diversity from many perspectives. We paid particular attention to three variables—biographical characteristics, abilities, and diversity programs. Diversity management must be an ongoing commitment that crosses all levels of the organization. Policies to improve the climate for diversity can be effective, and diversity management can be learned.

IMPLICATIONS FOR MANAGERS

- Understand your organization's antidiscrimination policies thoroughly and share them with all employees.
- Assess and challenge your stereotype beliefs to increase your objectivity.
- Look beyond readily observable biographical characteristics and consider the individual's capabilities before making management decisions; remain open and encouraging for individuals to disclose any hidden disabilities.
- Fully evaluate what accommodations a person with disabilities will need and then fine-tune the job to that person's abilities.
- Seek to understand and respect the unique biographical characteristics of each individual; a fair but individualistic approach yields the best performance.

⭐ TRY IT!

If your professor has assigned this, go to the Assignments section of **mymanagementlab .com** to complete the **Simulation: Human Resources**.

⭐ PERSONAL INVENTORY ASSESSMENTS

Ⓟ Ⓘ Ⓐ
PERSONAL INVENTORY ASSESSMENTS

Intercultural Sensitivity Scale

Are you aware of intercultural dynamics? Take this PIA to assess your intercultural sensitivity.

2-1. What is the most diverse group you have worked in? List all the ways in which this group was diverse.

3

Attitudes and Job Satisfaction

LEARNING OBJECTIVES

After studying this chapter, you should be able to:

1. Contrast the three components of an attitude.
2. Summarize the relationship between attitudes and behavior.
3. Compare the major job attitudes.
4. Identify the two approaches for measuring job satisfaction.
5. Summarize the main causes of job satisfaction.
6. Identify three outcomes of job satisfaction.
7. Identify four employee responses to job dissatisfaction.

⭐ **Chapter Warm-up**

If your professor has chosen to assign this, go to the Assignments section of **mymanagementlab.com** to complete the chapter warm-up.

ATTITUDES

Attitudes

Evaluative statements or judgments concerning objects, people, or events.

Attitudes are evaluative statements—either favorable or unfavorable—about objects, people, or events. They reflect how we feel about something. When you say "I like my job," you are expressing your attitude about your work.

Attitudes are complex. If you ask people about their attitudes toward religion, Lady Gaga, or an organization, you may get simple responses, but the underlying reasons are probably complicated. To fully understand attitudes, we must consider their fundamental properties or components.

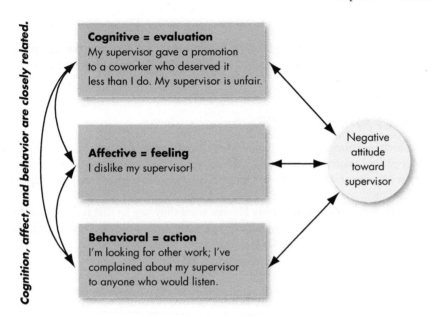

EXHIBIT 3-1
**The Components
of an Attitude**

Typically, researchers assume attitudes have three components: cognition, affect, and behavior.[1] The statement "My pay is low" is a **cognitive component** of an attitude—a description of or belief in the way things are. It sets the stage for the more critical part of an attitude—its **affective component**. Affect is the emotional or feeling segment of an attitude reflected in the statement "I am angry over how little I'm paid." Affect can lead to behavioral outcomes. The **behavioral component** of an attitude describes an intention to behave a certain way toward someone or something—as in, "I'm going to look for another job that pays better."

Viewing attitudes as having three components—cognition, affect, and behavior—helps us understand their complexity and the potential relationship between attitudes and behavior. For example, imagine you just realized that someone treated you unfairly. Aren't you likely to have feelings about this, occurring virtually instantaneously along with the realization? Thus, cognition and affect are intertwined.

Exhibit 3-1 illustrates how the three components of an attitude are related. In this example, an employee didn't get a promotion he thought he deserved. His attitude toward his supervisor is illustrated as follows: The employee thought he deserved the promotion (cognition); he strongly dislikes his supervisor (affect); and he has complained and taken action (behavior). Although we often think cognition causes affect, which then causes behavior, in reality these components are difficult to separate.

In organizations, attitudes are important for their behavioral component. If workers believe, for example, that managers, auditors, and engineers are in a conspiracy to make employees work harder for less money, we should try to understand how this attitude formed, how it impacts job behavior, and how it might be changed.

Cognitive component
The opinion or belief segment of an attitude.

Affective component
The emotional or feeling segment of an attitude.

Behavioral component
An intention to behave in a certain way toward someone or something.

✪ WATCH IT

If your professor has assigned this, go to the Assignments section of **mymanagementlab .com** to complete the video exercise titled **Gawker Media: Attitudes and Job Satisfaction**.

ATTITUDES AND BEHAVIOR

Early research on attitudes assumed they were causally related to behavior—that is, the attitudes people hold determine what they do. However, one researcher—Leon Festinger—argued that attitudes *follow* behavior. Other researchers have agreed that attitudes predict future behavior.[2]

Did you ever notice how people change what they say so that it doesn't contradict what they do? Perhaps a friend of yours consistently argued that her apartment complex was better than yours until another friend in your complex asked her to move in with him; once she moved to your complex, you noticed her attitude toward her former apartment became more critical. Cases of attitude following behavior illustrate the effects of **cognitive dissonance**,[3] contradictions individuals might perceive between their attitudes and their behavior.

Cognitive dissonance
Any incompatibility between two or more attitudes or between behavior and attitudes.

People seek consistency among their attitudes, and between their attitudes and their behavior.[4] Any form of inconsistency is uncomfortable, and individuals will therefore attempt to reduce it. People seek a stable state, which is a minimum of dissonance. When there is dissonance, people will alter either the attitudes or the behavior, or they will develop a rationalization for the discrepancy. Recent research found, for instance, that the attitudes of employees who experienced emotionally challenging work events improved after they talked about their experiences with coworkers. Social sharing helped these employees adjust their attitudes to behavioral expectations.[5]

No individual can avoid dissonance. You know texting while walking is unsafe, but you do it anyway and hope nothing bad happens. Or you give someone advice you have trouble following yourself. The desire to reduce dissonance depends on three factors, including the *importance* of the elements creating dissonance and the degree of *influence* we believe we have over those elements. The third factor is the *rewards* of dissonance; high rewards accompanying high dissonance tend to reduce tension inherent in the dissonance (dissonance is less distressing if accompanied by something good, such as a higher pay raise than expected). Individuals are more motivated to reduce dissonance when the attitudes are important or when they believe the dissonance is due to something they can control.

The most powerful moderators of the attitudes relationship are the *importance* of the attitude, its *correspondence to behavior*, its *accessibility*, the presence of *social pressures*, and whether a person has *direct experience* with the attitude.[6] Important attitudes reflect our fundamental values, self-interest, or identification with individuals or groups we value. These attitudes tend to show a strong relationship to our behavior. However, discrepancies between attitudes and behaviors tend to occur when social pressures to behave in certain ways hold exceptional power, as in most organizations. You're more likely to remember attitudes you frequently express, and attitudes that our memories can easily access are more likely to predict our behavior. The attitude–behavior relationship is also likely to be much stronger if an attitude refers to something with which we have direct personal experience.

JOB ATTITUDES

We have thousands of attitudes, but OB focuses on a very limited number that form positive or negative evaluations employees hold about their work environments. Much of the research has looked at three attitudes: job satisfaction, job involvement, and organizational commitment.[7] Other important attitudes include perceived organizational support and employee engagement.

Job Satisfaction and Job Involvement

When people speak of employee attitudes, they usually mean **job satisfaction**, a positive feeling about a job resulting from an evaluation of its characteristics. A person with high job satisfaction holds positive feelings about the work, while a person with low satisfaction holds negative feelings. Because OB researchers give job satisfaction high importance, we review this attitude in detail later.

Related to job satisfaction is **job involvement**, the degree to which people identify psychologically with their jobs and consider their perceived performance levels important to their self-worth.[8] Employees with high job involvement strongly identify with and really care about the kind of work they do. Another closely related concept is **psychological empowerment**—employees' beliefs regarding the degree to which they influence their work environment, their competencies, the meaningfulness of their job, and their perceived autonomy.[9]

Research suggests that empowerment initiatives need to be tailored to desired behavioral outcomes. Research in Singapore found that good leaders empower their employees by fostering their self-perception of competence—through involving them in decisions, making them feel their work is important, and giving them discretion to "do their own thing."[10]

Organizational Commitment

An employee with **organizational commitment** identifies with a particular organization and its goals and wishes to remain a member. Emotional attachment to an organization and belief in its values is the "gold standard" for employee commitment.[11]

Employees who are committed will be less likely to engage in work withdrawal even if they are dissatisfied because they have a sense of organizational loyalty or attachment.[12] Even if employees are not currently happy with their work, they are willing to make sacrifices for the organization if they are committed enough.

Perceived Organizational Support

Perceived organizational support (POS) is the degree to which employees believe the organization values their contributions and cares about their well-being. An excellent example is Research and Development (R&D) engineer John Greene, whose POS is sky-high because when he was diagnosed with leukemia, CEO Marc Benioff and 350 fellow Salesforce.com employees covered all his medical expenses and stayed in touch with him throughout his recovery. No doubt stories like this are part of the reason Salesforce.com was the eighth of *Fortune*'s 100 Best Companies to Work For in 2015.[13]

People perceive their organizations as supportive when rewards are deemed fair, when employees have a voice in decisions, and when they see their supervisors as supportive.[14]

Job satisfaction
A positive feeling about one's job resulting from an evaluation of its characteristics.

Job involvement
The degree to which a person identifies with a job, actively participates in it, and considers performance important to their self-worth.

Psychological empowerment
Employees' belief in the degree to which they affect their work environment, their competence, the meaningfulness of their job, and their perceived autonomy in their work.

Organizational commitment
The degree to which an employee identifies with a particular organization and its goals and wishes to maintain membership in the organization.

Perceived organizational support (POS)
The degree to which employees believe an organization values their contribution and cares about their well-being.

Power distance
A national culture attribute that describes the extent to which a society accepts that power in institutions and organizations is distributed unequally.

Employee engagement
An individual's involvement with, satisfaction with, and enthusiasm for the work he or she does.

POS is a predictor of employment outcomes, but there are some cultural influences. POS is important in countries where the **power distance**—the degree to which people in a country accept that power in institutions and organizations is distributed unequally—is lower. In low power-distance countries like the United States, people are more likely to view work as an exchange than as a moral obligation, so employees look for reasons to feel supported by their organizations. In high power-distance countries like China, employee POS perceptions are not as deeply based on employer demonstrations of fairness, support, and encouragement. The difference is in the level of expectation by employees.

Employee Engagement

Employee engagement is an individual's involvement with, satisfaction with, and enthusiasm for the work he or she does. To evaluate engagement, we might ask employees whether they have access to resources and opportunities to learn new skills, whether they feel their work is important and meaningful, and whether interactions with coworkers and supervisors are rewarding.[15] Highly engaged employees have a passion for their work and feel a deep connection to their companies; disengaged employees have essentially checked out, putting time but not energy or attention into their work. Engagement becomes a real concern for most organizations because so few employees—between 17 percent and 29 percent, surveys indicate—are highly engaged by their work. Employee engagement is related to job engagement, which we discuss in detail in Chapter 7.

Engagement levels determine many measurable outcomes. Promising research findings have earned employee engagement a following in many business organizations and management consulting firms. However, the concept generates active debate about its usefulness, partly because of the difficulty of identifying what creates engagement. The two top reasons for engagement that participants gave in a recent study were: (1) having a good manager they enjoy working for; and (2) feeling appreciated by their supervisor. However, most of their other reasons didn't relate to the engagement construct.[16] Another study in Australia found that emotional intelligence was linked to employee engagement.[17] Other research suggested that engagement fluctuates partially due to daily challenges and demands.[18]

There is some distinctiveness among attitudes, but they overlap greatly for various reasons, including the employee's personality. Altogether, if you know someone's level of job satisfaction, you know most of what you need to know about how that person sees the organization. Let's next dissect the concept more carefully. How do we measure job satisfaction? How satisfied are employees with their jobs?

MEASURING JOB SATISFACTION

Our definition of job satisfaction—a positive feeling about a job resulting from an evaluation of its characteristics—is broad. Yet that breadth is appropriate. A job is more than just shuffling papers, writing programming code, waiting on customers, or driving a truck. Jobs require interacting with coworkers and bosses, following organizational rules and policies, determining the power structure, meeting performance standards, living with less-than-ideal working conditions, adapting to new technologies, and so forth. An employee's assessment of satisfaction with the job is thus a complex summation of many discrete elements. How, then, do we measure it?

Approaches to Measurement

Two approaches are popular. The single global rating is a response to one question, such as "All things considered, how satisfied are you with your job?" Respondents circle a number between 1 and 5 on a scale from "highly satisfied" to "highly dissatisfied." The second method, the summation of job facets, is more sophisticated. It identifies key elements in a job, such as the type of work, skills needed, supervision, present pay, promotion opportunities, culture, and relationships with coworkers. Respondents rate these on a standardized scale, and researchers add the ratings to create an overall job satisfaction score.

Is one of these approaches superior? Intuitively, summing up responses to a number of job factors seems likely to achieve a more accurate evaluation of job satisfaction. Research, however, doesn't support the intuition.[19] This is one of those rare instances in which simplicity seems to work as well as complexity, making one method essentially as valid as the other. Both methods can be helpful. The single global rating method isn't very time consuming, while the summation of job facets helps managers zero in on problems and deal with them faster and more accurately.

Measured Job Satisfaction Levels

Are most people satisfied with their jobs? Generally, yes, to the tune of 49–69 percent of employees worldwide.[20] Job satisfaction levels can remain quite consistent over time. For instance, average job satisfaction levels in the United States were consistently high from 1972 to 2006.[21] However, economic conditions tend to influence job satisfaction rates. In late 2007, the economic contraction precipitated a drop-off in job satisfaction; the lowest point was in 2010, when only 42.6 percent of U.S. workers reported satisfaction with their jobs.[22] Thankfully, the job satisfaction rate increased to 47.7 percent in 2014,[23] but the level was still far off the 1987 level of 61.1 percent.[24] Job satisfaction rates tend to vary in different cultures worldwide, and of course there are always competing measurements that offer alternative viewpoints.

The facets of job satisfaction levels can vary widely. As shown in Exhibit 3-2, people have typically been more satisfied with their jobs overall, the work itself, and their supervisors and coworkers than they have been with their pay and promotion opportunities.

Regarding cultural differences in job satisfaction, Exhibit 3-3 provides the results of a global study of job satisfaction levels of workers in 15 countries, with the highest levels in Mexico and Switzerland. Do employees in these cultures have better jobs? Or are they simply more positive (and less self-critical)? Conversely, the lowest levels in the study were from South Korea. Autonomy is low in South Korean culture, and businesses tend to be rigidly hierarchical in structure. Does this make for lower job satisfaction?[25] It is difficult to discern all the factors influencing the scores, but exploring how businesses are responding to changes brought on by globalization may give us clues.

WHAT CAUSES JOB SATISFACTION?

Think about the best job you've ever had. What made it the best? The reasons can differ greatly. Let's consider some characteristics that likely influence job satisfaction, starting with job conditions.

EXHIBIT 3-2
Average Job Satisfaction Levels by Facet

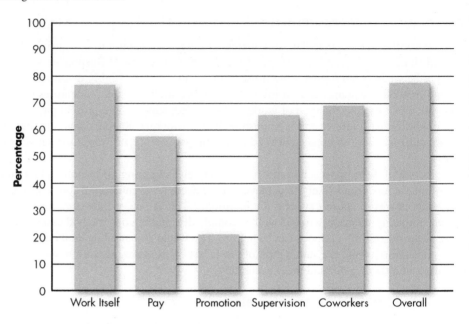

EXHIBIT 3-3
Average Levels of Employee Job Satisfaction by Country

Source: J. H. Westover, "The Impact of Comparative State-Directed Development on Working Conditions and Employee Satisfaction," *Journal of Management & Organization* 19, no. 4 (2012), 537–554.

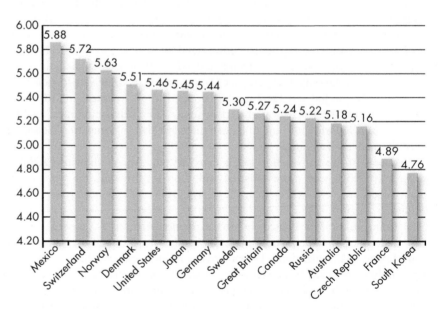

Job Conditions

Generally, interesting jobs that provide training, variety, independence, and control satisfy most employees. Interdependence, feedback, social support, and interaction with coworkers outside the workplace are also strongly related to job satisfaction, even after accounting for characteristics of the work itself.[26] As you may have guessed, managers also play a big role in employees' job satisfaction. Employees who feel empowered by their leaders experience higher job satisfaction, according to one study of a large Hong Kong telecommunications corporation.[27] Research in Israel further suggested that a manager's attentiveness, responsiveness, and support increase the employee's job satisfaction.[28]

Thus, job conditions—especially the intrinsic nature of the work itself, social interactions, and supervision—are important predictors of job satisfaction. Although each is important, and although their relative value will vary across employees, the intrinsic nature of the work is most important.[29] In other words, you have to like *what* you do.

Personality

As important as job conditions are to job satisfaction, personality also plays an important role. People who have positive **core self-evaluations** (**CSEs**; see Chapter 5 for further discussion)—who believe in their inner worth and basic competence—are more satisfied with their jobs than people with negative CSEs. Additionally, in the context of commitment to one's career, CSE influences job satisfaction. People with high levels of both CSE and career commitment may realize particularly high job satisfaction.[30]

Core self-evaluation (CSE)
Believing in one's inner worth and basic competence.

Pay

You've probably noticed that pay comes up often when people discuss job satisfaction. Pay does correlate with job satisfaction and overall happiness for many people, but the effect can be smaller once an individual reaches a standard level of comfortable living. As a corollary, money does *motivate* people, as we discover in Chapter 8. But what motivates us is not necessarily the same as what makes us happy.

Corporate Social Responsibility (CSR)

Would you be as happy to work for an organization with a stated social welfare mission as you would for an organization without one? An organization's commitment to **corporate social responsibility** (**CSR**), or its self-regulated actions to benefit society or the environment beyond what is required by law, increasingly affects employee job satisfaction. Organizations practice CSR through environmental sustainability initiatives, nonprofit work, charitable giving, and other globally attuned philanthropy.

Corporate social responsibility (CSR)
An organization's self-regulated actions to benefit society or the environment beyond what is required by law.

CSR is good for the planet and good for people. Employees whose personal values fit with the organization's CSR mission are often more satisfied. In fact, of 59 large and small organizations recently surveyed, 86 percent reported they have happier employees as a result of their CSR programs.[31]

The relationship between CSR and job satisfaction is particularly strong for millennials. "The next generation of employees is seeking out employers that are focused on the triple bottom line: people, planet, and revenue," said Susan Cooney, founder of philanthropy firm Givelocity.[32] CSR allows workers to serve a higher purpose or contribute to a mission. According to researcher Amy Wrzesniewski, people who view their work as part of a higher purpose often realize higher job satisfaction.[33] However, an organization's CSR efforts must be well governed and its initiatives must be sustainable for long-term job satisfaction benefits.[34]

Although the link between CSR and job satisfaction is strengthening, not all employees find value in CSR.[35] However, when managed well it can also significantly contribute to increased employee job satisfaction. Therefore, organizations need to address a few issues in order to be most effective. First, not all projects are equally meaningful for every person's job satisfaction, yet participation for all employees is sometimes expected. Second, some organizations require employees to contribute in a prescribed manner. Pressuring people to go "above and beyond" in ways that are not natural for them can burn them out for future CSR projects[36] and lower their job satisfaction, particularly when CSR projects provide direct benefits to the organization (such as positive press coverage).[37] People want CSR to be genuine and authentic.

Lastly, CSR measures can seem disconnected from the employee's actual work,[38] providing no increase to job satisfaction. In sum, CSR is a needed, positive trend of accountability and serving.

OUTCOMES OF JOB SATISFACTION

Having discussed some of the causes of job satisfaction, we now turn to some specific outcomes.

Job Performance

As a general rule, happy workers are more likely to be productive workers. Some researchers used to believe the relationship between job satisfaction and job performance was a myth, but a review of 300 studies suggested the correlation is quite robust.[39] Individuals with higher job satisfaction perform better, and organizations with more satisfied employees tend to be more effective than those with fewer.

Organizational Citizenship Behavior (OCB)

It seems logical that job satisfaction should be a major determinant of an employee's organizational citizenship behavior (known as OCB or citizenship behavior, see Chapter 1).[40] OCBs include people talking positively about their organizations, helping others, and going beyond the normal expectations of their jobs. Evidence suggests job satisfaction *is* moderately correlated with OCB; people who are more satisfied with their jobs are more likely to engage in citizenship behavior.[41]

Why does job satisfaction lead to OCB? One reason is trust. Research in 18 countries suggests that managers reciprocate employees' OCBs with trusting behaviors of their own.[42] Individuals who feel their coworkers support them are also more likely to engage in helpful behaviors than those who have antagonistic coworker relationships.[43] Personality matters, too. Individuals with certain personality traits (agreeableness and conscientiousness, for example; see Chapter 5) are more satisfied with their work, which in turn leads them to engage in more OCB.[44] Finally, individuals who receive positive feedback on their OCBs from their peers are more likely to continue their citizenship activities.[45]

Customer Satisfaction

Because service organization managers should be concerned with pleasing customers, it's reasonable to ask whether employee satisfaction is related to positive customer outcomes. For frontline employees who have regular customer contact, the answer is "yes." Satisfied employees appear to increase customer satisfaction and loyalty.[46]

A number of companies are acting on this evidence. Online shoe retailer Zappos is so committed to finding customer service employees who are satisfied with the job that it offers a $2,000 bribe to quit the company after training, figuring the least satisfied will take the cash and go.[47] Zappos employees are empowered to "create fun and a little weirdness" to ensure that customers are satisfied, and it works: of the company's more than 24 million customers, 75 percent are repeat buyers. For Zappos, employee satisfaction has a direct effect on customer satisfaction.

Life Satisfaction

Until now, we've treated job satisfaction as if it were separate from life satisfaction, but they may be more related than you think.[48] Research in Europe indicates that job satisfaction is positively correlated with life satisfaction, and our attitudes and experiences in life spill over into our job approaches and experiences.[49] Furthermore, life satisfaction decreases when people become unemployed, according to research in Germany, and not just because of the loss of income.[50] For most individuals, work is an important part of life, and therefore it makes sense that our overall happiness depends in no small part on our happiness in our work (our job satisfaction).

THE IMPACT OF JOB DISSATISFACTION

What happens when employees dislike their jobs? One theoretical model—the exit–voice–loyalty–neglect framework—is helpful for understanding the consequences of dissatisfaction. The framework's four responses differ along two dimensions: constructive/destructive and active/passive. The responses are as follows:[51]

- **Exit.** The **exit response** directs behavior toward leaving the organization, including looking for a new position or resigning. To measure the effects of this response to dissatisfaction, researchers study individual terminations and *collective turnover*—the total loss to the organization of employee knowledge, skills, abilities, and other characteristics.[52]
- **Voice.** The **voice response** includes actively and constructively attempting to improve conditions, including suggesting improvements, discussing problems with superiors, and undertaking union activity.
- **Loyalty.** The **loyalty response** means passively but optimistically waiting for conditions to improve, including speaking up for the organization in the face of external criticism and trusting the organization and its management to "do the right thing."
- **Neglect.** The **neglect response** passively allows conditions to worsen and includes chronic absenteeism or lateness, reduced effort, and an increased error rate.

Exit and neglect behaviors are linked to performance variables such as productivity, absenteeism, and turnover. But this model expands employee responses to include voice and loyalty—constructive behaviors that allow individuals to tolerate unpleasant situations or improve working conditions. As helpful as this framework is, it's quite general. We next address behavioral responses to job dissatisfaction.

Exit
Dissatisfaction expressed through behavior directed toward leaving the organization.

Voice
Dissatisfaction expressed through active and constructive attempts to improve conditions.

Loyalty
Dissatisfaction expressed by passively waiting for conditions to improve.

Neglect
Dissatisfaction expressed through allowing conditions to worsen.

Counterproductive Work Behavior (CWB)

Substance abuse, stealing at work, undue socializing, gossiping, absenteeism, and tardiness are examples of behaviors that are destructive to organizations. They are indicators

Counterproductive work behavior (CWB)
Intentional employee behavior that is contrary to the interests of the organization.

of a broader syndrome called **counterproductive work behavior** (**CWB**; related terms are deviant behavior in the workplace, or simply withdrawal behavior; see Chapter 1).[53] Like other behaviors we have discussed, CWB doesn't just happen—the behaviors often follow negative and sometimes long-standing attitudes. Therefore, if we can identify the predictors of CWB, we may lessen the probability of its effects.

Generally, job dissatisfaction predicts CWB. People who are not satisfied with their work become frustrated, which lowers their performance[54] and makes them more likely to commit CWB.[55] Other research suggests that, in addition to vocational misfit (being in the wrong line of work), lack of fit with the organization (working in the wrong kind of organizational culture; see person–organization fit, Chapter 5) predicts CWB.[56] Our immediate social environment also matters. One German study suggests that we are influenced toward CWB by the norms of our immediate work environment, such that individuals in teams with high absenteeism are more likely to be absent themselves.[57] CWB can, furthermore, be a response to abusive supervision from managers, which then spurs further abuse, starting a vicious cycle.[58]

One important point about CWB is that dissatisfied employees often choose one or more specific behaviors due to idiosyncratic factors. One worker might quit. Another might use work time to surf the Internet or take work supplies home for personal use. In short, workers who don't like their jobs "get even" in various ways. Because those ways can be quite creative, controlling only one behavior with policies and punishments leaves the root cause untouched. Employers should seek to correct the source of the problem—the dissatisfaction—rather than try to control the different responses.

According to U.K. research, sometimes CWB is an emotional reaction to perceived unfairness, a way to try to restore an employee's sense of equity exchange.[59] It therefore has complex ethical implications. For example, is someone who takes a box of markers home from the office for his children acting unethically? Some people consider this stealing. Others may want to look at moderating factors such as the employee's contribution to the organization before they decide. Does the person generously give extra time and effort to the organization, with little thanks or compensation? If so, they might see CWB behavior as part of an attempt to "even the score."

As a manager, you can take steps to mitigate CWB. You can poll employee attitudes, for instance, and identify areas for workplace improvement. If there is no vocational fit, the employee will not be fulfilled,[60] so you can try to screen for that to avoid a mismatch. Tailoring tasks to a person's abilities and values should increase job satisfaction and reduce CWB.[61] Furthermore, creating strong teams, integrating supervisors with them, providing formalized team policies, and introducing team-based incentives may help lower the CWB "contagion" that lowers the standards of the group.[62]

ABSENTEEISM   We find a consistent negative relationship between satisfaction and absenteeism, but the relationship is moderate to weak.[63] Generally, when numerous alternative jobs are available, dissatisfied employees have high absence rates, but when there are few alternatives, dissatisfied employees have the same (low) rate of absence as satisfied employees.[64] Organizations that provide liberal sick leave benefits are encouraging all their employees—including those who are highly satisfied—to take days off. You may find work satisfying yet still want to enjoy a three-day weekend if those days come free with no penalties.

TURNOVER The relationship between job satisfaction and turnover is stronger than between satisfaction and absenteeism.[65] Overall, a pattern of lowered job satisfaction is the best predictor of intent to leave. Turnover has a workplace environment connection too. If the climate within an employee's immediate workplace is one of low job satisfaction leading to turnover, there will be a contagion effect. This suggests managers should consider the job satisfaction (and turnover) patterns of coworkers when assigning workers to a new area.[66] Employees' **job embeddedness**—connections to the job and community that result in an increased commitment to the organization—can be closely linked to their job satisfaction and the probability of turnover such that where job embeddedness is high, the probability of turnover decreases, particularly in collectivist (group-centered; see Chapter 4) cultures where membership in an organization is of high personal value. Job embeddedness also negatively predicts important employment outcomes of OCB, CWB, and absenteeism, and positively predicts job performance.[67] Embedded employees thus seem more satisfied with their jobs and are less likely to want to consider alternative job prospects.

Job embeddedness The extent to which an employee's connections to the job and community result in an increased commitment to the organization.

Lastly, the satisfaction–turnover relationship is affected by alternative job prospects. If an employee accepts an unsolicited job offer, job dissatisfaction was less predictive of turnover because the employee more likely left in response to "pull" (the lure of the other job) than "push" (the unattractiveness of the current job). Similarly, job dissatisfaction is more likely to translate into turnover when other employment opportunities are plentiful. Furthermore, when employees have high "human capital" (high education, high ability), job dissatisfaction is more likely to translate into turnover because they have, or perceive, many available alternatives.[68]

Understanding the Impact

Given the evidence we've just reviewed, it should come as no surprise that job satisfaction can affect the bottom line. One study by a management consulting firm separated large organizations into those with high morale (more than 70 percent of employees expressed overall job satisfaction) and medium or low morale (fewer than 70 percent). The stock prices of companies in the high-morale group grew 19.4 percent, compared with 10 percent for the medium- or low-morale group. Despite these results, many managers are unconcerned about employee job satisfaction. Others overestimate how satisfied employees are, so they don't think there's a problem when there is one. For example, in one study of 262 large employers, 86 percent of senior managers believed their organizations treated employees well, but only 55 percent of employees agreed; another study found 55 percent of managers, compared to only 38 percent of employees, thought morale was good in their organization.[69]

Regular surveys can reduce gaps between what managers *think* employees feel and what they *really* feel. A gap in understanding can affect the bottom line in small franchise sites as well as in large companies. As manager of a KFC restaurant in Houston, Jonathan McDaniel surveyed his employees every three months. Results led him to make changes, such as giving employees greater say about which workdays they had off. McDaniel believed the process itself was valuable. "They really love giving their opinions," he said. "That's the most important part of it—that they have a voice and that they're heard." Surveys are no panacea, but if job attitudes are as important as we believe, organizations need to use every reasonable method find out how they can be improved.[70]

SUMMARY

Managers should be interested in their employees' attitudes because attitudes influence behavior and indicate potential problems. Creating a satisfied workforce is hardly a guarantee of successful organizational performance, but evidence strongly suggests managers' efforts to improve employee attitudes will likely result in positive outcomes, including greater organizational effectiveness, higher customer satisfaction, and increased profits.

IMPLICATIONS FOR MANAGERS

- Of the major job attitudes—job satisfaction, job involvement, organizational commitment, perceived organizational support (POS), and employee engagement—remember that an employee's job satisfaction level is the best single predictor of behavior.
- Pay attention to your employees' job satisfaction levels as determinants of their performance, turnover, absenteeism, and withdrawal behaviors.
- Measure employee job attitudes objectively and at regular intervals in order to determine how employees are reacting to their work.
- To raise employee satisfaction, evaluate the fit between the employee's work interests and the intrinsic parts of the job; then create work that is challenging and interesting to the individual.
- Consider the fact that high pay alone is unlikely to create a satisfying work environment.

⭐ TRY IT!

If your professor has assigned this, go to the Assignments section of **mymanagementlab.com** to complete the **Simulation: Attitudes & Job Satisfaction**.

⭐ PERSONAL INVENTORY ASSESSMENTS

Core Self-Evaluation (CSE) Scale

You probably have a general awareness of your CSE, or how you candidly view your capabilities. This PIA can provide you with further insight.

3-1. Based on your own experiences, can you identify situations in which your job attitudes directly influenced your behavior?

4

Emotions and Moods

MyManagementLab®
⭐ Improve Your Grade!
When you see this icon ⭐, visit **mymanagementlab.com** for activities that are applied, personalized, and offer immediate feedback.

LEARNING OBJECTIVES

After studying this chapter, you should be able to:

1. Differentiate between emotions and moods.
2. Identify the sources of emotions and moods.
3. Show the impact emotional labor has on employees.
4. Describe affective events theory.
5. Describe emotional intelligence.
6. Identify strategies for emotion regulation.
7. Apply concepts about emotions and moods to specific OB issues.

⭐ Chapter Warm-up
If your professor has chosen to assign this, go to the Assignments section of **mymanagementlab.com** to complete the chapter warm-up.

WHAT ARE EMOTIONS AND MOODS?

In our analysis of the role of emotions and moods in the workplace, we need three terms that are closely intertwined: *affect*, *emotions*, and *moods*. **Affect** is a generic term that covers a broad range of feelings, including both emotions and moods.[1] **Emotions** are intense feelings directed at someone or something.[2] **Moods** are less intense feelings than emotions and often arise without a specific event acting as a stimulus.[3] Exhibit 4-1 shows the relationships among affect, emotions, and moods.

First, as the exhibit shows, *affect* is a broad term that encompasses emotions and moods. Second, there are differences between emotions and moods. Emotions are more

Affect
A broad range of feelings that people experience.

Emotions
Intense feelings that are directed at someone or something.

Moods
Feelings that tend to be less intense than emotions and that lack a contextual stimulus.

EXHIBIT 4-1
Affect, Emotions, and Moods

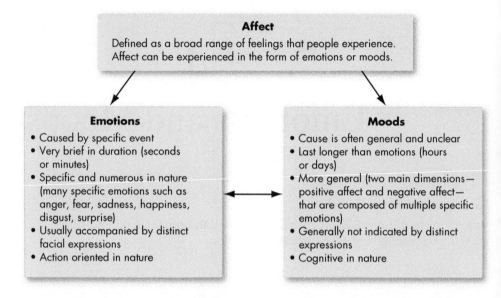

Affect
Defined as a broad range of feelings that people experience. Affect can be experienced in the form of emotions or moods.

Emotions
- Caused by specific event
- Very brief in duration (seconds or minutes)
- Specific and numerous in nature (many specific emotions such as anger, fear, sadness, happiness, disgust, surprise)
- Usually accompanied by distinct facial expressions
- Action oriented in nature

Moods
- Cause is often general and unclear
- Last longer than emotions (hours or days)
- More general (two main dimensions—positive affect and negative affect—that are composed of multiple specific emotions)
- Generally not indicated by distinct expressions
- Cognitive in nature

likely to be caused by a specific event and are more fleeting than moods. Also, some researchers speculate that emotions may be more action-oriented—they may lead us to some immediate action—while moods may be more cognitive, meaning they may cause us to think or brood for a while.[4]

Affect, emotions, and moods are separable in theory; in practice, the distinction isn't always defined. When we review the OB topics on emotions and moods, you may see more information about emotions in one area and more about moods in another. This is simply the state of the research. Let's start with a review of the basic emotions.

The Basic Emotions

How many emotions are there? There are dozens, including anger, contempt, enthusiasm, envy, fear, frustration, disappointment, embarrassment, disgust, happiness, hate, hope, jealousy, joy, love, pride, surprise, and sadness. Numerous researchers have tried to limit them to a fundamental set.[5] Other scholars argue that it makes no sense to think in terms of "basic" emotions, because even emotions we rarely experience, such as shock, can have a powerful effect on us.[6] It's unlikely psychologists or philosophers will ever completely agree on a set of basic emotions, or even on whether there is such a thing. Still, many researchers agree on six universal emotions—anger, fear, sadness, happiness, disgust, and surprise. We sometimes mistake happiness for surprise, but rarely do we confuse happiness and disgust.

Psychologists have tried to identify basic emotions by studying how we express them. Of our myriad ways of expressing emotions, facial expressions have proved one of the most difficult to interpret.[7] One problem is that some emotions are too complex to be easily represented on our faces. Second, people may not interpret emotions from vocalizations (such as sighs or screams) the same way across cultures. One study found that while vocalizations conveyed meaning in all cultures, the specific emotions people perceived varied. For example, Himba participants (from northwestern Namibia) did not agree with Western participants that crying meant sadness or a growl meant anger.[8] Lastly, cultures have norms that govern emotional expression, so the way we *experience* an emotion isn't always the same as the way we *show* it. For example, people in the Middle East and the United States recognize a smile as indicating happiness, but in the Middle East, a smile is also often interpreted as a sign of sexual attraction, so women have learned not to smile at men.

Cultural differences regarding emotions can be apparent between countries that are individualistic and collectivistic—broad terms that describe the general outlook of people in a society. **Individualistic** countries are those in which people see themselves as independent and desire personal goals and personal control. Individualistic values are present in North America and Western Europe, for example. **Collectivistic** countries are those in which people see themselves as interdependent and seek community and group goals. Collectivistic values are found in Asia, Africa, and South America, for example.[9] For this application, we find that in collectivist countries, people are more likely to believe another's emotional displays are connected to their personal relationship, while people in individualistic cultures don't think others' emotional expressions are directed at them.

Moral Emotions

Researchers have been studying what are called **moral emotions**; that is, emotions that have moral implications because of our instant judgment of the situation that evokes them. Examples of moral emotions include sympathy for the suffering of others, guilt about our own immoral behavior, anger about injustice done to others, and contempt for those who behave unethically.

Another example is the disgust we feel about violations of moral norms, called *moral disgust*. Moral disgust is different from disgust. Say you stepped in cow dung by mistake—you might feel disgusted by it, but not moral disgust—you probably wouldn't make a moral judgment. In contrast, say you watched a video of a police officer making a sexist or racist slur. You might feel disgusted in a different way because it offends your sense of right and wrong. In fact, you might feel a variety of emotions based on your moral judgment of the situation.[10]

The Basic Moods: Positive and Negative Affect

Emotions can be fleeting, but moods can endure... for quite a while. As a first step toward studying the effect of moods and emotions in the workplace, we classify emotions into two categories: positive and negative. Positive emotions—such as joy and gratitude—express a favorable evaluation or feeling. Negative emotions—such as anger and guilt—express the opposite. Keep in mind that emotions can't be neutral. Being neutral is being nonemotional.[11]

The two categories of emotions represent overall mood states, known as positive and negative affect (see Exhibit 4-2). We can think of **positive affect** as a mood dimension consisting of positive emotions such as excitement, enthusiasm, and elation at the high end (high positive affect) and boredom, depression, and fatigue at the low end (low positive affect, or lack of positive affect). **Negative affect** is a mood dimension consisting of nervousness, stress, and anxiety at the high end (high negative affect) and contentedness, calmness, and serenity at the low end (low negative affect, or lack of negative affect).

Individualistic
Countries/cultures in which people see themselves as independent and desire personal goals and personal control. Individualistic values are present in North America and Western Europe, for example.

Collectivistic
Cultural difference regarding emotions can be apparent between countries that are individualistic and collectivistic—broad terms that describe the general outlook of people in a society (which are discussed in greater detail in the next chapter, Chapter 5).

Moral emotions
Emotions that have moral implications because of our instant judgment of the situation that evokes them.

Positive affect
A mood dimension that consists of specific positive emotions such as excitement, self-assurance, and cheerfulness at the high end and boredom, sluggishness, and tiredness at the low end.

Negative affect
A mood dimension that consists of emotions such as nervousness, stress, and anxiety at the high end and relaxation, tranquility, and poise at the low end.

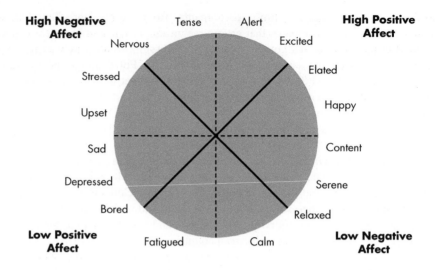

EXHIBIT 4-2
The Affective Circumplex

While we rarely experience both positive and negative affect at the same time, over time people do differ in how much they experience of each. Some people (we might call them emotional or intense) may experience quite a bit of high positive and high negative affect over, say, a week's time. Others (we might call them unemotional or phlegmatic) experience little of either. And still others may experience one much more predominately than the other.

Experiencing Moods and Emotions

Positivity offset
The tendency of most individuals to experience a mildly positive mood at zero input (when nothing in particular is going on).

As if it weren't complex enough to consider the many distinct emotions and moods a person might identify, the reality is that we each experience moods and emotions differently. For most people, positive moods are somewhat more common than negative moods. Indeed, research finds a **positivity offset**, meaning that at zero input (when nothing in particular is going on), most individuals experience a mildly positive mood.[12] This appears to be true for employees in a wide range of job settings. For example, one study of customer-service representatives in a British call center revealed that people reported experiencing positive moods 58 percent of the time, despite the stressful environment.[13] Another research finding is that negative emotions lead to negative moods.

There is much to be learned in exploring cultural differences. Some cultures embrace negative emotions, such as Japan and Russia, while others emphasize positive emotions and expressions, such as Mexico and Brazil.[14] There may also be a difference in the value of negative emotions between collectivist and individualist countries, and this difference may be the reason negative emotions are less detrimental to the health of Japanese than Americans.[15] For example, the Chinese consider negative emotions—while not always pleasant—as potentially more useful and constructive than do Americans.

The Function of Emotions

Emotions may be a mystery, but they can be critical to an effectively functioning workplace. For example, employees with more positive emotions demonstrate higher performance and organizational citizenship behavior (OCB; see Chapter 1), less turnover and counterproductive work behavior (CWB; see Chapter 3), particularly when they feel supported by their organizations in their effort to do well in their jobs.[16] Gratefulness and awe have also been shown to positively predict OCB,[17] which in turn increases trust and emotional expressions of concern.[18] Let's discuss two critical areas—rationality and ethicality—in which emotions can enhance performance.

DO EMOTIONS MAKE US IRRATIONAL? How often have you heard someone say, "Oh, you're just being emotional?" You might have been offended. Observations like this suggest that rationality and emotion are in conflict, and by exhibiting emotion, you are acting irrationally. The perceived association between the two is so strong that some researchers argue displaying emotions such as sadness to the point of crying is so toxic to a career that we should leave the room rather than allow others to witness it.[19] This perspective suggests the demonstration or even experience of emotions can make us seem weak, brittle, or irrational. However, this is wrong.

Research increasingly indicates that emotions are critical to rational thinking. Brain injury studies in particular suggest we must have the ability to experience emotions to be rational. Why? Because our emotions provide a context for how we understand the world around us. For instance, a recent study indicated that individuals in a negative mood are better able to discern truthful information than people in a happy mood.[20] Therefore, if we have a concern about someone telling the truth, shouldn't we conduct an inquiry while we are actively concerned, rather than wait until we cheer up? There may be benefits to this, or maybe not, depending on all the factors including the range of our emotions. The keys are to acknowledge the effect that emotions and moods are having on us, and to not discount our emotional responses as irrational or invalid.

DO EMOTIONS MAKE US ETHICAL? A growing body of research has begun to examine the relationship between emotions and moral attitudes.[21] It was previously believed that, like decision making in general, most ethical decision making was based on higher-order cognitive processes, but the research on moral emotions increasingly questions this perspective. Numerous studies suggest that moral judgments are largely based on feelings rather than on cognition, even though we tend to see our moral boundaries as logical and reasonable, not as emotional.

To some degree, our beliefs are shaped by our peer, interest, and work groups which influence our perceptions of others, resulting in unconscious responses and a feeling that our shared emotions are "right." Unfortunately, this feeling sometimes allows us to justify purely emotional reactions as rationally "ethical."[22] We also tend to judge out-group members (anyone who is not in our group) more harshly for moral transgressions than in-group members, even when we are trying to be objective.[23] In addition, perhaps to restore an emotional sense of fair play, we are likely to spitefully want outgroup members to be punished.[24]

SOURCES OF EMOTIONS AND MOODS

Have you ever said, "I got up on the wrong side of the bed today." Have you ever snapped at a coworker or family member for no reason? If you have, you probably wonder where those emotions and moods originated. Here we discuss some of the most commonly accepted influences.

Personality

Moods and emotions have a personality trait component, meaning that some people have built-in, natural tendencies to experience certain moods and emotions more frequently than others do. People also experience the same emotions with different intensities; the degree to which they experience them is called their **affect intensity**.[25] Affectively intense people experience both positive and negative emotions deeply: when they're sad, they're really sad, and when they're happy, they're really happy.

Affect intensity
Individual differences in the strength with which individuals experience their emotions.

Time of Day

Moods vary by the time of day. A fascinating study assessed patterns by analyzing millions of Twitter messages from across the globe.[26] The researchers noted the presence of words connoting positive affect (happy, enthused, excited) and negative affect (sad, angry, anxious). You can see the trends they observed in the positive affect part of Exhibit 4-3. Daily fluctuations in mood followed a similar pattern in most countries. These results are comparable to previous research. A major difference, though, happens in the evening. Whereas most research suggests that positive affect tends to drop after 7 P.M., this study suggests that it *increases* before the midnight decline. We have to wait for further research to see which description is accurate. The negative affect trends in this study were more consistent with past research, showing that negative affect is lowest in the morning and tends to increase over the course of the day and evening.

Day of the Week

Are people in their best moods on the weekends? In most cultures that is true—for example, U.S. adults tend to experience their highest positive affect on Friday, Saturday, and Sunday, and their lowest on Monday.[27] As shown in Exhibit 4-3, again based on the study of Twitter messages, that tends to be true in several other cultures as well. For Germans and Chinese, positive affect is highest from Friday to Sunday and lowest on Monday. This isn't the case in all cultures, however. As the exhibit shows, in Japan positive affect is higher on Monday than on either Friday or Saturday.

As for negative affect, Monday is the highest negative-affect day across most cultures. However, in some countries, negative affect is lower on Friday and Saturday than on Sunday. It may be that while Sunday is enjoyable as a day off (and thus we have higher positive affect), we also get a bit stressed about the week ahead (which is why negative affect is higher).

Weather

When do you think you would be in a better mood—when it's 70 degrees and sunny, or on a gloomy, cold, rainy day? Many people believe their mood is tied to the weather. However, a fairly large and detailed body of evidence suggests weather has little effect on mood, at least for most people.[28] **Illusory correlation**, which occurs when we associate two events that in reality have no connection, explains why people tend to *think* weather influences them. For example, employees may be more productive on bad weather days, a study in Japan and the United States recently indicated, but not because of mood—instead, the worse weather removed some work distractions.[29]

Illusory correlation
The tendency of people to associate two events when in reality there is no connection.

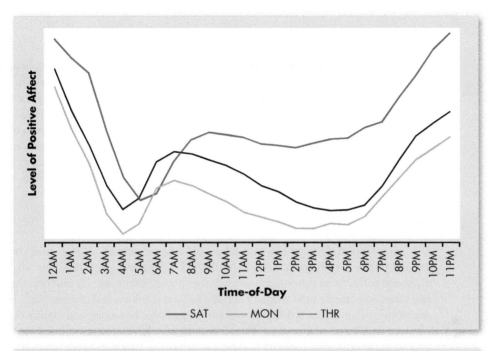

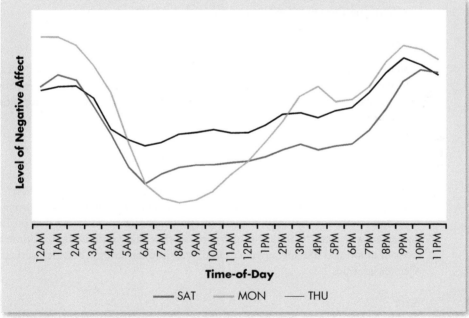

EXHIBIT 4-3

Time-of-Day Effects on Mood of U.S. Adults as Rated from Twitter Postings

Sources: Based on S. A. Golder and M. W. Macy, "Diurnal and Seasonal Mood Vary with Work, Sleep, and Daylength Across Diverse Cultures," *Science* 333 (2011), 1878–1881; A. Elejalde-Ruiz, "Seize the day," *Chicago Tribune* (September 5, 2012), downloaded June 20, 2013 from http://articles.chicagotribune.com/.

Note: Based on analysis of U.S. Twitter postings and coding of words that represent positive feelings (delight, enthusiasm) and negative feelings (fear, guilt). Lines represent percent of total words in Twitter post that convey these moods.

Stress

As you might imagine, stressful events at work (a nasty e-mail, impending deadline, loss of a big sale, reprimand from the boss, etc.) can negatively affect moods. The effects of stress also build over time. As the authors of one study noted, "A constant diet of even low-level stressful events has the potential to cause workers to experience gradually increasing levels of strain over time."[30] Mounting levels of stress can worsen our moods, as we experience more negative emotions. Although sometimes we thrive on it, most of us find stress usually takes a toll on our mood. In fact, when situations are overly emotionally charged and stressful, we have a natural response to disengage, to literally look away.[31]

Sleep

U.S. adults report sleeping less than adults did a generation ago.[32] According to researchers and public health specialists, 41 million U.S. workers sleep less than six hours per night and suffer from sleep deprivation. Sleep quality affects moods and decision making, and increased fatigue puts workers at risk of disease, injury, and depression.[33] Poor or reduced sleep also makes it difficult to control emotions. Even one bad night's sleep makes us more angry and risk-prone.[34] Poor sleep impairs job satisfaction[35] and makes us less able to make ethical judgments.[36] On the positive side, increased regular sleep enhances creativity, performance, and career success.

Exercise

You often hear that people should exercise to improve their mood. Does "sweat therapy" really work? It appears so. Research consistently shows exercise enhances people's positive moods.[37] While not terribly strong overall, the effects are strongest for those who are depressed.

Age

Do young people experience more extreme positive emotions (so-called youthful exuberance) than older people? Surprisingly, no. What about age and satisfaction? Regarding life satisfaction, there is a cultural assumption that older people are more prone to depression and loneliness. Actually, a study of adults ages 18 to 94 found that positive moods increased with age. "Contrary to the popular view that youth is the best time of life, the peak of emotional life may not occur until well into the seventh decade," researcher Laura Carstensen said.[38]

Sex

Many people believe women are more emotional than men. Is there any truth to this? Evidence does confirm women experience emotions more intensely, tend to "hold onto" emotions longer than men, and display more frequent expressions of both positive and negative emotions, except anger.[39] One study of participants from 37 different countries found that men consistently reported higher levels of powerful emotions like anger, whereas women reported more powerless emotions like sadness and fear. Thus, there are some sex differences in the experience and expression of emotions.[40]

Let's put together what we've learned about emotions and moods with workplace coping strategies, beginning with emotional labor.

EMOTIONAL LABOR

Employees expend physical and mental labor by putting body and mind, respectively, into their jobs. But jobs also require **emotional labor**, an employee's expression of organizationally desired emotions during interpersonal transactions at work. Emotional labor is a key component of effective job performance. We expect flight attendants to be cheerful, funeral directors to be sad, and doctors to be emotionally neutral. At the least, your managers expect you to be courteous, not hostile, in your interactions with coworkers.

Emotional labor
A situation in which an employee expresses organizationally desired emotions during interpersonal transactions at work.

Controlling Emotional Displays

The way we experience an emotion is obviously not always the same as the way we show it. To analyze emotional labor, we divide emotions into *felt* or *displayed emotions*.[41] **Felt emotions** are our actual emotions. In contrast, **displayed emotions** are those the organization requires workers to show and considers appropriate in a given job. They're not innate; they're learned, and they may or may not coincide with felt emotions. For instance, research suggests that in U.S. workplaces, it is expected that employees should typically display positive emotions like happiness and excitement, and suppress negative emotions like fear, anger, disgust, and contempt.[42]

Felt emotions
An individual's actual emotions.

Displayed emotions
Emotions that are organizationally required and considered appropriate in a given job.

Displaying fake emotions requires us to suppress real ones. **Surface acting** is hiding inner feelings and emotional expressions in response to display rules. Surface acting is literally "putting on a face" of appropriate response to a given situation, like smiling at a customer when you don't feel like it. Surface acting on a daily basis can also lead to emotional exhaustion at home, work-family conflict, and insomnia.[43] In the workplace, daily surface acting leads to exhaustion, fewer OCBs,[44] increased stress, and decreased job satisfaction.[45] Perhaps due to the costs of creatively expressing what we don't feel, individuals who *vary* their surface-acting responses may have lower job satisfaction and higher levels of work withdrawal than those who consistently give the same responses.[46] Employees who engage in surface displays should be given a chance to relax and recharge. For example, a study that looked at how cheerleading instructors spent their breaks from teaching found those who used the time to rest and relax were more effective after their breaks than those who did chores during their breaks.[47]

Surface acting
Hiding one's inner feelings and forgoing emotional expressions in response to display rules.

Deep acting is trying to modify our true inner feelings based on display rules. Surface acting deals with *displayed* emotions, and deep acting deals with *felt* emotions. Deep acting is less psychologically costly than surface acting because we are actually trying to experience the emotion, so we experience less emotional exhaustion. In the workplace, deep acting can have a positive impact. For example, one study in the Netherlands and Germany found that individuals in service jobs earned significantly more direct pay (tips) after they received training in deep acting.[48] Deep acting has a positive relationship with job satisfaction and job performance.[49] Employees who can depersonalize or standardize their work interactions that require emotional labor may be able to successfully carry on their acting while thinking of other tasks, thus bypassing the emotional impact.[50]

Deep acting
Trying to modify one's true inner feelings based on display rules.

Emotional Dissonance and Mindfulness

Emotional dissonance
Inconsistencies between the emotions people feel and the emotions they project.

When employees have to project one emotion *while feeling another*, this disparity is called **emotional dissonance**. Bottled-up feelings of frustration, anger, and resentment can lead to emotional exhaustion. Long-term emotional dissonance is a predictor for job burnout, declines in job performance, and lower job satisfaction.[51]

Mindfulness
Objectively and deliberately evaluating the emotional situation in the moment.

It is important to counteract the effects of emotional labor and emotional dissonance. Research in the Netherlands and Belgium indicates that while surface acting was stressful to employees, **mindfulness**—objectively and deliberately evaluating our emotional situation in the moment—was negatively correlated with emotional exhaustion and positively affected job satisfaction.[52] When people become non-judgmentally aware of the emotions they are experiencing, they are better able to look at situations more clearly. Mindfulness has been shown to increase the ability to shape our behavioral responses to emotions.[53]

The concepts within emotional labor make intuitive and organizational sense. Affective events theory, discussed next, fits a job's emotional labor requirements into a construct with implications for work events, emotional reactions, job satisfaction, and job performance.

AFFECTIVE EVENTS THEORY

Affective events theory (AET)
A model that suggests that workplace events cause emotional reactions on the part of employees, which then influence workplace attitudes and behaviors.

We've seen that emotions and moods are an important part of our personal and work lives. But how do they influence our job performance and satisfaction? **Affective events theory (AET)** proposes that employees react emotionally to things that happen to them at work, and this reaction influences their job performance and satisfaction.[54] Say you just found out your company is downsizing. You might experience a variety of negative emotions, causing you to worry that you'll lose your job. Because it is out of your hands, you may feel insecure and fearful, and spend much of your time worrying rather than working. Needless to say, your job satisfaction will also be down.

Work events trigger positive or negative emotional reactions, to which employees' personalities and moods predispose them to respond with greater or lesser intensity.[55] People who score low on emotional stability (see Chapter 5) are more likely to react strongly to negative events, and an emotional response to a given event can depend on mood. Finally, emotions influence a number of performance and satisfaction variables, such as OCB, organizational commitment, level of effort, intention to quit, and workplace deviance.

In sum, AET offers two important messages.[56] First, emotions provide valuable insights into how workplace events influence employee performance and satisfaction. Second, employees and managers shouldn't ignore emotions or the events that cause them, even when they appear minor, because they accumulate. The AET framework highlights the emotionality of the workplace and its real outcomes. Emotional intelligence is another framework that may help us understand the impact of emotions on job performance, so we look at that next.

EMOTIONAL INTELLIGENCE

As the CEO of an international talent company, Terrie Upshur-Lupberger was at a career pinnacle. So why was she resentful and unhappy? A close friend observed, "Terrie, you were out on the skinny branch—you know, the one that breaks easily in a strong wind. You

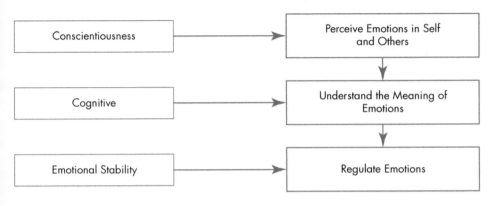

EXHIBIT 4-4
A Cascading Model of Emotional Intelligence

were so busy and overwhelmed and out of touch with your own values, cares, and guiding beliefs that you failed to pay attention to the branch that was about to break."[57] According to Upshur-Lupberger, she had failed to notice that her moods constantly swung toward frustration and exhaustion. Her job satisfaction, productivity, relationships, and results suffered. Worst, she was too busy to realize the deficiencies until she was completely depleted. She said, "I learned that, as a leader, you either pay attention to and manage the moods (including your own) in the organization, or . . . . you ignore them and pay the price."[58] Upshur-Lupberger learned the value of emotional intelligence.

Emotional intelligence (EI) is a person's ability to: (1) perceive emotions in him or herself and others; (2) understand the meaning of these emotions; and (3) regulate his or her own emotions accordingly, as shown in Exhibit 4-4. People who know their own emotions and are good at reading emotional cues—for instance, knowing why they're angry and how to express themselves without violating norms—are most likely to have high EI.[59]

Several studies suggest EI plays an important role in job performance. One study that used functional magnetic resonance imaging (fMRI) technology found that executive MBA students who performed best on a strategic decision-making task were more likely to incorporate emotion centers of the brain into their choice processes.[60] One simulation study showed that students who were good at identifying and distinguishing among their own feelings were able to make more profitable investment decisions.[61]

Although organizational behavior (OB) is progressing in its understanding of EI, and several studies suggest it plays an important role in job performance, many questions remain unanswered. One relates to proving what EI may predict. For example, while evidence indicates that EI correlates with job performance, the correlation isn't high and is explained to a large degree by traits such as emotional stability. A second question is about the reliability of EI testing. For example, part of the reason EI has only a modest correlation with job effectiveness is that it is hard to measure—mostly it is measured with self-report inventories, which of course are often far from objective!

All questions aside, EI is wildly popular among consulting firms and in the popular press, and it has accumulated some support in the research literature. Love it or hate it, one thing is for sure—EI is here to stay. So might be our next topic—emotion regulation—an independent concept from emotional labor and emotional intelligence, although they are related.[62]

Emotional intelligence (EI) The ability to detect and to manage emotional cues and information.

EMOTION REGULATION

Emotion regulation
The process of identifying and modifying felt emotions.

Have you ever tried to cheer yourself up when you're feeling down, or calm yourself when you're feeling angry? If so, you have engaged in **emotion regulation**. The central idea behind emotion regulation is to identify and modify the emotions you feel. Recent research suggests that emotion management ability is a strong predictor of task performance for some jobs and for OCB.[63] Therefore, in our study of OB, we are interested in *whether* and *how* emotion regulation should be used in the workplace. We begin by identifying which individuals might naturally employ it.

Emotion Regulation Influences and Outcomes

As you might suspect, not everyone is equally good at regulating emotions. Individuals who are higher in the personality trait of neuroticism (see Chapter 5) have more trouble doing so and often find their moods are beyond their ability to control. Individuals who have lower levels of self-esteem are also less likely to try to improve their sad moods, perhaps because they are less likely than others to feel they deserve to be in a good mood.[64]

The workplace environment has an effect on an individual's tendency to employ emotion regulation. In general, diversity in work groups increases the likelihood that you will regulate your emotions. For example, younger employees are likely to regulate their emotions when their work groups include older members.[65] Racial diversity also has an effect: if diversity is low, the minority may engage in emotion regulation, perhaps to "fit in" with the majority race as much as possible; if diversity is high and many different races are represented, the majority race will employ emotion regulation, perhaps to integrate themselves with the whole group.[66] These findings suggest a beneficial outcome of diversity—it may cause us to regulate our emotions more consciously and effectively.

While regulating your emotions might seem beneficial, research suggests there is a downside to trying to change the way you feel. Changing your emotions takes effort, and as we noted when discussing emotional labor, this effort can be exhausting. Sometimes attempts to change an emotion actually make the emotion stronger; for example, trying to talk yourself out of being afraid can make you focus more on what scares you, which makes you more afraid.[67] From another perspective, research suggests that avoiding negative emotional experiences is less likely to lead to positive moods than does seeking out positive emotional experiences.[68] For example, you're more likely to experience a positive mood if you have a pleasant conversation with a friend than if you avoid an unpleasant conversation with a hostile coworker.

Emotion Regulation Techniques

Researchers of emotion regulation often study the strategies people employ to change their emotions. One related technique of emotion regulation is *emotional suppression*, literally suppressing—blocking or ignoring—initial emotional responses to situations. This response seems to facilitate practical thinking in the short term. However, it appears to be helpful only when a strongly negative event would elicit a distressed emotional reaction in a crisis situation.[69] For example, a portfolio manager might suppress an emotional reaction to a sudden drop in the value of a stock and therefore be able to clearly decide how to plan. Suppression used in crisis situations appears to help an individual recover from the event emotionally, while suppression used as an everyday emotion regulation technique can take a toll on mental ability, emotional ability, health, and relationships.[70]

While emotion regulation techniques can help us cope with difficult workplace situations, research indicates that the effect varies. For example, one study in Taiwan found that all participants who worked for abusive supervisors reported emotional exhaustion and work withdrawal tendencies, but to different degrees based on the emotion regulation strategies they employed. Thus, while there is much promise in emotion regulation techniques, the best route to a positive workplace is to recruit positive-minded individuals and train leaders to manage their moods, job attitudes, and performance.[71] The best leaders manage emotions as much as they do tasks and activities. The best employees can use their knowledge of emotion regulation to decide when to speak up and how to express themselves effectively.[72]

Ethics of Emotion Regulation

Emotion regulation has important ethical implications. On one end of the continuum, some people might argue that controlling your emotions is unethical because it requires a degree of acting. On the other end, people might argue that all emotions should be controlled so you can take a dispassionate perspective. Both arguments—and all arguments in between—have ethical pros and cons you will have to decide for yourself. Consider the reasons for emotion regulation and the outcomes. Are you regulating your emotions so you don't react inappropriately, or are you regulating your emotions so no one knows what you are thinking? Finally, consider this: you may be able to "fake it 'til you make it." Acting like you are in a good mood might *put* you in a good mood. In one study, a group of participants was asked to hold only a conversation with a barista serving them at Starbucks, while another group was asked to act happy. The happy actors reported later that they were in much better moods.[73]

Now that we have studied the role of emotions and moods in OB, let's consider the opportunities for more specific applications that our understanding provides.

⊗WATCH IT

If your professor has assigned this, go to the Assignments section of **mymanagementlab .com** to complete the video exercise titled **East Haven Fire Department: Emotions and Moods**.

OB APPLICATIONS OF EMOTIONS AND MOODS

Our understanding of emotions and moods can affect many aspects of OB. Let's think through some of them.

Selection

One implication from the evidence on EI is that employers should consider it a factor in hiring employees, especially for jobs that demand a high degree of social interaction. In fact, more employers *are* starting to use EI measures to hire people. For example, a study of U.S. Air Force recruiters showed that top-performing recruiters exhibited high levels of EI. Using these findings, the Air Force revamped its selection criteria. A follow-up investigation found hires who had high EI scores became 2.6 times more successful than those with lower scores.

Decision Making

Moods and emotions have effects on decision making that managers should understand. Positive emotions and moods seem to help people make sound decisions. Positive emotions also enhance problem-solving skills, so positive people find better solutions.[74]

OB researchers continue to debate the role of negative emotions and moods in decision making. One recent study suggested that people who are saddened by events may make the same decisions as they would have, absent those events, while people who are angered by events might make stronger (though not necessarily better) choices.[75] Another study found that participants made choices reflecting more original thinking when in a negative mood.[76] Still other research indicated that individuals in a negative mood may take higher risks than when in a positive mood.[77] Taken together, these and other studies suggest negative (and positive) emotions impact decision making, but that there are other variables which require further research.[78]

Creativity

As we see throughout this text, one goal of leadership is to maximize employee productivity through creativity. Creativity is influenced by emotions and moods, but there are two schools of thought on the relationship. Much research suggests that people in good moods tend to be more creative than people in bad moods.[79] People in good moods produce more ideas and more options, and others find their ideas original.[80] It seems that people experiencing positive moods or emotions are more flexible and open in their thinking, which may explain why they're more creative.[81] All the activating moods, whether positive *or* negative, seem to lead to more creativity, whereas deactivating moods lead to less.[82] For example, we discussed earlier that other factors such as fatigue may boost creativity. A study of 428 students found they performed best on a creative problem-solving task when they were fatigued, suggesting that tiredness may free the mind to consider novel solutions.[83]

Motivation

Several studies have highlighted the importance of moods and emotions on motivation. Giving people performance feedback—whether real or fake—influences their mood, which then influences their motivation.[84] For example, one study looked at the moods of insurance sales agents in Taiwan.[85] Agents in a good mood were found to be more helpful toward their coworkers and also felt better about themselves. These factors in turn led to superior performance in the form of higher sales and better supervisor reports of performance.

Leadership

Research indicates that putting people in a good mood makes good sense. Leaders who focus on inspirational goals generate greater optimism, cooperation, and enthusiasm in employees, leading to more positive social interactions with coworkers and customers.[86] A study with Taiwanese military participants indicated that by sharing emotions, transformational leaders inspire positive emotions in their followers that lead to higher task performance.[87]

Leaders are perceived as more effective when they share positive emotions, and followers are more creative in a positive emotional environment. What about when leaders are sad? Research found that leader displays of sadness increased the analytic performance of followers, perhaps because followers attended more closely to tasks to help the leaders.[88]

Customer Service

Workers' emotional states influence the level of customer service they give, which in turn influences levels of repeat business and customer satisfaction.[89] This result is primarily due to **emotional contagion**—the "catching" of emotions from others.[90] When someone experiences positive emotions and laughs and smiles at you, you tend to respond positively. Of course, the opposite is true as well.

> **Emotional contagion**
> The process by which people's emotions are caused by the emotions of others.

Studies indicate a matching effect between employee and customer emotions. In the employee-to-customer direction, research finds that customers who catch the positive moods or emotions of employees shop longer. In the other direction, when an employee feels unfairly treated by a customer, it's harder for the employee to display the positive emotions the organization expects.[91] High-quality customer service places demands on employees because it often puts them in a state of emotional dissonance, which can be damaging to the employee and the organization. Managers can interrupt negative contagion by fostering positive moods.

Job Attitudes

Ever hear the advice "Never take your work home with you," meaning you should forget about work once you go home? That's easier said than done. The good news is that it appears a positive mood at work can spill over to your off-work hours, and a negative mood at work can be restored to a positive mood after a break. Several studies have shown people who had a good day at work tend to be in a better mood at home that evening, and vice versa. Other research has found that although people do emotionally take their work home with them, by the next day the effect is usually gone.[92] The bad news is that the moods of the people in your household may affect yours. As you might expect, one study found if one member of a couple was in a negative mood during the workday, the negative mood spilled over to the spouse at night.[93] The relationship between moods and job attitudes is reciprocal—the way our workday goes colors our moods, but our moods also affect the way we see our jobs.

Deviant Workplace Behaviors

Anyone who has spent much time in an organization realizes people can behave in ways that violate established norms and threaten the organization, its members, or both.[94] These counterproductive work behaviors (CWBs; see Chapter 3) can be traced to negative emotions and can take many forms. People who feel negative emotions are more likely than others to engage in short-term deviant behavior at work, such as gossiping or surfing the Internet,[95] though negative emotions can also lead to more serious forms of CWB.

For instance, envy is an emotion that occurs when you resent someone for having something you don't have but strongly desire—such as a better work assignment, larger office, or higher salary. It can lead to malicious deviant behaviors. An envious employee could undermine other employees and take all the credit for things others accomplished. Angry people look for other people to blame for their bad mood, interpret other people's behavior as hostile, and have trouble considering others' points of view.[96] It's not hard to see how these thought processes can lead directly to verbal or physical aggression.

One study in Pakistan found that anger correlated with more aggressive CWBs such as abuse against others and production deviance, while sadness did not. Interestingly, neither anger nor sadness predicted workplace deviance, which suggests that managers need to take employee expressions of anger seriously; employees may stay with an organization and continue to act aggressively toward others.[97] Once aggression starts, it's likely that other people will become angry and aggressive, so the stage is set for a serious escalation of negative behavior. Managers therefore need to stay connected with their employees to gauge emotions and emotional intensity levels.

Safety and Injury at Work

Research relating negative affectivity to increased injuries at work suggests employers might improve health and safety (and reduce costs) by ensuring workers aren't engaged in potentially dangerous activities when they're in a bad mood. Bad moods can contribute to injury at work in several ways.[98] Individuals in negative moods tend to be more anxious, which can make them less able to cope effectively with hazards. A person who is always fearful will be more pessimistic about the effectiveness of safety precautions because she feels she'll just get hurt anyway, or she might panic or freeze up when confronted with a threatening situation. Negative moods also make people more distractable, and distractions can obviously lead to careless behaviors.

Selecting positive team members can contribute towards a positive work environment because positive moods transmit from team member to team member. One study of 130 leaders and their followers found that leaders who are charismatic transfer their positive emotions to their followers through a contagion effect.[99] It makes sense, then, to choose team members predisposed to positive moods.

SUMMARY

Emotions and moods are similar in that both are affective in nature. But they're also different—moods are more general and less contextual than emotions. The time of day, stressful events, and sleep patterns are some of the many factors that influence emotions and moods. OB research on emotional labor, affective events theory, emotional intelligence, and emotional regulation helps us understand how people deal with emotions. Emotions and moods have proven relevant for virtually every OB topic we study, with implications for managerial practices.

IMPLICATIONS FOR MANAGERS

- Recognize that emotions are a natural part of the workplace and good management does not mean creating an emotion-free environment.
- To foster effective decision making, creativity, and motivation in employees, model positive emotions and moods as much as is authentically possible.

- Provide positive feedback to increase the positivity of employees. Of course, it also helps to hire people who are predisposed to positive moods.
- In the service sector, encourage positive displays of emotion, which make customers feel more positive and thus improve customer service interactions and negotiations.
- Understand the role of emotions and moods to significantly improve your ability to explain and predict your coworkers' and others' behavior.

⭐ TRY IT!

If your professor has assigned this, go to the Assignments section of **mymanagementlab.com** to complete the **Simulation: Emotions & Moods**.

⭐ PERSONAL INVENTORY ASSESSMENTS

Emotional Intelligence Assessment

Have you always been able to "read" others well? Do people say you seem to have "the right thing to say" for every occasion? Complete this PIA to determine your emotional intelligence (EI).

4-1. Do you think it is possible to reliably construct good emotions and moods in people? Why or why not?

5

Personality and Values

MyManagementLab®

⭐ Improve Your Grade!

When you see this icon ⭐, visit **mymanagementlab.com** for activities that are applied, personalized, and offer immediate feedback.

LEARNING OBJECTIVES

After studying this chapter, you should be able to:

1. Describe personality, the way it is measured, and the factors that shape it.
2. Describe the strengths and weaknesses of the Myers-Briggs Type Indicator (MBTI) personality framework and the Big Five Model.
3. Discuss how the concepts of core self-evaluation (CSE), self-monitoring, and proactive personality contribute to the understanding of personality.
4. Describe how the situation affects whether personality predicts behavior.
5. Contrast terminal and instrumental values.
6. Describe the differences between person–job fit and person–organization fit.
7. Compare Hofstede's five value dimensions and the GLOBE framework.

⭐ Chapter Warm-up

If your professor has chosen to assign this, go to the Assignments section of **www.mymanagementlab.com** to complete the chapter warm-up.

PERSONALITY

Why are some people quiet and passive, while others are loud and aggressive? Are certain personality types better adapted than others for certain jobs? Before we can answer these questions, we need to address a more basic one: what is personality?

What Is Personality?

When we speak of someone's personality, we use many adjectives to describe how they act and seem to think; in fact, research participants used 624 distinct adjectives to describe people they knew.[1] As organizational behaviorists, however, we organize characteristics by overall traits describing the growth and development of a person's personality.

DEFINING PERSONALITY For our purposes, think of **personality** as the sum of ways in which an individual reacts to and interacts with others. We most often describe personality in terms of the measurable traits a person exhibits.

> **Personality**
> The sum total of ways in which an individual reacts to and interacts with others.

Early work on personality tried to identify and label enduring characteristics that describe an individual's behavior including shy, aggressive, submissive, lazy, ambitious, loyal, and timid. When someone exhibits these characteristics in a large number of situations and they are relatively enduring over time, we call them **personality traits**.[2] The more consistent the characteristic over time and the more frequently it occurs in diverse situations, the more important the trait is in describing the individual.

> **Personality traits**
> Enduring characteristics that describe an individual's behavior.

ASSESSING PERSONALITY Personality assessments have been increasingly used in diverse organizational settings. In fact, 8 of the top 10 U.S. private companies and 57 percent of all large U.S. companies use them,[3] including Xerox, McDonald's, and Lowe's.[4] Schools such as DePaul University have also begun to use personality tests in their admissions process.[5] Personality tests are useful in hiring decisions and help managers forecast who is best for a job.[6]

MEASURING RESULTS The most common means of measuring personality is through self-report surveys in which individuals evaluate themselves on a series of factors, such as "I worry a lot about the future." In general, when people know their personality scores are going to be used for hiring decisions, they rate themselves as about half a standard deviation more conscientious and emotionally stable than if they are taking the test to learn more about themselves.[7] Another problem is accuracy; for example, a candidate who is in a bad mood when taking a survey may very well receive inaccurate scores.

CULTURE AND RATINGS Research indicates our culture influences the way we rate ourselves. People in individualistic countries (see Chapter 4) like the United States and Australia trend toward self-enhancement, while people in collectivistic countries (see Chapter 4) like Taiwan, China, and South Korea trend toward self-diminishment. Self-enhancement does not appear to harm a person's career in individualistic countries, but it does in collectivist countries, where humility is valued. Interestingly, underrating (self-diminishment) may harm a person's career in both collectivistic and individualistic communities.[8]

SELF-REPORTS AND OBSERVER-RATINGS Observer-ratings surveys provide an independent assessment of personality. Here, a coworker or another observer does the rating. Though the results of self-reports and observer-ratings surveys are strongly correlated, research suggests observer-ratings surveys predict job success more than self-ratings alone.[9] However, each can tell us something unique about an individual's behavior, so a combination of self-reports and observer-ratings predicts performance better than any one type of information. The implication is clear: Use both self-reports and observers-ratings (per SS) of personality when making important employment decisions.

PERSONALITY DETERMINANTS   An early debate centered on whether an individual's personality is the result of heredity or environment. Personality appears to be a result of both; however, research tends to support the importance of heredity over environment. **Heredity** refers to factors determined at conception. Physical stature, facial features, gender, temperament, muscle composition and reflexes, energy level, and biological rhythms are either completely or substantially influenced by parentage—by your biological parents' genetic, physiological, and inherent psychological makeup. The heredity approach argues that the ultimate explanation of an individual's personality is the molecular structure of the genes, located on the chromosomes. This is not to suggest that personality never changes. For example, people's scores on dependability tend to increase over time, as when young adults start families and establish careers. Personality is also more changeable in adolescence and more stable among adults.[10] However, strong individual differences in dependability remain; everyone tends to change by about the same amount, so their rank order stays roughly the same.[11]

Heredity
Factors determined at conception; one's biological, physiological, and inherent psychological makeup.

PERSONALITY FRAMEWORKS

Throughout history, people have sought to understand what makes individuals behave in myriad ways. Many of our behaviors stem from our personalities, so understanding the components of personality helps us predict behavior. Important theoretical frameworks and assessment tools, discussed next, help us categorize and study the dimensions of personality.

The Myers-Briggs Type Indicator

Myers-Briggs Type Indicator (MBTI)
A personality test that taps 4 characteristics and classifies people into 1 of 16 personality types.

The **Myers-Briggs Type Indicator (MBTI)** is the most widely used personality-assessment instrument in the world.[12] It is a 100-question personality test that asks people how they usually feel or act in situations. Respondents are classified as extraverted or introverted (E or I), sensing or intuitive (S or N), thinking or feeling (T or F), and judging or perceiving (J or P):

- **Extraverted (E) versus Introverted (I).** Extraverted individuals are outgoing, sociable, and assertive. Introverts are quiet and shy.
- **Sensing (s) versus Intuitive (N).** Sensing types are practical and prefer routine and order, and they focus on details. Intuitives rely on unconscious processes and look at the "big picture."
- **Thinking (T) versus Feeling (F).** Thinking types use reason and logic to handle problems. Feeling types rely on their personal values and emotions.
- **Judging (J) versus Perceiving (P).** Judging types want control and prefer order and structure. Perceiving types are flexible and spontaneous.

The MBTI describes personality types by identifying one trait from each of the four pairs. For example, Introverted/Intuitive/Thinking/Judging people (INTJs) are visionaries with original minds and great drive. They are skeptical, critical, independent, determined, and often stubborn. ENFJs are natural teachers and leaders. They are relational, motivational, intuitive, idealistic, ethical, and kind. ESTJs are organizers. They are realistic, logical, analytical, and decisive, perfect for business or mechanics. The ENTP type is innovative, individualistic, versatile, and attracted to entrepreneurial ideas. This person tends to be resourceful in solving challenging problems but may neglect routine assignments.

One problem with the MBTI is that the model forces a person into one type or another; that is, you're either introverted or extraverted. There is no in-between. Another problem is with the reliability of the measure: When people retake the assessment, they often receive different results. An additional problem is in the difficulty of interpretation. There are levels of importance for each of the MBTI facets, and separate meanings for certain combinations of facets, all of which require trained interpretation that can leave room for error. Finally, results from the MBTI tend to be unrelated to job performance.

The Big Five Personality Model

The MBTI may lack strong supporting evidence, but an impressive body of research supports the **Big Five Model**, which proposes that five basic dimensions underlie all others and encompass most of the significant variation in human personality.[13] Test scores of these traits do a very good job of predicting how people behave in a variety of real-life situations[14] and remain relatively stable for an individual over time, with some daily variations.[15] These are the Big Five factors:

- **Conscientiousness.** The **conscientiousness** dimension is a measure of reliability. A highly conscientious person is responsible, organized, dependable, and persistent. Those who score low on this dimension are easily distracted, disorganized, and unreliable.

- **Emotional stability.** The **emotional stability** dimension taps a person's ability to withstand stress. People with emotional stability tend to be calm, self-confident, and secure. High scorers are more likely to be positive and optimistic; they are generally happier than low scorers. Emotional stability is sometimes discussed as its converse, neuroticism. Low scorers (those with high neuroticism) are hypervigilant and vulnerable to the physical and psychological effects of stress. Those with high neuroticism tend to be nervous, anxious, depressed, and insecure.

- **Extraversion.** The **extraversion** dimension captures our comfort level with relationships. Extraverts tend to be gregarious, assertive, and sociable. They are generally happier and are often ambitious.[16] On the other hand, introverts (low extraversion) tend to be more thoughtful, reserved, timid, and quiet.

- **Openness to experience.** The **openness to experience** dimension addresses the range of a person's interests and their fascination with novelty. Open people are creative, curious, and artistically sensitive. Those at the low end of the category are conventional and find comfort in the familiar.

- **Agreeableness.** The **agreeableness** dimension refers to an individual's propensity to defer to others. Agreeable people are cooperative, warm, and trusting. You might expect agreeable people to be happier than disagreeable people. They are, but only slightly. When people choose organizational team members, agreeable individuals are usually their first choice. In contrast, people who score low on agreeableness can be cold and antagonistic.

Big Five Model
A personality assessment model that taps five basic dimensions.

Conscientiousness
A personality dimension that describes someone who is responsible, dependable, persistent, and organized.

Emotional stability
A personality dimension that characterizes someone as calm, self-confident, and secure (positive) versus nervous, depressed, and insecure (negative).

Extraversion
A personality dimension describing someone who is sociable, gregarious, and assertive.

Openness to experience
A personality dimension that characterizes someone in terms of imagination, sensitivity, and curiosity.

Agreeableness
A personality dimension that describes someone who is good natured, cooperative, and trusting.

How Do the Big Five Traits Predict Behavior at Work?

There are many relationships between the Big Five personality dimensions and job performance,[17] and we are learning more about them every day. Let's explore one trait at a time, beginning with the strongest predictor of job performance—conscientiousness.

CONSCIENTIOUSNESS AT WORK   Conscientiousness is key. As researchers recently stated, "Personal attributes related to conscientiousness and agreeableness are important for success across many jobs, spanning across low to high levels of job complexity, training, and experience."[18] Employees who score higher in conscientiousness develop higher levels of job knowledge, probably because highly conscientious people learn more (conscientiousness may be related to GPA),[19] and these levels correspond with higher levels of job performance. Conscientious people are also more able to maintain their job performance when faced with abusive supervision, according to a study in India.[20]

Like any trait, conscientiousness has its pitfalls. Highly conscientious individuals can prioritize work over family, resulting in more conflict between their work and family roles (termed work-family conflict).[21] They may also become too focused on their own work to help others in the organization,[22] and they don't adapt well to changing contexts. Furthermore, conscientious people may have trouble learning complex skills early in a training process because their focus is on performing well rather than on learning. Finally, they are often less creative, especially artistically.[23]

Despite pitfalls, conscientiousness is the best overall predictor of job performance. However, the other Big Five traits are also related to aspects of performance and have other implications for work and for life. Exhibit 5-1 summarizes these other relations.

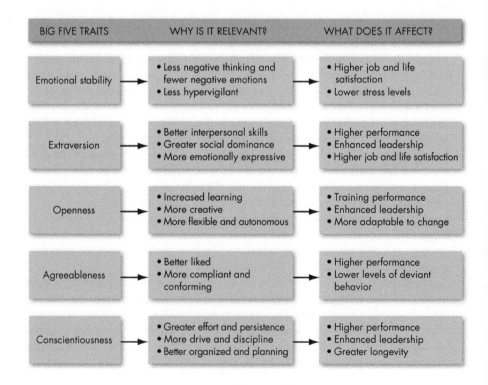

EXHIBIT 5-1
Model of How Big Five Traits Influence OB Criteria

EMOTIONAL STABILITY AT WORK Of the Big Five traits, emotional stability is most strongly related to life satisfaction, job satisfaction, and low stress levels. People with high emotional stability can adapt to unexpected or changing demands in the workplace.[24] At the other end of the spectrum, neurotic individuals who are unable to cope with these demands may experience burnout.[25] These people also tend to experience work-family conflict, which can affect work outcomes.[26]

EXTRAVERSION AT WORK Extraverts perform better in jobs with significant interpersonal interaction. They are socially dominant, "take charge" people.[27] Extraversion is a relatively strong predictor of leadership emergence in groups. Some negatives are that extraverts are more impulsive than introverts, are more likely to be absent from work, and may be more likely than introverts to lie during job interviews.[28]

OPENNESS AT WORK Open people are more likely to be effective leaders—and more comfortable with ambiguity. They cope better with organizational change and are more adaptable. While openness isn't related to initial performance on a job, individuals higher in openness are less susceptible to a decline in performance over a longer time period.[29] Open people also experience less work-family conflict.[30]

AGREEABLENESS AT WORK Agreeable individuals are better liked than disagreeable people; they tend to do better in interpersonally oriented jobs such as customer service. They're more compliant and rule abiding, less likely to get into accidents, and more satisfied in their jobs. They also contribute to organizational performance by engaging in organizational citizenship behavior (OCB; see Chapter 1).[31] Disagreeable people, on the other hand, are more likely to engage in counterproductive work behavior (CWB; see Chapter 3), as are people low in conscientiousness.[32] Low agreeableness also predicts involvement in work accidents.[33] Lastly, agreeableness is associated with lower levels of career success (especially earnings), perhaps because highly agreeable people consider themselves less marketable and are less willing to assert themselves.[34]

In general, the Big Five personality factors appear in almost all cross-cultural studies,[35] including China, Israel, Germany, Japan, Spain, Nigeria, Norway, Pakistan, and the United States. However, a study of illiterate indigenous people in Bolivia suggested the Big Five framework may be less applicable when studying the personalities of small, remote groups.[36]

The Dark Triad

With the exception of neuroticism, the Big Five traits are what we call socially desirable, meaning we would be glad to score high on them. They also have the most verifiable links to important organizational outcomes. Researchers have identified three other socially *undesirable* traits, which we all have in varying degrees and which are also relevant to organizational behavior (OB): Machiavellianism, narcissism, and psychopathy. Owing to their negative nature, researchers have labeled these the **Dark Triad**—though they do not always occur together.[37]

The Dark Triad may sound sinister, but these traits are not clinical pathologies hindering everyday functioning. They might be expressed particularly strongly when an individual is under stress and unable to moderate any inappropriate responses. Sustained

Dark Triad
A constellation of negative personality traits consisting of Machiavellianism, narcissism, and psychopathy.

high levels of dark personality traits can cause individuals to derail their careers and personal lives.[38]

MACHIAVELLIANISM   Hao is a young bank manager in Shanghai. He's received three promotions in the past four years and makes no apologies for the aggressive tactics he's used. "My name means clever, and that's what I am—I do whatever I have to do to get ahead," he says. Hao would be termed Machiavellian.

Machiavellianism
The degree to which an individual is pragmatic, maintains emotional distance, and believes that ends can justify means.

The personality characteristic of **Machiavellianism** (often abbreviated *Mach*) is named after Niccolo Machiavelli, who wrote in the sixteenth century on how to gain and use power. An individual high in Machiavellianism is pragmatic, maintains emotional distance, and believes that ends can justify means. "If it works, use it" is consistent with a high-Mach perspective. High Machs manipulate more, win more, are persuaded less by others, but persuade others more than do low Machs.[39] They are more likely to act aggressively and engage in CWBs as well. Surprisingly, Machiavellianism does not significantly predict overall job performance.[40] High-Mach employees, by manipulating others to their advantage, win in the short term at a job, but lose those gains in the long term because they are not well liked.

Machiavellian tendencies may have ethical implications. One study showed high-Mach job seekers were less positively affected by the knowledge that an organization engaged in a high level of corporate social responsibility (CSR; see Chapter 3),[41] suggesting that high-Mach people may care less about sustainability issues. Another study found Machs' ethical leadership behaviors were less likely to translate into followers' work engagement because followers see through these behaviors and realize they are cases of surface acting.[42]

Narcissism
The tendency to be arrogant, have a grandiose sense of self-importance, require excessive admiration, and have a sense of entitlement.

NARCISSISM   Sabrina likes to be the center of attention. She often looks at herself in the mirror, has extravagant dreams about her future, and considers herself a person of many talents. Sabrina is a narcissist. The trait is named for the Greek myth of Narcissus, a youth so vain and proud he fell in love with his own image. In psychology, **narcissism** describes a person who has a grandiose sense of self-importance, requires excessive admiration, and is arrogant. Narcissists often have fantasies of grand success, a tendency to exploit situations and people, a sense of entitlement, and a lack of empathy.[43] However, narcissists can be hypersensitive and fragile people.[44] They also may experience more anger.[45]

While narcissism seems to have little relationship to job effectiveness or OCB,[46] it is one of the largest predictors of increased CWB in individualistic cultures—but not in collectivist cultures that discourage self-promotion.[47] Narcissists commonly think they are overqualified for their positions.[48] When they receive feedback about their performance, they often tune out information that conflicts with their positive self-perception, but they will work harder if rewards are offered.[49]

On the bright side, narcissists may be more charismatic than others.[50] They also might be found in business more often than in other fields. They are more likely to be chosen for leadership positions, and medium ratings of narcissism (neither extremely high nor extremely low) are positively correlated with leadership effectiveness.[51] Some evidence suggests that narcissists are more adaptable and make better business decisions than others when the issue is complex.[52] Furthermore, a study of Norwegian bank employees found those scoring high on narcissism enjoyed their work more.[53]

PSYCHOPATHY   Psychopathy is part of the Dark Triad, but in OB, it does not connote clinical mental illness. In the OB context, **psychopathy** is defined as a lack of concern for others, and a lack of guilt or remorse when actions cause harm.[54] Measures of psychopathy attempt to assess motivation to comply with social norms, impulsivity, willingness to use deceit to obtain desired ends, and disregard, that is, the lack of empathic concern for others.

    The literature is not consistent about whether psychopathy is important to work behavior. One review found little correlation between measures of psychopathy and job performance or CWB. Another found antisocial personality, which is closely related to psychopathy, was positively related to advancement in the organization but unrelated to other aspects of career success and effectiveness.[55] Still other research suggests psychopathy is related to the use of hard influence tactics (threats, manipulation) and bullying work behavior (physical or verbal threatening).[56] The cunning displayed by people who score high on psychopathy may thus help them gain power in an organization but keep them from using it toward healthy ends for themselves or their organizations.

Psychopathy
The tendency for a lack of concern for others and a lack of guilt or remorse when actions cause harm.

OTHER TRAITS   The Dark Triad is a helpful framework for studying the three dominant dark-side traits in current personality research, and researchers are exploring other traits as well. One emerging framework incorporates five additional aberrant compound traits based on the Big Five. First, *antisocial* people are indifferent and callous toward others. They use their extraversion to charm people, but they may be prone to violent CWBs and risky decision making. Second, *borderline* people have low self-esteem and high uncertainty. They are unpredictable in their interactions at work, are inefficient, and may have low job satisfaction.[57] Third, *schizotypal* individuals are eccentric and disorganized. In the workplace, they can be highly creative, although they are susceptible to work stress. Fourth, *obsessive-compulsive* people are perfectionists and can be stubborn, yet they attend to details, carry a strong work ethic, and may be motivated by achievement. Fifth, *avoidant* individuals feel inadequate and hate criticism. They can function only in environments requiring little interaction.[58]

OTHER PERSONALITY ATTRIBUTES RELEVANT TO OB

As we've discussed, studies of traits have much to offer the field of OB. Now we'll look at other attributes that are powerful predictors of behavior in organizations: core self-evaluations, self-monitoring, and proactive personality.

Core Self-Evaluation (CSE)

As discussed in Chapter 3, core self-evaluations (CSEs) are bottom-line conclusions individuals have about their capabilities, competence, and worth as a person. People with positive CSEs like themselves and see themselves as effective and in control of their environment. Those with negative CSEs tend to dislike themselves, question their capabilities, and view themselves as powerless over their environment.[59] Recall that CSEs relate to job satisfaction, because people who are positive on this trait see more challenge in their jobs and actually attain more complex jobs.

    People with positive CSEs perform better than others because they set more ambitious goals, are more committed to their goals, and persist longer in attempting to reach them. People who have high CSEs provide better customer service, are more popular coworkers, and may have careers that begin on better footing and ascend more rapidly over time.[60] They perform especially well if they feel their work provides meaning and is helpful to others.[61] Therefore, people with high CSEs may thrive in organizations with high CSR.

Self-Monitoring

Zoe is always in trouble at work. Although she's competent, hardworking, and productive, she receives average ratings in performance reviews, and seems to have made a career out of irritating her bosses. Zoe's problem is that she's politically inept and unable to adjust her behavior to fit changing situations. As she says, "I'm true to myself. I don't remake myself to please others." Zoe is a low self-monitor.

Self-monitoring
A personality trait that measures an individual's ability to adjust his or her behavior to external, situational factors.

   Self-monitoring describes an individual's ability to adjust behavior to external, situational factors.[62] High self-monitors show considerable adaptability in adjusting their behavior to external situational factors. They are highly sensitive to external cues and can behave differently in varying situations, sometimes presenting striking contradictions between their public personae and their private selves. Evidence indicates high self-monitors pay closer attention to the behavior of others and are more capable of conforming than are low self-monitors.[63] Low self-monitors like Zoe can't disguise themselves in that way. They tend to display their true dispositions and attitudes in every situation; hence, there is high behavioral consistency between who they are and what they do.

Proactive Personality

Did you ever notice that some people actively take the initiative to improve their current circumstances or create new ones? These are proactive personalities.[64] Those with a **proactive personality** identify opportunities, show initiative, take action, and persevere until meaningful change occurs, compared to others who generally react to situations. Proactive individuals have many desirable behaviors that organizations covet. They have higher levels of job performance[65] and do not need much oversight.[66] They are receptive to changes in job demands and thrive when they can informally tailor their jobs to their strengths. Proactive individuals often achieve career success.[67]

Proactive personality
People who identify opportunities, show initiative, take action, and persevere until meaningful change occurs.

   Proactive personality may be important for work teams. One study of 95 R&D teams in 33 Chinese companies revealed that teams with high average levels of proactive personality were more innovative.[68] Proactive individuals are also more likely to exchange information with others in a team, which builds trust relationships.[69] Like other traits, proactive personality is affected by the context. One study of bank branch teams in China found that if a team's leader was not proactive, the potential benefits of the team's proactivity became dormant, or worse, their proactivity was suppressed by the leader.[70] In terms of pitfalls, one study of 231 Flemish unemployed individuals found that proactive individuals abandoned their job searches sooner. It may be that proactivity includes stepping back in the face of failure.[71]

PERSONALITY AND SITUATIONS

Earlier we discussed how research shows heredity is more important than the environment in developing our personalities. The environment is not irrelevant, though. Some personality traits, such as the Big Five, tend to be effective in almost any environment or situation. However, we are learning that the effect of particular traits on behavior depends on the situation. Two theoretical frameworks, situation strength and trait activation, help explain how this works.

Situation Strength Theory

Imagine you are in a meeting with your department. How likely are you to walk out, shout at a colleague, or turn your back on everyone? Probably highly unlikely. Now imagine working from home. You might work in your pajamas, listen to loud music, or take a catnap.

Situation strength theory proposes that the way personality translates into behavior depends on the strength of the situation. By *situation strength*, we mean the degree to which norms, cues, or standards dictate appropriate behavior. Strong situations show us what the right behavior is, pressure us to exhibit it, and discourage the wrong behavior. In weak situations, conversely, "anything goes," and thus we are freer to express our personality in behavior. Personality traits better predict behavior in weak situations than in strong ones.

Situation strength theory
A theory indicating that the way personality translates into behavior depends on the strength of the situation.

COMPONENTS OF SITUATION STRENGTH   Researchers have analyzed situation strength in organizations in terms of four elements:[72]

1. *Clarity*, or the degree to which cues about work duties and responsibilities are available and clear—jobs high in clarity produce strong situations because individuals can readily determine what to do. For example, the job of janitor probably provides higher clarity about each task than the job of nanny.
2. *Consistency*, or the extent to which cues regarding work duties and responsibilities are compatible with one another—jobs with high consistency represent strong situations because all the cues point toward the same desired behavior. The job of acute care nurse, for example, probably has higher consistency than the job of manager.
3. *Constraints*, or the extent to which individuals' freedom to decide or act is limited by forces outside their control—jobs with many constraints represent strong situations because an individual has limited discretion. Bank examiner, for example, is probably a job with stronger constraints than forest ranger.
4. *Consequences*, or the degree to which decisions or actions have important implications for the organization or its members, clients, supplies, and so on—jobs with important consequences represent strong situations because the environment is probably heavily structured to guard against mistakes. A surgeon's job, for example, has higher consequences than a foreign-language teacher's.

ORGANIZATIONAL SITUATIONS   Some researchers have speculated that organizations are, by definition, strong situations because they impose rules, norms, and standards that govern behavior. These constraints are usually appropriate. For example, we would not want an employee to feel free to engage in sexual harassment, follow questionable accounting procedures, or come to work only when the mood strikes.

The elements of situation strength are often determined by organizational rules and guidelines, which adds some objectivity to them. However, the perception of these rules influences how the person will respond to the situation's strength. For instance, a person who is usually self-directed may view step-by-step instructions (high clarity) for a simple task as a lack of faith in his ability. Another person who is a rule follower might appreciate the detailed instructions. Their responses (and work attitudes) will reflect their perception of the situation.[73]

Creating strong rules to govern diverse systems might be not only difficult but also unwise. In sum, managers need to recognize the role of situation strength in the workplace and find the appropriate balance.

Trait Activation Theory

Trait Activation Theory (TAT)
A theory that predicts that some situations, events, or interventions "activate" a trait more than others.

Another important theoretical framework toward understanding personality and situations is **Trait Activation Theory (TAT)**. TAT predicts that some situations, events, or interventions "activate" a trait more than others. Using TAT, we can foresee which jobs suit certain personalities. For example, a commission-based compensation plan would likely activate individual differences because extraverts are more reward-sensitive, than, say, open people. Conversely, in jobs that encourage creativity, differences in openness may better predict desired behavior than differences in extraversion. See Exhibit 5-2 for specific examples.

TAT also applies to personality tendencies. For example, a recent study found people learning online responded differently when their behavior was electronically monitored. Those who had a high fear of failure had higher apprehension from the monitoring than others, and consequently learned significantly less. In this case, a feature of the environment (electronic monitoring) activated a trait (fear of failing), and the combination of the two meant lowered job performance.[74] TAT can also work in a positive way. One study found that, in a supportive environment, everyone behaved prosocially, but in a harsh environment, only people with prosocial tendencies exhibited them.[75]

Together, situation strength and trait activation theories show that the debate over nature versus nurture might best be framed as nature *and* nurture. Not only do both affect behavior, but they interact with one another. Put another way, personality and the situation both affect work behavior, but when the situation is right, the power of personality to predict behavior is even higher.

Detail Orientation Required	Social Skills Required	Competitive Work	Innovation Required	Dealing with Angry People	Time Pressure (Deadlines)
Jobs scoring high (the traits listed here should predict behavior in these jobs)					
Air traffic controller	Clergy	Coach/scout	Actor	Correctional officer	Broadcast news analyst
Accountant	Therapist	Financial manager	Systems analyst	Telemarketer	Editor
Legal secretary	Concierge	Sales representative	Advertising writer	Flight attendant	Airline pilot
Jobs scoring low (the traits listed here should not predict behavior in these jobs)					
Forester	Software engineer	Postal clerk	Court reporter	Composer	Skincare specialist
Masseuse	Pump operator	Historian	Archivist	Biologist	Mathematician
Model	Broadcast technician	Nuclear reactor operator	Medical technician	Statistician	Fitness trainer
Jobs that score high activate these traits (make them more relevant to predicting behavior)					
Conscientiousness (+)	Extraversion (+) Agreeableness (+)	Extraversion (+) Agreeableness (−)	Openness (+)	Extraversion (+) Agreeableness (+) Neuroticism (−)	Conscientiousness (+) Neuroticism (−)

EXHIBIT 5-2

Trait Activation Theory: Jobs in Which Certain Big Five Traits Are More Relevant

Note: A plus (+) sign means individuals who score high on this trait should do better in this job. A minus (−) sign means individuals who score low on this trait should do better in this job.

VALUES

Having discussed personality traits, we now turn to values. Values are often very specific and describe belief systems rather than behavioral tendencies. Some beliefs or values reflect a person's personality, but we don't always act consistently with our values. Is capital punishment right or wrong? Is a desire for power good or bad? The answers to these questions are value-laden.

Values represent basic convictions that "a specific mode of conduct or end-state of existence is personally or socially preferable to an opposite or converse mode of conduct or end-state of existence."[76] Values contain a judgmental element because they carry an individual's ideas about what is right, good, or desirable. They have both content and intensity attributes. The content attribute says a mode of conduct or end-state of existence is *important*. The intensity attribute specifies *how important* it is. When we rank values in terms of intensity, we obtain that person's **value system**. We all have a hierarchy of values according to the relative importance we assign to values such as freedom, pleasure, self-respect, honesty, obedience, and equality. Values tend to be relatively stable and enduring.[77]

Values lay the foundation for understanding attitudes and motivation, and they influence our perceptions. We enter an organization with preconceived notions of what "ought" and "ought not" to be. These notions contain our interpretations of right and wrong and our preferences for certain behaviors or outcomes. Regardless of whether they clarify or bias our judgment, our values influence our attitudes and behaviors at work.

While values can sometimes augment decision making, at times they can cloud objectivity and rationality.[78] Suppose you enter an organization with the view that allocating pay on the basis of performance is right, while allocating pay on the basis of seniority is wrong. How will you react if you find the organization you've just joined rewards seniority and not performance? You're likely to be disappointed—this can lead to job dissatisfaction and a decision not to exert a high level of effort because "It's probably not going to lead to more money anyway." Would your attitudes and behavior be different if your values aligned with the organization's pay policies? Most likely.

Values
Basic convictions that a specific mode of conduct or end-state of existence is personally or socially preferable to an opposite or converse mode of conduct or end-state of existence.

Value system
A hierarchy based on a ranking of an individual's values in terms of their intensity.

⭐ WATCH IT

If your professor has assigned this, go to the Assignments section of **mymanagementlab .com** to complete the video exercise titled **Honest Tea: Ethics—Company Mission and Values**.

Terminal versus Instrumental Values

How can we organize values? One researcher—Milton Rokeach—argued that we can separate them into two categories. One set, called **terminal values**, refers to desirable end-states. These are the goals a person would like to achieve during a lifetime. The other set, called **instrumental values**, refers to preferable modes of behavior, or means of achieving the terminal values. Each of us places value on both the ends (terminal values) and the means (instrumental values). Some examples of terminal values are prosperity and economic success, freedom, health and well-being, world peace, and meaning in life. Examples of instrumental values are autonomy and self-reliance, personal discipline, kindness, and goal-orientation. A balance between terminal and instrumental values is important, as well as an understanding of how to strike this balance.

Terminal values
Desirable end-states of existence; the goals a person would like to achieve during his or her lifetime.

Instrumental values
Preferable modes of behavior or means of achieving one's terminal values.

Generational Values

Researchers have integrated several analyses of work values into groups that attempt to capture the shared views of different cohorts or generations in the U.S. workforce.[79] You will surely be familiar with the labels—for example, baby boomers, gen xers, millennials—some of which are used internationally. It is important to remember that while categories are helpful, they represent trends... not the beliefs of individuals.

Though it is fascinating to think about generational values, remember these classifications lack solid research support. Early research was plagued by methodological problems that made it difficult to assess whether differences actually exist. Reviews suggest many of the generalizations are either overblown or incorrect.[80] True differences across generations often do not support popular conceptions of how generations differ. For example, the value placed on leisure has increased over generations from the baby boomers to the millennials and work centrality has declined, but research did not find that millennials had more altruistic work values than their predecessors.[81] Generational classifications may help us understand our own and other generations better, but we must also appreciate their limits.

LINKING AN INDIVIDUAL'S PERSONALITY AND VALUES TO THE WORKPLACE

Thirty years ago, organizations were concerned with personality in order to match individuals to specific jobs. That concern has expanded to include how well the individual's personality *and* values match the organization. Why? Because managers today are less interested in an applicant's ability to perform a *specific* job than with his or her *flexibility* to meet changing situations and maintain commitment to the organization. Still, one of the first types of fit managers look for is person–job fit.

Personality–job fit theory

A theory that identifies six personality types and proposes that the fit between personality type and occupational environment determines satisfaction and turnover.

Person–Job Fit

The effort to match job requirements with personality characteristics is described by John Holland's **personality–job fit theory**, one of the more proven theories in use internationally.[82] The Vocational Preference Inventory questionnaire contains 160 occupational titles. Respondents indicate which they like or dislike, and their answers form personality profiles. Holland presented six personality types and proposed that satisfaction and the propensity to leave a position depend on how well individuals match their personalities to a job. Exhibit 5-3 describes the six types, their personality characteristics, and examples of congruent occupations for each.

There are cultural implications for person–job fit that speak to workers' expectations that jobs will be tailored to them. In individualistic countries where workers expect to be heard and respected by management, increasing person–job fit by tailoring the job to the person increases the individual's job satisfaction. However, in collectivistic countries, person–job fit is a weaker predictor of job satisfaction because people do not expect to have jobs tailored to them, so they value person–job fit efforts less. Therefore, managers in collectivistic cultures should not violate cultural norms by designing jobs for individuals; rather they should seek people who will likely thrive in jobs that have already been structured.[83]

Type	Personality Characteristics	Congruent Occupations
Realistic: Prefers physical activities that require skill, strength, and coordination	Shy, genuine, persistent, stable, conforming, practical	Mechanic, drill press operator, assembly-line worker, farmer
Investigative: Prefers activities that involve thinking, organizing, and understanding	Analytical, original, curious, independent	Biologist, economist, mathematician, news reporter
Social: Prefers activities that involve helping and developing others	Sociable, friendly, cooperative, understanding	Social worker, teacher, counselor, clinical psychologist
Conventional: Prefers rule-regulated, orderly, and unambiguous activities	Conforming, efficient, practical, unimaginative, inflexible	Accountant, corporate manager, bank teller, file clerk
Enterprising: Prefers verbal activities in which there are opportunities to influence others and attain power	Self-confident, ambitious, energetic, domineering	Lawyer, real estate agent, public relations specialist, small business manager
Artistic: Prefers ambiguous and unsystematic activities that allow creative expression	Imaginative, disorderly, idealistic, emotional, impractical	Painter, musician, writer, interior decorator

EXHIBIT 5-3

Holland's Typology of Personality and Congruent Occupations

Person–Organization Fit

We've noted that researchers have looked at matching people to organizations and jobs. If an organization has a dynamic and changing environment and needs employees who are able to readily change tasks and move easily between teams, it's more important that employees' personalities fit with the overall organization's culture than with the characteristics of any specific job.

Person–organization fit essentially means people are attracted to and selected by organizations that match their values, and they leave organizations that are not compatible with their personalities.[84] Using the Big Five terminology, for instance, we could expect that extraverts fit well with aggressive and team-oriented cultures; people high on agreeableness match better with a supportive organizational climate; and highly open people fit better in organizations that emphasize innovation rather than standardization.[85] Following these guidelines when hiring should yield employees who fit better with the organization's culture, which should, in turn, result in higher employee satisfaction and reduced turnover. Research on person–organization fit has also looked at whether people's values match the organization's culture. A match predicts job satisfaction, commitment to the organization, and low turnover.[86]

In pursuit of fit, it is more important than ever for organizations to manage their image online since job seekers view company websites as part of their pre-application process. Applicants want to see a user-friendly website that provides information about company philosophies and policies. For example, millennials in particular may react positively when they perceive an organization is committed to work–life balance. The website is so important to the development of perceived person–organization fit that improvements to its style (usability) and substance (policies) can lead to more applicants.[87]

Person–organization fit
A theory that people are attracted to and selected by organizations that match their values, and leave when there is not compatibility.

Other Dimensions of Fit

Although person–job fit and person–organization fit are considered the most salient dimensions for workplace outcomes, other avenues of fit are worth examining. These include *person–group fit* and *person–supervisor fit*. Person–group fit is important in team settings, where the dynamics of team interactions significantly affect work outcomes. Person–supervisor fit has become an important area of research since poor fit in this dimension can lead to lower job satisfaction and reduced performance.

All dimensions of fit are sometimes broadly referred to as person–environment fit. Each dimension can predict work attitudes, which are partially based on culture. A recent meta-analysis of person–environment fit in East Asia, Europe, and North America suggested the dimensions of person–organization and person–job fit are the strongest predictors of positive work attitudes and performance in North America. These dimensions are important to a lesser degree in Europe, and they are least important in East Asia.[88]

CULTURAL VALUES

Unlike personality, which is largely genetically determined, values are learned. They are passed down through generations and they vary by cultures. As researchers have sought to understand cultural value differences, two important frameworks have emerged from Geert Hofstede and the GLOBE studies.

Hofstede's Framework

One of the most widely referenced approaches for analyzing variations among cultures was done by Geert Hofstede.[89] Hofstede surveyed more than 116,000 IBM employees in 40 countries about their work-related values and found managers and employees varied on five value dimensions of national culture:

Power distance
A national culture attribute that describes the extent to which a society accepts that power in institutions and organizations is distributed unequally.

Individualism
A national culture attribute that describes the degree to which people prefer to act as individuals rather than as members of groups.

Collectivism
A national culture attribute that describes a tight social framework in which people expect others in groups of which they are a part to look after them and protect them Collectivistic countries/cultures in which people see themselves as interdependent and seek community and group goals. Collectivistic values are found in Asia, Africa, and South America, for example.

Masculinity
A national culture attribute that describes the extent to which the culture favors traditional masculine work roles of achievement, power, and control. Societal values are characterized by assertiveness and materialism.

- **Power distance. Power distance** describes the degree to which people in a country accept that power in institutions and organizations is distributed unequally. A high rating on power distance means large inequalities of power and wealth exist and are tolerated in the culture, as in a class or caste system that discourages upward mobility. A low power distance rating characterizes societies that stress equality and opportunity.
- **Individualism versus collectivism. Individualism** is the degree to which people prefer to act as individuals rather than as members of groups and believe in an individual's rights above all else. **Collectivism** emphasizes a tight social framework in which people expect others in groups of which they are a part to look after them and protect them. In OB, we tend to refer to the terms in the framework of individualist(ic) and collectivist(ic) countries/cultures.
- **Masculinity versus femininity.** Hofstede's construct of **masculinity** is the degree to which the culture favors traditional masculine roles such as achievement, power, and control, as opposed to viewing men and women as equals. A high masculinity rating indicates the culture has separate roles for men and women, with men dominating the society. A high **femininity** rating means the culture sees little differentiation between male and female roles and treats women as the equals of men in all respects.
- **Uncertainty avoidance.** The degree to which people in a country prefer structured over unstructured situations defines their **uncertainty avoidance**. In cultures scoring high on uncertainty avoidance, people have increased anxiety about uncertainty and ambiguity and use laws and controls to reduce uncertainty. People in cultures low on uncertainty avoidance are more accepting of ambiguity, are less rule oriented, take more risks, and more readily accept change.

- **Long-term versus short-term orientation.** This typology measures a society's devotion to traditional values. People in a culture with **long-term orientation** look to the future and value thrift, persistence, and tradition. In a **short-term orientation**, people value the here and now; they also accept change more readily and don't see commitments as impediments to change.

How do different countries score on Hofstede's dimensions? Exhibit 5-4 shows the ratings of the countries for which data are available. For example, power distance is higher in Malaysia than in any other country. The United States is very individualistic; in fact, it's the most individualistic nation of all (closely followed by Australia and Great Britain). Guatemala is the most collectivistic nation. The country with the highest masculinity rank by far is Japan, and the country with the highest femininity rank is Sweden. Greece scores the highest in uncertainty avoidance, while Singapore scores the lowest. Hong Kong has one of the longest-term orientations; Pakistan has the shortest-term orientation.

Research across 598 studies with more than 200,000 respondents has investigated the relationship of Hofstede's cultural values and a variety of organizational criteria at both the individual and national levels of analysis.[90] Overall, the five original culture dimensions were found to be equally strong predictors of relevant outcomes. The researchers also found measuring individual scores resulted in much better predictions of most outcomes than assigning all people in a country the same cultural values. In sum, this research suggests Hofstede's framework may be a valuable way of thinking about differences among people, but we should be cautious about assuming all people from a country have the same values.

The GLOBE Framework

Founded in 1993, the Global Leadership and Organizational Behavior Effectiveness (GLOBE) research program is an ongoing cross-cultural investigation of leadership and national culture. Using data from 825 organizations in 62 countries, the GLOBE team identified 9 dimensions on which national cultures differ.[91] Some dimensions—such as power distance, individualism/collectivism, uncertainty avoidance, gender differentiation (similar to masculinity versus femininity), and future orientation (similar to long-term versus short-term orientation)—resemble the Hofstede dimensions. The main difference is that the GLOBE framework added dimensions, such as humane orientation (the degree to which a society rewards individuals for being altruistic, generous, and kind to others) and performance orientation (the degree to which a society encourages and rewards group members for performance improvement and excellence).

Comparison of Hofstede's Framework and the GLOBE Framework

Which framework is better, Hofstede's or the GLOBE? That's hard to say, and each has its supporters. We give more emphasis to Hofstede's dimensions here because they have stood the test of time and the GLOBE study confirmed them. For example, a review of the organizational commitment literature shows both the Hofstede and GLOBE individualism/collectivism dimensions operated similarly. Specifically, both frameworks showed organizational commitment tends to be lower in individualistic countries.[92] Both frameworks have a great deal in common, and each has something to offer.

Femininity
A national culture attribute that indicates little differentiation between male and female roles; a high rating indicates that women are treated as the equals of men in all aspects of the society.

Uncertainty avoidance
A national culture attribute that describes the extent to which a society feels threatened by uncertain and ambiguous situations and tries to avoid them.

Long-term orientation
A national culture attribute that emphasizes the future, thrift, and persistence.

Short-term orientation
A national culture attribute that emphasizes the present and accepts change.

Country	Power Distance Index	Power Distance Rank	Individualism versus Collectivism Index	Individualism versus Collectivism Rank	Masculinity versus Femininity Index	Masculinity versus Femininity Rank	Uncertainty Avoidance Index	Uncertainty Avoidance Rank	Long- versus Short-Term Orientation Index	Long- versus Short-Term Orientation Rank
Argentina	49	35–36	46	22–23	56	20–21	86	10–15		
Australia	36	41	90	2	61	16	51	37	31	22–24
Austria	11	53	55	18	79	2	70	24–25	31	22–24
Belgium	65	20	75	8	54	22	94	5–6	38	18
Brazil	69	14	38	26–27	49	27	76	21–22	65	6
Canada	39	39	80	4–5	52	24	48	41–42	23	30
Chile	63	24–25	23	38	28	46	86	10–15		
Colombia	67	17	13	49	64	11–12	80	20		
Costa Rica	35	42–44	15	46	21	48–49	86	10–15		
Denmark	18	51	74	9	16	50	23	51	46	10
Ecuador	78	8–9	8	52	63	13–14	67	28		
El Salvador	66	18–19	19	42	40	40	94	5–6		
Finland	33	46	63	17	26	47	59	31–32	41	14
France	68	15–16	71	10–11	43	35–36	86	10–15	39	17
Germany	35	42–44	67	15	66	9–10	65	29	31	22–24
Great Britain	35	42–44	89	3	66	9–10	35	47–48	25	28–29
Greece	60	27–28	35	30	57	18–19	112	1		
Guatemala	95	2–3	6	53	37	43	101	3		
Hong Kong	68	15–16	25	37	57	18–19	29	49–50	96	2
India	77	10–11	48	21	56	20–21	40	45	61	7
Indonesia	78	8–9	14	47–48	46	30–31	48	41–42		
Iran	58	29–30	41	24	43	35–36	59	31–32		
Ireland	28	49	70	12	68	7–8	35	47–48	43	13
Israel	13	52	54	19	47	29	81	19		
Italy	50	34	76	7	70	4–5	75	23	34	19
Jamaica	45	37	39	25	68	7–8	13	52		
Japan	54	33	46	22–23	95	1	92	7	80	4
Korea (South)	60	27–28	18	43	39	41	85	16–17	75	5
Malaysia	104	1	26	36	50	25–26	36	46		
Mexico	81	5–6	30	32	69	6	82	18		
The Netherlands	38	40	80	4–5	14	51	53	35	44	11–12
New Zealand	22	50	79	6	58	17	49	39–40	30	25–26
Norway	31	47–48	69	13	8	52	50	38	44	11–12
Pakistan	55	32	14	47–48	50	25–26	70	24–25	0	34
Panama	95	2–3	11	51	44	34	86	10–15		
Peru	64	21–23	16	45	42	37–38	87	9		
Philippines	94	4	32	31	64	11–12	44	44	19	31–32
Portugal	63	24–25	27	33–35	31	45	104	2	30	25–26
Singapore	74	13	20	39–41	48	28	8	53	48	9
South Africa	49	35–36	65	16	63	13–14	49	39–40		
Spain	57	31	51	20	42	37–38	86	10–15	19	31–32
Sweden	31	47–48	71	10–11	5	53	29	49–50	33	20
Switzerland	34	45	68	14	70	4–5	58	33	40	15–16
Taiwan	58	29–30	17	44	45	32–33	69	26	87	3
Thailand	64	21–23	20	39–41	34	44	64	30	56	8
Turkey	66	18–19	37	28	45	32–33	85	16–17		
United States	40	38	91	1	62	15	46	43	29	27
Uruguay	61	26	36	29	38	42	100	4		
Venezuela	81	5–6	12	50	73	3	76	21–22		
Yugoslavia	76	12	27	33–35	21	48–49	88	8		
Regions:										
Arab countries	80	7	38	26–27	53	23	68	27		
East Africa	64	21–23	27	33–35	41	39	52	36	25	28–29
West Africa	77	10–11	20	39–41	46	30–31	54	34	16	33

EXHIBIT 5-4

Hofstede's Cultural Values by Nation

Source: Copyright Geert Hofstede BV, hofstede@bart.nl. Reprinted with permission.

SUMMARY

Personality matters to OB. It does not explain all behavior, but it sets the stage. Emerging theory and research reveal how personality matters more in some situations than others. The Big Five has been a particularly important advancement, though the Dark Triad and other traits matter as well. Every trait has advantages and disadvantages for work behavior, and there is no perfect constellation of traits that is ideal in every situation. Personality can help you to understand why people (including yourself!) act, think, and feel the way we do, and the astute manager can put that understanding to use by taking care to place employees in situations that best fit their personalities.

Values often underlie and explain attitudes, behaviors, and perceptions. Values tend to vary internationally along dimensions that can predict organizational outcomes; however, an individual may or may not hold values that are consistent with the values of the national culture.

IMPLICATIONS FOR MANAGERS

- Consider screening job candidates for conscientiousness—and the other Big Five traits, depending on the criteria your organization finds most important. Other aspects, such as core self-evaluation or narcissism, may be relevant in certain situations.
- Although the MBTI has faults, you can use it in training and development to help employees better understand each other, open up communication in work groups, and possibly reduce conflicts.
- Evaluate jobs, work groups, and your organization to determine the optimal personality fit.
- Take into account situational factors when evaluating observable personality traits, and lower the situation strength to better ascertain personality characteristics.
- The more you consider people's cultural differences, the better you will be able to determine their work behavior and create a positive organizational climate that performs well.

⭐ PERSONAL INVENTORY ASSESSMENTS

PERSONAL INVENTORY ASSESSMENTS

Personality Style Indicator

What's your personality? You've probably been wondering as you read this chapter. Take this PIA to obtain some indications of your personality style.

5-1. Do you think the personalities of businesspeople may be more alike than different?

6

Perception and Individual Decision Making

MyManagementLab®
⭐ Improve Your Grade!
When you see this icon ⭐, visit **mymanagementlab.com** for activities that are applied, personalized, and offer immediate feedback.

After studying this chapter, you should be able to:

1. Explain the factors that influence perception.
2. Describe attribution theory.
3. Explain the link between perception and decision making.
4. Contrast the rational model of decision making with bounded rationality and intuition.
5. Explain how individual differences and organizational constraints affect decision making.
6. Contrast the three ethical decision criteria.
7. Describe the three-stage model of creativity.

⭐ Chapter Warm-up
If your professor has chosen to assign this, go to the Assignments section of **mymanagementlab.com** to complete the chapter warm-up.

Perception
A process by which individuals organize and interpret their sensory impressions in order to give meaning to their environment.

WHAT IS PERCEPTION?

Perception is a process by which we organize and interpret sensory impressions in order to give meaning to their environment. What we perceive can be substantially different from objective reality. For example, all employees in a firm may view it as a great place to work—favorable working conditions, interesting job assignments, good pay, excellent benefits, understanding and responsible management—but, as most of us know, it's very unusual to find universal agreement.

Why is perception important in the study of OB? Simply because people's behavior is based on their perception of what reality is, not on reality itself. *The world as it is perceived is the world that is behaviorally important.* In other words, our perception becomes the reality from which we act.

Factors That Influence Perception

A number of factors shape and sometimes distort perception. These factors can reside in the *perceiver*, the object or *target* being perceived, or the *situation* in which the perception is made.

PERCEIVER When you look at a target, your interpretation of what you see is influenced by your personal characteristics—attitudes, personality, motives, interests, past experiences, and expectations. In some ways, we hear what we want to hear[1] and see what we want to see—not because it's the truth, but because it conforms to our thinking. For instance, research indicated that supervisors perceived employees who started work earlier in the day as more conscientious and therefore as higher performers; however, supervisors who were night owls themselves were less likely to make that erroneous assumption.[2] Some perceptions *created* by attitudes like these can be counteracted by objective evaluation, but others can be insidious. Consider, for instance, observer perceptions of a recent shooting in New York. There were two eyewitnesses—one said a police officer chased and shot a fleeing man; the other said a handcuffed man lying on the ground was shot. Neither perceived the situation correctly: The man was actually attempting to attack a police officer with a hammer when he was shot by another officer.[3]

TARGET The characteristics of the target also affect what we perceive. Because we don't look at targets in isolation, the relationship of a target to its background influences perception, as does our tendency to group close things and similar things together. We can perceive women, men, Whites, African Americans, Asians, or members of any other group that shares some surface characteristics (see Chapter 2) as alike in other, unrelated ways as well. Often, these assumptions are harmful, as when people who have criminal records are prejudged in the workplace as a result (whether or not it is known that they were wrongly arrested).[4] Sometimes differences can work in our favor, though, such as when we are drawn to those that are different from what we expect. For instance, one study found that participants respected a professor wearing a T-shirt and sneakers in the classroom more than the same professor dressed traditionally. The professor stood out from the norm in the classroom setting and was therefore perceived as an individualist.[5]

CONTEXT Context matters too. The time at which we see an object or event can influence our attention, as can location, light, heat, or situational factors. For instance, at a club on Saturday night you may not notice someone "decked out." Yet that same person so attired for your Monday morning management class would certainly catch your attention. Neither the perceiver nor the target has changed between Saturday night and Monday morning, but the situation is different.

People are usually not aware of the factors that influence their view of reality. In fact, people are not even that perceptive about their *own* abilities.[6] Thankfully, awareness and objective measures can reduce our perceptual distortions. For instance, when people are asked to ponder specific aspects of their ability, they become more realistic in their self-perceptions.[7] Let's next consider *how* we make perceptions of others.

✪ WATCH IT

If your professor has assigned this, go to the Assignments section of **mymanagementlab .com** to complete the video exercise titled **Orpheus Group Casting: Social Perception and Attribution**.

PERSON PERCEPTION: MAKING JUDGMENTS ABOUT OTHERS

The perception concepts most relevant to OB include *person perceptions*, or the perceptions people form about each other. Many of our perceptions of others are formed by first impressions and small cues that have little supporting evidence. Let's unravel some of our human tendencies that interfere with correct person perception, beginning with the evidence behind attribution theory.

Attribution Theory

Nonliving objects such as desks, machines, and buildings are subject to the laws of nature, but they have no beliefs, motives, or intentions. People do. When we observe people, we attempt to explain their behavior. Our perception and judgment of a person's actions are influenced by the assumptions we make about that person's state of mind.

Attribution theory
An attempt to determine whether an individual's behavior is internally or externally caused.

Attribution theory tries to explain the ways we judge people differently, depending on the meaning we attribute to a behavior.[8] For instance, consider what you think when people smile at you. Do you think they are cooperative, exploitative, or competitive? We assign meaning to smiles and other expressions in many different ways.[9]

INTERNAL AND EXTERNAL CAUSATION   Attribution theory suggests that when we observe an individual's behavior, we attempt to determine whether it was internally or externally caused. That determination depends largely on three factors: (1) distinctiveness, (2) consensus, and (3) consistency. Let's clarify the differences between internal and external causation, and then we'll discuss the determining factors.

Internally caused behaviors are those an observer believes to be under the personal behavioral control of another individual. *Externally* caused behavior is what we imagine the situation forced the individual to do. If an employee is late for work, you might attribute that to his overnight partying and subsequent oversleeping. This is an internal attribution. But if you attribute his lateness to a traffic snarl, you are making an external attribution.

DISTINCTIVENESS, CONSENSUS, AND CONSISTENCY   *Distinctiveness* refers to whether an individual displays different behaviors in different situations. Is the employee who arrives late today also one who regularly "blows off" other kinds of commitments? What we want to know is whether this behavior is unusual. If it is, we are likely to give it an external attribution. If it's not, we will probably judge the behavior to be internal.

If everyone who faces a similar situation responds in the same way, we can say the behavior shows *consensus*. The behavior of our tardy employee meets this criterion if all employees who took the same route were also late. From an attribution perspective, if consensus is high, you would probably give an external attribution to the employee's tardiness, whereas if other employees who took the same route made it to work on time, you would attribute his lateness to an internal cause.

Finally, an observer looks for *consistency* in a person's actions. Does the person respond the same way over time? Coming in 10 minutes late for work is not perceived the same for an employee who hasn't been late for several months as for an employee who is late three times a week. The more consistent the behavior, the more we are inclined to attribute it to internal causes.

Exhibit 6-1 summarizes the key elements in attribution theory. It tells us, for instance, that if an employee, Katelyn, generally performs at about the same level on related tasks as she does on her current task (low distinctiveness); other employees frequently perform differently—better or worse—than Katelyn on that task (low consensus); and Katelyn's performance on this current task is consistent over time (high consistency), anyone judging Katelyn's work will likely hold her primarily responsible for her task performance (internal attribution).

ERRORS AND BIASES   Errors or biases distort attributions. When we make judgments about the behavior of other people, we tend to underestimate the influence of external factors and overestimate the influence of internal or personal factors.[10] This **fundamental attribution error** can explain why a sales manager attributes the poor performance of her sales agents to laziness rather than to a competitor's innovative product line. Individuals and organizations tend to attribute their own successes to internal factors such as ability or effort, while blaming failure on external factors such as bad luck or difficult coworkers. Similarly, people tend to attribute ambiguous information as relatively flattering, accept positive feedback, and reject negative feedback. This is called **self-serving bias**.[11]

Fundamental attribution error
The tendency to underestimate the influence of external factors and overestimate the influence of internal factors when making judgments about the behavior of others.

Self-serving bias
The tendency for individuals to attribute their own successes to internal factors and put the blame for failures on external factors.

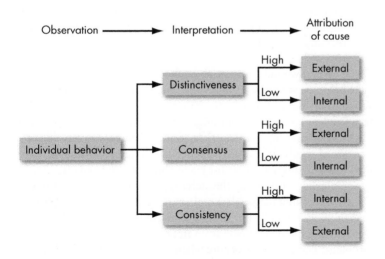

EXHIBIT 6-1
Attribution Theory

Self-serving biases may be less common in East Asian cultures, but evidence suggests they still operate there.[12] Studies indicate Chinese managers assess blame for mistakes using the same distinctiveness, consensus, and consistency cues used by Western managers.[13] They also become angry and punish those deemed responsible for failure, a reaction shown in many studies of Western managers. It might just take more evidence for Asian managers to conclude someone else should be blamed.

Common Shortcuts in Judging Others

Shortcuts for judging others often allow us to make accurate perceptions rapidly and provide valid data for making predictions. As we've seen, they can and do sometimes result in significant distortions. Let's explore this further.

SELECTIVE PERCEPTION   Any characteristic that makes a person, an object, or an event stand out will increase the probability we will perceive it. Why? Because it is impossible for us to assimilate everything we see; we can only take in certain stimuli. Thus, you are more likely to notice cars like your own, and your boss may reprimand some people, but not others, for doing the same thing. Because we can't observe everything going on around us, we use **selective perception**. We don't choose randomly: we select according to our interests, background, experience, and attitudes. Seeing what we want to see, we sometimes draw unwarranted conclusions from an ambiguous situation.

HALO EFFECT   When we draw an impression about an individual on the basis of a single characteristic, such as intelligence, sociability, or appearance, a **halo effect** is operating.[14] The halo effect is easy to demonstrate. If you knew someone was, say, gregarious, what else would you infer? You probably wouldn't say the person was introverted, right? You might assume the person was loud, happy, or quick-witted, when in fact gregarious does not include those other attributes. As managers, we need to be careful not to draw inferences from small clues.

CONTRAST EFFECTS   An old adage among entertainers is "Never follow an act that has kids or animals in it." Why? Audiences love children and animals so much that you'll look bad in comparison. This example demonstrates how the **contrast effect** can distort perceptions. We don't evaluate a person in isolation. Our reaction is influenced by other people we have recently encountered.

STEREOTYPING   When we judge someone on the basis of our perception of the group to which he or she belongs, we are **stereotyping**.[15] Stereotypes can be deeply ingrained and powerful enough to influence life-and-death decisions. One study, controlling for a wide array of factors (such as aggravating or mitigating circumstances), showed that the degree to which Black defendants in murder trials looked "stereotypically black" essentially doubled their odds of receiving a death sentence if convicted.[16] Another study found that students tended to assign higher scores for leadership potential and effective leadership to Whites than to minorities, supporting the stereotype of Whites as better leaders.[17]

We deal with the unmanageable number of stimuli of our complex world by using stereotypes or shortcuts called *heuristics* to make decisions quickly. For example, it does make sense to assume that Allison from finance will be able to help you figure out a forecasting problem. The challenge occurs when we generalize inaccurately or too much.

Selective perception
The tendency to selectively interpret what one sees on the basis of one's interests, background, experience, and attitudes.

Halo effect
The tendency to draw a general impression about an individual on the basis of a single characteristic.

Contrast effect
Evaluation of a person's characteristics that is affected by comparisons with other people recently encountered who rank higher or lower on the same characteristics.

Stereotyping
Judging someone on the basis of one's perception of the group to which that person belongs.

THE LINK BETWEEN PERCEPTION AND INDIVIDUAL DECISION MAKING

Individuals make **decisions**, choices from among two or more alternatives. Ideally, decision making would be an objective process, but the way individuals make decisions and the quality of their choices are largely influenced by their perceptions. Individual decision making is an important factor of behavior at all levels of an organization.

> **Decisions**
> Choices made from among two or more alternatives.

Decision making occurs as a reaction to a **problem**. That is, a discrepancy exists between the current state of affairs and some desired state, requiring us to consider alternative courses of action. If your car breaks down and you rely on it to get to work, you have a problem that requires a decision on your part.[18] Unfortunately, most problems don't come neatly labeled. One person's *problem* is another person's *satisfactory state of affairs.* One manager may view her division's 2 percent decline in quarterly sales to be a serious problem requiring immediate action on her part. Her counterpart in another division, who also had a 2 percent sales decrease, might consider it quite acceptable. So awareness that a problem exists and that a decision might or might not be needed is a perceptual issue.

> **Problem**
> A discrepancy between the current state of affairs and some desired state.

Every decision requires us to interpret and evaluate information. We typically receive data from multiple sources that we need to screen, process, and interpret. Which data are relevant to the decision, and which are not? Our perceptions will answer that question. We also need to develop alternatives and evaluate their strengths and weaknesses. Again, our perceptual process will affect the outcome. Finally, we have to consider how our perceptions of the situation influence our decisions. For instance, how good are you at saying no? Research indicates that we perceive that saying no is uncomfortable, and often after saying no we will feel obligated to say yes to subsequent requests. In fact, people are so uncomfortable saying no that they may agree to unethical acts. When student participants in a study asked 108 strangers to write "pickle" in library books, half of them did it![19]

DECISION MAKING IN ORGANIZATIONS

Business schools train students to follow rational decision-making models. While such rationalistic models have merit, they don't always describe how people make decisions. OB improves the way we make decisions in organizations by addressing the decision-making errors people commit in addition to the perception errors we've discussed. First, we describe some decision-making constructs, and then outline a few of the most common errors.

The Rational Model, Bounded Rationality, and Intuition

In OB, there are generally accepted constructs of decision making each of us employs to make determinations: rational decision making, bounded rationality, and intuition. Though their processes make sense, they may not lead to the most accurate (or best) decisions. More importantly, there are times when one strategy may lead to a better outcome than another in a given situation.

EXHIBIT 6-2
Steps in the
Rational
Decision-Making
Model

1. Define the problem.
2. Identify the decision criteria.
3. Allocate weights to the criteria.
4. Develop the alternatives.
5. Evaluate the alternatives.
6. Select the best alternative.

Rational
Characterized by making consistent, value-maximizing choices within specified constraints.

Rational decision-making model
A decision-making model that describes how individuals should behave in order to maximize some outcome.

RATIONAL DECISION MAKING   We often think the best decision maker is **rational** and makes consistent, value-maximizing choices within specified constraints.[20] Rational decisions follow a six-step **rational decision-making model**[21] (see Exhibit 6-2).

The rational decision-making model assumes the decision maker has complete information, is able to identify all relevant options in an unbiased manner, and chooses the option with the highest utility.[22] In reality, though, most decisions don't follow the rational model; people are usually content to find an acceptable or reasonable solution to a problem rather than an optimal one. We tend to limit our choices to the neighborhood of the problem's symptom and the current alternative at hand. As one expert in decision making put it, "Most significant decisions are made by judgment, rather than by a defined prescriptive model."[23] People are remarkably unaware of making suboptimal decisions.[24]

Bounded rationality
A process of making decisions by constructing simplified models that extract the essential features from problems without capturing all their complexity.

BOUNDED RATIONALITY   Often, we don't follow the rational decision-making model for a reason: Our limited information-processing capability makes it impossible to assimilate all the information necessary to optimize, even if the information is readily obtainable.[25] Because we cannot formulate and solve complex problems with full rationality, we operate within the confines of **bounded rationality**. We construct simplified models that extract the essential features from problems without capturing all their complexity. We can then behave rationally within the limits of the simple model.

One outcome of bounded rationality is a tendency to satisfice, or seek solutions that are satisfactory and sufficient ("good enough" in our estimation). While the satisficing answer is acceptable but not necessarily optimal, it's not always a bad method. Often, a simple process may frequently be more sensible than the traditional rational decision-making model.[26] To use the rational model, you need to gather a great deal of information about all the options, compute applicable weights, and then calculate values across a huge number of criteria. All these processes can cost time, energy, and money. If there are many unknown weights and preferences, the fully rational model may not be any more accurate than a best guess. Sometimes a fast-and-frugal process of solving problems might be your best option.

Intuitive decision making
An unconscious process created out of distilled experience.

INTUITION   Perhaps the least rational way of making decisions is **intuitive decision making**, an unconscious process created from distilled experience.[27] Intuitive decision making occurs outside conscious thought; relies on holistic associations, or links between disparate pieces of information; is fast; and is *affectively charged,* meaning it engages the emotions.[28] While intuition isn't rational, it isn't necessarily wrong. Nor does it always contradict rational analysis; the two can complement each other.

Does intuition help effective decision making? Researchers are divided, but most experts are skeptical, in part because intuition is hard to measure and analyze. Probably the best advice from one expert is: "Intuition can be very useful as a way of setting up a hypothesis but is unacceptable as 'proof.'" Use hunches derived from your experience to speculate, yes, but test those hunches with objective data and rational, dispassionate analysis.[29]

Common Biases and Errors in Decision Making

Decision makers engage in bounded rationality, but systematic biases and errors can creep into their judgments.[30] To minimize effort and avoid trade-offs, people tend to rely too heavily on experience, impulses, gut feelings, and convenient rules of thumb. Shortcuts can distort rationality. Exhibit 6-3 provides some suggestions for how to avoid falling into these biases and errors.

OVERCONFIDENCE BIAS   We tend to be overconfident about our abilities and the abilities of others; also, we are usually not aware of this bias.[31] For example, when people say they're 90 percent confident about the range a certain number might take, their estimated ranges contain the correct answer only about 50 percent of the time—and experts are no more accurate in setting up confidence intervals than are novices.[32]

Individuals whose intellectual and interpersonal abilities are *weakest* are most likely to overestimate their performance and ability.[33] There's also a negative relationship between entrepreneurs' optimism and performance of their new ventures: the more optimistic, the less successful.[34] The tendency to be too confident about their ideas might keep some from planning how to avoid problems that arise.

ANCHORING BIAS   **Anchoring bias** is a tendency to fixate on initial information and fail to adequately adjust for subsequent information.[35] As we discussed earlier in the chapter in relationship to employment interviews, the mind appears to give a disproportionate amount of emphasis to the first information it receives. Anchors are widely used by people in professions in which persuasion skills are important—advertising, management, politics, real estate, and law.

Anchoring bias
A tendency to fixate on initial information, from which one then fails to adequately adjust for subsequent information.

Focus on Goals. Without goals, you can't be rational, you don't know what information you need, you don't know which information is relevant and which is irrelevant, you'll find it difficult to choose between alternatives, and you're far more likely to experience regret over the choices you make. Clear goals make decision making easier and help you eliminate options that are inconsistent with your interests.

Look for Information That Disconfirms Your Beliefs. One of the most effective means for counteracting overconfidence and the confirmation and hindsight biases is to actively look for information that contradicts your beliefs and assumptions. When we overtly consider various ways we could be wrong, we challenge our tendencies to think we're smarter than we actually are.

Don't Try to Create Meaning out of Random Events. The educated mind has been trained to look for cause-and-effect relationships. When something happens, we ask why. And when we can't find reasons, we often invent them. You have to accept that there are events in life that are outside your control. Ask yourself if patterns can be meaningfully explained or whether they are merely coincidence. Don't attempt to create meaning out of coincidence.

Increase Your Options. No matter how many options you've identified, your final choice can be no better than the best of the option set you've selected. This argues for increasing your decision alternatives and for using creativity in developing a wide range of diverse choices. The more alternatives you can generate, and the more diverse those alternatives, the greater your chance of finding an outstanding one.

EXHIBIT 6-3
Reducing Biases and Errors

Source: S. P. Robbins, *Decide & Conquer: Making Winning Decisions and Taking Control of Your Life* (Upper Saddle River, NJ: Financial Times/ Prentice Hall, 2004), 81–84.

Any time a negotiation takes place, so does anchoring. When a prospective employer asks how much you made in your prior job, your answer typically anchors the employer's offer. (Remember this when you negotiate your salary, but set the anchor only as high as you truthfully can.) The more precise your anchor is, the smaller the adjustment. Some research suggests people think of making an adjustment after an anchor is set as rounding off a number: If you suggest a salary of $55,000, your boss will consider $50,000 to $60,000 a reasonable range for negotiation, but if you mention $55,650, your boss is more likely to consider $55,000 to $56,000 the range of likely values.[36]

Confirmation bias
The tendency to seek out information that reaffirms past choices and to discount information that contradicts past judgments.

CONFIRMATION BIAS   The rational decision-making process assumes we objectively gather information. But we don't. We *selectively* gather it. **Confirmation bias** represents a case of selective perception: we seek out information that reaffirms our past choices, and we discount information that contradicts them.[37] We also tend to accept at face value information that confirms our preconceived views, while we are skeptical of information that challenges them. We even tend to seek sources most likely to tell us what we want to hear, and we give too much weight to supporting information and too little to that which is contradictory. Fortunately, those who feel there is a strong need to be accurate in making a decision are less prone to confirmation bias.

Availability bias
The tendency for people to base their judgments on information that is readily available to them.

AVAILABILITY BIAS   People tend to fear flying more than driving in a car. But if flying on a commercial airline were as dangerous as driving, the equivalent of two 747s filled to capacity would crash every week, killing all aboard. Because the media give more attention to air accidents, we tend to overstate the risk of flying and understate the risk of driving.

Availability bias is our tendency to base judgments on readily available information. A combination of readily available information and our previous direct experience with similar information has a particularly strong impact on our decision making. Also, events that evoke emotions, are particularly vivid, or are more recent tend to be more available in our memory, leading us to overestimate the chances of unlikely events such as being in an airplane crash, suffering complications from medical treatment, or getting fired.[38] Availability bias can also explain why managers give more weight in performance appraisals to recent employee behaviors than to behaviors of 6 or 9 months earlier.[39]

Escalation of commitment
An increased commitment to a previous decision in spite of negative information.

ESCALATION OF COMMITMENT   Another distortion that creeps into decisions is a tendency to escalate commitment, often for increasingly nonrational reasons.[40] **Escalation of commitment** refers to our staying with a decision even if there is clear evidence it's wrong. When is escalation most likely to occur? Evidence indicates it occurs when individuals view themselves as responsible for the outcome. The fear of personal failure even biases the way we search for and evaluate information so that we choose only information that supports our dedication. It doesn't appear to matter whether we chose the failing course of action or if it was assigned to us—we feel responsible and escalate in either case. Also, the sharing of decision authority—such as when others review the choice we made—can lead to higher escalation.[41]

We usually think of escalation of commitment as ungrounded. However, persistence in the face of failure is responsible for a great many of history's greatest feats, including the building of the Pyramids, the Great Wall of China, the Panama Canal, and the Empire State Building among others. Researchers suggest a balanced approach includes frequent evaluation of the spent costs and whether the next step is worth the anticipated costs.[42] As such, what we want to combat is the tendency to *automatically* escalate commitment.

RANDOMNESS ERROR Most of us like to think we have some control over our world. Our tendency to believe we can predict the outcome of random events is the **randomness error**.

Decision making suffers when we try to create meaning from random events, particularly when we turn imaginary patterns into superstitions.[43] These can be completely contrived ("I never make important decisions on Friday the 13th") or they can evolve from a reinforced past pattern of behavior (wearing a lucky T-shirt).

Randomness error
The tendency of individuals to believe that they can predict the outcome of random events.

RISK AVERSION Mathematically speaking, we should find a 50–50 flip of the coin for $100 to be worth as much as a sure promise of $50. After all, the expected value of the gamble over a number of trials is $50. However, nearly everyone but committed gamblers would rather have the sure thing than a risky prospect.[44] For many people, a 50–50 flip of a coin even for $200 might not be worth as much as a sure promise of $50, even though the gamble is mathematically worth twice as much! This tendency to prefer a sure thing over a risky outcome is **risk aversion**.

Risk aversion has important business implications. For example, to offset the inherent risk employees accept in a commission-based wage, companies may pay commissioned employees considerably more than they do those on straight salaries. Second, risk-averse employees will stick with the established way of doing their jobs rather than take a chance on innovative methods. Continuing with a strategy that has worked in the past minimizes risk, but it will lead to stagnation. Third, ambitious people with power that can be taken away (most managers) appear to be especially risk averse, perhaps because they don't want to gamble with everything they've worked so hard to achieve.[45] CEOs at risk of termination are exceptionally risk averse, even when a riskier investment strategy is in their firms' best interests.[46]

Risk aversion
The tendency to prefer a sure gain of a moderate amount over a riskier outcome, even if the riskier outcome might have a higher expected payoff.

HINDSIGHT BIAS **Hindsight bias** is the tendency to believe falsely, after the outcome is known, that we would have accurately predicted it.[47] When we have feedback on the outcome, we seem good at concluding it was obvious.

For instance, the original home video rental industry in which movies were rented at brick-and-mortar stores collapsed as online distribution outlets ate away at the market.[48] Some have suggested that if rental companies like Blockbuster had leveraged their brand to offer online streaming and kiosks, they could have avoided failure. While that seems obvious now in hindsight, tempting us to think we would have predicted it, many experts failed to predict industry trends in advance. Though criticisms of decision makers may have merit,[49] as Malcolm Gladwell, author of *Blink* and *The Tipping Point,* writes, "What is clear in hindsight is rarely clear before the fact."[50]

Hindsight bias
The tendency to believe falsely, after an outcome of an event is actually known, that one would have accurately predicted that outcome.

INFLUENCES ON DECISION MAKING: INDIVIDUAL DIFFERENCES AND ORGANIZATIONAL CONSTRAINTS

We turn here to factors that influence the way people make decisions and the degree to which they are susceptible to errors and biases. We discuss individual differences and then organizational constraints.

Individual Differences

As we discussed, decision making in practice is characterized by bounded rationality, common biases and errors, and the use of intuition. Individual differences such as personality also create deviations from the rational model.

PERSONALITY   Specific facets of conscientiousness—particularly achievement striving and dutifulness—may affect escalation of commitment.[51] First, achievement-oriented people hate to fail, so they escalate their commitment, hoping to forestall failure. Dutiful people, however, are more inclined to do what they see as best for the organization, so they are less likely to escalate their commitment. Second, achievement-striving individuals appear more susceptible to hindsight bias, perhaps because they have a need to justify their actions.[52] We don't have evidence yet on whether dutiful people are immune to this bias.

GENDER   Who makes better decisions, men or women? It depends on the situation. When the situation isn't stressful, decision making by men and women is about equal in quality. In stressful situations, it appears that men become more egocentric and make more risky decisions, while women become more empathetic and their decision making improves.[53]

GENERAL MENTAL ABILITY   We know people with higher levels of general mental ability (GMA; see Chapter 5) are able to process information more quickly, solve problems more accurately, and learn faster, so you might expect them to be less susceptible to common decision errors. However, GMA appears to help people avoid only some of them.[54] Smart people are just as likely to fall prey to anchoring, overconfidence, and escalation of commitment; probably because being smart doesn't alert you to the possibility you're too confident or emotionally defensive. It's not that intelligence never matters. Once warned about decision-making errors, more intelligent people learn more quickly to avoid them.

CULTURAL DIFFERENCES   Cultures differ in time orientation, the value they place on rationality, their belief in the ability of people to solve problems, and their preference for collective decision making. Differences in time orientation help us understand, for instance, why managers in Egypt make decisions at a much slower and more deliberate pace than their U.S. counterparts. Second, while rationality is valued in North America, that's not true elsewhere. A North American manager might make a decision intuitively but know it's important to appear to proceed in a rational fashion because rationality is highly valued in the West. In countries such as Iran, where rationality is not paramount to other factors, efforts to appear rational are not necessary.

Third, some cultures emphasize solving problems, while others focus on accepting situations as they are. The United States falls in the first category; Thailand and Indonesia are examples of the second. Because problem-solving managers believe they can and should change situations to their benefit, U.S. managers might identify a problem long before their Thai or Indonesian counterparts would choose to recognize it as such. Fourth, decision making in Japan, a collectivistic society (see Chapter 4), is much more group-oriented than in the United States, an individualistic society (see Chapter 4). The Japanese value conformity and cooperation, so before Japanese CEOs make an important decision, they collect a large amount of information to use in consensus-forming group decisions.

NUDGING   Anyone who has ever seen a commercial knows about nudging. Commercials represent one of the most outright forms of an organization's attempt to influence our perceptions (of a product) and our decision (to acquire that product). Nudging has also been used positively in the development of corporate social responsibility (CSR; see Chapter 3) initiatives to change people's expectations for organizations.[55] People differ in their susceptibility to suggestion, but it is probably fair to say we are all receptive to nudging to some degree.

Organizational Constraints

Organizations can constrain decision makers, which is both good (to help prevent biases) and bad (to circumvent rational evaluation). For instance, managers shape decisions to reflect the organization's performance evaluation and reward systems, to comply with formal regulations, and to meet organizationally imposed time constraints. Precedents can also limit decisions.

PERFORMANCE EVALUATION SYSTEMS   Managers are influenced by the criteria on which they are evaluated. If a division manager believes the manufacturing plants under his responsibility are operating best when he hears nothing negative, the plant managers will spend a good part of their time ensuring that negative information doesn't reach him.

REWARD SYSTEMS   The organization's reward systems influence decision makers by suggesting which choices have better personal payoffs. For example, if the organization rewards risk aversion, managers are more likely to make conservative decisions.

FORMAL REGULATIONS   David, a shift manager at a Taco Bell restaurant in San Antonio, Texas, describes constraints he faces on his job: "I've got rules and regulations covering almost every decision I make—from how to make a burrito to how often I need to clean the restrooms. My job doesn't come with much freedom of choice." David's situation is not unique. All but the smallest organizations create rules and policies to program decisions and get individuals to act in the intended manner. In doing so, they limit decision choices.

SYSTEM-IMPOSED TIME CONSTRAINTS   Almost all important decisions come with explicit deadlines. For example, a report on new product development may have to be ready for executive committee review by the first of the month. Such conditions often make it difficult, if not impossible, for managers to gather all information before making a final choice.

HISTORICAL PRECEDENTS   Decisions aren't made in a vacuum; they have context. For example, it's common knowledge that the largest determinant of the size of any given year's budget is last year's budget. Choices made today are largely a result of choices made over the years.

WHAT ABOUT ETHICS IN DECISION MAKING?

Ethical considerations should be important to all organizational decision making. In this section, we present three ways to frame decisions ethically. We also address the important issue of how lying affects decision making.

Three Ethical Decision Criteria

Utilitarianism
A system in which decisions are made to provide the greatest good for the greatest number.

The first ethical yardstick is **utilitarianism**, which proposes making decisions solely on the basis of their *outcomes,* ideally to provide the greatest good for the greatest number.[56] This view dominates business decision making and is consistent with goals such as efficiency, productivity, and high profits. Keep in mind that utilitarianism is not always as objective as it sounds. One study indicated that the ethicality of utilitarianism is influenced in ways we don't realize. Participants were given a moral dilemma: The weight of five people bends a footbridge so it is low to some train tracks. A train is about to hit the bridge. The choice is to let all five people perish, or push the one heavy man off the bridge to save four people. In the United States, South Korea, France, and Israel, 20 percent of respondents chose to push the man off the bridge, in Spain, 18 percent, and in Korea, none. This might speak to cultural utilitarian values, but a minor change, asking people to answer in a non-native language they knew, caused more participants to push the man overboard: in one group, 33 percent pushed the man, and in another group 44 percent did.[57] The emotional distance of answering in a non-native language thus seemed to foster a utilitarian viewpoint. It appears that even our view of what we consider pragmatic is changeable.

A second ethical criterion is to make decisions consistent with fundamental liberties and privileges, as set forth in documents such as the U.S. Bill of Rights. An emphasis on *rights* in decision making means respecting and protecting the basic rights of individuals, such as the right to privacy, free speech, and due process. This criterion protects **whistle-blowers**[58] when they reveal an organization's unethical practices to the press or government agencies, using their right to free speech.

Whistle-blowers
Individuals who report unethical practices by their employer to outsiders.

A third criterion is to impose and enforce rules fairly and impartially to ensure *justice* or an equitable distribution of benefits and costs.[59] Justice perspectives are sometimes used to justify paying people the same wage for a given job regardless of performance differences and using seniority as the primary determinant in layoff decisions.

Choosing between Criteria

Decision makers, particularly in for-profit organizations, feel comfortable with utilitarianism. The "best interests" of the organization and its stockholders can justify a lot of questionable actions, such as large layoffs. But many critics feel this perspective needs to change. Public concern about individual rights and social justice suggests managers should develop ethical standards based on nonutilitarian criteria. This presents a challenge because satisfying individual rights and social justice creates far more ambiguities than utilitarian effects on efficiency and profits. However, while raising prices, selling products with questionable effects on consumer health, closing down inefficient plants, laying off large numbers of employees, and moving production overseas to cut costs can be justified in utilitarian terms, there may no longer be a single measure by which good decisions are judged.

This is where CSR comes in to affect a positive change. As we can see by looking at utilitarian ideals, organizations are not motivated to respond equitably when they are looking only at a balance sheet. However, public pressure on organizations to behave responsibly has meant sustainability issues now affect the bottom line: consumers increasingly choose to purchase goods and services from organizations with effective CSR initiatives, high performers are attracted to work for CSR organizations, governments offer incentives to organizations for sustainability efforts, and so forth. CSR is now beginning to make good business sense, folding ethics into utilitarian computations.

Behavioral Ethics

Increasingly, researchers are turning to **behavioral ethics**—an area of study that analyzes how people behave when confronted with ethical dilemmas. Their research tells us that while ethical standards exist collectively in societies and organizations, and individually in the form of personal ethics, we do not always follow ethical standards promoted by our organizations, and we sometimes violate our own standards. Our ethical behavior varies widely from one situation to the next.

Behavioral ethics
Analyzing how people actually behave when confronted with ethical dilemmas.

Lying

Are you a liar? Many of us would not like to be labeled as a liar. But if a liar is merely someone who lies, we are all liars. We lie to ourselves, and we lie to others. We lie consciously and unconsciously. We tell big lies and create small deceptions. Lying is one of the top unethical activities we may indulge in daily, and it undermines all efforts toward sound decision making.

The truth is that one of the reasons we lie is because lying is difficult for others to detect. In more than 200 studies, individuals correctly identified people who were lying only 47 percent of the time, which is less than random picking.[60] This seems to be true no matter what lie-detection technique is employed. For example, one technique police officers use is based on the theory that people look up and to the right when they lie. Unfortunately, researchers who tested the technique could not substantiate the underlying theory.[61]

Lying is deadly to decision making, whether we detect the lies or not. Managers— and organizations—simply cannot make good decisions when facts are misrepresented and people give false motives for their behaviors. Lying is a big ethical problem as well. From an organizational perspective, using fancy lie-detection techniques and entrapping liars when possible yields unreliable results.[62] The most lasting solution comes from OB, which studies ways to prevent lying by working with our natural propensities to create environments that are non-conducive to lying.

CREATIVITY, CREATIVE DECISION MAKING, AND INNOVATION IN ORGANIZATIONS

Models will often improve our decisions, but a decision maker also needs **creativity**, the ability to produce novel and useful ideas. Novel ideas are different from what's been done before but which are appropriate for the problem.

Creativity allows the decision maker to fully appraise and understand problems, including seeing problems others can't see. Although all aspects of OB are complex, that is especially true for creativity. To simplify, Exhibit 6-4 provides a **three-stage model of creativity** in organizations. The core of the model is *creative behavior*, which has both *causes* (predictors of creative behavior) and *effects* (outcomes of creative behavior).

Creativity
The ability to produce novel and useful ideas.

Three-stage model of creativity
The proposition that creativity involves three stages: causes (creative potential and creative environment), creative behavior, and creative outcomes (innovation).

**EXHIBIT 6-4
Three-Stage
Model of
Creativity in
Organizations**

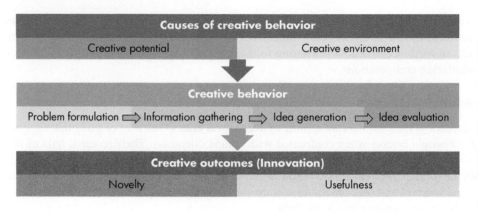

Problem formulation
The stage of creative
behavior that involves
identifying a problem
or opportunity
requiring a solution
that is as yet unknown.

Information gathering
The stage of creative
behavior when
possible solutions to a
problem incubate in an
individual's mind.

Idea generation
The process of
creative behavior that
involves developing
possible solutions to a
problem from relevant
information and
knowledge.

Idea evaluation
The process of creative
behavior involving the
evaluation of potential
solutions to problems
to identify the best one.

Creative Behavior

Creative behavior occurs in four steps, each of which leads to the next:[63]

1. **Problem formulation.** Any act of creativity begins with a problem that the behavior is designed to solve. Thus, **problem formulation** is the stage of creative behavior in which we identify a problem or opportunity that requires a solution that is as yet unknown.

2. **Information gathering.** Given a problem, the solution is rarely directly at hand. We need time to learn more and to process that learning. Thus, **information gathering** is the stage of creative behavior when knowledge is sought and possible solutions to a problem incubate in an individual's mind. Information gathering leads us to identifying innovation opportunities.[64]

3. **Idea generation. Idea generation** is the process of creative behavior in which we develop possible solutions to a problem from relevant information and knowledge. Sometimes we do this alone, when tricks like taking a walk[65] and doodling[66] can jump-start the process. Increasingly, though, idea generation is collaborative.

4. **Idea evaluation.** Finally, it's time to choose from the ideas we have generated. Thus, **idea evaluation** is the process of creative behavior in which we evaluate potential solutions problems to identify the best one.

Causes of Creative Behavior

Having defined creative behavior, the main stage in the three-stage model, we now look back to the causes of creativity: creative potential and creative environment.

CREATIVE POTENTIAL   Is there such a thing as a creative personality? Indeed. While creative genius is rare—whether in science (Stephen Hawking), the performing arts (Martha Graham), or business (Steve Jobs)—most people have some of the characteristics shared by exceptionally creative people. The more of these characteristics we have, the higher our creative potential. Innovation is one of the top organizational goals for leaders, with the facets of:

1. **Intelligence and Creativity** Intelligence is related to creativity. Smart people are more creative because they are better at solving complex problems. However, they may also be more creative because they have greater "working memory," that is, they can recall more information related to the task at hand.[67] Along the same lines, recent research in the Netherlands indicates that an individual's high need for cognition (desire to learn) is correlated with greater creativity.[68]

2. **Personality and Creativity** The Big Five personality trait of openness to experience (see Chapter 5) correlates with creativity, probably because open individuals are less conformist in behavior and more divergent in thinking.[69] Other traits of creative people include proactive personality, self-confidence, risk taking, tolerance for ambiguity, and perseverance.[70] Hope, self-efficacy (belief in your capabilities), and positive affect also predict an individual's creativity.[71] Furthermore, research in China suggests that people with high core self-evaluations are better able than others to maintain creativity in negative situations.[72] Perhaps counterintuitively, some research supports the "mad genius" theory that some people with mental illness are wildly creative partially due to their psychopathology; history certainly provides examples, such as Vincent van Gogh, John Forbes Nash, and others. However, the converse isn't true—people who are creative may have less psychopathology as a group than the general population.[73]

3. **Expertise and Creativity** *Expertise* is the foundation for all creative work and thus is the single most important predictor of creative potential. For example, film writer, producer, and director Quentin Tarantino spent his youth working in a video rental store, where he built up an encyclopedic knowledge of movies. The expertise of others is important, too. People with larger social networks have greater exposure to diverse ideas and informal access to the expertise and resources of others.[74]

4. **Ethics and Creativity** Although creativity is linked to many desirable individual characteristics, it is not correlated with ethicality. People who cheat may actually be more creative than those who behave ethically, according to recent research. It may be that dishonesty and creativity can both stem from a rule-breaking desire.[75]

CREATIVE ENVIRONMENT   Most of us have creative potential we can learn to apply, but as important as creative potential is, by itself it is not enough. We need to be in an environment where creative potential can be realized. Of the many environmental factors, perhaps most important is *motivation*. If you aren't motivated to be creative, it is unlikely you will be. Intrinsic motivation, or the desire to work on something because it's interesting, exciting, satisfying, and challenging (discussed in more detail in Chapter 7), correlates fairly strongly with creative outcomes.[76] However, it is also valuable to work in an environment that rewards and recognizes creative work. A study of health care teams found that team creativity translated into innovation only when the climate actively supported innovation.[77] The organization should foster the free flow of ideas, including providing fair and constructive judgment. Freedom from excessive rules also encourages creativity; employees should have the freedom to decide what work is to be done and how to do it. One study in China revealed that both structural empowerment (in which the structure of the work unit allows sufficient employee freedom) and psychological empowerment (which lets the individual feel personally enabled to decide) were related to employee creativity.[78] However, research in Slovenia found that creating a competitive climate where achievement at any cost is valued will stymie creativity.[79]

Teams matter to creativity too. As we will learn in Chapter 10, more work today is being done in teams, and many people believe diversity will increase team creativity. Past research has suggested that diverse teams are not more creative. More recently, however, one study of Dutch teams revealed that when team members were explicitly asked to understand and consider the point of view of the other team members (an exercise called perspective taking), diverse teams *were* more creative than those with less diversity.[80] Leadership might make the difference. One study of 68 Chinese teams reported that diversity was positively related to team creativity only when the team's leader was inspirational and instilled members with confidence.[81]

Creative Outcomes (Innovation)

The final stage in our model of creativity is the outcome. We can define *creative outcomes* as ideas or solutions judged to be novel and useful by relevant stakeholders. Novelty itself does not generate a creative outcome if it isn't useful. Thus, "off-the-wall" solutions are creative only if they help solve the problem. The usefulness of the solution might be self-evident (the iPad), or it might be considered successful by only the stakeholders initially.[82]

An organization may harvest many creative ideas from its employees and call itself innovative. However, as one expert stated, "Ideas are useless unless used." Soft skills help translate ideas into results. One researcher found that in a large agribusiness company, creative ideas were most likely to be implemented when an individual was motivated to translate the idea into practice—and had strong networking ability.[83] These studies highlight an important fact: creative ideas do not implement themselves; translating them into creative outcomes is a social process that requires utilizing other concepts addressed in this text, including power and politics, leadership, and motivation.

SUMMARY

Individuals base their behavior not on the way their external environment actually is, but rather on the way they see it or believe it to be. An understanding of the way people make decisions can help us explain and predict behavior, but few important decisions are simple or unambiguous enough for the rational model's assumptions to apply. We find individuals looking for solutions that satisfice rather than optimize, injecting biases and prejudices into the decision process, and relying on intuition. Managers should encourage creativity in employees and teams to create a route to innovative decision making.

IMPLICATIONS FOR MANAGERS

- Behavior follows perception, so to influence behavior at work, assess how people perceive their work. Often behaviors we find puzzling can be explained by understanding the initiating perceptions.
- Make better decisions by recognizing perceptual biases and decision-making errors we tend to commit. Learning about these problems doesn't always prevent us from making mistakes, but it does help.

- Adjust your decision-making approach to the national culture you're operating in and to the criteria your organization values. If you're in a country that doesn't value rationality, don't feel compelled to follow the decision-making model or to try to make your decisions appear rational. Adjust your decision approach to ensure compatibility with the organizational culture.
- Combine rational analysis with intuition. These are not conflicting approaches to decision making. By using both, you can actually improve your decision-making effectiveness.
- Try to enhance your creativity. Actively look for novel solutions to problems, attempt to see problems in new ways, use analogies, and hire creative talent. Try to remove work and organizational barriers that might impede creativity.

⭐TRY IT!

If your professor has assigned this, go to the Assignments section of **mymanagementlab.com** to complete the **Simulation: Perception & Individual Decision Making**

⭐ PERSONAL INVENTORY ASSESSMENTS

How Creative Are You?

Everyone is innovative, to some degree. Take this PIA to find out if you are wildly or mildly creative.

6-1. How do you think our perceptions influence our creativity?

7

Motivation Concepts

MOTIVATION

Some individuals seem driven to succeed. The same young student who struggles to read a textbook for more than 20 minutes may devour a *Harry Potter* book in a day. The difference is the situation. As we analyze the concept of motivation, keep in mind that levels of motivation vary both between individuals and within individuals at different times.

Motivation
The processes that account for an individual's intensity, direction, and persistence of effort toward attaining a goal.

We define **motivation** as the processes that account for an individual's *intensity*, *direction*, and *persistence* of effort toward attaining a goal.[1] While general motivation is concerned with effort toward *any* goal, we'll narrow the focus to *organizational* goals.

Intensity describes how hard a person tries. This is the element most of us focus on when we talk about motivation. However, high intensity is unlikely to lead to favorable job-performance outcomes unless the effort is channeled in a *direction* that benefits the organization. Therefore, we consider the quality of effort as well as its intensity. Effort directed toward, and consistent with, the organization's goals is the kind of effort we should be seeking. Finally, motivation has a *persistence* dimension. This measures how long a person can maintain effort. Motivated individuals stay with a task long enough to achieve their goals.

⭐ WATCH IT

If your professor has assigned this, go to the Assignments section of **mymanagementlab.com** to complete the video exercise titled **Motivation (TWZ Role Play)**.

EARLY THEORIES OF MOTIVATION

Three theories of employee motivation formulated during the 1950s are probably the best known. Although they are now of questionable validity (as we'll discuss), they represent a foundation, and practicing managers still use their terminology.

Hierarchy of Needs Theory

The best-known theory of motivation is Abraham Maslow's **hierarchy of needs**,[2] which hypothesizes that within every human being there is a hierarchy of five needs. Recently, a sixth need has been proposed for a highest level—intrinsic values—which is said to have originated from Maslow, but it has yet to gain widespread acceptance.[3] The original five needs are:

1. **Physiological.** Includes hunger, thirst, shelter, sex, and other bodily needs.
2. **Safety-security.** Security and protection from physical and emotional harm.
3. **Social-belongingness.** Affection, belongingness, acceptance, and friendship.
4. **Esteem.** Internal factors such as self-respect, autonomy, and achievement, and external factors such as status, recognition, and attention.
5. **Self-actualization.** Drive to become what we are capable of becoming; includes growth, achieving our potential, and self-fulfillment.

> **Hierarchy of needs** Abraham Maslow's hierarchy of five needs—physiological, safety, social, esteem, and self-actualization—in which, as each need is substantially satisfied, the next need becomes dominant.

According to Maslow, as each need becomes substantially satisfied, the next one becomes dominant. So if you want to motivate someone, you need to understand what level of the hierarchy that person is currently on and focus on satisfying needs at or above that level. We depict the hierarchy as a pyramid in Exhibit 7-1 since this is its best-known representation, but Maslow referred to the needs only in terms of levels.

Maslow's theory has received long-standing wide recognition, particularly among practicing managers. It is intuitively logical and easy to understand, and some research has validated it.[4] Unfortunately, however, most research has not, especially when the theory is applied to diverse cultures,[5] with the possible exception of physiological needs.[6] But old theories, especially intuitively logical ones, die hard. It is thus important to be aware of the prevailing public acceptance of the hierarchy when discussing motivation.

EXHIBIT 7-1
Maslow's
Hierarchy of
Needs

Source: H. Skelsey,
"Maslow's
Hierarchy of
Needs—the Sixth
Level," *Psychologist*
(2014): 982–83.

Two-Factor Theory

Two-factor theory
A theory that relates
intrinsic factors
to job satisfaction
and associates
extrinsic factors with
dissatisfaction. Also
called motivation-
hygiene theory.

Believing an individual's relationship to work is basic, and that the attitude toward work can determine success or failure, psychologist Frederick Herzberg wondered, "What do people want from their jobs?" He asked people to describe, in detail, situations in which they felt exceptionally *good* or *bad* about their jobs. The responses differed significantly and led Herzberg to his **two-factor theory** (also called *motivation-hygiene theory*, but this term is not used much today).[7]

According to a recent survey reported in the Harvard Business Review which identified thousands of events that lead to extreme satisfaction and dissatisfaction.[8]

Conditions such as quality of supervision, pay, company policies, physical work conditions, relationships with others, and job security are *hygiene factors*. When they're adequate, people will not be dissatisfied; neither will they be satisfied. If we want to *motivate* people on their jobs, we should emphasize factors associated with the work itself or with outcomes directly derived from it such as promotional opportunities, personal growth opportunities, recognition, responsibility, and achievement. These are the characteristics people find intrinsically rewarding. Note that Herzberg proposed a dual continuum: The opposite of "satisfaction" is "no satisfaction," and the opposite of "dissatisfaction" is "no dissatisfaction" (see Exhibit 7-2).

Two-factor theory has not been well supported in research. Criticisms center on Herzberg's original methodology and his assumptions, such as the statement that satisfaction is strongly related to productivity. Subsequent research has also shown that if hygiene and motivational factors are equally important to a person, both are capable of motivating.

Regardless of the criticisms, Herzberg's theory has been quite influential and is currently very much in use in research in Asia.[9] Most managers worldwide are familiar with its recommendations.

McClelland's Theory of Needs

You have one beanbag and five targets set up in front of you, each farther away than the last. Target A sits almost within arm's reach. If you hit it, you get $2. Target B is a bit farther out and pays $4, but only about 80 percent of the people who try can hit it. Target C pays $8, and about half the people who try can hit it. Very few people can hit Target D, but the payoff is $16 for those who do. Finally, Target E pays $32, but it's almost impossible to achieve. Which would you try for? If you selected C, you're likely to be a high achiever. Why? Read on.

Traditional view

Satisfaction   Dissatisfaction

Herzberg's view

Motivators

Satisfaction   No satisfaction

Hygiene factors

No dissatisfaction   Dissatisfaction

EXHIBIT 7-2
Contrasting
View of
Satisfaction and
Dissatisfaction

McClelland's theory of needs was developed by David McClelland and his associates.[10] As opposed to Maslow's hierarchy, these needs are more like motivating factors than strict needs for survival. There are three:

- **Need for achievement (nAch)** is the drive to excel, to achieve in relationship to a set of standards.
- **Need for power (nPow)** is the need to make others behave in a way they would not have otherwise.
- **Need for affiliation (nAff)** is the desire for friendly and close interpersonal relationships.

McClelland and subsequent researchers focused most of their attention on nAch. High achievers perform best when they perceive their probability of success as 0.5—that is, a 50–50 chance. They dislike gambling with high odds because they get no achievement satisfaction from success that comes by pure chance. Similarly, they dislike low odds (high probability of success) because then there is no challenge to their skills. They like to set goals that require stretching themselves a little. The view that high nAch acts as an internal motivator presupposes two cultural characteristics—willingness to accept a moderate degree of risk (which excludes countries with strong uncertainty-avoidance characteristics, see Chapter 5), and concern with performance (which applies to countries with strong achievement characteristics). This combination is found predominantly in Anglo-American countries such as the United States, Canada, and Great Britain, and much less in collectivistic countries like Chile and Portugal.

The three needs are linked to important job outcomes. First, when jobs have a high degree of personal responsibility and feedback, along with an intermediate degree of risk, high achievers are strongly motivated. Second, high nAch does not necessarily make someone a good manager, especially in large organizations. People with high nAch are interested in how well they do personally, and not in influencing others to do well. Third, the most effective leaders are high in nPow and nAff, according to recent research[11]—the "rough edges" of nPow may be tempered by the nAff desire to be included.

McClelland's theory has research support, particularly cross-culturally (when cultural dimensions including power distance [see Chapter 5] are taken into account).[12]

McClelland's theory of needs
A theory that achievement, power, and affiliation are three important needs that help explain motivation.

Need for achievement (nAch)
The drive to excel, to achieve in relationship to a set of standards, and to strive to succeed.

Need for power (nPow)
The need to make others behave in a way in which they would not have behaved otherwise.

Need for affiliation (nAff)
The desire for friendly and close interpersonal relationships.

First, the concept of nAch has received a great deal of research attention and acceptance in a wide array of fields, including organizational behavior (OB), psychology, and general business.[13] Second, the nPow concept also has research support, but it may be more familiar to people in broad terms than in relation to the original definition.[14] We will discuss power much more in Chapter 13. Third, the nAff concept is well established and accepted in research. Although it may seem like an updated version of Maslow's social need, it is actually quite separate. Many people take for granted the idea that human beings have a drive toward relationships, so none of us may completely lack this motivation. Fourth, personality characteristics influence our need pursuit, too. Recent research of Cameroonian and German adults indicates high neuroticism may constrain the drive toward establishing relationships (see Chapter 5). Agreeableness supports our pursuit of affiliation, while extraversion has no significant effect.[15]

CONTEMPORARY THEORIES OF MOTIVATION

Contemporary theories of motivation have one thing in common: Each has a reasonable degree of valid supporting documentation. We call them "contemporary theories" because they represent the latest thinking in explaining employee motivation. This doesn't mean they are unquestionably right.

Self-Determination Theory

"It's strange," said Marcia. "I started work at the Humane Society as a volunteer. I put in 15 hours a week helping people adopt pets. And I loved coming to work. Then, three months ago, they hired me full-time at $11 an hour. I'm doing the same work I did before. But I'm not finding it as much fun."

Self-determination theory
A theory of motivation that is concerned with the beneficial effects of intrinsic motivation and the harmful effects of extrinsic motivation.

Does Marcia's reaction seem counterintuitive? There's an explanation for it. It's called **self-determination theory**, which proposes that people prefer to feel they have control over their actions, so anything that makes a previously enjoyed task feel more like an obligation than a freely chosen activity will undermine motivation.[16] The theory is widely used in psychology, management, education, and medical research, and has given rise to several corollaries including organizational evaluation theory and self-concordance theory, discussed next.

Cognitive evaluation theory
A version of self-determination theory in which allocating extrinsic rewards for behavior that had been previously intrinsically rewarding tends to decrease the overall level of motivation if the rewards are seen as controlling.

COGNITIVE EVALUATION THEORY   Much research on self-determination theory in OB has focused on **cognitive evaluation theory**, a complementary theory hypothesizing that extrinsic rewards will reduce intrinsic interest in a task. When people are paid for work, it feels less like something they *want* to do and more like something they *have* to do. Self-determination theory proposes that in addition to being driven by a need for autonomy, people seek ways to achieve competence and make positive connections with others. Its major implications relate to work rewards.

What does self-determination theory suggest about providing rewards? It suggests that some caution in the use of extrinsic rewards to motivate is wise, and that pursuing goals from intrinsic motives (such as a strong interest in the work itself) is more sustaining to human motivation than are extrinsic rewards. Similarly, cognitive evaluation theory suggests that providing extrinsic incentives may, in many cases, undermine intrinsic motivation. For example, if a computer programmer values writing code because she likes to solve problems, a bonus for writing a certain number of lines of code every day could feel coercive, and her intrinsic motivation could suffer. She may or may not increase her number of lines of code per day in response to the extrinsic motivator. In support of the theory, one meta-analysis confirmed that intrinsic motivation contributes to the quality of work, while incentives contribute to the quantity of work. Although intrinsic motivation predicts performance whether or not there are incentives, it may therefore be less of a predictor when incentives are tied to performance directly (such as with monetary bonuses) rather than indirectly.[17]

SELF-CONCORDANCE A more recent outgrowth of self-determination theory is **self-concordance**, which considers how strongly people's reasons for pursuing goals are consistent with their interests and core values. OB research suggests that people who pursue work goals for intrinsic reasons are more satisfied with their jobs, feel they fit into their organizations better, and perform better.[18] Across cultures, if individuals pursue goals because of intrinsic interest, they are more likely to attain goals, are happier when they do, and are happy even if they do not.[19] Why? Because the process of striving toward goals is fun whether or not the goal is achieved. Recent research reveals that when people do not enjoy their work for intrinsic reasons, those who work because they feel obligated to do so can still perform acceptably, though they experience higher levels of strain as a result.[20]

What does all this mean? For individuals, it means you should choose your job for reasons other than extrinsic rewards. For organizations, it means managers should provide intrinsic as well as extrinsic incentives. Managers need to make the work interesting, provide recognition, and support employee growth and development. Employees who feel that what they do is within their control and a result of free choice are likely to be more motivated by their work and committed to their employers.[21]

Self-concordance
The degree to which people's reasons for pursuing goals are consistent with their interests and core values.

Goal-Setting Theory

You've likely heard the sentiment a number of times: "Just do your best. That's all anyone can ask." But what does "do your best" mean? Do we ever know whether we've achieved that vague goal? Research on **goal-setting theory**, proposed by Edwin Locke, reveals the impressive effects of goal specificity, challenge, and feedback on performance. Under the theory, intentions to work toward a goal are considered a major source of work motivation.[22]

Goal-setting theory
A theory that specific and difficult goals, with feedback, lead to higher performance.

DIFFICULTY AND FEEDBACK DIMENSIONS Goal-setting theory is well supported. First, evidence strongly suggests that *specific* goals increase performance; that *difficult* goals, when accepted, produce higher performances than do easy goals; and that *feedback* leads to higher performance than does non-feedback.[23] Second, the more difficult the goal is, the higher the level of performance. Once a hard task has been accepted, we can expect the employee to exert a high level of effort to try to achieve it. Third, people do better when they get feedback on how well they are progressing toward their goals—that is, feedback guides behavior. But all feedback is not equally potent. Self-generated feedback—with which employees are able to monitor their own progress or receive feedback from the task process itself—is more powerful than externally generated feedback.[24]

If employees can participate in the setting of their own goals, will they try harder? The evidence is mixed. In some studies, participatively set goals yielded superior performance; in others, individuals performed best when assigned goals by their boss. One study in China found, for instance, that participative team goal setting improved team outcomes.[25] Another study found that participation results in more achievable goals for individuals.[26] Without participation, the individual pursuing the goal needs to clearly understand its purpose and importance.[27]

GOAL COMMITMENT, TASK CHARACTERISTICS, AND NATIONAL CULTURE FACTORS
Three personal factors influence the goals–performance relationship: *goal commitment*, *task characteristics*, and *national culture*.

1. **Goal commitment.** Goal-setting theory assumes an individual is committed to the goal and determined not to lower or abandon it. The individual (1) believes he or she can achieve the goal and (2) wants to achieve it.[28] Goal commitment is most likely to occur when goals are made public, when the individual has an internal locus of control, when the goals are self-set rather than assigned, and when they are based at least partially on individual ability.[29]

2. **Task characteristics.** Goals themselves seem to affect performance more strongly when tasks are simple rather than complex, well learned rather than novel, independent rather than interdependent, and on the high end of achievable.[30] On interdependent tasks, group goals are more effective.

3. **National characteristics.** Goals may have different effects in different cultures. In collectivistic and high power-distance cultures, achievable moderate goals can be more motivating than difficult ones.[31] However, research has not shown group-based goals to be effective in collectivist than in individualist cultures (see Chapter 4). More research is needed to assess how goal constructs might differ across cultures.

Promotion focus
A self-regulation strategy that involves striving for goals through advancement and accomplishment.

Prevention focus
A self-regulation strategy that involves striving for goals by fulfilling duties and obligations.

INDIVIDUAL AND PROMOTION FOCI   Research has found that people differ in the way they regulate their thoughts and behaviors during goal pursuit. Generally, people fall into one of two categories, though they can belong to both. Those with a **promotion focus** strive for advancement and accomplishment, and approach conditions that move them closer toward desired goals. This concept is similar to the approach side of the approach-avoidance framework discussed in Chapter 5. Those with a **prevention focus** strive to fulfill duties and obligations, as well as avoid conditions, that pull them away from desired goals. Aspects of this concept are similar to the avoidance side of the approach-avoidance framework. Although you would be right to note that both strategies are in the service of goal accomplishment, the manner in which they get there is quite different. As an example, consider studying for an exam. You could engage in promotion-focused activities such as reading class materials, or you could engage in prevention-focused activities such as refraining from doing things that would get in the way of studying, such as playing video games.

Ideally, it's probably best to be both promotion *and* prevention oriented.[32] Keep in mind a person's job satisfaction will be more heavily impacted by failure when that person has an avoidance (prevention) outlook,[33] so set achievable goals, remove distractions, and provide structure to reduce the potential for missing a goal.[34]

GOAL-SETTING IMPLEMENTATION How do managers make goal-setting theory operational? That's often left up to the individual. Some managers set aggressive performance targets—what General Electric called "stretch goals." Some leaders, such as U.S. Secretary of Veterans Affairs (and former Procter & Gamble CEO) Robert McDonald and Best Buy's CEO Hubert Joly, are known for their demanding performance goals. But many managers don't set goals. When asked whether their jobs had clearly defined goals, a minority of respondents to a survey said yes.[35]

A more systematic way to utilize goal setting is with **management by objectives (MBO)**, an initiative most popular in the 1970s but still used today. MBO emphasizes participatively set goals that are tangible, verifiable, and measurable. As in Exhibit 7-3, the organization's overall objectives are translated into specific cascading objectives for each level (divisional, departmental, individual). Because lower-unit managers jointly participate in setting their own goals, MBO works from the bottom up as well as from the top down. The result is a hierarchy that links objectives at one level to those at the next. For the individual employee, MBO provides specific personal performance objectives.

Management by objectives (MBO)
A program that encompasses specific goals, participatively set, for an explicit time period and including feedback on goal progress.

Many elements in MBO programs match the propositions of goal-setting theory. You'll find MBO programs in many business, health care, educational, government, and nonprofit organizations.[36] A version of MBO, called Management by Objectives and Results (MBOR), has been used for over 30 years in the governments of Denmark, Norway, and Sweden.[37] However, the popularity of these programs does not mean they always work.[38] When MBO fails, the culprits tend to be unrealistic expectations, lack of commitment by top management, and inability or unwillingness to allocate rewards based on goal accomplishment.

GOAL SETTING AND ETHICS The relationship between goal setting and ethics is quite complex: If we emphasize the attainment of goals, what is the cost? The answer is probably found in the standards we set for goal achievement. For example, when money

Overall organizational objectives	XYZ Company					
Divisional objectives	Consumer products division			Industrial products division		
Departmental objectives	Production	Sales	Customer service	Marketing	Research	Development
Individual objectives	ooo	oo	oo	oo	ooo	oo

EXHIBIT 7-3
Cascading of Objectives

is tied to goal attainment, we may focus on getting the money and become willing to compromise ourselves ethically. If instead we are primed with thoughts about how we are spending our time when we are pursuing the goal, we are more likely to act ethically.[39] However, this result is limited to thoughts about how we are spending our time. If we are put under time pressure and worry about that, thoughts about time turn against us. Time pressure also increases as we are nearing a goal, which can tempt us to act unethically to achieve it.[40] Specifically, we may forego mastering tasks and adopt avoidance techniques so we don't look bad,[41] both of which can incline us toward unethical choices.

OTHER CONTEMPORARY THEORIES OF MOTIVATION

Self-determination theory and goal-setting theory are well supported contemporary theories of motivation. But they are far from the only noteworthy OB theories on the subject. Self-efficacy, reinforcement, equity/organizational justice, and expectancy theories reveal different aspects of our motivational processes and tendencies.

Self-Efficacy Theory

Self-efficacy theory
An individual's belief that he or she is capable of performing a task.

Self-efficacy theory, also known as *social cognitive theory* or *social learning theory,* refers to an individual's belief that he or she is capable of performing a task.[42] The higher your self-efficacy, the more confidence you have in your ability to succeed. So, in difficult situations people with low self-efficacy are more likely to lessen their effort or give up altogether, while those with high self-efficacy will try harder to master the challenge.[43] Self-efficacy can create a positive spiral in which those with high efficacy become more engaged in their tasks and then, in turn, increase performance, which increases efficacy further.[44] One study introduced the additional explanation that self-efficacy may be associated with a higher level of focused attention, which may lead to increased task performance.[45]

Goal-setting theory and self-efficacy theory don't compete; they complement each other. As Exhibit 7-4 shows, employees whose managers set difficult goals for them will have a higher level of self-efficacy and set higher goals for their own performance. Why? Setting difficult goals for people communicates your confidence in them.

INCREASING SELF-EFFICACY IN YOURSELF The researcher who developed self-efficacy theory, Albert Bandura, proposes four ways self-efficacy can be increased:[46]

1. Enactive mastery.
2. Vicarious modeling.
3. Verbal persuasion.
4. Arousal.

The most important source of increasing self-efficacy is *enactive mastery*—that is, gaining relevant experience with the task or job. The second source is *vicarious modeling*—becoming more confident because you see someone else doing the task. Vicarious modeling is most effective when you see yourself as similar to the person you are observing. The third source is *verbal persuasion*: we become more confident when someone convinces us we have the skills necessary to be successful. Motivational speakers use this tactic. Finally, *arousal* increases self-efficacy. Arousal leads to an energized state so we get "psyched up," feel up to the task, and perform better. But if the task

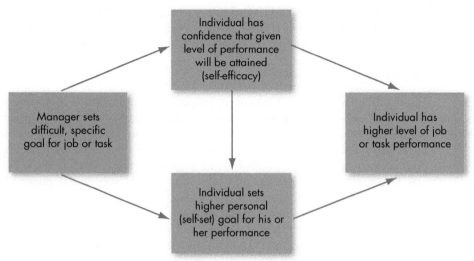

EXHIBIT 7-4
Joint Effects of Goals and Self-Efficacy on Performance"

Source: Based on E. A. Locke and G. P. Latham, "Building a Practically Useful Theory of Goal Setting and Task Motivation: A 35-Year Odyssey," *American Psychologist* 57, no. 9 (2002): 705–17.

requires a steady, lower-key perspective (say, carefully editing a manuscript), arousal may in fact hurt performance even as it increases self-efficacy because we might hurry through the task.

Intelligence and personality are absent from Bandura's list, but they too can increase self-efficacy.[47] People who are intelligent, conscientious, and emotionally stable are so much more likely to have high self-efficacy that some researchers argue self-efficacy is less important than prior research suggested.[48] They believe it is partially a by-product in a smart person with a confident personality.

INFLUENCING SELF-EFFICACY IN OTHERS   The best way for a manager to use verbal persuasion is through the *Pygmalion effect*, a term based on the Greek myth about a sculptor (Pygmalion) who fell in love with a statue he carved. The Pygmalion effect is a form of *self-fulfilling prophecy* in which believing something can make it true. Here, it is often used to describe "that what one person expects can come to serve a self-fulfilling prophecy."[49] An example from research should make this clear. In studies, teachers were told their students had very high IQ scores when, in fact, they spanned a range from high to low. Consistent with the Pygmalion effect, the teachers spent more time with the students they *thought* were smart, gave them more challenging assignments, and expected more of them—all of which led to higher student self-efficacy and better achievement outcomes.[50] This strategy has been used in the workplace too, with replicable results and enhanced effects when leader-subordinate relationships are strong.[51]

Training programs often make use of enactive mastery by having people practice and build their skills. In fact, one reason training works is that it increases self-efficacy, particularly when the training is interactive and feedback is given afterward.[52] Individuals with higher levels of self-efficacy also appear to reap more benefits from training programs and are more likely to use their training on the job.[53]

Reinforcement Theory

Reinforcement theory
A theory that behavior is a function of its consequences.

Goal setting is a cognitive approach, proposing that individuals' purposes direct their actions. **Reinforcement theory**, in contrast, takes a behavioristic view, arguing that reinforcement conditions behavior. The two theories are clearly philosophically at odds. Reinforcement theorists see behavior as environmentally caused. You need not be concerned, they would argue, with internal cognitive events; what controls behavior are reinforcers—any consequences that, when they immediately follow responses, increase the probability that the behavior will be repeated.

Reinforcement theory ignores the inner state of the individual and concentrates solely on what happens when he or she takes some action. Because it is not concerned with what initiates behavior, it is not, strictly speaking, a theory of motivation. But it does provide a powerful means of analyzing what controls behavior, and this is why we typically consider reinforcement concepts in discussions of motivation.[54]

OPERANT CONDITIONING/BEHAVIORISM AND REINFORCEMENT *Operant conditioning theory*, probably the most relevant component of reinforcement theory for management, argues that people *learn* to behave a certain way to either get something they want or to avoid something they don't want. Unlike reflexive or unlearned behavior, operant behavior is influenced by the reinforcement or lack of reinforcement brought about by consequences. Reinforcement strengthens a behavior and increases the likelihood it will be repeated.[55]

Behaviorism
A theory that behavior follows stimuli in a relatively unthinking manner.

B. F. Skinner, one of the most prominent advocates of operant conditioning, demonstrated that people will most likely engage in desired behaviors if they are positively reinforced for doing so; that rewards are most effective if they immediately follow the desired response; and that behavior that is not rewarded, or is punished, is less likely to be repeated. The concept of operant conditioning was part of Skinner's broader concept of **behaviorism**, which argues that behavior follows stimuli in a relatively unthinking manner. Skinner's form of radical behaviorism rejects feelings, thoughts, and other states of mind as causes of behavior. In short, under behaviorism people learn to associate stimulus and response, but their conscious awareness of this association is irrelevant.[56]

Social-learning theory
The view that we can learn through both observation and direct experience.

SOCIAL-LEARNING THEORY AND REINFORCEMENT Individuals can learn by being told or by observing what happens to other people, as well as through direct experience. Much of what we have learned comes from watching models—parents, teachers, peers, film and television performers, bosses, and so forth. The view that we can learn through both observation and direct experience is called **social-learning theory**.[57]

Although social-learning theory is an extension of operant conditioning—that is, it assumes behavior is a function of consequences—it also acknowledges the effects of observational learning and perception. People respond to the way they perceive and define consequences, not to the objective consequences themselves.

Equity Theory/Organizational Justice

Ainsley is a student working toward a bachelor's degree in finance. In order to gain some work experience and increase her marketability, she has accepted a summer internship in the finance department at a pharmaceutical company. She is quite pleased with the pay: $15 an hour is more than other students in her cohort receive for their summer internships. At work she meets Josh, a recent graduate working as a middle manager in the same finance department. Josh makes $30 an hour and is dissatisfied. Specifically, he tells Ainsley that, compared to managers at other pharmaceutical companies, he makes much less. "It isn't fair," he complains. "I work just as hard as they do, yet I don't make as much. Maybe I should go work for the competition."

How could someone making $30 an hour be less satisfied with his pay than someone making $15 an hour and be less motivated as a result? The answer lies in **equity theory** and, more broadly, in principles of organizational justice. According to equity theory, employees compare what they get from their jobs (their outcomes such as pay, promotions, recognition, or a bigger office) to what they put into it (their inputs such as effort, experience, and education). Employees therefore take the ratio of their Outcomes (O) to their Inputs (I) and compare it to the ratio of others, usually someone similar like a coworker or someone doing the same job. This is shown in Exhibit 7-5. If we believe our ratio is equal to those with whom we compare ourselves, a state of equity exists and we perceive our situation as fair.

Equity theory
A theory that individuals compare their job inputs and outcomes with those of others and then respond to eliminate any inequities.

Based on equity theory, employees who perceive inequity will make one of six choices:[58]

1. Change inputs (exert less effort if underpaid or more if overpaid).
2. Change outcomes (individuals paid on a piece-rate basis can increase their pay by producing a higher quantity of units of lower quality).
3. Distort perceptions of self ("I used to think I worked at a moderate pace, but now I realize I work a lot harder than everyone else").
4. Distort perceptions of others ("Mike's job isn't as desirable as I thought").
5. Choose a different referent ("I may not make as much money as my brother-in-law, but I'm doing a lot better than my Dad did when he was my age").
6. Leave the field (quit the job).

Equity theory has support from some researchers, but not from all.[59] However, although equity theory's propositions have not all held up, the hypothesis served as an important precursor to the study of **organizational justice**, or more simply fairness, in

Organizational justice
An overall perception of what is fair in the workplace, composed of distributive, procedural, informational, and interpersonal justice.

Ratio Comparisons*	Perception
$\dfrac{O}{I_A} < \dfrac{O}{I_B}$	Inequity due to being underrewarded
$\dfrac{O}{I_A} = \dfrac{O}{I_B}$	Equity
$\dfrac{O}{I_A} > \dfrac{O}{I_B}$	Inequity due to being overrewarded

*Where $\dfrac{O}{I_A}$ represents the employee and $\dfrac{O}{I_B}$ represents relevant others

EXHIBIT 7-5
Equity Theory

EXHIBIT 7-6
Model of Organizational Justice

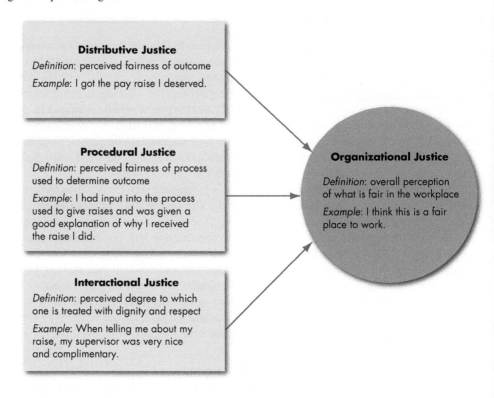

Distributive Justice

Definition: perceived fairness of outcome

Example: I got the pay raise I deserved.

Procedural Justice

Definition: perceived fairness of process used to determine outcome

Example: I had input into the process used to give raises and was given a good explanation of why I received the raise I did.

Interactional Justice

Definition: perceived degree to which one is treated with dignity and respect

Example: When telling me about my raise, my supervisor was very nice and complimentary.

Organizational Justice

Definition: overall perception of what is fair in the workplace

Example: I think this is a fair place to work.

the workplace.[60] Organizational justice is concerned broadly with how employees feel authorities and decision makers at work treat them. For the most part, employees evaluate how fairly they are treated, as shown in Exhibit 7-6. Let's discuss some of the topics related to organizational justice next.

Distributive justice
Perceived fairness of the amount and allocation of rewards among individuals.

DISTRIBUTIVE JUSTICE   **Distributive justice** is concerned with the fairness of outcomes, such as the pay and recognition that employees receive. Outcomes can be allocated in many ways. For example, raises can be distributed equally among employees, or they can be based on which employees need money the most. However, as we discussed about equity theory, employees tend to perceive their outcomes are fairest when they are distributed equitably.

Does the same logic apply to teams? At first glance, it would seem that distributing rewards equally among team members is best for boosting morale and teamwork—that way, no one is favored. However, a study of U.S. National Hockey League teams suggests otherwise. Differentiating the pay of team members on the basis of their inputs (how well they performed in games) attracted better players to the team, made it more likely they would stay, and increased team performance.[61]

Procedural justice
The perceived fairness of the process used to determine the distribution of rewards.

PROCEDURAL JUSTICE   Although employees care a lot about *what* outcomes are distributed (distributive justice), they also care about *how* they are distributed. While distributive justice looks at *what* outcomes are allocated, **procedural justice** examines *how*.[62] For one, employees perceive that procedures are fairer when they are given a say in the decision-making process. Having direct influence over how decisions are made, or at the very least being able to present our opinion to decision makers, creates a sense of control and helps us to feel empowered (we discuss empowerment more in the next chapter).

If outcomes are favorable and individuals get what they want, they care less about the process, so procedural justice doesn't matter as much when distributions are perceived to be fair. It's when outcomes are unfavorable that people pay close attention to the process. If the process is judged to be fair, then employees are more accepting of unfavorable outcomes.[63] Why is this the case? Think about it. If you are hoping for a raise and your manager informs you that you did not receive one, you'll probably want to know how raises were determined. If it turns out your manager allocated raises based on merit and you were simply outperformed by a coworker, then you're more likely to accept your manager's decision than if raises were based on favoritism. Of course, if you get the raise in the first place, then you'll be less concerned with how the decision was made.

INFORMATIONAL JUSTICE   Beyond outcomes and procedures, research has shown that employees care about two other types of fairness that have to do with the way they are treated during interactions with others. The first type is **informational justice**, which reflects whether managers provide employees with explanations for key decisions and keep them informed of important organizational matters. The more detailed and candid managers are with employees, the more fairly treated those employees feel.

Informational justice The degree to which employees are provided truthful explanations for decisions.

Though it may seem obvious that managers should be honest with their employees and not keep them in the dark about organizational matters, many managers are hesitant to share information. This is especially the case with bad news, which is uncomfortable for both the manager delivering it and the employee receiving it. Explanations for bad news are beneficial when they take the form of excuses after the fact ("I know this is bad, and I wanted to give you the office, but it wasn't my decision") rather than justifications ("I decided to give the office to Sam, but having it isn't a big deal").[64]

INTERPERSONAL JUSTICE   The second type of justice relevant to interactions between managers and employees is **interpersonal justice**, which reflects whether employees are treated with dignity and respect. Compared to the other forms of justice we've discussed, interpersonal justice is unique in that it can occur in everyday interactions between managers and employees.[65] This quality allows managers to take advantage of (or miss out on) opportunities to make their employees feel fairly treated. Many managers may view treating employees politely and respectfully as too "soft," choosing more aggressive tactics out of a belief that doing so will be more motivating. Although displays of negative emotions such as anger may be motivating in some cases,[66] managers sometimes take this too far. Consider former Rutgers University men's basketball coach Mike Rice, who was caught on video verbally and even physically abusing players, and was subsequently fired.[67]

Interpersonal justice The degree to which employees are treated with dignity and respect.

JUSTICE OUTCOMES   After all this talk about types of justice, how much does justice really matter to employees? A great deal, as it turns out. When employees feel fairly treated, they respond in a number of positive ways. All the types of justice discussed in this section have been linked to higher levels of task performance and citizenship behaviors such as helping coworkers, as well as lower levels of counterproductive behaviors such as shirking job duties. Distributive and procedural justice are more strongly associated with task performance, while informational and interpersonal justice are more strongly associated with citizenship behavior. Even more physiological outcomes, such as how well employees sleep and the state of their health, have been linked to fair treatment.[68]

Despite all attempts to enhance fairness, perceived injustices are still likely to occur. Fairness is often subjective; what one person sees as unfair, another may see as perfectly appropriate. In general, people see allocations or procedures favoring themselves as fair.[69] So, when addressing perceived injustices, managers need to focus their actions on the source of the problem. In addition, if employees feel they have been treated unjustly, opportunities to express frustration have been shown to reduce the desire for retribution.[70]

ENSURING JUSTICE   How can an organization affect the justice perceptions and rule adherence of its managers? This depends upon the motivation of each manager. Some managers are likely to calculate justice by their degree of adherence to the justice rules of the organization. These managers will try to gain greater subordinate compliance with behavioral expectations, create an identity of being fair to their employees, or establish norms of fairness. Other managers may be motivated in justice decisions by their emotions. When they have a high positive affect and/or a low negative affect, these managers are most likely to act fairly.

It might be tempting for organizations to adopt strong justice guidelines in attempts to mandate managerial behavior, but this isn't likely to be universally effective. In cases where managers have more rules and less discretion, those who calculate justice are more likely to act fairly, but managers whose justice behavior follows from their affect may act more fairly when they have greater discretion.[71]

CULTURE AND JUSTICE   Across nations, the same basic principles of procedural justice are respected, in that workers around the world prefer rewards based on performance and skills over rewards based on seniority.[72] However, inputs and outcomes are valued differently in various cultures.[73]

We may think of justice differences in terms of Hofstede's cultural dimensions (see Chapter 5). One large-scale study of over 190,000 employees in 32 countries and regions suggested that justice perceptions are most important to people in countries with individualistic, feminine, uncertainty-avoidance, and low power-distance values.[74] Organizations can tailor programs to meet these justice expectations. For example, in countries that are highest in individualism, such as Australia and the United States, competitive pay plans and rewards for superior individual performance may enhance feelings of justice. In countries dominated by uncertainty avoidance, such as France, fixed-pay compensation and employee participation may help employees feel more secure. The dominant dimension in Sweden is femininity, so relational concerns are considered important there. Swedish organizations may therefore want to provide work–life balance initiatives and social recognition. Austria, in contrast, has a strong low power-distance value. Ethical concerns may be foremost to individuals in perceiving justice in Austrian organizations, so organizations there may want to openly justify inequality between leaders and workers and provide symbols of ethical leadership.

Expectancy Theory

One of the most widely accepted explanations of motivation is Victor Vroom's expectancy theory.[75] Although it has critics, most evidence supports the theory.[76]

Expectancy theory argues that the strength of our tendency to act a certain way depends on the strength of our expectation of a given outcome and its attractiveness. In practical terms, employees are motivated to exert a high level of effort when they believe that it will lead to a good performance appraisal, that a good appraisal will lead to organizational rewards such as salary increases and/or intrinsic rewards, and that the rewards will satisfy their personal goals. The theory, therefore, focuses on three relationships (see Exhibit 7-7):

> **Expectancy theory**
> A theory that the strength of a tendency to act in a certain way depends on the strength of an expectation that the act will be followed by a given outcome and on the attractiveness of that outcome to the individual.

1. **Effort–performance relationship.** The probability perceived by the individual that exerting a given amount of effort will lead to performance.
2. **Performance–reward relationship.** The degree to which the individual believes performing at a particular level will lead to the attainment of a desired outcome.
3. **Rewards–personal goals relationship.** The degree to which organizational rewards satisfy an individual's personal goals or needs and the attractiveness of those potential rewards for the individual.[77] Expectancy theory helps explain why a lot of workers aren't motivated on their jobs and do only the minimum necessary to get by.

As a vivid example of how expectancy theory can work, consider stock analysts. They make their living trying to forecast a stock's future price; the accuracy of their buy, sell, or hold recommendations is what keeps them in work or gets them fired. But the dynamics are not simple. Analysts place few sell ratings on stocks, although in a steady market as many stocks are falling as are rising. Expectancy theory provides an explanation: Analysts who place a sell rating on a company's stock have to balance the benefits they receive from their accuracy against the risks they run by drawing that company's ire. What are these risks? They include public rebuke, professional blackballing, and exclusion from information. When analysts place a buy rating on a stock, they face no such trade-off because, obviously, companies love it when analysts recommend that investors buy their stock. So the incentive structure suggests the expected outcome of buy ratings is higher than the expected outcome of sell ratings, and that's why buy ratings vastly outnumber sell ratings.[78]

Does expectancy theory tend to work? Some critics suggest it has only limited use and is more valued where individuals clearly perceive effort–performance, and performance–reward, linkages.[79] Because few individuals do, the theory tends to be idealistic. If organizations actually rewarded individuals for performance rather than seniority, effort, skill level, and job difficulty, expectancy theory might be more valid.

① Effort–performance relationship
② Performance–reward relationship
③ Rewards–personal goals relationship

EXHIBIT 7-7
Expectancy Theory

However, rather than invalidating it, this criticism can explain why a significant segment of the workforce exerts low effort on the job.

JOB ENGAGEMENT

When Joseph reports to his job as a hospital nurse, it seems that everything else in his life goes away, and he becomes completely absorbed in what he is doing. His emotions, thoughts, and behavior are all directed toward patient care. In fact, he can get so caught up in his work that he isn't even aware of how long he's been there. As a result of this total commitment, he is more effective in providing patient care and feels uplifted by his time at work.

Job engagement

The investment of an employee's physical, cognitive, and emotional energies into job performance.

Joseph has a high level of **job engagement**, the investment of an employee's physical, cognitive, and emotional energies into job performance.[80] Practicing managers and scholars have become interested in facilitating job engagement, believing factors deeper than liking a job or finding it interesting drives performance. Researchers attempt to measure this deeper level of commitment. Job engagement is linked with employee engagement, which we discussed in Chapter 3.

Over the past 30 years, the Gallup organization has been studying the extent to which engagement is linked to positive work outcomes for millions of employees.[81] The results indicate there are far more engaged employees in highly successful organizations than in average ones, and groups with more engaged employees have higher levels of productivity, fewer safety incidents, and lower turnover. Academic studies have also found positive outcomes. For instance, one review found levels of engagement were associated with task performance and organizational citizenship behavior (OCB; see Chapter 1).[82]

What makes people more likely to be engaged in their jobs? One key is the degree to which an employee believes it is meaningful to engage in work. This is partially determined by job characteristics and access to sufficient resources to work effectively.[83] Another factor is a match between the individual's values and those of the organization.[84] Leadership behaviors that inspire workers to a greater sense of mission also increase employee engagement.[85]

INTEGRATING CONTEMPORARY THEORIES OF MOTIVATION

Our job might be simpler if, after presenting a half-dozen theories, we could say only one was found valid. But many of the theories in this chapter are complementary. We now tie them together to help you understand their interrelationships. To help, Exhibit 7-8 integrates much of what we know about motivation. Its basic foundation is the expectancy model that was shown in Exhibit 7-7. Let's walk through Exhibit 7-8. (We will look at job design closely in Chapter 8.)

We begin by explicitly recognizing that opportunities can either aid or hinder individual effort. Note that the individual effort box on the left also has another arrow leading into it, from the person's goals. Consistent with goal-setting theory, the goals–effort loop is meant to remind us that goals direct behavior.

Expectancy theory predicts employees will exert a high level of effort if they perceive strong relationships between effort and performance, performance and reward, and rewards and satisfaction of personal goals. Each of these relationships is, in turn, influenced by other factors. For effort to lead to good performance, the individual must have the ability to perform and perceive the performance appraisal system as fair and objective. The performance–reward relationship will be strong if the individual perceives that performance (rather than seniority, personal favorites, or other criteria) is rewarded. If cognitive evaluation theory were fully valid in the actual workplace, we would predict that basing rewards on performance should decrease the individual's intrinsic motivation. The final link in expectancy theory is the rewards–goals relationship. Motivation is high if the rewards for high performance satisfy the dominant needs consistent with individual goals.

A closer look at Exhibit 7-8 also reveals that the model considers achievement motivation, job design, reinforcement, and equity theories/organizational justice. A high achiever is not motivated by an organization's assessment of performance or organizational rewards, hence the jump from effort to personal goals for those with high nAch. Remember, high achievers are internally driven as long as their jobs provide them with personal responsibility, feedback, and moderate risks. They are not as concerned with the effort–performance, performance–reward, or rewards–goal linkages.

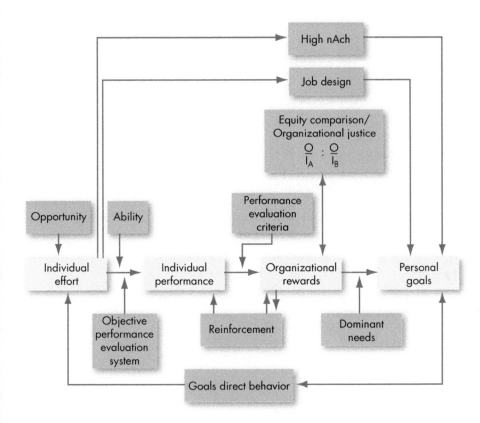

EXHIBIT 7-8
Integrating Contemporary Theories of Motivation

Reinforcement theory enters the model by recognizing that the organization's rewards reinforce the individual's performance. If employees see a reward system as "paying off" for good performance, the rewards will reinforce and encourage good performance. Rewards also play a key part in organizational justice research. Individuals will judge the favorability of their outcomes (for example, their pay) relative to what others receive but also with respect to how they are treated: When people are disappointed by their rewards, they are likely to be sensitive to the perceived fairness of the procedures used and the consideration given to them by their supervisors.

SUMMARY

The motivation theories in this chapter differ in their predictive strength. Maslow's hierarchy, two-factor theory, and McClelland's theory focus on needs. Self-determination theory and related theories have merits to consider. Goal-setting theory can be helpful but does not cover absenteeism, turnover, or job satisfaction. Self-efficacy theory contributes to our understanding of personal motivation. Reinforcement theory can also be helpful, but not regarding employee satisfaction or the decision to quit. Equity theory provided the spark for research on organizational justice. Expectancy theory can be helpful, but assumes employees have few constraints on decision making, and this limits its applicability. Job engagement goes a long way toward explaining employee commitment. Together, these concepts provide a theoretical foundation of what is known about motivation in the workplace.

IMPLICATIONS FOR MANAGERS

- Make sure extrinsic rewards for employees are not viewed as coercive, but instead provide information about competence and relatedness.
- Consider goal-setting theory: Clear and difficult goals often lead to higher levels of employee productivity.
- Consider reinforcement theory regarding quality and quantity of work, persistence of effort, absenteeism, tardiness, and accident rates.
- Consult equity theory to help understand productivity, satisfaction, absence, and turnover variables.
- Expectancy theory offers a powerful explanation of performance variables such as employee productivity, absenteeism, and turnover.

⭐ TRY IT!

If your professor has assigned this, go to the Assignments section of **mymanagementlab.com** to complete the **Simulation: Motivation**.

⭐ PERSONAL INVENTORY ASSESSMENTS

Work Motivation Indicator

Do you find that some jobs motivate you more than others? Take this PIA to determine your work motivation.

7-1. What do you think are the most important motivational aspects for a manager to keep in mind for managing a small group of employees? Why?

8

Motivation: From Concepts to Applications

MyManagementLab®

⭐ **Improve Your Grade!**

When you see this icon ⭐, visit **mymanagementlab.com** for activities that are applied, personalized, and offer immediate feedback.

⭐ **Chapter Warm-up**

If your professor has chosen to assign this, go to the Assignments section of **mymanagementlab.com** to complete the chapter warm-up.

MOTIVATING BY JOB DESIGN: THE JOB CHARACTERISTICS MODEL (JCM)

The way work is structured has a bigger impact on an individual's motivation than how it might first appear. **Job design** suggests that the way elements in a job are organized can influence employee effort, and the model discussed next can serve as a framework to identify opportunities for changes to those elements. Developed by J. Richard Hackman and Greg Oldham, the **job characteristics model** (**JCM**) describes jobs in terms of five core job dimensions:[1]

1. **Skill variety** is the degree to which a job requires different activities using specialized skills and talents. The work of a garage owner-operator who does electrical repairs, rebuilds engines, does bodywork, and interacts with customers scores high on skill variety. The job of a body shop worker who sprays paint eight hours a day scores low on this dimension.
2. **Task identity** is the degree to which a job requires completion of a whole and identifiable piece of work. A cabinetmaker who designs furniture, selects the wood, builds the objects, and finishes them has a job that scores high on task identity. A job scoring low on this dimension is operating a lathe solely to make table legs.
3. **Task significance** is the degree to which a job affects the lives or work of other people. The job of a nurse helping patients in a hospital intensive care unit scores high on task significance; sweeping floors in a hospital scores low.
4. **Autonomy** is the degree to which a job provides the worker freedom, independence, and discretion in scheduling work and determining the procedures for carrying it out. A sales manager who schedules her own work and tailors her sales approach to each customer without supervision has a highly autonomous job. An account representative who is required to follow a standardized sales script with potential customers has a job low on autonomy.
5. **Feedback** is the degree to which carrying out work activities generates direct and clear information about your own performance. A job with high feedback is testing and inspecting iPads. Installing components of iPads as they move down an assembly line provides low feedback.

Elements of the JCM

Exhibit 8-1 presents the JCM. The JCM proposes that individuals obtain internal rewards when they learn (knowledge of results in the model) that they personally have performed well (experienced responsibility) on a task they care about (experienced meaningfulness). The more these three psychological states are present, the greater will be employees' motivation, performance, and satisfaction, and the lower their absenteeism and likelihood of leaving. As Exhibit 8-1 indicates, individuals with a high growth need are more likely to experience the critical psychological states when their jobs are enriched—and respond to them more positively.

Efficacy of the JCM

Much evidence supports the JCM concept that the presence of these job characteristics generates higher job satisfaction and organizational commitment through increased motivation.[2] One study suggested that when employees were "other oriented" (concerned

Job design
The way the elements in a job are organized.

Job characteristics model (JCM)
A model that proposes any job can be described in terms of five core job dimensions: skill variety, task identity, task significance, autonomy, and feedback.

Skill variety
The degree to which a job requires a variety of different activities.

Task identity
The degree to which a job requires completion of a whole and identifiable piece of work.

Task significance
The degree to which a job has a substantial impact on the lives or work of other people.

Autonomy
The degree to which a job provides substantial freedom and discretion to the individual in scheduling the work and in determining the procedures to be used in carrying it out.

Feedback
The degree to which carrying out the work activities required by a job results in the individual obtaining direct and clear information about the effectiveness of his or her performance.

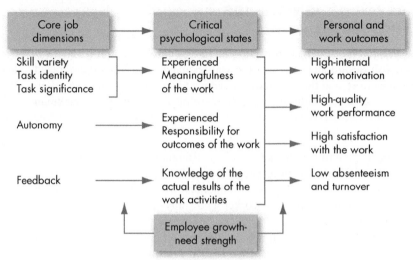

EXHIBIT 8-1
The Job Characteristics Model

Source: Hackman, J. R. & Oldham, G. R. (1975). Development of job diagnostic survey. *Journal of Applied Psychology,* 60, 159-170

with the welfare of others at work), the relationship between intrinsic job characteristics and job satisfaction was weaker,[3] meaning that our job satisfaction comes less from these characteristics when we care about others. Another study proposed that the degree of psychological ownership we feel toward our work enhances our motivation, particularly if the feelings of ownership are shared among a work group.[4] Other research has explored the JCM in unique settings such as virtual work situations, finding that if individuals work together online but not in person, their experience of meaningfulness, responsibility, and knowledge of results can suffer. Thankfully, managers can mitigate these outcomes for employees by consciously developing personal relationships with them and increasing their sense of task significance, autonomy, and feedback.[5]

Motivating Potential Score (MPS)

We can combine the core dimensions of the JCM into a single predictive index, called the **motivating potential score (MPS)** and calculated as follows:

Motivating potential score (MPS)
A predictive index that suggests the motivating potential in a job.

$$\text{MPS} = \frac{\text{Skill variety} + \text{Task identity} + \text{Task significance}}{3} \times \text{Autonomy} \times \text{Feedback}$$

To be high on motivating potential, jobs must be high in at least one of the three factors that lead to experienced meaningfulness and high in both autonomy and feedback. If jobs score high on motivating potential, the model predicts that motivation, performance, and satisfaction will improve, while absence and turnover will be reduced. But we can better calculate motivating potential by simply adding characteristics rather than using the formula. Think about your job. Do you have the opportunity to work on different tasks, or is your day routine? Are you able to work independently, or do you constantly have a supervisor or co-worker looking over your shoulder? Your answers indicate your job's motivating potential.

Cultural Generalizability of the JCM

A few studies have tested the JCM in different cultures, but the results aren't consistent. The fact that the model is relatively individualistic (it considers the relationship between the employee and his or her work) suggests job enrichment strategies may not have the same effects in collectivistic cultures as in individualistic cultures (such as the United States, see Chapter 4). Indeed, one study in Nigeria, which has a highly collectivistic culture, found that while the MPS was highly influenced by job dimensions, the correlations were different than the general data gathered from predominately individualistic countries.[6] In contrast, another study suggested the degree to which jobs had intrinsic job motivators predicted job satisfaction and job involvement equally well for U.S., Japanese, and Hungarian employees.[7] More research is needed in this area.

USING JOB REDESIGN TO MOTIVATE EMPLOYEES

"Every day was the same thing," Frank said. "Stand on that assembly line. Wait for an instrument panel to be moved into place. Unlock the mechanism and drop the panel into the Jeep Liberty as it moved by on the line. Then I plugged in the harnessing wires. I repeated that for eight hours a day. I don't care that they were paying me 24 dollars an hour. I was going crazy. Finally, I just said this isn't going to be the way I'm going to spend the rest of my life. My brain was turning to JELL-O. So I quit. Now I work in a print shop and I make less than 15 dollars an hour. But let me tell you, the work I do is really interesting. The job changes all the time, I'm continually learning new things, and the work really challenges me! I look forward every morning to going to work again."

The repetitive tasks in Frank's job at the Jeep plant provided little variety, autonomy, or motivation. In contrast, his job in the print shop is challenging and stimulating. From an organizational perspective, the failure of Frank's first employer to redesign his job into a more satisfying one led to increased turnover. Redesigning jobs therefore has important practical implications—reduced turnover and increased job satisfaction among them. Let's look at some ways to put the JCM into practice to make jobs more motivating.

Job Rotation

If employees suffer from over-routinization of their work, one alternative is **job rotation**, or the periodic shifting of an employee from one task to another with similar skill requirements at the same organizational level (also called *cross-training*). Manufacturers also use job rotation as needed to respond more flexibly to the volume of incoming orders. New managers are sometimes rotated through jobs, too, to help them get a picture of a whole organization.[8] For these reasons, job rotation can be applied in any setting where cross-training is feasible, from manufacturing floors to hospital wards. At Singapore Airlines, for instance, a ticket agent may temporarily take on the duties of a baggage handler, both for cross-training and to get exposure to different aspects of the organization. Extensive job rotation is among the reasons Singapore Airlines is rated one of the best airlines in the world.[9]

Job rotation
The periodic shifting of an employee from one task to another.

The use of job rotation has been shown to increase job satisfaction and organizational commitment.[10] Additionally, evidence from Italy, Britain, and Turkey indicated that job rotation is associated with higher levels of organizational performance in manufacturing settings.[11] It reduces boredom, increases motivation, and helps employees understand how their work contributes to the organization. It may also increase safety and reduce repetitive-based work injuries, but that is currently a topic of much study and debate, with mixed findings.[12]

Job rotation does have its drawbacks. Work that is done repeatedly may become habitual and routine, which does make decision making more automatic and efficient, but less thoughtfully considered. Second, training costs increase when each rotation necessitates that an employee learn new skills. Third, moving a worker into a new position reduces overall productivity for that role. Fourth, job rotation creates disruptions when members of the work group have to adjust to new employees. Finally, supervisors may have to spend more time answering questions and monitoring the work of recently rotated employees.

Relational Job Design

Relational job design
Constructing jobs so employees see the positive difference they can make in the lives of others directly through their work.

While redesigning jobs on the basis of job characteristics theory is likely to make work more intrinsically motivating, research is also exploring how to make jobs more *prosocially* motivating to people. In other words, how can managers design work so employees are motivated to promote the well-being of the organization's beneficiaries (customers, clients, patients, and employees)? This view, **relational job design**, shifts the spotlight from the employee to those whose lives are affected by the job that employee performs.[13] It also motivates individuals toward increased job performance.[14]

One way to make jobs more prosocially motivating is to better connect employees with the beneficiaries of their work. This can be done by, for example, relating stories from customers who have found the company's products or services to be helpful. Meeting beneficiaries firsthand—or even just seeing pictures of them—allows employees to see that their actions affect real people and have tangible consequences. It makes customers or clients more memorable and emotionally vivid, which leads employees to consider the effects of their work actions more. Lastly, connections allow employees to better understand the perspective of beneficiaries, which fosters higher levels of commitment.

Relational job design, with its focus on prosocial motivation, is an especially salient topic for organizations with corporate social responsibility (CSR) initiatives. As we discussed in Chapter 3, CSR efforts often include invitations for employees to volunteer their time and effort, sometimes using the skills they gained on the job (like Home Depot employees when they help rebuild homes) but often not (such as when bank employees help rebuild homes with groups like Habitat for Humanity). In both cases, the employees may be able to interact with the beneficiaries of their efforts. Research also indicates that corporate-sponsored volunteer programs enhanced in the JCM dimensions of meaningfulness and task significance motivate employees to volunteer.[15] But while this motivation for prosocial behavior is noteworthy, it is not the same as relational job design: for one, the CSR efforts are through volunteering (not on-the-job); and for another, the work they are providing is not usually the same work they do at their jobs (Home Depot workers do not build homes on the job). However, relational job design holds intriguing possibilities for CSR initiatives.

USING ALTERNATIVE WORK ARRANGEMENTS TO MOTIVATE EMPLOYEES

As you surely know, there are many approaches toward motivating people, and we've discussed some of them. Another approach to motivation is to consider alternative work arrangements such as flextime, job sharing, and telecommuting. These are likely to be especially important for a diverse workforce of dual-earner couples, single parents, and employees caring for sick or aging relatives.

Flextime

Susan is the classic "morning person." Every day she rises at 5:00 A.M. sharp, full of energy. However, as she puts it, "I'm usually ready for bed right after the 7:00 P.M. news." Her flexible work schedule as a claims processor at The Hartford Financial Services Group is perfect for her situation: her office opens at 6:00 A.M. and closes at 7:00 P.M., and she schedules her 8-hour day within this 13-hour period.

Susan's schedule is an example of **flextime**, short for "flexible work time." Flextime employees must work a specific number of hours per week but may vary their hours of work within limits. As in Exhibit 8-2, each day consists of a common core, usually six hours, with a flexibility band surrounding it. The core may be 9:00 A.M. to 3:00 P.M., with the office actually opening at 6:00 A.M. and closing at 6:00 P.M. Employees must be at their jobs during the common core period, but they may accumulate their other two hours

Flextime
Flexible work hours.

Schedule 1	
Percent Time:	100% = 40 hours per week
Core Hours:	9:00 A.M.–5:00 P.M., Monday through Friday (1 hour lunch)
Work Start Time:	Between 8:00 A.M. and 9:00 A.M.
Work End Time:	Between 5:00 P.M. and 6:00 P.M.

Schedule 2	
Percent Time:	100% = 40 hours per week
Work Hours:	8:00 A.M.–6:30 P.M., Monday through Thursday (1/2 hour lunch)
	Friday off
Work Start Time:	8:00 A.M.
Work End Time:	6:30 P.M.

Schedule 3	
Percent Time:	90% = 36 hours per week
Work Hours:	8:30 A.M.–5:00 P.M., Monday through Thursday (1/2 hour lunch)
	8:00 A.M.–Noon, Friday (no lunch)
Work Start Time:	8:30 A.M. (Monday–Thursday); 8:00 A.M. (Friday)
Work End Time:	5:00 P.M. (Monday–Thursday); Noon (Friday)

Schedule 4	
Percent Time:	80% = 32 hours per week
Work Hours:	8:00 A.M.–6:00 P.M., Monday through Wednesday (1/2 hour lunch)
	8:00 A.M.–11:30 A.M. Thursday (no lunch)
	Friday off
Work Start Time:	Between 8:00 A.M. and 9:00 A.M.
Work End Time:	Between 5:00 P.M. and 6:00 P.M.

EXHIBIT 8-2
Possible Flextime Staff Schedules

around that. Some flextime programs allow employees to accumulate extra hours and turn them into days off.

Flextime has become extremely popular. According to a recent survey, a majority (60 percent) of U.S. organizations offer some form of flextime.[16] This is not just a U.S. phenomenon, though. In Germany, for instance, 73 percent of businesses offer flextime, and such practices are becoming more widespread in Japan as well.[17] In Germany, Belgium, the Netherlands, and France, by law employers are not allowed to refuse an employee's request for either a part-time or a flexible work schedule as long as the request is reasonable, such as to care for an infant child.[18]

Most of the evidence stacks up favorably. Perhaps most important from the organization's perspective, flextime increases profitability. Interestingly, though, this effect seems to occur only when flextime is promoted as a work–life balance strategy (not when it is for the organization's gain).[19] Flextime also tends to reduce absenteeism,[20] probably for several reasons. Employees can schedule their work hours to align with personal demands, reducing tardiness and absences, and they can work when they are most productive. Flextime can also help employees balance work and family lives; in fact, it is a popular criterion for judging how "family friendly" a workplace is.

However, flextime is not applicable to every job or every worker. It is not a viable option for anyone whose service job requires being at a workstation at certain hours, for example. It also appears that people who have a strong desire to separate their work and family lives are less apt to want flextime, so it's not a motivator for everyone.[21] Also of note, research in the United Kingdom indicated that employees in organizations with flextime do not realize a reduction in their levels of stress, suggesting that this option may not truly improve work–life balance.[22]

Job Sharing

Job sharing
An arrangement that allows two or more individuals to split a traditional full-time job.

Job sharing allows two or more individuals to split a traditional full-time job. One employee might perform the job from 8:00 A.M. to noon, perhaps, and the other from 1:00 P.M. to 5:00 P.M., or the two could work full but alternate days. For example, top Ford engineers Julie Levine and Julie Rocco engaged in a job-sharing program that allowed both of them to spend time with their families while redesigning the Explorer crossover. Typically, one of them would work late afternoons and evenings while the other worked mornings. They both agreed that the program worked well, although making it feasible required a great deal of time and preparation.[23]

Only 18 percent of U.S. organizations offered job sharing in 2014, a 29 percent decrease since 2008.[24] Reasons it is not more widely adopted include the difficulty of finding compatible partners to job share and the historically negative perceptions of job share individuals as not completely committed to their jobs and employers. However, eliminating job sharing for these reasons might be short-sighted. Job sharing allows an organization to draw on the talents of more than one individual for a given job. It opens the opportunity to acquire skilled workers—for instance, parents with young children and retirees—who might not be available on a full-time basis. From the employee's perspective, job sharing can increase motivation and satisfaction.

An employer's decision to use job sharing is often based on economics and national policy. Two part-time employees sharing a job can be less expensive in terms of salary and benefits than one full-timer because training, coordination, and administrative costs can be high. On the other hand, in the United States the Affordable Care Act may create a financial incentive for companies to increase job-sharing arrangements in order to avoid the requirement to provide health care to full-time employees.[25] Many German and Japanese[26] firms have been using job sharing—but for a very different reason. Germany's Kurzarbeit program, which is now close to 100 years old, kept employment levels from plummeting throughout the economic crisis by switching full-time workers to part-time job-sharing work.[27]

Telecommuting

It might be close to the ideal job for many people: no rush hour traffic, flexible hours, freedom to dress as you please, and few interruptions. **Telecommuting** refers to working at home—or anywhere else the employee chooses that is outside the workplace—at least two days a week on a computer linked to the employer's office.[28] (A closely related concept—working from a *virtual office*—describes working outside the workplace on a relatively permanent basis.) A sales manager working from home is telecommuting, but a sales manager working from her car on a business trip is not because the location is not by choice.

Telecommuting
Working from home at least two days a week on a computer that is linked to the employer's office.

While the movement away from telecommuting by some companies makes headlines, it appears that for most organizations, it remains popular. For example, almost 50 percent of managers in Germany, the United Kingdom, and the United States are permitted telecommuting options. Telecommuting is less of a practice in China, but there, too, it is growing.[29] In developing countries, the telecommuting percentage is between 10 and 20 percent.[30] Organizations that actively encourage telecommuting include Amazon, IBM, American Express,[31] Intel, Cisco Systems,[32] and a number of U.S. government agencies.[33]

From the employee's standpoint, telecommuting can increase feelings of isolation and reduce job satisfaction.[34] Research indicates it does not reduce work–family conflicts, though perhaps it is because telecommuting often increases work hours beyond the contracted workweek.[35] Telecommuters are also vulnerable to the "out of sight, out of mind" effect: Employees who aren't at their desks, miss impromptu meetings in the office, and don't share in day-to-day informal workplace interactions may be at a disadvantage when it comes to raises and promotions because they're perceived as not putting in the requisite "face time."[36] As for a CSR benefit of reducing car emissions by allowing telecommuting, research indicates that employees actually drive over 45 miles more per day, due to increased personal trips, when they telecommute![37]

USING EMPLOYEE INVOLVEMENT AND PARTICIPATION (EIP) TO MOTIVATE EMPLOYEES

Employee involvement and participation (EIP)[38] is a process that uses employees' input to increase their commitment to organizational success. If workers are engaged in decisions that increase their autonomy and control over their work lives, they will become more motivated, committed to the organization, productive, and satisfied with their jobs. These benefits don't stop with individuals—when teams are given more control over their work, morale and performance increase as well.[39]

Employee involvement and participation (EIP)
A participative process that uses the input of employees to increase employee commitment to organizational success.

Cultural EIP

To be successful, EIP programs should be tailored to local and national norms.[40] Employees in many traditional cultures that value formal hierarchies do not especially value EIP programs, but this is changing. In China, for instance, some employees are becoming less high power–distance oriented. In one study, Chinese workers who were very accepting of traditional Chinese cultural values showed few benefits from participative decision making. However, Chinese workers who were less traditional were more satisfied and had higher performance ratings under participative management.[41] Another study conducted in China showed that involvement increased employees' thoughts and feelings of job security, enhancing their well-being.[42] These differences within China may well reflect the current transitional nature of that culture. Research in urban China indicated that some EIP programs, namely, those that favor consultation and expression but not participation in decision making, yielded higher job satisfaction.[43]

Forms of Employee Involvement Programs

Let's look at two major forms of employee involvement—participative management and representative participation—in more detail.

Participative management
A process in which subordinates share a significant degree of decision-making power with their immediate superiors.

PARTICIPATIVE MANAGEMENT Common to all **participative management** programs is joint decision making, in which subordinates share a significant degree of decision-making power with their immediate superiors. This sharing can occur either formally through, say, briefings or surveys, or informally through daily consultations, as a way to enhance motivation through trust and commitment.[44] Participative management has, at times, been considered a panacea for poor morale and low productivity. In reality, for participative management to be effective, followers must have trust and confidence in their leaders. Leaders should avoid coercive techniques and instead stress the organizational consequences of decision making to their followers.[45]

Studies of the participation–performance relationship have yielded mixed findings.[46] Organizations that institute participative management may realize higher stock returns, lower turnover rates, and higher labor productivity, although these effects are typically not large.[47] Research at the individual level indicates participation typically has only a modest influence on employee productivity, motivation, and job satisfaction. This doesn't mean participative management isn't beneficial. However, it is not a sure means for improving performance.

Representative participation
A system in which workers participate in organizational decision making through a small group of representative employees.

REPRESENTATIVE PARTICIPATION Most countries in western Europe require companies to practice **representative participation**. Representative participation redistributes power within an organization, putting labor's interests on a more equal footing with the interests of management and stockholders by including a small group of employees as participants in decision making. The two most common forms of representation are works councils and board representatives. Works councils are groups of nominated or elected employees who must be consulted when management makes decisions about employees. Board representatives are employees who sit on a company's board of directors and represent employees' interests. In the United Kingdom, Ireland, Australia, and New Zealand, representative participation was originally the only EIP program; it was formed to allow employee representatives to discuss issues outside union agreements and the representatives were all from the union. However, representative groups are now increasingly a mix of union and non-union, or separate from the union arrangement.[48]

The influence of representative participation on working employees seems to be mixed, but generally an employee would need to feel his or her interests were well represented and make a difference to the organization in order for motivation to increase. Thus representative participation as a motivational tool is surpassed by more direct participation methods.

USING EXTRINSIC REWARDS TO MOTIVATE EMPLOYEES

As we saw in Chapter 3, pay is not the only factor driving job satisfaction. However, it does motivate people, and companies often underestimate its importance. One study found that while 45 percent of *employers* thought pay was a key factor in losing top talent, 71 percent of *top performers* called it a foremost reason.[49]

Given that pay is so important, will the organization lead, match, or lag the market in pay? How will individual contributions be recognized? In this section, we consider (1) what to pay employees (decided by establishing a pay structure), and (2) how to pay individual employees (decided through variable-pay plans).

What to Pay: Establishing a Pay Structure

There are many ways to pay employees. The process of initially setting pay levels entails balancing *internal equity*—the worth of the job to the organization (usually established through a technical process called job evaluation), and *external equity*—the competitiveness of an organization's pay relative to pay in its industry (usually established through pay surveys). Obviously, the best pay system reflects what the job is worth, while also staying competitive relative to the labor market.

Pay more, and you may get better-qualified, more highly motivated employees who will stay with the organization longer. A study covering 126 large organizations found employees who believed they were receiving a competitive pay level had higher morale and were more productive, and customers were more satisfied as well.[50] But pay is often the highest single operating cost for an organization, which means paying too much can make the organization's products or services too expensive. It's a strategic decision an organization must make, with clear trade-offs.

In the case of Walmart, it appears that its strategic decision on pay did not work. While annual growth in U.S. stores slowed to around 1 percent in 2011, one of Walmart's larger competitors, Costco, grew around 8 percent. The average worker at Costco made approximately $45,000, compared to approximately $17,500 for the average worker at Walmart-owned Sam's Club. Costco's strategy was that it will get more if it pays more—and higher wages resulted in increased employee productivity and reduced turnover. Given the subsequent Walmart decision to increase worker wages throughout the organization, perhaps its executives agree.[51]

How to Pay: Rewarding Individual Employees through Variable-Pay Programs

Variable-pay program
A pay plan that bases a portion of an employee's pay on some individual and/or organizational measure of performance.

Piece rate, merit based, bonus, profit sharing, and employee stock ownership plans are all forms of a **variable-pay program** (also known as *pay-for-performance*), which bases a portion of an employee's pay on some individual and/or organizational measure of performance. The variable portion may be all or part of the paycheck, and it may be paid annually or upon attainment of benchmarks. It can also be either optional for the employee or an accepted condition of employment.[52] Variable-pay plans have long been used to compensate salespeople and executives, but the scope of variable-pay jobs has broadened as the motivational potential has been realized.

Globally, around 80 percent of companies offer some form of variable-pay plan. In the United States, 91 percent of companies offer a variable-pay program.[53] In Latin America, more than 90 percent of companies offer some form of variable-pay plan. Latin American companies also have the highest percentage of total payroll allocated to variable pay, at nearly 18 percent. European and U.S. companies are lower, at about 12 percent.[54] When it comes to executive compensation, Asian companies are outpacing western companies in their use of variable pay.[55]

Unfortunately, not all employees see a strong connection between pay and performance. The results of pay-for-performance plans vary. For instance, one study of 415 companies in South Korea suggested that group-based pay-for-performance plans may have a strong positive effect on organizational performance.[56] On the other hand, research in Canada indicated that variable-pay plans increase job satisfaction only if employee *effort* is rewarded as well as performance.[57]

Secrecy also pays a role in the motivational success of variable-pay plans. Although in some government and not-for-profit agencies pay amounts are either specifically or generally made public, most U.S. organizations encourage or require pay secrecy.[58] Is this good or bad? Unfortunately, it's bad: pay secrecy has a detrimental effect on job performance. Even worse, it adversely affects high performers more than other employees. It very likely increases employees' perception that pay is subjective, which can be demotivating. While individual pay amounts may not need to be broadcast to restore the balance, if general pay categories are made public and employees feel variable pay is linked objectively to their performance, the motivational effects of variable pay can be retained.[59]

Do variable-pay programs increase motivation and productivity? Generally yes, but that doesn't mean everyone is equally motivated by them.[60] Many organizations have more than one variable pay element in operation, such as an Employee Stock Option Plan (ESOP) and bonuses, so managers should evaluate the effectiveness of the overall plan in terms of the employee motivation gained from each element separately and from all elements together. Managers should monitor their employees' performance–reward expectancy, since a combination of elements that makes employees feel that their greater performance will yield them greater rewards will be the most motivating.[61]

Let's examine the different types of variable-pay programs in more detail.

Piece-rate pay plan
A pay plan in which workers are paid a fixed sum for each unit of production completed.

PIECE-RATE PAY The **piece-rate pay plan** has long been popular as a means of compensating production workers with a fixed sum for each unit of production completed, but it can be used in any organizational setting where the outputs are similar enough to be evaluated by quantity. A pure piece-rate plan provides no base salary and pays the employee only for what he or she produces. Ballpark workers selling peanuts and soda are frequently paid piece-rate. If they sell 40 bags of peanuts at $1 each for their earnings, their take is $40. The more peanuts they sell, the more they earn. Alternatively, piece-rate plans are sometimes distributed to sales teams, so a ballpark worker makes money on a portion of the total number of bags of peanuts sold by the group during a game.

Piece-rate plans are known to produce higher productivity and wages, so they can be attractive to organizations and motivating for workers.[62] In fact, one major Chinese university increased its piece-rate pay for articles by professors and realized 50 percent increased research productivity.[63] The chief concern of both individual and team piece-rate workers is financial risk. A recent experiment in Germany found that 68 percent of risk-averse individuals prefer an individual piece-rate system, and that lower performers prefer team piece-rate pay. Why? The authors suggested risk-averse and high-performing individuals would rather take their chances on pay based on what they can control (their own work) because they are concerned others will slack off in a team setting.[64] This is a valid concern, as we will discuss in the next chapter.

Organizations should verify that their piece-rate plans are indeed motivating to individuals. European research has suggested that when the pace of work is determined by uncontrollable outside factors such as customer requests, rather than internal factors such as coworkers, targets, and machines, a piece-rate plan is not motivating.[65] Either way, managers must be mindful of the motivation for workers to decrease quality in order to increase their speed of output. They should also be aware that by rewarding volume, piece-rate plans increase the probability of workplace injuries.[66]

MERIT-BASED PAY   A **merit-based pay plan** pays for individual performance based on performance appraisal ratings. A main advantage is that high performers can get bigger raises. If designed correctly, merit-based plans let individuals perceive a strong relationship between their performance and their rewards.[67]

Merit-based pay plan
A pay plan based on performance appraisal ratings.

Most large organizations have merit-based pay plans, especially for salaried employees. Merit pay is slowly taking hold in the public sector. For example, New York City's public hospital system pays doctors based on how well they reduce costs, increase patient satisfaction, and improve the quality of care.[68] A move away from merit pay, on the other hand, is coming from some organizations that don't feel it separates high and low performers enough. When the annual review and raise are months away, the motivation of this reward for high performers diminishes. Even companies that have retained merit pay are rethinking the allocation.[69]

Despite their intuitive appeal, merit-based pay plans have several limitations. One is that they are typically based on an annual performance appraisal and thus are only as valid as the performance ratings, which are often subjective. This brings up issues of discrimination, as we discussed in Chapter 2. Research indicates that African American employees receive lower performance ratings than White employees, women's ratings are higher than men's, and there are demographic differences in the distribution of salary increases, even with all other factors being equal.[70] Another limitation is that the pay-raise pool of available funds fluctuates on economic or other conditions that have little to do with individual performance. For instance, a colleague at a top university who performed very well in teaching and research was given a pay raise of $300. Why? Because the pay-raise pool was very small. Yet that amount is more of a cost-of-living increase than pay-for-performance. Lastly, unions typically resist merit-based pay plans. For example, relatively few U.S. teachers are covered by merit pay for this reason. Instead, seniority-based pay, which gives all employees the same raises, predominates.

BONUS   An annual **bonus** is a significant component of total compensation for many jobs. Once reserved for upper management, bonus plans are now routinely offered to employees in all levels of the organization. The incentive effects should be higher than those of merit pay because rather than paying for previous performance now rolled into

Bonus
A pay plan that rewards employees for recent performance rather than historical performance.

base pay, bonuses reward recent performance (merit pay is cumulative, but the increases are generally much smaller than bonus amounts). When times are bad, firms can cut bonuses to reduce compensation costs. Workers on Wall Street, for example, saw their average bonus drop by more than a third as their firms faced greater scrutiny.[71]

Bonus plans have a clear upside: they are motivating for workers. As an example, a recent study in India found that when a higher percentage of overall pay was reserved for the potential bonuses of managers and employees, productivity increased.[72] This example also highlights the downside of bonuses: they leave employees' pay more vulnerable to cuts. This is problematic, especially when employees depend on bonuses or take them for granted. "People have begun to live as if bonuses were not bonuses at all but part of their expected annual income," said Jay Lorsch, a Harvard Business School professor. KeySpan Corp., a 9,700-employee utility company in New York, combined yearly bonuses with a smaller merit-pay raise. Elaine Weinstein, KeySpan's senior vice president of HR, credits the plan with changing the culture from "entitlement to meritocracy."[73]

Profit-sharing plan
An organization-wide program that distributes compensation based on some established formula designed around a company's profitability.

PROFIT-SHARING PLAN   A **profit-sharing plan** distributes compensation based on some established formula designed around a company's profitability. Compensation can be direct cash outlays or, particularly for top managers, allocations of stock options. When you read about executives like Mark Zuckerberg, who accepts an absurdly modest $1 salary, remember that many executives are granted generous stock options. In fact, Zuckerberg has made as much as $2.3 billion after cashing out some of his stock options.[74] Of course, the vast majority of profit-sharing plans are not so grand in scale. Jacob Luke started his own lawn-mowing business at age 13. He employed his brother Isaiah and friend Marcel and paid them each 25 percent of the profits he made on each yard.

Studies generally support the idea that organizations with profit-sharing plans have higher levels of profitability than those without them.[75] These plans have also been linked to higher levels of employee commitment, especially in small organizations.[76] Profit sharing at the organizational level appears to have positive impacts on employee attitudes; employees report a greater feeling of psychological ownership.[77] Recent research in Canada indicates that profit-sharing plans motivate individuals to higher job performance when they are used in combination with other pay-for-performance plans.[78] Obviously, profit sharing does not work when there is no reported profit per se, such as in nonprofit organizations, or often in the public sector.

Employee stock ownership plan (ESOP)
A company-established benefits plan in which employees acquire stock, often at below-market prices, as part of their benefits.

EMPLOYEE STOCK OWNERSHIP PLAN   An **employee stock ownership plan (ESOP)** is a company-established benefit plan in which employees acquire stock, often at below-market prices, as part of their benefits. Research on ESOPs indicates they increase employee satisfaction and innovation;[79] however, they have the potential to increase job satisfaction only when employees psychologically experience ownership.[80] Even so, ESOPs may not inspire lower absenteeism or greater motivation,[81] perhaps because the employee's actual monetary benefit comes with cashing in the stock at a later date. Thus, employees need to be kept regularly informed of the status of the business and have the opportunity to positively influence it in order to feel motivated toward higher personal performance.[82]

ESOPs for top management can reduce unethical behavior. For instance, CEOs are less likely to manipulate firm earnings reports to make themselves look good in the short run when they have an ownership share.[83] Of course, not all companies want ESOPs, and they won't work in all situations.

USING BENEFITS TO MOTIVATE EMPLOYEES

Like pay, benefits are both a provision and a motivator. Todd E. is married and has three young children; his wife is at home full time. His Citigroup colleague Allison M. is married too, but her husband has a high-paying job with the federal government, and they have no children. Todd is concerned about having a good medical plan and enough life insurance to support his family in case it's needed. In contrast, Allison's husband already has her medical needs covered on his plan, and life insurance is a low priority. Allison is more interested in extra vacation time and long-term financial benefits, such as a tax-deferred savings plan.

A standardized benefits package would be unlikely to meet the needs of Todd and Allison well. Citigroup can, however, cover both sets of needs with flexible benefits.

Consistent with expectancy theory's thesis that organizational rewards should be linked to each employee's goals, **flexible benefits** individualize rewards by allowing each employee to choose the compensation package that best satisfies his or her current needs and situation. Flexible benefits can accommodate differences in employee needs based on age, marital status, partner's benefit status, and number and age of dependents.

Benefits in general can be a motivator for a person to go to work, and for a person to choose one organization over another. But are flexible benefits more motivating than traditional plans? It's difficult to tell. Some organizations that have moved to flexible plans report increased employee retention, job satisfaction, and productivity. However, flexible benefits may not substitute for higher salaries when it comes to motivation.[84] Furthermore, as more organizations worldwide adopt flexible benefits, the individual motivation they produce will likely decrease (the plans will be seen as a standard work provision). The downsides of flexible benefit plans may be obvious: They may be more costly to manage, and identifying the motivational impact of different provisions is challenging.

Given the intuitive motivational appeal of flexible benefits, however, it may be surprising that their usage is not yet global. In China, only a limited percentage of companies offer flexible plans,[85] as is true for many other Asian countries.[86] Almost all major corporations in the United States offer them, and a recent survey of 211 Canadian organizations found that 60 percent offer flexible benefits, up from 41 percent in 2005.[87] A similar survey of firms in the United Kingdom found that nearly all major organizations were offering flexible benefits programs, with options ranging from supplemental medical insurance to holiday trading (with coworkers), discounted bus travel, and child care assistance.[88]

Flexible benefits
A benefits plan that allows each employee to put together a benefits package individually tailored to his or her own needs and situation.

USING INTRINSIC REWARDS TO MOTIVATE EMPLOYEES

We have discussed motivating employees through job design and by the extrinsic rewards of pay and benefits. On an organizational level, are those the only ways to motivate employees? Not at all! We would be remiss if we overlooked intrinsic rewards organizations can provide, such as employee recognition programs. Let's start with an example. Laura makes $8.50 per hour working at her fast-food job in Pensacola, Florida, and the job isn't very challenging or interesting. Yet Laura talks enthusiastically about the job, her boss, and the company that employs her. "What I like is the fact that Guy [her supervisor] appreciates the effort I make. He compliments me regularly in front of the other people on my shift, and I've been chosen Employee of the Month twice in the past six months. Did you see my picture on that plaque on the wall?"

Employee recognition program
A plan to encourage specific employee behaviors by formally appreciating specific employee contributions.

Organizations are increasingly realizing what Laura knows: Recognition programs increase an employee's intrinsic motivation for work. An **employee recognition program** is a plan to encourage specific behaviors by formally appreciating specific employee contributions. Employee recognition programs range from a spontaneous and private thank-you to widely publicized formal programs in which the procedures for attaining recognition are clearly identified.

A few years ago, 1,500 employees were surveyed in a variety of work settings to find out what they considered the most powerful workplace motivator. Their response? Recognition, recognition, and more recognition. Other research suggests financial incentives may be more motivating in the short term, but in the long run nonfinancial incentives work best.[89] Surprisingly, there is not a lot of research on the motivational outcomes or global usage of employee recognition programs. However, studies indicated that employee recognition programs are associated with self-esteem, self-efficacy, and job satisfaction,[90] and the broader outcomes from intrinsic motivation are well documented.

An obvious advantage of recognition programs is that they are inexpensive: praise is free![91] With or without financial rewards, they can be highly motivating to employees. Despite the increased popularity of such programs, though, critics argue they are highly susceptible to political manipulation by management. When applied to jobs for which performance factors are relatively objective, such as sales, recognition programs are likely to be perceived by employees as fair. In most jobs, however, performance criteria aren't self-evident, which allows managers to manipulate the system and recognize their favorites. Abuse can undermine the value of recognition programs and demoralize employees. Therefore, where formal recognition programs are used, care must be taken to ensure fairness. Where they are not, it is important to motivate employees by consistently recognizing their performance efforts.

✪ WATCH IT

If your professor has assigned this, go to the Assignments section of **mymanagementlab .com** to complete the video exercise titled **Zappos: Motivating Employees through Company Culture**.

SUMMARY

As we've seen in the chapter, understanding what motivates individuals is ultimately key to organizational performance. Employees whose differences are recognized, who feel valued, and who have the opportunity to work in jobs tailored to their strengths and interests will be motivated to perform at the highest levels. Employee participation can also increase employee productivity, commitment to work goals, motivation, and job satisfaction. However, we cannot overlook the powerful role of organizational rewards in influencing motivation. Pay, benefits, and intrinsic rewards must be carefully and thoughtfully designed in order to enhance employee motivation toward positive organizational outcomes.

IMPLICATIONS FOR MANAGERS

- Recognize individual differences. Spend the time necessary to understand what's important to each employee. Design jobs to align with individual needs to maximize their motivation potential.
- Use goals and feedback. You should give employees firm, specific goals, and employees should get feedback on how well they are faring in pursuit of those goals.
- Allow employees to participate in decisions that affect them. Employees can contribute to setting work goals, choosing their own benefits packages, and solving productivity and quality problems.
- Link rewards to performance. Rewards should be contingent on performance, and employees must perceive the link between the two.
- Check the system for equity. Employees should perceive that individual effort and outcomes explain differences in pay and other rewards.

⭐TRY IT!

If your professor has assigned this, go to the Assignments section of **mymanagementlab.com** to complete the **Motivation: From Concepts to Applications.**

⭐ PERSONAL INVENTORY ASSESSMENTS

Diagnosing the Need for Team Building

We might be tempted to think that assembling a group for a project is team building, but intentional team building is much different. Take this PIA to find out how to diagnose the need for planned team building.

8-1. What compensation and benefits plan would motivate you most in your next job? In a job five years from now? What are the similarities and differences between these two points in time, and why?

9

Foundations of Group Behavior

MyManagementLab®
⭐ Improve Your Grade!
When you see this icon ⭐, visit **mymanagementlab.com** for activities that are applied, personalized, and offer immediate feedback.

LEARNING OBJECTIVES

After studying this chapter, you should be able to:

1. Distinguish between the different types of groups.
2. Describe the punctuated-equilibrium model of group development.
3. Show how role requirements change in different situations.
4. Demonstrate how norms exert influence on an individual's behavior.
5. Show how status and size differences affect group performance.
6. Describe how issues of cohesiveness and diversity can be integrated for group effectiveness.
7. Contrast the strengths and weaknesses of group decision making.

⭐ Chapter Warm-up
If your professor has chosen to assign this, go to the Assignments section of **mymanagementlab.com** to complete the chapter warm-up.

GROUPS AND GROUP IDENTITY

Groups have their strengths—and their pitfalls. How do we get the best out of group situations? Let's dissect the anatomy of group life, starting with the basics. In organizational behavior (OB), a **group** consists of two or more individuals, interacting and interdependent, who have come together to achieve particular objectives. Groups can be either formal or informal. A **formal group** is defined by the organization's structure, with designated work assignments and established tasks. In formal groups, the behaviors team members should engage in are stipulated by and directed toward organizational goals. The six members of an airline flight crew are a formal group, for example. In contrast, an **informal group** is neither formally structured nor organizationally determined. Informal groups in the work environment meet the need for social contact. Three employees from different departments who regularly have lunch or coffee together are an informal group. These types of interactions among individuals, though informal, deeply affect their behavior and performance.

Social Identity

Have you noticed that people often feel strongly about their groups? This is partly because shared experiences amplify our perception of events.[1] As you would expect, positive shared experiences enhance our bond with our groups. According to research in Australia, sharing painful experiences also increases our felt bond and trust with others.[2] Consider the aftermath of a sports national championship game. Fan groups of the winning team are elated, and sales of team-related shirts, jackets, and hats skyrocket. Conversely, fans of the losing team feel dejected, even embarrassed. Why? Even though fans have little to do with the actual performance of the sports team, their self-image can be wrapped up in their identification with the group. Our tendency to personally invest in the accomplishments of a group is the territory of **social identity theory**.

People develop many group identities throughout the course of their lives. You might define yourself in terms of the organization you work for, the city you live in, your profession, your religious background, your ethnicity, and/or your gender. Over time, some groups you belong to may become more significant to you than others. A U.S. expatriate working in Rome might be very aware of being from the United States, for instance, but doesn't give national identity a second thought when transferring from Tulsa to Tucson.[3] We may thus pick and choose which of our social identities are salient to the situation, or we may find that our social identities are in conflict, such as the identities of business leader and parent.[4] In the workplace, our identification with our workgroups is often stronger than with our organizations, but both are important to positive outcomes in attitudes and behaviors. If we have low identification with our organizations, we may experience decreased satisfaction and engage in fewer organizational citizenship behaviors (OCBs; see Chapter 1).[5]

Ingroups and Outgroups

Ingroup favoritism occurs when we see members of our group as better than other people and people not in our group as all the same. Recent research suggests that people with low openness and/or low agreeableness (see Chapter 5) are more susceptible to ingroup favoritism.[6]

Whenever there is an ingroup, there is by necessity an **outgroup**, which is sometimes everyone else, but it is usually an identified group known by the ingroup's members. For example, if my ingroup is the Republican party in U.S. politics, my outgroup

Group
Two or more individuals, interacting and interdependent, who have come together to achieve particular objectives.

Formal group
A designated work group defined by an organization's structure.

Informal group
A group that is neither formally structured nor organizationally determined; such a group appears in response to the need for social contact.

Social identity theory
A perspective that considers when and why individuals consider themselves members of groups.

Ingroup favoritism
Perspective in which we see members of our ingroup as better than other people, and people not in our group as all the same.

Outgroup
The inverse of an ingroup; an outgoup can mean anyone outside the group, but more usually it is an identified other group.

might be anyone in the world who is not a Republican, but it's more likely to be the other U.S. political parties, or perhaps just Democrats.

When there are ingroups and outgroups, there is often animosity between them. One of the most powerful sources of ingroup–outgroup feelings regards the practice of religion, even in the workplace. One global study, for instance, found that when groups became heavily steeped in religious rituals and discussions, they became especially discriminatory toward outgroups and aggressive if the outgroups had more resources.[7] Consider an example from another study of a U.K. Muslim organization that supported Al-Qaeda and identified moderate U.K. Muslims as its outgroup. The Al-Qaeda ingroup was not neutral toward the moderate outgroup; instead, the ingroup denounced the moderates, denigrating them as deviant and threatening outward aggression.[8]

STAGES OF GROUP DEVELOPMENT

⬡ WATCH IT

If your professor has assigned this, go to the Assignments section of **mymanagementlab .com** to complete the video exercise titled **Witness.org: Managing Groups & Teams**.

Temporary groups with finite deadlines pass through a unique sequencing of actions (or inaction):

1. The first meeting sets the group's direction.
2. The first phase of group activity is one of inertia and thus makes slower progress.
3. A transition takes place exactly when the group has used up half its allotted time.
4. This transition initiates major changes.
5. A second phase of inertia follows the transition.
6. The group's last meeting is characterized by markedly accelerated activity.[9]

Punctuated-equilibrium model
A set of phases that temporary groups go through that involves transitions between inertia and activity.

This pattern, called the **punctuated-equilibrium model**, is illustrated by Exhibit 9-1. Let's discuss each stage of the model. At the first meeting, the group's general purpose and direction is established, and then a framework emerges of behavioral patterns and assumptions through which the group will approach its project, sometimes in the first few seconds of the group's existence. Once set, the group's direction is solidified and is unlikely to be reexamined throughout the first half of its life. This is a period of inertia—the group tends to stand still or become locked into a fixed course of action even if it gains new insights that challenge initial patterns and assumptions.

One of the most interesting discoveries in studies was that groups experienced a transition precisely halfway between the first meeting and the official deadline—whether members spent an hour on their project or six months. The midpoint appears to work like an alarm clock, heightening members' awareness that their time is limited and they need to get moving. This transition ends Phase 1 and is characterized by a concentrated burst of changes, dropping of old patterns, and adoption of new perspectives. The transition sets a revised direction for Phase 2, a new equilibrium or period of inertia in which the group executes plans created during the transition period. Lastly, the group's last meeting is characterized by a final burst of activity to finish its work. In summary, the punctuated-equilibrium model characterizes groups as exhibiting long periods of inertia interspersed with brief revolutionary changes triggered primarily by members' awareness of time and deadlines.

EXHIBIT 9-1
The Punctuated-Equilibrium Model

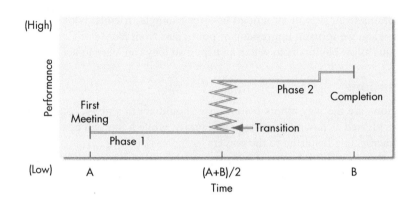

There are many models of group stages, but this one is a dominant theory with strong support. Keep in mind, however, that this model doesn't apply to all groups, but is suited to the finite quality of temporary task groups working under a time deadline.[10]

GROUP PROPERTY 1: ROLES

Workgroups shape members' behavior, and they also help explain individual behavior as well as the performance of the group itself. Some defining group properties are *roles*, *norms*, *status*, *size*, *cohesiveness*, and *diversity*. We'll discuss each in the sections that follow. Let's begin with the first group property, roles.

Shakespeare said, "All the world's a stage, and all the men and women merely players."[11] Using the same metaphor, all group members are actors, each playing a **role**, a set of expected behavior patterns attributed to someone occupying a given position in a social unit. We are required to play a number of diverse roles, both on and off our jobs. As we'll see, one of the tasks in understanding behavior is grasping the role a person is currently playing.

Role
A set of expected behavior patterns attributed to someone occupying a given position in a social unit.

Bill is a plant manager with EMM Industries, a large electrical equipment manufacturer in Phoenix. He fulfills a number of roles—employee, member of middle management, and electrical engineer. Off the job, Bill holds more roles: husband, father, Catholic, tennis player, member of the Thunderbird Country Club, and president of his homeowners' association. Many of these roles are compatible; some create conflicts. How does Bill's religious commitment influence his managerial decisions regarding layoffs, expense padding, and provision of accurate information to government agencies? A recent offer of promotion requires Bill to relocate, yet his family wants to stay in Phoenix. Can the role demands of his job be reconciled with the demands of his husband and father roles?

Different groups impose different role requirements on individuals. Like Bill, we all play a number of roles, and our behavior varies with each. But how do we know each role's requirements? We draw upon our *role perceptions* to frame our ideas of appropriate behaviors, and learn the *expectations* of our groups. We also seek to understand the parameters of our roles to minimize *role conflict*. Let's discuss each of these facets.

Role Perception

Role perception
An individual's view
of how he or she is
supposed to act in a
given situation.

Our view of how we're supposed to act in a given situation is a **role perception**. We get role perceptions from stimuli all around us—for example, friends, books, films, and television, like when we form an impression of politicians from *House of Cards*. Apprenticeship programs allow beginners to watch an expert so they can learn to act as expected.

Role Expectations

Role expectations
How others believe a
person should act in a
given situation.
**Psychological
contract**
An unwritten
agreement that sets
out what management
expects from an
employee and vice
versa.

Role expectations are the way others believe you should act in a given context. A U.S. federal judge is viewed as having propriety and dignity, while a football coach is seen as aggressive, dynamic, and inspiring to the players.

In the workplace, we look at role expectations through the perspective of the **psychological contract**: an unwritten agreement that exists between employees and employers. This agreement sets out mutual expectations.[12] Management is expected to treat employees justly, provide acceptable working conditions, clearly communicate what is a fair day's work, and give feedback on how well an employee is doing. Employees are expected to demonstrate a good attitude, follow directions, and show loyalty to the organization.

What happens if management is derelict in its part of the bargain? We can expect negative effects on employee performance and satisfaction. One study among restaurant managers found that violations of the psychological contract were related to greater intentions to quit, while another study of a variety of different industries found broken psychological contracts were associated with lower levels of productivity, higher levels of theft, and greater work withdrawal.[13]

Role Conflict

Role conflict
A situation in
which an individual
is confronted by
divergent role
expectations.
Interrole conflict
A situation in which
the expectations of an
individual's different,
separate groups are in
opposition.

When compliance with one role requirement makes it difficult to comply with another, the result is **role conflict**.[14] At the extreme, two or more role expectations may be contradictory. For example, if as a manager you were to provide a performance evaluation of a person you mentored, your roles as evaluator and mentor may conflict. Similarly, we can experience **interrole conflict**[15] when the expectations of our different, separate groups are in opposition. An example can be found in work-family conflict, which Bill experienced when expectations placed on him as a husband and father differed from those placed on him as an executive with EMM Industries. Bill's wife and children want to remain in Phoenix, while EMM expects its employees to be responsive to the company's needs and requirements. Although it might be in Bill's financial and career interests to accept a relocation, the conflict centers on choosing between family and work-role expectations. Indeed, a great deal of research demonstrates that work-family conflict is one of the most significant sources of stress for most employees.[16]

GROUP PROPERTY 2: NORMS

Norms
Acceptable standards of
behavior within a group
that are shared by the
group's members.

Did you ever notice that golfers don't speak while their partners are putting? Why not? The answer is norms.

All groups have established **norms**—acceptable standards of behavior shared by members that express what they ought and ought not to do under certain circumstances.

It's not enough for group leaders to share their opinions—even if members adopt the leaders' views, the effect may last only three days![17] When agreed to by the group, norms influence behavior with a minimum of external controls. Different groups, communities, and societies have different norms, but they all have them.[18]

Norms and Emotions

Have you ever noticed how the emotions of one member of your family, especially strong emotions, can influence the emotions of the other members? A family can be a highly normative group. So can a task group whose members work together on a daily basis, because frequent communication can increase the power of norms. A recent study found that, in a task group, individuals' emotions influenced the group's emotions and vice versa. This may not be surprising, but researchers also found that norms dictated the *experience* of emotions for the individuals and for the groups—in other words, people grew to interpret their shared emotions in the same way.[19] As we discovered in Chapter 4, our emotions and moods can shape our perspective, so the normative effect of groups can powerfully influence group attitudes and outcomes.

Norms and Conformity

As a member of a group, you desire acceptance by the group. Thus, you are susceptible to conforming to group norms. Considerable evidence suggests that groups can place strong pressures on individual members to change their attitudes and behaviors to match the group's standard.[20]

The impact that group pressures for **conformity** can have on an individual member's judgment was demonstrated in studies by Solomon Asch and others.[21] Asch made up groups of seven or eight people who were asked to compare two cards. One card had one line, and the other had three lines of varying length, one of which was identical to the line on the one-line card, as Exhibit 9-2 shows. The difference in line length was obvious; in fact, under ordinary conditions, subjects were incorrect less than 1 percent of the time in announcing which of the three lines matched the single line.

The experiment began with sets of matching exercises. Everyone gave the right answers. On the third set, however, the first subject, who was part of the research team, gave an obviously wrong answer—for example, saying "C" in Exhibit 9-2. The next subject, also on the research team, gave the same wrong answer, and so forth. Now the dilemma confronting the subject, who didn't know any of the subjects were on the research team, was this: publicly state a perception that differed from the announced position of the others, or give an incorrect answer that agreed with the others.

The results over many experiments showed 75 percent of subjects gave at least one answer that conformed—that they knew was wrong but was consistent with the replies of

Conformity
The adjustment of one's behavior to align with the norms of the group.

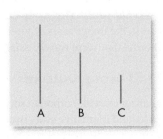

EXHIBIT 9-2
Examples of Cards Used in Asch's Study

other group members—and the average conformer gave wrong answers 37 percent of the time. But does that mean we are mere robots? Certainly not. Do individuals conform to the pressures of all groups to which they belong? Again, obviously not. People conform most to their **reference groups**, important groups in which a person is aware of other members, defines himself or herself as a member or would like to be a member, and feels group members are significant to him or her.

Reference groups
Important groups to which individuals belong or hope to belong and with whose norms individuals are likely to conform.

Norms and Behavior

Norms can cover any aspect of group behavior.[22] As we've mentioned, norms in the workplace significantly influence employee behavior. This may seem intuitive, but full appreciation of the influence of norms on worker behavior did not occur until the Hawthorne Studies conducted between 1924 and 1932 with production workers at the Western Electric Company's Hawthorne Works in Chicago.[23] Subsequent studies have reinforced the general findings, so next we detail the Hawthorne experiments for you.

The researchers first examined the relationship between the physical environment—specifically, the amount of light on the shop floor—and productivity. As they increased the light level for the experimental group of workers, output rose for that unit and the control group. But as they dropped the light level, productivity continued to increase. In fact, productivity in the experimental group decreased only when the light intensity had been reduced to that of moonlight, leading researchers to believe that group dynamics, rather than the environment, influenced behavior.

The researchers next isolated a small group of women assembling telephones so their behavior could be more carefully observed. Over the next several years, this small group's output increased steadily, and the number of personal and sick absences was approximately one-third of that in the regular production department. It became evident this group's performance was significantly influenced by its "special" status. The members thought they were in an elite group, and that management showed concern about their interests by engaging in experimentation. In essence, workers in both the illumination and assembly experiments were really reacting to the increased attention they received.

A wage-incentive plan was then introduced in the bank wiring observation room. The most important finding was that employees did not individually maximize their output. Rather, their role performance became controlled by a group norm. Members were afraid that if they significantly increased their output, the unit incentive rate might be cut, the expected daily output might be increased, layoffs might occur, or slower workers might be reprimanded. So the group established its idea of a fair output—neither too much nor too little. Members helped each other ensure their reports were nearly level, and the norms the group established included a number of behavioral "don'ts." *Don't* be a rate-buster—turning out too much work. *Don't* be a chiseler—turning out too little work. *Don't* squeal on any of your peers. The group enforced its norms with name-calling, ridicule, and even punches to the upper arms of violators. The group thus operated well below its capability, using norms that were tightly established and strongly enforced.

Positive Norms and Group Outcomes

One goal of every organization with corporate social responsibility (CSR; see Chapter 3) initiatives is for its values to hold normative sway over employees. After all, if employees aligned their thinking with positive norms, these norms would become stronger and the probability of positive impact would grow exponentially. We might expect the same outcomes from political correctness (PC) norms. But what *is* the effect of strong positive norms on group outcomes? The popular thinking is that to increase creativity in groups, for instance, norms should be loosened. However, research on gender-diverse groups indicates that strong PC norms increase group creativity. Why? The clear expectations about male–female interactions usually present in high PC environments reduce uncertainty about group expectations,[24] which allows the members to more easily express their creative ideas without combating stereotype norms.

Positive group norms may well beget positive outcomes, but only if other factors are present, too. For instance, in a recent study a high level of group extraversion predicted helping behaviors more strongly when there were positive cooperation norms.[25] As powerful as norms can be, though, not everyone is equally susceptible to positive group norms. Individual personalities factor in, too, as well as the level of a person's social identity with the group. Also, a recent study in Germany indicated that the more satisfied people were with their groups, the more closely they followed group norms.[26]

Negative Norms and Group Outcomes

LeBron is frustrated by a coworker who constantly spreads malicious and unsubstantiated rumors about him. Lindsay is tired of a member of her workgroup who, when confronted with a problem, takes out his frustration by yelling and screaming at her and other members. And Mi-Cha recently quit her job as a dental hygienist after being sexually harassed by her employer.

What do these illustrations have in common? They represent employees exposed to acts of deviant workplace behavior.[27] As we discussed in Chapter 3, counterproductive work behavior (CWB) or **deviant workplace behavior** is voluntary behavior that violates significant organizational norms and, in so doing, threatens the well-being of the organization or its members. Exhibit 9-3 provides a typology of deviant workplace behaviors, with examples of each.

Deviant workplace behavior
Voluntary behavior that violates significant organizational norms and, in so doing, threatens the well-being of the organization or its members. Also called antisocial behavior or workplace incivility.

Category	Examples
Production	Leaving early Intentionally working slowly Wasting resources
Property	Sabotage Lying about hours worked Stealing from the organization
Political	Showing favoritism Gossiping and spreading rumors Blaming coworkers
Personal aggression	Sexual harassment Verbal abuse Stealing from coworkers

EXHIBIT 9-3
Typology of Deviant Workplace Behavior

Source: Based on S. L. Robinson and R. J. Bennett, "A Typology of Deviant Workplace Behaviors: A Multidimensional Scaling Study," *Academy of Management Journal* 38, no. 2 (1995), p. 565. Copyright 1995 by Academy of Management (NY); S. H. Appelbaum, G. D. Iaconi, and A. Matousek, "Positive and Negative Deviant Workplace Behaviors: Causes, Impacts, and Solutions," *Corporate Governance* 7, no. 5 (2007), 586–598; and R. W. Griffin, and A. O'Leary-Kelly, *The Dark Side of Organizational Behavior* (New York: Wiley, 2004)."

Few organizations will admit to creating or condoning conditions that encourage or sustain deviant behaviors. Yet they exist. For one, as we discussed before, a workgroup can become characterized by positive or negative attributes. When those attributes are negative, such as when a workgroup is high in psychopathy and aggression, the characteristics of deceit, amorality, and intent to harm others are pronounced.[28] Second, employees have been reporting an increase in rudeness and disregard toward others by bosses and coworkers in recent years. Workplace incivility, like many other deviant behaviors, has many negative outcomes for those on the receiving end.[29] Nearly half of employees who have suffered this incivility say it has led them to think about changing jobs; 12 percent actually quit because of it.[30] Also, a study of nearly 1,500 respondents found that in addition to increasing their intentions to leave, incivility at work increased reports of psychological stress and physical illness.[31] Third, research suggests that a lack of sleep, which is often caused by heightened work demands and which hinders a person's ability to regulate emotions and behaviors, can lead to deviant behavior. As organizations have tried to do more with less and pushing their employees to work extra hours, they may indirectly be facilitating deviant behavior.[32]

Norms and Culture

Do people in collectivist cultures have different norms than people in individualist cultures? Of course they do. But did you know that our orientation may be changed, even after years of living in one society? In one recent experiment, an organizational role-playing exercise was given to a neutral group of subjects; the exercise stressed either collectivist or individualist (see Chapter 4) norms. Subjects were then given a task of their personal choice or were assigned one by an ingroup or outgroup person. When the individualist-primed subjects were allowed personal choice of the task, or the collectivist-primed subjects were assigned the task by an ingroup person, they became more highly motivated.[33]

GROUP PROPERTY 3: STATUS, AND GROUP PROPERTY 4: SIZE

We've discussed how the roles we play and the norms we internalize tend to dictate our behavior in groups. However, those are not the only two factors that influence who we are in a group and how the group functions. Have you ever noticed how groups tend to stratify into higher- and lower-status members? Sometimes the status of members reflects their status outside the group setting, but not always. Also, status often varies between groups of different sizes. Let's examine how these factors affect a workgroup's efficacy.

Group Property 3: Status

Status
A socially defined position or rank given to groups or group members by others.

Status characteristics theory
A theory that states that differences in status characteristics create status hierarchies within groups.

Status—a socially defined position or rank given to groups or group members by others—permeates every society. Even the smallest group will show differences in member status over time. Status is a significant motivator and has major behavioral consequences when individuals perceive a disparity between what they believe their status is and what others perceive it to be.

WHAT DETERMINES STATUS? According to **status characteristics theory**, status tends to derive from one of three sources:[34]

1. **The power a person wields over others.** Because they likely control the group's resources, people who control group outcomes tend to be perceived as high status.

2. **A person's ability to contribute to a group's goals.** People whose contributions are critical to the group's success tend to have high status.
3. **An individual's personal characteristics.** Someone whose personal characteristics are positively valued by the group (good looks, intelligence, money, or a friendly personality) typically has higher status than someone with fewer valued attributes.

STATUS AND NORMS   Status has some interesting effects on the power of norms and pressures to conform. High-status individuals may be more likely to deviate from norms when they have low identification (social identity) with the group.[35] They also eschew pressure from lower-ranking members of other groups. High-status people are also better able to resist conformity pressures than are their lower-status peers. An individual who is highly valued by a group but doesn't need or care about the group's social rewards is particularly able to disregard conformity norms.[36] In general, bringing high-status members into a group may improve performance, but only up to a point, perhaps because these members may introduce counterproductive norms.[37]

STATUS AND GROUP INTERACTION   People tend to become more assertive when they seek to attain higher status in a group.[38] They speak out more often, criticize more, state more commands, and interrupt others more often. Lower-status members tend to participate less actively in group discussions; when they possess expertise and insights that could aid the group, failure to fully utilize these members reduces the group's overall performance. But that doesn't mean a group of only high-status individuals would be preferable. Adding *some* high-status individuals to a group of mid-status individuals may be advantageous because group performance suffers when too many high-status people are in the mix.[39]

STATUS INEQUITY   It is important for group members to believe the status hierarchy is equitable. Perceived inequity creates disequilibrium, which inspires various types of corrective behaviors. Hierarchical groups can lead to resentment among those at the lower end of the status continuum. Large differences in status within groups are also associated with poorer individual performance, lower health, and higher intentions for the lower-status members to leave the group.[40]

STATUS AND STIGMATIZATION   Although it's clear that your own status affects the way people perceive you, the status of people with whom you are affiliated can also affect others' views of you. Studies have shown that people who are stigmatized can "infect" others with their stigma. This "stigma by association" effect can result in negative opinions and evaluations of the person affiliated with the stigmatized individual, even if the association is brief and purely coincidental. Of course, many of the foundations of cultural status differences have no merit in the first place.

GROUP STATUS   Early in life, we acquire an "us and them" mentality.[41] You may have correctly surmised that if you are in an outgroup, your group is of lower status in the eyes of the associated ingroup's members. Culturally, sometimes ingroups represent the dominant forces in a society and are given high status, which can create discrimination against their outgroups. Low-status groups, perhaps in response to this discrimination, are likely to leverage ingroup favoritism to compete for higher status.[42] When high-status groups then feel the discrimination from low-status groups, they may increase their bias against the outgroups.[43] With each cycle, the groups become more polarized.

Group Property 4: Size

Does the size of a group affect the group's overall behavior? Yes, but the effect depends on what dependent variables we examine. Groups with a dozen or more members are good for gaining diverse input. If the goal is fact-finding or idea-generating, then larger groups should be more effective. Smaller groups of about seven members are better at doing something productive.

Social loafing
The tendency for individuals to expend less effort when working collectively than when working individually.

One of the most important findings about the size of a group concerns **social loafing**, the tendency for individuals to expend less effort when working collectively than when alone.[44] Social loafing directly challenges the assumption that the productivity of the group as a whole should at least equal the sum of the productivity of the individuals in it, no matter what the group size. The implications for OB are significant. When managers use collective work situations, they must also be able to identify individual efforts. Furthermore, greater performance diversity creates greater social loafing the longer a group is together, which decreases satisfaction and performance.[45]

Social loafing appears to have a Western bias. It's consistent with individualistic cultures, such as those found in the United States and Canada, which are dominated by self-interest. It is *not* consistent with collectivistic societies, in which individuals are motivated by group goals. For example, in studies comparing U.S. employees with employees from China and Israel (both collectivistic societies), Chinese and Israelis showed no propensity to engage in social loafing and actually performed better in a group than alone.

Research indicates that the stronger an individual's work ethic is, the less likely that person is to engage in social loafing.[46] Also, the greater the level of conscientiousness and agreeableness (see Chapter 5) in a group, the more likely that performance will remain high whether there is social loafing or not.[47] There are ways to prevent social loafing:

1. Set group goals, so the group has a common purpose to strive toward.
2. Increase intergroup competition, which focuses on the shared group outcome.
3. Engage in peer evaluations.
4. Select members who have high motivation and prefer to work in groups.
5. Base group rewards in part on each member's unique contributions.[48]

Recent research indicates that social loafing can also be counteracted by publicly posting individual performance ratings for group members, too.[49]

GROUP PROPERTY 5: COHESIVENESS, AND GROUP PROPERTY 6: DIVERSITY

For a group to be highly functioning, it must act cohesively as a unit, but not because all the group members think and act alike. In some ways, the properties of cohesiveness and diversity need to be valued at the initial tacit establishment of roles and norms—will the group be inclusive of all its members, regardless of differences in backgrounds? Let's discuss the importance of group cohesiveness first.

Group Property 5: Cohesiveness

Groups differ in their **cohesiveness**—the degree to which members are attracted to each other and motivated to stay in the group. Some workgroups are cohesive because the members have spent a great deal of time together, the group's small size or purpose facilitates high interaction, or external threats have brought members close together.

Cohesiveness affects group productivity. Studies consistently show that the relationship between cohesiveness and productivity depends on the group's performance-related norms.[50] If norms for quality, output, and cooperation with outsiders are high, a cohesive group will be more productive than a less cohesive group. But if cohesiveness is high and performance norms are low, productivity will be low. If cohesiveness is low and performance norms are high, productivity increases, but less than in the high-cohesiveness/high-norms situation. When cohesiveness and performance-related norms are both low, productivity tends to fall into the low-to-moderate range. These conclusions are summarized in Exhibit 9-4.

What can you do to encourage group cohesiveness?

1. Make the group smaller.
2. Encourage agreement with group goals.
3. Increase the time members spend together.
4. Increase the group's status and the perceived difficulty of attaining membership.
5. Stimulate competition with other groups.
6. Give rewards to the group rather than to individual members.
7. Physically isolate the group.[51]

Cohesiveness
The degree to which group members are attracted to each other and are motivated to stay in the group.

Group Property 6: Diversity

The final property of groups we consider is **diversity** in the group's membership, or the degree to which members of the group are similar to, or different from, one another. Overall, studies identify both costs and benefits from group diversity.

Diversity appears to increase group conflict, especially in the early stages of a group's tenure, which often lowers group morale and raises dropout rates. One study compared groups that were culturally diverse and homogeneous (composed of people from the same country). On a wilderness survival test, the groups performed equally well, but the members from the diverse groups were less satisfied with their groups, were less cohesive, and had more conflict.[52] Groups in which members' values or opinions differ

Diversity
The extent to which members of a group are similar to, or different from, one another.

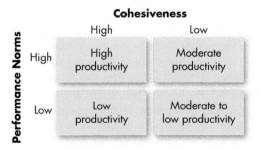

**EXHIBIT 9-4
The Impact of Cohesiveness and Performance Norms on Productivity**

tend to experience more conflict, but leaders who can get the group to focus on the task at hand and encourage group learning are able to reduce these conflicts and enhance discussion of group issues.[53] Gender diversity can also be a challenge to a group, but if inclusiveness is stressed, group conflict and dissatisfaction are lowered.[54]

TYPES OF GROUP DIVERSITY You may have correctly surmised that the type of group diversity matters. Surface-level diversity—in observable characteristics such as national origin, race, and gender—alerts people to possible deep-level diversity—in underlying attitudes, values, and opinions. Right or wrong, one researcher argues, "The mere presence of diversity you can see, such as a person's race or gender, actually cues a team that there's likely to be differences of opinion."[55] Surface-level diversity may subconsciously cue team members to be more open-minded in their views.[56] For example, two studies of MBA student groups found surface-level diversity led to greater openness.

The effects of deep-level diversity are less understood. Research in Korea indicates that putting people with a high need for power (nPow; see Chapter 8) with those with a low need for power can reduce unproductive group competition, whereas putting individuals with a similar need for achievement may increase task performance.[57]

CHALLENGES OF GROUP DIVERSITY Although differences can lead to conflict, they also provide an opportunity to solve problems in unique ways. One study of jury behavior found diverse juries were more likely to deliberate longer, share more information, and make fewer factual errors when discussing evidence. Altogether, the impact of diversity on groups is mixed. It is difficult to be in a diverse group in the short term. However, if members can weather their differences, over time diversity may help them to be more open-minded and creative and to do better. But even positive effects are unlikely to be especially strong. As one review stated, "The business case (in terms of demonstrable financial results) for diversity remains hard to support based on the extant research."[58] Yet, other researchers argue that we shouldn't overlook the effects of homogeneity, many of which can be detrimental.[59]

Faultlines

The perceived divisions that split groups into two or more subgroups based on individual differences such as sex, race, age, work experience, and education.

One possible negative effect of diverse teams—especially those that are diverse in terms of surface-level characteristics—is **faultlines**, or perceived divisions that split groups into two or more subgroups based on individual differences such as sex, race, age, work experience, and education.

For example, let's say Group A is composed of three men and three women. The three men have approximately the same amount of work experience and backgrounds in marketing. The three women have about the same amount of work experience and backgrounds in finance. Group B has three men and three women, but they all differ in terms of their experience and backgrounds. Two of the men are experienced, while the other is new. One of the women has worked at the company for several years, while the other two are new. In addition, two of the men and one woman in Group B have backgrounds in marketing, while the other man and the remaining two women have backgrounds in finance. It is thus likely that a faultline will result in the subgroups of males and females in Group A but not in Group B, based on the differentiating characteristics.

Research on faultlines has shown that splits are generally detrimental to group functioning and performance. Subgroups may compete with each other, which takes time away from core tasks and harms group performance. Groups that have subgroups learn more slowly, make more risky decisions, are less creative, and experience higher levels of conflict. Subgroups may not trust each other. Finally, satisfaction with subgroups is generally high, but the overall group's satisfaction is lower when faultlines are present.[60] However, faultlines regarding skill, knowledge, and expertise may be beneficial in a results-driven organizational culture.[61] Furthermore, problems stemming from strong faultlines may be overcome when the group is given a common goal to strive for. Altogether, forced collaboration between members of subgroups and focus on accomplishing a goal may transcend the faultlines.[62]

GROUP DECISION MAKING

The belief—characterized by juries—that two heads are better than one has long been accepted as a basic component of the U.S. legal system and those of many other countries. Many decisions in organizations are made by groups, teams, or committees. We'll discuss the advantages of group decision making, along with the unique challenges group dynamics bring to the decision-making process. Finally, we'll offer some techniques for maximizing the group decision-making opportunity.

Groups versus the Individual

Decision-making groups may be widely used in organizations, but are group decisions preferable to those made by an individual alone? The answer depends on a number of factors. Groups are an excellent vehicle for performing many steps in the decision-making process and offer both breadth and depth of input for information gathering. If group members have diverse backgrounds, the alternatives generated should be more extensive and the analysis more critical. When the final solution is agreed on, there are more people in a group decision to support and implement it. These pluses, however, may be more than offset by the time consumed by group decisions, the internal conflicts they create, and the pressures they generate toward conformity.

We must be careful to define the types of conflicts, however. Research in Korea indicates that group conflicts about tasks may increase group performance, while conflicts in relationships may decrease performance.[63] In some cases, therefore, we can expect individuals to make better decisions than groups. Let's look at the considerations of group decision making.

STRENGTHS OF GROUP DECISION MAKING Groups generate *more complete information and knowledge.* By aggregating the resources of several individuals, groups bring more input as well as heterogeneity into the decision process. They offer *increased diversity of views.* This opens up the opportunity to consider more approaches and alternatives. Finally, groups lead to increased *acceptance of a solution.* Group members who participate in making a decision are more likely to enthusiastically support and encourage others to accept it later.

WEAKNESSES OF GROUP DECISION MAKING Group decisions are time-consuming because groups typically take more time to reach a solution. There are *conformity pressures.* The desire by group members to be accepted and considered an asset to the group can squash any overt disagreement. Group discussion can be *dominated by one or a few members.* If they're low- and medium-ability members, the group's overall effectiveness will suffer. Finally, group decisions suffer from *ambiguous responsibility.*

In an individual decision, it's clear who is accountable for the final outcome. In a group decision, the responsibility of any single member is diluted.

EFFECTIVENESS AND EFFICIENCY   Whether groups are more effective than individuals depends on how you define effectiveness. Group decisions are generally more *accurate* than the decisions of the average individual in a group, but generally less accurate than the judgments of the most accurate person.[64] In terms of *speed*, individuals are superior. If *creativity* is important, groups tend to be more effective. And if effectiveness means the degree of *acceptance* of achievable solutions, the nod again goes to the group.[65]

We cannot consider effectiveness without also assessing efficiency. With few exceptions, group decision making consumes more work hours than does having an individual tackle the same problem. The exceptions tend to be instances in which, to achieve comparable quantities of diverse input, the single decision maker must spend a great deal of time reviewing files and talking to other people. In deciding whether to use groups, then, managers must assess whether increases in effectiveness are more than enough to offset the reductions in efficiency.

Groupthink

Groupthink, a by-product of a decision, can affect a group's ability to appraise alternatives objectively and achieve high-quality solutions. **Groupthink** relates to norms and describes situations in which group pressures for conformity deter the group from critically appraising unusual, minority, or unpopular views.

Groupthink
A phenomenon in which the norm for consensus overrides the realistic appraisal of alternative courses of action.

GROUPTHINK   Groupthink appears closely aligned with the conclusions Solomon Asch drew in his experiments with a lone dissenter. Individuals who hold a position different from that of the dominant majority are under pressure to suppress, withhold, or modify their true feelings and beliefs. As members of a group, we find it more pleasant to be in agreement—to be a positive part of the group—than to be a disruptive force, even if disruption would improve effectiveness. Groups that are more focused on performance than on learning are especially likely to fall victim to groupthink and to suppress the opinions of those who do not agree with the majority.[66] Groupthink seems to occur most often when there is a clear group identity, when members hold a positive image of their group they want to protect, and when the group perceives a collective threat to its positive image.[67]

What can managers do to minimize groupthink?[68] First, they can monitor group size. People grow more intimidated and hesitant as group size increases, and although there is no magic number that will eliminate groupthink, individuals are likely to feel less personal responsibility when groups get larger than about 10 members. Managers should also encourage group leaders to play an impartial role. Leaders should actively seek input from all members and avoid expressing their own opinions, especially in the early stages of deliberation. In addition, managers should appoint one group member to play the role of devil's advocate, overtly challenging the majority position and offering divergent perspectives. Yet another suggestion is to use exercises that stimulate active discussion of diverse alternatives without threatening the group or intensifying identity protection. Have group members delay discussion of possible gains so they can first talk about the dangers or risks inherent in a decision. Requiring members to initially focus on the negatives of an alternative makes the group less likely to stifle dissenting views and more likely to gain an objective evaluation.

Groupshift or Group Polarization

Groupshift describes the way group members tend to exaggerate their initial positions when discussing a given set of alternatives to arrive at a solution. In some situations, caution dominates and there is a conservative shift, while in other situations, groups tend toward a risky shift. There are differences between group decisions and the individual decisions of group members.[69] In groups, discussion leads members toward a more extreme view of the position they already held. Conservatives become more cautious, and more aggressive types take on more risk. We can view this group polarization as a special case of groupthink. The group's decision reflects the dominant decision-making norm—toward greater caution or more risk—that develops during discussion.

Groupshift
A change between a group's decision and an individual decision that a member within the group would make; the shift can be toward either conservatism or greater risk but it generally is toward a more extreme version of the group's original position.

The shift toward polarization has several explanations.[70] It's been argued, for instance, that discussion makes the members more comfortable with each other and thus more willing to express extreme versions of their original positions. Another argument is that the group diffuses responsibility. Group decisions free any single member from accountability for the group's final choice, so a more extreme position can be taken. It's also likely that people take extreme positions because they want to demonstrate how different they are from the outgroup.[71] People on the fringes of political or social movements may take on ever-more-extreme positions just to prove they are really committed to the cause, whereas those who are more cautious tend to take moderate positions to demonstrate how reasonable they are.

We now turn to the techniques by which groups make decisions. These reduce some of the dysfunctional aspects of group decision making.

Group Decision-Making Techniques

The most common form of group decision making takes place in **interacting groups**. Members meet face to face and rely on both verbal and nonverbal interactions to communicate. But as our discussion of groupthink demonstrated, interacting groups often censor themselves and pressure individual members toward conformity of opinion. Brainstorming and the nominal group technique (discussed below) can reduce problems inherent in the traditional interacting group.

Interacting groups
Typical groups in which members interact with each other face to face.

BRAINSTORMING **Brainstorming** can overcome the pressures for conformity that dampen creativity[72] by encouraging any and all alternatives while withholding criticism. In a typical brainstorming session, a half-dozen to a dozen people sit around a table. The group leader states the problem in a clear manner so all participants understand. Members then freewheel as many alternatives as they can in a given length of time. To encourage members to "think the unusual," no criticism is allowed, even of the most bizarre suggestions, and all ideas are recorded for later discussion and analysis.

Brainstorming
An idea-generation process that specifically encourages any and all alternatives while withholding any criticism of those alternatives.

Brainstorming may indeed generate ideas—but not in a very efficient manner. Research consistently shows individuals working alone generate more ideas than a group in a brainstorming session does. One reason for this is "production blocking." When people are generating ideas in a group, many are talking at once, which blocks individuals' thought process and eventually impedes the sharing of ideas.[73]

Nominal group technique
A group decision-making method in which individual members meet face to face to pool their judgments in a systematic but independent fashion.

NOMINAL GROUP TECHNIQUE   The **nominal group technique** may be more effective. This technique restricts discussion and interpersonal communication during the decision-making process. Group members are all physically present, as in a traditional meeting, but they operate independently. Specifically, a problem is presented and then the group takes the following steps:

1. Before any discussion takes place, each member independently writes down ideas about the problem.
2. After this silent period, each member presents one idea to the group. No discussion takes place until all ideas have been presented and recorded.
3. The group discusses the ideas for clarity and evaluates them.
4. Each group member silently and independently rank-orders the ideas. The idea with the highest aggregate ranking determines the final decision.

The chief advantage of the nominal group technique is that it permits a group to meet formally but does not restrict independent thinking. Research generally shows nominal groups outperform brainstorming groups.[74]

Each of the group-decision techniques has its own set of strengths and weaknesses. The choice depends on the criteria you want to emphasize and the cost-benefit trade-off. As Exhibit 9-5 indicates, an interacting group is good for achieving commitment to a solution; brainstorming develops group cohesiveness; and the nominal group technique is an inexpensive means for generating a large number of ideas.

SUMMARY

We can draw several implications from our discussion of groups. First, norms control behavior by establishing standards of right and wrong. Second, status inequities create frustration and can adversely influence productivity and willingness to remain with an organization. Third, the impact of size on a group's performance depends on the type of task. Fourth, cohesiveness may influence a group's level of productivity, depending on the group's performance-related norms. Fifth, diversity appears to have a mixed impact on group performance, with some studies suggesting that diversity can help performance and others suggesting the opposite. Sixth, role conflict is associated with job-induced tension and job dissatisfaction.[75] Groups can be carefully managed toward positive organizational outcomes and optimal decision making. The next chapter will explore several of these conclusions in greater depth.

Effectiveness Criteria	Type of Group		
	Interacting	Brainstorming	Nominal
Number and quality of ideas	Low	Moderate	High
Social pressure	High	Low	Moderate
Money costs	Low	Low	Low
Speed	Moderate	Moderate	Moderate
Task orientation	Low	High	High
Potential for interpersonal conflict	High	Low	Moderate
Commitment to solution	High	Not applicable	Moderate
Development of group cohesiveness	High	High	Moderate

EXHIBIT 9-5
Evaluating Group Effectiveness

IMPLICATIONS FOR MANAGERS

- Recognize that groups can dramatically affect individual behavior in organizations, to either a positive or negative effect. Therefore, pay special attention to roles, norms, and cohesion—to understand how these are operating within a group is to understand how the group is likely to behave.
- To decrease the possibility of deviant workplace activities, ensure that group norms do not support antisocial behavior.
- Pay attention to the status aspect of groups. Because lower-status people tend to participate less in group discussions, groups with high-status differences are likely to inhibit input from lower-status members and reduce their potential.
- Use larger groups for fact-finding activities and smaller groups for action-taking tasks. With larger groups, provide measures of individual performance.
- To increase employee satisfaction, ensure people perceive their job roles accurately.

 TRY IT!

If your professor has assigned this, go to the Assignments section of **mymanagementlab.com** to complete the **Simulation: Group Behavior**.

PERSONAL INVENTORY ASSESSMENTS

Communicating Supportively

Are you a supportive person? Take this PIA to find out if you communicate supportively.

9-1. Which of the concepts in this chapter apply to experiences you've had in groups?

10

Understanding Work Teams

MyManagementLab®

⭐ Improve Your Grade!

When you see this icon ⭐, visit **mymanagementlab.com** for activities that are applied, personalized, and offer immediate feedback.

LEARNING OBJECTIVES

After studying this chapter, you should be able to:

1. Analyze the continued popularity of teams in organizations.
2. Contrast groups and teams.
3. Contrast the five types of team arrangements.
4. Identify the characteristics of effective teams.
5. Explain how organizations can create team players.
6. Decide when to use individuals instead of teams.

⭐ Chapter Warm-up

If your professor has chosen to assign this, go to the Assignments section of **mymanagementlab.com** to complete the chapter warm-up.

WHY HAVE TEAMS BECOME SO POPULAR?

Why are teams popular? In short, because we believe they are effective. "A team of people happily committed to the project and to one another will outperform a brilliant individual every time," writes *Forbes* publisher Rich Karlgaard.[1] In some ways, he's right. Teams can sometimes achieve feats an individual could never accomplish.[2] Teams are more flexible and responsive to changing events than traditional departments or other forms of permanent groups can be. They can quickly assemble, deploy, refocus, and disband. They are an effective means to democratize organizations and increase employee involvement. And finally, research indicates that our involvement in teams positively shapes the way we think as individuals, introducing a collaborative mind-set about even our own personal decision making.[3]

The fact that organizations have embraced teamwork doesn't necessarily mean teams are always effective. Team members, being human, can be swayed by fads and herd mentality that can lead them astray from the best decisions. What conditions affect their potential? How do members work together? Do we even like teams? Maybe not. To answer these questions, let's first distinguish between groups and teams.

DIFFERENCES BETWEEN GROUPS AND TEAMS

Groups and teams are not the same thing. In Chapter 9, we defined a *group* as two or more individuals, interacting and interdependent, who work together to achieve particular objectives. A **work group** is a group that interacts primarily to share information and make decisions to help each member perform within his or her area of responsibility.

Workgroups have no need or opportunity to engage in collective work with joint effort, so the group's performance is merely the summation of each member's individual contribution. There is no positive synergy that would create an overall level of performance greater than the sum of the inputs. A workgroup is a collection of individuals doing their work, albeit with interaction and/or dependency.

A **work team**, on the other hand, generates positive synergy through coordination. The individual efforts result in a level of performance greater than the sum of the individual inputs.

In both workgroups and work teams, there are often behavioral expectations of members, collective normalization efforts, active group dynamics, and some level of decision making (even if just informally about the scope of membership). Both may generate ideas, pool resources, or coordinate logistics such as work schedules; for the workgroup, however, this effort will be limited to information gathering for decision makers outside the group.

Whereas we can think of a work team as a subset of a workgroup, the team is constructed to be purposeful (symbiotic) in its member interaction. The distinction between a workgroup and a work team should be kept even when the terms are mentioned interchangeably in differing contexts. Exhibit 10-1 highlights the differences between them.

Workgroup
A group that interacts primarily to share information and make decisions to help each group member perform within his or her area of responsibility.

Work team
A group whose individual efforts result in performance that is greater than the sum of the individual inputs.

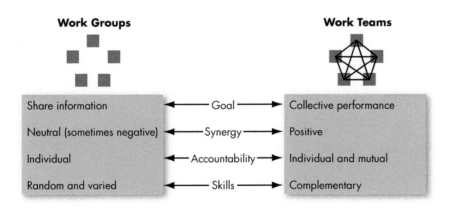

Work Groups		Work Teams
Share information	← Goal →	Collective performance
Neutral (sometimes negative)	← Synergy →	Positive
Individual	← Accountability →	Individual and mutual
Random and varied	← Skills →	Complementary

EXHIBIT 10-1
Comparing Work Groups and Work Teams

The definitions help clarify why organizations structure work processes by teams. Management is looking for positive synergy that will create increased performance. The extensive use of teams creates the *potential* for an organization to generate greater outputs with no increase in employee headcount. Notice, however, that we said *potential*. There is nothing magical that ensures the achievement of positive synergy in the creation of teams. Merely calling a *group* a *team* doesn't automatically improve its performance. As we show later, effective teams have certain common characteristics. If management hopes to gain increases in organizational performance through the use of teams, the teams must possess these characteristics.

TYPES OF TEAMS

Teams can make products, provide services, negotiate deals, coordinate projects, offer advice, and make decisions.[4] In this section, we first describe four common types of teams in organizations: *problem-solving teams*, *self-managed work teams*, *cross-functional teams*, and *virtual teams* (see Exhibit 10-2). Then we will discuss *multiteam systems*, which utilize a "team of teams" and are becoming increasingly widespread as work increases in complexity.

Problem-Solving Teams

Quality-control teams have been in use for many years. Originally seen most often in manufacturing plants, these were permanent teams that generally met at a regular time, sometimes weekly or daily, to address quality standards and any problems with the products made. The use of quality-control teams has since expanded into other arenas such as the medical field, where they are used to improve patient care services. **Problem-solving teams** like these rarely have the authority to unilaterally implement their suggestions, but if their recommendations are paired with implementation processes, some significant improvements can be realized.

Self-Managed Work Teams

As we discussed, problem-solving teams only make recommendations. Some organizations have gone further and created teams that also implement solutions and take responsibility for outcomes. **Self-managed work teams** are groups of employees (typically 10 to 15 in number) who perform highly related or interdependent jobs; these teams take on some supervisory responsibilities.[5] Typically, the responsibilities include planning and scheduling work, assigning tasks to members, making operating decisions, taking

Problem-solving teams
Groups of 5 to 12 employees from the same department who meet for a few hours each week to discuss ways of improving quality, efficiency, and the work environment.

Self-managed work teams
Groups of 10 to 15 people who take on responsibilities of their former supervisors.

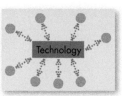

**EXHIBIT 10-2
Four Types of Teams**

Problem-solving   Self-managed   Cross-functional   Virtual

action on problems, and working with suppliers and customers. Fully self-managed work teams even select their own members who evaluate each other's performance. When these teams are established, former supervisory positions become less important and are sometimes eliminated.

Research results on the effectiveness of self-managed work teams have not been uniformly positive. Some research indicates that self-managed teams may be more or less effective based on the degree to which team-promoting behaviors are rewarded. For example, one study of 45 self-managing teams found that when team members perceived that economic rewards such as pay were dependent on input from their teammates, performance improved for both individuals and the team as a whole.[6]

A second area of research focus has been the impact of conflict on self-managed team effectiveness. Some research indicated that self-managed teams are not effective when there is conflict. When disputes arise, members often stop cooperating and power struggles ensue, which lead to lower group performance.[7] However, other research indicates that when members feel confident they can speak up without being embarrassed, rejected, or punished by other team members—in other words, when they feel psychologically safe, conflict can be beneficial and boost team performance.[8]

Thirdly, research has explored the effect of self-managed work teams on member behavior. Here again the findings are mixed. Although individuals on teams report higher levels of job satisfaction than other individuals, studies indicate they sometimes also have higher absenteeism and turnover rates. Furthermore, one large-scale study of labor productivity in British establishments found that although using teams improved individual (and overall) labor productivity, no evidence supported the claim that self-managed teams performed better than traditional teams with less decision-making authority.[9]

Cross-Functional Teams

Starbucks created a team of individuals from production, global PR, global communications, and U.S. marketing to develop the Via brand of instant coffee. The team's suggestions resulted in a product that would be cost-effective to produce and distribute, and that was marketed with a tightly integrated, multifaceted strategy.[10] This example illustrates the use of **cross-functional teams**, teams made up of employees from about the same hierarchical level, but from different work areas, who come together to accomplish a task.

Cross-functional teams are an effective means of allowing people from diverse areas within or even between organizations to exchange information, develop new ideas, solve problems, and coordinate complex projects. However, due to the high need for coordination, cross-functional teams are not simple to manage. Why? First, power shifts occur as different expertise is needed because the members are at roughly the same level in the organization, which creates leadership ambiguity. A climate of trust thus needs to be developed before shifts can happen without undue conflict.[11] Second, the early stages of development are often long since members need to learn to work with higher levels of diversity and complexity. Third, it takes time to build trust and teamwork, especially among people with different experiences and perspectives.

In sum, the strength of traditional cross-functional teams is the collaborative effort of individuals with diverse skills from a variety of disciplines. When the unique perspectives of these members are considered, these teams can be very effective.

Cross-functional teams
Employees from about the same hierarchical level, but from different work areas, who come together to accomplish a task.

Virtual Teams

Virtual teams
Teams that use computer technology to tie together physically dispersed members in order to achieve a common goal.

The teams described in the preceding section do their work face-to-face, whereas **virtual teams** use computer technology to unite physically dispersed members in an effort to achieve a common goal.[12] Members collaborate online using communication links such as wide area networks, corporate social media, videoconferencing, and e-mail; whether members are nearby or continents apart. Nearly all teams do at least some of their work remotely.

Virtual teams should be managed differently than face-to-face teams in an office, partially because virtual team members may not interact along traditional hierarchical patterns. Because of the complexity of interactions, research indicated that shared leadership of virtual teams may significantly enhance team performance, although the concept is still in development.[13] For virtual teams to be effective, management should ensure that: (1) trust is established among members (one inflammatory remark in an e-mail can severely undermine team trust); (2) progress is monitored closely (so the team doesn't lose sight of its goals and no team member "disappears"); and (3) the efforts and products of the team are publicized throughout the organization (so the team does not become invisible).[14]

Multiteam Systems

The types of teams we've described so far are typically smaller, stand-alone teams, though their activities relate to the broader objectives of the organization. As tasks become more complex, teams often grow in size. Increases in team size are accompanied by higher coordination demands, creating a tipping point at which the addition of another member does more harm than good. To solve this problem, organizations use **multiteam systems**, collections of two or more interdependent teams that share a superordinate goal. In other words, a multiteam system is a "team of teams."[1]

Multiteam system
A collection of two or more interdependent teams that share a superordinate goal; a team of teams.

To picture a multiteam system, imagine the coordination of response needed after a major car accident. There is the emergency medical services team, which responds first and transports the injured people to the hospital. An emergency room team then takes over, providing medical care, followed by a recovery team. Although the emergency services team, emergency room team, and recovery team are technically independent, their activities are interdependent, and the success of one depends on the success of the others. Why? Because they all share the higher goal of saving lives.

Some factors that make smaller, more traditional teams effective do not necessarily apply to multiteam systems and can even hinder their performance. One study showed that multiteam systems performed better when they had "boundary spanners" whose jobs were to coordinate efforts with all constituents. This reduced the need for some team member communication, which was helpful because it reduced coordination demands.[16] Leadership of multiteam systems is also much different than for stand-alone teams. While leadership of all teams affects team performance, a multiteam leader must both facilitate coordination between teams and lead them. Research indicated teams that received more attention and engagement from the organization's leaders felt more empowered, which made them more effective as they sought to solve their own problems.[17]

In general, a multiteam system is the best choice either when a team has become too large to be effective, or when teams with distinct functions need to be highly coordinated.

⭐ WATCH IT

If your professor has assigned this, go to the Assignments section of **mymanagementlab .com** to complete the video exercise titled **Teams (TWZ Role Play)**.

CREATING EFFECTIVE TEAMS

Teams are often created deliberately but sometimes evolve organically. Take the rise of the team "hive" over the past five years as an example of organic evolution. The hive process typically begins with freelancers. Freelancing is typically the solo work of people who are highly specialized in their fields and can provide expertise to organizations on a short-term basis. The difficulty is for the freelancers to effectively market themselves to organizations, and for organizations to find freelancers who fit their needs. To bridge this gap, freelancers form teams with other freelancers from complementary specialties to present a cohesive working unit—a hive—to clients. This team-based approach has proven very successful.[18]

Many people have tried to identify factors related to team effectiveness. To help, some studies have organized what was once a large list of characteristics into a relatively focused model.[19] Exhibit 10-3 summarizes what we currently know about what makes teams effective. As you'll see, it builds on many of the group concepts introduced in Chapter 9.

We can organize the key components of effective teams into three general categories. First are the resources and other *contextual* influences that make teams effective. The second relates to the team's *composition*. Finally, *process* variables are events within the team that influence effectiveness. We will explore each of these components next.

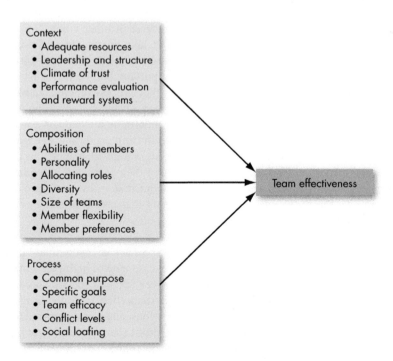

EXHIBIT 10-3
Team Effectiveness Model

Team Context: What Factors Determine Whether Teams Are Successful?

The four contextual factors most significantly related to team performance, discussed next, are *adequate resources*, *leadership and structure*, a *climate of trust*, and a *performance evaluation and reward system* that reflects team contributions.

ADEQUATE RESOURCES   Teams are part of a larger organization system; every work team relies on resources outside the group to sustain it. A scarcity of resources directly reduces the ability of a team to perform its job effectively and achieve its goals. Important resources include timely information, proper equipment, adequate staffing, encouragement, and administrative assistance.

LEADERSHIP AND STRUCTURE   Teams can't function if they can't agree on who is to do what and ensure all members share the workload. Agreeing on the specifics of work and how they fit together to integrate individual skills requires leadership and structure, either from management or from team members themselves. In self-managed teams, members absorb many of the duties typically assumed by managers. A manager's job then becomes managing *outside* (rather than inside) the team.

As mentioned before, leadership is especially important in multiteam systems. Here, leaders need to delegate responsibility to teams and play the role of facilitator, making sure the teams work together rather than against one another.[20]

CLIMATE OF TRUST   Trust is the foundation of leadership; it allows a team to accept and commit to the leader's goals and decisions. Members of effective teams exhibit trust in their leaders.[21] They also trust each other. Interpersonal trust among team members facilitates cooperation, reduces the need to monitor each other's behavior, and bonds individuals through the belief that members won't take advantage of them. Members are more likely to take risks and expose vulnerabilities when they can trust others on their team. The overall level of trust in a team is important, but the way trust is dispersed among team members also matters. Trust levels that are asymmetric and imbalanced between team members can mitigate the performance advantages of a high overall level of trust—in such cases, coalitions form that often undermine the team as a whole.[22]

Trust is a perception that can be vulnerable to shifting conditions in a team environment. For instance, research in Singapore found that, in high-trust teams, individuals are less likely to claim and defend personal ownership of their ideas, but individuals who do still claim personal ownership are rated as lower contributors by *team members*.[23] This "punishment" by the team may reflect resentments that create negative relationships, increased conflicts, and reduced performance.

PERFORMANCE EVALUATION AND REWARD SYSTEM   Individual performance evaluations and incentives may interfere with the development of high-performance teams. So, in addition to evaluating and rewarding employees for their individual contributions, management should utilize hybrid performance systems that incorporate an individual member component to recognize individual contributions, and a group reward to recognize positive team outcomes.[24] Group-based appraisals, profit sharing, small-group incentives, and other system modifications can reinforce team effort and commitment.

Team Composition

Maria Contreras-Sweet, head of the U.S. Small Business Administration, suggests that when she is building a team, she looks for a variety of qualities in potential team members including resourcefulness, flexibility, and discreetness (which also reflects integrity).[25] These are good qualities, but not all that we should consider when staffing teams. The team composition category includes variables that relate to how teams should be staffed: the *abilities* and *personalities* of team members, *allocation of roles*, *diversity*, *cultural differences*, *size* of the team, and *members' preferences* for teamwork.

ABILITIES OF MEMBERS It's true we occasionally read about an athletic team of mediocre players who, because of excellent coaching, determination, and precision teamwork, beat a far more talented group. But such cases make the news precisely because they are unusual. A team's performance depends in part on the knowledge, skills, and abilities of individual members.[26] Abilities set limits on what members can do and how effectively they will perform on a team.

Research revealed insights into team composition and performance. First, when solving a complex problem such as reengineering an assembly line, high-ability teams—composed of mostly intelligent members—do better than lower-ability teams. High-ability teams are also more adaptable to changing situations; they can more effectively apply existing knowledge to new problems.

Finally, the ability of the team's leader matters. Smart team leaders help less intelligent team members when they struggle with a task. A less intelligent leader can, conversely, neutralize the effect of a high-ability team.[27]

PERSONALITY OF MEMBERS We demonstrated in Chapter 5 that personality significantly influences individual behavior. Some dimensions identified in the Big Five personality model are particularly relevant to team effectiveness.[28] Conscientiousness is especially important to teams. Conscientious people are good at backing up other team members and sensing when their support is truly needed. Conscientious teams also have other advantages—one study found that behavioral tendencies such as organization, achievement orientation, and endurance were all related to higher levels of team performance.[29]

Team composition can be based on individual personalities to good effect. Suppose an organization needs to create 20 teams of 4 people each and has 40 highly conscientious people and 40 who score low on conscientiousness. Would the organization be better off: (1) forming 10 teams of highly conscientious people and 10 teams of members low on conscientiousness; or (2) "seeding" each team with two people who score high and two who score low on conscientiousness? Perhaps surprisingly, evidence suggests Option 1 is the best choice; performance across the teams will be higher if the organization forms 10 highly conscientious teams and 10 teams low in conscientiousness. The reason is that a team with varying conscientiousness levels will not work to the peak performance of its highly conscientious members. Instead, a group normalization dynamic (or simple resentment) will complicate interactions and force the highly conscientious members to lower their expectations, thus reducing the group's performance.[30]

What about the other traits? Teams with a high level of openness to experience tend to perform better, and research indicates that constructive task conflict *enhances* the effect. Open team members communicate better with one another and throw out more ideas, which makes teams with open people more creative and innovative.[31] Task conflict also enhances performance for teams with high levels of emotional stability.[32] It's not so much that the conflict itself improves performance for these teams, but that teams characterized by openness and emotional stability are able to handle conflict and leverage it to improve performance. The minimum level of team member agreeableness matters, too: teams do worse when they have one or more highly disagreeable members, and a wide span in individual levels of agreeableness can lower productivity. Research is not clear on the outcomes of extraversion, but one study indicated that a high mean level of extraversion in a team can increase the level of helping behaviors, particularly in a climate of cooperation.[33] Thus, the personality traits of individuals are as important to teams as the overall personality characteristics of the team.

ALLOCATION OF ROLES   Teams have different needs, and members should be selected to ensure all the various roles are filled. A study of 778 major league baseball teams over a 21-year period highlighted the importance of assigning roles appropriately.[34] As you might expect, teams with more experienced and skilled members performed better. However, the experience and skill of those in core roles—those who handled more of the workflow of the team and were central to all work processes (in this case, pitchers and catchers)—were especially vital.[35] In other words, put your most able, experienced, and conscientious workers in the most central roles in a team.

We can identify nine potential team member roles (see Exhibit 10-4). Successful work teams have selected people to play all these roles based on their skills and

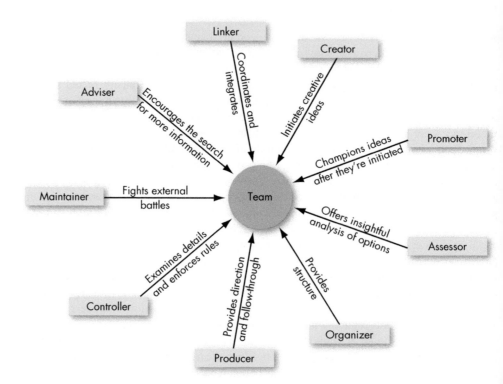

EXHIBIT 10-4
Potential Team
Member Roles

preferences. (On many teams, individuals will play multiple roles.) To increase the likelihood team members will work well together, managers need to understand the individual strengths each person can bring to a team, select members with their strengths in mind, and allocate work assignments that fit with members' preferred styles.

DIVERSITY OF MEMBERS   In Chapter 9, we discussed the effect of diversity on groups. How does *team* diversity affect *team* performance? The degree to which members of a work unit (group, team, or department) share a common demographic attribute, such as age, sex, race, educational level, or length of service in the organization, is the subject of **organizational demography**. Organizational demography suggests that attributes such as age or the date of joining should help predict turnover. The logic goes like this: Turnover will be greater among those with dissimilar experiences because communication is more difficult and conflict is more likely. Increased conflict makes membership less attractive, so employees are more likely to quit. Similarly, the losers of a conflict are more apt to leave voluntarily or be forced out.[36] The conclusion is that diversity negatively affects team performance.

> **Organizational demography**
> The degree to which members of a work unit share a common demographic attribute; such as age, sex, race, educational level, or length of service in an organization; and the impact of this attribute on turnover.

Many of us hold the optimistic view that diversity should be a good thing—diverse teams should benefit from differing perspectives. Two meta-analytic reviews showed, however, that demographic diversity was essentially unrelated to team performance, while a third review suggested that race and gender diversity were actually negatively related to team performance.[37] Other research findings are mixed. One qualifier is that gender and ethnic diversity have more negative effects in occupations dominated by White or male employees, but in more demographically balanced occupations, diversity is less of a problem. Diversity in function, education, and expertise are positively related to team performance, but these effects are small and depend on the situation.

CULTURAL DIFFERENCES   We have discussed research on team diversity regarding a number of differences. But what about cultural differences? Evidence indicates cultural diversity interferes with team processes, at least in the short term,[38] but let's dig a little deeper: what about differences in cultural status? Though it's debatable, people with higher cultural status are usually in the majority or ruling race group of their nations. Researchers in the United Kingdom, for example, found that cultural status differences affected team performance, noting that teams with more high cultural-status members than low cultural-status members realized improved performance... for *every* member on the team.[39] This suggests not that diverse teams should be filled with individuals who have high cultural status in their countries, but that we should be aware of how people identify with their cultural status even in diverse group settings.

In general, cultural diversity seems to be an asset for tasks that call for a variety of viewpoints. But culturally heterogeneous teams have more difficulty learning to work with each other and solving problems. The good news is that these difficulties seem to dissipate with time.

SIZE OF TEAMS   Most experts agree that keeping teams small is key to improving group effectiveness.[40] Amazon CEO Jeff Bezos uses the "two-pizza" rule, saying, "If it takes more than two pizzas to feed the team, the team is too big."[41] Psychologist George Miller claimed "the magical number [is] seven, plus or minus two," for the ideal team size.[42]

Author and *Forbes* publisher Rich Karlgaard writes, "Bigger teams almost never correlate with a greater chance of success" because the potential connections between people grow exponentially as team size increases, complicating communications.[43]

Generally speaking, the most effective teams have five to nine members. Experts suggest using the smallest number of people who can do the task. Unfortunately, managers often err by making teams too large. It may require only four or five members to develop an array of views and skills, while coordination problems can increase as others are added. When teams have excess members, cohesiveness and mutual accountability decline, social loafing increases, and people communicate less. Members of large teams have trouble coordinating with one another, especially under time pressure. When a natural working unit is larger and you want a team effort, consider breaking the group into subteams.[44]

MEMBER PREFERENCES   Not every employee is a team player. Given the option, many employees will select themselves *out* of team participation. When people who prefer to work alone are required to team up, there is a direct threat to the team's morale and to individual member satisfaction.[45] This suggests that, when selecting team members, managers should consider individual preferences along with abilities, personalities, and skills. High-performing teams are likely to be composed of people who prefer working as part of a group.

Team Processes

The final category related to team effectiveness includes process variables such as member commitment to a *common plan and purpose*, *specific team goals*, *team efficacy*, *team identity*, *team cohesion*, *mental models*, *conflict levels*, and *social loafing*. These will be especially important in larger teams and in teams that are highly interdependent.[46]

Why are processes important to team effectiveness? Teams should create outputs greater than the sum of their inputs. Exhibit 10-5 illustrates how group processes can have an impact on a group's actual effectiveness.[47] Teams are often used in research laboratories because they can draw on the diverse skills of various individuals to produce more meaningful research than researchers working independently—that is, they produce positive synergy, and their process gains exceed their process losses.

COMMON PLAN AND PURPOSE   Effective teams begin by analyzing the team's mission, developing goals to achieve that mission, and creating strategies for achieving the goals. Teams that consistently perform better have a clear sense of what needs to be done and how.[48] This sounds obvious, but many teams ignore this fundamental process. Effective teams show **reflexivity**, meaning they reflect on and adjust their purpose when necessary. A team must have a good plan, but it needs to be willing and able to adapt when conditions call for it.[49] Interestingly, some evidence suggests that teams high in reflexivity are better able to adapt to conflicting plans and goals among team members.[50]

Reflexivity
A team characteristic of reflecting on and adjusting the master plan when necessary.

EXHIBIT 10-5
Effects of Group Processes

Potential group effectiveness + Process gains − Process losses = Actual group effectiveness

SPECIFIC GOALS   Successful teams translate their common purpose into specific, measurable, and realistic performance goals. Specific goals facilitate clear communication. They help teams maintain their focus on getting results. Consistent with the research on individual goals, team goals should be challenging. Difficult but achievable goals raise team performance on those criteria for which they're set. So, for instance, goals for quantity tend to increase quantity, goals for accuracy increase accuracy, and so on.[51]

TEAM EFFICACY   Effective teams have confidence in themselves; they believe they can succeed. We call this **team efficacy**.[52] Teams that have been successful raise their beliefs about future success, which, in turn, motivates them to work harder. In addition, teams that have a shared knowledge of individual capabilities can strengthen the link between team members' self-efficacy and their individual creativity because members can more effectively solicit informed opinions from their teammates.[53] What can management do to increase team efficacy? Two options are helping the team achieve small successes that build confidence, and providing training to improve members' technical and interpersonal skills. The greater the abilities of team members, the more likely the team will develop confidence and the ability to deliver on that confidence.

Team efficacy
A team's collective belief among team members that they can succeed at their tasks.

TEAM IDENTITY   In Chapter 9, we discussed the important role of social identity in people's lives. When people connect emotionally with the groups they're in, they are more likely to invest in their relationship with those groups. It's the same with teams. For example, research with soldiers in the Netherlands indicated that individuals who felt included and respected by team members became more willing to work hard for their teams, even though as soldiers they were already called upon to be dedicated to their units. Therefore, by recognizing individuals' specific skills and abilities, as well as creating a climate of respect and inclusion, leaders and members can foster positive **team identity** and realize improved team outcomes.[54]

Organizational identity is important, too. Rarely do teams operate in a vacuum—more often teams interact with other teams, requiring interteam coordination. Individuals with a positive team identity but without a positive organizational identity can become fixed to their teams and unwilling to coordinate with other teams within the organization.[55]

Team identity
A team member's affinity for and sense of belongingness to his or her team.

TEAM COHESION   Have you ever been a member of a team that really "gelled," one in which team members felt connected? The term **team cohesion** means members are emotionally attached to one another and motivated toward the team because of their attachment. Team cohesion is a useful tool to predict team outcomes. For example, a large study in China indicated that if team cohesion is high and tasks are complex, costly investments in promotions, rewards, training, and so forth yield greater profitable team creativity. Teams with low cohesion and simple tasks, on the other hand, are not likely to respond to incentives with greater creativity.[56]

Team cohesion is a strong predictor of team performance such that when cohesion is harmed, performance may be too. Negative relationships are one driver of reduced cohesion. To mitigate this effect, teams can foster high levels of interdependence and high-quality interpersonal interactions.

Team cohesion
A situation when team members are emotionally attached to one another and motivated toward the team because of their attachment.

Mental models
Team members' knowledge and beliefs about how the work gets done by the team.

MENTAL MODELS Effective teams share accurate **mental models**—organized mental representations of the key elements within a team's environment that team members share (If the team mission and goals pertain to *what* a team needs to be effective, mental models pertain to *how* a team does its work).[57] If team members have the wrong mental models, which is particularly likely in teams under acute stress, their performance suffers.[58] One review of 65 independent studies found that teams with shared mental models engaged in more frequent interactions with one another, were more motivated, had more positive attitudes toward their work, and had higher levels of objectively rated performance.[59] If team members have different ideas about how to do things, however, the team will fight over methods rather than focus on what needs to be done.[60]

An anesthetic team in a hospital is one example of an action team with shared mental models. Research in Switzerland found that anesthetic teams communicated two distinct types of messages while in an operation: vocally monitoring each other's performance (not to criticize but to keep a vocal record of events), and "talking to the room" (announcements to everyone such as, "Patient's blood pressure is dropping"). The study found that high- and low-performing teams communicated in these ways equally often; what mattered to performance was the sequencing of the communication to maintain a shared mental model. High-performing teams followed up monitoring dialogue with assistance and instructions, and talking-to-the-room dialogue with further team dialogue.[61] The message seems simple: to maintain shared mental models and to share in conversations about what is happening while the team is in operation!

CONFLICT LEVELS Conflict has a complex relationship with team performance, and it's not necessarily bad (see Chapter 14). *Relationship conflicts*—those based on interpersonal incompatibility, tension, and animosity toward others—are almost always dysfunctional. However, when teams are performing nonroutine activities, disagreements about task content—called *task conflicts*—stimulate discussion, promote critical assessment of problems and options, and can lead to better team decisions. According to one study conducted in China, moderate levels of task conflict during the initial phases of team performance were positively related to team creativity, but both very low and very high levels of task conflict were negatively related to team performance.[62] In other words, both too much and too little disagreement about how a team should initially perform a creative task can inhibit performance.

SOCIAL LOAFING As we noted earlier, individuals can engage in social loafing and coast on the group's effort when their particular contributions (or lack thereof) can't be identified. Effective teams undermine this tendency by making members individually and jointly accountable for the team's purpose, goals, and approach.[63] Therefore, members should be clear on what they are individually and jointly responsible for on the team.

TURNING INDIVIDUALS INTO TEAM PLAYERS

We've made a case for the value and growing popularity of teams. But many people are not inherently team players, and many organizations have historically nurtured individual accomplishments. Teams often fit well in countries that score high on collectivism, but what if an organization wants to introduce teams into a work population of individuals born and raised in an individualistic society? Let's consider each phase of organizational team building.

Selecting: Hiring Team Players

Some people already possess the interpersonal skills to be effective team players. Therefore, managers, when hiring team members, can make certain that candidates can fulfill their team roles as well as technical requirements.[64] Creating teams often means resisting the urge to hire the best talent no matter what. For example, the New York Knicks professional basketball team pays Carmelo Anthony well because he scores a lot of points for his team; but statistics show he takes more shots than other highly paid players in the league, which means fewer shots for his teammates.[65] Personal traits appear to make some people better candidates for working in diverse teams. Teams made of members who like to work through difficult mental puzzles also seem more effective and able to capitalize on the multiple points of view that arise from diversity in age and education.[66]

Training: Creating Team Players

Training specialists conduct exercises that allow employees to experience the satisfaction teamwork can provide. Workshops help employees improve their problem-solving, communication, negotiation, conflict-management, and coaching skills. L'Oréal, for example, found that successful sales teams required much more than a staff of high-ability salespeople. "What we didn't account for was that many members of our top team in sales had been promoted because they had excellent technical and executional skills," said L'Oréal's senior VP David Waldock. As a result of introducing purposeful team training, Waldock said, "We are no longer a team just on paper, working independently. We have a real group dynamic now, and it's a good one."[67] An effective team doesn't develop overnight—it takes time.

Rewarding: Providing Incentives to Be a Good Team Player

A traditional organization's reward system must be reworked to encourage cooperative efforts rather than competitive ones.[68] Hallmark Cards Inc. added to its basic individual-incentive system an annual bonus based on the achievement of team goals. Whole Foods directs most of its performance-based rewards toward team performance. As a result, teams select new members carefully so they will contribute to team effectiveness (and, thus, team bonuses).[69] It is usually best to set a cooperative tone as soon as possible in the life of a team. As we already noted, teams that switch from competitive to cooperative do not immediately share information, and they still tend to make rushed, poor-quality decisions.[70] The low trust typical of the competitive group will not be readily replaced by high trust with a quick change in reward systems. Promotions, pay raises, and other forms of recognition should be given to individuals who work effectively as team members by training new colleagues, sharing information, helping resolve team conflicts, and mastering needed new skills. This doesn't mean individual contributions should be ignored; rather, they should be balanced with selfless contributions to the team.

Finally, don't forget the intrinsic rewards, such as camaraderie, that employees can receive from teamwork. It's exciting to be part of a successful team. The opportunity for personal development of self and teammates can be a very satisfying and rewarding experience.

BEWARE! TEAMS AREN'T ALWAYS THE ANSWER

Teamwork takes more time and often more resources than individual work. Teams have increased communication demands, conflicts to manage, and meetings to run. So, the benefits of using teams have to exceed the costs, and that's not always possible.[71] How do you know whether the work of your group would be better done in teams? You can apply three tests.[72] First, can the work be done better by more than one person? Good indicators are the complexity of the work and the need for different perspectives. Simple tasks that don't require diverse inputs are probably better left to individuals. Second, does the work create a common purpose or set of goals for the people in the group that is more than the aggregate of individual goals? Many service departments of new vehicle dealers have introduced teams that link customer-service people, mechanics, parts specialists, and sales representatives. Such teams can better manage collective responsibility for ensuring customer needs are properly met.

The final test is to determine whether the members of the group are interdependent. Using teams makes sense when there is interdependence among tasks—the success of the whole depends on the success of each one, *and* the success of each one depends on the success of the others. Soccer, for instance, is an obvious *team* sport. Success requires a great deal of coordination among interdependent players. Conversely, except possibly for relays, swim teams are not really teams. They're groups of individuals performing individually, whose total performance is merely the aggregate summation of their individual performances.

SUMMARY

Few trends have influenced jobs as much as the massive movement to teams into the workplace. Working on teams requires employees to cooperate with others, share information, confront differences, and sublimate personal interests for the greater good of the team.

Understanding the distinctions between problem-solving, self-managed, cross-functional, and virtual teams as well as multiteam systems helps determine the appropriate applications for team-based work. Concepts such as reflexivity, team efficacy, team identity, team cohesion, and mental models bring to light important issues relating to team context, composition, and processes. For teams to function optimally, careful attention must be given to hiring, creating, and rewarding team players. Still, effective organizations recognize that teams are not always the best method for getting the work done efficiently. Careful discernment and an understanding of organizational behavior are needed.

IMPLICATIONS FOR MANAGERS

- Effective teams have adequate resources, effective leadership, a climate of trust, and a performance evaluation and reward system that reflects team contributions. These teams have individuals with technical expertise, and the right traits and skills.
- Effective teams tend to be small. They have members who fill role demands and who prefer to be part of a group.
- Effective teams have members who believe in the team's capabilities, are committed to a common plan and purpose, and have an accurate shared mental model of what it is to be accomplished.

- Select individuals who have the interpersonal skills to be effective team players; provide training to develop teamwork skills; and reward individuals for cooperative efforts.
- Do not assume that teams are always needed. When tasks will not benefit from interdependency, individuals may be the better choice.

⭐ TRY IT!

If your professor has assigned this, go to the Assignments section of **mymanagementlab.com** to complete the **Simulation: Teams**.

⭐ PERSONAL INVENTORY ASSESSMENTS

PERSONAL INVENTORY ASSESSMENTS

Team Development Behaviors

Take this assessment to learn more about behavior in teams.

10-1. From your understanding of the chapter, list the characteristics of an optimally successful team.

11

Communication

MyManagementLab®

⭐ Improve Your Grade!

When you see this icon ⭐, visit **mymanagementlab.com** for activities that are applied, personalized, and offer immediate feedback.

LEARNING OBJECTIVES

After studying this chapter, you should be able to:

1. Describe the functions and process of communication.
2. Contrast downward, upward, and lateral communication through small-group networks and the grapevine.
3. Contrast oral, written, and nonverbal communication.
4. Describe how channel richness underlies the choice of communication channel.
5. Differentiate between automatic and controlled processing of persuasive messages.
6. Identify common barriers to effective communication.
7. Discuss how to overcome potential problems of cross-cultural communication.

⭐ Chapter Warm-up

If your professor has chosen to assign this, go to the Assignments section of **mymanagementlab.com** to complete the chapter warm-up.

COMMUNICATION

Communication is powerful: no group or organization can exist without sharing meaning among its members. In this chapter, we'll analyze communication and ways we can make it more effective.

Communication must include both the *transfer* and the *understanding* of meaning. Communicating is more than merely imparting meaning; that meaning must also be understood. It is only thus that we can convey information and ideas. In perfect communication, if it existed, a thought would be transmitted so the receiver understood the same mental picture the sender intended. Though it sounds elementary, perfect communication is never achieved in practice. Increased understanding of the functions and processes of communication can lead to positive changes in organizational behavior.

Communication
The transfer and the understanding of meaning.

Functions of Communication

Communication serves five major functions within a group or organization: *management, feedback, emotional sharing, persuasion*, and *information exchange*.[1] Almost every communication interaction that takes place in a group or organization performs one or more of these functions, and none of the five is more important than any of the others.

MANAGING BEHAVIOR Communication acts to *manage* member behavior in several ways. Organizations have authority hierarchies and formal guidelines for employees that guide communication flow. When employees follow their job descriptions or comply with company policies, communication performs a management function. Informal communication controls behavior too. When work groups tease or harass a member who produces too much (and makes the rest of the members look bad), they are informally communicating, and managing, the member's behavior.

FEEDBACK Communication creates *feedback* by clarifying to employees what they must do, how well they are doing it, and how they can improve their performance. We saw this operating in goal-setting theory in Chapter 7. Formation of goals, feedback on progress, and reward for desired behavior all require communication and stimulate motivation.

EMOTIONAL SHARING The workgroup is a primary source of social interaction for many employees. Communication within the group is a fundamental mechanism by which members show satisfaction and frustration. Communication, therefore, provides for the *emotional sharing* of feelings and fulfillment of social needs. For example, after a White police officer shot an unarmed Black man in Ferguson, Missouri, in 2015, software engineer Carl Jones wanted to process his feelings through talking with his coworkers at his corporation. As a second example, Starbucks had baristas write "Race Together" on coffee cups to start conversations about race relations. In both cases, the initial communications were awkward, so awkward that Starbucks pulled the campaign, but Jones and others have forged solid relationships from their emotional sharing.[2]

PERSUASION Like emotional sharing, *persuasion* can be good or bad depending on if, say, a leader is trying to persuade a workgroup to commit to the organization's corporate social responsibility (CSR) initiatives or to, conversely, persuade the workgroup to break the law to meet an organizational goal. These may be extreme examples, but it's important to remember that persuasion can benefit or harm an organization.

INFORMATION EXCHANGE The final function of communication is *information exchange* to facilitate decision making. Communication provides the information individuals and groups need to make decisions by transmitting the data needed to identify and evaluate choices.

The Communication Process

Before communication can take place it needs a purpose, a message to be conveyed between a sender and a receiver. The sender encodes the message (converts it to a symbolic form) and passes it through a medium (channel) to the receiver, who decodes it. The result is a transfer of meaning from one person to another.[3]

Communication process
The steps between a source and a receiver that result in the transfer and understanding of meaning.

Exhibit 11-1 depicts this **communication process**. The key parts of this model are (1) the sender, (2) encoding, (3) the message, (4) the channel, (5) decoding, (6) the receiver, (7) noise, and (8) feedback.

The *sender* initiates a message by encoding a thought. The *message* is the actual physical product of the sender's *encoding*. When we speak, the speech is the message. When we write, the writing is the message. When we gesture, the movements of our arms and the expressions on our faces are the message. The *channel* is the medium through which the message travels. The sender selects it, determining whether to use a formal or informal channel. **Formal channels** are established by the organization and transmit messages that are related to the professional activities of members. They traditionally follow the authority chain within the organization. Other forms of messages, such as those that are personal or social, follow **informal channels**, which are spontaneous and subject to individual choice.[4] The *receiver* is the person(s) to whom the message is directed, who must first translate the symbols into understandable form. This step is the *decoding* of the message. *Noise* represents communication barriers that distort the clarity of the message, such as perceptual problems, information overload, semantic difficulties, or cultural differences. The final link in the communication process is a feedback loop. *Feedback* is the check on how successful we have been in transferring our messages as originally intended. It determines whether understanding has been achieved.

Formal channels
Communication channels established by an organization to transmit messages related to the professional activities of members.

Informal channels
Communication channels that are created spontaneously and that emerge as responses to individual choices.

DIRECTION OF COMMUNICATION

Communication can flow vertically or laterally, through formal small-group networks or the informal grapevine. We subdivide the vertical dimension into downward and upward directions.[5]

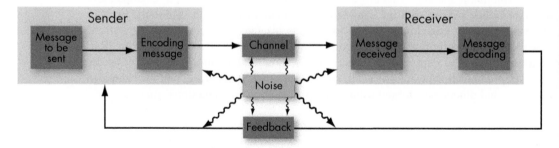

EXHIBIT 11-1
The Communication Process

Downward Communication

Communication that flows from one level of a group or organization to a lower level is *downward communication*. Group leaders and managers use it to assign goals, provide job instructions, explain policies and procedures, point out problems that need attention, and offer feedback.

In downward communication, the delivery mode and the context of the information are of high importance. We will talk more about communication methods later, but consider the ultimate downward communication: the performance review. Alan Buckelew, CEO of Carnival Cruise Lines says, "A review is probably the one time when you want to be physically present." The Samsonite CEO agrees: "A conference call cannot substitute for face-to-face interactions." Automated performance reviews have allowed managers to review their subordinates without discussions, which is efficient but misses critical opportunities for growth, motivation, and relationship-building.[6] In general, employees subjected to less direct, personalized communication are less likely to understand the intentions of the message correctly. The best communicators explain the reasons behind their downward communications but also solicit communication from the employees they supervise.

Upward Communication

Upward communication flows to a higher level in the group or organization. It's used to provide feedback to higher-ups, inform them of progress toward goals, and relay current problems. Upward communication keeps managers aware of how employees feel about their jobs, coworkers, and the organization in general. Managers also rely on upward communication for ideas on how conditions can be improved.

Given that most managers' job responsibilities have expanded, upward communication is increasingly difficult because managers can be overwhelmed and easily distracted. To engage in effective upward communication, try to communicate in short summaries rather than long explanations, support your summaries with actionable items, and prepare an agenda to make sure you use your boss's attention well.[7] And watch what you say, especially if you are communicating something to your manager that will be unwelcome. If you're turning down an assignment, for example, be sure to project a "can do" attitude while asking advice about your workload dilemma or inexperience with the assignment.[8] Your delivery can be as important as the content of your communication.

Lateral Communication

When communication occurs between members of the same workgroup, members at the same level in separate workgroups, or any other horizontally equivalent workers, we describe it as *lateral communication.*

Lateral communication saves time and facilitates coordination. Some lateral relationships are formally sanctioned. More often, they are informally created to short-circuit the vertical hierarchy and expedite action. So from management's viewpoint, lateral communications can be good or bad. Because strictly adhering to the formal vertical structure for all communications can be inefficient, lateral communication occurring with management's knowledge and support can be beneficial. But dysfunctional conflict can result when formal vertical channels are breached, when members go above or around their superiors, or when bosses find actions have been taken or decisions made without their knowledge.

EXHIBIT 11-2
Three Common Small Group Networks

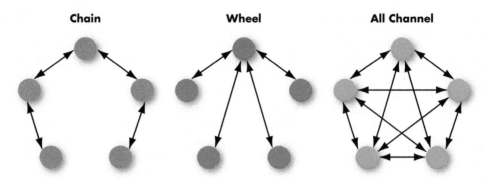

Formal Small-Group Networks

Formal organizational networks can be complicated, including hundreds of people and a half-dozen or more hierarchical levels. We've condensed these networks into three common small groups of five people each (see Exhibit 11-2): chain, wheel, and all channel.

The *chain* rigidly follows the formal chain of command; this network approximates the communication channels you might find in a rigid three-level organization. The *wheel* relies on a central figure to act as the conduit for all group communication; it simulates the communication network you might find on a team with a strong leader. The *all-channel* network permits group members to actively communicate with each other; it's most often characterized by self-managed teams, in which group members are free to contribute and no one person takes on a leadership role. Many organizations today like to consider themselves all channel, meaning that anyone can communicate with anyone (but sometimes they shouldn't).

As Exhibit 11-3 demonstrates, the effectiveness of each network is determined by the dependent variable that concerns you. The structure of the wheel facilitates the emergence of a leader, the all-channel network is best if you desire high member satisfaction, and the chain is best if accuracy is most important. Exhibit 11-3 leads us to the conclusion that no single network will be best for all occasions.

The Grapevine

Grapevine
An organization's informal communication network.

The informal communication network in a group or organization is called the **grapevine**.[9] Although rumors and gossip transmitted through the grapevine may be informal, it's still an important source of information for employees and candidates. Grapevine or word-of-mouth information from peers about a company has important effects on whether job applicants join an organization,[10] even over and above informal ratings on websites like Glassdoor.

EXHIBIT 11-3
Small Group Networks and Effectiveness Criteria

Criteria	Chain	Wheel	All Channel
		Networks	
Speed	Moderate	Fast	Fast
Accuracy	High	High	Moderate
Emergence of a leader	Moderate	High	None
Member satisfaction	Moderate	Low	High

The grapevine is an important part of any group or organization communication network. It serves employees' needs: small talk creates a sense of closeness and friendship among those who share information, although research suggests it often does so at the expense of those in the outgroup.[11] It also gives managers a feel for the morale of their organization, the issues employees consider important, and employee anxieties. Evidence indicates that managers can study the gossip driven largely by employee social networks to learn more about how positive and negative information is flowing through the organization.[12] Furthermore, managers can identify influencers (highly networked people trusted by their coworkers[13]) by noting which individuals are small talkers (those who regularly communicate about insignificant, unrelated issues). Small talkers tend to be influencers. One study found that social talkers are so influential that they were significantly more likely to retain their jobs during layoffs.[14] Thus, while the grapevine may not be sanctioned or controlled by the organization, it can be understood and leveraged a bit.

MODES OF COMMUNICATION

How do group members transfer meaning among each other? They rely on oral, written, and nonverbal communication. This much is obvious, but as we will discuss, the choice between modes can greatly enhance or detract from the way the perceiver reacts to the message. Certain modes are highly preferred for specific types of communication. We will cover the latest thinking and practical application.

Oral Communication

A primary means of conveying messages is oral communication. Speeches, formal one-on-one and group discussions, and the informal rumor mill or grapevine are popular forms of oral communication.

The advantages of oral communication are *speed*, *feedback*, and *exchange*. Regarding *speed*, we can convey a verbal message and receive a response in minimal time. As one professional put it, "Face-to-face communication on a consistent basis is still the best way to get information to and from employees."[15] If the receiver is unsure of the message, rapid *feedback* allows the sender to quickly detect and correct it. Unfortunately, we should acknowledge that we are usually bad listeners. Researchers indicate that we are prone to "listener burnout" in which we tune the other person out and rush to offer advice. "Good listeners overcome their natural inclination to fix the other's problems and to keep the conversation brief," said Professor Graham Bodie.[16] Active listening; in which we remove distractions, lean in, make eye contact, paraphrase, and encourage the talker to continue[17]—helps us learn more and build trust if we are genuine and not judgmental.[18] The *exchange* given through oral communication has social, cultural, and emotional components. Cultural social exchange, in which we purposefully share exchanges that transcend cultural boundaries, can build trust, cooperation, and agreement between individuals and teams.[19]

One major disadvantage of oral communication surfaces whenever a message has to pass through a number of people: the more people, the greater the potential distortion. If you've ever played "Telephone," you know the problem. Each person who receives a whispered message in this pass-along game interprets the message in his or her own way. The message's content, when it reaches its destination, is often very different from the original, even when we think the message is simple and straightforward. Therefore, oral-communication "chains" are generally more of a liability than an effective tool in organizations.

Written Communication

Written communication includes letters, e-mail, instant messaging, organizational periodicals, and any other method that conveys written words or symbols. The advantages depend on what written mode is used. Written business communication today is usually conducted via letters, PowerPoint®, e-mail, instant messaging, text messaging, social media, apps, and blogs. Some of these create a digital or physical long-term record, while the advantage of others is quick, fleeting information exchange. The disadvantages are also specific to each written mode. We will therefore discuss the applications more in a bit.

Nonverbal Communication

Every time we deliver a verbal message, we also impart an unspoken message.[20] Sometimes the nonverbal component may stand alone as a powerful message of our business communication. No discussion of communication would thus be complete without consideration of *nonverbal communication*; which includes body movements, the intonations or emphasis we give to words, facial expressions, and the physical distance between the sender and receiver.

We could argue that every *body movement* has meaning, and no movement is accidental (though some are unconscious). We act out our state of being with nonverbal body language. For example, we smile to project trustworthiness, uncross our arms to appear approachable, and stand to signal authority.[21]

If you read the minutes of a meeting, you wouldn't grasp the impact of what was said the same way as if you had been there or could see the meeting on video. Why not? There is no record of nonverbal communication, and the emphasis given to words or phrases (*intonation*) is missing. Both make the meaning clear. Intonations can change the meaning of a message. *Facial expressions* also convey meaning. Facial expressions, along with intonations, can show arrogance, aggressiveness, fear, shyness, and other characteristics.

Physical distance also has meaning. What is considered proper spacing between people largely depends on cultural norms. A businesslike distance in some European countries feels intimate in many parts of North America. If someone stands closer to you than is considered appropriate, it may indicate aggressiveness or sexual interest; if farther away, it may signal disinterest or displeasure with what is being said.

CHOICE OF COMMUNICATION CHANNEL

Why do people choose one channel of communication over another? A model of media richness helps explain channel selection among managers.[22]

Channel Richness

Channel richness
The amount of information that can be transmitted during a communication episode.

Channels differ in their capacity to convey information. Some are *rich* in that they can (1) handle multiple cues simultaneously, (2) facilitate rapid feedback, and (3) be very personal. Others are *lean*, in that they score low on these factors. Face-to-face conversation scores highest in **channel richness** because it transmits the most information per communication episode–multiple information cues (words, postures, facial expressions, gestures, intonations), immediate feedback (both verbal and nonverbal), and the personal touch of being present. Other examples of media with high channel richness (in descending order) include video conferences, telephone conversations, live speeches, and voice mail. Impersonal written media such as formal reports and bulletins score lowest in richness as well as memos, letters, prerecorded speeches, and e-mail.[23]

In sum, rich channels give us the chance to observe. The unconscious aspects of communication help us understand the full meaning of a message. When these aspects are missing, we must look for other clues to deduce the sender's emotions and attitudes.

Choosing Communication Methods

The choice of channel depends on whether the message is routine. Routine messages tend to be straightforward and have minimal ambiguity; channels low in richness can carry them efficiently. Nonroutine communications are likely to be complicated and have the potential for misunderstanding. Managers can communicate them effectively only by selecting rich channels.

CHOOSING ORAL COMMUNICATION   Whenever you need to gauge the receiver's receptivity, *oral communication* is usually the better choice. The marketing plan for a new product, for instance, may need to be worked out with clients in person, so you can see their reactions to each idea you propose. Also consider the receiver's preferred mode of communication; some individuals focus on content better in written form and others prefer discussion. For example, if your manager requests a meeting with you, you may not want to ask for an e-mail exchange instead. The pace of your work environment matters too. A fast-paced workplace may thrive on pop-by meetings, while a deadline-heavy team project may progress faster with scheduled Skype videoconferences.

Much of what we communicate face-to-face is in the delivery, so also consider your speaking skills when choosing your communication method. Research indicates the sound of your voice is twice as important as what you are saying. A good speaking voice, clear and moderated, can be a help to your career; while loud, questioning, irritating, immature, falsetto, breathy, or monotone voice tones can hinder you. If your voice is problematic, your work teams can help you raise your awareness so you can make changes, or you may benefit from the help of a voice coach.[24]

CHOOSING WRITTEN COMMUNICATION   *Written communication* is generally the most reliable mode for complex and lengthy communications, and it can be the most efficient method for short messages when, for instance, a two-sentence text can take the place of a 10-minute phone call. But keep in mind that written communication can be limited in its emotional expression.

Choose written communication when you want the information to be tangible, verifiable, and "on the record." *Letters* are used in business primarily for networking and record-keeping purposes, and when signatures need to be authentic. Also, a handwritten thank-you note is never a wrong choice for an applicant to send after an employment interview, and handwritten envelopes are often put right on the receiver's desk unopened by administrative staff. In general, you should respond to *instant messages* only when they are professional and initiate them only when you know they will be welcome; remember that your conversation will not be stored for later reference. *Texts* are cheap to send and receive, and the willingness to be available for quick communications from clients and managers is conducive to good business. However, some users—and managers—view text messaging as intrusive and distracting, so establish some protocols first. Some of the most spectacular gains in *social media* are in the sales arena, both business-to-public and business-to-business. For instance, one sales representative for virtual meetings company PGi landed his fastest sale ever by instantly connecting with a potential client after TweetDeck alerted him that a CEO was tweeting his frustration about Web conferencing.[25] Finally, curtail usage of blogs, posting, and commenting; both options are more public than you may think, and your words are easily found by your name via search engines like Google.

CHOOSING NONVERBAL COMMUNICATION   It's important to be alert to *nonverbal* aspects of communication; look for these cues as well as the literal meaning of a sender's words. You should particularly be aware of contradictions between the messages. For example, someone who frequently glances at her wristwatch is giving the message that she would prefer to terminate the conversation no matter what she actually says. We misinform others when we express one message verbally, such as trust, but nonverbally communicate a contradictory message that reads, "I don't have confidence in you."

Information Security

Security is a huge concern for nearly all organizations with private or proprietary information about clients, customers, and employees. Organizations worry about the security of the electronic information they need to protect such as hospital patient data, physical information they still keep in file cabinets, and information they entrust their employees with knowing. Most companies actively monitor employee Internet use and e-mail records, and some even use video surveillance and record phone conversations. Necessary though they may be, such practices can seem invasive to employees. An organization can relieve employee concerns by engaging them in the creation of information-security policies and giving them some control over how their personal information is used.[26]

PERSUASIVE COMMUNICATION

We've discussed a number of methods for communication up to this point. Now we turn our attention to one of the functions of communication—persuasion—and the features that might make messages more or less persuasive to an audience.

Automatic and Controlled Processing

To understand the process of persuasion, it is useful to consider two different ways we process information.[27] Think about the last time you bought a can of soda. Did you carefully research brands, or did you reach for the can that had the most appealing advertising? If we're honest, we'll admit glitzy ads and catchy slogans have an influence on our choices as consumers. We often rely on **automatic processing**, a relatively superficial consideration of evidence and information, making use of heuristics like those we discussed in Chapter 6. Automatic processing takes little time and low effort, so it makes sense to use it for processing persuasive messages related to topics you don't care much

Automatic processing
A relatively superficial consideration of evidence and information making use of heuristics.

about. The disadvantage is that it lets us be easily fooled by a variety of tricks, like a cute jingle or glamorous photo.

Now consider the last time you chose a place to live. You probably sourced experts who knew something about the area, gathered information about prices, and considered the costs and benefits of renting versus buying. You were engaging in more effortful **controlled processing**, a detailed consideration of evidence and information, relying on facts, figures, and logic. Controlled processing requires effort and energy, and it's harder to fool someone who has taken the time and effort to engage in it. So what makes someone engage in either shallow or deep processing? Let's explore how we might determine what types of processing an audience will use.

> **Controlled processing** A detailed consideration of evidence and information relying on facts, figures, and logic.

INTEREST LEVEL   One of the best predictors of whether people will use an automatic or controlled process for reacting to a persuasive message is their level of interest in it.[28] Interest levels reflect the impact a decision is going to have on your life. When people are very interested in the outcome of a decision, they're more likely to process information carefully. That's probably why people look for so much more information when deciding about something important (like where to live) than something relatively unimportant (like which soda to drink).

PRIOR KNOWLEDGE   People who are well informed about a subject area are more likely to use controlled processing strategies. They have already thought through various arguments for or against a specific course of action, and therefore won't readily change their position unless very good, thoughtful reasons are provided. On the other hand, people who are poorly informed about a topic can change their minds more readily, even in the face of fairly superficial arguments presented without a great deal of evidence. A better-informed audience is likely to be much harder to persuade.

PERSONALITY   Do you always read at least five reviews of a movie before deciding whether to see it? Perhaps you even research films by the same stars and director. If so, you are probably high in **need for cognition**, a personality trait of individuals who are most likely to be persuaded by evidence and facts.[29] Those who are lower in their need for cognition are more likely to use automatic processing strategies, relying on intuition and emotion to guide their evaluation of persuasive messages.

> **Need for cognition** A personality trait of individuals depicting the ongoing desire to think and learn.

MESSAGE CHARACTERISTICS   Another factor that influences whether people use an automatic or controlled processing strategy is the characteristics of the message itself. Messages provided through relatively lean communication channels, with little opportunity for users to interact with the content of the message, encourage automatic processing. Conversely, messages provided through richer communication channels encourage more deliberative processing.

Tailoring the Message

The most important implication is to match your persuasive message to the type of processing your audience is likely to use. When the audience is not interested in a persuasive message topic, when they are poorly informed, when they are low in need for cognition, and when information is transmitted through relatively lean channels, they'll be more likely to use automatic processing. In these cases, use messages that are more emotionally laden and associate positive images with your preferred outcome. On the other hand, when the audience is interested in a topic, when they are high in need for cognition, or when the information is transmitted through rich channels, then it is a better idea to focus on rational arguments and evidence to make your case.

BARRIERS TO EFFECTIVE COMMUNICATION

A number of barriers can slow or distort effective communication, barriers that we need to recognize and reduce. In this section, we highlight the most important.

Filtering

Filtering
A sender's manipulation of information so that it will be seen more favorably by the receiver.

Filtering refers to a sender's purposely manipulating information so the receiver will see it more favorably. A manager who tells his boss what he feels the boss wants to hear is filtering information.

The more vertical levels in the organization's hierarchy, the more opportunities there are for filtering. But some filtering will occur wherever there are status differences. Factors such as fear of conveying bad news and the desire to please the boss often lead employees to tell their superiors what they think they want to hear, thus distorting upward communications.

Selective Perception

Selective perception is important because the receivers in the communication process selectively see and hear based on their needs, motivations, experience, background, and other personal characteristics. Receivers also project their interests and expectations into communications as they decode them. For example, an employment interviewer who expects a female job applicant to put her family ahead of her career is likely to see that characteristic in all female applicants, regardless of whether any of the women actually feel that way. As we said in Chapter 6, we don't see reality; we interpret what we see and call it reality.

Information Overload

Information overload
A condition in which information inflow exceeds an individual's processing capacity.

Individuals have a finite capacity for processing data. When the information we have to work with exceeds our processing capacity, the result is **information overload**. We've seen in this text that dealing with it has become a huge challenge for individuals and for organizations. It's a challenge you can manage, to some degree, by following the steps outlined earlier in this chapter.

What happens when individuals have more information than they can sort and use? They tend to select, ignore, pass over, or forget it. Or they may put off further processing until the overload situation ends. In any case, lost information and less effective communication results, making it all the more important to deal well with overload.

More generally, as an Intel study shows, it may make sense to connect less frequently to technology, to, in the words of one article, "avoid letting the drumbeat of digital missives constantly shake up and reorder to-do lists."[30] One radical way is to limit the number of devices you access. For example, Coors Brewing executive Frits van Paasschen jettisoned his desktop computer in favor of mobile devices only, and Eli Lilly & Co. moved its sales teams from laptops plus other devices to just iPads. Both these moves have resulted in increased productivity.[31]

Emotions

You may interpret the same message differently when you're angry or distraught than when you're happy. For example, individuals in positive moods are more confident about their opinions after reading a persuasive message, so well-designed arguments have a stronger impact on their opinions.[32] People in negative moods are more likely to scrutinize messages in greater detail, whereas those in positive moods tend to accept communications at face value.[33] Extreme emotions such as jubilation or depression are most likely to hinder effective communication. In such instances, we are most prone to disregard our rational and objective thinking processes and substitute emotional judgments.

Language

Even when we're communicating in the same language, words mean different things to different people. Age and context are two of the biggest factors that influence such differences. For example, when business consultant Michael Schiller asked his 15-year-old daughter where she was going with friends, he said, "You need to recognize your ARAs and measure against them." Schiller said that in response, his daughter "looked at him like he was from outer space."[34] (ARA stands for accountability, responsibility, and authority.) Those new to corporate lingo may find acronyms such as ARA, words such as *deliverables* (verifiable outcomes of a project), and phrases such as *get the low-hanging fruit* (deal with the easiest parts first) bewildering, in the same way parents may be mystified by teen slang.[35]

Silence

It's easy to ignore silence or lack of communication because it is defined by the absence of information. This is often a mistake—silence itself can be the message to communicate non-interest or inability to deal with a topic. Silence can also be a simple outcome of information overload, or a delaying period for considering a response. For whatever reasons, research suggests using silence and withholding communication are common and problematic.[36] One survey found that more than 85 percent of managers reported remaining silent about at least one issue of significant concern.[37] The impact of silence can be organizationally detrimental. Employee silence can mean managers lack information about ongoing operational problems; management silence can leave employees bewildered. Silence regarding discrimination, harassment, corruption, and misconduct means top management cannot take action to eliminate problematic behavior.

Communication Apprehension

An estimated 5 to 20 percent of the population suffers debilitating **communication apprehension**, or social anxiety.[38] These people experience undue tension and anxiety in oral communication, written communication, or both.[39] They may find it extremely difficult to talk with others face to face or become extremely anxious when they have to use the phone, relying on memos or e-mails when a phone call would be faster and more appropriate.

    Oral-communication apprehensives avoid situations, such as teaching, for which oral communication is a dominant requirement.[40] But almost all jobs require *some* oral

Communication apprehension
Undue tension and anxiety about oral communication, written communication, or both.

communication. Of greater concern is evidence that high oral-communication apprehensives distort the communication demands of their jobs in order to minimize the need for communication. Be aware that some people severely limit their oral communication and rationalize their actions by telling themselves communicating isn't necessary for them to do their job effectively.

Lying

The final barrier to effective communication is outright misrepresentation of information, or lying. People differ in their definition of a lie. For example, is deliberately withholding information about a mistake a lie, or do you have to actively deny your role in the mistake to pass the threshold? While the definition of a lie befuddles ethicists and social scientists, there is no denying the prevalence of lying. People may tell one to two lies per day, with some individuals telling considerably more.[41] Compounded across a large organization, this is an enormous amount of deception happening every day. Evidence shows people are more comfortable lying over the phone than face-to-face, and more comfortable lying in e-mails than when they have to write with pen and paper.[42]

CULTURAL FACTORS

Effective communication is difficult under the best of conditions. Cross-cultural factors clearly create the potential for increased communication problems. A gesture that is well understood and acceptable in one culture can be meaningless or lewd in another. Unfortunately, only 18 percent of companies have documented strategies for communicating with employees across cultures, and only 31 percent require that corporate messages be customized for consumption in other cultures.

Cultural Barriers

There are a number of problems related to language difficulties in cross-cultural communications. First are *barriers caused by semantics*. Words mean different things to different people, particularly people from different national cultures. Some words don't translate between cultures. For instance, the Finnish word *sisu* means something akin to "guts" or "dogged persistence" but is essentially untranslatable into English. Similarly, capitalists in Russia may have difficulty communicating with their British or Canadian counterparts because English terms such as *efficiency*, *free market*, and *regulation* have no direct Russian equivalents.

Second are *barriers caused by word connotations*. Words imply different things in different languages. Negotiations between U.S. and Japanese executives can be difficult because the Japanese word *hai* translates as "yes," but its connotation is "Yes, I'm listening" rather than "Yes, I agree."

Third are *barriers caused by tone differences*. In some cultures, language is formal; in others, it's informal. In some cultures, the tone changes depending on the context: People speak differently at home, in social situations, and at work. Using a personal, informal style when a more formal style is expected can be inappropriate.

Fourth are *differences in tolerance for conflict and methods for resolving conflicts*. People from individualist cultures tend to be more comfortable with direct conflict and will make the source of their disagreements overt. Collectivists are more likely to

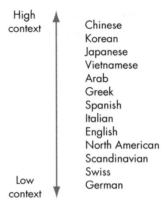

High
context

Chinese
Korean
Japanese
Vietnamese
Arab
Greek
Spanish
Italian
English
North American
Scandinavian
Swiss
German

Low
context

EXHIBIT 11-4
Continuum of
Countries with
High and Low
Context Cultures

acknowledge conflict only implicitly and avoid emotionally charged disputes. They may attribute conflicts to the situation more than to the individuals and therefore may not require explicit apologies to repair relationships, whereas individualists prefer explicit statements, accepting responsibility for conflicts and public apologies to restore relationships.

Cultural Context

Cultures tend to differ in the degree to which context influences the meaning individuals take from communication.[43] In **high-context cultures** such as China, Korea, Japan, and Vietnam, people rely heavily on nonverbal and subtle situational cues in communicating with others, and a person's official status, place in society, and reputation carry considerable weight. What is *not* said may be more significant than what *is* said. In contrast, people from Europe and North America reflect their **low-context cultures**. They rely essentially on spoken and written words to convey meaning; body language and formal titles are secondary (see Exhibit 11-4).

High-context cultures
Cultures that rely heavily on nonverbal and subtle situational cues in communication.

Low-context cultures
Cultures that rely heavily on words to convey meaning in communication.

Contextual differences mean quite a lot in terms of communication. Communication in high-context cultures implies considerably more trust by both parties. What may appear to be casual and insignificant conversation, in fact reflects the desire to build a relationship and create trust. Oral agreements imply strong commitments in high-context cultures. And who you are—your age, seniority, rank in the organization—is highly valued and heavily influences your credibility. Managers can therefore "make suggestions" rather than give orders. But in low-context cultures, enforceable contracts tend to be in writing, precisely worded, and highly legalistic. Similarly, low-context cultures value directness. Managers are expected to be explicit and precise in conveying intended meaning.

A Cultural Guide

There is much to be gained from business intercultural communications. It is safe to assume every one of us has a different viewpoint that is culturally shaped. Because we do have differences, we have an opportunity to reach the most creative solutions possible with the help of others if we communicate effectively.

According to Fred Casmir, a leading expert in intercultural communication research, we often do not communicate well with people outside of our culture because we tend to generalize from only their cultural origin. This can be insensitive and potentially disastrous, especially when we make assumptions based on observable characteristics. Many of us have a richly varied ethnic background and would be offended if someone addressed us according to what culture our physical features might favor, for instance. Also, attempts to be culturally sensitive to another person are often based on stereotypes propagated by media. These stereotypes usually do not have a correct or current relevance.

Casmir noted that because there are far too many cultures for anyone to understand completely, and individuals interpret their own cultures differently, intercultural communication should be based on sensitivity and pursuit of common goals. He found the ideal condition is an ad hoc "third culture" where a group can form when they seek to incorporate aspects of each member's cultural communication preferences. The norms this subculture establishes through appreciating individual differences create a common ground for effective communication. Intercultural groups that communicate effectively can be highly productive and innovative.

When communicating with people from a different culture, what can you do to reduce misinterpretations? Casmir and other experts offer the following suggestions:

1. *Know yourself.* Recognizing your own cultural identity and biases is critical to understanding the unique viewpoints of other people.
2. *Foster a climate of mutual respect, fairness, and democracy.* Clearly establish an environment of equality and mutual concern. This will be your "third culture" context for effective intercultural communication that transcends each person's cultural norms.
3. *State facts, not your interpretation.* Interpreting or evaluating what someone has said or done draws more on your own culture and background than on the observed situation. If you state only facts, you will have the opportunity to benefit from the other person's interpretation. Delay judgment until you've had sufficient time to observe and interpret the situation from the differing perspectives of all concerned.
4. *Consider the other person's viewpoint.* Before sending a message, put yourself in the recipient's shoes. What are his or her values, experiences, and frames of reference? What do you know about his or her education, upbringing, and background that can give you added insight? Try to see the people in the group as they really are first, and take a collaborative problem-solving approach whenever potential conflicts arise.
5. *Proactively maintain the identity of the group.* Like any culture, the establishment of a common-ground "third culture" for effective intercultural communication takes time and nurturing. Remind members of the group of your common goals, mutual respect, and need to adapt to individual communication preferences.[44]

⭐ WATCH IT

If your professor has assigned this, go to the Assignments section of **mymanagementlab .com** to complete the video exercise titled **Communication (TWZ Role Play)**.

SUMMARY

You've probably discovered the link between communication and employee satisfaction in this chapter: the less uncertainty, the greater the satisfaction. Distortions, ambiguities, and incongruities between verbal and nonverbal messages all increase uncertainty and reduce satisfaction. Careful attention to the methods and modes for each communication better ensures that the message is properly interpreted by the receiver.

IMPLICATIONS FOR MANAGERS

- Remember that your communication mode will partly determine your communication effectiveness.
- Obtain feedback to make certain your messages—however, they are communicated—are understood.
- Remember that written communication creates more misunderstandings than oral communication does; communicate with employees through in-person meetings when possible.
- Make sure you use communication strategies appropriate to your audience and the type of message you're sending.
- Keep in mind communication barriers such as gender and culture.

✪ TRY IT!

If your professor has assigned this, go to the Assignments section of **mymanagementlab.com** to complete the **Simulation: Communication**.

✪ PERSONAL INVENTORY ASSESSMENTS

Communication Styles

What is your preferred communication style? Take this PIA to learn more about various communication styles.

11-1. What is your favorite method of communication, and how might you incorporate your preference into your business communications now that you've read the chapter?

12

Leadership

MyManagementLab®

⭐ Improve Your Grade!

When you see this icon ⭐, visit **mymanagementlab.com** for activities that are applied, personalized, and offer immediate feedback.

LEARNING OBJECTIVES

After studying this chapter, you should be able to:

1. Summarize the conclusions of trait theories of leadership.
2. Identify the central tenets and main limitations of behavioral theories.
3. Contrast contingency theories of leadership.
4. Describe the contemporary theories of leadership and their relationship to foundational theories.
5. Discuss the roles of leaders in creating ethical organizations.
6. Describe how leaders can have a positive impact on their organizations through building trust and mentoring.
7. Identify the challenges to our understanding of leadership.

⭐ Chapter Warm-up

If your professor has chosen to assign this, go to the Assignments section of **mymanagementlab.com** to complete the chapter warm-up.

⭐ WATCH IT

If your professor has assigned this, go to the Assignments section of **mymanagementlab.com** to complete the video exercise titled **Leadership (TWZ Role Play)**.

TRAIT THEORIES OF LEADERSHIP

We define **leadership** as the ability to influence a group toward the achievement of a vision or set of goals. Surely you've noticed, though, that not all leaders are managers, nor are all managers leaders. Nonsanctioned leadership—the ability to influence that arises outside the formal structure of the organization—is sometimes more important than formal influence. What makes a person a leader? Since strong leaders have been described by their traits throughout history, leadership research has sought to identify the personality, social, physical, or intellectual attributes that differentiate leaders from nonleaders. As we will see in the chapter, there are a number of different approaches toward analyzing leadership. Keep in mind that none of the concepts is mutually exclusive—in fact, research is not clear yet about which variables in combination yield the best leadership. But we're getting there.

To begin, the **trait theories of leadership** focus on personal qualities, including personality traits like those in the Big Five (see Chapter 5), and characteristics that predict two distinct outcomes: leadership emergence and leadership effectiveness. Based on the latest research literature, we offer two conclusions about personality traits and leadership: one, traits can predict leadership; and two, traits do a better job in predicting the emergence of leaders and the appearance of leadership than in distinguishing between effective and ineffective leaders.[1] The fact that an individual exhibits the right traits and others consider that person a leader does not necessarily mean he or she will be effective, successful at getting the group to achieve its goals. That said, there are some strong links between traits and leadership we should consider.

> **Leadership**
> The ability to influence a group toward the achievement of a vision or set of goals.

> **Trait theories of leadership**
> Theories that consider personal qualities and characteristics that differentiate leaders from nonleaders.

Personality Traits and Leadership

What constitutes a great leader? In general, individuals who like being around people and who are able to assert themselves (extraverted), disciplined and able to keep commitments they make (conscientious), and creative and flexible (open) have an apparent advantage when it comes to leadership. Let's break that down a bit.

BIG FIVE TRAITS In examining personality traits, researchers have consistently found extraversion to be the most predictive trait of effective leadership.[2] However, extraversion sometimes relates more to the way leaders emerge than to their effectiveness. Sociable and dominant people are more likely to assert themselves in group situations, which can help extraverts be identified as leaders, but effective leaders are not domineering. One study found leaders who scored very high in assertiveness, a facet of extraversion, were less effective than those who were moderately high.[3] So although extraversion can predict effective leadership, the relationship may be due to unique facets of the trait.

Unlike agreeableness and emotional stability, which do not seem to predict leadership, conscientiousness and openness to experience may predict leadership, especially leader effectiveness. For example, one study indicated that top management teams that were high in conscientiousness positively influenced organizational performance through their leadership.[4] Conscientiousness and extraversion are positively related to leaders' self-efficacy (see Chapter 7),[5] and since people are more likely to follow someone who is confident he or she is going in the right direction, these leaders tend to emerge.

DARK-SIDE TRAITS   What about the Dark-Side personality traits of machiavellianism, narcissism, and psychopathy (see Chapter 5)? Research indicates they're not all bad for leadership. A study in Europe and the United States found that normative (mid-range) scores on the Dark-Side personality traits were optimal, and low (and high) scores were associated with ineffective leadership. Furthermore, the study suggested that high emotional stability may actually accentuate ineffective behaviors.[6] However, higher scores on Dark-Side traits and emotional stability can contribute to leadership emergence. Thankfully, both this study and other international research indicate that building self-awareness and self-regulation skills may be helpful for leaders to control the effects of their Dark-Side traits.[7]

Emotional Intelligence (EI) and Leadership

Another trait that may indicate effective leadership is emotional intelligence (EI). As discussed in Chapter 4, a core component of EI is empathy. Empathetic leaders can sense others' needs, listen to what followers say (and don't say), and read the reactions of others. A leader who effectively displays and manages emotions will find it easier to influence the feelings of followers by expressing genuine sympathy and enthusiasm for good performance, and by showing irritation when employees fail to perform.[8] The link between EI and leadership effectiveness may be worth investigating in greater detail.[9] Research has also demonstrated that people high in EI are more likely to emerge as leaders, even after taking cognitive ability and personality into account.[10]

BEHAVIORAL THEORIES

Trait theories help us *predict* leadership, but they don't fully help us *explain* leadership. What do successful leaders do that makes them effective? Are different types of leader behaviors equally effective? Behavioral theories, discussed next, help us define the parameters of leadership. Another way to look at this is by examining the utility of these theories. Trait research provides a basis for *selecting* the right people for leadership. **Behavioral theories of leadership**, in contrast, imply we can *train* people to be leaders.

> **Behavioral theories of leadership**
> Theories proposing that specific behaviors differentiate leaders from nonleaders.

The most comprehensive behavioral theories of leadership resulted from the Ohio State Studies,[11] which sought to identify independent dimensions of leader behavior. Beginning with more than a thousand dimensions, the studies narrowed the list to two that substantially accounted for most of the leadership behavior described by employees: *initiating structure* and *consideration*.

Initiating Structure

> **Initiating structure**
> The extent to which a leader is likely to define and structure his or her role and those of subordinates in the search for goal attainment.

Initiating structure is the extent to which a leader is likely to define and structure his or her role and those of employees in the search for goal attainment. It includes behavior that attempts to organize work, work relationships, and goals. A leader high in initiating structure is someone who assigns followers particular tasks, sets definite standards of performance, and emphasizes deadlines. According to a review of the leadership literature, initiating structure is more strongly related to higher levels of group and organization productivity, and to more positive performance evaluations.

Consideration

Consideration is the extent to which a person's job relationships are characterized by mutual trust, respect for employees' ideas, and regard for their feelings. A leader high in consideration helps employees with personal problems, is friendly and approachable, treats all employees as equals, and expresses appreciation and support (people-oriented). Most of us want to work for considerate leaders—when asked to indicate what most motivated them at work, 66 percent of U.S. employees surveyed mentioned appreciation.[12] Indeed, one review found the followers of leaders high in consideration were more satisfied with their jobs, were more motivated, and had more respect for their leaders.

Consideration
The extent to which a leader is likely to have job relationships characterized by mutual trust, respect for subordinates' ideas, and regard for their feelings.

Cultural Differences

Mixed results from behavioral theory tests may lie partly in follower preferences, particularly cultural preferences. Research from the GLOBE program—a study of 18,000 leaders from 825 organizations in 62 countries, discussed in Chapter 5—suggested there are international differences in the preference for initiating structure and consideration.[13] The study found that leaders high in consideration succeeded best in countries where cultural values did not favor unilateral decision making, such as Brazil. As one Brazilian manager noted, "We do not prefer leaders who take self-governing decisions and act alone without engaging the group. That's part of who we are." A U.S. manager leading a team in Brazil would therefore need to be high in consideration—team-oriented, participative, and humane—to be effective. In contrast, the French have a more bureaucratic view of leaders and are less likely to expect them to be humane and considerate. A leader high in initiating structure (relatively task-oriented) will do best there and can make decisions in a relatively autocratic manner. A manager who scores high in consideration (people-oriented) may find her style backfires in France. In other cultures, both dimensions may be important—for example, Chinese culture emphasizes being polite, considerate, and unselfish, but it has a high performance orientation. Thus, consideration and initiating structure may both be important for a manager to be effective in China.

CONTINGENCY THEORIES

Some tough-minded leaders seem to gain a lot of admirers when they take over struggling companies and lead them out of crises. However, predicting leadership success is more complex than finding a few hero examples. Also, the leadership style that works in very bad times doesn't necessarily translate into long-term success. When researchers looked at situational influences, it appeared that under condition a, leadership style x would be appropriate, whereas style y was more suitable for condition b, and style z for condition c. But what *were* conditions a, b, and c? We next consider the Fiedler model, one approach to isolating situational variables.

Fiedler contingency model
The theory that effective groups depend on a proper match between a leader's style of interacting with subordinates and the degree to which the situation gives control and influence to the leader.

The Fiedler Model

Fred Fiedler developed the first comprehensive contingency model for leadership.[14] The **Fiedler contingency model** proposes that group performance depends on the proper match between the leader's style and the degree to which the situation gives the leader control. With the model, the individual's leadership style is assumed to be permanent.

Least preferred coworker (LPC) questionnaire
An instrument that measures whether a person is task- or relationship-oriented.

As a first step, the **least preferred coworker (LPC) questionnaire** identifies whether a person is *task-oriented* or *relationship-oriented* by asking respondents to think of all the coworkers they ever had and describe the one they *least enjoyed* working with. If you describe this person in favorable terms (a high LPC score), you are relationship-oriented. If you see your least-preferred coworker in unfavorable terms (a low LPC score), you are primarily interested in productivity and are task-oriented.

After finding a score, a fit must be found between the organizational situation and the leader's style for leadership effectiveness to be predicted. We can assess the situation in terms of three contingency or situational dimensions:

Leader–member relations
The degree of confidence, trust, and respect subordinates have in their leader.

Task structure
The degree to which job assignments are procedurized.

Position power
Influence derived from one's formal structural position in the organization; includes power to hire, fire, discipline, promote, and give salary increases.

1. **Leader–member relations** is the degree of confidence, trust, and respect members have in their leader.
2. **Task structure** is the degree to which the job assignments are procedurized (that is, structured or unstructured).
3. **Position power** is the degree of influence a leader has over power variables such as hiring, firing, discipline, promotions, and salary increases.

According to the model, the higher the task structure becomes, the more procedures are added; and the stronger the position power, the more control the leader has. The favorable situations are on the left side of the model in Exhibit 12-1. A very favorable situation (in which the leader has a great deal of control) might include a payroll manager who has the respect and confidence of his or her employees (good leader–member relations); activities that are clear and specific—such as wage computation, check writing,

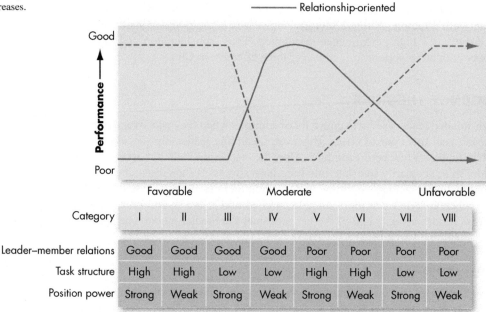

Category	I	II	III	IV	V	VI	VII	VIII
Leader–member relations	Good	Good	Good	Good	Poor	Poor	Poor	Poor
Task structure	High	High	Low	Low	High	High	Low	Low
Position power	Strong	Weak	Strong	Weak	Strong	Weak	Strong	Weak

EXHIBIT 12-1
Findings From the Fiedler Model

and report filing (high task structure); and considerable freedom to reward and punish employees (strong position power). An unfavorable situation, to the right in the model, might be that of the disliked chairperson of a volunteer United Way fundraising team (low leader–member relations, low task structure, low position power). In this job, the leader has very little control. When faced with a category I, II, III, VII, or VIII situation, task-oriented leaders perform better. Relationship-oriented leaders, however, perform better in moderately favorable situations—categories IV, V, and VI.

Studies testing the overall validity of the Fiedler model were initially supportive, but the model hasn't been studied much in recent years. Therefore, while it provides some insights we should consider, its strict practical application is problematic.

Situational Leadership Theory

Situational leadership theory (**SLT**) focuses on the followers. It says successful leadership depends on selecting the right leadership style contingent on the followers' *readiness*, the extent to which followers are willing and able to accomplish a specific task. A leader should choose one of four behaviors depending on follower readiness.

Situational leadership theory (SLT)
A contingency theory that focuses on followers' readiness.

If followers are *unable* and *unwilling* to do a task, the leader needs to give clear and specific directions; if they are *unable* but *willing*, the leader needs to display a high task orientation to compensate for followers' lack of ability, and a high relationship orientation to get them to "buy into" the leader's desires. If followers are *able* but *unwilling,* the leader needs to use a supportive and participative style; if they are both *able* and *willing*, the leader doesn't need to do much.

SLT has intuitive appeal. It acknowledges the importance of followers and builds on the logic that leaders can compensate for followers' limited ability and motivation. Yet research efforts to test and support the theory have generally been disappointing.[15] Why? Possible explanations include internal ambiguities and inconsistencies in the model itself as well as problems with research methodology. So, despite its intuitive appeal and wide popularity, any endorsement must be cautious for now.

Path–Goal Theory

Developed by Robert House, **path–goal theory** extracts elements from the research on initiating structure and consideration, and on the expectancy theory of motivation.[16] Path–goal theory suggests it's the leader's job to provide followers with information, support, or other resources necessary to achieve goals (the term *path–goal* implies that effective leaders clarify followers' paths to their work goals and make the journey easier by reducing roadblocks). The theory predicts:

Path–goal theory
A theory that states that it is the leader's job to assist followers in attaining their goals and to provide the necessary direction and/or support to ensure that their goals are compatible with the overall objectives of the group or organization.

- Directive leadership yields greater employee satisfaction when tasks are ambiguous or stressful than when they are highly structured and well laid out.
- Supportive leadership results in high employee performance and satisfaction when employees are performing structured tasks.
- Directive leadership is likely to be perceived as redundant among employees with high ability or considerable experience.

Of course, this is a simplification. The match between leadership style and situation can be individualistic and mercurial. Some tasks might be both stressful and highly structured, and employees may have high ability or experience in some tasks and not others. Other research has found that goal-focused leadership can lead to higher levels of emotional exhaustion for subordinates who are low in conscientiousness and emotional stability.[17] This suggests that leaders who set goals enable conscientious followers to achieve higher performance but may cause stress for workers who are low in conscientiousness.

Like SLT, path–goal theory has intuitive appeal, especially from a goal attainment perspective. Also like SLT, the theory can be only cautiously adopted for application, but it is a useful framework in examining the important role of leadership.[18]

Leader-Participation Model

Leader-participation model
A leadership theory that provides a set of rules to determine the form and amount of participative decision making in different situations.

The final contingency theory we cover argues that *the way* the leader makes decisions is as important as *what* he or she decides. The **leader-participation model** relates leadership behavior to subordinate participation in decision making.[19] Like path–goal theory, it says leader behavior must adjust to reflect the task structure (such as routine, nonroutine, or in between), but it does not cover all leadership behaviors and is limited to recommending what types of decisions might be best made with subordinate participation. It lays the groundwork for the situations and leadership behaviors most likely to elicit acceptance from subordinates.

As one leadership scholar noted, "Leaders do not exist in a vacuum;" leadership is a symbiotic relationship between leaders and followers.[20] But the theories we've covered to this point assume leaders use a fairly homogeneous style with everyone in their work units. Think about your experiences in groups. Did leaders often act very differently toward different people? It's common.

CONTEMPORARY THEORIES OF LEADERSHIP

Leaders are important—to organizations and to employees. The understanding of leadership is a constantly evolving science. Contemporary theories have built upon the foundation we've just established to discover the unique ways leaders emerge, influence, and guide their employees and organizations. Let's explore some of the leading current concepts, and look for aspects of the theories we've discussed already.

Leader–Member Exchange (LMX) Theory

Leader–member exchange (LMX) theory
A theory that supports leaders' creation of ingroups and outgroups; subordinates with ingroup status will likely have higher performance ratings, less turnover, and greater job satisfaction.

Think of a leader you know. Does this leader have favorites who make up an ingroup? If you answered "yes," you're acknowledging **leader–member exchange (LMX) theory**.[21] LMX argues that, because of time pressures, leaders establish a special relationship with a small group of their followers. These followers make up the ingroup—they are trusted, get a disproportionate amount of the leader's attention, and are more likely to receive special privileges. Other followers fall into the outgroup.

LMX theory proposes that early in the history of the interaction between a leader and a given follower, the leader implicitly categorizes the follower as an "in" or an "out;" that relationship becomes relatively stable over time. Leaders induce LMX by rewarding employees with whom they want a closer linkage and punishing those with whom they do not.[22] For the LMX relationship to remain intact, the leader and the follower must invest in the relationship.

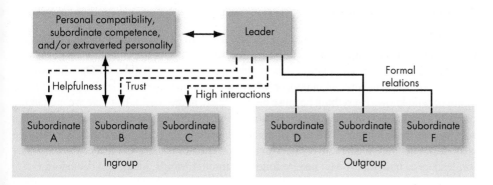

EXHIBIT 12-2
**Similarity with
and Interactions
between the
Leader, Ingroup,
and Outgroup**

Just how the leader chooses who falls into each category is unclear, but there is evidence ingroup members have demographic, attitude, and personality characteristics similar to those of their leaders or a higher level of competence than outgroup members[23] (see Exhibit 12-2). Leaders and followers of the same gender tend to have closer (higher LMX) relationships than those of different genders.[24] Even though the leader does the choosing, the follower's characteristics drive the categorizing decision.

Research to test LMX theory has been generally supportive, with substantive evidence that leaders do differentiate among followers; these disparities are far from random; and followers with ingroup status receive higher performance ratings, engage in more helping or citizenship behaviors at work, and report greater satisfaction with their superiors.[25]

One study conducted in Portugal and the United States found that LMX was associated strongly with followers' commitment to the organization when leaders were seen as embodying the values and identity of the organization.[26] Other research suggested that employees of leaders who provided family support (helping employees achieve work–life balance) in the LMX relationship were more committed and performed better.[27] These findings shouldn't be surprising given our knowledge of self-fulfilling prophecy (see Chapter 6). Leaders invest resources in those whom they expect to perform best. Believing ingroup members are the most competent, leaders treat them as such and unwittingly fulfill their prophecy.

For all the positive outcomes the ingroup receives, research indicates that both the ingroup and the outgroup realize negative effects from LMX. For example, a study in Turkey demonstrated that when leaders differentiated strongly among their followers in terms of their relationships (some followers had very positive LMX, others very poor), employees from both groups responded with more negative work attitudes and higher levels of withdrawal behavior.[28] One study in China and the United States indicated that differential leadership treatment hurts team trust and perceptions of procedural justice, especially when the team members work closely together.[29] Other research indicated that, although ingroup team members showed increased performance, the team as a whole became uncoordinated in the LMX environment and overall performance suffered.[30] Close-knit teams may be able to help outgroup members retain their confidence and self-efficacy by offering a supportive environment,[31] but this is often to the detriment of the relationship between employees and leaders.

Charismatic Leadership

Do you think leaders are born not made, or made not born? True, an individual may be literally born into a leadership position (think family heirs with surnames like Ford and Hilton), endowed with a leadership position due to past accomplishments (like CEOs who worked their way up the organizational ranks), or informally acknowledged as a leader (like a Twitter employee who knows everything because he was "there at the start"). But here we are talking not about the inputs into leadership role attainment; rather, we are focused on what makes great leaders extraordinary. Two contemporary leadership theories—charismatic leadership and transformational leadership—share a common theme in the great leader debate: They view leaders as individuals who inspire followers through words, ideas, and behaviors.

WHAT IS CHARISMATIC LEADERSHIP?   Sociologist Max Weber defined *charisma* (from the Greek for "gift") as "a certain quality of an individual personality, by virtue of which he or she is set apart from ordinary people and treated as endowed with supernatural, superhuman, or at least specifically exceptional powers or qualities. These are not accessible to the ordinary person and are regarded as of divine origin or as exemplary, and on the basis of them the individual concerned is treated as a leader."[32]

The first researcher to consider charismatic leadership in terms of organizational behavior (OB) was Robert House. According to his **charismatic leadership theory**, followers attribute heroic or extraordinary leadership abilities when they observe certain behaviors, and tend to give these leaders power.[33] A number of studies have attempted to identify the characteristics of charismatic leaders: they have a vision, are willing to take personal risks to achieve that vision, are sensitive to follower needs, and exhibit extraordinary behaviors[34] (see Exhibit 12-3). Recent research in Greece suggested that charismatic leadership increases follower organizational identification (commitment) by building a shared group identity among followers.[35] Other research indicates that charismatic leadership may predict follower job satisfaction.[36]

Charismatic leadership theory
A leadership theory that states that followers make attributions of heroic or extraordinary leadership abilities when they observe certain behaviors.

ARE CHARISMATIC LEADERS BORN OR MADE?   Are charismatic leaders born with their qualities? Or can people actually learn to be charismatic leaders? Yes, and yes.

Individuals *are* born with traits that make them charismatic. In fact, studies of identical twins found they scored similarly on charismatic leadership measures, even if they were raised in different households and never met. Personality is also related to charismatic leadership; charismatic leaders are likely to be extraverted, self-confident, and achievement-oriented.[37] Consider the legendary qualities of U.S. presidents Barack Obama, Bill Clinton, and Ronald Reagan, and U.K. Prime Minister Margaret Thatcher, when they were in office: whether you liked them or not, they are often compared because they all exhibited the qualities of charismatic leaders.

EXHIBIT 12-3
Key Characteristics of a Charismatic Leader

Source: Based on J. A. Conger and R. N. Kanungo, *Charismatic Leadership in Organizations* (Thousand Oaks, CA: Sage, 1998), p. 94.

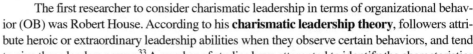

1. *Vision and articulation.* Has a vision—expressed as an idealized goal—that proposes a future better than the status quo; and is able to clarify the importance of the vision in terms that are understandable to others.
2. *Personal risk.* Willing to take on high personal risk, incur high costs, and engage in self-sacrifice to achieve the vision.
3. *Sensitivity to follower needs.* Perceptive of others' abilities and responsive to their needs and feelings.
4. *Unconventional behavior.* Engages in behaviors that are perceived as novel and counter to norms.

Research indicates that charismatic leadership is not only the province of world leaders—all of us can develop, within our own limitations, a more charismatic leadership style. If you stay active and central in your leadership roles, you will naturally communicate your vision for achieving goals to your followers, which increases the likelihood you will be seen as charismatic.[38] To further develop an aura of charisma, use your passion as a catalyst for generating enthusiasm. Speak in an animated voice, reinforce your message with eye contact and facial expressions, and gesture for emphasis. Bring out the potential in followers by tapping into their emotions, and create a bond that inspires them. Remember, enthusiasm is contagious!

HOW CHARISMATIC LEADERS INFLUENCE FOLLOWERS How do charismatic leaders actually influence followers? By articulating an appealing **vision**, a long-term strategy for attaining a goal by linking the present with a better future for the organization. Desirable visions fit the times and circumstances, and reflect the uniqueness of the organization. Thus, followers are inspired not only by how passionately the leader communicates, but also to an appealing message.

Vision
A long-term strategy for attaining a goal or goals.

A vision needs an accompanying **vision statement**, a formal articulation of an organization's vision or mission. Charismatic leaders may use vision statements to imprint on followers an overarching goal and purpose. These leaders also set a tone of cooperation and mutual support. They build followers' self-esteem and confidence with high performance expectations and the belief that followers can attain them. Through words and actions, the leader conveys a new set of values and sets an example for followers to imitate. Finally, the charismatic leader engages in emotion-inducing and often unconventional behavior to demonstrate courage and conviction about the vision.

Vision statement
A formal articulation of an organization's vision or mission.

Research indicates that charismatic leadership works as followers "catch" the emotions their leader is conveying.[39] One study found employees had a stronger sense of personal belonging at work when they had charismatic leaders which, in turn, increased their willingness to engage in helping and compliance-oriented behavior.[40]

DOES EFFECTIVE CHARISMATIC LEADERSHIP DEPEND ON THE SITUATION? Charismatic leadership has positive effects across many contexts. There are, however, characteristics of followers, and of the situation, that enhance or somewhat limit its effects.

One factor that enhances charismatic leadership is stress. People are especially receptive to charismatic leadership when they sense a crisis, when they are under stress, or when they fear for their lives. We may be more receptive to charismatic leadership under crises because we think bold leadership is needed. Some of it, however, may be more primal. When people are psychologically aroused, even in laboratory studies, they are more likely to respond to charismatic leaders.[41]

Some personalities are especially susceptible to charismatic leadership.[42] For instance, an individual who lacks self-esteem and questions his or her self-worth is more likely to absorb a leader's direction rather than establish an individual way of leading or thinking. For these people, the situation may matter much less than the desired charismatic qualities of the leader.

THE DARK-SIDE OF CHARISMATIC LEADERSHIP Unfortunately, charismatic leaders who are larger than life don't necessarily act in the best interests of their organizations.[43] Commensurate with this research observation, studies have indicated that individuals who are narcissistic are higher in some behaviors associated with charismatic leadership.[44] Many charismatic—but corrupt—leaders have allowed their personal goals to override the goals of their organizations. For example, leaders at Enron, Tyco, WorldCom, and HealthSouth recklessly used organizational resources for their personal benefit, violated laws and ethics to inflate stock prices, and then cashed in millions of dollars in personal stock options. Some charismatic leaders—Hitler, for example—are all too successful at convincing their followers to pursue a disastrous vision. If charisma is power, then that power can be used for good . . . and for ill.

It's not that charismatic leadership isn't effective; overall, it is. But a charismatic leader isn't always the answer. Success depends, to some extent, on the situation and on the leader's vision, and on the organizational checks and balances in place to monitor the outcomes.

Transactional and Transformational Leadership

Transactional leaders
Leaders who guide or motivate their followers in the direction of established goals by clarifying role and task requirements.

Transformational leaders
Leaders who inspire followers to transcend their own self-interests and who are capable of having a profound and extraordinary effect on followers.

Charismatic leadership theory relies on leaders' ability to inspire followers to believe in them. In contrast, Fiedler's model, situational leadership theory, and path–goal theory describe **transactional leaders**, leaders who guide their followers toward established goals by clarifying role and task requirements. A stream of research has focused on differentiating transactional from **transformational leaders**,[45] who inspire followers to transcend their self-interests for the good of the organization. Transformational leaders can have an extraordinary effect on their followers, who respond with increased levels of commitment.[46] Richard Branson of the Virgin Group is a good example of a transformational leader. He pays attention to the concerns and needs of individual followers, changes followers' awareness of issues by helping them look at old problems in new ways, and excites and inspires followers to put forth extra effort to achieve group goals. Research suggests that transformational leaders are most effective when their followers are able to see the positive impact of their work through direct interaction with customers or other beneficiaries.[47] Exhibit 12-4 briefly identifies and defines characteristics that differentiate transactional from transformational leaders.

Transactional Leader

Contingent Reward: Contracts exchange of rewards for effort, promises rewards for good performance, recognizes accomplishments.

Management by Exception (active): Watches and searches for deviations from rules and standards, takes corrective action.

Management by Exception (passive): Intervenes only if standards are not met.

Laissez-Faire: Abdicates responsibilities, avoids making decisions.

Transformational Leader

Idealized Influence: Provides vision and sense of mission, instills pride, gains respect and trust.

Inspirational Motivation: Communicates high expectations, uses symbols to focus efforts, expresses important purposes in simple ways.

Intellectual Stimulation: Promotes intelligence, rationality, and careful problem solving.

Individualized Consideration: Gives personal attention, treats each employee individually, coaches, advises.

EXHIBIT 12-4
Characteristics of Transactional and Transformational Leaders

Source: Based on A. H. Eagly, M. C. Johannesen-Schmidt, and M. L. Van Engen, "Transformational, Transactional, and Laissez-faire Leadership Styles: A Meta-Analysis Comparing Women and Men," *Psychological Bulletin* 129, no. 4 (2003), 569–591; and T. A. Judge and J. E. Bono, "Five Factor Model of Personality and Transformational Leadership," *Journal of Applied Psychology* 85, no. 5 (2000), 751–765."

Transactional and transformational leadership complement each other; they aren't opposing approaches to getting things done.[48] The best leaders are transactional *and* transformational. Transformational leadership *builds on* transactional leadership and produces levels of follower effort and performance beyond what transactional leadership alone can do. But the reverse isn't true. If you are a good transactional leader but do not have transformational qualities, you'll likely only be a mediocre leader.

FULL RANGE OF LEADERSHIP MODEL   Exhibit 12-5 shows the **full range of leadership model**. Laissez-faire, which literally means "let it be" (do nothing), is the most passive and therefore least effective of leader behaviors.[49] Management by exception, in which leaders primarily "put out fires" when there are crisis exceptions to normal operating procedures, means leaders are often too late to be effective. Contingent reward leadership, which gives predetermined rewards for employee efforts, can be an effective style of leadership but will not get employees to go above and beyond the call of duty.

Only with the four remaining styles—all aspects of transformational leadership—are leaders able to motivate followers to perform above expectations and transcend their self-interest for the sake of the organization. Individualized consideration, intellectual stimulation, inspirational motivation, and idealized influence (known as the "four I's") all result in extra effort from workers, higher productivity, higher morale and satisfaction, higher organizational effectiveness, lower turnover, lower absenteeism, and greater

Full range of leadership model
A model that depicts seven management styles on a continuum: laissez-faire, management by exception, contingent reward leadership, individualized consideration, intellectual stimulation, inspirational motivation, and idealized influence.

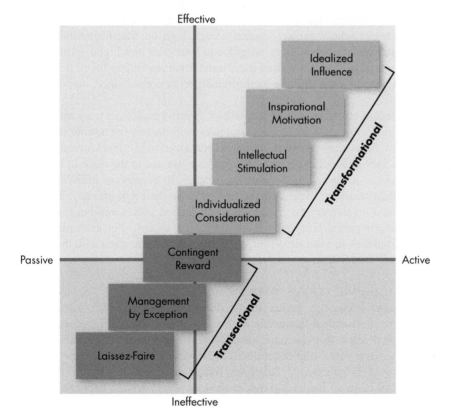

EXHIBIT 12-5
Full Range of Leadership Model

organizational adaptability. Based on this model, leaders are most effective when they regularly use the four I's.

 HOW TRANSFORMATIONAL LEADERSHIP WORKS Organizations with transformational leaders generally have greater decentralization of responsibility, managers with a higher propensity to take risks, and compensation plans geared toward long-term results—all of which facilitate corporate entrepreneurship.[50] There are other ways transformational leadership works, as well. One study of information technology workers in China found empowering leadership behavior led to feelings of positive personal control among workers, which increased their creativity at work.[51] Other research in Germany found that transformational leadership positively influenced workers' creativity, but suggested leaders need to guard against dependent leader relationships, which lower employee creativity.[52]

 Companies with transformational leaders often show greater agreement among top managers about the organization's goals, which yields superior organizational performance.[53] The Israeli military has seen similar results, showing that transformational leaders improve performance by building consensus among group members.[54]

 EVALUATION OF TRANSFORMATIONAL LEADERSHIP Transformational leadership has been supported at diverse job levels and occupations (including school principals, teachers, marine commanders, ministers, presidents of MBA associations, military cadets, union shop stewards, sales reps). In general, organizations perform better when they have transformational leaders. For example, one study of research and development (R&D) firms found teams whose project leaders scored high on transformational leadership produced better-quality products as judged one year later and higher profits five years later.[55] A review of 117 studies testing transformational leadership found it was related to higher levels of individual follower performance, team performance, and organizational performance.[56]

 The effect of transformational leadership on performance can vary by the situation. In general, transformational leadership has a greater impact on the bottom line in smaller, privately held firms than in more complex organizations.[57] Transformational leadership can also vary depending on whether work is evaluated at the team or the individual level.[58] Individual-focused transformational leadership empowers individual followers to develop ideas, enhance their abilities, and increase their self-efficacy. Team-focused transformational leaders emphasize group goals, shared values and beliefs, and unified efforts. Transformational leadership is not foolproof, though. For example, research in China suggested that, in team situations, the members' identification with the group could override the effects of transformational leadership.[59]

TRANSFORMATIONAL VERSUS TRANSACTIONAL LEADERSHIP We have seen that transformational leadership yields many desirable organizational outcomes. When comparing transformational leadership with transactional leadership, research indicates transformational leadership is more strongly correlated than transactional leadership with lower turnover rates, higher productivity, lower employee stress and burnout, and higher employee satisfaction.[60] However, transformational leadership theory is not perfect; the full range of leadership model shows a clear division between transactional and transformational leadership that may not fully exist in effective leadership. And contrary to the full range of leadership model, the four I's of transformational leadership are not always superior in effectiveness to transactional leadership; contingent reward leadership—in which leaders dole out rewards as certain goals are reached by employees—sometimes works as well as transformational leadership. More research is needed, but the general supportable conclusion is that transformational leadership is desirable and effective, given the right application.

TRANSFORMATIONAL VERSUS CHARISMATIC LEADERSHIP In considering transformational and charismatic leadership, you surely noticed some commonalities. There are differences, too. Charismatic leadership places somewhat more emphasis on the way leaders communicate (are they passionate and dynamic?), while transformational leadership focuses more on what they are communicating (is it a compelling vision?). Still, the theories are more alike than different. At their heart, both focus on the leader's ability to inspire followers, and sometimes they do so in the same way. Because of this, some researchers believe the concepts are somewhat interchangeable.

RESPONSIBLE LEADERSHIP

Although theories have increased our understanding of effective leadership, they do not explicitly deal with the roles of ethics and trust, which some argue are essential to complete the picture. Here, we consider contemporary concepts that explicitly address the role of leaders in creating ethical organizations. These and the theories we discussed earlier are not mutually exclusive ideas (a transformational leader may also be a responsible one), but we could argue that most leaders generally appear to be stronger in one category than another.

Authentic Leadership

Authentic leadership focuses on the moral aspects of being a leader. **Authentic leaders** know who they are, know what they believe in, and act on those values and beliefs openly and candidly. Their followers consider them ethical people. The primary quality produced by authentic leadership is trust. Authentic leaders share information, encourage open communication, and stick to their ideals. The result: People come to have faith in them. Related to this behavior is the concept of humility, another characteristic of being authentic. Research indicates that leaders who model humility help followers to understand the growth process for their own development.[61]

Authentic leaders Leaders who know who they are, know what they believe in and value, and act on those values and beliefs openly and candidly. Their followers consider them to be ethical people.

Authentic leadership, especially when shared among top management team members, can create a positive energizing effect that heightens firm performance.[62] Transformational or charismatic leaders can have a vision and communicate it persuasively, but sometimes the vision is wrong (as in the case of Hitler), or the leader is more concerned with his or her own needs or pleasures, as were Dennis Kozlowski (ex-CEO of Tyco), Jeff Skilling (ex-CEO of Enron), and Raj Rajaratnam (founder of the Galleon Group).[63] Authentic leaders do not exhibit these behaviors. They may also be more likely to promote corporate social responsibility (CSR; see Chapter 3).

Ethical Leadership

Leadership is not value-free. In assessing its effectiveness, we need to address the *means* a leader uses to achieve goals as well as the content of those goals. The role of the leader in creating the ethical expectations for all members is crucial.[64] Ethical top leadership influences not only direct followers, but all the way down the command structure as well, because top leaders create an ethical culture and expect lower-level leaders to behave along ethical guidelines.[65] Leaders rated as highly ethical tend to have followers who engage in more organizational citizenship behaviors (OCBs; see Chapter 1) and who are more willing to bring problems to the leaders' attention.[66] Research also found that ethical leadership reduced interpersonal conflicts.[67]

Ethical and authentic leadership intersect at a number of junctures. Leaders who treat their followers ethically and authentically—with fairness, especially by providing honest, frequent, and accurate information—are seen as more effective.[68] Transformational leadership has ethical implications since these leaders change the way followers think. Charisma, too, has an ethical component. Unethical leaders use their charisma to enhance power over followers, directed toward self-serving ends. To integrate ethical and charismatic leadership, scholars have advanced the idea of **socialized charismatic leadership**—conveying other-centered (not self-centered) values through leaders who model ethical conduct.[69] These leaders are able to bring employee values in line with their own values through their words and actions.[70]

Although every member of an organization is responsible for ethical behavior, many initiatives aimed at increasing organizational ethical behavior are focused on the leaders. Because top executives set the moral tone for an organization, they need to set high ethical standards, demonstrate them through their own behavior, and encourage and reward integrity in others while avoiding abuses of power. One research review found that role modeling by top leaders positively influenced managers throughout their organizations to behave ethically and fostered a climate that reinforced group-level ethical conduct. The findings suggest that organizations should invest in ethical leadership training programs, especially in industries with few ethical regulations. Leadership training programs that incorporate cultural values should be especially mandated for leaders who take foreign assignments or manage multicultural work teams.[71]

Servant Leadership

Scholars have recently considered ethical leadership from a new angle by examining **servant leadership**.[72] Servant leaders go beyond their self-interest and focus on opportunities to help followers grow and develop. Characteristic behaviors include listening, empathizing, persuading, accepting stewardship, and actively developing followers' potential. Because servant leadership is based on the value of serving the needs of others, research has focused on its outcomes for the well-being of followers. Perhaps not surprisingly, a study of 126 CEOs found that servant leadership was negatively correlated with the trait of narcissism.[73]

What are the effects of servant leadership? One study of 123 supervisors found it resulted in higher levels of commitment to the supervisor, self-efficacy, and perceptions of justice, which all were related to OCB.[74] This relationship between servant leadership and follower OCB appears to be stronger when followers are encouraged to focus on being dutiful and responsible.[75] Second, servant leadership increases team potency (a belief

Socialized charismatic leadership
A leadership concept that states that leaders convey values that are other-centered versus self-centered and who role-model ethical conduct.

Servant leadership
A leadership style marked by going beyond the leader's own self-interest and instead focusing on opportunities to help followers grow and develop.

that your team has above-average skills and abilities), which in turn leads to higher levels of group performance.[76] Third, a study with a nationally representative sample found higher levels of citizenship were associated with a focus on growth and advancement, which in turn was associated with higher levels of creative performance.[77] Other research found that servant leadership and a resulting culture of service increased employee job performance and creativity while reducing turnover intentions.[78]

Servant leadership may be more prevalent and effective in certain cultures.[79] When asked to draw images of leaders, for example, U.S. subjects tended to draw them in front of the group, giving orders to followers. Participants from Singapore tended to draw leaders at the back of the group, acting more to gather a group's opinions together and then unify the group from the rear. This suggests the East Asian prototype is more like a servant leader, which might mean servant leadership is more effective in these cultures.

POSITIVE LEADERSHIP

In each of the theories we've discussed, you can see opportunities for the practice of good, bad, or mediocre leadership. Now let's think about the intentional development of positive leadership environments.

Trust

Trust is a psychological state that exists when you agree to make yourself vulnerable to another person because you have positive expectations about how things are going to turn out.[80] Although you aren't completely in control of the situation, you are willing to take a chance that the other person will come through for you. Followers who trust a leader are confident their rights and interests will not be abused.[81] As you might expect, transformational leaders generate a higher level of trust from their followers, which in turn is related to higher levels of team confidence and, ultimately, higher levels of team performance.[82] Trust is a primary attribute associated with leadership; breaking it can have serious adverse effects on a group's performance.[83]

Trust
A positive expectation that another person will not act opportunistically.

THE OUTCOMES OF TRUST   Trust between supervisors and employees has a number of specific advantages. Here are just a few from research:

- **Trust encourages taking risks.** Whenever employees decide to deviate from the usual way of doing things, or to take their supervisor's word on a new direction, they are taking a risk. In both cases, a trusting relationship can facilitate that leap.
- **Trust facilitates information sharing.** When managers demonstrate they will give employees' ideas a fair hearing and actively make changes, employees are more willing to speak out.[84]
- **Trusting groups are more effective.** When a leader sets a trusting tone in a group, members are more willing to help each other and exert extra effort, which increases trust.
- **Trust enhances productivity.** Employees who trust their supervisors tend to receive higher performance ratings, indicating higher productivity.[85]

TRUST DEVELOPMENT   What key characteristics lead us to believe a leader is trustworthy? Evidence has identified three: *integrity*, *benevolence*, and *ability* (see Exhibit 12-6).[86]

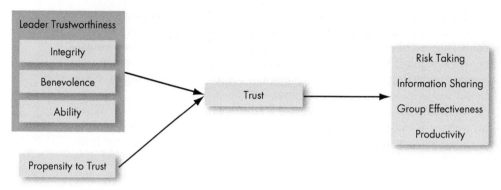

EXHIBIT 12-6
Model of Trust in Organizations

Integrity refers to honesty and truthfulness. When 570 white-collar employees were given a list of 28 attributes related to leadership, they rated honesty the most important by far.[87] Integrity also means maintaining consistency between what you do and say.

Benevolence means the trusted person has your interests at heart, even if your interests aren't necessarily in line with theirs. Caring and supportive behavior is part of the emotional bond between leaders and followers.

Ability encompasses an individual's technical and interpersonal knowledge and skills. You're unlikely to depend on someone whose abilities you don't believe in even if the person is highly principled and has the best intentions.

Trust propensity
How likely an employee is to trust a leader.

TRUST PROPENSITY   **Trust propensity** refers to how likely a particular employee is to trust a leader. Some people are simply more likely to believe others can be trusted.[88] Trust propensity is closely linked to the personality trait of agreeableness and people with lower self-esteem are less likely to trust others.[89]

TRUST AND CULTURE   Does trust look the same in every culture? Using the basic definition of trust, it certainly does. However, in the work context, trust in an employment relationship may be built on very different perceptions from culture to culture. For example, a recent study in Taiwan indicated that employees responded to paternalistic leadership, when it was benevolent and ethical, with increased trust.[90] This positive response to paternalism may be unique to the collectivistic context of Taiwan, where the Confucian values of hierarchy and relationship predominate. In individualistic societies (see Chapter 4), we might expect that paternalistic leadership will rankle many employees who prefer not to see themselves as part of a hierarchical family work group. Employees in individualistic cultures may build trust according to the degree of leadership support and consistency instead.

THE ROLE OF TIME   We come to trust people by observing their behavior over a period of time.[91] To help, leaders need to demonstrate integrity, benevolence, and ability in situations where trust is important—say, where they could behave opportunistically or let employees down. Second, trust can be won in the ability domain by demonstrating competence. Third, research with 100 companies around the world suggested that leaders can build trust by shifting their communication style from top-down commands to ongoing organizational dialogue. Lastly, when leaders regularly create interpersonal conversations with their employees that are intimate, interactive, inclusive, and that intentionally follow an agenda, followers demonstrate trust with high levels of engagement.[92]

REGAINING TRUST   Managers who break the psychological contract with workers, demonstrating they aren't trustworthy leaders, will find employees are less satisfied and less committed, have a higher intent toward turnover, engage in less OCB, and have lower levels of task performance.[93] Leaders who betray trust are especially likely to be evaluated negatively by followers if there is already a low level of LMX.[94]

Once it has been violated, trust can be regained, but only in certain situations and depending on the type of violation.[95] If the cause is lack of ability, it's usually best to apologize and recognize you should have done better. When lack of integrity is the problem, apologies don't do much good. Regardless of the violation, saying nothing or refusing to confirm or deny guilt is never an effective strategy for regaining trust. Trust can be restored when we observe a consistent pattern of trustworthy behavior by the transgressor. However, if the transgressor used deception, trust never fully returns, not even after apologies, promises, or a consistent pattern of trustworthy actions.[96]

Mentoring

Leaders often take responsibility for developing future leaders. A **mentor** is a senior employee who sponsors and supports a less-experienced employee, a protégé. Successful mentors are good teachers. They present ideas clearly, listen well, and empathize with protégés' problems. Mentoring relationships serve career and psychosocial functions.[97]

Are all employees in an organization likely to participate in a mentoring relationship? Unfortunately, no. However, research continues to indicate that employers should establish mentoring programs because they benefit both mentors and protégés. For example, one study in Korea found that mentors achieved higher levels of transformational leadership as a result of the mentoring process, while organizational commitment and well-being increased for both mentors and protégés.[98]

You might assume mentoring is valuable for objective outcomes like compensation and job performance, but research suggests the gains are primarily psychological. Thus, while mentoring can have an impact on career success, it is not as much of a contributing factor as ability and personality. It may *feel* nice to have a mentor, but it doesn't appear that having a good mentor, or any mentor, is critical to your career. Rather, mentorship is a boost to your confidence.

> **Mentor**
> A senior employee who sponsors and supports a less-experienced employee, called a protégé.

CHALLENGES TO OUR UNDERSTANDING OF LEADERSHIP

Management expert Jim Collins said, "In the 1500s, people ascribed all events they didn't understand to God. Why did the crops fail? God. Why did someone die? God. Now our all-purpose explanation is leadership." This may be an astute observation from management consulting, but of course much of an organization's success or failure is due to factors outside the influence of leadership. Sometimes it's a matter of being in the right or wrong place at a given time. In this section, we present challenges to the accepted beliefs about the value of leadership.

Leadership as an Attribution

As you may remember from Chapter 6, attribution theory examines how people try to make sense of cause-and-effect relationships. The **attribution theory of leadership** says leadership

> **Attribution theory of leadership**
> A leadership theory that says that leadership is merely an attribution that people make about other individuals.

is merely an attribution people make about other individuals.[99] We attribute the following to leaders: intelligence, outgoing personality, strong verbal skills, aggressiveness, understanding, and industriousness.[100] At the organizational level, we tend, rightly or wrongly, to see leaders as responsible for both extremely negative and extremely positive performance.[101]

Perceptions of leaders by their followers strongly affect leaders' ability to be effective. First, one study of 128 major U.S. corporations found that whereas perceptions of CEO charisma did not lead to objectively better company performance, company performance did lead to perceptions of charisma.[102] Second, perceptions of leaders' behaviors are significant predictors of whether employees blame their leaders for failure, regardless of how the leaders assess themselves.[103] Third, a study of more than 3,000 employees from western Europe, the United States, and the Middle East found that people who tended to "romanticize" leadership in general were more likely to believe their own leaders were transformational.[104]

Attribution theory suggests what's important is projecting the *appearance* of being a leader rather than focusing on *actual accomplishments*. Leader-wannabes who can shape the perception that they're smart, personable, verbally adept, aggressive, hardworking, and consistent in their style can increase the probability their bosses, colleagues, and employees will view them as effective leaders.

Substitutes for and Neutralizers of Leadership

Substitutes
Attributes, such as experience and training, that can replace the need for a leader's support or ability to create structure.

Neutralizers
Attributes that make it impossible for leader behavior to make any difference to follower outcomes.

One theory of leadership suggests that in many situations, leaders' actions are irrelevant.[105] Experience and training are among the **substitutes** that can replace the need for a leader's support or ability to create structure. Organizations such as video game producer Valve Corporation, Gore-Tex maker W. L. Gore, and collaboration-software firm GitHub have experimented with eliminating leaders and management. Governance in the "bossless" work environment is achieved through accountability to coworkers, who determine team composition and sometimes even pay.[106] Organizational characteristics such as explicit formalized goals, rigid rules and procedures, and cohesive workgroups can replace formal leadership, while indifference to organizational rewards can neutralize its effects. **Neutralizers** make it impossible for leader behavior to make any difference to follower outcomes (see Exhibit 12-7).

Defining Characteristics	Relationship-Oriented Leadership	Task-Oriented Leadership
Individual		
Experience/training	No effect on	Substitutes for
Professionalism	Substitutes for	Substitutes for
Indifference to rewards	Neutralizes	Neutralizes
Job		
Highly structured task	No effect on	Substitutes for
Provides its own feedback	No effect on	Substitutes for
Intrinsically satisfying	Substitutes for	No effect on
Organization		
Explicit formalized goals	No effect on	Substitutes for
Rigid rules and procedures	No effect on	Substitutes for
Cohesive work groups	Substitutes for	Substitutes for

EXHIBIT 12-7
Substitutes for and Neutralizers of Leadership

Source: Based on S. Kerr and J. M. Jermier, "Substitutes for Leadership: Their Meaning and Measurement," *Organizational Behavior and Human Performance* (1978), p. 378."

Sometimes the difference between substitutes and neutralizers is fuzzy. If I'm working on a task that's intrinsically enjoyable, theory predicts leadership will be less important because the task provides motivation. But does that mean intrinsically enjoyable tasks neutralize leadership effects, or substitute for them, or both? Another problem is that while substitutes for leadership (such as employee characteristics and the nature of the task) matter to performance, that doesn't necessarily mean leadership is irrelevant.[107] It's simplistic to think employees are guided to goal accomplishments solely by the actions of their leaders. We've introduced a number of variables—such as attitudes, personality, ability, and group norms; that affect employee performance and satisfaction. Leadership is simply another independent variable in our overall OB model.

Online Leadership

How do you lead people who are physically separated from you when you primarily communicate electronically? This question needs attention from OB researchers.[108] Today's managers and employees are increasingly linked by networks rather than geographic proximity.

We propose that online leaders have to think carefully about what actions they want their digital messages to initiate. These leaders confront unique challenges, the greatest of which appears to be developing and maintaining trust. **Identification-based trust**, based on a mutual understanding of each other's intentions and appreciation of the other's wants and desires, is particularly difficult to achieve without face-to-face interaction.[109] Online negotiations can also be hindered because parties tend to express lower levels of trust.[110]

We believe good leadership skills will soon include the ability to communicate support, trust, and inspiration through electronic communication and to accurately read emotions in others' messages. In electronic communication, writing skills are likely to become an extension of interpersonal skills in ways that are not yet defined.

Identification-based trust
Trust based on a mutual understanding of each other's intentions and appreciation of each other's wants and desires.

SUMMARY

Leadership plays a central part in understanding group behavior because it's the leader who usually directs us toward our goals. Knowing what makes a good leader should thus be valuable toward improving group performance. The Big Five personality framework shows strong and consistent relationships between personality and leadership. The behavioral approach's major contribution was narrowing leadership into task-oriented (initiating structure) and people-oriented (consideration) styles. By evaluating the situation in which a leader operates, contingency theories promised to improve on the behavioral approach. Contemporary theories have made major contributions to our understanding of leadership effectiveness, and studies of ethics and positive leadership offer exciting promise.

IMPLICATIONS FOR MANAGERS

- For maximum leadership effectiveness, ensure that your preferences on the initiating structure and consideration dimensions are a match for your work dynamics and culture.
- Hire candidates who exhibit transformational leadership qualities and who have demonstrated success in working through others to meet a long-term vision.

Personality tests can reveal candidates higher in extraversion, conscientiousness, and openness, which may indicate leadership readiness.

- Hire candidates whom you believe are ethical and trustworthy for management roles and train current managers in your organization's ethical standards in order to increase leadership effectiveness.
- Seek to develop trusting relationships with followers because, as organizations have become less stable and predictable, strong bonds of trust are replacing bureaucratic rules in defining expectations and relationships.
- Consider investing in leadership training such as formal courses, workshops, and mentoring.

⭐ TRY IT!

If your professor has assigned this, go to the Assignments section of **mymanagementlab.com** to complete the **Simulation: Leadership**.

PERSONAL INVENTORY ASSESSMENTS

⭐ PERSONAL INVENTORY ASSESSMENTS

Ethical Leadership Assessment

If you've ever worked for someone who was an unethical leader, you know the importance of ethical leadership for positive outcomes. Take this PIA to explore ethical leadership further.

12-1. Describe the qualities of your ideal leader in terms of the concepts in this chapter.

13

Power and Politics

MyManagementLab®

⭐ Improve Your Grade!

When you see this icon ⭐, visit **mymanagementlab.com** for activities that are applied, personalized, and offer immediate feedback.

LEARNING OBJECTIVES

After studying this chapter, you should be able to:

1. Contrast leadership and power.
2. Explain the three bases of formal power and the two bases of personal power.
3. Explain the role of dependence in power relationships.
4. Identify power or influence tactics and their contingencies.
5. Identify the causes and consequences of abuse of power.
6. Describe how politics work in organizations.
7. Identify the causes, consequences, and ethics of political behavior.

⭐ Chapter Warm-up

If your professor has chosen to assign this, go to the Assignments section of **mymanagementlab.com** to complete the chapter warm-up.

⭐ WATCH IT

If your professor has assigned this, go to the Assignments section of **mymanagementlab.com** to complete the video exercise titled **Power and Political Behavior.**

POWER AND LEADERSHIP

Power

A capacity that *A* has to influence the behavior of *B* so that *B* acts in accordance with *A*'s wishes.

Dependence

B's relationship to *A* when *A* possesses something that *B* requires.

We often talk about power abstractly—with either respect, pride, or deference. In organizational behavior (OB), **power** simply refers to a capacity that *A* has to influence the behavior of *B* so *B* acts in accordance with *A*'s wishes.[1] Someone can thus have power but not use it; it is a capacity or potential. Probably the most important aspect of power is that it is a function of **dependence**. The greater *B*'s dependence on *A,* the greater *A*'s power in the relationship. Dependence, in turn, is based on alternatives that *B* perceives and the importance *B* places on the alternative(s) *A* controls. A person can have power over you only if he or she controls something you desire. If you want a college degree and have to pass a certain course to get it, and your current instructor is the only faculty member in the college who teaches that course, she has power over you because your alternatives are highly limited and you place a high degree of importance on the outcome. Similarly, if you're attending college on funds provided by your parents, you probably recognize the power they hold over you. But once you're out of school, have a job, and are making a good income; your parents' power is reduced significantly.

A careful comparison of our description of power with our description of leadership in Chapter 12 reveals that the concepts are closely intertwined. *Leaders* use *power* as a means of attaining group goals. How are the two terms different? Power does not require goal compatibility, just dependence. Leadership, on the other hand, requires some congruence between the goals of the leader and those being led. A second difference relates to the direction of influence. Leadership research focuses on the downward influence on followers. It minimizes the importance of lateral and upward influence patterns. Power research takes all factors into consideration. For a third difference, leadership research often emphasizes style. It seeks answers to questions such as: How supportive should a leader be? How much decision making should be shared with followers? In contrast, the research on power focuses on tactics for gaining compliance. Lastly, leadership concentrates on the individual leader's influence, while the study of power acknowledges that groups as well as individuals can use power to control other individuals or groups.

You may have noted that for a power situation to exist, one person or group needs to have control over resources the other person or group values. This is usually the case in established leadership situations. However, power relationships are possible in all areas of life, and power can be obtained in many ways. Let's explore the various sources of power next.

BASES OF POWER

Where does power come from? What gives an individual or a group influence over others? We answer by dividing the bases or sources of power into two general groupings, formal and personal, and breaking each of these down into more specific categories.[2]

Formal Power

Formal power is based on an individual's position in an organization. It can come from the ability to coerce or reward, or from formal authority.

Coercive power

A power base that is dependent on fear of the negative results from failing to comply.

COERCIVE POWER   The **coercive power** base depends on the target's fear of negative results from failing to comply. On the physical level, coercive power rests on the application, or the threat of application, of bodily distress through the infliction of pain, the restriction of movement, or the withholding of basic physiological or safety needs.

At the organizational level, *A* has coercive power over *B* if *A* can dismiss, suspend, or demote *B*, assuming *B* values the job. If *A* can assign *B* work activities *B* finds unpleasant, or treat *B* in a manner *B* finds embarrassing, *A* possesses coercive power over *B*. Coercive power comes also from withholding key information. People in an organization who have data or knowledge others need can make others dependent on them.

REWARD POWER   The opposite of coercive power is **reward power**, with which people comply because it produces positive benefits; someone who can distribute rewards others view as valuable will have power over them. These rewards can be financial—such as controlling pay rates, raises, and bonuses—or nonfinancial, including recognition, promotions, interesting work assignments, friendly colleagues, and preferred work shifts or sales territories.[3]

Reward power
Compliance achieved based on the ability to distribute rewards that others view as valuable.

LEGITIMATE POWER   In formal groups and organizations, probably the most common access to one or more of the power bases is through **legitimate power**. It represents the formal authority to control and use organizational resources based on the person's structural position in the organization.

Legitimate power is broader than the power to coerce and reward. Specifically, it includes members' acceptance of the authority of a hierarchical position. We associate power so closely with the concept of hierarchy that just drawing longer lines in an organization chart leads people to infer the leaders are especially powerful.[4] In general, when school principals, bank presidents, or army captains speak; teachers, tellers, and first lieutenants usually comply.

Legitimate power
The power a person receives as a result of his or her position in the formal hierarchy of an organization.

Personal Power

Many of the most competent and productive chip designers at Intel have power, but they aren't managers and they have no formal power. What they have is *personal power*, which comes from an individual's unique characteristics. There are two bases of personal power: expertise and the respect and admiration of others. Personal power is not mutually exclusive from formal power, but it can be independent.

EXPERT POWER   **Expert power** is influence wielded as a result of expertise, special skills, or knowledge. As jobs become more specialized, we become dependent on experts to achieve goals. It is generally acknowledged that physicians have expertise and hence expert power: most of us follow our doctor's advice. Computer specialists, tax accountants, economists, industrial psychologists, and other specialists wield power as a result of their expertise.

Expert power
Influence based on special skills or knowledge.

REFERENT POWER   **Referent power** is based on identification with a person who has desirable resources or personal traits. If I like, respect, and admire you; you can exercise power over me because I want to please you.

Referent power develops out of admiration of another and a desire to be like that person. It helps explain, for instance, why celebrities are paid millions of dollars to endorse products in commercials. Marketing research shows people such as LeBron James and Tom Brady have the power to influence your choice of athletic shoes and credit cards. With a little practice, you and I could probably deliver as smooth a sales pitch as these celebrities, but the buying public doesn't identify with us. Some people who are not in formal leadership positions have referent power and exert influence over others because of their charismatic dynamism, likability, and emotional appeal.

Referent power
Influence based on identification with a person who has desirable resources or personal traits.

Which Bases of Power Are Most Effective?

Of the three bases of formal power (coercive, reward, legitimate) and two bases of personal power (expert, referent), which are most important? Research suggests the personal sources of power are most effective. Both expert and referent power are positively related to employees' satisfaction with supervision, their organizational commitment, and their performance, whereas reward and legitimate power seem to be unrelated to these outcomes. One source of formal power, coercive power, can be damaging.

Referent power can be a powerful motivator. Consider Steve Stoute's company, Translation, which matches pop-star spokespersons with corporations that want to promote their brands. Stoute has paired Justin Timberlake with McDonald's, Beyoncé with Tommy Hilfiger, and Jay-Z with Reebok. Stoute's business seems to be all about referent power. The success of these well-known companies attests to Stoute's expectation that the buying public identifies with and emulates his spokespersons and therefore thinks highly of the brands they represent. Stoute's business seems to be all about referent power, using the credibility of artists and performers to reach youth culture.[5]

DEPENDENCE: THE KEY TO POWER

The most important aspect of power is that it is a function of dependence. In this section, we show how understanding dependence helps us understand degrees of power.

The General Dependence Postulate

Let's begin with a general postulate: *The greater B's dependence on A, the more power A has over B.* When you possess anything others require that you alone control, you make them dependent on you, and therefore you gain power over them.[6] As the old saying goes, "In the land of the blind, the one-eyed man is king!" But if something is plentiful, possessing it will not increase your power. Therefore, the more you can expand your own options, the less power you place in the hands of others. This explains why most organizations develop multiple suppliers rather than give their business to only one. It also explains why so many people aspire to financial independence. Independence reduces the power others can wield to limit our access to opportunities and resources.

What Creates Dependence?

Dependence increases when a resource you control is important, scarce, and nonsubstitutable.[7]

IMPORTANCE   If nobody wants what you have, it's not going to create dependence. However, note that there are many degrees of importance, from needing the resource for survival to wanting a resource that is in fashion or adds to convenience.

SCARCITY   We see the scarcity-dependence relationship in the power situation of employment. When the supply of labor is low relative to demand, workers can negotiate compensation and benefits packages that are far more attractive than those in occupations with an abundance of candidates. For example, college administrators have no problem today finding English instructors since there is a high supply and low demand. The market for network systems analysts, in contrast, is comparatively tight, with demand high and supply limited. The resulting bargaining power of computer-engineering faculty allows them to negotiate higher salaries, lighter teaching loads, and other benefits.

NONSUBSTITUTABILITY The fewer viable substitutes for a resource, the more power a person controlling that resource has. At universities that value faculty publishing, for example, the more recognition the faculty member receives through publication, the more control that person has because other universities also want faculty who are highly published and visible.

Social Network Analysis: A Tool for Assessing Resources

One tool to assess the exchange of resources and dependencies within an organization is *social network analysis*.[8] This method examines patterns of communication among organizational members to identify how information flows between them. Within a social network, or connections between people who share professional interests, each individual or group is called a node, and the links between nodes are called ties. When nodes communicate or exchange resources frequently, they are said to have very strong ties. Other nodes that are not engaged in direct communication with one another achieve resource flows through intermediary nodes. In other words, some nodes act as brokers between otherwise unconnected nodes. A graphical illustration of the associations among individuals in a social network is called a *sociogram*, which functions like an informal version of an organization chart. The difference is that a formal organization chart shows how authority is supposed to flow, whereas a sociogram shows how resources *really* flow in an organization. An example of a sociogram is shown in Exhibit 13-1.

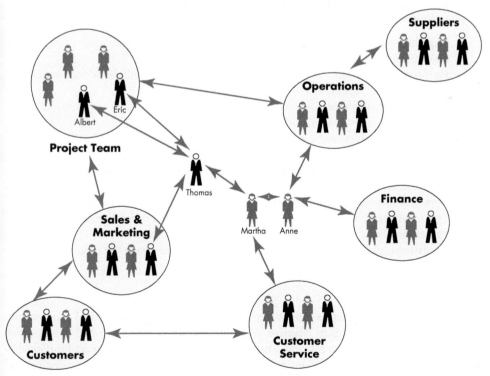

EXHIBIT 13-1
Example of a
Sociogram

Networks can create substantial power dynamics. Those in the position of brokers tend to have more power because they can leverage the unique resources they can acquire from different groups. In other words, many people are dependent upon brokers, which gives the brokers more power. For example, organizational culture changes such as corporate social responsibility (CSR) awareness will often begin in a single connected group of individuals, grow in strength, and slowly move to other connected groups through brokers over time.[9] Data from the United Kingdom's National Health Service shows that change agents, people entrusted with helping an organization to make a significant change, have more success if they are information brokers.[10] These functions are not without cost, however. One study found that people identified as central to advice networks were more likely to quit their jobs, possibly because they did a great deal of extra work without reward.[11]

There are many ways to implement a social network analysis in an organization.[12] Some organizations keep track of the flow of e-mail communications or document sharing across departments. These big data tools are an easy way to gather objective information about how individuals exchange information. Other organizations look at data from human resources (HR) information systems, analyzing how supervisors and subordinates interact with one another. These data sources can produce sociograms showing how resources and power flow. Leaders can then identify powerful brokers who exert the strongest influence on many groups, and address these key individuals.

POWER TACTICS

Power tactics
Ways in which individuals translate power bases into specific actions.

What **power tactics** do people use to translate power bases into specific action? What options do they have for influencing their bosses, coworkers, or employees? Research has identified nine distinct influence tactics:[13]

- **Legitimacy.** Relying on your authority position or saying a request accords with organizational policies or rules.
- **Rational persuasion.** Presenting logical arguments and factual evidence to demonstrate a request is reasonable.
- **Inspirational appeals.** Developing emotional commitment by appealing to a target's values, needs, hopes, and aspirations.
- **Consultation.** Increasing support by involving the target in deciding how to accomplish your plan.
- **Exchange.** Rewarding the target with benefits or favors in exchange for acceding to a request.
- **Personal appeals.** Asking for compliance based on friendship or loyalty.
- **Ingratiation.** Using flattery, praise, or friendly behavior prior to making a request.
- **Pressure.** Using warnings, repeated demands, and threats.
- **Coalitions.** Enlisting the aid or support of others to persuade the target to agree.

Using Power Tactics

Some tactics are more effective than others. Rational persuasion, inspirational appeals, and consultation tend to be the most effective, especially when the audience is highly interested in the outcomes of a decision process. The pressure tactic tends to backfire and is typically the least effective of the nine.[14] You can increase your chance of success by using two or more tactics together or sequentially, as long as your choices are compatible.[15] Using ingratiation and legitimacy together can lessen negative reactions, but only when the audience does not really care about the outcome of a decision process or the policy is routine.[16]

Let's consider the most effective way of getting a raise. You can start with a rational approach—figure out how your pay compares to that of your organizational peers, land a competing job offer, gather data that testify to your performance, or use salary calculators like Salary.com to compare your pay with others in your occupation—then share your findings with your manager. The results can be impressive. Kitty Dunning, a vice president at Don Jagoda Associates, landed a 16 percent raise when she e-mailed her boss numbers showing she had increased sales.[17]

While rational persuasion may work in this situation, the effectiveness of some influence tactics depends on the direction of influence,[18] and of course on the audience. As Exhibit 13-2 shows, rational persuasion is the only tactic effective across organizational levels. Inspirational appeals work best as a downward-influencing tactic with subordinates. When pressure works, it's generally downward only. Personal appeals and coalitions are most effective as lateral influence. Other factors relating to the effectiveness of influence include the sequencing of tactics, a person's skill in using the tactic, and the organizational culture.

In general, you're more likely to be effective if you begin with "softer" tactics that rely on personal power, such as personal and inspirational appeals, rational persuasion, and consultation. If these fail, you can move to "harder" tactics, such as exchange, coalitions, and pressure, which emphasize formal power and incur greater costs and risks.[19] A single soft tactic is more effective than a single hard tactic, and combining two soft tactics or a soft tactic and rational persuasion is more effective than any single tactic or combination of hard tactics.[20]

As we mentioned, the effectiveness of tactics depends on the audience.[21] People especially likely to comply with soft power tactics tend to be more reflective and intrinsically motivated; they have high self-esteem and a greater desire for control. Those likely to comply with hard power tactics are more action-oriented and extrinsically motivated, and are more focused on getting along with others than on getting their own way.

Cultural Preferences for Power Tactics

Preference for power tactics varies across cultures.[22] Those from individualistic countries tend to see power in personalized terms and as a legitimate means of advancing their personal ends, whereas those in collectivistic countries see power in social terms and as a legitimate means of helping others.[23] Managers in the United States seem to prefer rational appeal, whereas Chinese managers may prefer coalition tactics.[24] Reason-based tactics are consistent with the U.S. preference for direct confrontation, and rational persuasion to influence others and resolve differences, while coalition tactics align with the Chinese preference for meeting difficult or controversial requests with indirect approaches.

Upward Influence	Downward Influence	Lateral Influence
Rational persuasion	Rational persuasion	Rational persuasion
	Inspirational appeals	Consultation
	Pressure	Ingratiation
	Consultation	Exchange
	Ingratiation	Legitimacy
	Exchange	Personal appeals
	Legitimacy	Coalitions

EXHIBIT 13-2
Preferred Power Tactics by Influence Direction

Applying Power Tactics

Political skill
The ability to influence others in such a way as to enhance one's objectives.

People differ in their **political skill**, or their ability to influence others to enhance their own objectives. The politically skilled are more effective users of all the influence tactics. Political skill is also more effective when the stakes are high, such as when the individual is accountable for important organizational outcomes. Finally, the politically skilled are able to exert their influence without others detecting it, a key element in effectiveness (it's damaging to be labeled political).[25] These individuals are able to use their political skills in environments with low levels of procedural and distributive justice. When an organization has fairly applied rules, free of favoritism or biases, political skill is actually negatively related to job performance ratings.[26]

Lastly, we know cultures within organizations differ markedly; some are warm, relaxed, and supportive; others are formal and conservative. Some encourage participation and consultation, some encourage reason, and still others rely on pressure. People who fit the culture of the organization tend to obtain more influence.[27] Specifically, extraverts tend to be more influential in team-oriented organizations, and highly conscientious people are more influential in organizations that value working alone on technical tasks. People who fit the culture are influential because they can perform especially well in the domains deemed most important for success. Thus, the organization itself will influence which subset of power tactics is viewed as acceptable for use.

HOW POWER AFFECTS PEOPLE

To this point, we've discussed what power is and how it is acquired. But we've not yet answered one important question: does power corrupt?

There is certainly evidence that there are corrupting aspects of power. Power leads people to place their own interests ahead of others' needs or goals. Why does this happen? Interestingly, power not only leads people to focus on their self-interests because they can, it also liberates them to focus inward and thus come to place greater weight on their own aims and interests. Power also appears to lead individuals to "objectify" others (to see them as tools to obtain their instrumental goals) and to see relationships as more peripheral.[28]

That's not all. Powerful people react—especially negatively—to any threats to their competence. People in positions of power hold on to it when they can, and individuals who face threats to their power are exceptionally willing to take actions to retain it whether their actions harm others or not. Those given power are more likely to make self-interested decisions when faced with a moral hazard (such as when hedge fund managers take more risks with other people's money because they're rewarded for gains but punished less often for losses). People in power are more willing to denigrate others. Power also leads to overconfident decision making.[29]

Power Variables

As we've discussed, power does appear to have some important disturbing effects on us. But that is hardly the whole story—power is more complicated than that. It doesn't affect everyone in the same way, and there are even positive effects of power. Let's consider each of these in turn.

First, the toxic effects of power depend on the wielder's personality. Research suggests that if you have an anxious personality, power does not corrupt you because you are less likely to think that using power benefits yourself.[30] Second, the corrosive effect of power can be contained by organizational systems. For example, one study found that while power made people behave in a self-serving manner, the self-serving behavior stopped when accountability for the behavior was initiated. Third, we have the means to blunt the negative effects of power. One study showed that simply expressing gratitude toward powerful others makes them less likely to act aggressively against us. Finally, remember the saying that those with little power abuse what little they have? There seems to be some truth to this in that the people most likely to abuse power are those who start low in status and gain power. Why is this the case? It appears that having low status is threatening, and the fear this creates is used in negative ways if power is given later.[31]

As you can see, some factors can moderate the negative effects of power. But there can also be general positive effects. Power energizes and increases motivation to achieve goals. It also can enhance our motivation to help others. One study found, for example, that a desire to help others translated into actual work behavior when people felt a sense of power.[32]

This study points to an important insight about power. It is not so much that power corrupts as it *reveals what we value*. Supporting this line of reasoning, another study found that power led to self-interested behavior only in those with a weak moral identity (the degree to which morals are core to someone's identity). In those with a strong moral identity, power enhanced their moral awareness and willingness to act.[33]

Sexual Harassment: Unequal Power in the Workplace

Sexual harassment is defined as any unwanted activity of a sexual nature that affects an individual's employment or creates a hostile work environment. According to the U.S. Equal Employment Opportunity Commission (EEOC), sexual harassment happens when a person encounters "unwelcome sexual advances, requests for sexual favors, and other verbal or physical conduct of a sexual nature" on the job that disrupts work performance or that creates an "intimidating, hostile, or offensive" work environment.[34] Although the definition changes from country to country, most nations have at least some policies to protect workers. Whether the policies or laws are followed is another question, however. Equal employment opportunity legislation is established in Pakistan, Bangladesh, and Oman, for example, but studies suggest it might not be well implemented.[35]

Sexual harassment
Any unwanted activity of a sexual nature that affects an individual's employment and creates a hostile work environment.

Generally, sexual harassment is more prevalent in male-dominated societies. For example, a study in Pakistan found that up to 93 percent of female workers were sexually harassed.[36] In Singapore, up to 54 percent of workers (women and men) reported they were sexually harassed.[37] The percentages in the United States and some other countries are generally much lower but still troubling. Surveys indicate about one-quarter of U.S. women and 10 percent of men have been sexually harassed.[38] Data from the EEOC suggest that sexual harassment is decreasing: sexual harassment claims now make up 10 percent of all discrimination claims, compared with 20 percent in the mid-1990s. Of this percentage, though, claims from men have increased from 11 percent of total claims in 1997 to 17.5 percent today.[39] Sexual harassment is disproportionately prevalent for women in certain types of jobs. In the restaurant industry, for instance, 80 percent of female waitstaff in a study reported having been sexually harassed by coworkers or customers, compared to 70 percent of male waitstaff.[40]

The bottom line is that managers have a responsibility to protect their employees from a hostile work environment. They may easily be unaware that one of their employees is being sexually harassed, but being unaware does not protect them or their organization. If investigators believe a manager could have known about the harassment, both the manager and the company can be held liable.

POLITICS: POWER IN ACTION

Whenever people get together in groups, power will be exerted. People in organizations want to carve out a niche to exert influence, earn rewards, and advance their careers. If they convert their power into action, we describe them as being engaged in *politics*. Those with good political skills have the ability to use their bases of power effectively.[41] Politics are not only inevitable; they might be essential, too.

Definition of Organizational Politics

There is no shortage of definitions of *organizational politics*. Essentially, this type of politics focuses on the use of power to affect decision making in an organization, sometimes for self-serving and organizationally unsanctioned behaviors.[42] For our purposes, **political behavior** in organizations consists of activities that are not required as part of an individual's formal role but that influence, or attempt to influence, the distribution of advantages and disadvantages within the organization.[43]

Political behavior
Activities that are not required as part of a person's formal role in the organization but that influence, or attempt to influence, the distribution of advantages and disadvantages within the organization.

This definition encompasses what most people mean when they talk about organizational politics. Political behavior is outside specified job requirements. It requires some attempt to use power bases. It includes efforts to influence the goals, criteria, or processes used for decision making. Our definition is broad enough to include varied political behaviors such as withholding key information from decision makers, joining a coalition, whistle-blowing, spreading rumors, leaking confidential information to the media, exchanging favors with others for mutual benefit, and lobbying on behalf of or against a particular individual or decision alternative. In this way, political behavior is often negative, but not always.

The Reality of Politics

Interviews with experienced managers show most believe political behavior is a major part of organizational life.[44] Many managers report some use of political behavior is ethical, as long as it doesn't directly harm anyone else. They describe politics as necessary and believe someone who never uses political behavior will have a hard time getting things done. Most also indicate they have never been trained to use political behavior effectively. But why, you may wonder, must politics exist? Isn't it possible for an organization to be politics-free? It's *possible*—if all members of that organization hold the same goals and interests, if organizational resources are not scarce, and if performance outcomes are completely clear and objective. But that doesn't describe the organizational world in which most of us live.

Maybe the most important factor leading to politics within organizations is the realization that most of the "facts" used to allocate limited resources are open to interpretation. When allocating pay based on performance, for instance, what is *good* performance? What's an *adequate* improvement? What constitutes an *unsatisfactory* job? The manager of any major league baseball team knows a .400 hitter is a high performer and a .125 hitter is a poor performer. You don't need to be a baseball genius to know you should play your .400 hitter and send the .125 hitter back to the minors. But what if you have to choose between players who hit .280 and .290? Then less objective factors come into play: fielding expertise, attitude, potential, ability to perform in a clutch, loyalty to the team, and so on. More managerial decisions resemble the choice between a .280 and a .290 hitter than between a .125 hitter and a .400 hitter. It is in this large and ambiguous middle ground of organizational life—where the facts don't speak for themselves—that politics flourish.

Finally, because most decisions have to be made in a climate of ambiguity—where facts are rarely objective and thus open to interpretation—people within organizations will use whatever influence they can to support their goals and interests. That, of course, creates the activities we call *politicking.* One person's "selfless effort to benefit the organization" is seen by another as a "blatant attempt to further his or her interest."[45]

CAUSES AND CONSEQUENCES OF POLITICAL BEHAVIOR

Now that we've discussed the constant presence of politicking in organizations, let's discuss the causes and consequences of these behaviors.

Factors Contributing to Political Behavior

Not all groups or organizations are equally political. In some organizations, politicking is overt and rampant, while in others politics play a small role in influencing outcomes. What causes this variation? Research and observation have identified a number of factors that appear to encourage political behavior. Some are individual characteristics, derived from the qualities of the people the organization employs; others are a result of the organization's culture or internal environment. Exhibit 13-3 illustrates how both individual and organizational factors can increase political behavior and provide favorable outcomes (increased rewards and averted punishments) for individuals and groups in the organization.

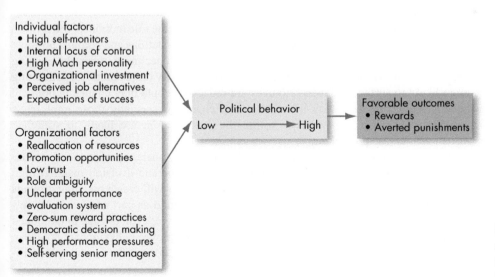

Individual factors
• High self-monitors
• Internal locus of control
• High Mach personality
• Organizational investment
• Perceived job alternatives
• Expectations of success

Organizational factors
• Reallocation of resources
• Promotion opportunities
• Low trust
• Role ambiguity
• Unclear performance evaluation system
• Zero-sum reward practices
• Democratic decision making
• High performance pressures
• Self-serving senior managers

Political behavior
Low ———→ High

Favorable outcomes
• Rewards
• Averted punishments

EXHIBIT 13-3
Antecedents and Outcomes of Political Behavior

INDIVIDUAL FACTORS   At the individual level, researchers have identified certain personality traits, needs, and other factors likely to be related to political behavior. In terms of traits, we find that employees who are high self-monitors, possess an internal locus of control, and have a high need for power (nPow; see Chapter 7) are more likely to engage in political behavior. The high self-monitor is more sensitive to social cues, exhibits higher levels of social conformity, and is more likely to be skilled in political behavior than the low self-monitor. Because they believe they can control their environment, individuals with an internal locus of control are more prone to take a proactive stance and attempt to manipulate situations in their favor. Not surprisingly, the Machiavellian personality (see Chapter 5)—characterized by the will to manipulate and the desire for power—is consistent with using politics as a means to further personal interests.

An individual's investment in the organization and perceived alternatives influence the degree to which he or she will pursue illegitimate means of political action.[46] The more a person expects increased future benefits from the organization, and the more that person has to lose if forced out, the less likely he or she is to use illegitimate means. Conversely, the more alternate job opportunities an individual has—due to a favorable job market, possession of scarce skills or knowledge, prominent reputation, or influential contacts outside the organization—the more likely the person is to employ politics.

Finally, some individuals engage in political behavior simply because they are better at it. Such individuals read interpersonal interactions well, fit their behavior to situational needs, and excel at networking.[47] These people are often indirectly rewarded for their political efforts. For example, a study of a construction firm in southern China found that politically skilled subordinates were more likely to receive recommendations for rewards from their supervisors, and politically oriented supervisors were especially likely to respond positively to politically skilled subordinates.[48] Other studies from countries around the world have similarly shown that higher levels of political skill are associated with higher levels of perceived job performance.[49]

ORGANIZATIONAL FACTORS   Although we acknowledge the role individual differences can play, the evidence more strongly suggests that certain situations and cultures promote politics. Specifically, when an organization's resources are declining, when the existing pattern of resources is changing, and when there is opportunity for promotions, politicking is more likely to surface.[50] When resources are reduced, people may engage in political actions to safeguard what they have. Also, *any* changes, especially those implying a significant reallocation of resources within the organization, are likely to stimulate conflict and increase politicking.

Cultures characterized by low trust, role ambiguity, unclear performance evaluation systems, win–lose reward allocation practices, democratic decision making, high pressure for performance, and self-serving senior managers will create breeding grounds for politicking.[51] Because political activities are not required as part of the employee's formal role, the greater the role ambiguity, the more employees can engage in unnoticed political activity. Role ambiguity means the prescribed employee behaviors are not clear. In this situation, there are fewer limits to the scope and functions of the employee's political actions.

THE ZERO-SUM APPROACH The more an organizational culture emphasizes the zero-sum or win–lose approach to reward allocations, the more employees will be motivated to engage in politicking. The **zero-sum approach** treats the reward "pie" as fixed, so any gain one person or group achieves comes at the expense of another person or group. For example, if $15,000 is distributed among five employees for raises, any employee who gets more than $3,000 takes money away from one or more of the others. Such a practice encourages making others look bad and increasing the visibility of what you do.

INTER-ORGANIZATIONAL FACTORS There are also political forces at work in the relationships *between* organizations, where politics work differently depending on the organizational cultures.[52] One study showed that when two organizations with very political environments interacted with one another, the political interactions between them hurt performance in collaborative projects. On the other hand, when companies with less internal political behavior interacted with one another, even political disputes between them did not lead to lower performance in collaborative projects. This study shows companies should be wary of forming alliances with organizations that have high levels of internal political behavior.

Zero-sum approach
A negotiation approach that treats the reward "pie" as fixed, so any gain one person or group achieves comes at the expense of another person or group.

How Do People Respond to Organizational Politics?

For most people who have modest political skills or who are unwilling to play the politics game, outcomes tend to be predominantly negative in terms of decreased job satisfaction, increased anxiety and stress, increased turnover, and reduced performance. However, very strong evidence indicates perceptions of organizational politics are negatively related to job satisfaction.[53] Politics may lead to self-reported declines in employee performance, perhaps because employees perceive political environments to be unfair, which demotivates them.[54] Not surprisingly, when politicking becomes too much to handle, it can lead employees to quit.[55] The negative effects from politicking seem to be universal to most cultures. When employees of two agencies in a study in Nigeria viewed their work environments as political, for example, they reported higher levels of job distress and were less likely to help their coworkers. Thus, although developing countries such as Nigeria present perhaps more ambiguous and therefore more political environments in which to work, the negative consequences of politics appear to be the same as in the United States.[56]

There are some qualifiers to keep in mind when considering the effects of politicking. First, the politics–performance relationship appears to be moderated by an individual's understanding of the "hows" and "whys" of organizational politics. Researchers have noted, "An individual who has a clear understanding of who is responsible for making decisions and why they were selected to be the decision makers would have a better understanding of how and why things happen the way they do than someone who does not understand the decision-making process in the organization."[57] When both politics and understanding are high, performance is likely to increase because these individuals see political activity as an opportunity. This is consistent with what you might expect for individuals with well-honed political skills. But when understanding is low, individuals are more likely to see politics as a threat, which can have a negative effect on job performance.[58]

Second, political behavior at work moderates the effects of ethical leadership.[59] One study found male employees were more responsive to ethical leadership and showed the most citizenship behavior when levels of both politics and ethical leadership were high. Women, on the other hand, appeared most likely to engage in citizenship behavior when the environment was consistently ethical and *apolitical.*

Defensive behaviors
Reactive and protective behaviors to avoid action, blame, or change.

Third, when employees see politics as a threat, they often respond with **defensive behaviors**—reactive and protective behaviors to avoid action, blame, or change.[60] (Exhibit 13-4 provides some examples.) In the short run, employees may find that defensiveness protects their self-interest, but in the long run it wears them down. People who consistently rely on defensiveness find that eventually it is the only way they know how to behave. At that point, they lose the trust and support of their peers, bosses, employees, and clients.

Impression Management

We know people have an ongoing interest in how others perceive and evaluate them. For example, North Americans spend billions of dollars on diets, health club memberships, cosmetics, and plastic surgery—all intended to make them more attractive to others. Being perceived positively by others has benefits in an organizational setting. It might, for instance, help us initially to get the jobs we want in an organization and, once hired, to get favorable evaluations, superior salary increases, and more rapid promotions. The process

Avoiding Action

Overconforming. Strictly interpreting your responsibility by saying things like "The rules clearly state ..." or "This is the way we've always done it."

Buck passing. Transferring responsibility for the execution of a task or decision to someone else.

Playing dumb. Avoiding an unwanted task by falsely pleading ignorance or inability.

Stretching. Prolonging a task so that one person appears to be occupied—for example, turning a two-week task into a four-month job.

Stalling. Appearing to be more or less supportive publicly while doing little or nothing privately.

Avoiding Blame

Bluffing. Rigorously documenting activity to project an image of competence and thoroughness, known as "covering your rear."

Playing safe. Evading situations that may reflect unfavorably. It includes taking on only projects with a high probability of success, having risky decisions approved by superiors, qualifying expressions of judgment, and taking neutral positions in conflicts.

Justifying. Developing explanations that lessen one's responsibility for a negative outcome and/or apologizing to demonstrate remorse, or both.

Scapegoating. Placing the blame for a negative outcome on external factors that are not entirely blameworthy.

Misrepresenting. Manipulation of information by distortion, embellishment, deception, selective presentation, or obfuscation.

Avoiding Change

**EXHIBIT 13-4
Defensive
Behaviors**

Prevention. Trying to prevent a threatening change from occurring.

Self-protection. Acting in ways to protect one's self-interest during change by guarding information or other resources.

by which individuals attempt to control the impression others form of them is called **impression management (IM)**.[61] See Exhibit 13-5 for examples.

Most of the studies to test the effectiveness of IM techniques have related IM to two criteria: interview success and performance evaluations. Let's consider each of these.

Conformity

Agreeing with someone else's opinion to gain his or her approval is a form of *ingratiation.*

Example: A manager tells his boss, "You're absolutely right on your reorganization plan for the western regional office. I couldn't agree with you more.

Favors

Doing something nice for someone to gain that person's approval is a form of *ingratiation.*

Example: A salesperson says to a prospective client, "I've got two tickets to the theater tonight that I can't use. Take them. Consider it a thank-you for taking the time to talk with me."

Excuses

Explaining a predicament-creating event aimed at minimizing the apparent severity of the predicament is a *defensive IM technique.*

Example: A sales manager says to her boss, "We failed to get the ad in the paper on time, but no one responds to those ads anyway."

Apologies

Admitting responsibility for an undesirable event and simultaneously seeking to get a pardon for the action is a *defensive IM technique.*

Example: An employee says to his boss, "I'm sorry I made a mistake on the report. Please forgive me."

Self-Promotion

Highlighting your best qualities, downplaying your deficits, and calling attention to your achievements is a *self-focused IM technique.*

Example: A salesperson tells his boss, "Matt worked unsuccessfully for three years to try to get that account. I sewed it up in six weeks. I'm the best closer this company has."

Enhancement

Claiming that something you did is more valuable than most other members of the organizations would think is a *self-focused IM technique.*

Example: A journalist tells his editor, "My work on this celebrity divorce story was really a major boost to our sales" (even though the story only made it to page 3 in the entertainment section).

Flattery

Complimenting others about their virtues in an effort to make yourself appear perceptive and likeable is an *assertive IM technique.*

Example: A new sales trainee says to her peer, "You handled that client's complaint so tactfully! I could never have handled that as well as you did."

Exemplification

Doing more than you need to in an effort to show how dedicated and hardworking you are is an *assertive IM technique.*

Example: An employee sends e-mails from his work computer when he works late so that his supervisor will know how long he's been working.

Impression management (IM)
The process by which individuals attempt to control the impression others form of them.

EXHIBIT 13-5
Impression Management (IM) Techniques

Source: Based on B. R. Schlenker, *Impression Management* (Monterey, CA: Brooks/Cole, 1980); M. C. Bolino, K. M. Kacmar, W. H. Turnley, and J. B. Gilstrap, "A Multi-Level Review of Impression Management Motives and Behaviors," *Journal of Management* 34, no. 6 (2008), 1080–1109; and R. B. Cialdini, "Indirect Tactics of Image Management Beyond Basking," in R. A. Giacalone and P. Rosenfeld (eds.), *Impression Management in the Organization* (Hillsdale, NJ: Lawrence Erlbaum, 1989), 45–71.

INTERVIEWS AND IM The evidence indicates most job applicants use IM techniques in interviews and that it works.[62] To develop a sense of how effective different IM techniques are in interviews, one study grouped data from thousands of recruiting and selection interviews into appearance-oriented efforts (efforts toward looking professional), explicit tactics (such as flattering the interviewer or talking up your own accomplishments), and verbal cues (such as using positive terms and showing general enthusiasm).[63] Across all the dimensions, it was quite clear that IM was a powerful predictor of how well people did. However, there was a twist. When interviews were highly structured, meaning the interviewer's questions were written out in advance and focused on applicant qualifications, the effects of IM were substantially weaker. Manipulative behaviors like IM are more likely to have an effect in ambiguous and unstructured interviews.

PERFORMANCE EVALUATIONS AND IM In terms of performance evaluations, the picture is quite different. Ingratiation is positively related to performance ratings, meaning those who ingratiate with their supervisors get higher performance evaluations. However, self-promotion appears to backfire: Those who self-promote actually may receive *lower* performance ratings.[64] There is an important qualifier to these general findings. It appears that individuals high in political skill are able to translate IM into higher performance appraisals, whereas those lower in political skill are more likely to be hurt by their IM attempts.[65] One study of 760 boards of directors found that individuals who ingratiated themselves to current board members (expressed agreement with the director, pointed out shared attitudes and opinions, complimented the director) increased their chances of landing on a board.[66] Another study found that interns who attempted to use ingratiation with their supervisors were usually disliked— unless they had high levels of political skill. For those who had this ability, ingratiation led to higher levels of liking from supervisors, and higher performance ratings.[67]

IM BY CULTURE Are our conclusions about responses to politics globally valid? Should we expect people in Israel, for instance, to respond the same way to impression management that people in the United States do? Almost all our conclusions on employee reactions to organizational politics and impression management are based on studies conducted in North America. The few studies that have included other countries suggest some minor modifications.[68] One study of managers in the U.S. culture and three Chinese cultures (People's Republic of China, Hong Kong, and Taiwan) found that U.S. managers evaluated "gentle persuasion" tactics such as consultation and inspirational appeal as more effective than did their Chinese counterparts.[69] This finding may have implications for the effectiveness of impression management techniques in individualistic and collectivistic countries. Other research suggests effective U.S. leaders achieve influence by focusing on the personal goals of group members and the tasks at hand (an analytical approach), whereas influential East Asian leaders focus on relationships among group members and meeting the demands of people around them (a holistic approach). Further research is needed in this area.[70]

The Ethics of Behaving Politically

Although there are no clear-cut ways to differentiate ethical from unethical politicking, there are some questions you should consider. For example, what is the utility of engaging in politicking? Sometimes we do it for little good reason. Major league baseball player Al Martin claimed he played football at USC when in fact he never did. As a baseball player, he had little to gain by pretending to have played football! Outright lies like this may be rather rare and extreme examples of impression management, but many of us have at least distorted information to make a favorable impression. One thing to keep in mind is whether it's worth the risk. Another question is this: How does the utility of engaging in the political behavior balance out harm (or potential harm) it will do to others? Complimenting a supervisor on her appearance in order to curry favor is probably much less harmful than grabbing credit that others deserve.

Finally, does the political activity conform to standards of equity and justice? Sometimes it is difficult to weigh the costs and benefits of a political action, but the ethicality is clear. The department head who inflates the performance evaluation of a favored employee and deflates the evaluation of a disfavored employee—and then uses the evaluations to justify giving the former a big raise and the latter nothing—has treated the disfavored employee unfairly.

Unfortunately, powerful people can become very good at explaining self-serving behaviors in terms of the organization's best interests. They can persuasively argue that unfair actions are really fair and just. Those who are powerful, articulate, and persuasive are most vulnerable to ethical lapses because they are more likely to get away with them. When faced with an ethical dilemma regarding organizational politics, try to consider whether playing politics is worth the risk and whether others might be harmed in the process. If you have a strong power base, recognize the ability of power to corrupt. Remember it's a lot easier for people who are in a powerless position to act ethically, if for no other reason than they typically have very little political discretion to exploit.

Mapping Your Political Career

As we have seen, politics is not just for politicians. You can use the concepts presented in this chapter in some very tangible ways we have outlined in your organization. However, they also have another application: You.

One of the most useful ways to think about power and politics is in terms of your own career. What are your ambitions? Who has the power to help you achieve them? What is your relationship to these people? The best way to answer these questions is with a political map, which can help you sketch out your relationships with the people upon whom your career depends. Exhibit 13-6 contains such a political map.[71] Let's walk through it.

Assume your future promotion depends on five people, including Jamie, your immediate supervisor. As you can see in the exhibit, you have a close relationship with Jamie (you would be in real trouble otherwise). You also have a close relationship with Zack in finance. However, with the others you have either a loose relationship (Lane) or none at all (Jia, Marty). One obvious implication of this map is the need to formulate a plan to gain more influence over, and a closer relationship with, these people. How might you do that?

One of the best ways to influence people is indirectly. What if you played in a tennis league with Mark, Jamie's former coworker who you know remains friends with Jamie? To influence Mark, in many cases, may also be to influence Marty. Why not post an entry on CJ's blog? You can complete a similar analysis for the other four decision makers and their networks.

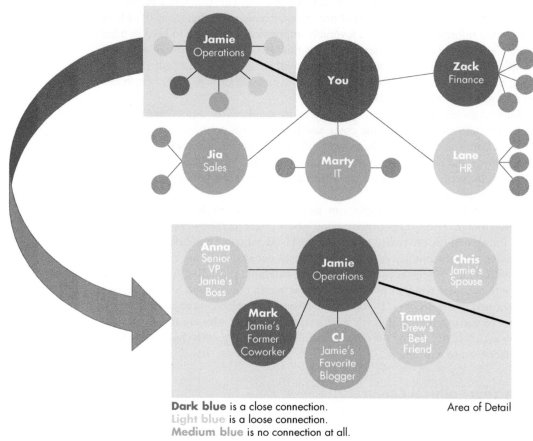

Dark blue is a close connection.   Area of Detail
Light blue is a loose connection.
Medium blue is no connection at all.

EXHIBIT 13-6
Drawing Your Political Map

Source: Based on D. Clark, "A Campaign Strategy for Your Career," *Harvard Business Review,* November 2012, 131-134.

All of this may seem a bit Machiavellian to you. However, remember that only one person gets the promotion, and your competition may have a map of his or her own. As we noted in the early part of the chapter, power and politics are a part of organizational life.

SUMMARY

Few employees relish being powerless in their jobs and organizations. People respond differently to the various power bases. Expert and referent power are derived from an individual's personal qualities. In contrast, coercion, reward, and legitimate power are essentially organizationally granted. Competence especially appears to offer wide appeal, and its use as a power base results in high performance by group members.

An effective manager accepts the political nature of organizations. Some people are more politically astute than others, meaning they are aware of the underlying politics and can manage impressions. Those who are good at playing politics can be expected to get higher performance evaluations and, hence, larger salary increases and more promotions than the politically naïve or inept. The politically astute are also likely to exhibit higher job satisfaction and be better able to neutralize job stressors. A political map can provide a good schematic from which to identify positive politicking opportunities. Finally, power and politics present significant ethical considerations. To accept the reality of these dimensions in organizations is to accept the responsibility for awareness and ethical behavior.

IMPLICATIONS FOR MANAGERS

- To maximize your power, increase others' dependence on you. For instance, increase your power in relation to your boss by developing a needed knowledge or skill for which there is no ready substitute.
- You will not be alone in attempting to build your power bases. Others, particularly employees and peers, will be seeking to increase your dependence on them, while you are trying to minimize it and increase their dependence on you.
- Try to avoid putting others in a position where they feel they have no power.
- By assessing behavior in a political framework, you can better predict the actions of others and use that information to formulate political strategies that will gain advantages for you and your work unit.
- Consider that employees who have poor political skills or are unwilling to play the politics game generally relate perceived organizational politics to lower job satisfaction and self-reported performance, increased anxiety, and higher turnover. Therefore, if you are adept at organizational politics, help others understand the importance of becoming politically savvy.

✪ TRY IT!

If your professor has assigned this, go to the Assignments section of **mymanagementlab.com** to complete the **Simulation: Power & Politics**.

✪ PERSONAL INVENTORY ASSESSMENTS

PERSONAL INVENTORY ASSESSMENTS

Gaining Power and Influence

Do you like power and influence? Take this PIA to learn more about gaining both.

13-1. If a person has more power, do you think his or her need for politics becomes greater or less? Why?

14
Conflict and Negotiation

MyManagementLab®
⭐ Improve Your Grade!
When you see this icon ⭐, visit **mymanagementlab.com** for activities that are applied, personalized, and offer immediate feedback.

LEARNING OBJECTIVES

After studying this chapter, you should be able to:

1. Describe the three types of conflict and the three loci of conflict.
2. Outline the conflict process.
3. Contrast distributive and integrative bargaining.
4. Apply the five steps of the negotiation process.
5. Show how individual differences influence negotiations.
6. Describe the social factors that influence negotiations.
7. Assess the roles and functions of third-party negotiations.

⭐ Chapter Warm-up
If your professor has chosen to assign this, go to the Assignments section of **mymanagementlab.com** to complete the chapter warm-up.

A DEFINITION OF CONFLICT

Conflict
A process that begins when one party perceives that another party has negatively affected, or is about to negatively affect, something that the first party cares about.

There has been no shortage of definitions of *conflict*,[1] but common to most is the idea that conflict is a perception of differences or opposition. If no one is aware of a conflict, then it is generally agreed no conflict exists. Opposition or incompatibility, as well as interaction, are also needed to begin the conflict process.

We define **conflict** broadly as a process that begins when one party perceives another party has affected or is about to negatively affect something the first party cares about. Conflict describes the point in ongoing activity when interaction becomes disagreement. People experience a wide range of conflicts in organizations over an incompatibility of goals, differences in interpretations of facts, disagreements over behavioral expectations, and the like. Our definition covers the full range of conflict levels, from overt and violent acts to subtle forms of disagreement.

Contemporary perspectives differentiate types of conflict based on their effects. **Functional conflict** supports the goals of the group and improves its performance, and is thus a constructive form of conflict. For example, a debate among members of a work team about the most efficient way to improve production can be functional if unique points of view are discussed and compared openly. Conflict that hinders group performance is destructive or **dysfunctional conflict**. A highly personal struggle for control that distracts from the task at hand in a team is dysfunctional. Exhibit 14-1 provides an overview depicting the effect of levels of conflict. To understand different types of conflict, we will discuss next the *types* of conflict and the *loci* of conflict.

Functional conflict
Conflict that supports the goals of the group and improves its performance.

Dysfunctional conflict
Conflict that hinders group performance.

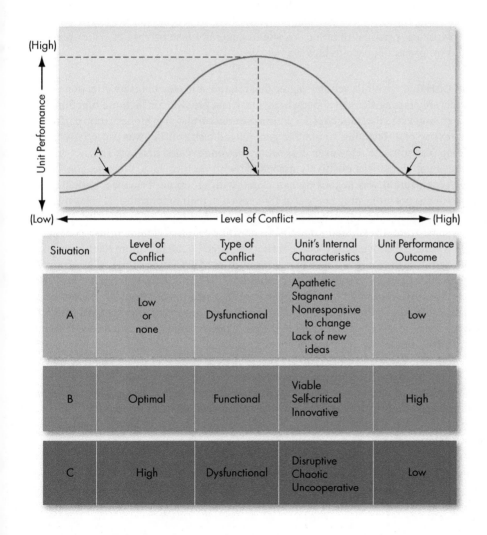

Situation	Level of Conflict	Type of Conflict	Unit's Internal Characteristics	Unit Performance Outcome
A	Low or none	Dysfunctional	Apathetic Stagnant Nonresponsive to change Lack of new ideas	Low
B	Optimal	Functional	Viable Self-critical Innovative	High
C	High	Dysfunctional	Disruptive Chaotic Uncooperative	Low

EXHIBIT 14-1
The Effect of Levels of Conflict

Types of Conflict

One means of understanding conflict is to identify the *type* of disagreement, or what the conflict is about. Is it a disagreement about goals? Is it about people who just rub one another the wrong way? Or is it about the best way to get things done? Although each conflict is unique, researchers have classified conflicts into three categories: relationship, task, or process. **Relationship conflict** focuses on interpersonal relationships. **Task conflict** relates to the content and goals of the work. **Process conflict** is about how the work gets done.

Relationship conflict
Conflict based on interpersonal relationships.

Task conflict
Conflict over content and goals of the work.

Process conflict
Conflict over how work gets done.

RELATIONSHIP CONFLICT   Studies demonstrate that relationship conflicts, at least in work settings, are almost always dysfunctional. Why? It appears that the friction and interpersonal hostilities inherent in relationship conflicts increase personality clashes and decrease mutual understanding, which hinders the completion of organizational tasks. Of the three types, relationship conflicts also appear to be the most psychologically exhausting to individuals. Because they tend to revolve around personalities, you can see how relationship conflicts can become destructive. After all, we can't expect to change our coworkers' personalities, and we would generally take offense at criticisms directed at who we *are* as opposed to how we behave.

TASK CONFLICT   While scholars agree that relationship conflict is dysfunctional, there is considerably less agreement about whether task and process conflicts are functional. Early research suggested that task conflict within groups correlated to higher group performance, but a review of 116 studies found that generalized task conflict was essentially unrelated to group performance. However, close examination revealed that task conflict among top management teams was positively associated with performance, whereas conflict lower in the organization was negatively associated with group performance, perhaps because people in top positions may not feel as threatened in their organizational roles by conflict. This review also found that it mattered whether other types of conflict were occurring at the same time. If task and relationship conflict occurred together, task conflict more likely was negative, whereas if task conflict occurred by itself, it more likely was positive. Other scholars have argued that the strength of conflict is important: if task conflict is very low, people aren't really engaged or addressing the important issues; if task conflict is too high, infighting will quickly degenerate into relationship conflict. Moderate levels of task conflict may thus be optimal. Supporting this argument, one study in China found that moderate levels of task conflict in the early development stage increased creativity in groups, but high levels decreased team performance.[2]

Finally, the personalities of the teams appear to matter. One study demonstrated that teams of individuals who are, on average, high in openness and emotional stability are better able to turn task conflict into increased group performance. The reason may be that open and emotionally stable teams can put task conflict in perspective and focus on how the variance in ideas can help solve the problem, rather than letting it degenerate into relationship conflicts.

PROCESS CONFLICT   What about process conflict? Researchers found that process conflicts are about delegation and roles. Conflicts over delegation often revolve around the perception that some members as shirking, and conflicts over roles can leave some group members feeling marginalized. Thus, process conflicts often become highly personalized and quickly devolve into relationship conflicts. It's also true, of course, that arguing about how to do something takes time away from actually doing it. We've all been part of groups in which the arguments and debates about roles and responsibilities seem to go nowhere.

Loci of Conflict

Another way to understand conflict is to consider its *locus*, or the framework within which the conflict occurs. Here, too, there are three basic types. **Dyadic conflict** is conflict between two people. **Intragroup conflict** occurs *within* a group or team. **Intergroup conflict** is conflict *between* groups or teams.

> **Dyadic conflict**
> Conflict that occurs between two people.
>
> **Intragroup conflict**
> Conflict that occurs within a group or team.
>
> **Intergroup conflict**
> Conflict between different groups or teams.

Nearly all the literature on relationship, task, and process conflicts considers intragroup conflict (within the group). That makes sense given that groups and teams often exist only to perform a particular task. However, it doesn't necessarily tell us all we need to know about the context and outcomes of conflict. For example, research has found that for intragroup task conflict to positively influence performance within the team, it is important that the team has a supportive climate in which mistakes aren't penalized and every team member "[has] the other's back."[3] But is this concept applicable to the effects of intergroup conflict? Think about, say, NFL football. As we said, for a team to adapt and improve, perhaps a certain amount of intragroup conflict (but not too much) is good for team performance, especially when the team members support one another. But would we care whether members from one team supported members from another team? Probably not. In fact, if groups are competing with one another so that only one team can "win," conflict seems almost inevitable. Still, it must be managed. Intense intergroup conflict can be quite stressful to group members and might well affect the way they interact. One study found, for example, that high levels of conflict between teams caused individuals to focus on complying with norms within their teams.[4]

It may surprise you how certain individuals become most important during intergroup conflicts. One study that focused on intergroup conflict found an interplay between an individual's position within a group and the way that individual managed conflict between groups. Group members who were relatively peripheral in their own group were better at resolving conflicts between their group and another one. But this happened only when those peripheral members were still accountable to their groups, and the effect can be confounded by dyadic conflicts.[5] Thus, being at the core of your work group does not necessarily make you the best person to manage conflict with other groups.

Altogether, understanding functional and dysfunctional conflict requires not only that we identify the type of conflict; we also need to know where it occurs. It's possible that while the concepts of relationship, task, and process conflicts are useful in understanding intragroup or even dyadic conflict, they are less useful in explaining the effects of intergroup conflict. But how do we make conflict as productive as possible? A better understanding of the conflict process, discussed next, will provide insight about potential controllable variables.

> **Conflict process**
> A process that has five stages: potential opposition or incompatibility, cognition and personalization, intentions, behavior, and outcomes.

THE CONFLICT PROCESS

The **conflict process** has five stages: potential opposition or incompatibility, cognition and personalization, intentions, behavior, and outcomes (see Exhibit 14-2).

EXHIBIT 14-2
The Conflict
Process

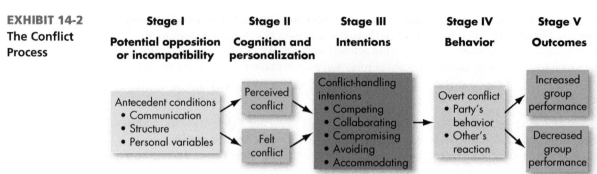

Stage I	Stage II	Stage III	Stage IV	Stage V
Potential opposition or incompatibility	**Cognition and personalization**	**Intentions**	**Behavior**	**Outcomes**

Stage I: Potential Opposition or Incompatibility

The first stage of conflict is the appearance of conditions—causes or sources—that create opportunities for it to arise. These conditions *need not* lead directly to conflict, but one of them is necessary if it is to surface. We group the conditions into three general categories: communication, structure, and personal variables.

COMMUNICATION   Communication can be a source of conflict.[6] There are opposing forces that arise from semantic difficulties, misunderstandings, and "noise" in the communication channel (see Chapter 11). These factors, along with jargon and insufficient information, can be barriers to communication and potential antecedent conditions to conflict. The potential for conflict has also been found to increase with too little or *too much* communication. Communication is functional up to a point, after which it is possible to overcommunicate, increasing the potential for conflict.

STRUCTURE   The term *structure* in this context includes variables such as size of group, degree of specialization in tasks assigned to group members, jurisdictional clarity, member–goal compatibility, leadership styles, reward systems, and degree of dependence between groups. The larger the group and the more specialized its activities, the greater the likelihood of conflict. Tenure and conflict are inversely related, meaning that the longer a person stays with an organization, the less likely conflict becomes. Therefore, the potential for conflict is greatest when group members are newer to the organization and when turnover is high.

PERSONAL VARIABLES   Our last category of potential sources of conflict is personal variables, which include personality, emotions, and values. People high in the personality traits of disagreeableness, neuroticism, or self-monitoring (see Chapter 5) are prone to tangle with other people more often—and to react poorly when conflicts occur.[7] Emotions can cause conflict even when they are not directed at others. For example, an employee who shows up to work irate from her hectic morning commute may carry that anger into her workday, which can result in a tension-filled meeting.[8] Furthermore, differences in preferences and values can generate increased levels of conflict. For example, a study in Korea found that when group members didn't agree about their desired achievement levels, there was more task conflict; when group members didn't agree about their desired interpersonal closeness levels, there was more relationship conflict; and when group members didn't have similar desires for power, there was more conflict over status.[9]

Stage II: Cognition and Personalization

If the conditions cited in Stage I negatively affect something one party cares about, then the potential for opposition or incompatibility becomes actualized in the second stage.

As we noted in our definition of conflict, one or more of the parties must be aware that antecedent conditions exist. However, just because a disagreement is a **perceived conflict** does not mean it is personalized. It is at the **felt conflict** level, when individuals become emotionally involved, that they experience anxiety, tension, frustration, or hostility.

Stage II is important because it's where conflict issues tend to be defined, where the parties decide what the conflict is about.[10] The definition of conflict is important because it delineates the set of possible settlements. Most evidence suggests that people tend to default to cooperative strategies in interpersonal interactions unless there is a clear signal that they are faced with a competitive person. However, if our disagreement regarding, say, your salary is a zero-sum situation (the increase in pay you want means there will be that much less in the raise pool for me), I am going to be far less willing to compromise than if I can frame the conflict as a potential win–win situation (the dollars in the salary pool might be increased so both of us could get the added pay we want).

Second, emotions play a major role in shaping perceptions.[11] Negative emotions allow us to oversimplify issues, lose trust, and put negative interpretations on the other party's behavior.[12] In contrast, positive feelings increase our tendency to see potential relationships among elements of a problem, take a broader view of the situation, and develop innovative solutions.[13]

> **Perceived conflict**
> Awareness by one or more parties of the existence of conditions that create opportunities for conflict to arise.
>
> **Felt conflict**
> Emotional involvement in a conflict that creates anxiety, tenseness, frustration, or hostility.

Stage III: Intentions

Intentions intervene between people's perceptions and emotions, and their overt behavior. They are decisions to act in a given way.[14] There is slippage between intentions and behavior, so behavior does not always accurately reflect a person's intentions.

Using two dimensions—*assertiveness* (the degree to which one party attempts to satisfy his or her own concerns) and *cooperativeness* (the degree to which one party attempts to satisfy the other party's concerns)—we can identify five conflict-handling intentions: *competing* (assertive and uncooperative), *collaborating* (assertive and cooperative), *avoiding* (unassertive and uncooperative), *accommodating* (unassertive and cooperative), and *compromising* (mid-range on both assertiveness and cooperativeness).[15]

Intentions are not always fixed. During the course of a conflict, intentions might change if a party is able to see the other's point of view or to respond emotionally to the other's behavior. People generally have preferences among the five conflict-handling intentions. We can predict a person's intentions rather well from a combination of intellectual and personality characteristics.

> **Intentions**
> Decisions to act in a given way.

COMPETING When one person seeks to satisfy his or her own interests regardless of the impact on the other parties in the conflict, that person is **competing**. We are more apt to compete when resources are scarce.

> **Competing**
> A desire to satisfy one's interests, regardless of the impact on the other party to the conflict.

Collaborating
A situation in which the parties to a conflict each desire to satisfy fully the concerns of all parties.

Avoiding
The desire to withdraw from or suppress a conflict.

Accommodating
The willingness of one party in a conflict to place the opponent's interests above his or her own.

Compromising
A situation in which each party to a conflict is willing to give up something.

COLLABORATING When parties in conflict each desire to fully satisfy the concerns of all parties, there is cooperation and a search for a mutually beneficial outcome. In **collaborating**, parties intend to solve a problem by clarifying differences rather than by accommodating various points of view. If you attempt to find a win–win solution that allows both parties' goals to be completely achieved, that's collaborating.

AVOIDING A person may recognize a conflict exists and want to withdraw from or suppress it. Examples of **avoiding** include trying to ignore a conflict and keeping away from others with whom you disagree.

ACCOMMODATING A party who seeks to appease an opponent may be willing to place the opponent's interests above his or her own, sacrificing to maintain the relationship. We refer to this intention as **accommodating**. Supporting someone else's opinion despite your reservations about it, for example, is accommodating.

COMPROMISING In **compromising**, there is no winner or loser. Rather, there is a willingness to ration the object of the conflict and accept a solution with incomplete satisfaction of both parties' concerns. The distinguishing characteristic of compromising, therefore, is that each party intends to give up something.

A review that examined the effects of the four sets of behaviors across multiple studies found that openness and collaborating were both associated with superior group performance, whereas avoiding and competing strategies were associated with significantly worse group performance.[16] These effects were nearly as large as the effects of relationship conflict. This further demonstrates that it is not just the existence of conflict or even the type of conflict that creates problems, but rather the ways people respond to conflict and manage the process once conflicts arise.

Stage IV: Behavior

Stage IV is a dynamic process of interaction. For example, you make a demand on me, I respond by arguing, you threaten me, I threaten you back, and so on. Exhibit 14-3 provides a way of visualizing conflict behavior. Each behavioral stage in a conflict is built upon a foundation. At the lowest point are perceptions, misunderstandings, and differences of opinions. These may grow to subtle, indirect, and highly controlled forms

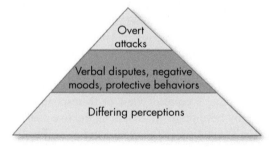

EXHIBIT 14-3
Dynamic Escalation of Conflict

Sources: P. T. Coleman, R. R. Vallacher, A. Nowak, and L. Bui-Wrzosinska, "Intractable Conflict as an Attractor: A Dynamical Systems Approach to Conflict Escalation and Intractability," *The American Behavioral Scientist* 50, no. 11 (2007): 1545–75; K. K. Petersen, "Conflict Escalation in Dyads with a History of Territorial Disputes," *International Journal of Conflict Management* 21, no. 4 (2010): 415–33.

of tension, such as a student challenging a point the instructor has made. Conflict can intensify until it becomes highly destructive. Strikes, riots, and wars clearly fall in this upper range. Conflicts that reach the upper ranges of the continuum are almost always dysfunctional. Functional conflicts are typically confined to the lower levels.

In conflict, intentions are translated into certain likely behaviors. *Competing* brings out active attempts to contend with team members, and greater individual effort to achieve ends without working together. *Collaborating* efforts create an investigation of multiple solutions with other members of the team and trying to find a solution that satisfies all parties as much as possible. *Avoidance* is seen in behavior like refusals to discuss issues and reductions in effort toward group goals. People who *accommodate* put their relationships ahead of the issues in the conflict, deferring to others' opinions and sometimes acting as a subgroup with them. Finally, when people *compromise*, they both expect to (and do) sacrifice parts of their interests, hoping that if everyone does the same, an agreement will sift out.

If a conflict is dysfunctional, what can the parties do to de-escalate it? Or, conversely, what options exist if conflict is too low to be functional and needs to be increased? This brings us to techniques of **conflict management**. We have already described several techniques in terms of conflict-handling intentions. Under ideal conditions, a person's intentions should translate into comparable behaviors.

Conflict management
The use of resolution and stimulation techniques to achieve the desired level of conflict.

Stage V: Outcomes

The action–reaction interplay between conflicting parties creates consequences. As our model demonstrates (see Exhibit 14-1), these outcomes may be functional if the conflict improves the group's performance, or dysfunctional if it hinders performance.

FUNCTIONAL OUTCOMES Conflict is constructive when it improves the quality of decisions, stimulates creativity and innovation, encourages interest and curiosity among group members, provides the medium for problems to be aired and tensions released, and fosters self-evaluation and change. Mild conflicts also may generate energizing emotions so members of groups become more active and engaged in their work.[17]

Conflict is an antidote for groupthink (see Chapter 9). Conflict doesn't allow the group to passively rubber-stamp decisions that may be based on weak assumptions, inadequate consideration of relevant alternatives, or other debilities. Conflict challenges the status quo and furthers the creation of new ideas, promotes reassessment of group goals and activities, and increases the probability that the group will respond to change. An open discussion focused on higher-order goals can make functional outcomes more likely. Groups that are extremely polarized do not manage their underlying disagreements effectively and tend to accept suboptimal solutions, or they avoid making decisions altogether rather than work out the conflict.[18] Research studies in diverse settings confirm the functionality of active discussion. Team members with greater differences in work styles and experience tend to share more information with one another.[19]

DYSFUNCTIONAL OUTCOMES The destructive consequences of conflict on the performance of a group or an organization are generally well known: Uncontrolled opposition breeds discontent, which acts to dissolve common ties and eventually leads to the destruction of the group. A substantial body of literature documents how dysfunctional conflicts can reduce group effectiveness.[20] Among the undesirable consequences are poor communication, reductions in group cohesiveness, and subordination of group goals to the primacy of infighting among members. All forms of conflict—even the functional varieties—appear to reduce group member satisfaction and trust.[21] When active discussions turn into open conflicts between members, information sharing between members decreases significantly.[22] At the extreme, conflict can bring group functioning to a halt and threaten the group's survival.

MANAGING CONFLICT   One of the keys to minimizing counterproductive conflicts is recognizing when there really is a disagreement. Many apparent conflicts are due to people using different verbiage to discuss the same general course of action. For example, someone in marketing might focus on "distribution problems," while someone from operations talks about "supply chain management" to describe essentially the same issue. Successful conflict management recognizes these different approaches and attempts to resolve them by encouraging open, frank discussions focused on interests rather than issues. Another approach is to have opposing groups pick parts of the solution that are most important to them and then focus on how each side can get its top needs satisfied. Neither side may get exactly what it wants, but each side will achieve the most important parts of its agenda.[23] Third, groups that resolve conflicts successfully discuss differences of opinion openly and are prepared to manage conflict when it arises.[24] An open discussion makes it much easier to develop a shared perception of the problems at hand; it also allows groups to work toward a mutually acceptable solution. Fourth, managers need to emphasize shared interests in resolving conflicts, so groups that disagree with one another don't become too entrenched in their points of view and start to take the conflicts personally. Groups with cooperative conflict styles and a strong underlying identification with the overall group goals are more effective than groups with a competitive style.[25]

CULTURAL INFLUENCES   Differences across countries in conflict resolution strategies may be based on collectivistic versus individualistic (see Chapter 4) tendencies and motives. Collectivistic cultures see people as deeply embedded in social situations, whereas individualistic cultures see them as autonomous. As a result, collectivists are more likely to seek to preserve relationships and promote the good of the group as a whole, and they prefer indirect methods for resolving differences of opinion. One study suggests that top management teams in Chinese high-technology firms prefer collaboration even more than compromising and avoiding. Collectivists may also be more interested in demonstrations of concern and working through third parties to resolve disputes, whereas individualists will be more likely to confront differences of opinion directly and openly.

Cross-cultural negotiations can create issues of trust.[26] One study of Indian and U.S. negotiators found that respondents reported having less trust in their cross-culture negotiation counterparts. The lower level of trust was associated with less discovery of common interests between parties, which occurred because cross-culture negotiators were less willing to disclose and solicit information. Another study found that both U.S. and Chinese negotiators tended to have an ingroup bias, which led them to favor negotiating partners from their own cultures. For Chinese negotiators, this was particularly true when accountability requirements were high.

Having considered conflict—its nature, causes, and consequences—we now turn to negotiation, which often resolves conflict.

⭐ WATCH IT

If your professor has assigned this, go to the Assignments section of **mymanagementlab.com** to complete the video exercise titled **Gordon Law Group: Conflict and Negotiation.**

NEGOTIATION

Negotiation permeates the interactions of almost everyone in groups and organizations. There's the obvious: Labor bargains with management. There's the not-so-obvious: managers negotiate with employees, peers, and bosses; salespeople negotiate with customers; purchasing agents negotiate with suppliers. Then there's the subtle: an employee agrees to cover for a colleague for a few minutes in exchange for a future favor. In today's loosely structured organizations, in which members often work with colleagues over whom they have no direct authority and with whom they may not even share a common boss, negotiation skills are critical.

We can define **negotiation** as a process that occurs when two or more parties decide how to allocate scarce resources.[27] Although we commonly think of the outcomes of negotiation in one-shot economic terms, like negotiating over the price of a car, every negotiation in organizations also affects the relationship between negotiators and the way negotiators feel about themselves.[28] Depending on how much the parties are going to interact with one another, sometimes maintaining the social relationship and behaving ethically will be just as important as achieving an immediate outcome of bargaining. Note that we use the terms *negotiation* and *bargaining* interchangeably.

Negotiation
A process in which two or more parties exchange goods or services and attempt to agree on the exchange rate for them.

Bargaining Strategies

There are two general approaches to negotiation—*distributive bargaining* and *integrative bargaining*.[29] As Exhibit 14-4 shows, they differ in their goals and motivation, focus, interests, information sharing, and duration of relationship. Let's define each and illustrate the differences.

Bargaining Characteristic	Distributive Bargaining	Integrative Bargaining
Goal	Get as much of the pie as possible	Expand the pie so that both parties are satisfied
Motivation	Win–lose	Win–win
Focus	Positions ("I can't go beyond this point on this issue.")	Interests ("Can you explain why this issue is so important to you?")
Interests	Opposed	Congruent
Information sharing	Low (Sharing information will only allow other party to take advantage)	High (Sharing information will allow each party to find ways to satisfy interests of each party)
Duration of relationship	Short term	Long term

EXHIBIT 14-4
Distributive Versus Integrative Bargaining

DISTRIBUTIVE BARGAINING   You see a used car advertised for sale online that looks great. You go see the car. It's perfect, and you want it. The owner tells you the asking price. You don't want to pay that much. The two of you negotiate. The negotiating strategy you're engaging in is called **distributive bargaining**. Its identifying feature is that it operates under zero-sum conditions—that is, any gain I make is at your expense, and vice versa (see Chapter 13). Every dollar you can get the seller to cut from the car's price is a dollar you save, and every dollar the seller can get from you comes at your expense. The essence of distributive bargaining is negotiating over who gets what share of a fixed pie. By **fixed pie**, we mean a set amount of goods or services to be divvied up. When the pie is fixed, or the parties believe it is, they tend to bargain distributively.

The essence of distributive bargaining is depicted in Exhibit 14-5. Parties A and B represent two negotiators. Each has a *target point* that defines what he or she would like to achieve. Each also has a *resistance point*, which marks the lowest acceptable outcome— the point beyond which the party would break off negotiations rather than accept a less favorable settlement. The area between these two points makes up each party's *aspiration range*. As long as there is some overlap between A's and B's aspiration ranges, there exists a settlement range in which each one's aspirations can be met.

When you are engaged in distributive bargaining, one of the best things you can do is make the first offer and make it an aggressive one. Making the first offer shows power; individuals in power are much more likely to make initial offers, speak first at meetings, and thereby gain the advantage. Another reason this is a good strategy is the anchoring bias, mentioned in Chapter 6. People tend to fixate on initial information. Once that anchoring point has been set, they fail to adequately adjust it based on subsequent information. A savvy negotiator sets an anchor with the initial offer, and scores of negotiation studies show that such anchors greatly favor the person who sets them.[30]

INTEGRATIVE BARGAINING   Jake was a Chicago luxury boutique owned by Jim Wetzel and Lance Lawson. In the early days of the business, Wetzel and Lawson moved millions of dollars of merchandise from many up-and-coming designers. They developed such a good rapport that many designers would send allotments to Jake without requiring advance payment. When the economy soured in 2008, Jake had trouble selling inventory, and designers were not being paid for what they had shipped to the store. Despite the fact that many designers were willing to work with the store on a delayed payment plan, Wetzel and Lawson stopped returning their calls. Lamented one designer, Doo-Ri Chung, "You kind of feel this familiarity with people who supported you for so long. When they have cash-flow issues, you want to make sure you are there for them as well."[31] Chung's attitude shows the promise of **integrative bargaining**. In contrast to distributive bargaining, integrative bargaining assumes that one or more of

Distributive bargaining
Negotiation that seeks to divide up a fixed amount of resources; a win–lose situation.

Fixed pie
The belief that there is only a set amount of goods or services to be divvied up between the parties.

Integrative bargaining
Negotiation that seeks one or more settlements that can create a win–win solution.

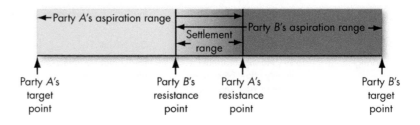

EXHIBIT 14-5
Staking Out the Bargaining Zone

Party A's aspiration range — Settlement range — Party B's aspiration range

Party A's target point — Party B's resistance point — Party A's resistance point — Party B's target point

the possible settlements can create a win–win solution. Of course, as the Jake example shows, both parties must be engaged for integrative bargaining to work.

CHOOSING BARGAINING METHODS In terms of intraorganizational behavior, integrative bargaining is preferable to distributive bargaining because the former builds long-term relationships. Integrative bargaining bonds negotiators and allows them to leave the bargaining table feeling they have achieved a victory. Distributive bargaining, however, leaves one party a loser. It tends to build animosity and deepen divisions when people have to work together on an ongoing basis. Research shows that over repeated bargaining episodes, a losing party who feels positively about the negotiation outcome is much more likely to bargain cooperatively in subsequent negotiations.

Why, then, don't we see more integrative bargaining in organizations? The answer lies in the conditions necessary for it to succeed. These include opposing parties who are open with information and candid about concerns, are sensitive to the other's needs and trust, and maintain flexibility. Because these conditions seldom exist in organizations, negotiations often take a win-at-any-cost dynamic.

Compromise and accommodation may be your worst enemy in negotiating a win–win agreement. Both reduce the pressure to bargain integratively. After all, if you or your opponent caves in easily, no one needs to be creative to reach a settlement. Consider a classic example in which two siblings are arguing over who gets an orange. Unknown to them, one sibling wants the orange to drink the juice, whereas the other wants the orange peel to bake a cake. If one capitulates and gives the other the orange, they will not be forced to explore their reasons for wanting the orange, and thus they will never find the win–win solution: They could *each* have the orange because they want different parts.

THE NEGOTIATION PROCESS

Exhibit 14-6 provides a simplified model of the negotiation process. It views negotiation as made up of five steps: (1) preparation and planning, (2) definition of ground rules,

EXHIBIT 14-6
The Negotiation Process

(3) clarification and justification, (4) bargaining and problem solving, and (5) closure and implementation.[32]

PREPARATION AND PLANNING   This may be the most important part of the process. Before you start negotiating, do your homework. What's the nature of the conflict? What's the history leading up to this negotiation? Who's involved and what are their perceptions of the conflict? Then consider your goals, in writing, with a range of outcomes from "most helpful" to "minimally acceptable." If you're a supply manager at Dell Computer, for instance, and your goal is to get a significant cost reduction from your keyboard supplier, make sure this goal stays paramount in discussions and doesn't get overshadowed by other issues. Next, assess what you think are the other party's goals. What intangible or hidden interests may be important to them? On what might they be willing to settle? Think carefully about what the other side might be willing to give up. People who underestimate their opponent's willingness to give on key issues before the negotiation even starts end up with lower outcomes.[33]

BATNA
The best alternative to a negotiated agreement; the least the individual should accept.

Once you've gathered your information, develop a strategy. You should determine your and the other side's **b**est **a**lternative **t**o a **n**egotiated **a**greement, or **BATNA**. Your BATNA determines the lowest value acceptable to you for a negotiated agreement. Any offer you receive that is higher than your BATNA is better than an impasse. Conversely, you shouldn't expect success in your negotiation effort unless you're able to make the other side an offer it finds more attractive than its BATNA.

In nearly all cases, the party with superior alternatives will do better in a negotiation, so experts advise negotiators to solidify their BATNA prior to any interaction.[34] Therefore, be equipped to counter arguments with facts and figures that support your position. There is an interesting exception to this general rule—negotiators with absolutely no alternative to a negotiated agreement sometimes "go for broke" since they don't even consider what would happen if the negotiation falls through.[35]

DEFINITION OF GROUND RULES   Once you've done your planning and developed a strategy, you're ready to define with the other party the ground rules and procedures of the negotiation itself. Who will do the negotiating? Where will it take place? What time constraints, if any, will apply? To what issues will negotiation be limited? Will you follow a specific procedure if an impasse is reached? During this phase, the parties will exchange their initial proposals or demands.

CLARIFICATION AND JUSTIFICATION   When you have exchanged initial positions, you and the other party will explain, amplify, clarify, bolster, and justify your original demands. This step needn't be confrontational. Rather, it's an opportunity for educating each other on the issues, why they are important, and how you arrived at your initial demands. Provide the other party with any documentation that supports your position.

BARGAINING AND PROBLEM SOLVING   The essence of the negotiation process is the actual give-and-take in trying to hash out an agreement. This is where both parties need to make concessions. Relationships change as a result of negotiation, so take that into consideration. If you could "win" a negotiation but push the other side into resentment or animosity, it might be wiser to pursue a more compromising style. If preserving the relationship will make you seem easily exploited, you may consider a more aggressive style. As an example of how the tone of a relationship in negotiations matters, people who feel good about the *process* of a job offer negotiation are more satisfied with their jobs and less likely to turn over a year later regardless of their actual *outcomes* from these negotiations.[36]

CLOSURE AND IMPLEMENTATION The final step in the negotiation process is formalizing your agreement and developing procedures necessary for implementing and monitoring it. For major negotiations—from labor–management negotiations to bargaining over lease terms—this requires hammering out the specifics in a formal contract. For other cases, closure of the negotiation process is nothing more formal than a handshake.

INDIVIDUAL DIFFERENCES IN NEGOTIATION EFFECTIVENESS

Are some people better negotiators than others? The answer is complex. Four factors influence how effectively individuals negotiate: personality, mood/emotions, culture, and gender.

PERSONALITY TRAITS IN NEGOTIATIONS Can you predict an opponent's negotiating tactics if you know something about his or her personality? Because personality and negotiation outcomes are related but only weakly, the answer is, at best, "sort of."[37] Most research has focused on the Big Five traits of agreeableness, for obvious reasons— agreeable individuals are cooperative, compliant, kind, and conflict-averse. We might think such characteristics make agreeable individuals easy prey in negotiations, especially distributive ones. The evidence suggests, however, that overall agreeableness is weakly related to negotiation outcomes.

Self-efficacy (see Chapter 7) is one individual-difference variable that consistently seems to relate to negotiation outcomes.[38] This is a fairly intuitive finding—it isn't too surprising to hear that those who believe they will be more successful in negotiation situations tend to perform more effectively. It may be that individuals who are more confident stake out stronger claims, are less likely to back down from their positions, and exhibit confidence that intimidates others. Although the exact mechanism is not yet clear, it does seem that negotiators may benefit from trying to get a boost in confidence before going to the bargaining table.

MOODS/EMOTIONS IN NEGOTIATIONS Do moods and emotions influence negotiation? They do, but the way they work depends on the emotion as well as the context. A negotiator who shows anger can induce concessions, for instance, because the other negotiator believes no further concessions from the angry party are possible. One factor that governs this outcome, however, is power—you should show anger in negotiations only if you have at least as much power as your counterpart. If you have less, showing anger actually seems to provoke "hardball" reactions from the other side.[39] "Faked" anger, or anger produced from surface acting, is not effective, but showing anger that is genuine (deep acting) is (see Chapter 4).[40] Having a history of showing anger, rather than sowing the seeds of revenge, actually induces more concessions because the other party perceives the negotiator as "tough."[41] Anger has a cultural context. For instance, one study found that when East Asian participants showed anger, it induced more concessions than when the negotiator expressing anger was from the United States or Europe, perhaps because of the stereotype of East Asians as refusing to show anger.[42]

Another relevant emotion is disappointment. Generally, a negotiator who perceives disappointment from his or her counterpart concedes more. Anxiety also may impact negotiation. For example, one study found that individuals who experienced more anxiety about a negotiation used more deceptions in dealing with others.[43] Another study found that anxious negotiators expect lower outcomes, respond to offers more quickly, and exit the bargaining process more quickly, leading them to obtain worse outcomes.[44] Even emotional unpredictability affects outcomes; researchers have found that negotiators who express positive and negative emotions in an unpredictable way extract more concessions because this behavior makes the other party feel less in control.[45] As one negotiator put it, "Out of the blue, you may have to react to something you have been working on in one way, and then something entirely new is introduced, and you have to veer off and refocus."[46]

CULTURE IN NEGOTIATIONS   Do people from different cultures negotiate differently? The simple answer is the obvious one: Yes, they do. In general, people negotiate more effectively within cultures than between them. For example, a Colombian is apt to do better negotiating with a Colombian than with a Sri Lankan.

It appears that for successful cross-cultural negotiations, it is especially important that the negotiators be high in openness. This suggests a good strategy is to choose cross-cultural negotiators who are high on openness, and it helps to avoid factors such as time pressure that tend to inhibit learning about the other party.[47] Second, because emotions are culturally sensitive, negotiators need to be especially aware of the emotional dynamics in cross-cultural negotiation. For example, individuals from East Asian cultures may feel that using anger to get their way in a negotiation is not a legitimate tactic, so they refuse to cooperate when their opponents become upset.[48]

GENDER IN NEGOTIATIONS   There are many areas of organizational behavior (OB) in which men and women are not that different. Negotiation is not one of them. It seems fairly clear that men and women negotiate differently, that men and women are treated differently by negotiation partners, and that these differences affect outcomes.

A popular stereotype is that women are more cooperative and pleasant in negotiations than men. Though this is controversial, there is some merit to it. Men tend to place a higher value on status, power, and recognition, whereas women tend to place a higher value on compassion and altruism. Moreover, women tend to value relationship outcomes more than men, and men tend to value economic outcomes more than women.[49]

These differences affect both negotiation behavior and negotiation outcomes. Compared to men, women tend to behave in a less assertive, less self-interested, and more accommodating manner. As one review concluded, women "are more reluctant to initiate negotiations, and when they do initiate negotiations, they ask for less, are more willing to accept [the] offer, and make more generous offers to their negotiation partners than men do."[50] A study of MBA students at Carnegie-Mellon University found that the male students took the step of negotiating their first offer 57 percent of the time, compared to 4 percent for the female students. The net result? A $4,000 difference in starting salaries.[51]

One comprehensive literature review suggested that the tendency for men to receive better negotiation outcomes in some situations did not cover *all* situations. Indeed, the evidence suggested women and men bargain more equally in certain situations, women sometimes outperform men, and both men and women obtain more nearly equal outcomes when negotiating on behalf of someone else.[52] In other words, everyone is better at advocating for others than they are at advocating for themselves. Factors that increased the predictability of negotiations also tended to reduce gender differences. When the range of negotiation settlements was well defined, men and women were more equal in outcomes. When more experienced negotiators were at the table, men and women were also nearly equivalent. The study authors proposed that when situations are more ambiguous, with less well-defined terms and less experienced negotiators, stereotypes may have stronger effects, leading to larger gender differences in outcomes.

NEGOTIATING IN A SOCIAL CONTEXT

We have mostly been discussing negotiations that occur among parties that meet only once, and in isolation from other individuals. However, in organizations, many negotiations are open-ended and public. When you are trying to figure out who in a work group should do a tedious task, negotiating with your boss to get a chance to travel internationally, or asking for more money for a project; there's a social component to the negotiation. You are probably negotiating with someone you already know and will work with again, and the negotiation and its outcome are likely to be topics people will talk about. To really understand negotiations in practice, then, we must consider the social factors of reputation and relationships.

Reputation

Your reputation is the way other people think and talk about you. When it comes to negotiation, having a reputation for being trustworthy matters. In short, trust in a negotiation process opens the door to many forms of integrative negotiation strategies that benefit both parties.[53] The most effective way to build trust is to behave in an honest way across repeated interactions. Then, others feel more comfortable making open-ended offers with many different outcomes. This helps to achieve win–win outcomes, since both parties can work to achieve what is most important to themselves while still benefiting the other party.

Sometimes we either trust or distrust people based on word-of-mouth about a person's characteristics. What characteristics help a person develop a trustworthy reputation? A combination of competence and integrity.[54] Negotiators higher in self-confidence and cognitive ability are seen as more competent by negotiation partners.[55] They are also considered better able to accurately describe a situation and their own resources, and are more credible when they make suggestions for creative solutions to impasses. Individuals who have a reputation for integrity can also be more effective in negotiations.[56] They are seen as more likely to keep their promises and present information accurately, so others are more willing to accept their promises as part of a bargain. This opens many options for the negotiator that wouldn't be available to someone who is not seen as trustworthy. Finally, individuals who have higher reputations are better liked and have more friends and allies—in other words, they have more social resources, which may give them more understood power in negotiations.

Relationships

There is more to repeated negotiations than just reputation. The social, interpersonal component of relationships with repeated negotiations means that individuals go beyond valuing what is simply good for themselves and instead start to think about what is best for the other party and the relationship as a whole.[57] Repeated negotiations built on a foundation of trust also broaden the range of options, since a favor or concession today can be offered in return for some repayment further down the road.[58] Repeated negotiations also facilitate integrative problem solving. This occurs partly because people begin to see their negotiation partners in a more personal way over time and come to share emotional bonds.[59] Repeated negotiations also make integrative approaches more workable because a sense of trust and reliability has been built up.[60]

THIRD-PARTY NEGOTIATIONS

To this point, we've discussed bargaining in terms of direct negotiations. Occasionally, however, individuals or group representatives reach a stalemate and are unable to resolve their differences through direct negotiations. In such cases, they may turn to a third party to help them find a solution. There are three basic third-party roles: mediator, arbitrator, and conciliator.

mediator
A neutral third party who facilitates a negotiated solution by using reasoning, persuasion, and suggestions for alternatives.

A **mediator** is a neutral third party who facilitates a negotiated solution by using reasoning and persuasion, suggesting alternatives, and the like. Mediators are widely used in labor–management negotiations and in civil court disputes. Their overall effectiveness is fairly impressive. For example, the Equal Employment Opportunity Commission (EEOC) reported a settlement rate through mediation at 72.1 percent.[61] But the situation is the key to whether mediation will succeed; the conflicting parties must be motivated to bargain and resolve their conflict. In addition, conflict intensity can't be too high; mediation is most effective under moderate levels of conflict. Finally, perceptions of the mediator are important; to be effective, the mediator must be perceived as neutral and noncoercive.

Arbitrator
A third party to a negotiation who has the authority to dictate an agreement.

An **arbitrator** is a third party with the authority to dictate an agreement. Arbitration can be voluntary (requested by the parties) or compulsory (forced on the parties by law or contract). The big plus of arbitration over mediation is that it always results in a settlement. Whether there is a downside depends on how heavy-handed the arbitrator appears. If one party is left feeling overwhelmingly defeated, that party is certain to be dissatisfied and the conflict may resurface at a later time.

A **conciliator** is a trusted third party who provides an informal communication link between the negotiator and the opponent. This role was made famous by Robert Duval in the first *Godfather* film. As Don Corleone's adopted son and a lawyer by training, Duval acted as an intermediary between the Corleones and the other Mafioso families. Comparing conciliation to mediation in terms of effectiveness has proven difficult because the two overlap a great deal. In practice, conciliators typically act as more than mere communication conduits. They also engage in fact-finding, interpreting messages, and persuading disputants to develop agreements.

Conciliator
A trusted third party who provides an informal communication link between the negotiator and the opponent.

SUMMARY

While many people assume conflict lowers group and organizational performance, this assumption is frequently incorrect. Conflict can be either constructive or destructive to the functioning of a group or unit. Levels of conflict can be either too high or too low to be constructive. Either extreme hinders performance. An optimal level is one that prevents stagnation, stimulates creativity, allows tensions to be released, and initiates the seeds of change without being disruptive or preventing the coordination of activities.

IMPLICATIONS FOR MANAGERS

- Choose an authoritarian management style in emergencies, when unpopular actions need to be implemented (such as cost cutting, enforcement of unpopular rules, and discipline), and when the issue is vital to the organization's welfare. Be certain to communicate your logic when possible to make certain others remain engaged and productive.
- Seek integrative solutions when your objective is to learn, when you want to merge insights from people with different perspectives, when you need to gain commitment by incorporating concerns into a consensus, and when you need to work through feelings that have interfered with a relationship.
- You can build trust by accommodating others when you find you're wrong, when you need to demonstrate reasonableness, when other positions need to be heard, when issues are more important to others than to yourself, when you want to satisfy others and maintain cooperation, when you can build social credits for later issues, to minimize loss when you are outmatched and losing, and when others should learn from their own mistakes.
- Consider compromising when goals are important but not worth potential disruption, when opponents with equal power are committed to mutually exclusive goals, and when you need temporary settlements to complex issues.
- Distributive bargaining can resolve disputes, but it often reduces the satisfaction of one or more negotiators because it is confrontational and focused on the short term. Integrative bargaining, in contrast, tends to provide outcomes that satisfy all parties and build lasting relationships.

PERSONAL INVENTORY ASSESSMENTS

⭐ PERSONAL INVENTORY ASSESSMENTS

Strategies for Handling Conflict

We all handle conflict, but few of us may have actual strategies in place. Take this PIA to further explore ways to handle conflict.

14-1. Do you think employee conflicts are, in general, bad? Why? In what ways do you think they might be constructive?

15

Foundations of Organization Structure

MyManagementLab®

⭐ Improve Your Grade!

When you see this icon ⭐, visit **mymanagementlab.com** for activities that are applied, personalized, and offer immediate feedback.

LEARNING OBJECTIVES

After studying this chapter, you should be able to:

1. Identify seven elements of an organization's structure.
2. Identify the characteristics of the functional structure, the divisional structure, and the matrix structure.
3. Identify the characteristics of the virtual structure, the team structure, and the circular structure.
4. Describe the effects of downsizing on organizational structures and employees.
5. Contrast the reasons for mechanistic and organic structural models.
6. Analyze the behavioral implications of different organizational designs.

⭐ Chapter Warm-up

If your professor has chosen to assign this, go to the Assignments section of **mymanagementlab.com** to complete the chapter warm-up.

WHAT IS ORGANIZATIONAL STRUCTURE?

**Organizational
structure**
The way in which
job tasks are formally
divided, grouped, and
coordinated.

Have you ever noticed how different work situations affect people's behavior? We know
that not all situations are equally conducive to effective organizational behavior (OB).
Careful analysis reveals that the structure of an organization has a large impact on behavior. An **organizational structure** defines how job tasks are formally divided, grouped,
and coordinated. Managers should address seven key elements when they design their organization's structure: work specialization, departmentalization, chain of command, span
of control, centralization and decentralization, formalization, and boundary spanning.[1]
Exhibit 15-1 presents each element as the answer to an important structural question, and
the following sections describe them.

Work Specialization

Work specialization
The degree to
which tasks in an
organization are
subdivided into
separate jobs.

Early in the twentieth century, Henry Ford became rich by building automobiles on an assembly line. Every worker was assigned a specific, specialized task such as putting on the
right front door. By dividing jobs into small standardized tasks that could be performed
repeatedly and quickly, the Ford Motor Company was able to produce a car every 10 seconds, using employees with relatively limited skills. **Work specialization**, or *division of
labor*, describes the degree to which activities in any organization are divided into separate jobs. The essence of work specialization is to divide a job into a number of steps, each
completed by a separate individual. Individuals thus specialize in doing part of an activity
rather than the entirety. Overall, specialization is a means of making the most efficient use
of employee skills and even successfully improving them through repetition. Less time
is spent changing tasks, putting away tools and equipment from a prior step, and getting
ready for another.

By the 1960s, it increasingly seemed that the good news of specialization could be
carried too far. Human diseconomies began to surface in the form of boredom, fatigue,
stress, low productivity, poor quality, increased absenteeism, and high turnover, which

**EXHIBIT 15-1
Key Design
Questions
and Answers
for Designing
the Proper
Organizational
Structure**

The Key Question	The Answer Is Provided by
1. To what degree are activities subdivided into separate jobs?	Work specialization
2. On what basis will jobs be grouped together?	Departmentalization
3. To whom do individuals and groups report?	Chain of command
4. How many individuals can a manager efficiently and effectively direct?	Span of control
5. Where does decision-making authority lie?	Centralization and decentralization
6. To what degree will there be rules and regulations to direct employees and managers?	Formalization
7. Do individuals from different areas need to regularly interact?	Boundary spanning

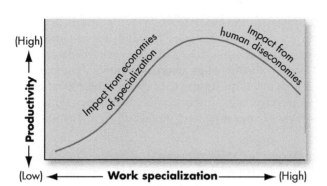

EXHIBIT 15-2
Economies and
Diseconomies
of Work
Specialization

more than offset the economic advantages (see Exhibit 15-2). Managers could increase productivity now by enlarging, rather than narrowing, the scope of job activities. Giving employees a variety of activities to do, allowing them to do a whole and complete job, and putting them into teams with interchangeable skills often achieved significantly higher output, with increased employee satisfaction.

Most managers today recognize the economies specialization provides in certain jobs and the problems when it's carried too far. Wherever job roles can be broken down into specific tasks or projects, specialization is possible. As you may have guessed, specialization is often used in manufacturing, but may confer new advantages outside manufacturing, particularly where job sharing and part-time work are prevalent.[2] Amazon's Mechanical Turk program, TopCoder, and others like it have facilitated a new trend in microspecialization in which extremely small pieces of programming, data processing, or evaluation tasks are delegated to a global network of individuals by a program manager who then assembles the results.[3] Thus, whereas specialization of yesteryear focused on breaking manufacturing tasks into specific duties within the same plant, today's specialization judiciously breaks complex tasks into specific elements by technology, expertise, and region. Yet the core principle is the same.

Departmentalization

Once jobs have been divided through work specialization, they must be grouped so common tasks can be coordinated. The basis by which jobs are grouped is called **departmentalization**.

Departmentalization
The basis by which jobs in an organization are grouped together.

FUNCTIONAL DEPARTMENTALIZATION One of the most popular ways to group activities is by the *functions* performed. A manufacturing manager might organize a plant into engineering, accounting, manufacturing, human resources (HR), and supply chain departments. A hospital might have departments for research, surgery, intensive care, accounting, and so forth. The major advantage of this type of functional departmentalization is efficiencies gained from putting like specialists together.

PRODUCT OR SERVICE DEPARTMENTALIZATION We can also departmentalize jobs by the type of *product* or *service* the organization produces. Procter & Gamble places each major product—such as Tide, Pampers, Charmin, and Pringles—under an executive who has complete global responsibility for it. The major advantage here is increased accountability for performance because all activities related to a specific product or service are under the direction of a single manager.

GEOGRAPHICAL DEPARTMENTALIZATION   When a firm is departmentalized on the basis of *geography* (or territory); the sales function, for instance, may have western, southern, midwestern, and eastern regions which are each a department organized around geography. This form is valuable when an organization's customers are scattered over a large geographic area and have similar needs within their locations. For this reason, Toyota changed its management structure into geographic regions "so that they may develop and deliver ever better products," said CEO Akio Toyoda.[4]

PROCESS AND CUSTOMER DEPARTMENTALIZATION   *Process* departmentalization works for processing customers as well as products. If you've ever been to a state motor vehicle office to get a driver's license, you probably went through several departments before receiving your license. In one typical state, applicants go through three steps, each handled by a separate department: (1) validation by the motor vehicles division, (2) processing by the licensing department, and (3) payment collection by the treasury department. A final category of departmentalization uses the particular type of *customer* the organization seeks to reach.

IMPLICATIONS FOR OB   Interestingly, organizations do not always stay with the basis of departmentalization they first adopt. Microsoft, for instance, used customer departmentalization for years, organizing around its customer bases: consumers, large corporations, software developers, and small businesses. However, in a June 2013 letter from CEO Steve Ballmer to all employees, he announced a restructuring to functional departmentalization, citing a need to foster continuing innovation. The new departments grouped jobs by traditional functions including engineering, marketing, business development, strategy and research, finance, HR, and legal.[5]

Ballmer expected the change in Microsoft's organizational structure would "re-shape how we interact with our customers, developers, and key innovation partners, delivering a more coherent message and family of product offerings."[6] As we see throughout this text, whenever changes are deliberately made in organizations to align practices with organizational goals, particularly the goals of strong leaders, a good execution of the changes creates a much higher probability for improvement. In Microsoft's case, the results are not yet determined—Ballmer, who is a strong leader, announced his retirement two months later (he officially left Microsoft in 2014), and further changes ensued. Microsoft continued to struggle with the reorganization, announcing further changes in its leadership personnel and team structure less than a year later.[7]

Chain of command
The unbroken line of authority that extends from the top of the organization to the lowest echelon and clarifies who reports to whom.

Chain of Command

While the chain of command was once a basic cornerstone in the design of organizations, it has far less importance today. But managers should still consider its implications, particularly in industries that deal with potential life-or-death situations when people need to quickly rely on decision makers. The **chain of command** is an unbroken line of authority that extends from the top of the organization to the lowest echelon and clarifies who reports to whom.

Authority
The rights inherent in a managerial position to give orders and to expect the orders to be obeyed.

AUTHORITY   We can't discuss the chain of command without also discussing *authority* and *unity of command*. **Authority** refers to the rights inherent in a managerial position to give orders and expect them to be obeyed. To facilitate coordination, each managerial position is given a place in the chain of command, and each manager is given a degree of authority in order to meet his or her responsibilities.

UNITY OF COMMAND   The principle of **unity of command** helps preserve the concept of an unbroken line of authority. It says a person should have one and only one superior to whom he or she is directly responsible. If the unity of command is broken, an employee might have to cope with conflicting demands or priorities from several superiors, as is often the case in organization charts' dotted-line reporting relationships depicting an employee's accountability to multiple managers.

Unity of command
The idea that a subordinate should have only one superior to whom he or she is directly responsible.

IMPLICATIONS FOR OB   Times change, and so do the basic tenets of organizational design. A low-level employee today can access information in seconds that was available only to top managers a generation ago, and many employees are empowered to make decisions previously reserved for management. Add the popularity of self-managed and cross-functional teams as well as structural designs that include multiple bosses, and you can see why authority and unity of command may appear to hold less relevance. Yet many organizations still find they can be most productive by enforcing the chain of command. Indeed, one survey of more than 1,000 managers found that 59 percent agreed with the statement, "There is an imaginary line in my company's organizational chart. Strategy is created by people above this line, while strategy is executed by people below the line."[8] However, this same survey found that lower-level employees' buy-in (agreement and active support) to the organization's overall, big picture strategy was inhibited by their reliance on the hierarchy for decision making.

Span of Control

How many employees can a manager efficiently and effectively direct? The **span of control** describes the number of levels and managers an organization has. All things being equal, the wider or larger the span, with fewer levels and more employees at each level, the more efficient the organization can be.

Span of control
The number of subordinates a manager can efficiently and effectively direct.

Assume two organizations each have about 4,100 operative-level employees. One has a uniform span of 4 and the other a span of 8. As Exhibit 15-3 illustrates, the wider

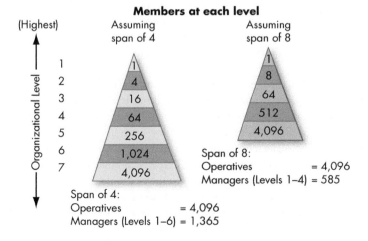

EXHIBIT 15-3

Contrasting Spans of Control

span of 8 will have two fewer levels and approximately 800 fewer managers. If the average manager makes $50,000 a year, the wider span will save $40 million a year in management salaries! Obviously, wider spans are more efficient in terms of cost. However, at some point when supervisors no longer have time to provide subordinates with the necessary leadership and support, effectiveness declines and employee performance suffers.

Narrow or small spans have their advocates. Narrow spans of control with, perhaps, five or six members are sometimes preferred to minimize ambiguity, but narrow spans have three major drawbacks. First, they're expensive because they add levels of management. Second, they make vertical communication in the organization more complex. The added levels of hierarchy slow down decision making and can isolate upper management. Third, narrow spans encourage overly tight supervision and discourage employee autonomy.

The trend in recent years has been toward wider spans of control. They're consistent with firms' efforts to reduce costs, cut overhead, speed decision making, increase flexibility, get closer to customers, and empower employees. However, to ensure performance doesn't suffer because of these wider spans, organizations have been investing heavily in employee training. Managers recognize they can handle a wider span best when employees know their jobs inside and out or can turn to coworkers with questions.

Centralization and Decentralization

Centralization
The degree to which decision making is concentrated at a single point in an organization.

Decentralized decision making
The degree to which decision making is pushed down to the managers closest to the action or to workgroups.

Centralization refers to the degree to which decision making is concentrated at a single point in the organization. In *centralized* organizations, top managers make all the decisions, and lower-level managers merely carry out their directives. In organizations at the other extreme, *decentralized* **decision making** is pushed down to the managers closest to the action or to workgroups. The concept of centralization includes only formal authority—that is, the rights inherent to a position.

IMPLICATIONS FOR OB   An organization characterized by centralization is different structurally from one that's decentralized. A decentralized organization can act more quickly to solve problems, more people provide input into decisions, and employees are less likely to feel alienated from those who make decisions that affect their work lives. The effects of centralization and decentralization can be predicted: centralized organizations are better for avoiding commission errors (bad choices), while decentralized organizations are better for avoiding omission errors (lost opportunities).[9]

Management efforts to make organizations more flexible and responsive have produced a trend toward decentralized decision making by lower-level managers, who are closer to the action and typically have more detailed knowledge about problems than top managers. For example, Sears and JCPenney have given their store managers considerably more discretion in choosing what merchandise to stock in individual stores. This allows the stores to compete more effectively against local merchants. Similarly, when Procter & Gamble empowered small groups of employees to make decisions about new-product development independent of the usual hierarchy, it was able to rapidly increase the proportion of new products ready for market.[10] Concerning creativity, research investigating a large number of Finnish organizations demonstrated that companies with decentralized research and development (R&D) offices in multiple locations were better at producing innovation than companies that centralized all R&D in a single office.[11]

Decentralization is often necessary for companies with offshore sites because localized decision making is needed to respond to each region's profit opportunities, client base, and specific laws, while centralized oversight is needed to hold regional managers accountable. Failure to successfully balance these priorities can harm not only the organization, but also its relationships with foreign governments.[12]

Formalization

Formalization refers to the degree to which jobs within the organization are standardized. If a job is highly formalized, the employee has a minimal amount of discretion over what to do and when and how to do it, resulting in consistent and uniform output. There are explicit job descriptions, lots of organizational rules, and clearly defined procedures covering work processes. Formalization not only eliminates the possibility of employees engaging in alternative behaviors; it removes the need for them to consider alternatives. Conversely, where formalization is low, job behaviors are relatively unprogrammed and employees have a great deal of freedom to exercise discretion in their work.

> **Formalization**
> The degree to which jobs within an organization are standardized.

The degree of formalization can vary widely between and within organizations. Research from 94 high-technology Chinese firms indicated that formalization is a detriment to team flexibility in decentralized organization structures, suggesting that formalization does not work as well where duties are inherently interactive, or where there is a need to be flexible and innovative.[13] For example, publishing representatives who call on college professors to inform them of their company's new publications have a great deal of freedom in their jobs. They have only a general sales pitch, which they tailor as needed, and rules and procedures governing their behavior may be little more than suggestions on what to emphasize about forthcoming titles and the requirement to submit a weekly sales report. At the other extreme, clerical and editorial employees in the same publishing houses may need to be at their desks by 8:00 A.M. and follow a set of precise procedures dictated by management.

Boundary Spanning

We've described ways that organizations create well-defined task structures and chains of authority. These systems facilitate control and coordination for specific tasks, but if there is too much division within an organization, attempts to coordinate across groups can be disastrous. One way to overcome compartmentalization and retain the positive elements of structure is to encourage or create boundary-spanning roles.

Within a single organization, **boundary spanning** occurs when individuals form relationships with people outside their formally assigned groups. An HR executive who frequently engages with the IT group is engaged in boundary spanning, as is a member of an R&D team who implements ideas from a production team. These activities help prevent formal structures from becoming too rigid and, not surprisingly, enhance organization and team creativity.[14]

> **Boundary spanning**
> When individuals form relationships outside their formally assigned groups.

Organizations can use formal mechanisms to facilitate boundary-spanning activities through their structures. One method is to assign formal liaison roles or develop committees of individuals from different areas of the organization. Development activities can also facilitate boundary spanning. Employees with experience in multiple functions, such as accounting and marketing, are more likely to engage in boundary spanning.[15] Many organizations try to set the stage for these sorts of positive relationships by creating job rotation programs so new hires get a better sense of different areas of the organization. A final method to encourage boundary spanning is to bring attention to overall organizational goals and shared identity concepts.

Boundary-spanning activities occur not only within but also between organizations. Gathering information from external knowledge sources is especially advantageous in highly innovative industries where keeping up with the competition is challenging. Positive results are especially strong in organizations that encourage extensive internal communication; in other words, external boundary spanning is most effective when it is followed up with internal boundary spanning.[16]

COMMON ORGANIZATIONAL FRAMEWORKS AND STRUCTURES

Organizational designs are known by many names and are constantly evolving in response to changes in the way work is done. We start with three of the more common organizational frameworks: the *simple structure*, the *bureaucracy*, and the *matrix structure*.

The Simple Structure

What do a small retail store, an electronics firm run by a hard-driving entrepreneur, and an airline's "war room" in the midst of a pilot's strike have in common? They probably all use the **simple structure**.

Simple structure
An organization structure characterized by a low degree of departmentalization, wide spans of control, authority centralized in a single person, and little formalization.

The simple structure has a low degree of departmentalization, wide spans of control, authority centralized in a single person, and little formalization. It is a flat organization; it usually has only two or three vertical levels, a loose body of employees, and one individual with decision-making authority. Most companies start as a simple structure, and many innovative technology-based firms with short life spans, like cell phone app development firms, remain compact by design.[17]

Consider a retail men's store owned and managed by Jack Gold. Jack employs five full-time salespeople, a cashier, and extra workers for weekends and holidays, but he runs the show. Though this is typical for a small business, in times of crisis large companies often simplify their structures (though not to this degree) as a means of focusing their resources.

The strength of the simple structure lies in its simplicity. It's fast, flexible, inexpensive to operate, and accountability is clear. One major weakness is that it becomes increasingly inadequate as an organization grows because its low formalization and high centralization tend to create information overload at the top. Decision making typically becomes slower as the single executive tries to continue doing it all. This proves the undoing of many small businesses. If the structure isn't changed and made more elaborate, the firm often loses momentum and can eventually fail. The simple structure's other weakness is that it's risky—everything depends on one person. An illness at the top can literally halt the organization's information and decision-making capabilities.

The Bureaucracy

Standardization! That's the key concept that underlies all bureaucracies. Consider the bank where you keep your checking account, the store where you buy clothes, or the government offices that collect your taxes, enforce health regulations, or provide local fire protection. They all rely on standardized work processes for coordination and control.

The **bureaucracy** is characterized by highly routine operating tasks achieved through specialization, strictly formalized rules and regulations, tasks grouped into units, centralized authority, narrow spans of control, and decision making that follows the chain of command. Bureaucracy incorporates all the strongest degrees of departmentalization described earlier.

Bureaucracy is a dirty word in many people's minds. However, it does have advantages, primarily the ability to perform standardized activities in a highly efficient manner. Putting like specialties together in units results in economies of scale, minimum duplication of people and equipment, and a common language employees all share. Bureaucracies can get by with less talented—and hence less costly—middle- and lower-level managers because rules and regulations substitute for managerial discretion. There is little need for innovative and experienced decision makers below the level of senior executives.

Listen in on a dialogue among four executives in one company: "You know, nothing happens in this place until we *produce* something," said the production executive. "Wrong," commented the R&D manager, "Nothing happens until we *design* something!" "What are you talking about?" asked the marketing executive, "Nothing happens until we *sell* something!" The exasperated accounting manager responded, "It doesn't matter what you produce, design, or sell. No one knows what happens until we *tally up the results*!" This conversation highlights that bureaucratic specialization can create conflicts in which the unit perspectives override the overall goals of the organization.

The other major weakness of a bureaucracy is something we've all witnessed: obsessive concern with following the rules. When cases don't precisely fit the rules, there is no room for modification. The bureaucracy is efficient only as long as employees confront familiar problems with programmed decision rules. There are two aspects of bureaucracies we should explore: functional and divisional structures.

Bureaucracy
An organization structure with highly routine operating tasks achieved through specialization, very formalized rules and regulations, tasks that are grouped into functional departments, centralized authority, narrow spans of control, and decision making that follows the chain of command.

THE FUNCTIONAL STRUCTURE The **functional structure** groups employees by their similar specialties, roles, or tasks.[18] An organization structured into production, marketing, HR, and accounting departments is an example. Many large organizations utilize this structure, although this is evolving to allow for quick changes in response to business opportunities. Still, there are advantages, including that the functional structure allows specialists to become experts more easily than if they worked in diversified units. Employees can also be motivated by a clear career path to the top of the organization chart specific to their specialties.

The functional structure works well if the organization is focused on one product or service. Unfortunately, it creates rigid, formal communications because the hierarchy dictates the communication protocol. Coordination among many units is a problem, and infighting in units and between units can lead to reduced motivation.

Functional structure
An organization structure that groups employees by their similar specialties, roles, or tasks.

Divisional structure
An organization structure that groups employees into units by product, service, customer, or geographical market area.

THE DIVISIONAL STRUCTURE The **divisional structure** groups employees into units by product, service, customer, or geographical market area.[19] It is highly departmentalized. Sometimes this structure is known by the type of division structure it uses: *product/service organizational structure* (like units for cat food, dog food, and bird food that report to an animal food producer); *customer organizational structure* (like units for outpatient care, inpatient care, and pharmacy that report to hospital administration); or *geographic organizational structure* (like units for Europe, Asia, and South America that report to corporate headquarters).[20]

The divisional structure has the opposite benefits and disadvantages of the functional structure. It facilitates coordination in units to achieve on-time completion, budget targets, and development and introduction of new products to market, while addressing the specific concerns of each unit. It provides clear responsibility for all activities related to a product, but with duplication of functions and costs. Sometimes this is helpful, say when the organization has a unit in Spain and another in China, and a marketing strategy is needed for a new product. Marketing experts in both places can incorporate the appropriate cultural perspectives into their region's marketing campaigns. However, having marketing function employees in two different countries may represent an increased cost for the organization, in that they are doing basically the same task in two different places.

The Matrix Structure

Matrix structure
An organization structure that creates dual lines of authority and combines functional and product departmentalization.

The **matrix structure** combines the functional and product structures, and we find it in advertising agencies, aerospace firms, R&D laboratories, construction companies, hospitals, government agencies, universities, management consulting firms, and entertainment companies.[21] Companies that use matrix-like structures include ABB, Boeing, BMW, IBM, and P&G.

The most obvious structural characteristic of the matrix is that it breaks the unity-of-command concept. Employees in the matrix have two bosses: their functional department managers and their product managers. Exhibit 15-4 shows the matrix for a college of business administration. The academic departments of accounting, decision and information systems, marketing, and so forth are functional

Programs Academic Departments	Undergraduate	Master's	Ph.D.	Research	Executive Development	Community Service
Accounting						
Finance						
Decision and Information Systems						
Management						
Marketing						

EXHIBIT 15-4
Matrix Structure for a College of Business Administration

units. Overlaid on them are specific programs (that is, products). Thus, members in a matrix structure have a dual chain of command: to their functional department and to their product groups. A professor of accounting teaching an undergraduate course may report to the director of undergraduate programs as well as to the chairperson of the accounting department.

The strength of the matrix is its ability to facilitate coordination when the organization has a number of complex and interdependent activities. The matrix reduces "bureau-pathologies"—its dual lines of authority limit people's tendency to protect their territories at the expense of the organization's goals.[22] The major disadvantages of the matrix lie in the confusion it creates, its tendency to foster power struggles, and the stress it places on individuals.[23] Without the unity-of-command concept, ambiguity about who reports to whom is significantly increased and often leads to conflict and power struggles between functional and product managers.

ALTERNATE DESIGN OPTIONS

In the ever-increasing trend toward flatter structures, many organizations have been developing new options with fewer layers of hierarchy and more emphasis on opening the boundaries of the organization.[24] In this section, we describe three such designs: the *virtual structure*, the *team structure*, and the *circular structure.*

The Virtual Structure

Why own when you can rent? That question captures the essence of the **virtual structure** (also sometimes called the *network*, or *modular*, structure), typically a small, core organization that outsources its major business functions.[25] The virtual structure is highly centralized, with little or no departmentalization.

Exhibit 15-5 shows a virtual structure in which management outsources all the primary functions of the business. The core of the organization is a small group of executives

Virtual structure
A small, core organization that outsources major business functions.

**EXHIBIT 15-5
A Virtual
Organization**

whose job is to oversee directly any activities done in-house and to coordinate relationships with organizations that manufacture, distribute, and perform other crucial functions. The dotted lines represent the relationships typically maintained under contracts. In essence, managers in virtual structures spend most of their time coordinating and controlling external relations.

The major advantage of the virtual structure is its flexibility, which allows individuals with an innovative idea and little money to successfully compete against larger, more established organizations. The structure also saves a great deal of money by eliminating permanent offices and hierarchical roles.[26] On the other hand, the drawbacks have become increasingly clear as popularity has grown.[27] Virtual organizations are in a state of perpetual flux and reorganization, which means roles, goals, and responsibilities are unclear, setting the stage for political behavior. Cultural alignment and shared goals can be lost because of the low degree of interaction among members. Team members who are geographically dispersed and communicate infrequently find it difficult to share information and knowledge, which can limit innovation and slow response time. Ironically, some virtual organizations are less adaptable and innovative than those with well-established communication and collaboration networks.

The Team Structure

Team structure
An organization structure that replaces departments with empowered teams, and which eliminates horizontal boundaries and external barriers between customers and suppliers.

The **team structure** seeks to eliminate the chain of command and replace departments with empowered teams.[28] This structure removes vertical and horizontal boundaries in addition to breaking down external barriers between the company and its customers and suppliers.

By removing vertical boundaries, management flattens the hierarchy and minimizes status and rank. Cross-hierarchical teams (which include top executives, middle managers, supervisors, and operative employees), participative decision-making practices, and the use of 360-degree performance appraisals (in which peers and others evaluate performance) can be used. For example, at the Danish firm Oticon A/S, the world's largest hearing aid manufacturer, all traces of hierarchy have disappeared. Everyone works at uniform mobile workstations, and project teams, not functions or departments, coordinate work.

When fully operational, the team structure may break down geographic barriers. Today, most large U.S. companies see themselves as team-oriented global corporations; many, like Coca-Cola and McDonald's, do as much business overseas as in the United States, and some struggle to incorporate geographic regions into their structure. In other cases, the team approach is need-based. Such is the case with Chinese companies that, together, made 93 acquisitions in the oil and gas industry in five years—incorporating each acquisition as a new team unit—to meet forecasted demand their resources in China could not meet.[29] The team structure provides a solution because it considers geography as more of a tactical, logistical issue than a structural one. In short, the goal may be to break down cultural barriers and open opportunities.

Some organizations create teams incorporating their employees and their customers or suppliers. For example, to ensure important product parts are reliably made to exacting specifications by its suppliers, Honeywell International partners some of its engineers with managers at those suppliers.

The Circular Structure

Picture the concentric rings of an archery target. In the center are the executives; radiating outward in rings grouped by function are the managers, then the specialists, then the workers. This is the **circular structure**.[30] Does it seem like organizational anarchy? Actually, there is still a hierarchy, but top management is at the very heart of the organization, with its vision spreading outward.

The circular structure has intuitive appeal for creative entrepreneurs, and some small innovative firms have claimed it. However, as in many of the current hybrid approaches, employees are apt to be unclear about whom they report to and who is running the show. We are still likely to see the popularity of the circular structure spread. The concept may have intuitive appeal for spreading a vision of corporate social responsibility (CSR) initiatives, for instance.

Circular structure An organization structure in which executives are at the center, spreading their vision outward in rings grouped by function (managers, then specialists, then workers).

THE LEANER ORGANIZATION: DOWNSIZING

The goal of some organizational structures we've described is to improve agility by creating a lean, focused, and flexible organization. *Downsizing* is a systematic effort to make an organization leaner by closing locations, reducing staff, or selling off business units that don't add value. Downsizing doesn't necessarily mean physically shrinking the size of your office, although that's been happening, too.

Some firms downsize to direct all their efforts toward their core competencies. American Express claims to have been doing this in a series of layoffs over more than a decade: 7,700 jobs in 2001; 6,500 jobs in 2002; 7,000 jobs (10 percent of its workforce) in 2008; 4,000 jobs in 2009. The 2013 cut of 5,400 jobs (8.5 percent of the remaining workforce) represented "its biggest retrenchment in a decade." An additional layoff of 4,000 jobs was slated for 2015. Each layoff was accompanied by a restructuring to reflect changing customer preferences, away from personal customer service and toward online customer service. According to CEO Ken Chennault, "Our business and industry continue to become transformed by technology. As a result of these changes, we have the need and the opportunity to evolve our organization and cost structure."[31]

Despite the advantages of being a lean organization, the impact of downsizing on organizational performance is not without controversy. Reducing the size of the workforce has an immediately positive outcome in the form of lower wage costs, and companies downsizing to improve strategic focus often see positive effects on stock prices after the announcement. An example is Russia's Gorky Automobile Factory (GAZ), which realized a profit for the first time in many years after President Bo Andersson fired 50,000 workers, half the workforce.[32] On the other hand, among companies that only cut employees but don't restructure, profits and stock prices usually decline. Part of the problem is the effect of downsizing on employee attitudes. Employees who remain often feel worried about future layoffs and may be less committed to the organization. Stress reactions can lead to increased sickness absences, lower concentration on the job, and lower creativity. Downsizing can also lead to more voluntary turnover, so vital human capital is lost. The result is a company that is more anemic than lean.

In short, companies that make themselves lean can be more agile, efficient, and productive—but only if they make cuts carefully and help employees through the process through investing in people, communicating more, inviting employee participation, and assisting dislocated employees.

WHY DO STRUCTURES DIFFER?

Mechanistic model
A structure characterized by extensive departmentalization, high formalization, a limited information network, and centralization.

Organic model
A structure that is flat, uses cross-hierarchical and cross-functional teams, has low formalization, possesses a comprehensive information network, and relies on participative decision making.

We've described many organization design options. Exhibit 15-6 recaps our discussions by presenting two extreme models of organizational design. One we call the **mechanistic model**. It's generally synonymous with the bureaucracy in that it has highly standardized processes for work, high formalization, and more managerial hierarchy. The other extreme is the **organic model**. It's flat, has fewer formal procedures for making decisions, has multiple decision makers, and favors flexible practices.[33]

With these two models in mind, let's ask a few questions: Why are some organizations structured along more mechanistic lines whereas others follow organic characteristics? What forces influence the choice of design? In this section, we present major causes or determinants of an organization's structure.[34]

Organizational Strategies

Because structure is a means to achieve objectives, and objectives derive from the organization's overall strategy, it's only logical that structure should follow strategy. If management significantly changes the organization's strategy or its values, the structure must also change to accommodate. For example, recent research indicates that aspects of organizational culture may influence the success of CSR initiatives.[35] If the culture is supported by the structure, the initiatives are more likely to have clear

The Mechanistic Model

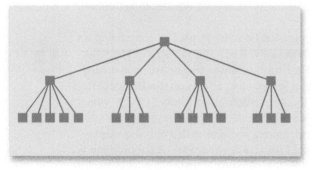

- High specialization
- Rigid departmentalization
- Clear chain of command
- Narrow spans of control
- Centralization
- High formalization

The Organic Model

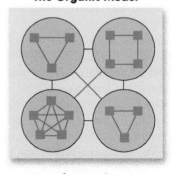

- Cross-functional teams
- Cross-hierarchical teams
- Free flow of information
- Wide spans of control
- Decentralization
- Low formalization

EXHIBIT 15-6
Mechanistic vs. Organic Models

paths toward application. Most current strategy frameworks focus on three strategy dimensions—innovation, cost minimization, and imitation—and a structural design that works best with each.[36]

INNOVATION STRATEGY   To what degree does an organization introduce major new products or services? An **innovation strategy** strives to achieve meaningful and unique innovations. Obviously, not all firms pursue innovation. Apple and 3M do, but conservative retailer Marks & Spencer doesn't. Innovative firms use competitive pay and benefits to attract top candidates and motivate employees to take risks. Some degree of the mechanistic structure can actually benefit innovation. Well-developed communication channels, policies for enhancing long-term commitment, and clear channels of authority all may make it easier for rapid changes to occur smoothly.

Innovation strategy
A strategy that emphasizes the introduction of major new products and services.

COST-MINIMIZATION STRATEGY   An organization pursuing a **cost-minimization strategy** tightly controls costs, refrains from incurring unnecessary expenses, and cuts prices in selling a basic product. This describes the strategy pursued by Walmart and the makers of generic or store-label grocery products. Cost-minimizing organizations usually pursue fewer policies meant to develop commitment among their workforce.

Cost-minimization strategy
A strategy that emphasizes tight cost controls, avoidance of unnecessary innovation or marketing expenses, and price cutting.

IMITATION STRATEGY   Organizations following an **imitation strategy** try to both minimize risk and maximize opportunity for profit, moving new products or entering new markets only after innovators have proven their viability. Mass-market fashion manufacturers that copy designer styles follow this strategy, as do firms such as Hewlett-Packard and Caterpillar. They follow smaller and more innovative competitors with superior products, but only after competitors have demonstrated the market is there. Italy's Moleskine SpA, a small maker of fashionable notebooks, is another example of imitation strategy but in a different way: looking to open more retail shops around the world, it imitates the expansion strategies of larger, successful fashion companies Salvatore Ferragamo SpA and Brunello Cucinelli.[37]

Imitation strategy
A strategy that seeks to move into new products or new markets only after their viability has already been proven.

STRUCTURAL MATCHES   Exhibit 15-7 describes the structural option that best matches each strategy. Innovators need the flexibility of the organic structure (although, as we noted, they may use some elements of the mechanistic structure as well), whereas cost minimizers seek the efficiency and stability of the mechanistic structure. Imitators combine the two structures. They use a mechanistic structure to maintain tight controls and low costs in their current activities but create organic subunits in which to pursue new opportunities.

Strategy	Structural Option
Innovation	**Organic:** A loose structure; low specialization, low formalization, decentralized
Cost minimization	**Mechanistic:** Tight control; extensive work specialization, high formalization, high centralization
Imitation	**Mechanistic and organic:** Mix of loose with tight properties; tight controls over current activities and looser controls for new undertakings

EXHIBIT 15-7
The Optimal Structural Option for Each Organizational Strategy

Organization Size

An organization's size significantly affects its structure. Organizations that employ 2,000 or more people tend to have more specialization, more departmentalization, more vertical levels, and more rules and regulations than do small organizations. However, size becomes less important as an organization expands. Why? At around 2,000 employees, an organization is already fairly mechanistic; 500 more employees won't have much impact. But adding 500 employees to an organization of only 300 is likely to significantly shift it toward a more mechanistic structure.

Technology

Technology
The way in which an organization transfers its inputs into outputs.

Technology describes the way an organization transfers inputs into outputs. Every organization has at least one technology for converting financial, human, and physical resources into products or services. For example, the Chinese consumer electronics company Haier uses an assembly-line process for mass-produced products, which is complemented by more flexible and innovative structures to respond to customers and design new products.[38] Also, colleges may use a number of instructional technologies—the ever-popular lecture, case analysis, experiential exercise, programmed learning, online instruction, and distance learning. Regardless, organizational structures adapt to their technology.

Environment

Environment
Forces outside an organization that potentially affect the organization's structure.

An organization's **environment** includes outside institutions or forces that can affect its structure, such as suppliers, customers, competitors, and public pressure groups. Dynamic environments create significantly more uncertainty for managers than do static ones. To minimize uncertainty in key market arenas, managers may broaden their structure to sense and respond to threats. Most companies, for example Pepsi and Southwest Airlines, have added social networking departments to counter negative information posted on blogs. Or companies may form strategic alliances.

Any organization's environment has three dimensions: capacity, volatility, and complexity.[39] Let's discuss each separately.

CAPACITY   *Capacity* refers to the degree to which the environment can support growth. Rich and growing environments generate excess resources, which can buffer the organization in times of relative scarcity.

VOLATILITY   *Volatility* describes the degree of instability in the environment. A dynamic environment with a high degree of unpredictable change makes it difficult for management to make accurate predictions. Because information technology changes at such a rapid place, more organizations' environments are becoming volatile.

COMPLEXITY   Finally, *complexity* is the degree of heterogeneity and concentration among environmental elements. Simple environments—like the tobacco industry where the methods of production, competitive and regulatory pressures, and the like haven't changed in quite some time—are homogeneous and concentrated. Environments characterized by heterogeneity and dispersion—like the broadband industry—are complex and diverse, with numerous competitors.

THREE-DIMENSIONAL MODEL Exhibit 15-8 summarizes our definition of the environment along its three dimensions. The arrows indicate movement toward higher uncertainty. Thus, organizations that operate in environments characterized as scarce, dynamic, and complex face the greatest degree of uncertainty because they have high unpredictability, little room for error, and a diverse set of elements in the environment to monitor constantly.

Given this three-dimensional definition of *environment*, we can offer some general conclusions about environmental uncertainty and structural arrangements. The more scarce, dynamic, and complex the environment, the more organic a structure should be. The more abundant, stable, and simple the environment, the more the mechanistic structure will be preferred.

Institutions

Another factor that shapes organizational structure is **institutions**. These are cultural factors that act as guidelines for appropriate behavior.[40] Institutional theory describes some of the forces that lead many organizations to have similar structures and, unlike the theories we've described so far, focuses on pressures that aren't necessarily adaptive. In fact, many institutional theorists try to highlight the ways corporate behaviors sometimes *seem* to be performance oriented but are actually guided by unquestioned social norms and conformity.

The most obvious institutional factors come from regulatory pressures; certain industries under government contracts, for instance, must have clear reporting relationships and strict information controls. Sometimes simple inertia determines an organizational form—companies can be structured in a particular way just because that's the way things have always been done. Organizations in countries with high power distance might have a structural form with strict authority relationships because it's seen as more legitimate in that culture. Some have attributed problems in adaptability in Japanese organizations to the institutional pressure to maintain authority relationships.

Sometimes organizations start to have a particular structure because of fads or trends. Organizations can try to copy other successful companies just to look good to investors, and not because they need that structure to perform better. Many companies have recently tried to copy the organic form of a company like Google only to find that such structures

Institutions
Cultural factors that lead many organizations to have similar structures, especially those factors that might not lead to adaptive consequences.

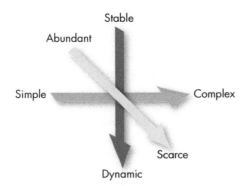

EXHIBIT 15-8
The Environment Along Three Dimensions

are a very poor fit with their operating environment. Institutional pressures are often difficult to see specifically because we take them for granted, but that doesn't mean they aren't powerful.

ORGANIZATIONAL DESIGNS AND EMPLOYEE BEHAVIOR

We opened this chapter by implying an organization's structure can have significant effects on its members. What might those effects be?

A review of the evidence leads to a pretty clear conclusion: You can't generalize! Not everyone prefers the freedom and flexibility of organic structures. Different factors stand out in different structures as well. In highly formalized, heavily structured, mechanistic organizations, the level of fairness in formal policies and procedures (organizational justice) is a very important predictor of satisfaction. In more personal, individually adaptive organic organizations, employees value interpersonal justice more.[41] Some people are most productive and satisfied when work tasks are standardized and ambiguity is minimized—that is, in mechanistic structures. So, any discussion of the effect of organizational design on employee behavior has to address individual differences. To do so, let's consider employee preferences for work specialization, span of control, centralization, and predictability versus autonomy, as well as preferences specific to certain cultures.[42]

Work Specialization

The evidence generally indicates that *work specialization* contributes to higher employee productivity—but at the price of job satisfaction. However, work specialization is not an unending source of higher productivity. Problems start to surface, and productivity begins to suffer, when the human diseconomies of doing repetitive and narrow tasks overtake the economies of specialization. As the workforce has become more highly educated and desirous of jobs that are intrinsically rewarding, we seem to reach the point at which productivity begins to decline as a function of specialization more quickly than in the past. While decreased productivity often prompts companies to add oversight and inspection roles, the better answer may be to reorganize work functions and accountability.[43]

Span of Control

It is probably safe to say no evidence supports a relationship between *span of control* and employee satisfaction or performance. Although it is intuitively attractive that large spans might lead to higher employee performance because they provide more distant supervision and more opportunity for personal initiative, research fails to support this notion. Some people like to be left alone; others prefer the security of a boss who is quickly available at all times. Consistent with several of the contingency theories of leadership discussed in Chapter 12, we would expect factors such as employees' experiences and abilities, and the degree of structure in their tasks, to explain when wide or narrow spans of control are likely to contribute to performance and job satisfaction. However, some evidence indicates that a *manager's* job satisfaction increases as the number of employees supervised increases.

Centralization

We find fairly strong evidence linking *centralization* and job satisfaction. In general, less centralized organizations have a greater amount of autonomy, and autonomy appears positively related to job satisfaction. But again, while one employee may value freedom, another may find autonomous environments frustratingly ambiguous.

Predictability versus Autonomy

We can draw one obvious insight: people don't select employers randomly. They are attracted to, are selected by, and stay with organizations that suit their personal characteristics.[44] Job candidates who prefer predictability are likely to seek out and take employment in mechanistic structures, and those who want autonomy are more likely to end up in organic structures. Thus, the effect of structure on employee behavior is undoubtedly reduced when the selection process facilitates proper matching of individual characteristics with organizational characteristics. Furthermore, companies should strive to establish, promote, and maintain the unique identity of their structures since skilled employees may quit as a result of dramatic changes.[45]

National Culture

Research suggests national culture influences the preference for structure.[46] Organizations that operate with people from high power-distance cultures, such as Greece, France, and most of Latin America, often find their employees are much more accepting of mechanistic structures than are employees from low power-distance countries. So consider cultural differences along with individual differences when predicting how structure will affect employee performance and satisfaction.

Finally, the changing landscape of organizational structure designs has implications for the individual progressing on a career path. Research with managers in Japan, the United Kingdom, and the United States indicated that employees who weathered downsizing and resulting hybrid organizational structures considered their future career prospects diminished. While this may or may not have been correct, their thinking shows that organizational structure does affect the employee and thus must be carefully designed.[47]

⭐ WATCH IT

If your professor has assigned this, go to the Assignments section of **mymanagementlab.com** to complete the video exercise titled **ZipCar: Organizational Structure**.

SUMMARY

The theme of this chapter is that an organization's internal structure contributes to explaining and predicting behavior. That is, in addition to individual and group factors, the structural relationships in which people work have a bearing on employee attitudes and behavior. What's the basis for this argument? To the degree that an organization's structure reduces ambiguity for employees and clarifies concerns such as "What am I supposed to do?" "How am I supposed to do it?" "To whom do I report?" and "To whom do I go if I have a problem?" it shapes their attitudes and facilitates and motivates them to higher levels of performance.

IMPLICATIONS FOR MANAGERS

- Specialization can make operations more efficient, but remember that excessive specialization can create dissatisfaction and reduced motivation.
- Avoid designing rigid hierarchies that overly limit employees' empowerment and autonomy.
- Balance the advantages of remote work against the potential pitfalls before adding flexible workplace options into the organization's structure.
- Downsize your organization to realize major cost savings, and focus the company around core competencies—but only if necessary, because downsizing can have a significant negative impact on employee affect.
- Consider the scarcity, dynamism, and complexity of the environment, and balance organic and mechanistic elements when designing an organizational structure.

⭐ TRY IT!

If your professor has assigned this, go to the Assignments section of **mymanagementlab.com** to complete the **Simulation: Organizational Structure**.

⭐ PERSONAL INVENTORY ASSESSMENTS

Organizational Structure Assessment

To learn about how organizations are structured, complete this PIA.

15-1. Which organizational designs do you think are best suited to incorporate employees who work from home? Why?

16

Organizational Culture

MyManagementLab®

⭐ Improve Your Grade!

When you see this icon ⭐, visit **mymanagementlab.com** for activities that are applied, personalized, and offer immediate feedback.

⭐ Chapter Warm-up

If your professor has assigned this, go to the Assignments section of **mymanagementlab.com** to complete the chapter warm-up.

⭐ WATCH IT

If your professor has assigned this, go to the Assignments section of **mymanagementlab .com** to complete the video exercise titled **Organizational Culture (TWZ Role Play)**.

WHAT IS ORGANIZATIONAL CULTURE?

An executive was once asked what he thought *organizational culture* meant. He gave essentially the same answer U.S. Supreme Court Justice Potter Stewart gave in defining pornography: "I can't define it, but I know it when I see it." We have all felt an indescribable essence about the organizations we've experienced. The pervasive atmosphere can have a strong and measurable impact on behavior. Let's begin discussing this important element of organizational behavior (OB) by exploring the parameters of the phenomenon.

A Definition of Organizational Culture

Organizational culture
A system of shared meaning held by members that distinguishes the organization from other organizations.

Organizational culture refers to a system of shared meaning held by members that distinguishes the organization from other organizations.[1] Seven primary characteristics seem to capture the essence of an organization's culture:[2]

1. **Innovation and risk taking.** The degree to which employees are encouraged to be innovative and take risks.
2. **Attention to detail.** The degree to which employees are expected to exhibit precision, analysis, and attention to detail.
3. **Outcome orientation.** The degree to which management focuses on results or outcomes rather than on the techniques and processes used to achieve them.
4. **People orientation.** The degree to which management decisions take into consideration the effect of outcomes on people within the organization.
5. **Team orientation.** The degree to which work activities are organized around teams rather than individuals.
6. **Aggressiveness.** The degree to which people are aggressive and competitive rather than easygoing.
7. **Stability.** The degree to which organizational activities emphasize maintaining the status quo in contrast to growth.

Each of these characteristics exists on a continuum from low to high. Appraising an organization on the strength of each provides a basis for the shared understanding members have about the organization, how things are done in it, and the way they are supposed to behave. Organizational culture shows how employees perceive the characteristics of an organization, not whether they like them—that is, it's a *descriptive* term. Research on organizational culture has sought to measure how employees see their organization: Does it encourage teamwork? Does it reward innovation? Does it stifle initiative? In contrast, job satisfaction is an *evaluative* term: it seeks to measure how employees feel about the organization's expectations, reward practices, and the like. See Exhibit 16-1 for a contrast of two companies with very different organizational cultures.

Dominant culture
A culture that expresses the core values that are shared by a majority of the organization's members.

Core values
The primary or dominant values that are accepted throughout the organization.

Do Organizations Have Uniform Cultures?

Organizational culture represents a perception the organization's members hold in common. Statements about organizational culture are valid only if individuals with different backgrounds or at different levels in the organization describe the culture in similar terms.[3]

Within the organization, the **dominant culture** expresses the **core values** a majority of members share and that give the organization its distinct personality.[4] That's what

EXHIBIT 16-1
Contrasting
Organizational
Cultures

Organization A

This organization is a manufacturing firm. Managers are expected to fully document all decisions, and "good managers" are those who can provide detailed data to support their recommendations. Creative decisions that incur significant change or risk are not encouraged. Because managers of failed projects are openly criticized and penalized, managers try not to implement ideas that deviate much from the status quo. One lower-level manager quoted an often-used phrase in the company: "If it ain't broke, don't fix it."

There are extensive rules and regulations in this firm that employees are required to follow. Managers supervise employees closely to ensure there are no deviations. Management is concerned with high productivity, regardless of the impact on employee morale or turnover.

Work activities are designed around individuals. There are distinct departments and lines of authority, and employees are expected to minimize formal contact with other employees outside their functional area or line of command. Performance evaluations and rewards emphasize individual effort, although seniority tends to be the primary factor in the determination of pay raises and promotions.

Organization B

This organization is also a manufacturing firm. Here, however, management encourages and rewards risk taking and change. Decisions based on intuition are valued as much as those that are well rationalized. Management prides itself on its history of experimenting with new technologies and its success in regularly introducing innovative products. Managers or employees who have a good idea are encouraged to "run with it." And failures are treated as "learning experiences." The company prides itself on being market driven and rapidly responsive to the changing needs of its customers.

There are few rules and regulations for employees to follow, and supervision is loose because management believes that its employees are hardworking and trustworthy. Management is concerned with high productivity but believes that this comes through treating its people right. The company is proud of its reputation as being a good place to work.

Job activities are designed around work teams, and team members are encouraged to interact with people across functions and authority levels. Employees talk positively about the competition between teams. Individuals and teams have goals, and bonuses are based on achievement of these outcomes. Employees are given considerable autonomy in choosing the means by which the goals are attained.

allows us to say, for example, that the Zappos culture values customer care and dedication over speed and efficiency, which explains the behavior of Zappos executives and employees.[5]

In addition to the dominant cultures of each organization, **subcultures** tend to develop in large organizations in response to common problems or experiences a group of members face in the same department or location. Most large organizations have a dominant culture and numerous subcultures.[6] For example, the purchasing department can have a subculture that includes the core values of the dominant culture, such as aggressiveness, plus additional values unique to members of that department, such as risk-taking. If organizations were composed only of subcultures, the dominant organizational culture would be significantly less powerful. It is the "shared meaning" aspect of culture that makes it a potent device for guiding and shaping behavior.

Subcultures Minicultures within an organization, typically defined by department designations and geographical separation.

Strong versus Weak Cultures

It's possible to differentiate between strong and weak cultures.[7] If most employees (responding to surveys) have the same opinions about the organization's mission and values, the culture is strong; if opinions vary widely, the culture is weak.

Strong culture
A culture in which
the core values are
intensely held and
widely shared.

In a **strong culture**, the organization's core values are both intensely held and widely shared.[8] The more members who accept the core values and the greater their commitment, the stronger the culture and the greater its influence on member behavior. The reason is that a high degree of shared values and intensity create a climate of high behavioral control. Nordstrom employees know in no uncertain terms what is expected of them, for example, and these expectations go a long way toward shaping their behavior.

A strong culture should reduce employee turnover because it demonstrates high agreement about what the organization represents. Such unanimity of purpose builds cohesiveness, loyalty, and organizational commitment. These qualities, in turn, lessen employees' propensity to leave.[9]

Culture versus Formalization

We've seen in this text that high formalization creates predictability, orderliness, and consistency. A strong culture modifies behavior similarly. Therefore, we should view formalization and culture as two different roads to a common destination. The stronger an organization's culture, the less management needs to be concerned with developing formal rules and regulations to guide employee behavior. Those guides will be internalized in employees when they adopt the organization's culture.

WHAT DO CULTURES DO?

Let's discuss the functions of culture and the role culture performs in relation to organizational climate, ethics, sustainability, and innovation. Then we will explore when culture is an asset... and when it is a distinct liability.

The Functions of Culture

Culture defines the rules of the game. First, it has a boundary-defining role: It creates distinctions between organizations. Second, it conveys a sense of identity for organization members. Third, culture facilitates commitment to something larger than individual self-interest. Fourth, it enhances the stability of the social system. Culture is the social glue that helps hold the organization together by providing standards for what employees should say and do. Finally, it is a sense-making and control mechanism that guides and shapes employees' attitudes and behavior. This last function is of particular interest to us in the study of OB.[10]

A strong culture supported by formal rules and regulations ensures employees will act in a relatively uniform and predictable way. Today's trend toward decentralized organizations makes culture more important than ever, but ironically, it also makes establishing a strong culture more difficult. When formal authority and control systems are reduced through decentralization, culture's *shared meaning* can point everyone in the same direction. However, employees organized in a team may show greater allegiance to their team and its values than to the organization as a whole. Furthermore, in virtual organizations, the lack of frequent face-to-face contact makes establishing a common set of norms very difficult. Strong leadership that fosters a strong culture by communicating frequently about common goals and priorities is especially important for innovative organizations.[11]

Individual–organization "fit"—that is, whether the applicant's or employee's attitudes and behavior are compatible with the culture—strongly influences who gets a job offer, a favorable performance review, or a promotion. It's no coincidence that Disney theme park employees appear almost universally attractive, clean, and wholesome with bright smiles. The company selects employees who will maintain that image.

Culture Creates Climate

If you've worked with someone whose positive attitude inspired you to do your best, or with a lackluster team that drained your motivation, you've experienced the effects of climate. **Organizational climate** refers to the shared perceptions organizational members have about their organization and work environment.[12] This aspect of culture is like team spirit at the organizational level. When everyone has the same general feelings about what's important or how well things are working, the effect of these attitudes will be more than the sum of the individual parts. One meta-analysis found that across dozens of different samples, psychological climate was strongly related to individuals' levels of job satisfaction, involvement, commitment, and motivation.[13] A positive workplace climate has been linked to higher customer satisfaction and organizational financial performance as well.[14]

> **Organizational climate**
> The shared perceptions organizational members have about their organization and work environment.

Dozens of dimensions of climate have been studied, including innovation, creativity, communication, warmth and support, involvement, safety, justice, diversity, and customer service.[15] There are a number of findings managers can use to improve their plans for organizational design and team building. For example, someone who encounters a diversity climate will feel more comfortable collaborating with coworkers regardless of their demographic backgrounds. Climates can interact with one another to produce behavior. For example, a climate of worker empowerment can lead to higher levels of performance in organizations that also have a climate of personal accountability.[16] Climate also influences the habits people adopt. If there is a climate of safety, everyone wears safety gear and follows safety procedures even if individually they wouldn't normally think very often about being safe—indeed, many studies have shown that a safety climate decreases the number of documented injuries on the job.[17]

The Ethical Dimension of Culture

Organizational cultures are not neutral in their ethical orientation, even when they are not openly pursuing ethical goals. Over time, an **ethical work climate** (**EWC**), which is the shared concept of right and wrong behavior, develops as part of the organizational climate. EWC reflects the true values of the organization and shapes the ethical decision making of its members.

> **Ethical work climate (EWC)**
> The shared concept of right and wrong behavior in the workplace that reflects the true values of the organization and shapes the ethical decision making of its members.

Researchers have developed *ethical climate theory* (*ECT*) and the *ethical climate index* (*ECI*) to categorize and measure the ethical dimensions of organizational cultures.[18] Of the nine identified ECT climate categories, five are most prevalent in organizations: *instrumental*, *caring*, *independence*, *law and code*, and *rules*. Each explains the general mind-set, expectations, and values of managers and employees in relationship to their organizations. For instance, in an *instrumental* ethical climate, managers may frame their decision making around the assumption that employees (and companies) are motivated by self-interest (egoistic). In a *caring* climate, conversely, managers may operate under the expectation that their decisions will positively affect the greatest number of stakeholders (employees, customers, suppliers) possible.

Ethical climates of *independence* rely on each individual's personal moral ideas to dictate his or her workplace behavior. *Law and code* climates require managers and employees to use an external standardized moral compass such as a professional code of conduct for norms, while *rules* climates tend to operate by internal standardized expectations from, perhaps, an organizational policy manual. Organizations often progress through different categories as they move through their business life cycle.

An organization's ethical climate powerfully influences the way its individual members feel they should behave, so much so that researchers have been able to predict organizational outcomes from the climate categories.[19] For example, instrumental climates are negatively associated with employee job satisfaction and organizational commitment, even though those climates appeal to self-interest (of the employee and the company). They are positively associated with turnover intentions, workplace bullying, and deviant behavior. Caring and rules climates may bring greater job satisfaction. Caring, independence, rules, and law and code climates reduce employee turnover intentions, workplace bullying, and dysfunctional behavior. Research indicates that ethical cultures take a long-term perspective and balance the rights of multiple stakeholders including employees, stockholders, and the community. Managers are supported for taking risks and innovating, discouraged from engaging in unbridled competition, and guided to heed not just *what* goals are achieved but *how* they are achieved.

Culture and Sustainability

Sustainability
Organization practices that can be sustained over a long period of time because the tools or structures that support them are not damaged by the processes.

As the name implies, **sustainability** refers to practices that can be maintained over very long periods of time[20] because the tools or structures that support the practices are not damaged by the processes. One survey found that a great majority of executives saw sustainability as an important part of future success.[21] Concepts of sustainable management have their origins in the environmental movement, so processes that are in harmony with the natural environment are encouraged. *Social sustainability* practices address the ways social systems are affected by an organization's actions over time, and in turn, how changing social systems may affect the organization.

For example, farmers in Australia have been working collectively to increase water use efficiency, minimize soil erosion, and implement tilling and harvesting methods that ensure long-term viability for their farm businesses.[22] In a very different context, 3M has an innovative pollution-prevention program rooted in cultural principles of conserving resources, creating products that have minimal effects on the environment, and collaborating with regulatory agencies to improve environmental effects.[23]

To create a truly sustainable business, an organization must develop a long-term culture and put its values into practice.[24] In other words, there needs to be a sustainable system for creating sustainability! In one workplace study, a company seeking to reduce energy consumption found that soliciting group feedback reduced energy use significantly more than simply issuing reading materials about the importance of conservation.[25] In other words, talking about energy conservation and building the value into the organizational culture resulted in positive employee behavioral changes. Like other cultural practices we've discussed, sustainability needs time and nurturing to grow.

Culture and Innovation

The most innovative companies are often characterized by their open, unconventional, collaborative, vision-driven, and accelerating cultures.[26] Start-up firms often have innovative cultures by definition because they are usually small, agile, and focused on solving problems in order to survive and grow. Consider digital music leader Echo Nest, recently bought by Spotify. As a start-up, Echo Nest was an unconventional, flexible, and open company; they would even host music app "hack" days for users, fostered a music culture within their organization.[27] All these are hallmarks of Spotify's culture, too, making the fit rather seamless.[28] Because of the similar organizational cultures, Echo Nest and Spotify may be able to continue their start-up level of innovation.

At the other end of the start-up spectrum, consider 30-year-old Intuit, one of the World's 100 Most Innovative Companies according to *Forbes*. Intuit employees attend workshops to teach them how to think creatively... and unconventionally. Sessions have led to managers talking through puppets and holding bake sales to sell prototype apps with their cupcakes. The culture stresses open accountability. "I saw one senior guy whose idea they'd been working on for nine months get disproved in a day because someone had a better way. He got up in front of everyone and said, 'This is my bad. I should have checked my hypothesis earlier,'" said Eric Ries, author of *The Lean Startup*. As a consultant for entrepreneurs, Ries considers the older software company equally innovative to start-ups because of its culture.[29]

Alexion Pharmaceuticals is also one of *Forbes'* Most Innovative and, like Intuit, it has been in operation long past the usual innovation life-cycle stage. Unlike Intuit, though, this maker of life-saving medicines is not known for management shenanigans. The key to Alexion's continuing innovation is a culture of caring, which drives it to develop medicines that save victims of rare diseases even when the patients affected are few, the cost of development is prohibitively high, and the probability of success is low.[30]

Culture as an Asset

As we have discussed, organizational culture can provide a positive ethical environment and foster innovation. Culture can also significantly contribute to an organization's bottom line in many ways.

One strong example can be found in the case of ChildNet. ChildNet is a nonprofit child welfare agency in Florida whose organizational culture was described as "grim" from 2000 (when one of its foster children disappeared) through 2007 (when the CEO was fired amid FBI allegations of fraud and forgery). "We didn't know if we would have jobs or who would take over," employee Maggie Tilelli said. However, after intense turnaround efforts aimed at changing the organizational culture, ChildNet became Florida's top-ranked agency within four years and *Workforce Management*'s Optima award winner for General Excellence in 2012. While ChildNet demonstrates how an organizational culture can positively affect outcomes, Dish Network illustrates the elusiveness of matching a particular culture to an industry or organization. By every measure, Dish Network is a business success story—it is the second-largest U.S. satellite TV provider and it has made founder Charlie Ergen one of the richest men in the world. Yet Dish was recently ranked as the worst U.S. company to work for, and employees say that this is due to the micromanaging culture Ergen created and enforces. Employees recounted arduous mandatory overtime, fingerprint scanners to record work hours to the minute, public berating (most notably from Ergen), management condescension and distrust, quarterly "bloodbath" layoffs, and no working from home. One employee advised another online, "You're part of a poisonous environment . . . go find a job where you can use your talents for good rather than evil."

Culture as a Liability

Culture can enhance organizational commitment and increase the consistency of employee behavior, which clearly benefits an organization. Culture is valuable to employees too, because it spells out how things are done and what's important. But we shouldn't ignore the potentially dysfunctional aspects of culture, especially a strong one, on an organization's effectiveness. Hewlett-Packard, once known as a premier computer manufacturer, rapidly lost market share and profits as dysfunction in its top management team trickled down, leaving employees disengaged, uncreative, unappreciated, and polarized.[31] Let's unpack some of the major factors that signal a negative organizational culture, beginning with institutionalization.

Institutionalization
A condition that occurs when an organization takes on a life of its own, apart from any of its members, and acquires immortality.

INSTITUTIONALIZATION   When an organization undergoes **institutionalization**—that is, it becomes valued for itself and not for the goods or services it produces—it takes on a life of its own, apart from its founders or members.[32] Institutionalized organizations often don't go out of business even if the original goals are no longer relevant. Acceptable modes of behavior become largely self-evident to members, and although this isn't entirely negative, it does mean behaviors and habits go unquestioned, which can stifle innovation and make maintaining the organization's culture an end in itself.

BARRIERS TO CHANGE   Culture is a liability when shared values don't agree with those that further the organization's effectiveness. This is most likely when an organization's environment is undergoing rapid change, and its entrenched culture may no longer be appropriate.[33] Consistency of employee behavior, which is an asset in a stable environment, may then burden the organization and make it difficult to respond to changes.

BARRIERS TO DIVERSITY   There are many barriers to diversity that are driven by organizational culture. Hiring new employees who differ from the majority in race, age, gender, disability, or other characteristics creates a paradox:[34] Management wants to demonstrate support for the differences these employees bring to the workplace, but newcomers who wish to fit in must accept the organization's core culture. The desire for quick assimilation creates one barrier to diversity. Second, because diverse behaviors and unique strengths are likely to diminish as people assimilate, strong cultures can become liabilities when they effectively eliminate the advantages of diversity. Third, a strong culture that condones prejudice, supports bias, or becomes insensitive to differences can undermine formal corporate diversity policies.

STRENGTHENING DYSFUNCTIONS   We've discussed cultures that generally cohere around a positive set of values and attitudes. This consensus can create a powerful forward momentum. However, coherence around negativity and dysfunctional management systems in a corporation can produce downward forces that are equally powerful. One study of thousands of hospitality-industry employees in hundreds of locations found that local organizational cultures marked by low or decreasing job satisfaction had higher levels of turnover regardless of a generally positive organization-wide culture.[35] As we know from this text, low job satisfaction and high turnover indicate dysfunction on the organization's part. Negative attitudes in groups add to negative outcomes, suggesting a powerful influence of culture on individuals.

BARRIERS TO ACQUISITIONS AND MERGERS   Historically, when management looked at acquisition or merger decisions, the key decision factors were potential financial advantage and product synergy. In recent years, cultural compatibility has become the primary concern.[36] All things being equal, whether the acquisition works seems to have much to do with how well the two organizations' cultures match up. When they don't mesh well, the organizational cultures of both become a liability to the whole new organization. For example, a study conducted by Bain and Company found that 70 percent of mergers failed to increase shareholder values, and Hay Group found that more than 90 percent of mergers in Europe failed to reach financial goals.[37] Considering this dismal rate of success, Lawrence Chia from Deloitte Consulting observed, "One of the biggest failings is people. The people at Company A have a different way of doing things from Company B . . . you can't find commonality in goals." Culture clash was also commonly argued to be one of the causes of AOL Time Warner's problems. The $183 billion merger between America Online (AOL) and Time Warner in 2001 was the largest in U.S. corporate history. It was a disaster. Only 2 years later, the new company saw its stock fall an astounding 90 percent, and it reported what was then the largest financial loss in U.S. history.

CREATING AND SUSTAINING CULTURE

An organization's culture doesn't pop out of thin air, and once established it rarely fades away. What influences the creation of a culture? What reinforces and sustains it once in place?

How a Culture Begins

An organization's customs, traditions, and general way of doing things are largely due to what it has done before and how successful it was in doing it. This leads us to the ultimate source of an organization's culture: the founders.[38] Founders have a vision of what the organization should be, and a firm's initially small size makes it easy to impose that vision on all members.

Culture creation occurs in three ways.[39] First, founders hire and keep only employees who think and feel the same way they do. Second, they indoctrinate and socialize employees to their way of thinking and feeling. And finally, the behavior of the founder(s) encourages employees to identify with them and internalize their beliefs, values, and assumptions. When the organization succeeds, the personality of the founder(s) becomes embedded in the culture. For example, the fierce, competitive style and disciplined, authoritarian nature of Hyundai, the giant Korean conglomerate, exhibits the same characteristics often used to describe founder Chung Ju-Yung. Other founders with sustaining impact on their organization's culture include Bill Gates at Microsoft, Ingvar Kamprad at IKEA, Herb Kelleher at Southwest Airlines, Fred Smith at FedEx, and Richard Branson at the Virgin Group.

Keeping a Culture Alive

Once a culture is in place, practices within the organization maintain it by giving employees a set of similar experiences.[40] The selection process, performance evaluation criteria, training and development activities, and promotion procedures ensure those hired fit in with the culture, reward those employees who support it, and penalize (or even expel) those who challenge it. Three forces play a particularly important part in sustaining a culture: selection practices, actions of top management, and socialization methods. Let's look at each.

SELECTION   The explicit goal of the selection process is to identify and hire individuals with the knowledge, skills, and abilities to perform successfully. The final decision, because it is significantly influenced by the decision maker's judgment of how well candidates will fit into the organization, identifies people whose values are consistent with at least a good portion of the organization's.[41] The selection process also provides information to applicants. Those who perceive a conflict between their values and those of the organization can remove themselves from the applicant pool. Selection thus becomes a two-way street, allowing employer and applicant to avoid a mismatch and sustaining an organization's culture by removing those who might attack or undermine its core values, for better or worse.

TOP MANAGEMENT   The actions of top management have a major impact on the organization's culture.[42] Through words and behavior, senior executives establish norms that filter through the organization about, for instance, whether risk taking is desirable, how much freedom managers give employees, what is appropriate dress, and what actions earn pay raises, promotions, and other rewards.

Socialization
A process that adapts employees to the organization's culture.

SOCIALIZATION   No matter how good a job the organization does in recruiting and selection, new employees need help adapting to the prevailing culture. That help is **socialization**.[43] Socialization can help alleviate the problem many employees report when their new jobs are different than they expected. For example, Clear Channel Communications, Facebook, Google, and other companies are adopting fresh onboarding (new hire assimilation) procedures, including assigning "peer coaches," holding socializing events, personalizing orientation programs, and giving out immediate work assignments. "When we can stress the personal identity of people, and let them bring more of themselves at work, they are more satisfied with their job and have better results," researcher Francesca Gino of Harvard said.[44]

We can think of socialization as a process with three stages: prearrival, encounter, and metamorphosis.[45] This process, shown in Exhibit 16-2, has an impact on the new employee's work productivity, commitment to the organization's objectives, and decision to stay with the organization.

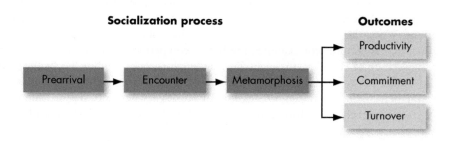

EXHIBIT 16-2
A Socialization Model

1. *Prearrival stage.* The **prearrival stage** recognizes that each individual arrives with a set of values, attitudes, and expectations about both the work and the organization. One major purpose of a business school, for example, is to socialize students to the attitudes and behaviors companies want. Newcomers to high-profile organizations with strong market positions have their own assumptions about what it's like to work there.[46] Most new recruits will expect Nike to be dynamic and exciting and a stock brokerage firm to be high in pressure and rewards. How accurately people judge an organization's culture before they join the organization, and how proactive their personalities are, become critical predictors of how well they adjust.[47]

   Prearrival stage
   The period of learning in the socialization process that occurs before a new employee joins the organization.

2. *Encounter stage.* The selection process can help inform prospective employees about the organization as a whole. Upon entry into the organization, the new member enters the **encounter stage** and confronts the possibility that expectations—about the job, coworkers, boss, and organization in general—may differ from reality. If expectations were fairly accurate, this stage merely cements earlier perceptions. However, this is not often the case. At the extreme, a new member may become disillusioned enough to resign. Proper recruiting and selection should significantly reduce this outcome, along with encouraging friendship ties in the organization—newcomers are more committed when friendly coworkers help them "learn the ropes."[48]

   Encounter stage
   The stage in the socialization process in which a new employee sees what the organization is really like and confronts the possibility that expectations and reality may diverge.

3. *Metamorphosis stage.* Finally, to work out any problems discovered during the encounter stage, the new member changes or goes through the **metamorphosis stage**. The options presented in Exhibit 16-3 are alternatives designed to bring about metamorphosis. Most research suggests two major "bundles" of socialization

   Metamorphosis stage
   The stage in the socialization process in which a new employee changes and adjusts to the job, work group, and organization.

Formal vs. Informal The more a new employee is segregated from the ongoing work setting and differentiated in some way to make explicit his or her newcomer's role, the more socialization is formal. Specific orientation and training programs are examples. Informal socialization puts the new employee directly into the job, with little or no special attention.

Individual vs. Collective New members can be socialized individually. This describes how it's done in many professional offices. They can also be grouped together and processed through an identical set of experiences, as in military boot camp.

Fixed vs. Variable This refers to the time schedule in which newcomers make the transition from outsider to insider. A fixed schedule establishes standardized stages of transition. This characterizes rotational training programs. It also includes probationary periods, such as the 8- to 10-year "associate" status used by accounting and law firms before deciding on whether or not a candidate is made a partner. Variable schedules give no advance notice of their transition timetable. Variable schedules describe the typical promotion system, in which one is not advanced to the next stage until one is "ready."

Serial vs. Random Serial socialization is characterized by the use of role models who train and encourage the newcomer. Apprenticeship and mentoring programs are examples. In random socialization, role models are deliberately withheld. New employees are left on their own to figure things out.

Investiture vs. Divestiture Investiture socialization assumes that the newcomer's qualities and qualifications are the necessary ingredients for job success, so these qualities and qualifications are confirmed and supported. Divestiture socialization tries to strip away certain characteristics of the recruit. Fraternity and sorority "pledges" go through divestiture socialization to shape them into the proper role.

EXHIBIT 16-3
Entry Socialization Options

practices. The more management relies on formal, collective, fixed, and serial socialization programs while emphasizing divestiture, the more likely newcomers' differences will be stripped away and replaced by standardized predictable behaviors. These *institutional* practices are common in police departments, fire departments, and other organizations that value rule following and order. Programs that are informal, individual, variable, and random while emphasizing investiture are more likely to give newcomers an innovative sense of their roles and methods of working. Creative fields such as research and development, advertising, and filmmaking rely on these *individual* practices. Most research suggests high levels of institutional practices encourage person–organization fit and high levels of commitment, whereas individual practices produce more role innovation.[49]

Researchers examine how employee attitudes change during socialization by measuring it at several time points over the first few months. Several studies have now documented patterns of "honeymoons" and "hangovers" for new workers, showing that the period of initial adjustment is often marked by decreases in job satisfaction as idealized hopes come into contact with the reality of organizational life.[50] Newcomers may find that the level of social support they receive from supervisors and coworkers is gradually withdrawn over the first few weeks on the job, as everyone returns to "business as usual."[51] Role conflict and role overload may rise for newcomers over time, and workers with the largest increases in these role problems experience the largest decreases in commitment and satisfaction.[52] It may be that the initial adjustment period for newcomers presents increasing demands and difficulties, at least in the short term.

Summary: How Organizational Cultures Form

Exhibit 16-4 summarizes how an organization's culture is established and sustained. The original culture derives from the founders' philosophy and strongly influences hiring criteria as the firm grows. The success of socialization depends on the deliberateness of matching new employees' values to those of the organization in the selection process and on top management's commitment to socialization programs. Top managers' actions set the general climate, including what is acceptable behavior and what is not, and employees sustain and perpetuate the culture.

HOW EMPLOYEES LEARN CULTURE

Culture is transmitted to employees in a number of forms, the most potent being stories, rituals, material symbols, and language.

EXHIBIT 16-4
How Organizational Cultures Form

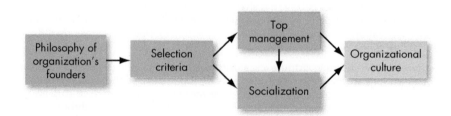

Stories

When Henry Ford II was chairman of Ford Motor Company, you would have been hard pressed to find a manager who hadn't heard how he reminded his executives when they got too arrogant, "It's my name that's on the building." The message was clear: Henry Ford II ran the company.

Today, a number of senior Nike executives spend much of their time serving as corporate storytellers.[53] When they tell how co-founder (and Oregon track coach) Bill Bowerman went to his workshop and poured rubber into a waffle iron to create a better running shoe, they're talking about Nike's spirit of innovation. When new hires hear tales of Oregon running star Steve Prefontaine's battles to make running a professional sport and attain better performance equipment, they learn of Nike's commitment to helping athletes.

Stories such as these circulate through many organizations, anchoring the present in the past and legitimizing current practices. They typically include narratives about the organization's founders, rule breaking, rags-to-riches successes, workforce reductions, relocations of employees, reactions to past mistakes, and organizational coping.[54] Employees also create their own narratives about how they came to either fit or not fit with the organization during the process of socialization, including first days on the job, early interactions with others, and first impressions of organizational life.[55]

Rituals

Rituals are repetitive sequences of activities that express and reinforce the key values of the organization—what goals are most important and/or which people are important versus which are expendable.[56] Some companies have nontraditional rituals to help support the values of their cultures. Kimpton Hotels & Restaurants, one of *Fortune*'s 100 Best Companies to Work For, maintains its customer-oriented culture with traditions like a Housekeeping Olympics that includes blindfolded bedmaking and vacuum races.[57] At marketing firm United Entertainment Group, employees work unusual hours a few times a year, arriving in the late afternoon and working until early morning. CEO Jarrod Moses does this to support a culture of creativity. He says, "You mess with somebody's internal clock, and some interesting ideas come out."[58]

Rituals
Repetitive sequences of activities that express and reinforce the key values of the organization, which goals are most important, which people are important, and which are expendable.

Symbols

The layout of corporate headquarters, the types of automobiles top executives are given, and the presence or absence of corporate aircraft are a few examples of **material symbols**. Others include the size of offices, the elegance of furnishings, perks, and attire.[59] These convey to employees who is important, the degree of egalitarianism top management desires, and the kinds of behavior that are appropriate, such as risk taking, conservative, authoritarian, participative, individualistic, or social.

One example of the intentional use of material symbols is Texas electric company Dynegy. Dynegy's headquarters doesn't look like your typical head-office operation. There are few individual offices, even for senior executives. The space is essentially made up of cubicles, common areas, and meeting rooms. This informality conveys to employees that Dynegy values openness, equality, creativity, and flexibility. While some organizations provide their top executives with chauffeur-driven limousines and a corporate jet,

Material symbols
What conveys to employees who is important, the degree of egalitarianism top management desires, and the kinds of behavior that are appropriate.

other CEOs drive the company car themselves and travel in the economy section. At some firms, like Chicago shirtmaker Threadless, an "anything goes" atmosphere helps emphasize a creative culture. Threadless meetings are held in an Airstream camper parked inside the company's converted FedEx warehouse, while employees in shorts and flip-flops work in bullpens featuring disco balls and garish decorations chosen by each team.[60]

Some cultures are known for the perks in their environments, such as Google's bocce courts, FACTSET Research's on-site pie/cheese/cupcake trucks, software designer Autodesk's bring-your-dog office, SAS's free health care clinic, Microsoft's organic spa, and adventure-gear specialist REI's free equipment rentals. Other companies communicate the values of their cultures through the gift of time to think creatively, either with leaders or off-site. For instance, Biotech leader Genentech and many other top companies provide paid sabbaticals. Genentech offers every employee 6 weeks' paid leave for every 6 years of service to support a culture of equitability and innovative thinking.[61]

Language

Many organizations and subunits within them use language to help members identify with the culture, attest to their acceptance of it, and help preserve it. Unique terms describe equipment, officers, key individuals, suppliers, customers, or products that relate to the business. New employees may at first be overwhelmed by acronyms and jargon that, once assimilated, act as a common denominator to unite members of a given culture or subculture.

INFLUENCING AN ORGANIZATIONAL CULTURE

As we discussed, the culture of an organization is set by its founders and is often difficult to change afterward. It's true that the ideal scenario is a strong founder (or founders) who carefully plans the organization's culture beforehand. That's seldom the case, though; organizational culture usually grows organically over time. When we think of the development of culture as ongoing and conducted through each employee, we can see ways to increase the ethical, positive, and/or spiritual aspects of the environment, as discussed next.

An Ethical Culture

Despite differences across industries and cultures, ethical organizational cultures share some common values and processes.[62] Therefore, managers can create a more ethical culture by adhering to the following principles:[63]

- **Be a visible role model.** Employees will look to the actions of top management as a benchmark for appropriate behavior, but everyone can be a role model to positively influence the ethical atmosphere. Send a positive message.
- **Communicate ethical expectations.** Whenever you serve in a leadership capacity, minimize ethical ambiguities by sharing a code of ethics that states the organization's primary values and the judgment rules employees must follow.
- **Provide ethical training.** Set up seminars, workshops, and training programs to reinforce the organization's standards of conduct, clarify what practices are permissible, and address potential ethical dilemmas.

- **Visibly reward ethical acts and punish unethical ones.** Evaluate subordinates on how their decisions measure up against the organization's code of ethics. Review the means as well as the ends. Visibly reward those who act ethically and conspicuously punish those who don't.
- **Provide protective mechanisms.** Seek formal mechanisms so everyone can discuss ethical dilemmas and report unethical behavior without fear of reprimand. These might include identifying ethical counselors, ombudspeople, or ethical officers for liaison roles.

A widespread positive ethical climate has to start at the top of the organization.[64] One study demonstrated that when top management emphasizes strong ethical values, supervisors are more likely to practice ethical leadership. Positive attitudes transfer down to line employees, who show lower levels of deviant behavior and higher levels of cooperation and assistance. Several other studies have come to the same general conclusion: The values of top management are a good predictor of ethical behavior among employees. One study involving auditors found perceived pressure from organizational leaders to behave unethically was associated with increased intentions to engage in unethical practices.[65] Clearly, the wrong type of organizational culture can negatively influence employee ethical behavior. Finally, employees whose ethical values are similar to those of their department are more likely to be promoted, so we can think of ethical culture as flowing from the bottom up as well.[66]

A Positive Culture

At first blush, creating a positive culture may sound hopelessly naïve or like a Dilbert-style conspiracy. The one thing that makes us believe this trend is here to stay, however, are signs that management practice and OB research are converging. A **positive organizational culture** emphasizes building on employee strengths, rewards more than it punishes, and encourages individual vitality and growth.[67] Let's consider each of these areas.

Positive organizational culture
A culture that emphasizes building on employee strengths, rewards more than it punishes, and encourages individual vitality and growth.

BUILDING ON EMPLOYEE STRENGTHS   Although a positive organizational culture does not ignore problems, it does emphasize showing workers how they can capitalize on their strengths. As management guru Peter Drucker said, "Most Americans do not know what their strengths are. When you ask them, they look at you with a blank stare, or they respond in terms of subject knowledge, which is the wrong answer." Wouldn't it be better to be in an organizational culture that helped you discover your strengths and how to make the most of them?

REWARDING MORE THAN PUNISHING   Although most organizations are sufficiently focused on extrinsic rewards such as pay and promotions, they often forget about the power of smaller (and cheaper) rewards such as praise. Part of creating a positive organizational culture is "catching employees doing something right." Many managers withhold praise because they're afraid employees will coast or because they think praise is not valued. Employees generally don't ask for praise, and managers usually don't realize the costs of failing to give it.

ENCOURAGING VITALITY AND GROWTH   No organization will get the best from employees who see themselves as mere cogs in the machine. A positive culture recognizes the difference between a job and a career. It supports not only what the employee contributes to organizational effectiveness but how the organization can make the employee more effective—personally and professionally.

RECOGNIZING OUTSIDE CONTEXT   Is a positive culture a cure-all? Though many companies have embraced aspects of a positive organizational culture, it is a new enough idea for us to be uncertain about how and when it works best.

Not all national cultures value being positive as much as the U.S. culture does and, even within U.S. culture, there surely are limits to how far organizations should go. The limits may need to be dictated by the industry and society. For example, Admiral, a British insurance company, has established a Ministry of Fun in its call centers to organize poem writing, foosball, conkers (a British game involving chestnuts), and fancy-dress days, which may clash with an industry value of more serious cultures. When does the pursuit of a positive culture start to seem coercive? As one critic notes, "Promoting a social orthodoxy of positiveness focuses on a particular constellation of desirable states and traits but, in so doing, can stigmatize those who fail to fit the template."[68] There may be benefits to establishing a positive culture, but an organization also needs to be objective and not pursue it past the point of effectiveness.

A Spiritual Culture

What do Southwest Airlines, Hewlett-Packard, Ford, The Men's Wearhouse, Tyson Foods, Wetherill Associates, and Tom's of Maine have in common? They're among a growing number of organizations that have embraced workplace spirituality.

Workplace spirituality
The recognition that people have an inner life that nourishes and is nourished by meaningful work that takes place in the context of community.

WHAT IS SPIRITUALITY?   Workplace spirituality is *not* about organized religious practices. It's not about God or theology. **Workplace spirituality** recognizes that people have an inner life that nourishes and is nourished by meaningful work in the context of community.[69] Organizations that support a spiritual culture recognize that people seek to find meaning and purpose in their work and desire to connect with other human beings as part of a community. Many of the topics we have discussed—ranging from job design to corporate social responsibility (CSR)—are well matched to the concept of organizational spirituality. When a company emphasizes its commitment to paying third-world suppliers a fair (above-market) price for their products to facilitate community development—as did Starbucks—or encourages employees to share prayers or inspirational messages through e-mail—as did Interstate Batteries—it may encourage a more spiritual culture.[70]

WHY SPIRITUALITY NOW?   As noted in our discussion of emotions in Chapter 4, the myth of rationality assumed the well-run organization eliminated people's feelings. Concern about an employee's inner life had no role in the perfectly rational model. But just as we realize that the study of emotions improves our understanding of OB, an awareness of spirituality can help us better understand employee behavior.

EXHIBIT 16-5
Reasons for the
Growing Interest
in Spirituality

- Spirituality can counterbalance the pressures and stress of a turbulent pace of life. Contemporary lifestyles—single-parent families, geographic mobility, the temporary nature of jobs, new technologies that create distance between people—underscore the lack of community many people feel and increase the need for involvement and connection.

- Formalized religion hasn't worked for many people, and they continue to look for anchors to replace a lack of faith and to fill a growing feeling of emptiness.

- Job demands have made the workplace dominant in many people's lives, yet they continue to question the meaning of work.

- People want to integrate personal life values with their professional lives.

- An increasing number of people are finding that the pursuit of more material acquisitions leaves them unfulfilled.

Of course, employees have always had an inner life. So why has the search for meaning and purposefulness in work surfaced now? We summarize the reasons in Exhibit 16-5.

CHARACTERISTICS OF A SPIRITUAL ORGANIZATION The concept of workplace spirituality draws on our previous discussions of values, ethics, motivation, and leadership. Although research remains preliminary, several cultural characteristics tend to be evident in spiritual organizations:[71]

- **Benevolence.** Spiritual organizations value kindness toward others and the happiness of employees and other organizational stakeholders.
- **Strong sense of purpose.** Spiritual organizations build their cultures around a meaningful purpose. Although profits may be important, they're not the primary value.
- **Trust and respect.** Spiritual organizations are characterized by mutual trust, honesty, and openness. Employees are treated with esteem and are valued, consistent with the dignity of each individual.
- **Open-mindedness.** Spiritual organizations value flexible thinking and creativity among employees.

ACHIEVING SPIRITUALITY IN THE ORGANIZATION Many organizations have grown interested in spirituality but have experienced difficulty putting principles into practice. Several types of practices can facilitate a spiritual workplace,[72] including those that support work–life balance. Leaders can demonstrate values, attitudes, and behaviors that trigger intrinsic motivation and a sense of fulfilling a calling through work. Second, encouraging employees to consider how their work provides a sense of purpose can help achieve a spiritual workplace; often this is done through group counseling and organizational development, a topic we take up in Chapter 17. Third, a growing number of companies, including Taco Bell and Sturdisteel, offer employees the counseling services of corporate chaplains. Many chaplains are employed by agencies, such as Marketplace Chaplains USA, while some corporations, such as R.J. Reynolds Tobacco and Tyson Foods, employ chaplains directly. The workplace presence of corporate chaplains, who are often ordained Christian ministers, is obviously controversial, although their role is not to increase spirituality but to help human resources departments serve the employees who already have Christian beliefs.[73] Similar roles for leaders of other faiths certainly must be encouraged.

CRITICISMS OF SPIRITUALITY Critics of the spirituality movement in organizations have focused on three issues. First is the question of scientific foundation. There is comparatively little research on workplace spirituality, and it has been defined so broadly in some sources that practices from job rotation to corporate retreats at meditation centers have been identified as spiritual. Second, an emphasis on spirituality can clearly make some employees uneasy. Critics have argued that secular institutions, especially business firms, should not impose spiritual values on employees.[74] This criticism is undoubtedly valid when spirituality is defined as bringing religion and God into the workplace. However, it seems less stinging when the goal is limited to helping employees find meaning and purpose in their work lives. Finally, whether spirituality and profits are compatible objectives is a relevant concern for managers and investors in business. The evidence, although limited, indicates they are. In one study, organizations that provided their employees with opportunities for spiritual development outperformed those that didn't.[75] Other studies reported that spirituality in organizations was positively related to creativity, employee satisfaction, job involvement, and organizational commitment.[76]

THE GLOBAL CONTEXT

We considered global cultural values (collectivism–individualism, power distance, and so on) in Chapter 5. Here our focus is a bit narrower: How is organizational culture affected by the global context? Organizational culture is so powerful that it often transcends national boundaries. But that doesn't mean organizations should, or could, ignore national and local culture.

One of the primary things U.S. managers can do is be culturally sensitive. The United States is a dominant force in business and in culture—and with that influence comes a reputation. "We are broadly seen throughout the world as arrogant people, totally self-absorbed and loud," says one U.S. executive. Some ways in which U.S. managers can be culturally sensitive include talking in a low tone of voice, speaking slowly, listening more, and avoiding discussions of religion and politics.

The management of ethical behavior is one area where national culture can rub against corporate culture.[77] U.S. managers endorse the supremacy of anonymous market forces as a moral obligation for business organizations. This worldview sees bribery, nepotism, and favoring personal contacts as highly unethical. They also value profit maximization, so any action that deviates from profit maximization may suggest inappropriate or corrupt behavior. In contrast, managers in developing economies are more likely to see ethical decisions as embedded in the social environment. That means doing special favors for family and friends is not only appropriate but possibly even an ethical responsibility. Managers in many nations view capitalism skeptically and believe the interests of workers should be put on a par with the interests of shareholders, which may limit profit maximization. Creating a multinational organizational culture can initiate strife between employees of traditionally competing countries. As national organizations seek to employ workers in overseas operations, management must decide whether to standardize many facets of organizational culture.

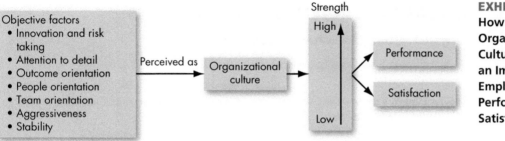

EXHIBIT 16-6
How
Organizational
Cultures Have
an Impact on
Employee
Performance and
Satisfaction

SUMMARY

Exhibit 16-6 depicts the impact of organizational culture. Employees form an overall subjective perception of the organization based on factors such as the degree of risk tolerance, team emphasis, and support of individuals. This overall perception represents, in effect, the organization's culture or personality and affects employee performance and satisfaction, with stronger cultures having greater impact.

IMPLICATIONS FOR MANAGERS

- Realize that an organization's culture is relatively fixed in the short term. To affect change, involve top management and strategize a long-term plan.
- Hire individuals whose values align with those of the organization; these employees will tend to remain committed and satisfied. Not surprisingly, "misfits" have considerably higher turnover rates.
- Understand that employees' performance and socialization depend to a considerable degree on their knowing what to do and not do. Train your employees well and keep them informed of changes to their job roles.
- You can shape the culture of your work environment, sometimes as much as it shapes you. All managers can especially do their part to create an ethical culture and to consider spirituality and its role in creating a positive organizational culture.
- Be aware that your company's organizational culture may not be "transportable" to other countries. Understand the cultural relevance of your organization's norms before introducing new plans or initiatives overseas.

⭐ TRY IT!

If your professor has assigned this, go to the Assignments section of
mymanagementlab.com to complete the **Simulation: Organizational Culture**.

⭐ PERSONAL INVENTORY ASSESSMENTS

Organizational Structure Assessment

To learn about how organizations are structured, complete this PIA.

16-1. What are the ways you would like to influence an organization's culture? How will you go about making a difference?

17

Organizational Change and Stress Management

MyManagementLab®

⭐ Improve Your Grade!

When you see this icon ⭐, visit **mymanagementlab.com** for activities that are applied, personalized, and offer immediate feedback.

LEARNING OBJECTIVES

After studying this chapter, you should be able to:

1. Contrast the forces for change and planned change.
2. Describe ways to overcome resistance to change.
3. Compare the four main approaches to managing organizational change.
4. Demonstrate three ways of creating a culture for change.
5. Identify the potential environmental, organizational, and personal sources of stress at work as well as the role of individual and cultural differences.
6. Identify the physiological, psychological, and behavioral symptoms of stress at work.
7. Describe individual and organizational approaches to managing stress at work.

⭐ Chapter Warm-up

If your professor has chosen to assign this, go to the Assignments section of **mymanagementlab.com** to complete the chapter warm-up.

CHANGE

If we want to realize positive outcomes for organizational behavior (OB), which after all is the purpose of this text in its entirety, we need to address two realities of organizational life: change and stress. Let's first discuss change, which often brings about increased stress. As we will find, change brought upon by many forces is either reactionary or planned.

Forces for Change

"Change or die!" is the rallying cry among today's managers worldwide. Change often occurs along one (or more) of six dimensions:

1. **The changing nature of the workforce.** Almost every organization must adjust to a multicultural environment, demographic changes, immigration, and outsourcing.
2. **Technology** is continually changing jobs and organizations. It is not difficult to imagine the idea of an office becoming an antiquated concept in the near future.
3. **Economic shocks** also have a huge impact on organizations. During the great recession of 2007 to 2009, millions of jobs were lost worldwide, home values dropped dramatically, and many large, well-known corporations like Merrill Lynch, Countrywide Financial, and Ameriquest disappeared or were acquired. Recovery has occurred in many countries, and with it, new job prospects and investments. Other countries, like Greece and Spain, struggle to regain their economic footing, limiting the economic viability of many Greek and Spanish organizations.
4. **Competition** is changing. Competitors are as likely to be across the ocean as across town. Successful organizations are fast on their feet, capable of developing new products rapidly and getting them to market quickly. In other words, they are flexible and require an equally flexible and responsive workforce.
5. **Social trends** don't remain static. Consumers who were strangers now meet and share product information in chat rooms and blogs. Organizations must therefore continually adjust product and marketing strategies to be sensitive to changing social trends. Consumers, employees, and organizational leaders are increasingly sensitive to environmental concerns. "Green" practices are quickly becoming expected rather than optional.
6. Not even globalization's strongest proponents could have imagined the change in world politics in recent years. We've seen a major set of financial crises that have rocked global markets, a dramatic rise in the power and influence of China, and intense shakeups in governments across the Arab world. Throughout the industrialized world, businesses—particularly in the banking and financial sectors—have come under new scrutiny.

Reactionary versus Planned Change

Change
Making things different.

Planned change
Change activities that are intentional and goal oriented.

Change agents
People who act as catalysts and assume the responsibility for managing change activities.

Change is simply making things different. However, only proactive situations describe **planned change**. Many changes are in direct reaction to, say, employee demands. Some organizations treat all change as an accidental occurrence. In this chapter, we address change as an intentional, goal-oriented activity.

What are the goals of planned change? First, it seeks to improve the ability of the organization to adapt to changes in its environment. Second, it seeks to change employee behavior.

Who is responsible for managing change activities in organizations? The answer is **change agents**.[1] They see a future for the organization others have not identified, and they are able to motivate, invent, and implement this vision. Change agents can be managers or non-managers, current or new employees, or outside consultants.

RESISTANCE TO CHANGE

Our egos are fragile, and we often see change as threatening. Even when employees are shown data that suggest they need to change, they latch onto whatever information they can find that suggest they are okay and don't need to change.[2] Employees who have negative feelings about a change cope by not thinking about it, increasing their use of sick time, or quitting. All of these reactions can sap the organization of vital energy when it is most needed.[3] Resistance to change doesn't just come from lower levels of the organization. In many cases, higher-level managers will resist changes proposed by subordinates, especially if these leaders are focused on immediate performance.[4] Conversely, when leaders are more focused on mastery and exploration, they are more willing to hear and adopt subordinates' suggestions for change.

Resistance to change can be positive if it leads to open discussion and debate.[5] These responses are usually preferable to apathy or silence and can indicate that members of the organization are engaged in the process, providing change agents an opportunity to explain the change effort. Change agents can also monitor resistance in order to modify the change to fit the preferences of members of the organization.

Resistance doesn't necessarily surface in standardized ways. It can be overt, implicit, immediate, or deferred. It's easiest for management to deal with overt and immediate resistance such as complaints, a work slowdown, or a strike threat. The greater challenge is managing resistance that is implicit or deferred because these responses— loss of loyalty or motivation, increased errors or absenteeism—are more subtle and more difficult to recognize for what they are. Deferred actions also cloud the link between the change and the reaction to it, sometimes surfacing weeks, months, or even years later. Or a single change of little inherent impact may be the straw that breaks the camel's back because resistance to earlier changes has been deferred and stockpiled.

Exhibit 17-1 summarizes major forces for resistance to change, categorized by their sources. Individual sources reside in human characteristics such as perceptions, personalities, and needs. Organizational sources reside in the structural makeup of organizations themselves.

Overcoming Resistance to Change

Eight tactics can help change agents deal with resistance to change.[6] Let's review them briefly.

COMMUNICATION   Communication is more important than ever in times of change. One study of German companies revealed changes are most effective when a company communicates a rationale that balances the interests of various stakeholders (shareholders, employees, community, customers) rather than those of shareholders only.[7] Other research on a changing organization in the Philippines found that formal information sessions decreased employees' anxiety about the change, and that providing high-quality information about the change increased their commitment to it.[8]

PARTICIPATION   It's difficult to resist a change decision in which we've participated. Assuming participants have the expertise to make a meaningful contribution, their involvement can reduce resistance, obtain commitment, and increase the quality of the change decision. However, against these advantages are the negatives: the potential for a poor solution and a great consumption of time.

EXHIBIT 17-1

Sources of Resistance to Change

Individual Sources

Habit—To cope with life's complexities, we rely on habits or programmed responses. But when confronted with change, this tendency to respond in our accustomed ways becomes a source of resistance.

Security—People with a high need for security are likely to resist change because it threatens their feelings of safety.

Economic factors—Changes in job tasks or established work routines can arouse economic fears if people are concerned that they won't be able to perform the new tasks or routines to their previous standards, especially when pay is closely tied to productivity.

Fear of the unknown—Change substitutes ambiguity and uncertainty for the unknown.

Selective information processing—Individuals are guilty of selectively processing information in order to keep their perceptions intact. They hear what they want to hear, and they ignore information that challenges the world they've created.

Organizational Sources

Structural inertia—Organizations have built-in mechanisms—such as their selection processes and formalized regulations—to produce stability. When an organization is confronted with change, this structural inertia acts as a counterbalance to sustain stability.

Limited focus of change—Organizations consist of a number of interdependent subsystems. One can't be changed without affecting the others. So limited changes in subsystems tend to be nullified by the larger system.

Group inertia—Even if individuals want to change their behavior, group norms may act as a constraint.

Threat to expertise—Changes in organizational patterns may threaten the expertise of specialized groups.

Threat to established power relationships—Any redistribution of decision-making authority can threaten long-established power relationships within the organization.

BUILDING SUPPORT AND COMMITMENT   When managers or employees have low emotional commitment to change, they resist it and favor the status quo.[9] Employees are also more accepting of changes when they are committed to the organization as a whole.[10] So, firing up employees and emphasizing their commitment to the organization overall can help them emotionally commit to the change rather than embrace the status quo. Counseling and therapy, new-skills training, or a short paid leave of absence may facilitate adjustment to change when employees' fear and anxiety are high.

DEVELOPING POSITIVE RELATIONSHIPS   People are more willing to accept changes if they trust the managers implementing them.[11] One study surveyed 235 employees from a large housing corporation in the Netherlands that was experiencing a merger. Those who had a more positive relationship with their supervisor, and who felt that the work environment supported development, were much more positive about the change process.[12] Underscoring the importance of social context, other work shows that even individuals who are generally resistant to change will be more willing to accept new and different ideas when they feel supported by their coworkers and believe the environment is safe for taking risks.[13] Another set of studies found that individuals who were dispositionally resistant to change felt more positive about change if they trusted the change agent.[14]

IMPLEMENTING CHANGES FAIRLY   One way organizations can minimize negative impact is to make sure change is implemented fairly. As we saw in Chapter 7, procedural fairness is especially important when employees perceive an outcome as negative, so it's crucial that employees see the reason for the change and perceive its implementation as consistent and fair.[15]

MANIPULATION AND COOPTATION   *Manipulation* refers to covert influence attempts. Twisting facts to make them more attractive, withholding information, and creating false rumors to get employees to accept change are all examples of manipulation. *Cooptation*, on the other hand, combines manipulation and participation. It seeks to buy off the leaders of a resistance group by giving them a key role, seeking their advice not to find a better solution but to get their endorsement. Both manipulation and cooptation are relatively inexpensive ways to gain the support of adversaries, but they can backfire if the targets become aware they are being tricked or used. Once that's discovered, the change agent's credibility may drop to zero.

SELECTING PEOPLE WHO ACCEPT CHANGE   Research suggests the ability to easily accept and adapt to *change* is related to personality—some people simply have more positive attitudes toward change.[16] Individuals who are open to experience, are willing to take risks, and are flexible in their behavior are prime candidates. This seems to be universal. One study of managers in the United States, Europe, and Asia found those with a positive self-concept and high risk tolerance coped better with organizational change. A study of 258 police officers found those who were higher in the need for growth/development and internal work motivation, and who also had an internal locus of control, held more positive attitudes about organizational change efforts.[17] Individuals higher in general mental ability are also better able to learn and adapt to changes in the workplace.[18] In sum, an impressive body of evidence shows organizations can facilitate change by selecting people predisposed to accept it.

COERCION   Last on the list of tactics is *coercion*, the application of direct threats or force on dissenters. If management is determined to close a manufacturing plant whose employees don't acquiesce to a pay cut, the company is using coercion. Other examples of coercion include threatening employees with forced transfers, blocked promotions, negative performance evaluations, and poor letters of recommendation. Coercion is most effective when some force or pressure is enacted on at least some resisters—for instance, if an employee is publicly refused a transfer request, the threat of blocked promotions will become a real possibility in the minds of other employees. The advantages and drawbacks of coercion are approximately the same as for manipulation and cooptation.

The Politics of Change

No discussion of resistance would be complete without a mention of the politics of change. Because change invariably threatens the status quo, it inherently implies political activity.

Politics suggests the impetus for change is more likely to come from outside change agents, employees new to the organization (who have less invested in the status quo), or managers who are slightly removed from the main power structure. Managers who have spent a long time with an organization and achieved a senior position in the hierarchy are often major impediments to change. Of course, as you might guess, these longtime power holders tend to implement incremental changes when they are forced to introduce change. Radical change is often considered too threatening. This explains why boards of directors that recognize the imperative for rapid and radical change frequently turn to outside candidates for new leadership.[19]

APPROACHES TO MANAGING ORGANIZATIONAL CHANGE

We now turn to several approaches to managing change: Lewin's classic three-step model of the change process, Kotter's eight-step plan, action research, and organizational development.

Lewin's Three-Step Model

Kurt Lewin argued that successful change in organizations should follow three steps: *unfreezing* the status quo, *movement* to a desired end state, and *refreezing* the new change to make it permanent[20] (see Exhibit 17-2).

By definition, status quo is an equilibrium state. To move from equilibrium—to overcome the pressures of both individual resistance and group conformity—unfreezing must happen in one of three ways (see Exhibit 17-3). For one, the **driving forces**, which direct behavior away from the status quo, can be increased. For another, the **restraining forces**, which hinder movement away from equilibrium, can be decreased. A third alternative is to combine the first two approaches. Companies that have been successful in the past are likely to encounter restraining forces because people question the need for change.[21]

Once the movement stage begins, it's important to keep the momentum going. Organizations that build up to change do less well than those that get to and move through the movement stage quickly. When change has been implemented, the new situation must be refrozen so it can be sustained over time. Without this last step, change will likely be short-lived and employees will attempt to revert to the previous equilibrium state. The objective of refreezing, then, is to stabilize the new situation by balancing the driving and restraining forces.

Driving forces
Forces that direct behavior away from the status quo (Lewin).

Restraining forces
Forces that hinder movement from the existing equilibrium (Lewin).

EXHIBIT 17-2
Lewin's Three-Step Change Model

Kotter's Eight-Step Plan

John Kotter built on Lewin's three-step model to create a more detailed approach for implementing change.[22] Kotter began by listing common mistakes managers make when trying to initiate change. They may fail to do one or more of the following: to create a sense of urgency about the need for change, to create a coalition for managing the change process, to have a vision for change and effectively communicate it, and/or to anchor the changes into the organization's culture. They also may fail to remove obstacles that could impede the vision's achievement and/or provide short-term and achievable goals. Finally, they may declare victory too soon.

EXHIBIT 17-3
Unfreezing the Status Quo

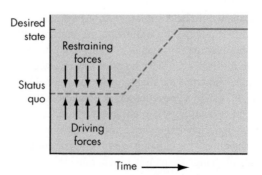

1. Establish a sense of urgency by creating a compelling reason for why change is needed.
2. Form a coalition with enough power to lead the change.
3. Create a new vision to direct the change and strategies for achieving the vision.
4. Communicate the vision throughout the organization.
5. Empower others to act on the vision by removing barriers to change and encouraging risk taking and creative problem solving.
6. Plan for, create, and reward short-term "wins" that move the organization toward the new vision.
7. Consolidate improvements, reassess changes, and make necessary adjustments in the new programs.
8. Reinforce the changes by demonstrating the relationship between new behaviors and organizational success.

EXHIBIT 17-4
Kotter's Eight-Step Plan for Implementing Change

Source: Based on M. du Plessis, "Re-implementing an Individual Performance Management System as a Change Intervention at Higher Education Institutions Overcoming Staff Resistance," *Proceedings of the 7th European Conference on Management Leadership and Governance,* 2011, 105–15.

Kotter established eight sequential steps to overcome these problems. They're listed in Exhibit 17-4. Notice how Kotter's first four steps essentially extrapolate Lewin's "unfreezing" stage. Steps 5, 6, and 7 represent "movement," and the final step works on "refreezing." So Kotter's contribution lies in providing managers and change agents with a more detailed guide for successfully implementing change.

Action Research

Action research is a change process based on the systematic collection of data and selection of a change action based on what the analyzed data indicate.[23] Its value is in providing a scientific methodology for managing planned change. Action research consists of five steps (note how they closely parallel the scientific method): diagnosis, analysis, feedback, action, and evaluation.

Action research provides at least two specific benefits. First, it's problem-focused. The change agent objectively looks for problems, and the type of problem determines the type of change action. A second benefit of action research is the lowering of resistance. Because action research engages employees so thoroughly in the process, it reduces resistance to change. Once employees have actively participated in the feedback stage, the change process typically takes on a momentum of its own.

Action research
A change process based on the systematic collection of data and the selection of a change action based on what the analyzed data indicate.

Organizational Development

Organizational development (OD) is a collection of change methods that try to improve organizational effectiveness and employee well-being.[24]

OD methods value human and organizational growth, collaborative and participative processes, and a spirit of inquiry.[25] Contemporary OD borrows heavily from postmodern philosophy in placing heavy emphasis on the subjective ways people see and make sense of their work environment. The change agent may take the lead in OD, but there is a strong emphasis on collaboration.

Organizational development (OD)
A collection of planned change interventions, built on humanistic–democratic values, that seeks to improve organizational effectiveness and employee well-being.

What are some OD techniques or interventions for bringing about change? Here are six.

Sensitivity training
Training groups that seek to change behavior through unstructured group interaction.

SENSITIVITY TRAINING   A variety of names—**sensitivity training**, laboratory training, encounter groups, and T-groups (training groups)—all refer to an early method of changing behavior through unstructured group interaction.[26] Current organizational interventions such as diversity training, executive coaching, and team-building exercises are descendants of this early OD intervention technique.

SURVEY FEEDBACK   One tool for assessing the attitudes of organizational members, identifying discrepancies among member perceptions, and solving differences is the **survey feedback** approach.[27] Basically, data collected from strategic surveys is then used to spur problem identification and discussion.

Survey feedback
The use of questionnaires to identify discrepancies among member perceptions; discussion follows and remedies are suggested.

The survey feedback approach can be helpful to keep decision makers informed about the attitudes of employees toward the organization. However, individuals are influenced by many factors when they respond to surveys, which may make some findings unreliable. Second, a high number of nonresponses may indicate organizational dysfunction or decreased job satisfaction, which the absence of data will not show. Managers who use the survey feedback approach should therefore monitor their organization's current events and employee response rates.

Process consultation (PC)
A meeting in which a consultant assists a client in understanding process events with which he or she must deal and identifying processes that need improvement.

PROCESS CONSULTATION   Managers often sense their unit's performance can be improved but are unable to identify what to improve and how. The purpose of **process consultation** (PC) is for an outside consultant to assist a client, usually a manager, "to perceive, understand, and act upon process events" with which the manager must deal.[28] These events might include those surrounding the workflow, informal relationships among unit members, and formal communication channels in the organization.

PC is similar to sensitivity training in assuming we can improve organizational effectiveness by dealing with interpersonal problems and in emphasizing involvement. But PC is more task-directed, and consultants do not solve the organization's problems, but rather guide or coach the client to solve his or her own problems after *jointly* diagnosing what needs improvement. The client develops the skill to analyze processes within his or her unit and can therefore use the skill long after the consultant is gone. Because the client actively participates in both the diagnosis and the development of alternatives, he or she arrives at a greater understanding of the process and the remedy, and becomes less resistant to the action plan chosen.

Team building
High interaction among team members to increase trust and openness.

TEAM BUILDING   We've noted throughout this text that organizations increasingly rely on teams to accomplish work tasks. **Team building** uses high-interaction group activities to increase trust and openness among team members, improve coordination efforts, and increase team performance.[29]

Team building typically includes goal-setting, development of interpersonal relations among team members, role analysis to clarify each member's role and responsibilities, and team process analysis. It may emphasize or exclude certain activities, depending on the purpose of the development effort and the specific problems the team is confronting. Basically, however, team building uses high interaction among members to increase trust and openness. In these times when organizations increasingly rely on teams, team building is an important topic.

INTERGROUP DEVELOPMENT A major area of concern in OD is dysfunctional conflict among groups. **Intergroup development** seeks to change groups' attitudes, stereotypes, and perceptions about each other. Here, training sessions closely resemble diversity training, except rather than focusing on demographic differences, they focus on differences among occupations, departments, or divisions within an organization. Among several approaches for improving intergroup relations, a popular one emphasizes problem solving.[30] Each group meets independently to list its perceptions of itself and another group and how it believes the other group perceives it. The groups then share their lists, discuss similarities and differences, and look for causes of disparities.

> **Intergroup development**
> Organizational development (OD) efforts to change the attitudes, stereotypes, and perceptions that groups have of each other.

Once they have identified the causes of discrepancies, the groups move to the integration phase—developing solutions to improve relations between them. Subgroups can be formed of members from each of the conflicting groups to conduct further diagnoses and formulate alternative solutions.

APPRECIATIVE INQUIRY Most OD approaches are problem-centered. They identify a problem or set of problems, then look for a solution. **Appreciative inquiry** (**AI**) instead accentuates the positive.[31] Rather than looking for problems to fix, it seeks to identify the unique qualities and special strengths of an organization, which members can build on to improve performance. That is, AI focuses on an organization's successes rather than its problems.

> **Appreciative inquiry (AI)**
> An approach that seeks to identify the unique qualities and special strengths of an organization, which can then be built on to improve performance.

The AI process consists of four steps—discovery, dreaming, design, and destiny—often played out in a large-group meeting over two to three days and overseen by a trained change agent. *Discovery* sets out to identify what people think are the organization's strengths. Employees recount times they felt the organization worked best or when they specifically felt most satisfied with their jobs. In *dreaming*, employees use information from the discovery phase to speculate on possible futures, such as what the organization will be like in five years. In *design*, participants find a common vision of how the organization will look in the future and agree on its unique qualities. For the fourth step, participants seek to define the organization's *destiny* or how to fulfill their dream, and they typically write action plans and develop implementation strategies.

CREATING A CULTURE FOR CHANGE

We've considered how organizations can *adapt* to change. But recently, some OB scholars have focused on a more proactive approach—how organizations can *embrace* change by transforming their cultures. In this section, we review three approaches: managing paradox, stimulating an innovative culture, and creating a learning organization. We also address the issue of organizational change and stress.

Managing Paradox

Managers can learn a few lessons from **paradox theory**,[32] which states the key paradox in management is that there is no final optimal status for an organization.[33] In a *paradox* situation, we are required to balance tensions across various courses of action. There is a constant process of finding a balancing point, a dynamic equilibrium, among shifting priorities over time. The first lesson is that as the environment and members of the organization change, different elements take on more or less importance. For example, sometimes a company needs to acknowledge past success and learn how it worked, while at other times looking

> **Paradox theory**
> The theory that the key paradox in management is that there is no final optimal status for an organization.

backward will only hinder progress. There is some evidence that managers who think holistically and recognize the importance of balancing paradoxical factors are more effective, especially in generating adaptive and creative behaviors in those they are managing.[34]

Stimulating a Culture of Innovation

How can an organization become more innovative? Although there is no guaranteed formula, certain characteristics—in structure, culture, and human resource (HR) policies—surface repeatedly when researchers study innovative organizations. Let's first clarify what we mean by innovation.

Innovation
A new idea applied to initiating or improving a product, process, or service.

DEFINITION OF *INNOVATION* We said change refers to making things different. **Innovation**, a specialized kind of change, is applied to initiating or improving a product, process, or service.[35] So all innovations imply change, but not all changes introduce new ideas or lead to significant improvements. Innovations can range from incremental improvements, such as tablets, to radical breakthroughs, such as Nissan's electric LEAF car.

SOURCES OF INNOVATION Structural variables are one potential source of innovation.[36] A comprehensive review of the structure–innovation relationship leads to the following conclusions:[37]

1. **Organic structures.** Because they're lower in vertical differentiation, formalization, and centralization; organic organizations facilitate the flexibility, adaptation, and cross-fertilization that make the adoption of innovations easier.
2. **Long tenure in management.** Managerial tenure can provide the legitimacy and knowledge of how to accomplish tasks and obtain desired outcomes through creative methods.
3. **Slack resources.** Having an abundance of resources allows an organization to afford to purchase or develop innovations, bear the cost of instituting them, and absorb failures.
4. **High interunit communication.**[38] These organizations are heavy users of committees, task forces, cross-functional teams, and other mechanisms that facilitate interaction across departmental lines.

CONTEXT AND INNOVATION. Innovative organizations tend to have similar cultures. They encourage experimentation and reward both successes and failures. Unfortunately, in too many organizations, people are rewarded for the absence of failures rather than for the presence of successes. Such cultures extinguish risk taking and innovation. Innovative organizations have policies to actively promote the training and development of their members so they keep current, offer high job security so employees don't fear getting fired for making mistakes, and encourage individuals to become champions of change. These practices should be mirrored for workgroups as well. One study of 1,059 individuals on over 200 different teams in a Chinese high-tech company found that work systems emphasizing commitment to employees increased creativity in teams.[39] These effects were even greater in teams where there was cohesion among coworkers.

IDEA CHAMPIONS AND INNOVATION Once a new idea has been developed, **idea champions** actively and enthusiastically promote it, build support, overcome resistance, and ensure it is implemented.[40] Champions often have similar personality characteristics:

extremely high self-confidence, persistence, energy, and a tendency to take risks. They usually display traits associated with transformational leadership—they inspire and energize others with their vision of an innovation's potential and their strong personal conviction about their mission. Situations can also influence the extent to which idea champions are forces for change. For example, passion for change among entrepreneurs is greatest when work roles and the social environment encourage them to put their creative identities forward.[41] On the flip side, work roles that push creative individuals to do routine management and administration tasks will diminish both the passion for and successful implementation of change. Idea champions are good at gaining the commitment of others, and their jobs should provide considerable decision-making discretion. This autonomy helps them introduce and implement innovations when the context is supportive.[42]

Idea champions
Individuals who take an innovation and actively and enthusiastically promote the idea, build support, overcome resistance, and ensure that the idea is implemented.

Do successful idea champions do things differently in varied cultures? Yes.[43] Generally, people in collectivist cultures prefer appeals for cross-functional support for innovation efforts; people in high power-distance cultures prefer champions to work closely with those in authority to approve innovative activities before work has begun; and the higher the uncertainty avoidance of a society, the more champions should work within the organization's rules and procedures to develop the innovation.

Creating a Learning Organization

Another way an organization can proactively manage change is to make continuous growth part of its culture—to become a learning organization.[44]

WHAT'S A LEARNING ORGANIZATION?   Just as individuals learn, so do organizations. A **learning organization** has developed the continuous capacity to adapt and change. The Dimensions of the Learning Organization Questionnaire (DLOQ) has been adopted and adapted internationally to assess the degree of commitment to learning organization principles.[45]

Learning organization
An organization that has developed the continuous capacity to adapt and change.

Exhibit 17-5 summarizes the five basic characteristics of a learning organization—one in which people put aside their old ways of thinking, learn to be open with each other, understand how their organization really works, form a plan or vision everyone can agree on, and work together to achieve that vision.[46]

1. There exists a shared vision that everyone agrees on.

2. People discard their old ways of thinking and the standard routines they use for solving problems or doing their jobs.

3. Members think of all organizational processes, activities, functions, and interactions with the environment as part of a system of interrelationships.

4. People openly communicate with each other (across vertical and horizontal boundaries) without fear of criticism or punishment.

5. People sublimate their personal self-interest and fragmented departmental interests to work together to achieve the organization's shared vision.

EXHIBIT 17-5
Characteristics of a Learning Organization

Source: Based on P. M. Senge, *The Fifth Discipline: The Art and Practice of the Learning Organization* (New York: Doubleday, 2006).

MANAGING LEARNING What can managers do to make their firms learning organizations? Here are some suggestions:

- **Establish a strategy.** Management needs to make explicit its commitment to change, innovation, and continuous improvement.
- **Redesign the organization's structure.** The formal structure can be a serious impediment to learning. Flattening the structure, eliminating or combining departments, and increasing the use of cross-functional teams reinforces interdependence and reduces boundaries.
- **Reshape the organization's culture.** To become a learning organization, managers must demonstrate by their actions that taking risks and admitting failures are desirable. This means rewarding people who take chances and make mistakes. Management needs to encourage functional conflict.

Organizational Change and Stress

Think about the times you have felt stressed during your work life. Look past the everyday stress factors that can spill over to the workplace, like a traffic jam that makes you late for work. What have been your more memorable and lasting stressful times at work? For many people, they were those caused by organizational change.

Not surprisingly, we also find the role of leadership is critical. One study indicates that transformational leaders can help shape employee affect so employees stay committed to the change and do not perceive it as stressful.[47] Other research indicates that a positive orientation toward change *before* new initiatives are planned will decrease employees' stress when they go through organizational changes and increase their positive attitudes. Managers can continually strive to increase employees' self-efficacy, change-related attitudes, and perceived control over the situation to create this positive change orientation. For instance, they can use role clarification and continual rewards to increase self-efficacy, and they can enhance employees' perceived control and positive attitudes toward change by including them throughout the planning stages to the application of new processes.[48] Another study adds the need for increasing the amount of communication to employees during change, assessing and enhancing employees' psychological resilience through offering social support, and training employees in emotional self-regulation techniques.[49] Through these methods, managers can help employees keep their stress levels low and their commitment high.

⊙ WATCH IT

If your professor has chosen to assign this, go to the Assignments section of **mymanagementlab.com** to complete the video exercise titled **East Haven Fire Department: Managing Stress**.

STRESS AT WORK

Friends say they're stressed from greater workloads and longer hours than ever before. Parents worry about the lack of job stability and reminisce about a time when a job with a large corporation implied lifetime security. Employees complain about the stress of trying to balance work and family responsibilities. Harris, Rothenberg International, a leading provider of employee assistance programs (EAPs), finds that employees are having mental

What area of your life causes you the most stress?

Area	Causes Most Stress
Financial worries	64%
Work	60%
Family responsibilities	47%
Health concerns	46%

EXHIBIT 17-6

Work Is a Top Source of Stress

Source: "Stress in America: Paying with Our Health," American Psychological Association, February 4, 2015, http://www.apa.org/news/press/releases/stress/2014/stress-report.pdf.

breakdowns and needing professional help at higher rates than ever.[50] Indeed, as Exhibit 17-6 shows, work is a major source of stress in most people's lives. What are the causes and consequences of stress, and what can individuals and organizations do to reduce it?

What Is Stress?

Stress is a dynamic condition in which an individual is confronted with an opportunity, demand, or resource related to what the individual desires and for which the outcome is perceived to be both uncertain and important.[51] Although stress is typically discussed in a negative context, it also has a positive purpose. Many professionals see the pressures of heavy workloads and deadlines as positive challenges that enhance the quality of their work and the satisfaction they get from their job. However, when the situation is negative, stress is harmful and may hinder your progress by elevating your blood pressure uncomfortably and creating an erratic heart rhythm as you struggle to speak and think logically.[52]

STRESSORS   Researchers have argued that **challenge stressors**—or stressors associated with workload, pressure to complete tasks, and time urgency—operate quite differently from **hindrance stressors**—or stressors that keep you from reaching your goals (for example, red tape, office politics, confusion over job responsibilities). Although research is just starting to accumulate, early evidence suggests challenge stressors produce less strain than hindrance stressors.[53]

Researchers have sought to differentiate the effects of challenge and hindrance stressors. When challenge stress increases, those with high levels of organizational support realize higher role-based performance, but those with low levels of organizational support do not.[54] There is also evidence that challenge stress improves job performance in a supportive work environment, whereas hindrance stress reduces job performance in all work environments.[55]

DEMANDS AND RESOURCES   Typically, stress is associated with **demands** and **resources**. Demands are responsibilities, pressures, obligations, and uncertainties individuals face in the workplace. Resources are things within an individual's control that he or she can use to resolve the demands. Let's discuss what this demands–resources model means.[56]

When you take a test at school or undergo your annual performance review at work, you feel stress because you confront opportunities and performance pressures. A good performance review may lead to a promotion, greater responsibilities, and a higher salary. A poor review may prevent you from getting a promotion. An extremely poor review might even result in your being fired. To the extent you can apply resources to the demands

Stress
An unpleasant psychological process that occurs in response to environmental pressures.

Challenge stressors
Stressors associated with workload, pressure to complete tasks, and time urgency.

Hindrance stressors
Stressors that keep you from reaching your goals (for example, red tape, office politics, confusion over job responsibilities).

Demands
Responsibilities, pressures, obligations, and even uncertainties that individuals face in the workplace.

Resources
Things within an individual's control that can be used to resolve demands.

on you—such as preparing for the review, putting the review in perspective (it's not the end of the world), or obtaining social support—you will feel less stress. In fact, this last resource—social support—may be more important on an ongoing basis than anything else. According to recent research, people with emotional support may experience lower stress levels, feel less depressed from stress, and be more likely to make lifestyle changes that may reduce stress.[57] Overall, under the demands–resources perspective, having resources to cope with stress is just as important in offsetting stress as demands are in increasing it.[58]

ALLOSTASIS So far, what was discussed may give you the impression that individuals are seeking a steady state in which demands perfectly match resources. While early research tended to emphasize such a *homeostatic*, or balanced equilibrium, perspective; it has now become clear that no single ideal state exists. Instead, it's more accurate to talk about *allostatic* models, in which demands shift, resources shift, and systems of addressing imbalances shift.[59] Through **allostasis**, we work to find stability by changing our behaviors and attitudes. It all depends on the allostatic load, or the cumulative effect of stressors on us given the resources we draw upon.[60] For example, if you're feeling especially confident in your abilities and have lots of support from others, you may increase your willingness to experience strain and be better able to mobilize coping resources. This would be a situation where the allostatic load was not too great; in other cases where the allostatic load is too great and too prolonged, we may experience psychological or physiological stress symptoms.

Allostasis
Working to change behavior and attitudes to find stability.

Potential Sources of Stress at Work

What causes stress? A meta-analysis of responses from more than 35,000 individuals showed role ambiguity, role conflict, role overload, job insecurity, environmental uncertainty, and situational constraints were all consistently negatively related to job performance.[61] To break it down, let's examine the model in Exhibit 17-7.

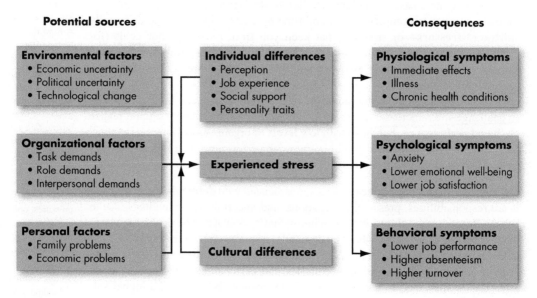

Potential sources

Environmental factors
- Economic uncertainty
- Political uncertainty
- Technological change

Organizational factors
- Task demands
- Role demands
- Interpersonal demands

Personal factors
- Family problems
- Economic problems

Individual differences
- Perception
- Job experience
- Social support
- Personality traits

Experienced stress

Cultural differences

Consequences

Physiological symptoms
- Immediate effects
- Illness
- Chronic health conditions

Psychological symptoms
- Anxiety
- Lower emotional well-being
- Lower job satisfaction

Behavioral symptoms
- Lower job performance
- Higher absenteeism
- Higher turnover

EXHIBIT 17-7
A Model of Stress

ENVIRONMENTAL FACTORS   Environmental uncertainty not only influences the design of an organization's structure, it also influences stress levels among employees in that organization. Indeed, uncertainty is the biggest reason people have trouble coping with organizational changes.[62] There are three main types of environmental uncertainty: economic, political, and technological.

Changes in the business cycle create *economic uncertainties*. When the economy is contracting, for example, people become increasingly anxious about their job security. *Political uncertainties* don't tend to create stress among North Americans as much as they do for employees in countries such as Haiti or Venezuela. The obvious reason is that the United States and Canada have more stable political systems, in which change is typically implemented in an orderly manner. Yet political threats and changes in all countries can induce stress. Because innovations can make an employee's skills and experience obsolete in a very short time, keeping up with new computer programs, robotics, automation, and similar forms of *technological change* are a further challenge to many people at work that cause them stress.

ORGANIZATIONAL FACTORS   There is no shortage of factors within an organization that can cause stress. Pressures to avoid errors or complete tasks in a limited time, work overload, a demanding and insensitive boss, and unpleasant coworkers are a few examples. We've categorized these factors around task, role, and interpersonal demands.

1. *Task demands* relate to a person's job. They include the design of the job (including its degree of autonomy, task variety, and automation), working conditions, and the physical work layout. The single factor most consistently related to stress in the workplace is the amount of work that needs to be done, followed closely by the presence of looming deadlines.[63] Working in an overcrowded room or visible location where noise and interruptions are constant can also increase anxiety and stress.[64]

2. *Role demands* relate to pressures placed on a person as a function of the particular role he or she plays in the organization. Role conflicts create expectations that may be hard to reconcile or satisfy. Role overload occurs when the employee is expected to take on too much. Role ambiguity means role expectations are not clearly understood and the employee is not sure what to do. Unfortunately, individuals who face high situational constraints by their roles (such as fixed work hours or demanding job responsibilities) are less able to engage in proactive coping behaviors, like taking a break, which can reduce stress levels.[65]

3. *Interpersonal demands* are pressures created by other employees. Some pressures are expected, but a rapidly growing body of research has shown that negative coworker and supervisor behaviors, including fights, bullying, incivility, racial harassment, and sexual harassment, are especially and strongly related to stress at work.[66] Interpersonal mistreatment can have effects at a physiological level, with one study finding that unfair treatment in a controlled setting triggered the release of cortisol, a hormone involved in the stress-reaction process.[67] Furthermore, individuals who believe they are experiencing a social climate of discrimination from multiple sources over time have higher levels of psychological strain, even after accounting for differing baseline levels of well-being.[68]

PERSONAL FACTORS   The typical individual may work between 40 and 50 hours a week. But the experiences and problems people encounter in the other 120-plus hours in the week can spill over to the job. The final category of sources of stress at work includes factors of an employee's personal life: family issues and personal economic problems.

National surveys consistently show people hold their families dear. *Family issues*, even good ones, can cause stress that significantly impacts individuals. Family issues are often closely related to work–life conflict.

The *personal economic problems* of overextended financial resources create stress and siphon attention away from work. Regardless of income level, some people are poor money managers or have wants and needs that exceed their earning capacity. People who make $100,000 per year seem to have as much trouble handling their finances as those who earn $20,000, although recent research indicates that those who make under $50,000 per year do experience more stress.[69]

STRESSORS ARE ADDITIVE   When we review stressors individually, it's easy to overlook that stress is an additive phenomenon—it builds up.[70] Each new and persistent stressor adds to an individual's stress level. A single stressor may be relatively unimportant in and of itself, but if added to an already high level of stress, it can be too much. To appraise the total amount of stress an individual is under, we have to sum up all of the sources and severity levels of that person's stress. Since this cannot be easily quantified or observed, managers should remain aware of the potential stress loads from organizational factors in particular. Many employees are willing to express their perceived stress load at work to a caring manager.

Individual Differences in Stress

Some people thrive on stressful situations, while others are overwhelmed by them. What differentiates people in terms of their ability to handle stress? What individual variables moderate the relationship between *potential* stressors and *experienced* stress? At least four are relevant—perception, job experience, social support, and personality traits.

PERCEPTION   In Chapter 6, we demonstrated that employees react in response to their perception of reality, rather than to reality itself. *Perception*, therefore, will moderate the relationship between a potential stress condition and an employee's reaction to it. Layoffs may cause one person to fear losing a job, while another sees it as an opportunity to get a large severance allowance and start a new business. So stress potential doesn't lie in objective conditions; rather, it lies in an employee's interpretation of those conditions.

JOB EXPERIENCE   *Experience* on the job tends to be negatively related to work stress. Why? Two explanations have been offered.[71] First is selective withdrawal. Voluntary turnover is more probable among people who experience more stress. Therefore, people who remain with an organization longer are those with more stress-resistant traits or those more resistant to the stress characteristics of the organization. Second, people eventually develop coping mechanisms to deal with stress. Because this takes time, senior members of the organization are more likely to be fully adapted and should experience less stress.

SOCIAL SUPPORT   *Social support*—collegial relationships with coworkers or supervisors—can buffer the impact of stress.[72] This is one of the best-documented relationships in the stress literature. Social support acts as a palliative, mitigating the negative effects of even high-strain jobs.

PERSONALITY TRAITS   Stress symptoms expressed on the job may originate from the person's personality.[73] Perhaps the most widely studied *personality trait* in research on stress is neuroticism, which we discussed in Chapter 5. As you might expect, neurotic individuals are more prone to experience psychological strain.[74] Evidence suggests that neurotic individuals are more likely to find stressors in their work environments, so they believe their environments are more threatening. They also tend to select less adaptive coping mechanisms, relying on avoidance as a way of dealing with problems rather than attempting to resolve them.[75]

Cultural Differences

Research suggests that the job conditions that cause stress show some differences across cultures. One study revealed that whereas U.S. employees were stressed by a lack of control, Chinese employees were stressed by job evaluations and lack of training. It doesn't appear that personality effects on stress are different across cultures, however. One study of employees in Hungary, Italy, the United Kingdom, Israel, and the United States found Type A personality traits (see Chapter 5) predicted stress equally well across countries.[76] A study of 5,270 managers from 20 countries found individuals from individualistic countries such as the United States, Canada, and the United Kingdom experienced higher levels of stress due to work interfering with family than did individuals from collectivist countries in Asia and Latin America.[77] The authors proposed that this may occur because, in collectivist cultures, working extra hours is seen as a sacrifice to help the family, whereas in individualistic cultures, work is seen as a means to personal achievement that takes away from the family.

Evidence suggests that stressors are associated with perceived stress and strains among employees in different countries. In other words, stress is equally bad for employees of all cultures.[78]

CONSEQUENCES OF STRESS AT WORK

Stress shows itself in a number of ways, such as high blood pressure, ulcers, irritability, difficulty making routine decisions, changes in appetite, accident proneness, and the like. Refer back to Exhibit 17-7. These symptoms can be fit under three general categories: physiological, psychological, and behavioral symptoms.

PHYSIOLOGICAL SYMPTOMS   Most early concerns with stress were directed at physiological symptoms because most researchers were specialists in the health and medical sciences. Their work led to the conclusion that stress could create changes in metabolism, increase heart and breathing rates and blood pressure, bring on headaches, and induce heart attacks.

Evidence now clearly suggests stress may have other harmful physiological effects. A long-term study conducted in the United Kingdom found that job strain was associated with higher levels of coronary heart disease.[79] Still another study conducted with Danish human services workers found that higher levels of psychological burnout at the work-unit level were related to significantly higher levels of sickness absence.[80] Many other studies have shown similar results linking work stress to a variety of indicators of poor health.

PSYCHOLOGICAL SYMPTOMS Job dissatisfaction is an obvious cause of stress. But stress shows itself in other psychological states—for instance, tension, anxiety, irritability, boredom, and procrastination. One study that tracked physiological responses of employees over time found that stress due to high workloads was related to lower emotional well-being.[81]

Jobs that make multiple and conflicting demands or that lack clarity about the incumbent's duties, authority, and responsibilities increase both stress and dissatisfaction.[82] Similarly, the less control people have over the pace of their work, the greater their stress and dissatisfaction. Jobs that provide a low level of variety, significance, autonomy, feedback, and identity appear to create stress and reduce satisfaction and involvement in the job.[83] Not everyone reacts to autonomy in the same way, however. For those with an external locus of control, increased job control increases the tendency to experience stress and exhaustion.[84]

BEHAVIORAL SYMPTOMS Research on behavior and stress has been conducted across several countries and over time, and the relationships appear relatively consistent. Behavior-related stress symptoms include reductions in productivity; increases in absences and turnover; and personal changes in eating habits, increased smoking or consumption of alcohol, rapid speech, fidgeting, and sleep disorders.[85]

A significant amount of research has investigated the stress–performance relationship. One study indicated that individuals with high emotional intelligence (EI, discussed in Chapter 4) may be able to mitigate the effects of job stress on performance.[86] Therefore, this model may be a good, neutral starting point from which to study differences.

MANAGING STRESS

It's not unlikely for employees and management to have different notions of what constitutes an acceptable level of stress on the job. What management may consider to be "a positive stimulus that keeps the adrenaline running" is very likely to be seen as "excessive pressure" by the employee. Keep this in mind as we discuss individual and organizational approaches toward managing stress.[87]

Individual Approaches

An employee can and should take personal responsibility for reducing stress levels. Individual strategies that have proven effective include time-management techniques, physical exercise, relaxation techniques, and social support networks.

TIME-MANAGEMENT TECHNIQUES Many people manage their time poorly. The well-organized employee, like the well-organized student, can often accomplish twice as much as the person who is poorly organized. Time-management skills can help minimize procrastination by focusing efforts on immediate goals and boosting motivation even in the face of tasks that are less enjoyable.[88]

PHYSICAL EXERCISE Physicians have recommended noncompetitive *physical exercise*, such as aerobics, walking, jogging, swimming, and riding a bicycle, as a way to deal with excessive stress levels. These activities decrease the detrimental physiological responses to stress and allow us to recover from stress more quickly.[89]

RELAXATION TECHNIQUES   Individuals can teach themselves to reduce tension through *relaxation techniques* such as meditation, hypnosis, and deep breathing. The objective is to reach a state of deep physical relaxation, in which you focus all your energy on the release of muscle tension.[90] Deep relaxation for 15 or 20 minutes a day releases strain and provides a pronounced sense of peacefulness, as well as significant changes in heart rate, blood pressure, and other physiological factors. A growing body of research shows that simply taking breaks from work at routine intervals can facilitate psychological recovery and reduce stress significantly and may improve job performance, and these effects are even greater if relaxation techniques are employed.[91]

SOCIAL SUPPORT NETWORKS   As we have noted, friends, family, or work colleagues can provide an outlet when stress levels become excessive. Expanding your *social support network* provides someone to hear your problems and offer a more objective perspective on a stressful situation than your own.

Organizational Approaches

Several organizational factors that cause stress—particularly task and role demands—are controlled by management and thus can be modified or changed. Strategies to consider include improving employee selection and job placement, goal-setting, redesign of jobs, increasing employee involvement, organizational communication, employee sabbaticals, and corporate wellness programs.

SELECTION AND PLACEMENT   Certain jobs are more stressful than others, but as we've seen, individuals differ in their response to stressful situations. We know individuals with little experience or an external locus of control tend to be more prone to stress. Obviously, management shouldn't hire only experienced individuals with an internal locus, but such individuals may adapt better to high-stress jobs and perform those jobs more effectively. Similarly, *training* can increase an individual's self-efficacy and thus lessen job strain.

GOAL-SETTING   As discussed in Chapter 7, individuals perform better when they have specific and challenging goals and receive feedback on their progress toward these goals. Goals can reduce stress as well as provide motivation.[92] Employees who are highly committed to their goals and see purpose in their jobs experience less stress because they are more likely to perceive stressors as challenges rather than hindrances. Specific goals perceived as attainable clarify performance expectations. In addition, goal feedback reduces uncertainties about actual job performance. The result is less employee frustration, role ambiguity, and stress.

REDESIGNING JOBS   *Redesigning jobs* to give employees more responsibility, more meaningful work, more autonomy, and increased feedback can reduce stress because these factors give employees greater control over work activities and lessen dependence on others. But not all employees want enriched jobs. The right redesign for employees with a low need for growth might include less responsibility and increased specialization. If individuals prefer structure and routine, reducing skill variety should reduce uncertainties and stress levels.

EMPLOYEE INVOLVEMENT Role stress is detrimental to a large extent because employees feel uncertain about goals, expectations, how they'll be evaluated, and the like. By giving these employees a voice in the decisions that directly affect their job performance, management can increase employee control and reduce role stress. Thus, managers should consider increasing *employee involvement* in decision making because evidence clearly shows that increases in employee empowerment reduce psychological strain.[93]

ORGANIZATIONAL COMMUNICATION Increasing formal *organizational communication* with employees reduces uncertainty by lessening role ambiguity and role conflict. Given the importance that perceptions play in moderating the stress–response relationship, management can also use effective communication as a means to shape employee perceptions. Remember that what employees categorize as demands, threats, or opportunities at work is an interpretation; that interpretation can be affected by the symbols and actions communicated by management.

EMPLOYEE SABBATICALS Some employees need an occasional escape from the frenetic pace of their work. Companies including Genentech, American Express, Intel, General Mills, Microsoft, Morningstar, DreamWorks Animation, and Adobe Systems have begun to provide extended voluntary leaves.[94] These *sabbaticals*—ranging in length from a few weeks to several months—can revive and rejuvenate workers who might otherwise be headed for burnout.

Wellness programs
Organizationally supported programs that focus on the employee's total physical and mental condition.

WELLNESS PROGRAMS Our final suggestion is to create organizationally supported **wellness programs**. These typically provide workshops to help people quit smoking, control alcohol use, lose weight, eat better, and develop a regular exercise program; they focus on the employee's total physical and mental condition.[95] Some programs help employees improve their psychological health as well. A meta-analysis of 36 programs designed to reduce stress (including wellness programs) showed that interventions that helped employees reframe stressful situations and use active coping strategies appreciably reduced stress levels.[96] Most wellness programs assume employees need to take personal responsibility for their physical and mental health and that the organization is merely a means to that end.

Most firms that have introduced wellness programs have observed significant benefits. Johnson & Johnson reported that their wellness program has saved the organization $250 million in health care costs in 10 years, and research has indicated that effective wellness programs significantly decreased turnover rates for most organizations.[97] Other research sponsored by the U.S. Department of Labor and Department of Health and Human Services indicates that organizational wellness programs create healthier employees with fewer health risk factors.[98]

SUMMARY

The need for change has been implied throughout this text. For instance, think about attitudes, motivation, work teams, communication, leadership, organizational structures, HR practices, and organizational cultures. Change was an integral part in our discussion of each. If environments were perfectly static, if employees' skills and abilities were always up to date and incapable of deteriorating, and if tomorrow were always exactly the same as today, organizational change would have little or no relevance to managers. But the real world is turbulent, requiring organizations and their members to undergo dynamic change if they are to perform at competitive levels. Coping with all of these changes can be a source of stress, but with effective management, challenge can enhance engagement and fulfillment, leading to high performance which, as you've discovered in this text, is one major goal of the study of OB.

IMPLICATIONS FOR MANAGERS

- Consider that, as a manager, you are a change agent in your organization. The decisions you make and your role-modeling behaviors will help shape the organization's change culture.
- Your management policies and practices will determine the degree to which the organization learns and adapts to changing environmental factors.
- Some stress is good. Increasing challenges brought by autonomy and responsibility at work will lead to some stress but also increase feelings of accomplishment and fulfillment. Hindrance stressors like bureaucracy and interpersonal conflicts, on the other hand, are entirely negative and should be eliminated.
- You can help alleviate harmful workplace stress for your employees by accurately matching workloads to employees, providing employees with stress-coping resources, and responding to their concerns.
- You can identify extreme stress in your employees when performance declines, turnover increases, health-related absenteeism increases, and engagement declines. However, by the time these symptoms are visible, it may be too late to be helpful, so stay alert for early indicators and be proactive.

⭐ TRY IT!

If your professor has chosen to assign this, go to the Assignments section of **mymanagementlab.com** to complete the **Simulation: Change**.

⭐ PERSONAL INVENTORY ASSESSMENTS

Tolerance of Ambiguity Scale

How well can you tolerate the ambiguity that change brings? Take this PIA to learn more about your tolerance level for this challenge.

17-1. What do you think are the best ways to prepare employees for organizational change? Support your answers.

EPILOGUE

The end of a book typically has the same meaning to an author that it has to the reader: it generates feelings of both accomplishment and relief. As both of us rejoice at having completed our tour of the essential concepts in organizational behavior, this is a good time to examine where we've been and what it all means.

The underlying theme of this book has been that the behavior of people at work is not a random phenomenon. Employees are complex entities, but their attitudes and behavior can nevertheless be explained and predicted with a reasonable degree of accuracy. Our approach has been to look at organizational behavior at three levels: the individual, the group, and the organization system.

We started with the individual and reviewed the major psychological contributions to understanding why individuals act as they do. We found that many of the individual differences among employees can be systematically labeled and categorized, and therefore generalizations can be made. For example, we know that individuals with a conventional type of personality are better matched to certain jobs in corporate management than are people with investigative personalities. So placing people into jobs that are compatible with their personality types should result in higher-performing and more satisfied employees.

Next, our analysis moved to the group level. We argued that the understanding of group behavior is more complex than merely multiplying what we know about individuals by the number of members in the group, because people act differently in a group than when they are alone. We demonstrated how roles, norms, leadership styles, power relationships, and other similar group factors affect the behavior of employees.

Finally, we overlaid system-wide variables on our knowledge of individual and group behavior to further improve our understanding of organizational behavior. Major emphasis was given to showing how an organization's structure, design, and culture affect both the attitudes and the behavior of employees.

It may be tempting to criticize the stress this book placed on theoretical concepts, but as noted psychologist Kurt Lewin is purported to have said, "There is nothing so practical as a good theory." Of course, it's also true that there is nothing so impractical as a good theory that leads nowhere. To avoid presenting theories that lead nowhere, this book included a wealth of examples and illustrations and we regularly stopped to inquire about the implications of theory for the practice of management. The result has been the presentation of numerous concepts that, individually, offer some insights into behavior; but when taken together, provide a complex system to help you explain, predict, and control organizational behavior.

ENDNOTES

CHAPTER 1

1. "Survey: Few CFOs Plan to Invest in Interpersonal Skills Development for Their Teams," Accountemps press release, June 19, 2013, on the Accountemps website, http://accountemps.rhi.mediaroom.com/2013-06-19-Survey-Few-CFOs-Plan-to-Invest-in-Interpersonal-Skills-Development-for-Their-Teams.
2. K. Dill, "The 20 Best Places to Work in 2015," *Forbes,* December 10, 2014, http://www.forbes.com/sites/kathryndill/2014/12/10/the-best-places-to-work-in-2015/.
3. I. S. Fulmer, B. Gerhart, and K. S. Scott, "Are the 100 Best Better? An Empirical Investigation of the Relationship between Being a 'Great Place to Work' and Firm Performance," *Personnel Psychology* 56, no. 4, (2003): 965–93.
4. S. E. Humphrey, J. D. Nahrgang, and F. P. Morgeson, "Integrating Motivational, Social, and Contextual Work Design Features: A Meta-Analytic Summary and Theoretical Extension of the Work Design Literature," *Journal of Applied Psychology* 92, no. 5 (2007): 1332–56.
5. E. R. Burris, "The Risks and Rewards of Speaking Up: Managerial Responses to Employee Voice," *Academy of Management Journal* 55, no. 4 (2012): 851–75.
6. T. L. Miller, C. L. Wesley II, and D. E. Williams, "Educating the Minds of Caring Hearts: Comparing the Views of Practitioners and Educators on the Importance of Social Entrepreneurship Competencies," *Academy of Management Learning & Education* 2, no. 3 (2012): 349–70.
7. H. Aguinis and A. Glavas, "What We Don't Know about Corporate Social Responsibility: A Review and Research Agenda," *Journal of Management* 38, no. 4 (2012): 932–68.
8. D. Meinert, "Background on Bosses," *HR Magazine,* August 2014, 29.
9. Ibid.
10. Ibid.
11. For a review of what one researcher believes *should* be included in organizational behavior, based on survey data, see J. B. Miner, "The Rated Importance, Scientific Validity, and Practical Usefulness of Organizational Behavior Theories: A Quantitative Review," *Academy of Management Learning & Education* 2, no. 3 (2003): 250–68.
12. For the original study, see F. Luthans, "Successful vs. Effective Real Managers," *Academy of Management Executive,* 2, no. 2 (1988): 127–32. A great deal of research has been built by Fred Luthans and others from this study. See, for example, M. M. Hopkins, D. A. O'Neil, and J. K. Stoller, "Distinguishing Competencies of Effective Physician Leaders," *Journal of Management Development* 34, no. 5 (2015): 566–84.
13. P. Wu, M. Foo, and D. B. Turban, "The Role of Personality in Relationship Closeness, Developer Assistance, and Career Success," *Journal of Vocational Behavior* 73, no. 3 (2008): 440–48.
14. L. Dragoni, H. Park, J. Soltis, and S. Forte-Trammell, "Show and Tell: How Supervisors Facilitate Leader Development Among Transitioning Leaders," *Journal of Applied Psychology* 99, no. 1 (2014): 66–86.
15. D. M. Rousseau, *The Oxford Handbook of Evidence-Based Management* (New York: Oxford University Press, 2014).
16. J. Welch and S. Welch, "When to Go with Your Gut," *LinkedInPulse* (blog post), November 12, 2013, https://www.linkedin.com/pulse/20131112125301-86541065-when-to-go-with-your-gut.
17. Z. Karabell, "Everyone Has a Data Point," *The Wall Street Journal,* February 19, 2014, A11.
18. E. Morozov, "Every Little Byte Counts," *The New York Times Book Review,* May 18, 2014, 23.
19. M. Taves, "If I Could Have More Data…", *The Wall Street Journal,* March 24, 2014, R5.
20. "The Future of Work—A Journey to 2022,", PricewaterhouseCoopers LLP Report, 2014, http://www.pwc.com/gx/en/issues/talent/future-of-work/journey-to-2022.html
21. N. Bloom, R. Sadun, and J. Van Reenan, "Does Management Really Work? How Three Essential Practices can Address Even the Most Complex Global Problems," *Harvard Business Review,* November 2012, 77–82.
22. C. Cole, Association for Psychological Science, "Changing Neurobiology with Behavior," *Observer* 27, no. 6 (2014): 29–32.
23. E. Dwoskin, "Big Data Knows When You Turn off the Lights," *The Wall Street Journal,* October 21, 2014, B1–B2.
24. S. Lohr, "Unblinking Eyes Track Employees," *The New York Times,* June 22, 2014, 1, 15.
25. R. Karlgaard, "Danger Lurking: Taylor's Ghost," *Forbes,* May 26, 2014, 34.
26. C. Karmin and S. Chaturvedi, "Grosvenor House Is Seized," *The Wall Street Journal,* March 4, 2015, C8.
27. V. McGrane, "The Downside of Lower Unemployment," *The Wall Street Journal,* February 3, 2014, A2.
28. A. Lowrey, "Long Out of Work, and Running Out of Options," *The New York Times,* April 4, 2014, B1, B4.
29. L. Weber and R. E. Silverman, "On-Demand Workers: 'We Are Not Robots,'" *The Wall Street Journal,* January 28, 2015, B1, B7.
30. C. Porter and M. Korn, "Can This Online Course Get Me a Job?" *The Wall Street Journal,* March 4, 2014, B7.
31. D. Belkin and M. Peters, "For New Grads, Path to a Career Is Bumpy," *The Wall Street Journal,* May 24–25, 2014, A5.
32. N. Kitsantonis, "A Hands-On Approach to the Greek Economy," *The New York Times,* March 25, 2014, B3.
33. G. Naik, "Global Life Expectancy Rises by Six Years," *The Wall Street Journal,* December 18, 2014, A10.
34. J. Greenwald, "Tips for Dealing with Employees Whose Social Media Posts Reflect Badly on Your Company," *Forbes,* March 6, 2015, www.forbes.com/sites/entrepreneursorganization/2015/03/06/tips-for-dealing-with-employees-whose-social-media-posts-reflect-badly-on-your-company/.
35. E. Jaffe, Association for Psychological Science, "Using Technology to Scale the Scientific Mountain," *Observer* 27, no. 6 (2014): 17–19.
36. N. Fallon, "No Face Time? No Problem: How to Keep Virtual Workers Engaged," *Business News Daily,* October 2, 2014, http://www.businessnewsdaily.com/7228-engaging-remote-employees.html.
37. E. J. Hirst, "Burnout on the Rise," *Chicago Tribune,* October 19, 2012, http://articles.chicagotribune.com/2012-10-29/business/ct-biz-1029-employee-burnout-20121029_1_employee-burnout-herbert-freudenberger-employee-stress.

38. F. Luthans and C. M. Youssef, "Emerging Positive Organizational Behavior," *Journal of Management* 33, no. 3 (2007): 321–49; C. M. Youssef and F. Luthans, "Positive Organizational Behavior in the Workplace: The Impact of Hope, Optimism, and Resilience," *Journal of Management* 33, no. 5 (2007): 774–800; and J. E. Dutton and S. Sonenshein, "Positive Organizational Scholarship," in *Encyclopedia of Positive Psychology*, eds. C. Cooper and J. Barling, (Thousand Oaks, CA: Sage, 2007).

39. "Five Jobs That Won't Exist in 10 Years... And One New Title You'll Start to See," *HR Magazine*, February 2014, 16.

40. Editorial Board, "NCAA Should Punish the University of North Carolina for Cheating Scandal," *Chicago Tribune*, November 7, 2014, http://www.chicagotribune.com/news/opinion/editorials/ct-north-carolina-sports-scandal-edit-1108-20141107-story.html, accessed March 11, 2015.

41. D. M. Mayer, M. Kuenzi, R. Greenbaum, M. Bardes, and R. Salvador, "How Low Does Ethical Leadership Flow? Test of a Trickle-Down Model," *Organizational Behavior and Human Decision Processes* 108, no. 1 (2009): 1–13; and A. Ardichvili, J. A. Mitchell, and D. Jondle, "Characteristics of Ethical Business Cultures," *Journal of Business Ethics* 85, no. 4 (2009): 445–51.

42. D. Meinert, "Managers' Influence," *HR Magazine*, April 2014, 25.

43. X. Zhao and A. S. Mattila, "Examining the Spillover Effect of Frontline Employees' Work-Family Conflict on Their Affective Work Attitudes and Customer Satisfaction," *International Journal of Hospitality Management* 33 (2013): 310–15.

CHAPTER 2

1. A. R. Davies and B. D. Frink, "The Origins of the Ideal Worker: The Separation of Work and Home in the United States from the Market Revolution to 1950," *Work and Occupations* 41, no. 1 (2014): 18–39.

2. U.S. Census Bureau, *Current Population Survey*, December 2014; S. Ricker, "The Changing Face of U.S. Jobs: Composition of Occupations by Gender, Race, and Age from 2001–2014," *The Hiring Site* (CareerBuilder blog) March 26, 2015, www.thehiringsite.careerbuilder.com/2015/03/26/9-findings-diversity-americas-workforce.

3. L. Colley, "Not Codgers in Cardigans! Female Workforce Participation and Ageing Public Services," *Gender Work and Organization* 20, no. 3 (2013): 327–48.

4. W. H. Frey, *Diversity Explosion: How New Racial Demographics are Remaking America* (Washington, DC: Brookings Institution Press, 2014).

5. M. Toossi, "Labor Force Projections to 2020: A More Slowly Growing Workforce," *Monthly Labor Review* 135, no. 1 (2012): 43–64.

6. C. T. Kulik, "Spotlight on the Context: How a Stereotype Threat Framework Might Help Organizations to Attract and Retain Older Workers," *Industrial and Organizational Psychology* 7, no. 3 (2014): 456–61.

7. A. H. Eagly and J. L. Chin, "Are Memberships in Race, Ethnicity, and Gender Categories Merely Surface Characteristics?" *American Psychologist* 65, no. 9 (2010): 934–35.

8. W. J. Casper, J. H. Wayne, and J. G. Manegold, "Who Will We Recruit? Targeting Deep- and Surface-Level Diversity with Human Resource Policy Advertising," *Human Resource Management* 52, no. 3 (2013): 311–32.

9. J. H. Carlson and J. D. Seacat, "Multiple Threat: Overweight/Obese Women in the Workforce," and B. J. Casad and S. M. Merritt, "The Importance of Stereotype Threat Mechanisms in Workplace Outcomes," *Industrial and Organizational Psychology* 7, no. 3 (2014): 413–18.

10. G. Czukor and M. Bayazit, "Casting a Wide Net? Performance Deficit, Priming, and Subjective Performance Evaluation in Organizational Stereotype Threat Research," *Industrial and Organizational Psychology* 7, no. 3 (2014): 409–12; K. S. Jones and N. C. Carpenter, "Toward a Sociocultural Psychological Approach to Examining Stereotype Threat in the Workplace," *Industrial and Organizational Psychology* 7, no. 3 (2014): 429–32; and C. T. Kulik, "Spotlight on the Context: How a Stereotype Threat Framework Might Help Organizations to Attract and Retain Older Workers," *Industrial and Organizational Psychology* 7, no. 3 (2014): 456–61.

11. L. M. Cortina, "Unseen Injustice: Incivility as Modern Discrimination in Organizations," *Academy of Management Review* 33, no. 1 (2008): 55–75; and C. M. Harold and B. C. Holtz, "The Effects of Passive Leadership on Workplace Incivility," *Journal of Organizational Behavior* 36, no. 1 (2015): 16–38.

12. J. P. Jamieson, K. Koslov, M. K. Nock, and W. B. Mendes, "Experiencing Discrimination Increases Risk Taking," *Psychological Science* 24, no. 2 (2012): 131–39.

13. C. T. Kulik, S. Ryan, S. Harper, and G. George, "Aging Populations and Management," *Academy of Management Journal* 57, no. 4 (2014): 929–35.

14. T. Lytle, "Benefits for Older Workers," *HR Magazine*, March 2012, 53–58.

15. A. Tergesen, "Why Everything You Know about Aging Is Probably Wrong," *The Wall Street Journal*, December 1, 2014, B1–B2.

16. L. Turner and A. Suflas, "Global Diversity—One Program Won't Fit All," *HR Magazine*, May 2014, 59–61.

17. L. Weber, "Americans Rip Up Retirement Plans," *The Wall Street Journal*, January 31, 2013, http://online.wsj.com/article/SB10001424127887323926104578276241741448064.html.

18. M. Chand and R. L. Tung, "The Aging of the World's Population and Its Effects on Global Business," *Academy of Management Perspectives* 28, no. 4 (2014): 409–29.

19. S. Shellenbarger, "Work & Family Mailbox," *The Wall Street Journal*, January 29, 2014, D2.

20. N. E. Wolfson, T. M. Cavanaugh, and K. Kraiger, "Older Adults and Technology-Based Instruction: Optimizing Learning Outcomes and Transfer," *Academy of Management Learning & Education* 13, no. 1 (2014): 26–44.

21. A. Tergesen, "Why Everything You Know about Aging Is Probably Wrong." The Wall Street Journal (November 30, 2014).

22. Ibid.

23. Ibid.

24. T. W. H. Ng and D. C. Feldman, "The Relationship of Age with Job Attitudes: A Meta-Analysis," *Personnel Psychology* 63, no. 3 (2010): 677–718.

25. E. Zell, Z. Krizan, and S. R. Teeter, "Evaluating Gender Similarities and Differences Using Metasynthesis," *American Psychologist* 70, no. 1 (2015): 10–20.

26. J. B. Allendorfer et al., "Females and Males Are Highly Similar in Language Performance and Cortical Activation Patterns during Verb Generation," *Cortex* 48, no. 9 (2012): 1218–33; and A. Ardila, M. Rosselli, E. Matute, and O. Inozemtseva, "Gender Differences in Cognitive Development," *Developmental Psychology* 47, no. 4 (2011): 984–90.

27. P. L. Roth, K. L. Purvis, and P. Bobko, "A Meta-Analysis of Gender Group Differences for Measures of Job Performance in Field Studies," *Journal of Management* 38, no. 2 (2012): 719–39.

28. S. C. Paustian-Underdahl, L. S. Walker, and D. J. Woehr, "Gender and Perceptions of Leadership Effectiveness: A Meta-Analysis of Contextual Moderators," *Journal of Applied Psychology* 99, no. 6 (2014): 1129–45.

29. R. E. Silverman, "Study Suggests Fix for Gender Bias on the Job," *The Wall Street Journal,* January 9, 2013, D4.

30. A. J. Koch, S. D. D'Mello, and P. R. Sackett, "A Meta-Analysis of Gender Stereotypes and Bias in Experimental Simulations of Employment Decision Making," *Journal of Applied Psychology* 100, no. 1 (2015): 128–61.

31. E. B. King et al., "Benevolent Sexism at Work: Gender Differences in the Distribution of Challenging Developmental Experiences," *Journal of Management* 38, no. 6 (2012): 1835–66.

32. L. Gartzia, M. K. Ryan, N. Balluerka, and A. Aritzeta, "Think Crisis-Think Female: Further Evidence," *European Journal of Work and Organizational Psychology* 21, no. 4 (2014): 603–28.

33. P. Wechsler, "58 Women CFOs in the Fortune 500: Is This Progress?" *Fortune,* February 24, 2015, http://fortune.com/2015/02/24/58-women-cfos-in-the-fortune-500-is-this-progress/.

34. L. Turner and A. Suflas, "Global Diversity—One Program Won't Fit All."

35. Ibid.

36. H. L. Kusterer, T. Lindholm, and H. Montgomery, "Gender Typing in Stereotypes and Evaluations of Actual Managers," *Journal of Managerial Psychology* 28, no. 5 (2013): 561–79; and W. B. Morgan, K. B. Elder, and E. B. King, "The Emergence and Reduction of Bias in Letters of Recommendation," *Journal of Applied Social Psychology* 43, no. 11 (2013): 2297–2306.

37. T. Vega, "With Diversity Still Lacking, Industry Focuses on Retention," *The New York Times,* September 4, 2012, B3.

38. D. R. Avery, P. F. McKay, and D. C. Wilson "What Are the Odds? How Demographic Similarity Affects the Prevalence of Perceived Employment Discrimination," *Journal of Applied Psychology* 93, no. 2 (2008): 235–49.

39. J. M. Sacco, C. R. Scheu, A. M. Ryan, and N. Schmitt, "An Investigation of Race and Sex Similarity Effects in Interviews: A Multilevel Approach to Relational Demography," *Journal of Applied Psychology* 88, no. 5 (2003): 852–65; and P. F. McKay and M. A. McDaniel, "A Reexamination of Black-White Mean Differences in Work Performance: More Data, More Moderators," *Journal of Applied Psychology* 91, no. 3 (2006): 538–54.

40. S. Mullainathan, "The Measuring Sticks of Racial Bias," *The New York Times,* January 4, 2015, 6.

41. L. Turner and A. Suflas, "Global Diversity—One Program Won't Fit All."

42. Information on the Americans with Disabilities Act can be found on their website at www.ada.gov.

43. S. G. Goldberg, M. B. Killeen, and B. O'Day, "The Disclosure Conundrum: How People with Psychiatric Disabilities Navigate Employment," *Psychology, Public Policy, and Law* 11, no. 3 (2005): 463–500; and M. L. Ellison, Z. Russinova, K. L. MacDonald-Wilson, and A. Lyass, "Patterns and Correlates of Workplace Disclosure among Professionals and Managers with Psychiatric Conditions," *Journal of Vocational Rehabilitation* 18, no. 1 (2003): 3–13.

44. B. S. Bell and K. J. Klein, "Effect of Disability, Gender, and Job Level on Ratings of Job Applicants," *Rehabilitation Psychology* 46, no. 3 (2001): 229–46; and E. Louvet, "Social Judgment Toward Job Applicants with Disabilities: Perception of Personal Qualities and Competences," *Rehabilitation Psychology* 52, no. 3 (2007): 297–303.

45. L. R. Ren, R. L. Paetzold, and A. Colella, "A Meta-Analysis of Experimental Studies on the Effects of Disability on Human Resource Judgments," *Human Resource Management Review* 18, no. 3 (2008): 191–203.

46. S. Almond and A. Healey, "Mental Health and Absence from Work: New Evidence from the UK Quarterly Labour Force Survey," *Work, Employment, and Society* 17, no. 4 (2003): 731–42.

47. P. T. J. H. Nelissen, K. Vornholt, G. M. C. Van Ruitenbeek, U. R. Hülsheger, and S. Uitdewilligen, "Disclosure or Nondisclosure—Is This the Question?" *Industrial and Organizational Psychology* 7, no. 2 (2014): 231–35.

48. A. M. Santuzzi, P. R. Waltz, and L. M. Finkelstein, "Invisible Disabilities: Unique Challenges for Employees and Organizations," *Industrial and Organizational Psychology* 7, no. 2 (2014): 204–19.

49. Ibid.

50. R. A. Schriber, R. W. Robins, and M. Solomon, "Personality and Self-Insight in Individuals with Autism Spectrum Disorder," *Journal of Personality and Social Psychology* 106, no. 1 (2014): 112–30.

51. C. L. Nittrouer, R. C. E. Trump, K. R. O'Brien, and M. Hebl, "Stand Up and Be Counted: In the Long Run, Disclosing Helps All," *Industrial and Organizational Psychology* 7, no. 2 (2014): 235–41.

52. L. Turner and A. Suflas, "Global Diversity—One Program Won't Fit All."

53. T. Audi, "A New Mosque Rises in Anchorage," *The Wall Street Journal,* August 15, 2014, A5.

54. E. B. King and A. S. Ahmad, "An Experimental Field Study of Interpersonal Discrimination Toward Muslim Job Applicants," *Personnel Psychology* 63, no. 4 (2010): 881–906.

55. A. Liptak, "In a Case of Religious Dress, Justices Explore the Obligations of Employers," *The New York Times,* February 25, 2015, http://www.nytimes.com/2015/02/26/us/in-a-case-of-religious-dress-justices-explore-the-obligations-of-employers.html?

56. A. Tilcsik, "Pride and Prejudice: Employment Discrimination against Openly Gay Men in the United States," *American Journal of Sociology* 117, no. 2 (2011): 586–626.

57. J. Browne, "What One CEO Learned by Being Outed," *The Wall Street Journal,* June 7–8, 2014, C3.

58. "Facts about Discrimination in Federal Government Employment Based on Marital Status, Political Affiliation, Status as a Parent, Sexual Orientation, or Transgender (Gender Identity) Status," U.S. Equal Employment Opportunity Commission (2013), www.eeoc.gov/federal/otherprotections.cfm.

59. L. Turner and A. Suflas, "Global Diversity—One Program Won't Fit All."

60. V. Priola, D. Lasio, S. De Simone, and F. Serri, "The Sound of Silence: Lesbian, Gay, Bisexual, and Transgender Discrimination in 'Inclusive Organizations'," *British Journal of Management* 25, no. 3 (2012): 488–502.

61. "Sex-Based Discrimination," U.S. Equal Employment Opportunity Commission (2013), www.eeoc.gov/laws/types/sex.cfm.

62. M. Keisling, "No Longer at Zero: An Update on ENDA," The *Huffington Post,* March 13, 2013, www.huffingtonpost.com/mara-keisling/no-longer-at-zero-an-upda_b_2861885.html; and J. Pike, "One-Year Anniversary of Senate ENDA Passage," Human Rights Campaign (blog), November 7, 2014, http://www.hrc.org/blog/entry/one-year-anniversary-of-senate-enda-passage), accessed March 26, 2015.

63. C. Burns, *The Costly Business of Discrimination* (Washington, D.C.: Center for American Progress, 2012), www.scribd.com/doc/81214767/The-Costly-Business-of-Discrimination.

64. D. Fidas and L. Cooper, *HRC Corporate Equality Index* (Washington, D.C.: Human Rights Campaign Foundation, 2015), http://hrc-assets.s3-website-us-east-1.amazonaws.com//files/documents/CEI-2015-rev.pdf

65. V. Priola, D. Lasio, S. De Simone, and F. Serri, "The Sound of Silence: Lesbian, Gay, Bisexual, and Transgender Discrimination in 'Inclusive Organizations'", *British Journal of Management* 25, no. 3 (2014): 488–502.

66. P. A. Freund and N. Kasten, "How Smart Do You Think You Are? A Meta-Analysis of the Validity of Self-Estimates of Cognitive Ability," *Psychological Bulletin* 138, no. 2 (2012): 296–321.

67. R. E. Nisbett et al., "Intelligence: New Findings and Theoretical Developments," *American Psychologist* 67, no. 2 (2012): 130–59.

68. L. S. Gottfredson, "The Challenge and Promise of Cognitive Career Assessment," *Journal of Career Assessment* 11, no. 2 (2003): 32–34.

69. M. D. Dunnette and E. A. Fleishman, eds., *Human Performance and Productivity: Human Capability Assessment* (New York and London: Psychology Press/Taylor & Francis Group, 2014).

70. J. W. B. Lang, M. Kersting, U. R. Hülscheger, and J. Lang, "General Mental Ability, Narrower Cognitive Abilities, and Job Performance: The Perspective of the Nested-Factors Model of Cognitive Abilities" *Personnel Psychology* 63, no. 3 (2010): 595–640.

71. N. Barber, "Educational and Ecological Correlates of IQ: A Cross-National Investigation," *Intelligence* 33, no. 3 (2005): 273–84.

72. "What Companies Will Make You Take a Wonderlic Test?" *Beat the Wonderlic* (blog) December 31, 2014, http://www.beatthewonderlic.com/blog/2014/12/31/what-companies-will-make-you-take-a-wonderlic-test.

73. Y. Ganzach, "Intelligence, Education, and Facets of Job Satisfaction," *Work and Occupations* 30, no. 1 (2003): 97–122.

74. J. J. Caughron, M. D. Mumford, and E. A. Fleishman, "The Fleishman Job Analysis Survey: Development, Validation, and Applications," in M. A. Wilson, W. Bennett Jr., S. G. Gibson, and G. M. Alliger, eds., *The Handbook of Work Analysis: Methods, Systems, Applications and Science of Work Measurement in Organizations* (New York: Routledge/Taylor & Francis Group, 2012); and P. D. Converse, F. L. Oswald, M. A. Gillespie, K. A. Field, and E. B. Bizot, "Matching Individuals to Occupations Using Abilities and the O*Net: Issues and an Application in Career Guidance," *Personnel Psychology* 57, no. 2 (2004): 451–87.

75. S. S. Wang, "Companies Find Autism Can Be a Job Skill," *The Wall Street Journal,* March 28, 2014, B1–B2.

76. B. R. Ragins, J. A. Gonzalez, K. Ehrhardt, and R. Singh, "Crossing the Threshold: The Spillover of Community Racial Diversity and Diversity Climate to the Workplace," *Personnel Psychology* 65, no. 4 (2012): 755–87.

77. P. F. McKay, D. R. Avery, and M. A. Morris, "Mean Racial-Ethnic Differences in Employee Sales Performance: The Moderating Role of Diversity Climate," *Personnel Psychology* 61, no. 2 (2008): 349–74.

78. D. R. Avery, J. A. Richeson, M. R. Hebl, and N. Ambady, "It Does Not Have to Be Uncomfortable: The Role of Behavioral Scripts in Black-White Interracial Interactions," *Journal of Applied Psychology* 94, no. 6 (2009): 1382–93.

79. N. Wingfield, "Microsoft Chief Backpedals on Women's Pay," *The Wall Street Journal,* October 10, 2014, B1, B7.

80. D. R. Avery, "Reactions to Diversity in Recruitment Advertising: Are the Differences Black and White?" *Journal of Applied Psychology* 88, no. 4 (2003): 672–79; P. F. McKay and D. R. Avery, "What Has Race Got to Do with It? Unraveling the Role of Racioethnicity in Job Seekers' Reactions to Site Visits," *Personnel Psychology* 59, no. 2 (2006): 395–429; and D. R. Avery and P. F. McKay, "Target Practice: An Organizational Impression Management Approach to Attracting Minority and Female Job Applicants," *Personnel Psychology* 59, no. 1 (2006): 157–87.

81. A. Overholt, "More Women Coders," *Fortune,* February 25, 2013, 14.

82. L. Kwoh, "McKinsey Tries to Recruit Mothers Who Left the Fold," *The Wall Street Journal,* February 20, 2013, B1, B7.

83. M. R. Buckley, K. A. Jackson, M. C. Bolino, J. G. Veres, and H. S. Field, "The Influence of Relational Demography on Panel Interview Ratings: A Field Experiment," *Personnel Psychology* 60, no. 3 (2007): 627–46; J. M. Sacco, C. R. Scheu, A. M. Ryan, and N. Schmitt, "An Investigation of Race and Sex Similarity Effects in Interviews: A Multilevel Approach to Relational Demography," *Journal of Applied Psychology* 88, no. 5 (2003): 852–65; and J. C. Ziegert and P. J. Hanges, "Employment Discrimination: The Role of Implicit Attitudes, Motivation, and a Climate for Racial Bias," *Journal of Applied Psychology* 90, no. 3 (2005): 553–62.

84. K. Bezrukova, K. A. Jehn, and C. S. Spell, "Reviewing Diversity Training: Where We Have Been and Where We Should Go," *Academy of Management Learning & Education* 11, no. 2 (2012): 207–27.

85. S. T. Bell, "Deep-Level Composition Variables as Predictors of Team Performance: A Meta-Analysis," *Journal of Applied Psychology* 92, no. 3 (2007): 595–615; S. K. Horwitz and I. B. Horwitz, "The Effects of Team Diversity on Team Outcomes: A Meta-Analytic Review of Team Demography," *Journal of Management* 33, no. 6 (2007): 987–1015; G. L. Stewart, "A Meta-Analytic Review of Relationships between Team Design Features and Team Performance," *Journal of Management* 32, no. 1 (2006): 29–54; and A. Joshi and H. Roh, "The Role of Context in Work Team Diversity Research: A Meta-Analytic Review," *Academy of Management Journal* 52, no. 3 (2009): 599–627.

86. G. Andrevski, O. C. Richard, J. D. Shaw, and W. J. Ferrier, "Racial Diversity and Firm Performance: The Mediating Role of Competitive Intensity," *Journal of Management* 40, no. 3 (2014): 820–44.

87. A. C. Homan, J. R. Hollenbeck, S. E. Humphrey, D. van Knippenberg, D. R. Ilgen, and G. A. Van Kleef, "Facing Differences with an Open Mind: Openness to Experience, Salience of Intragroup Differences, and Performance of Diverse Work Groups," *Academy of Management Journal* 51, no. 6 (2008): 1204–22.

88. E. Kearney and D. Gebert, "Managing Diversity and Enhancing Team Outcomes: The Promise of Transformational

Leadership," *Journal of Applied Psychology* 94, no. 1 (2009): 77–89.

89. C. L. Holladay and M. A. Quiñones, "The Influence of Training Focus and Trainer Characteristics on Diversity Training Effectiveness," *Academy of Management Learning and Education* 7, no. 3 (2008): 343–54; and R. Anand and M. Winters, "A Retrospective View of Corporate Diversity Training from 1964 to the Present," *Academy of Management Learning and Education* 7, no. 3 (2008): 356–72.

90. A. Sippola and A. Smale, "The Global Integration of Diversity Management: A Longitudinal Case Study," *International Journal of Human Resource Management* 18, no. 11 (2007): 1895–1916.

CHAPTER 3

1. A. Barsky, S. A. Kaplan, and D. J. Beal, "Just Feelings? The Role of Affect in the Formation of Organizational Fairness Judgments," *Journal of Management* 37, no. 1 (2011): 248–79; J. A. Mikels, S. J. Maglio, A. E. Reed, and L. J. Kaplowitz, "Should I Go with My Gut? Investigating the Benefits of Emotion-Focused Decision Making," *Emotion* 11, no. 4 (2011): 743–53; and A. J. Rojas Tejada, O. M. Lozano Rojas, M. Navas Luque, and P. J. Pérez Moreno, "Prejudiced Attitude Measurement Using the Rasch Scale Model," *Psychological Reports* 109, no. 2 (2011): 553–72.

2. See L. S. Glasman and D. Albarracín, "Forming Attitudes That Predict Future Behavior: A Meta-Analysis of the Attitude-Behavior Relation," *Psychological Bulletin* 132, no. 5 (2006): 778–822.

3. Y. L. Liu and C.-J. Keng, "Cognitive Dissonance, Social Comparison, and Disseminating Untruthful or Negative Truthful EWOM Messages," *Social Behavior and Personality* 24, no. 6 (2014): 979–94.

4. See, for instance, L. R. Fabrigar, R. E. Petty, S. M. Smith, and S. L. Crites, "Understanding Knowledge Effects on Attitude-Behavior Consistency: The Role of Relevance, Complexity, and Amount of Knowledge," *Journal of Personality and Social Psychology* 90, no. 4 (2006): 556–77; and D. J. Schleicher, J. D. Watt, and G. J. Greguras, "Reexamining the Job Satisfaction-Performance Relationship: The Complexity of Attitudes," *Journal of Applied Psychology* 89, no. 1 (2004): 165–77.

5. A. S. McCance, C. D. Nye, L. Wang, K. S. Jones, and C. Chiu, "Alleviating the Burden of Emotional Labor: The Role of Social Sharing," *Journal of Management* 39, no. 2 (2013): 392–415.

6. L. S. Glasman and D. Albarracin, "Forming Attitudes That Predict Future Behavior: A Meta-Analysis of the Attitude-Behavior Relation."

7. D. P. Moynihan and S. K. Pandey, "Finding Workable Levers over Work Motivation: Comparing Job Satisfaction, Job Involvement, and Organizational Commitment," *Administration & Society* 39, no. 7 (2007): 803–32.

8. S. Zhang, "Impact of Job Involvement on Organizational Citizenship Behaviors in China," *Journal of Business Ethics* 120, no. 2 (2014): 165–74.

9. G. Chen and R. J. Klimoski, "The Impact of Expectations on Newcomer Performance in Teams as Mediated by Work Characteristics, Social Exchanges, and Empowerment," *Academy of Management Journal* 46, no. 5 (2003): 591–607; A. Ergeneli, G. Saglam, and S. Metin, "Psychological Empowerment and Its Relationship to Trust in Immediate Managers," *Journal of Business Research* 60, no. 1 (2007): 41–49; and S. E. Seibert, S. R. Silver, and W. A. Randolph, "Taking Empowerment to the Next Level: A Multiple-Level Model of Empowerment, Performance, and Satisfaction," *Academy of Management Journal* 47, no. 3 (2004): 332–49.

10. B. J. Avolio, W. Zhu, W. Koh, and P. Bhatia, "Transformational Leadership and Organizational Commitment: Mediating Role of Psychological Empowerment and Moderating Role of Structural Distance," *Journal of Organizational Behavior* 25, no. 8 (2004): 951–68.

11. O. N. Solinger, W. van Olffen, and R. A. Roe, "Beyond the Three-Component Model of Organizational Commitment," *Journal of Applied Psychology* 93, no. 1 (2008): 70–83.

12. J. P. Hausknecht, N. J. Hiller, and R. J. Vance, "Work-Unit Absenteeism: Effects of Satisfaction, Commitment, Labor Market Conditions, and Time," *Academy of Management Journal* 51, no. 6 (2008): 1223–45.

13. "100 Best Companies to Work For," *Fortune,* February 2015, www.fortune.com/best-companies/2015/.

14. L. Rhoades, R. Eisenberger, and S. Armeli, "Affective Commitment to the Organization: The Contribution of Perceived Organizational Support," *Journal of Applied Psychology* 86, no. 5 (2001): 825–36.

15. B. L. Rich, J. A. Lepine, and E. R. Crawford, "Job Engagement: Antecedents and Effects on Job Performance," *Academy of Management Journal* 53, no. 3 (2010): 617–35.

16. "Employee Engagement," *Workforce Management* (February 2013): 19; and "The Cornerstone OnDemand 2013 U.S. Employee Report," *Cornerstone* (2013), www.cornerstoneondemand.com/resources/research/survey-2013.

17. Y. Brunetto, S. T. T. Teo, K. Shacklock, and R. Farr-Wharton, "Emotional Intelligence, Job Satisfaction, Well-being and Engagement: Explaining Organisational Commitment and Turnover Intentions in Policing," *Human Resource Management Journal* 22, no. 4 (2012): 428–41.

18. P. Petrou, E. Demerouti, M. C. W. Peeters, W. B. Schaufeli, and Jørn Hetland, "Crafting a Job on a Daily Basis: Contextual Correlates and the Link to Work Engagement," *Journal of Organizational Behavior* 33, no. 8 (2012): 1120–41.

19. C. L. Dolbier, J. A. Webster, K. T. McCalister, M. W. Mallon, and M. A. Steinhardt, "Reliability and Validity of a Single-Item Measure of Job Satisfaction," *American Journal of Health Promotion* 19, no. 3 (2005): 194–98.

20. *Employee's Job Satisfaction Worldwide 2012,* Distributed by New York, NY: Statista, 2012. http://www.statista.com/statistics/224508/employee-job-satisfaction-worldwide/; Kelly Services, Kelly Global Workforce Index, 2012, *Acquisition and Retention in the war for Talent.* http://www.kellyservices.no/NO/Om-oss/KGWI-APRIL-2012—Talent-Acquisiton-and-Retention/"

21. N. A. Bowling, M. R. Hoepf, D. M. LaHuis, and L. R. Lepisto, "Mean Job Satisfaction Levels over Time: Are Things Bad and Getting Worse?" *The Industrial-Organizational Psychologist* 50, no. 4 (2013): 57–64.

22. L. Weber, "U.S. Workers Can't Get No (Job) Satisfaction," *The Wall Street Journal: At Work* (blog), June 18, 2014, 12:01 AM, http://blogs.wsj.com/atwork/2014/06/18/u-s-workers-cant-get-no-job-satisfaction/.

23. B. Cheng, M. Kan, G. Levanon, and R. L. Ray. "Job Satisfaction: 2014 Edition," The Conference Board, https://

www.conference-board.org/topics/publicationdetail.cfm?publicationid=2785.

24. L. Weber, "U.S. Workers Can't Get No (Job) Satisfaction."

25. "Doing Business in South Korea," *World Business Culture*, accessed January 14, 2016, www.worldbusinessculture.com/Business-in-South-Korea.html.

26. S. E. Humphrey, J. D. Nahrgang, and F. P. Morgeson, "Integrating Motivational, Social, and Contextual Work Design Features: A Meta-Analytic Summary and Theoretical Extension of the Work Design Literature," *Journal of Applied Psychology* 92, no. 5 (2007): 1332–56; and D. S. Chiaburu and D. A. Harrison, "Do Peers Make the Place? Conceptual Synthesis and Meta-Analysis of Coworker Effect on Perceptions, Attitudes, OCBs, and Performance," *Journal of Applied Psychology* 93, no. 5 (2008): 1082–103.

27. K. H. Fong and E. Snape, "Empowering Leadership, Psychological Empowerment and Employee Outcomes: Testing a Multi-Level Mediating Model," *British Journal of Management* 26, no. 1 (2015): 126–38.

28. S. Ronen and M. Mikulincer, "Predicting Employees' Satisfaction and Burnout from Managers' Attachment and Caregiving Orientations," *European Journal of Work and Organizational Psychology* 21, no. 6 (2012): 828–49.

29. A. Calvo-Salguero, J.-M. Salinas Martinez-de-Lecea, and A.-M. Carrasco-Gonzalez, "Work-Family and Family-Work Conflict: Does Intrinsic-Extrinsic Satisfaction Mediate the Prediction of General Job Satisfaction?" *Journal of Psychology* 145, no. 5 (2011): 435–61.

30. J. Zhang, Q. Wu, D. Miao, X. Yan, and J. Peng, "The Impact of Core Self-Evaluations on Job Satisfaction: The Mediator Role of Career Commitment," *Social Indicators Research* 116, no. 3 (2014): 809–22.

31. D. Thorpe, "Why CSR? The Benefits of Corporate Social Responsibility Will Move You to Act," *Forbes,* May 18, 2013, http://www.forbes.com/sites/devinthorpe/2013/05/18/why-csr-the-benefits-of-corporate-social-responsibility-will-move-you-to-act/.

32. N. Fallon, "What Is Corporate Responsibility?" *Business News Daily,* December 22, 2014, http://www.businessnewsdaily.com/4679-corporate-social-responsibility.html.

33. R. Feintzeig, "I Don't Have a Job. I Have a Higher Calling," *The Wall Street Journal,* February 25, 2015, B1, B4.

34. See I. Filatotchev and C. Nakajima, "Corporate Governance, Responsible Managerial Behavior, and Corporate Social Responsibility: Organizational Efficiency versus Organizational Legitimacy?" *Academy of Management Perspectives* 28, no. 3 (2014): 289–306.

35. A. Hurst, "Being 'Good' Isn't the Only Way to Go," *The New York Times,* April 20, 2014, 4.

36. M. C. Bolino, H.-H. Hsiung, J. Harvey, and J. A. LePine, "Well, I'm Tired of Tryin'! Organizational Citizenship Behavior and Citizenship Fatigue," *Journal of Applied Psychology* 100, no. 1 (2015): 56–74.

37. Ge. E. Newman and D. M. Cain, "Tainted Altruism: When Doing Some Good Is Evaluated as Doing Worse Than Doing No Good at All," *Psychological Science* 25, no. 3 (2014): 648–55.

38. Ibid.

39. D. J. Schleicher, T. A. Smith, W. J. Casper, J. D. Watt, and G. J. Greguras, "It's All in the Attitude: The Role of Job Attitude Strength in Job Attitude-Outcome Relationships," *Journal of Applied Psychology* 100, no. 4 (2015): 1259–74.

40. N. P. Podsakoff, P. M. Podsakoff, and S. B. MacKenzie, "Consequences of Unit-Level Organizational Citizenship Behaviors: A Review and Recommendations for Future Research," *Journal of Organizational Behavior* 35, no. S1 (2014): S87–119.

41. B. J. Hoffman, C. A. Blair, J. P. Meriac, and D. J. Woehr, "Expanding the Criterion Domain? A Quantitative Review of the OCB Literature," *Journal of Applied Psychology* 92, no. 2 (2007): 555–66.

42. B. B. Reiche et al., "Why Do Managers Engage in Trustworthy Behavior? A Multilevel Cross-Cultural Study in 18 Countries," *Personnel Psychology* 67, no. 1 (2014): 61–98.

43. D. S. Chiaburu and D. A. Harrison, "Do Peers Make the Place? Conceptual Synthesis and Meta-Analysis of Coworker Effect on Perceptions, Attitudes, OCBs, and Performance," *Journal of Applied Psychology* 93, no. 5 (2008): 1082–103.

44. R. Ilies, I. S. Fulmer, M. Spitzmuller, and M. D. Johnson, "Personality and Citizenship Behavior: The Mediating Role of Job Satisfaction," *Journal of Applied Psychology* 94, no. 4 (2009): 945–59.

45. G. L. Lemoine, C. K. Parsons, and S. Kansara, "Above and Beyond, Again and Again: Self-Regulation in the Aftermath of Organizational Citizenship Behaviors," *Journal of Applied Psychology* 100, no. 1 (2015): 40–55.

46. C. Vandenberghe, K. Bentein, R. Michon, J. Chebat, M. Tremblay, and J. Fils, "An Examination of the Role of Perceived Support and Employee Commitment in Employee-Customer Encounters," *Journal of Applied Psychology* 92, no. 4 (2007): 1177–87; and M. Schulte, C. Ostroff, S. Shmulyian, and A. Kinicki, "Organizational Climate Configurations: Relationships to Collective Attitudes, Customer Satisfaction, and Financial Performance," *Journal of Applied Psychology* 94, no. 3 (2009): 618–34.

47. B. Taylor, "Why Amazon Is Copying Zappos and Paying Employees to Quit," *Harvard Business Review,* April 14, 2014, https://hbr.org/2014/04/why-amazon-is-copying-zappos-and-paying-employees-to-quit/.

48. J. Barling, E. K. Kelloway, and R. D. Iverson, "High-Quality Work, Job Satisfaction, and Occupational Injuries," *Journal of Applied Psychology* 88, no. 2 (2003): 276–83; and F. W. Bond and D. Bunce, "The Role of Acceptance and Job Control in Mental Health, Job Satisfaction, and Work Performance," *Journal of Applied Psychology* 88, no. 6 (2003): 1057–67.

49. Y. Georgellis and T. Lange, "Traditional versus Secular Values and the Job-Life Satisfaction Relationship across Europe," *British Journal of Management* 23, no. 4 (2012): 437–54.

50. O. Stavrova, T. Schlosser, and A. Baumert, "Life Satisfaction and Job-Seeking Behavior of the Unemployed: The Effect of Individual Differences in Justice Sensitivity," *Applied Psychology: An International Review* 64, no. 4 (2014): 643–70.

51. R. Gibney, T. J. Zagenczyk, and M. F. Masters, "The Negative Aspects of Social Exchange: An Introduction to Perceived Organizational Obstruction," *Group & Organization Management* 34, no. 6 (2009): 665–97.

52. C. Caldwell and M. Canuto-Carranco, "'Organizational Terrorism' and Moral Choices—Exercising Voice When the Leader Is the Problem," *Journal of Business Ethics* 97, no. 1 (2010): 159–71; and A. J. Nyberg and R. E. Ployhart, "Context-Emergent Turnover (CET) Theory: A Theory of Collective Turnover," *Academy of Management Review* 38, no. 1 (2013): 109–31.

53. P. E. Spector, S. Fox, L. M. Penney, K. Bruursema, A. Goh, and S. Kessler, "The Dimensionality of Counterproductivity:

Are All Counterproductive Behaviors Created Equal?" *Journal of Vocational Behavior* 68, no. 3 (2006): 446–60; and D. S. Chiaburu and D. A. Harrison, "Do Peers Make the Place? Conceptual Synthesis and Meta-Analysis of Coworker Effects on Perceptions, Attitudes, OCBs, and Performance," *Journal of Applied Psychology* 93, no. 5 (2008): 1082–103.

54. P. A. O'Keefe, "Liking Work Really Does Matter," *The New York Times,* September 7, 2014, 12.

55. D. Iliescu, D. Ispas, C. Sulea, and A. Ilie, "Vocational Fit and Counterproductive Work Behaviors: A Self-Regulation Perspective," *Journal of Applied Psychology* 100, no. 1 (2015): 21–39.

56. A. S. Gabriel, J. M. Diefendorff, M. M. Chandler, C. M. M. Pradco, and G. J. Greguras, "The Dynamic Relationships of Work Affect and Job Satisfaction with Perceptions of Fit," *Personnel Psychology* 67, no. 2 (2014): 389–420.

57. S. Diestel, J. Wegge, and K.-H. Schmidt, "The Impact of Social Context on the Relationship between Individual Job Satisfaction and Absenteeism: The Roles of Different Foci of Job Satisfaction and Work-Unit Absenteeism," *Academy of Management Journal* 57, no. 2 (2014): 353–82.

58. H. Lian, D. L. Ferris, R. Morrison, and D. J. Brown, "Blame It on the Supervisor or the Subordinate? Reciprocal Relations between Abusive Supervision and Organizational Deviance," *Journal of Applied Psychology* 99, no. 4 (2014): 651–64.

59. T. A. Beauregard, "Fairness Perceptions of Work-Life Balance Initiatives; Effects on Counterproductive Work Behavior," *British Journal of Management* 25, no. 4 (2014): 772–89.

60. D. Iliescu, D. Ispas, C. Sulea, and A. Ilie, "Vocational Fit and Counterproductive Work Behaviors: A Self-Regulation Perspective."

61. A. S. Gabriel, J. M. Diefendorff, M. M. Chandler, C. M. M. Pradco, and G. J. Greguras, "The Dynamic Relationships of Work Affect and Job Satisfaction with Perceptions of Fit."

62. S. Diestel, J. Wegge, and K.-H. Schmidt, "The Impact of Social Context on the Relationship between Individual Job Satisfaction and Absenteeism: The Roles of Different Foci of Job Satisfaction and Work-Unit Absenteeism."

63. J. F. Ybema, P. G. W. Smulders, and P. M. Bongers, "Antecedents and Consequences of Employee Absenteeism: A Longitudinal Perspective on the Role of Job Satisfaction and Burnout," *European Journal of Work and Organizational Psychology* 19, no. 1 (2010): 102–24.

64. J. P. Hausknecht, N. J. Hiller, and R. J. Vance, "Work-Unit Absenteeism: Effects of Satisfaction, Commitment, Labor Market Conditions, and Time," *Academy of Management Journal* 51, no. 6 (2008): 1123–245.

65. G. Chen, R. E. Ployhart, H. C. Thomas, N. Anderson, and P. D. Bliese, "The Power of Momentum: A New Model of Dynamic Relationships between Job Satisfaction Change and Turnover Intentions," *Academy of Management Journal* 54, no. 1 (2011): 159–81.

66. D. Liu, T. R. Mitchell, T. W. Lee, B. C. Holtom, and T. R. Hinkin, "When Employees Are Out of Step with Coworkers: How Job Satisfaction Trajectory and Dispersion Influence Individual- and Unit-Level Voluntary Turnover," *Academy of Management Journal* 55, no. 6 (2012): 1360–80.

67. K. Kiazad, B. C. Holtom, P. W. Hom, and A. Newman, "Job Embeddedness: A Multifoci Theoretical Extension," *Journal of Applied Psychology* 100, no. 3 (2015): 641–59.

68. T. H. Lee, B. Gerhart, I. Weller, and C. O. Trevor, "Understanding Voluntary Turnover: Path-Specific Job Satisfaction Effects and the Importance of Unsolicited Job Offers," *Academy of Management Journal* 51, no. 4 (2008): 651–71.

69. K. Holland, "Inside the Minds of Your Employees," *The New York Times,* January 28, 2007, B1; M. Schoeff Jr. "Study Sees Link between Morale and Stock Price," *Workforce Management* 85, no. 4 February 27, 2006: 15; and P. B. Brown "The Workplace as Solar System," *The New York Times,* October 28, 2006, B5.

70. E. White, "How Surveying Workers Can Pay Off," *The Wall Street Journal,* June 18, 2007, B3.

CHAPTER 4

1. S. G. Barsade and D. E. Gibson, "Why Does Affect Matter in Organizations?" *Academy of Management Perspectives,* 21, no. 1 (2007): 36–59.

2. *Oxford Advanced Learner's Dictionary,* s. v. emotion, accessed July 31, 2015, http://www.oxforddictionaries.com/us/definition/american_english/emotion.

3. *The American Heritage Medical Dictionary,* revised edition, s. v. mood, accessed April 27, 2015, http://medical-dictionary.thefreedictionary.com/mood.

4. *Farlex Partner Medical Dictionary,* s. v. mood, accessed April 27, 2015, http://medical-dictionary.thefreedictionary.com/mood.

5. See, for example, J. L. Tracy and R. W. Robins, "Emerging Insights into the Nature and Function of Pride," *Current Directions in Psychological Science* 16, no. 3 (2007): 147–50.

6. G. Nikolaidis, "Indeterminacy of Definitions and Criteria in Mental Health: Case Study of Emotional Disorders," *Journal of Evaluation in Clinical Practice* 19, no. 3 (2013): 531–36; and W. G. Parrott, "Ur-Emotions and Your Emotions: Reconceptualizing Basic Emotion," *Emotion Review* 2, no. 1 (2010): 14–21.

7. P. Ekman, *Emotions Revealed: Recognizing Faces and Feelings to Improve Communication and Emotional Life* (New York: Times Books/Henry Holt and Co., 2003).

8. M. Gendron, D. Roberson, J. M. van der Vyver, and L. F. Barrett, "Cultural Relativity of Perceiving Emotion from Vocalizations," *Psychological Science* 25, no. 4 (2014): 911–20.

9. R. M. Msetfi, D. E. Kornbrot, H. Matute, and R. A. Murphy, "The Relationship between Mood State and Perceived Control in Contingency Learning: Effects of Individualist and Collectivist Values," *Frontiers in Psychology* 6, no. 1430 (2015): 1–18; and M. Pfundmair, V. Graupmann, D. Frey, and N. Aydin, "The Different Behavioral Intentions of Collectivists and Individualists in Response to Social Exclusion," *Personality and Social Psychology Bulletin* 41, no. 3 (2015): 363–78.

10. P. S. Russell and R. Giner-Sorolla, "Bodily Moral Disgust: What It Is, How It Is Different from Anger, and Why It Is an Unreasoned Emotion," *Psychological Bulletin* 139, no. 2 (2013): 328–51.

11. J. Dvash, G. Gilam, A. Ben-Ze'ev, T. Hendler, and S. G. Shamay-Tsoory, "The Envious Brain: The Neural Basis of Social Comparison," *Human Brain Mapping* 31, no. 11 (2010): 1741–50.

12. T. A. Ito and J. T. Cacioppo, "Variations on a Human Universal: Individual Differences in Positivity Offset and Negativity Bias," *Cognition and Emotion* 19, no. 1 (2005): 1–26.

13. D. Holman, "Call Centres," in *The Essentials of the New Work Place: A Guide to the Human Impact of Modern Working*

Practices, eds. D. Holman, T. D. Wall, C. Clegg, P. Sparrow, and A. Howard (Chichester, UK: Wiley, 2005), 111–32.

14. S. D. Pressman, M. W. Gallagher, S. J. Lopez, and B. Campos, "Incorporating Culture into the Study of Affect and Health," *Psychological Science* 25, no. 12 (2014): 2281–83.

15. K. B. Curhan, T. Simms, H. R. Markus, … C. D. Ryff, "Just How Bad Negative Affect Is for Your Health Depends on Culture," *Psychological Science* 25, no. 12 (2014): 2277–80.

16. D. Xanthopoulou, A. B. Bakker, E. Demerouti, and W. B. Schaufeli, "A Diary Study on the Happy Worker: How Job Resources Relate to Positive Emotions and Personal Resources," *European Journal of Work and Organizational Psychology* 21, no. 4 (2012): 489–517.

17. J. R. Spence, D. J. Brown, L. M. Keeping, and H. Lian, "Helpful Today, But Not Tomorrow? Feeling Grateful as a Predictor of Daily Organizational Citizenship Behaviors," *Personnel Psychology* 67, no. 3 (2014): 705–38.

18. E. Bernstein, "Feeling Awesome: Studies Find an Emotion Has Myriad Benefits," *The Wall Street Journal*, February 24, 2015, D3.

19. L. M. Poverny and S. Picascia, "There Is No Crying in Business," *Womensmedia.com*, October 20, 2009, www.womensmedia.com/new/Crying-at-Work.shtml.

20. M.-A. Reinhard and N. Schwartz, "The Influence of Affective States on the Process of Lie Detection," *Journal of Experimental Psychology* 18, no. 4 (2012): 377–389.

21. J. Haidt, "The New Synthesis in Moral Psychology," *Science* 316, no. 5827, May 18, 2007, 998, 1002; I. E. de Hooge, R. M. A. Nelissen, S. M. Breugelmans, and M. Zeelenberg, "What Is Moral about Guilt? Acting 'Prosocially' at the Disadvantage of Others," *Journal of Personality and Social Psychology* 100, no. 3 (2011): 462–73; and C. A. Hutcherson and J. J. Gross, "The Moral Emotions: A Social-Functionalist Account of Anger, Disgust, and Contempt," *Journal of Personality and Social Psychology* 100, no. 4 (2011): 719–37.

22. T. Jacobs, "My Morals Are Better Than Yours," *Miller-McCune*, March/April 2012, 68–69.

23. A. Gopnik, "Even Children Get More Outraged at 'Them' and 'Us'," *The Wall Street Journal*, August 30–31, 2014, C2.

24. N. Angier, "Spite Is Good. Spite Works," *The Wall Street Journal*, April 1, 2014, D1, D3.

25. D. C. Rubin, R. M. Hoyle, and M. R. Leary, "Differential Predictability of Four Dimensions of Affect Intensity," *Cognition and Emotion* 26, no. 1 (2012): 25–41.

26. S. A. Golder and W. M. Macy, "Diurnal and Seasonal Mood Vary with Work, Sleep, and Daylength across Diverse Cultures," *Science* 333, no. 6051, September 30, 2011, 1878–81.

27. Ibid.

28. J. J. A. Denissen, L. Butalid, L. Penke, and M. A. G. van Aken, "The Effects of Weather on Daily Mood: A Multilevel Approach," *Emotion* 8, no. 5 (2008): 662–67; and M. C. Keller, B. L. Fredrickson, O. Ybarra, S. Côté, K. Johnson, J. Mikels, A. Conway, and T. Wagner, "A Warm Heart and a Clear Head: The Contingent Effects of Weather on Mood and Cognition," *Psychological Science* 16, no. 9 (2005): 724–31.

29. J. J. Lee, F. Gino, and B. R. Staats, "Rainmakers: Why Bad Weather Means Good Productivity," *Journal of Applied Psychology* 99, no. 3 (2014): 504–13.

30. J. A. Fuller, J. M. Stanton, G. G. Fisher, C. Spitzmüller, S. S. Russell, and P. C. Smith, "A Lengthy Look at the Daily Grind: Time Series Analysis of Events, Mood, Stress, and Satisfaction," *Journal of Applied Psychology* 88, no. 6 (2003): 1019–33.

31. G. Schaffer, Association for Psychological Science, "What's Good, When, and Why?", *The Observer* 25, no. 9 (2012): 27–29.

32. *Sleep in America Poll* (Washington, DC: National Sleep Foundation, 2005), https://sleepfoundation.org/sites/default/files/2005_summary_of_findings.pdf.

33. D. Meinert, "Sleepless in Seattle … and Cincinnati and Syracuse," *HR Magazine*, October 2012, 55–57.

34. E. Bernstein, "Changing the Clocks Wasn't Good for Your Relationships," *The Wall Street Journal*, March 10, 2015, D1, D2.

35. B. A. Scott and T. A. Judge, "Insomnia, Emotions, and Job Satisfaction: A Multilevel Study," *Journal of Management* 32, no. 5 (2006): 622–45.

36. E. Bernstein, "Changing the Clocks Wasn't Good for Your Relationships."

37. P. R. Giacobbi, H. A. Hausenblas, and N. Frye, "A Naturalistic Assessment of the Relationship between Personality, Daily Life Events, Leisure-Time Exercise, and Mood," *Psychology of Sport and Exercise* 6, no. 1 (2005): 67–81.

38. A. Tergesen, "Why Everything You Know about Aging is Probably Wrong," *The Wall Street Journal*, December 1, 2014, B1–B2.

39. M. G. Gard and A. M. Kring, "Sex Differences in the Time Course of Emotion," *Emotion* 7, no. 2 (2007): 429–37; and M. Jakupcak, K. Salters, K. L. Gratz, and L. Roemer, "Masculinity and Emotionality: An Investigation of Men's Primary and Secondary Emotional Responding," *Sex Roles* 49, no. 3 (2003): 111–20.

40. A. H. Fischer, P. M. Rodriguez Mosquera, A. E. M. van Vianen, and A. S. R. Manstead, "Gender and Culture Differences in Emotion," *Emotion* 4, no. 1 (2004): 84–7.

41. A. Caza, G. Zhang, L. Wang, and Y. Bai, "How Do You Really Feel? Effect of Leaders' Perceived Emotional Sincerity on Followers' Trust," *The Leadership Quarterly* 26, no. 4 (2015): 518–31; and A. S. Gabriel, M. A. Daniels, J. M. Diefendorff, and G. J. Greguras, "Emotional Labor Actors: A Latent Profile Analysis of Emotional Labor Strategies," *Journal of Applied Psychology* 100, no. 3 (2015): 863–79.

42. J. M. Diefendorff and G. J. Greguras, "Contextualizing Emotional Display Rules: Examining the Roles of Targets and Discrete Emotions in Shaping Display Rule Perceptions," *Journal of Management* 35, no. 4 (2009): 880–98.

43. D. T. Wagner, C. M. Barnes, and B. A. Scott, "Driving It Home: How Workplace Emotional Labor Harms Employee Home Life," *Personnel Psychology* 67, no. 2 (2014): 487–516.

44. J. P. Trougakos, D. J. Beal, B. H. Cheng, I. Hideg, and D. Zweig, "Too Drained to Help: A Resource Depletion Perspective on Daily Interpersonal Citizenship Behaviors," *Journal of Applied Psychology* 100, no. 1 (2015): 227–36.

45. J. D. Kammeyer-Mueller et al. "A Meta-Analytic Structural Model of Dispositional Affectivity and Emotional Labor," *Personnel Psychology* 66, no. 1 (2013): 47–90.

46. B. A. Scott, C. M. Barnes, and D. T. Wagner, "Chameleonic or Consistent? A Multilevel Investigation of Emotional Labor Variability and Self-Monitoring," *Academy of Management Journal* 55, no. 4 (2012): 905–26.

47. J. P. Trougakos, D. J. Beal, S. G. Green, and H. M. Weiss, "Making the Break Count: An Episodic Examination of Recovery Activities, Emotional Experiences, and Positive

Affective Displays," *Academy of Management Journal* 51, no. 1 (2008): 131–46.

48. U. R. Hülsheger, J. W. B. Lang, A. F. Schewe, and F. R. H. Zijlstra, "When Regulating Emotions at Work Pays Off: A Diary and an Intervention Study on Emotion Regulation and Customer Tips in Service Jobs," *Journal of Applied Psychology* 100, no. 2 (2015): 263–77.

49. J. D. Kammeyer-Mueller et al. "A Meta-Analytic Structural Model of Dispositionally Affectivity and Emotional Labor."

50. K. L. Wang and M. Groth, "Buffering the Negative Effects of Employee Surface Acting: The Moderating Role of Employee-Customer Relationship Strength and Personalized Services," *Journal of Applied Psychology* 99, no. 2 (2014): 341–50.

51. A. A. Grandey, "When 'The Show Must Go on': Surface Acting and Deep Acting as Determinants of Emotional Exhaustion and Peer-Rated Service Delivery," *Academy of Management Journal* 46, no. 1 (2003): 86–96.

52. U. R. HÜlsheger, H. J. E. Alberts, A. Feinholdt, and J. W. B. Lang, "Benefits of Mindfulness at Work: The Role of Mindfulness in Emotion Regulation, Emotional Exhaustion, and Job Satisfaction," *Journal of Applied Psychology* 98, no. 2 (2013): 310–25.

53. R. Teper, Z. V. Segal, and M. Inzlicht, "Inside the Mindful Mind: How Mindfulness Enhances Emotion Regulation through Improvements in Executive Control," *Current Directions in Psychological Science* 22, no. 6 (2013): 449–54.

54. H. Guenter, I. J. H. van Emmerik, and B. Schreurs, "The Negative Effects of Delays in Information Exchange: Looking at Workplace Relationships from an Affective Events Perspective," *Human Resource Management Review* 24, no. 4 (2014): 283–98; and F. K. Matta, H. T. Erol-Korkmaz, R. E. Johnson, and P. Biçaksiz, "Significant Work Events and Counterproductive Work Behavior: The Role of Fairness, Emotions, and Emotion Regulation," *Journal of Organizational Behavior* 35, no. 7 (2014): 920–44.

55. C. D. Fisher, A. Minbashian, N. Beckmann, and R. E. Wood, "Task Appraisals, Emotions, and Performance Goal Orientations," *Journal of Applied Psychology* 98, no. 2 (2013): 364–73.

56. K. L. Wang and M. Groth, "Buffering the Negative Effects of Employee Surface Acting: The Moderating Role of Employee-Customer Relationship Strength and Personalized Services," *Journal of Applied Psychology* 99, no. 2 (2014): 341–50.

57. T. Upshur-Lupberger, "Watch Your Mood: A Leadership Lesson," *The Huffington Post*, April 22, 2015, http://www .huffingtonpost.com/terrie-upshurlupberger/watch-your-mood-a-leaders_b_7108648.html.

58. Ibid.

59. P. Salovey and D. Grewal, "The Science of Emotional Intelligence," *Current Directions in Psychological Science* 14, no. 6 (2005): 281–85; and D. Geddes and R. R. Callister, "Crossing the Line(s): A Dual Threshold Model of Anger in Organizations," *Academy of Management Review* 32, no. 3 (2007): 721–46.

60. R. Gilkey, R. Caceda, and C. Kilts, "When Emotional Reasoning Trumps IQ," *Harvard Business Review*, September 2010, 27.

61. M. Seo and L. F. Barrett, "Being Emotional during Decision Making—Good or Bad? An Empirical Investigation," *Academy of Management Journal* 50, no. 4 (2007): 923–40.

62. S. L. Koole, "The Psychology of Emotion Regulation: An Integrative Review," *Cognition and Emotion* 23, no. 1

(2009): 4–41; and H. A. Wadlinger and D. M. Isaacowitz, "Fixing Our Focus: Training Attention to Regulate Emotion," *Personality and Social Psychology Review* 15, no. 1 (2011): 75–102.

63. D. H. Kluemper, T. DeGroot, and S. Choi, "Emotion Management Ability: Predicting Task Performance, Citizenship, and Deviance," *Journal of Management* 39, no. 4 (2013): 878–905.

64. J. V. Wood, S. A. Heimpel, L. A. Manwell, and E. J. Whittington, "This Mood Is Familiar and I Don't Deserve to Feel Better Anyway: Mechanisms Underlying Self-Esteem Differences in Motivation to Repair Sad Moods," *Journal of Personality and Social Psychology* 96, no. 2 (2009): 363–80.

65. E. Kim, D. P. Bhave, and T. M. Glomb, "Emotion Regulation in Workgroups: The Roles of Demographic Diversity and Relational Work Context," *Personnel Psychology* 66, no. 3 (2013): 613–44.

66. Ibid.

67. S. L. Koole, "The Psychology of Emotion Regulation: An Integrative Review," *Cognition and Emotion* 23, no. 1 (2009): 4–41.

68. L. K. Barber, P. G. Bagsby, and D. C. Munz, "Affect Regulation Strategies for Promoting (or Preventing) Flourishing Emotional Health," *Personality and Individual Differences* 49, no. 6 (2010): 663–66.

69. J. J. Lee and F. Gino, "Poker-Faced Morality: Concealing Emotions Leads to Utilitarian Decision Making," *Organizational Behavior and Human Decision Processes* 126 (2015): 49–64.

70. Ibid.

71. R. H. Humphrey, "How Do Leaders Use Emotional Labor?" *Journal of Organizational Behavior* 33, no. 5 (2012): 740–44.

72. A. M. Grant, "Rocking the Boat But Keeping It Steady: The Role of Emotion Regulation in Employee Voice," *Academy of Management Journal* 56, no. 6 (2013): 1703–23.

73. S. Reddy, "Walk This Way: Acting Happy Can Make It So," *The Wall Street Journal,* November 18, 2014, D3.

74. S. M. Carpenter, S. Peters, D. Vastfjall, and A. M. Isen, "Positive Feelings Facilitate Working Memory and Complex Decision Making among Older Adults," *Cognition and Emotion* 27, no. 1 (2013): 184–92; B. E. Hermalin and A. M. Isen, "A Model of Affect on Economic Decision Making," *QME-Quantitative Marketing and Economics* 6, no. 1 (2008): 17–40; and B. Scheibehenne and B. von Helversen, "Selecting Decision Strategies: The Differential Role of Affect," *Cognition and Emotion* 29, no. 1 (2015): 158–67.

75. N. Nunez, K. Schweitzer, C. A. Chai, and B. Myers, "Negative Emotions Felt during Trial: The Effect of Fear, Anger, and Sadness on Juror Decision Making," *Applied Cognitive Psychology* 29, no. 2 (2015): 200–9.

76. S. N. Mohanty and D. Suar, "Decision Making under Uncertainty and Information Processing in Positive and Negative Mood States," *Psychological Reports* 115, no. 1 (2014): 91–105.

77. S.-C. Chuang and H.-M. Lin, "The Effect of Induced Positive and Negative Emotion and Openness-to-Feeling in Student's Consumer Decision Making," *Journal of Business and Psychology* 22, no. 1 (2007): 65–78.

78. D. van Knippenberg, H. J. M. Kooij-De Bode, and W. P. van Ginkel, "The Interactive Effects of Mood and Trait Negative Affect in Group Decision Making," *Organization Science* 21, no. 3 (2010): 731–44.

79. S. Lyubomirsky, L. King, and E. Diener, "The Benefits of Frequent Positive Affect: Does Happiness Lead to Success?"

Psychological Bulletin 131, no. 6 (2005): 803–55; and M. Baas, C. K. W. De Dreu, and B. A. Nijstad, "A Meta-Analysis of 25 Years of Mood-Creativity Research: Hedonic Tone, Activation, or Regulatory Focus," *Psychological Bulletin* 134, no. 6 (2008): 779–806.

80. M. J. Grawitch, D. C. Munz, and E. K. Elliott, "Promoting Creativity in Temporary Problem-Solving Groups: The Effects of Positive Mood and Autonomy in Problem Definition on Idea-Generating Performance," *Group Dynamics* 7, no. 3 (2003): 200–13.

81. S. Lyubomirsky, L. King, and E. Diener, "The Benefits of Frequent Positive Affect: Does Happiness Lead to Success?"

82. C. K. W. De Dreu, M. Baas, and B. A. Nijstad, "Hedonic Tone and Activation Level in the Mood-Creativity Link: Toward a Dual Pathway to Creativity Model," *Journal of Personality and Social Psychology* 94, no. 5 (2008): 739–56; and J. M. George and J. Zhou, "Dual Tuning in a Supportive Context: Joint Contributions of Positive Mood, Negative Mood, and Supervisory Behaviors to Employee Creativity," *Academy of Management Journal* 50, no. 3 (2007): 605–22.

83. M. B. Wieth and R. T. Zacks, "Time of Day Effects on Problem Solving: When the Non-Optimal Is Optimal," *Thinking & Reasoning* 17, no. 4 (2011): 387–401.

84. R. Ilies and T. A. Judge, "Goal Regulation across Time: The Effect of Feedback and Affect," *Journal of Applied Psychology* 90, no. 3 (May 2005): 453–67.

85. W. Tsai, C.-C. Chen, and H. Liu, "Test of a Model Linking Employee Positive Moods and Task Performance," *Journal of Applied Psychology* 92, no. 6 (2007): 1570–83.

86. J. E. Bono, H. J. Foldes, G. Vinson, and J. P. Muros, "Workplace Emotions: The Role of Supervision and Leadership," *Journal of Applied Psychology* 92, no. 5 (2007): 1357–67.

87. S. G. Liang and S.-C. S. Chi, "Transformational Leadership and Follower Task Performance: The Role of Susceptibility to Positive Emotions and Follower Positive Emotions," *Journal of Business and Psychology* 28, no. 1 (2013): 17–29.

88. V. A. Visser, D. van Knippenberg, G. Van Kleef, and B. Wisse, "How Leader Displays of Happiness and Sadness Influence Follower Performance: Emotional Contagion and Creative versus Analytical Performance," *Leadership Quarterly* 24, no. 1 (2013): 172–88.

89. P. S. Christoforou and B. E. Ashforth, "Revisiting the Debate on the Relationship Between Display Rules and Performance: Considering the Explicitness of Display Rules," *Journal of Applied Psychology* 100, no. 1 (2015): 249–61; A. Grandey, D. Rupp, and W. N. Brice, "Emotional Labor Threatens Decent Work: A Proposal to Eradicate Emotional Display Rules," *Journal of Organizational Behavior* 36, no. 6 (2015): 770–85; and W.-M. Hur, T.-W. Moon, and Y. S. Jung, "Customer Response to Employee Emotional Labor: The Structural Relationship Between Emotional Labor, Job Satisfaction, and Customer Satisfaction," *Journal of Services Marketing* 29, no. 1 (2015): 71–80.

90. P. B. Barker and A. A. Grandey, "Service with a Smile and Encounter Satisfaction: Emotional Contagion and Appraisal Mechanisms," *Academy of Management Journal* 49, no. 6 (2006): 1229–38; and E. Y. J. Tee, "The Emotional Link: Leadership and the Role of Implicit and Explicit Emotional Contagion Processes across Multiple Organizational Levels," *Leadership Quarterly* 26, no. 4 (2015): 654–70.

91. D. E. Rupp and S. Spencer, "When Customers Lash Out: The Effects of Customer Interactional Injustice on Emotional Labor and the Mediating Role of Emotions," *Journal of Applied Psychology* 91, no. 4 (2006): 971–78; and W. C. Tsai and Y. M. Huang, "Mechanisms Linking Employee Affective Delivery and Customer Behavioral Intentions, *Journal of Applied Psychology* 87, no. 5 (2002): 1001–8.

92. T. A. Judge and R. Ilies, "Affect and Job Satisfaction: A Study of Their Relationship at Work and at Home," *Journal of Applied Psychology* 89, no. 4 (2004): 661–73.

93. Z. Song, M. Foo, and M. A. Uy, "Mood Spillover and Crossover among Dual-Earner Couples: A Cell Phone Event Sampling Study," *Journal of Applied Psychology* 93, no. 2 (2008): 443–52.

94. T. J. Zagenczyk, S. L. D. Restubog, C. Kiewitz, K. Kiazad, and R. L. Tang, "Psychological Contracts as a Mediator between Machiavellianism and Employee Citizenship and Deviant Behaviors," *Journal of Management* 40, no. 4 (2014): 1109–22.

95. T. A. Judge, B. A. Scott, and R. Ilies, "Hostility, Job Attitudes, and Workplace Deviance: Test of a Multilevel Mode," *Journal of Applied Psychology* 91, no. 1 (2006): 126–38; and S. Kaplan, J. C. Bradley, J. N. Luchman, and D. Haynes, "On the Role of Positive and Negative Affectivity in Job Performance: A Meta-Analytic Investigation," *Journal of Applied Psychology* 94, no. 1 (2009): 152–76.

96. S. C. Douglas, C. Kiewitz, M. Martinko, P. Harvey, Y. Kim, and J. U. Chun, "Cognitions, Emotions, and Evaluations: An Elaboration Likelihood Model for Workplace Aggression," *Academy of Management Review* 33, no. 2 (2008): 425–51.

97. A. K Khan, S. Ouratulain, and J. R. Crawshaw, "The Mediating Role of Discrete Emotions in the Relationship between Injustice and Counterproductive Work Behaviors: A Study in Pakistan," *Journal of Business and Psychology* 28, no. 1 (2013): 49–61.

98. S. Kaplan, J. C. Bradley, J. N. Luchman, and D. Haynes, "On the Role of Positive and Negative Affectivity in Job Performance: A Meta-Analytic Investigation;" and J. Maiti, "Design for Worksystem Safety Using Employees' Perception about Safety," *Work—A Journal of Prevention Assessment & Rehabilitation* 41 (2012): 3117–22.

99. J. E. Bono and R. Ilies, "Charisma, Positive Emotions and Mood Contagion," *Leadership Quarterly* 17, no. 4 (2006): 317–34.

CHAPTER 5

1. D. Leising, J. Scharloth, O. Lohse, and D. Wood, "What Types of Terms Do People Use When Describing an Individual's Personality?" *Psychological Science* 25, no. 9 (2014): 1787–94.

2. B. W. Roberts and D. Mroczek, "Personality Trait Change in Adulthood," *Current Directions in Psychological Science* 17, no. 1 (2008): 31–5.

3. L. Weber, "To Get a Job, New Hires Are Put to the Test," *The Wall Street Journal*, April 15, 2015, A1, A10.

4. L. Weber and E. Dwoskin, "As Personality Tests Multiply, Employers Are Split," *The Wall Street Journal*, September 30, 2014, A1, A10.

5. D. Belkin, "Colleges Put the Emphasis on Personality," *The Wall Street Journal*, January 9, 2015, A3.

6. K. I. van der Zee, J. N. Zaal, and J. Piekstra, "Validation of the Multicultural Personality Questionnaire in the Context of Personnel Selection," *European Journal of Personality* 17, no. S1 (2003): S77–S100.

7. S. A. Birkeland, T. M. Manson, J. L. Kisamore, M. T. Brannick, and M. A. Smith, "A Meta-Analytic Investigation of Job Applicant Faking on Personality Measures," *International Journal of Selection and Assessment* 14, no. 14 (2006): 317–35.

8. K. L. Cullen, W. A. Gentry, and F. J. Yammamarino, "Biased Self-Perception Tendencies: Self-Enhancement/Self-Diminishment and Leader Derailment in Individualistic and Collectivistic Cultures," *Applied Psychology: An International Review* 64, no. 1 (2015): 161–207.

9. D. H. Kluemper, B. D. McLarty, and M. N. Bing, "Acquaintance Ratings of the Big Five Personality Traits: Incremental Validity beyond and Interactive Effects with Self-Reports in the Prediction of Workplace Deviance," *Journal of Applied Psychology* 100, no. 1 (2015): 237–48; I. Oh, G. Wang, and M. K. Mount, "Validity of Observer Ratings of the Five-Factor Model of Personality Traits: A Meta-Analysis," *Journal of Applied Psychology* 96, no. 4 (2011): 762–73.

10. S. E. Hampson and L. R. Goldberg, "A First Large Cohort Study of Personality Trait Stability over the 40 Years between Elementary School and Midlife," *Journal of Personality and Social Psychology* 91, no. 4 (2006): 763–79.

11. S. Srivastava, O. P. John, and S. D. Gosling, "Development of Personality in Early and Middle Adulthood: Set Like Plaster or Persistent Change?" *Journal of Personality and Social Psychology* 84, no. 5 (2003): 1041–53; and B. W. Roberts, K. E. Walton, and W. Viechtbauer, "Patterns of Mean-Level Change in Personality Traits across the Life Course: A Meta-Analysis of Longitudinal Studies," *Psychological Bulletin* 132, no. 1 (2006): 1–25.

12. R. B. Kennedy and D. A. Kennedy, "Using the Myers-Briggs Type Indicator in Career Counseling," *Journal of Employment Counseling* 41, no. 1 (2004): 38–44.

13. See, for example, I. Oh, G. Wang, and M. K. Mount, "Validity of Observer Ratings of the Five-Factor Model of Personality Traits: A Meta-Analysis;" and M. R. Barrick and M. K. Mount, "Yes, Personality Matters: Moving on to More Important Matters," *Human Performance* 18, no. 4 (2005): 359–72.

14. W. Fleeson and P. Gallagher, "The Implications of Big Five Standing for the Distribution of Trait Manifestation in Behavior: Fifteen Experience-Sampling Studies and a Meta-Analysis," *Journal of Personality and Social Psychology* 97, no. 6 (2009): 1097–114.

15. T. A. Judge, L. S. Simon, C. Hurst, and K. Kelley, "What I Experienced Yesterday Is Who I Am Today: Relationship of Work Motivations and Behaviors to Within-Individual Variation in the Five-Factor Model of Personality," *Journal of Applied Psychology* 99, no. 2 (2014): 199–221.

16. R. D. Zimmerman, W. R. Boswell, A. J. Shipp, B. B. Dunford, and J. W. Boudreau, "Explaining the Pathways between Approach-Avoidance Personality Traits and Employees' Job Search Behavior," *Journal of Management* 38, no. 5 (2012): 1450–75.

17. See, for instance, I. Oh and C. M. Berry, "The Five-Factor Model of Personality and Managerial Performance: Validity Gains through the Use of 360 Degree Performance Ratings," *Journal of Applied Psychology* 94, no. 6 (2009): 1498–513; J. Hogan and B. Holland, "Using Theory to Evaluate Personality and Job-Performance Relations: A Socioanalytic Perspective," *Journal of Applied Psychology* 88, no. 1 (2003): 100–12; and M. R. Barrick and M. K. Mount, "Select on Conscientiousness and Emotional Stability," in *Handbook of Principles of Organizational Behavior*, ed. E. A. Locke (Malden, MA: Blackwell, 2004), 15–28.

18. P. R. Sackett and P. T. Walmsley, "Which Personality Attributes Are Most Important in the Workplace?" *Perspectives on Psychological Science* 9, no. 5 (2014): 538–51.

19. A. E. Poropat, "A Meta-Analysis of the Five-Factor Model of Personality and Academic Performance," *Psychological Bulletin* 135, no. 2 (2009): 322–38.

20. A. K. Nandkeolyar, J. A. Shaffer, A. Li, S. Ekkirala, and J. Bagger, "Surviving an Abusive Supervisor: The Joint Roles of Conscientiousness and Coping Strategies," *Journal of Applied Psychology* 99, no. 1 (2014): 138–50.

21. B. Wille, F. De Fruyt, and M. Feys, "Big Five Traits and Intrinsic Success in the New Career Era: A 15-Year Longitudinal Study on Employability and Work-Family Conflict," *Applied Psychology: An International Review* 62, no. 1 (2013): 124–56.

22. M. K. Shoss, K. Callison, and L. A. Witt, "The Effects of Other-Oriented Perfectionism and Conscientiousness on Helping at Work," *Applied Psychology: An International Review* 64, no. 1 (2015): 233–51.

23. C. Robert and Y. H. Cheung, "An Examination of the Relationship between Conscientiousness and Group Performance on a Creative Task," *Journal of Research in Personality* 44, no. 2 (2010): 222–31; and M. Batey, T. Chamorro-Premuzic, and A. Furnham, "Individual Differences in Ideational Behavior. Can the Big Five and Psychometric Intelligence Predict Creativity Scores?" *Creativity Research Journal* 22, no. 1 (2010): 90–97.

24. J. L. Huang, A. M. Ryan, K. L. Zabel, and A. Palmer, "Personality and Adaptive Performance at Work: A Meta-Analytic Investigation," *Journal of Applied Psychology* 99, no. 1 (2014): 162–79.

25. R. D. Zimmerman, W. R. Boswell, A. J. Shipp, B. B. Dunford, and J. W. Boudreau, "Explaining the Pathways between Approach-Avoidance Personality Traits and Employees' Job Search Behavior," *Journal of Management* 38, no. 5 (2012): 1450–75.

26. B. Wille, F. De Fruyt, and M. Feys, "Big Five Traits and Intrinsic Success in the New Career Era: A 15-Year Longitudinal Study on Employability and Work-Family Conflict."

27. R. J. Foti and M. A. Hauenstein, "Pattern and Variable Approaches in Leadership Emergence and Effectiveness," *Journal of Applied Psychology* 92, no. 2 (2007): 347–55.

28. B. Weiss and R. S. Feldman, "Looking Good and Lying to Do It: Deception as an Impression Management Strategy in Job Interviews," *Journal of Applied Social Psychology* 36, no. 4 (2006): 1070–86.

29. A. Minbashian, J. Earl, and J. E. H. Bright, "Openness to Experience as a Predictor of Job Performance Trajectories," *Applied Psychology: An International Review* 62, no. 1 (2013): 1–12.

30. B. Wille, F. De Fruyt, and M. Feys, "Big Five Traits and Intrinsic Success in the New Career Era: A 15-Year Longitudinal Study on Employability and Work-Family Conflict."

31. R. Ilies, I. S. Fulmer, M. Spitzmuller, and M. D. Johnson, "Personality and Citizenship Behavior: The Mediating Role of Job Satisfaction," *Journal of Applied Psychology* 94, no. 4 (2009): 945–59.

32. D. H. Kluemper, B. D. McLarty, and M. N. Bing, "Acquaintance Ratings of the Big Five Personality Traits: Incremental Validity beyond and Interactive Effects with Self-Reports in

the Prediction of Workplace Deviance," *Journal of Applied Psychology* 100, no. 1 (2015): 237–48.

33. S. Clarke and I. Robertson, "An Examination of the Role of Personality in Accidents Using Meta-Analysis," *Applied Psychology: An International Review* 57, no. 1 (2008): 94–108.

34. B. Wille, F. De Fruyt, and M. Feys, "Big Five Traits and Intrinsic Success in the New Career Era: A 15-Year Longitudinal Study on Employability and Work-Family Conflict."

35. See, for instance, S. Yamagata, et al., "Is the Genetic Structure of Human Personality Universal? A Cross-Cultural Twin Study from North America, Europe, and Asia," *Journal of Personality and Social Psychology* 90, no. 6 (2006): 987–98; and R. R. McCrae, et al., "Consensual Validation of Personality Traits across Cultures," *Journal of Research in Personality* 38, no. 2 (2004): 179–201.

36. M. Gurven, C. von Ruden, M. Massenkoff, H. Kaplan, and M. L. Vie, "How Universal Is the Big Five? Testing the Five-Factor Model of Personality Variation among Forager-Farmers in the Bolivian Amazon," *Journal of Personality and Social Psychology* 104, no. 2 (2013): 354–70.

37. J. F. Rauthmann, "The Dark Triad and Interpersonal Perception: Similarities and Differences in the Social Consequences of Narcissism, Machiavellianism, and Psychopathy," *Social Psychological and Personality Science* 3, no. 4 (2012): 487–96.

38. P. D. Harms and S. M. Spain, "Beyond the Bright Side: Dark Personality at Work," *Applied Psychology: An International Review* 64, no. 1 (2015): 15–24.

39. P. K. Jonason, S. Slomski, and J. Partyka, "The Dark Triad at Work: How Toxic Employees Get Their Way," *Personality and Individual Differences* 52, no. 3 (2012): 449–53.

40. E. H. O'Boyle, D. R. Forsyth, G. C. Banks, and M. A. McDaniel, "A Meta-Analysis of the Dark Triad and Work Behavior: A Social Exchange Perspective," *Journal of Applied Psychology* 97, no. 3 (2012): 557–79.

41. L. Zhang and M. A. Gowan, "Corporate Social Responsibility, Applicants' Individual Traits, and Organizational Attraction: A Person–Organization Fit Perspective," *Journal of Business and Psychology* 27, no. 3 (2012): 345–62.

42. D. N. Hartog and F. D. Belschak, "Work Engagement and Machiavellianism in the Ethical Leadership Process," *Journal of Business Ethics* 107, no. 1 (2012): 35–47.

43. E. Grijalva and P. D. Harms, "Narcissism: An Integrative Synthesis and Dominance Complementarity Model," *Academy of Management Perspectives* 28, no. 2 (2014): 108–27.

44. D. C. Maynard, E. M. Brondolo, C. E. Connelly, and C. E. Sauer, "I'm Too Good for This Job: Narcissism's Role in the Experience of Overqualification," *Applied Psychology: An International Review* 64, no. 1 (2015): 208–32.

45. E. Grijalva and P. D. Harms, "Narcissism: An Integrative Synthesis and Dominance Complementarity Model."

46. B. J. Brummel and K. N. Parker, "Obligation and Entitlement in Society and the Workplace," *Applied Psychology: An International Review* 64, no. 1 (2015): 127–60.

47. E. Grijalva and D. A. Newman, "Narcissism and Counterproductive Work Behavior (CWB): Meta-Analysis and Consideration of Collectivist Culture, Big Five Personality, and Narcissism's Facet Structure," *Applied Psychology: An International Review* 64, no. 1 (2015): 93–126.

48. D. C. Maynard, E. M. Brondolo, C. E. Connelly, and C. E. Sauer, "I'm Too Good for This Job: Narcissism's Role in the Experience of Overqualification."

49. E. Grijalva and P. D. Harms, "Narcissism: An Integrative Synthesis and Dominance Complementarity Model."

50. J. J. Sosik, J. U. Chun, and W. Zhu, "Hang on to Your Ego: The Moderating Role of Leader Narcissism on Relationships between Leader Charisma and Follower Psychological Empowerment and Moral Identity," *Journal of Business Ethics* 120, no. 1 (12, 2013); and B. M. Galvin, D. A. Waldman, and P. Balthazard, "Visionary Communication Qualities as Mediators of the Relationship between Narcissism and Attributions of Leader Charisma," *Personnel Psychology* 63, no. 3 (2010): 509–37.

51. D. Meinert, "Narcissistic Bosses Aren't All Bad, Study Finds," *HR Magazine,* March 2014, 18.

52. K. A. Byrne and D. A. Worthy, "Do Narcissists Make Better Decisions? An Investigation of Narcissism and Dynamic Decision-Making Performance," *Personality and Individual Differences* 55, no. 2 (2013): 112–17.

53. C. Andreassen, H. Ursin, H. Eriksen, and S. Pallesen, "The Relationship of Narcissism with Workaholism, Work Engagement, and Professional Position," *Social Behavior and Personality* 40, no. 6 (2012): 881–90.

54. O'Boyle, Forsyth, Banks, and McDaniel, "A Meta-Analysis of the Dark Triad and Work Behavior: A Social Exchange Perspective," 558.

55. B. Wille, F. De Fruyt, and B. De Clercq, "Expanding and Reconceptualizing Aberrant Personality at Work: Validity of Five-Factor Model Aberrant Personality Tendencies to Predict Career Outcomes," *Personnel Psychology* 66, no. 1 (2013): 173–223.

56. P. K. Jonason, S. Slomski, and J. Partyka, "The Dark Triad at Work: How Toxic Employees Get Their Way," *Personality and Individual Differences*; and H. M. Baughman, S. Dearing, E. Giammarco, and P. A. Vernon, "Relationships between Bullying Behaviours and the Dark Triad: A Study with Adults," *Personality and Individual Differences* 52, no. 5 (2012): 571–75.

57. U. Orth and R. W. Robins, "Understanding the Link between Low Self-Esteem and Depression," *Current Directions in Psychological Science* 22, no. 6 (2013): 455–60.

58. B. Wille, F. De Fruyt, and B. De Clercq, "Expanding and Reconceptualizing Aberrant Personality at Work: Validity of Five-Factor Model Aberrant Personality Tendencies to Predict Career Outcomes."

59. T. A. Judge, A. Erez, J. E. Bono, and C. J. Thoreson, "The Core Self-Evaluations Scale: Development of a Measure," *Personnel Psychology* 56, no. 2 (2003): 303–31.

60. A. N. Salvaggio, B. Schneider, L. H. Nishi, D. M. Mayer, A. Ramesh, and J. S. Lyon, "Manager Personality, Manager Service Quality Orientation, and Service Climate: Test of a Model," *Journal of Applied Psychology* 92, no. 6 (2007): 1741–50; B. A. Scott and T. A. Judge, "The Popularity Contest at Work: Who Wins, Why, and What Do They Receive?" *Journal of Applied Psychology* 94, no. 1 (2009): 20–33; and T. A. Judge and C. Hurst, "How the Rich (and Happy) Get Richer (and Happier): Relationship of Core Self-Evaluations to Trajectories in Attaining Work Success," *Journal of Applied Psychology* 93, no. 4 (2008): 849–63.

61. A. M. Grant and A. Wrzesniewksi, "I Won't Let You Down . . . or Will I? Core Self-Evaluations, Other-Orientation, Anticipated Guilt and Gratitude, and Job Performance," *Journal of Applied Psychology* 95, no. 1 (2010): 108–21.

62. L. Parks-Leduc, M. W. Pattie, F. Pargas, and R. G. Eliason, "Self-Monitoring as an Aggregate Construct: Relationships

with Personality and Values," *Personality and Individual Differences* 58 (2014): 3–8.

63. F. J. Flynn and D. R. Ames, "What's Good for the Goose May Not Be as Good for the Gander: The Benefits of Self-Monitoring for Men and Women in Task Groups and Dyadic Conflicts," *Journal of Applied Psychology* 91, no. 2 (2006): 272–81.

64. P.-Y. Liao, "The Role of Self-Concept in the Mechanism Linking Proactive Personality to Employee Work Outcomes," *Applied Psychology—An International Review* 64, no. 2 (2015): 421–43.

65. K. Tornau and M. Frese, "Construct Clean-up in Proactivity Research: A Meta-Analysis on the Nomological Net of Work-Related Proactivity Concepts and Their Incremental Values," *Applied Psychology: An International Review* 62, no. 1 (2013): 44–96.

66. W.-D. Li, D. Fay, M. Frese, P. D. Harms, and X. Y. Gao, "Reciprocal Relationship between Proactive Personality and Work Characteristics: A Latent Change Score Approach," *Journal of Applied Psychology* 99, no. 5 (2014): 948–65.

67. P. D. Converse, P. J. Pathak, A. M. DePaul-Haddock, T. Gotlib, and M. Merbedone, "Controlling Your Environment and Yourself: Implications for Career Success," *Journal of Vocational Behavior* 80, no. 1 (2012): 148–59.

68. G. Chen, J. Farh, E. M. Campbell-Bush, Z. Wu, and X. Wu, "Teams as Innovative Systems: Multilevel Motivational Antecedents of Innovation in R&D Teams," *Journal of Applied Psychology* 98, no. 6 (2013).

69. Y. Gong, S.-Y. Cheung, M. Wang, and J.-C. Huang, "Unfolding the Proactive Process for Creativity: Integration of the Employee Proactivity, Information Exchange, and Psychological Safety Perspectives," *Journal of Management* 38, no. 5 (2012): 1611–33.

70. Z. Zhang, M. Wang, and S. Junqi, "Leader-Follower Congruence in Proactive Personality and Work Outcomes: The Mediating Role of Leader-Member Exchange," *Academy of Management Journal* 55, no. 1 (2012): 111–30.

71. G. Van Hoye and H. Lootens, "Coping with Unemployment: Personality, Role Demands, and Time Structure," *Journal of Vocational Behavior* 82, no. 2 (2013): 85–95.

72. R. D. Meyer, R. S. Dalal, and R. Hermida, "A Review and Synthesis of Situational Strength in the Organizational Sciences," *Journal of Management* 36, no. 1 (2010): 121–40.

73. R. D. Meyer et al., "Measuring Job-Related Situational Strength and Assessing Its Interactive Effects with Personality on Voluntary Work Behavior," *Journal of Management* 40, no. 4 (2014): 1010–41.

74. A. M. Watson et al., "When Big Brother Is Watching: Goal Orientation Shapes Reactions to Electronic Monitoring during Online Training," *Journal of Applied Psychology* 98, no. 4 (2013): 642–57.

75. Y. Kim, L. Van Dyne, D. Kamdar, and R. E. Johnson, "Why and When Do Motives Matter? An Integrative Model of Motives, Role Cognitions, and Social Support as Predictors of OCB," *Organizational Behavior and Human Decision Processes* 121, no. 2 (2013): 231–45.

76. G. R. Maio, J. M. Olson, M. M. Bernard, and M. A. Luke, "Ideologies, Values, Attitudes, and Behavior," in *Handbook of Social Psychology*, ed. J. Delamater (New York: Springer, 2003), 283–308.

77. See, for instance, A. Bardi, J. A. Lee, N. Hofmann-Towfigh, and G. Soutar, "The Structure of Intraindividual Value Change," *Journal of Personality and Social Psychology* 97, no. 5 (2009): 913–29.

78. B. C. Holtz and C. M. Harold, "Interpersonal Justice and Deviance: The Moderating Effects of Interpersonal Justice Values and Justice Orientation," *Journal of Management* 39, no. 2 (2013): 339–65.

79. See, for example, N. R. Lockwood, F. R. Cepero, and S. Williams, *The Multigenerational Workforce* (Alexandria, VA: Society for Human Resource Management, 2009).

80. E. Parry and P. Urwin, "Generational Differences in Work Values: A Review of Theory and Evidence," *International Journal of Management Reviews* 13, no. 1 (2011): 79–96.

81. J. M. Twenge, S. M. Campbell, B. J. Hoffman, and C. E. Lance, "Generational Differences in Work Values: Leisure and Extrinsic Values Increasing, Social and Intrinsic Values Decreasing," *Journal of Management* 36, no. 5 (2010): 1117–42.

82. B. J. Dik, S. R. Strife, and J.-I. C. Hansen, "The Flip Side of Holland Type Congruence: Incongruence and Job Satisfaction," *Career Development Quarterly* 58, no. 4 (2010): 352–58; A. Rezaei, A. Qorbanpoor, T. A. Gatab, and A. Rezaei, "Comparative Research for Personality Types of Guilan University Physical Exercise and Counseling Students Based on Holland Theory," *Procedia—Social and Behavioral Sciences* 30 (2011): 2032–36; and D. L. Ohler and E. M. Levinson, "Using Holland's Theory in Employment Counseling: Focus on Service Occupations," *Journal of Employment Counseling* 49, no. 4 (2012): 148–59.

83. Y. Lee and J. Antonakis, "When Preference Is Not Satisfied But the Individual Is: How Power Distance Moderates Person-Job Fit," *Journal of Management* 40, no. 3 (2014): 641–57.

84. W. Arthur Jr., S. T. Bell, A. J. Villado, and D. Doverspike, "The Use of Person–Organization Fit in Employment Decision-Making: An Assessment of Its Criterion-Related Validity," *Journal of Applied Psychology* 91, no. 4 (2006): 786–801; and J. R. Edwards, D. M. Cable, I. O. Williamson, L. S. Lambert, and A. J. Shipp, "The Phenomenology of Fit: Linking the Person and Environment to the Subjective Experience of Person–Environment Fit," *Journal of Applied Psychology* 91, no. 4 (2006): 802–27.

85. E. E. Kausel and J. E. Slaughter, "Narrow Personality Traits and Organizational Attraction: Evidence for the Complementary Hypothesis," *Organizational Behavior and Human Decision Processes* 114, no. 1 (2011): 3–14; and A. Leung and S. Chaturvedi, "Linking the Fits, Fitting the Links: Connecting Different Types of PO Fit to Attitudinal Outcomes," *Journal of Vocational Behavior* 79, no. 2 (2011): 391–402.

86. M. L. Verquer, T. A. Beehr, and S. E. Wagner, "A Meta-Analysis of Relations between Person–Organization Fit and Work Attitudes," *Journal of Vocational Behavior* 63, no. 3 (2003): 473–89; and J. C. Carr, A. W. Pearson, M. J. Vest, and S. L. Boyar, "Prior Occupational Experience, Anticipatory Socialization, and Employee Retention", *Journal of Management* 32, no. 3 (2006): 343–59.

87. K. H. Ehrhart, D. M. Mayer, and J. C. Ziegert, "Web-Based Recruitment in the Millennial Generation: Work-Life Balance, Website Usability, and Organizational Attraction," *European Journal of Work and Organizational Psychology* 21, no. 6 (2012): 850–74.

88. I. -S. Oh et al. "Fit Happens Globally: A Meta-Analytic Comparison of the Relationships of Person-Environment Fit Dimensions with Work Attitudes and Performance across East

Asia, Europe, and North America," *Personnel Psychology* 67, no. 1 (2014): 99–152.

89. See The Hofstede Centre, G. Hofstede. *The Hofstede Centre* (website), http://www.geert-hofstede.com.

90. V. Taras, B. L. Kirkman, and P. Steel, "Examining the Impact of Culture's Consequences: A Three-Decade, Multilevel, Meta-Analytic Review of Hofstede's Cultural Value Dimensions," *Journal of Applied Psychology* 95, no. 5 (2010): 405–39.

91. R. J. House, P. J. Hanges, M. Javidan, and P. W. Dorfman, eds., *Leadership, Culture, and Organizations: The GLOBE Study of 62 Societies* (Thousand Oaks, CA: Sage, 2004); and O. Schloesser et al., "Human Orientation as a New Cultural Dimension of the GLOBE Project: A Validation Study of the GLOBE Scale and Out-Group Human Orientation in 25 Countries," *Journal of Cross-Cultural Psychology* 44, no. 4 (2012): 535–51.

92. J. P. Meyer et al., "Affective, Normative, and Continuance Commitment Levels across Cultures: A Meta-Analysis," *Journal of Vocational Behavior* 80, no. 2 (2012): 225–45.

CHAPTER 6

1. E. Bernstein, "'Honey, You Never Said…,'" *The Wall Street Journal,* March 24, 2015, D1, D4.

2. K. C. Yam, R. Fehr, and C. M. Barnes, "Morning Employees Are Perceived as Better Employees: Employees' Start Times Influence Supervisor Performance Ratings," *Journal of Applied Psychology* 99, no. 6 (2014): 1288–99.

3. J. Dwyer, "Witness Accounts in Midtown Hammer Attack Show the Power of False Memory," *The New York Times,* May 14, 2015, http://www.nytimes.com/2015/05/15/nyregion/witness-accounts-in-midtown-hammer-attack-show-the-power-of-false-memory.html?_r=1.

4. G. Fields and J. R. Emshwiller, "Long after Arrests, Records Live On," *The Wall Street Journal,* December 26, 2014, A1, A10.

5. S. S. Wang, "The Science of Standing Out," *The Wall Street Journal,* March 18, 2014, D1, D4.

6. E. Zell and Z. Krizan, "Do People Have Insight into Their Abilities? A Metasynthesis," *Perspectives on Psychological Science* 9, no. 2 (2014): 111–25.

7. E. Demerouti, D. Xanthopoulou, I. Tsaousis, and A. B. Bakker, "Disentangling Task and Contextual Performance," *Journal of Personnel Psychology* 13, no. 2 (2014): 59–69.

8. P. Harvey, K. Madison, M. Martinko, T. R. Crook, and T. A. Crook, "Attribution Theory in the Organizational Sciences: The Road Traveled and the Path Ahead," *Academy of Management Perspectives* 28, no. 2 (2014): 128–46; and M. J. Martinko, P. Harvey, and M. T. Dasborough, "Attribution Theory in the Organizational Sciences: A Case of Unrealized Potential," *Journal of Organizational Behavior* 32, no. 1 (2011): 144–49.

9. C. M. de Melo, P. J. Carnevale, S. J. Read, and J. Gratch, "Reading People's Minds from Emotion Expressions in Interdependent Decision Making," *Journal of Personality and Social Psychology* 106, no. 1 (2014): 73–88.

10. J. M. Moran, E. Jolly, and J. P. Mitchell, "Spontaneous Mentalizing Predicts the Fundamental Attribution Error," *Journal of Cognitive Neuroscience* 26, no. 3 (2014): 569–76; and D. R. Stadler, "Competing Roles for the Subfactors of Need for Closure in Committing the Fundamental Attribution Error,"

Personality and Individual Differences 47, no. 7 (2009): 701–5.

11. See, for instance, M. Goerke, J. Moller, S. Schulz-Hardt, U. Napiersky, and D. Frey, "'It's Not My Fault—But Only I Can Change It': Counterfactual and Prefactual Thoughts of Managers," *Journal of Applied Psychology* 89, no. 2 (2004): 279–92; and E. G. Hepper, R. H. Gramzow, and C. Sedikides, "Individual Differences in Self-Enhancement and Self-Protection Strategies: An Integrative Analysis," *Journal of Personality* 78, no. 2 (2010): 781–814.

12. J. D. Brown, "Across the (Not So) Great Divide: Cultural Similarities in Self-Evaluative Processes," *Social and Personality Psychology Compass* 4, no. 5 (2010): 318–30.

13. A. Zhang, C. Reyna, Z. Qian, and G. Yu, "Interpersonal Attributions of Responsibility in the Chinese Workplace: A Test of Western Models in a Collectivistic Context," *Journal of Applied Social Psychology* 38, no. 9 (2008): 2361–77; and A. Zhang, F. Xia, and C. Li, "The Antecedents of Help Giving in Chinese Culture: Attribution, Judgment of Responsibility, Expectation Change and the Reaction of Affect," *Social Behavior and Personality* 35, no. 1 (2007): 135–42.

14. See P. Rosenzweig, *The Halo Effect* (New York: The Free Press, 2007); I. Dennis, "Halo Effects in Grading Student Projects," *Journal of Applied Psychology* 92, no. 4 (2007): 1169–76; C. E. Naquin and R. O. Tynan, "The Team Halo Effect: Why Teams Are Not Blamed for Their Failures," *Journal of Applied Psychology* 88, no. 2 (2003): 332–40; and T. M. Bechger, G. Maris, and Y. P. Hsiao, "Detecting Halo Effects in Performance-Based Evaluations," *Applied Psychological Measurement* 34, no. 8 (2010): 607–19.

15. J. K. Clark, K. C. Thiem, J. Barden, J. O'Rourke Stuart, and A. T. Evans, "Stereotype Validation: The Effects of Activating Negative Stereotypes after Intellectual Performance," *Journal of Personality and Social Psychology* 108, no. 4 (2015): 531–52.

16. J. L. Eberhardt, P. G. Davies, V. J. Purdic-Vaughns, and S. L. Johnson, "Looking Deathworthy: Perceived Stereotypicality of Black Defendants Predicts Capital-Sentencing Outcomes," *Psychological Science* 17, no. 5 (2006): 383–86.

17. A. S. Rosette, G. J. Leonardelli, and K. W. Phillips, "The White Standard: Racial Bias in Leader Categorization," *Journal of Applied Psychology* 93, no. 4 (2008): 758–77.

18. D. A. Hofmann, "Overcoming the Obstacles to Cross-Functional Decision Making: Laying the Groundwork for Collaborative Problem Solving," *Organizational Dynamics* 44, no. 1 (2015): 17–25.

19. E. Bernstein, "The Right Answer is 'No,'" *The Wall Street Journal,* March 11, 2014, D1–D2.

20. See, for example, P. L. Curseu and S. G. L. Schruijer, "Decision Styles and Rationality: An Analysis of the Predictive Validity of the General Decision-Making Style Inventory," *Educational and Psychological Measurement* 72, no. 6 (2012): 1053–62.

21. For a review of the rational decision-making model, see M. Verweij, T. J. Senior, J. F. D. Dominguez, and R. Turner, "Emotion, Rationality, and Decision-Making: How to Link Affective and Social Neuroscience with Social Theory," *Frontiers in Neuroscience* 9, no. 332 (2015).

22. J. G. March, *A Primer on Decision Making* (New York: The Free Press, 2009); and D. Hardman and C. Harries, "How Rational Are We?" *The Psychologist* 15, no. 2 (2002): 76–79.

23. M. H. Bazerman and D. A. Moore, *Judgment in Managerial Decision Making* (Hoboken, NJ: John Wiley & Sons, 2013).

24. J. E. Russo, K. A. Carlson, and M. G. Meloy, "Choosing an Inferior Alternative," *Psychological Science* 17, no. 10 (2006): 899–904.

25. N. Halevy and E. Y. Chou, "How Decisions Happen: Focal Points and Blind Spots in Interdependent Decision Making," *Journal of Personality and Social Psychology* 106, no. 3 (2014): 398–417; D. Kahneman, "Maps of Bounded Rationality: Psychology for Behavioral Economics," *The American Economic Review* 93, no. 5 (2003): 1449–75; and J. Zhang, C. K. Hsee, and Z. Xiao, "The Majority Rule in Individual Decision Making," *Organizational Behavior and Human Decision Processes* 99, no. 1 (2006): 102–11.

26. G. Gigerenzer, "Why Heuristics Work," *Perspectives on Psychological Science* 3, no. 1 (2008): 20–29; and A. K. Shah and D. M. Oppenheimer, "Heuristics Made Easy: An Effort-Reduction Framework," *Psychological Bulletin* 134, no. 2 (2008): 207–22.

27. See A. W. Kruglanski and G. Gigerenzer, "Intuitive and Deliberate Judgments Are Based on Common Principles," *Psychological Review* 118, no. 1 (2011): 97–109.

28. E. Dane and M. G. Pratt, "Exploring Intuition and Its Role in Managerial Decision Making," *Academy of Management Review* 32, no. 1 (2007): 33–54; and J. A. Hicks, D. C. Cicero, J. Trent, C. M. Burton, and L. A. King, "Positive Affect, Intuition, and Feelings of Meaning," *Journal of Personality and Social Psychology* 98, no. 6 (2010): 967–79.

29. C. Akinci and E. Sadler-Smith, "Intuition in Management Research: A Historical Review," *International Journal of Management Reviews* 14, no. 1 (2012): 104–22.

30. S. P. Robbins, *Decide & Conquer: Making Winning Decisions and Taking Control of Your Life* (Upper Saddle River, NJ: Financial Times/Prentice Hall, 2004), 13.

31. S. Ludwig and J. Nafziger, "Beliefs about Overconfidence," *Theory and Decision* 70, no. 4 (2011): 475–500.

32. C. R. M. McKenzie, M. J. Liersch, and I. Yaniv, "Overconfidence in Interval Estimates: What Does Expertise Buy You," *Organizational Behavior and Human Decision Processes* 107, no. 2 (2008): 179–91.

33. R. P. Larrick, K. A. Burson, and J. B. Soll, "Social Comparison and Confidence: When Thinking You're Better Than Average Predicts Overconfidence (and When It Does Not)," *Organizational Behavior and Human Decision Processes* 102, no. 1 (2007): 76–94.

34. K. M. Hmieleski and R. A. Baron, "Entrepreneurs' Optimism and New Venture Performance: A Social Cognitive Perspective," *Academy of Management Journal* 52, no. 3 (2009): 473–88.

35. See, for instance, J. P. Simmons, R. A. LeBoeuf, and L. D. Nelson, "The Effect of Accuracy Motivation on Anchoring and Adjustment: Do People Adjust from Their Provided Anchors?" *Journal of Personality and Social Psychology* 99, no. 6 (2010): 917–32.

36. C. Janiszewski and D. Uy, "Precision of the Anchor Influences the Amount of Adjustment," *Psychological Science* 19, no. 2 (2008): 121–27.

37. See, for example, P. Frost, B. Casey, K. Griffin, L. Raymundo, C. Farrell, and R. Carrigan, "The Influence of Confirmation Bias on Memory and Source Monitoring," *Journal of General Psychology* 142, no. 4 (2015): 238–52; and W. Hart, D. Albarracín, A. H. Eagly, I. Brechan, M. Lindberg, and L. Merrill, "Feeling Validated versus Being Correct: A Meta-Analysis of Selective Exposure to Information," *Psychological Bulletin* 135, no. 4 (2009): 555–88.

38. T. Pachur, R. Hertwig, and F. Steinmann, "How Do People Judge Risks: Availability Heuristic, Affect Heuristic, or Both?" *Journal of Experimental Psychology: Applied* 18, no. 3 (2012): 314–30.

39. G. Morgenson, "Debt Watchdogs: Tamed or Caught Napping?" *The New York Times,* December 7, 2009, 1, 32.

40. K. Moser, H.-G. Wolff, and A. Kraft, "The De-Escalation of Commitment: Predecisional Accountability and Cognitive Processes," *Journal of Applied Social Psychology* 43, no. 2 (2013): 363–76.

41. D. J. Sleesman, D. E. Conlon, G. McNamara, and J. E. Miles, "Cleaning Up the Big Muddy: A Meta-Analytic Review of the Determinants of Escalation of Commitment," *Academy of Management Journal* 55, no. 3 (2012): 541–62.

42. H. Drummond, "Escalation of Commitment: When to Stay the Course?" *Academy of Management Perspectives* 28, no. 4 (2014): 430–46.

43. See, for instance, U. Hahn and P. A. Warren, "Perceptions of Randomness: Why Three Heads Are Better Than One," *Psychological Review* 116, no. 2 (2009): 454–61.

44. See, for example, D. J. Keys and B. Schwartz, "Leaky Rationality: How Research on Behavioral Decision Making Challenges Normative Standards of Rationality," *Psychological Science* 2, no. 2 (2007): 162–80; and U. Simonsohn, "Direct Risk Aversion: Evidence from Risky Prospects Valued below Their Worst Outcome," *Psychological Science* 20, no. 6 (2009): 686–92.

45. J. K. Maner, M. T. Gailliot, D. A. Butz, and B. M. Peruche, "Power, Risk, and the Status Quo: Does Power Promote Riskier or More Conservative Decision Making?" *Personality and Social Psychology Bulletin* 33, no. 4 (2007): 451–62.

46. A. Chakraborty, S. Sheikh, and N. Subramanian, "Termination Risk and Managerial Risk Taking," *Journal of Corporate Finance* 13, no. 1 (2007): 170–88.

47. R. L. Guilbault, F. B. Bryant, J. H. Brockway, and E. J. Posavac, "A Meta-Analysis of Research on Hindsight Bias," *Basic and Applied Social Psychology* 26, nos. 2–3 (2004): 103–17.

48. J. Bell, "The Final Cut?" *Oregon Business* 33, no. 5 (2010): 27.

49. E. Dash and J. Creswell, "Citigroup Pays for a Rush to Risk," *The New York Times,* November 20, 2008, 1, 28; S. Pulliam, S. Ng, and R. Smith, "Merrill Upped Ante as Boom in Mortgage Bonds Fizzled," *The Wall Street Journal,* April 16, 2008, A1, A14.

50. M. Gladwell, "Connecting the Dots," *The New Yorker,* March 10, 2003.

51. H. Moon, J. R. Hollenbeck, S. E. Humphrey, and B. Maue, "The Tripartite Model of Neuroticism and the Suppression of Depression and Anxiety within an Escalation of Commitment Dilemma," *Journal of Personality* 71, no. 3 (2003): 347–68.

52. J. Musch, "Personality Differences in Hindsight Bias," *Memory* 11, nos. 4–5 (2003): 473–89.

53. T. Huston, "Are Women Better Decision Makers?" *The New York Times,* October 19, 2014, 9.

54. K. E. Stanovich and R. F. West, "On the Relative Independence of Thinking Biases and Cognitive Ability," *Journal of Personality and Social Psychology* 94, no. 4 (2008): 672–95.

55. B. Burrough, "How Big Business Can Take the High Road," *The New York Times,* March 9, 2014, 10.

56. K. V. Kortenkamp and C. F. Moore, "Ethics under Uncertainty: The Morality and Appropriateness of Utilitarianism

When Outcomes Are Uncertain," *American Journal of Psychology* 127, no. 3 (2014): 367–82.

57. A. Lukits, "Hello and Bonjour to Moral Dilemmas," *The Wall Street Journal,* May 13, 2014, D4.

58. J. Hollings, "Let the Story Go: The Role of Emotion in the Decision-Making Process of the Reluctant, Vulnerable Witness or Whistle-Blower," *Journal of Business Ethics* 114, no. 3 (2013): 501–12.

59. D. E. Rupp, P. M. Wright, S. Aryee, and Y. Luo, "Organizational Justice, Behavioral Ethics, and Corporate Social Responsibility: Finally the Three Shall Merge," *Management and Organization Review* 11, no. 1 (2015): 15–24.

60. N. Klein and H. Zhou, "Their Pants Aren't on Fire," *The New York Times,* March 25, 2014, D3.

61. Ibid.

62. S. D. Levitt and S. J. Dubner, "Traponomics," *The Wall Street Journal,* May 10–11, 2014, C1, C2.

63. N. Anderson, K. Potocnik, and J. Zhou, "Innovation and Creativity in Organizations: A State-of-the-Science Review, Prospective Commentary, and Guiding Framework," *Journal of Management* 40, no. 5 (2014): 1297–333.

64. M. M. Gielnik, A.-C. Kramer, B. Kappel, and M. Frese, "Antecedents of Business Opportunity Identification and Innovation: Investigating the Interplay of Information Processing and Information Acquisition," *Applied Psychology: An International Review* 63, no. 2 (2014): 344–81.

65. G. Reynolds, "Want a Good Idea? Take a Walk," *The New York Times,* May 6, 2014, D6.

66. S. Shellenbarger, "The Power of the Doodle: Improve Your Focus and Memory," *The Wall Street Journal,* July 30, 2014, D1, D3.

67. C. K. W. De Dreu, B. A. Nijstad, M. Baas, I. Wolsink, and M. Roskes, "Working Memory Benefits Creative Insight, Musical Improvisation, and Original Ideation through Maintained Task-Focused Attention," *Personality and Social Psychology Bulletin* 38, no. 5 (2012): 656–69.

68. C.-H. Wu, S. K. Parker, and J. P. J. de Jong, "Need for Cognition as an Antecedent of Individual Innovation Behavior," *Journal of Management* 40, no. 6 (2014): 1511–34.

69. S. M. Wechsler, C. Vendramini, and T. Oakland, "Thinking and Creative Styles: A Validity Study," *Creativity Research Journal* 24, nos. 2-3 (2012): 235–42.

70. Y. Gong, S. Cheung, M. Wang, and J. Huang, "Unfolding the Proactive Processes for Creativity: Integration of the Employee Proactivity, Information Exchange, and Psychological Safety Perspectives," *Journal of Management* 38, no. 5 (2012): 1611–33.

71. A. Rego, F. Sousa, C. Marques, and M. P. E. Cunha, "Retail Employees' Self-Efficacy and Hope Predicting Their Positive Affect and Creativity," *European Journal of Work and Organizational Psychology* 21, no. 6 (2012): 923–45.

72. H. Zhang, H. K. Kwan, X. Zhang, and L.-Z. Wu, "High Core Self-Evaluators Maintain Creativity: A Motivational Model of Abusive Supervision," *Journal of Management* 40, no. 4 (2012): 1151–74.

73. D. K. Simonton, "The Mad-Genius Paradox: Can Creative People Be More Mentally Healthy But Highly Creative People More Mentally Ill?" *Perspectives on Psychological Science* 9, no. 5 (2014): 470–80.

74. C. Wang, S. Rodan, M. Fruin, and X. Xu, "Knowledge Networks, Collaboration Networks, and Exploratory Innovation," *Academy of Management Journal* 57, no. 2 (2014): 484–514.

75. F. Gino and S. S. Wiltermuth, "Evil Genius? Dishonesty Can Lead to Greater Creativity," *Psychological Science* 25, no. 4 (2014): 973–81.

76. S. N. de Jesus, C. L. Rus, W. Lens, and S. Imaginário, "Intrinsic Motivation and Creativity Related to Product: A Meta-Analysis of the Studies Published between 1990–2010," *Creativity Research Journal* 25, no. 1 (2013): 80–84.

77. A. Somech and A. Drach-Zahavy, "Translating Team Creativity to Innovation Implementation: The Role of Team Composition and Climate for Innovation," *Journal of Management* 39, no. 3 (2013): 684–708.

78. L. Sun, Z. Zhang, J. Qi, and Z. X. Chen, "Empowerment and Creativity: A Cross-Level Investigation," *Leadership Quarterly* 23, no. 1 (2012): 55–65.

79. M. Cerne, C. G. L. Nerstad, A. Dysvik, and M. Skerlavaj, "What Goes Around Comes Around: Knowledge Hiding, Perceived Motivational Climate, and Creativity," *Academy of Management Journal* 57, no. 1 (2014): 172–92.

80. I. J. Hoever, D. van Knippenberg, W. P. van Ginkel, and H. G. Barkema, "Fostering Team Creativity: Perspective Taking as Key to Unlocking Diversity's Potential," *Journal of Applied Psychology* 97, no. 5 (2012): 982–96.

81. S. J. Shin, T. Kim, J. Lee, and L. Bian, "Cognitive Team Diversity and Individual Team Member Creativity: A Cross-Level Interaction," *Academy of Management Journal* 55, no. 1 (2012): 197–212.

82. T. Montag, C. P. Maertz, and M. Baer, "A Critical Analysis of the Workplace Creativity Criterion Space," *Journal of Management* 38, no. 4 (2012): 1362–86.

83. M. Baer, "Putting Creativity to Work: The Implementation of Creative Ideas in Organizations," *Academy of Management Journal* 55, no. 5 (2012): 1102–19.

CHAPTER 7

1. C. C. Pinder, *Work Motivation in Organizational Behavior,* 2nd ed. (New York, NY: Psychology Press, 2008).

2. R. J. Taormina and J. H. Gao, "Maslow and the Motivation Hierarchy: Measuring Satisfaction of the Needs," *American Journal of Psychology* 126, no. 2 (2013): 155–57.

3. H. S. Guest "Maslow's Hierarchy of Needs—The Sixth Level," *Psychologist* 27, no. 12 (2014): 982–83.

4. Ibid.

5. S. H. Mousavi and H. Dargahi, "Ethnic Differences and Motivation Based on Maslow's Theory on Iranian Employees," *Iranian Journal of Public Health* 42, no. 5 (2013): 516–21.

6. D. Lester, "Measuring Maslow's Hierarchy of Needs," *Psychological Reports* 113, no. 1 (2013): 127–29.

7. J.-G. Choi and J.-K. Lee, "Testing the Applicability of the Herzberg's Motivation-Hygiene Theory to the Hotel Industry," *DaeHan Journal of Business* 25, no. 4 (2012): 2091–111.

8. F. Herzberg, "One More time: How do you Motivate Employees?," *Harvard Business Review,* January 2003, 1–12.

9. See, for instance, C.-S. Park and K.-S. Ko, "A Study on Factors of Job Satisfaction of Caregivers in Home Care Facilities Based on Herzberg's Motivation-Hygiene Theory," *Church Social Work* 19, no. 8 (2012): 123–58; and "Study on the Important Factors for Non-Commissioned Officer's Job Satisfaction in R.O.K. Army Based on Herzberg's Two Factor Theory," *Journal of Korean Public Police and Security Studies* 9, no. 2 (2012): 217–38.

10. D. McClelland, *The Achieving Society* (Princeton, NJ: Van Nostrand, 1961).

11. B. Steinmann, S. L. Doerr, O. C. Schultheiss, and G. W. Maier, "Implicit Motives and Leadership Performance Revisited: What Constitutes the Leadership Motive Pattern?" *Motivation and Emotion* 39, no. 2 (2015): 167–74.

12. H. van Emmerick, W. L. Gardner, H. Wendt, and D. Fischer, "Associations of Culture and Personality with McClelland's Motives: A Cross-Cultural Study of Managers in 24 Countries," *Group and Organization Management* 35, no. 3 (2010): 329–67.

13. See, for instance, F. Yang, J. E. Ramsay, O. C. Schultheiss, and J. S. Pang, "Need for Achievement Moderates the Effect of Motive-Relevant Challenge on Salivary Cortisol Changes," *Motivation and Emotion* 39, no. 3 (2015): 321–34; M. S. Khan, R. J. Breitnecker, and E. J. Schwarz, "Adding Fuel to the Fire: Need for Achievement Diversity and Relationship Conflict in Entrepreneurial Teams," *Management Decision* 53, no. 1 (2015): 75–79; M. G. Koellner and O. C. Schultheiss, "Meta-Analytic Evidence of Low Convergence between Implicit and Explicit Measures of the Needs for Achievement, Affiliation, and Power," *Frontiers in Psychology* 5, no. 826 (2014); and T. Bipp and K. van Dam, "Extending Hierarchical Achievement Motivation Models: The Role of Motivational Needs for Achievement Goals and Academic Performance," *Personality and Individual Differences* 64 (2014): 157–62.

14. M. G. Koellner and O. C. Schultheiss, "Meta-Analytic Evidence of Low Convergence between Implicit and Explicit Measures of the Needs for Achievement, Affiliation, and Power."

15. J. Hofer, H. Busch, and C. Schneider, "The Effect of Motive-Trait Interaction on Satisfaction of the Implicit Need for Affiliation among German and Cameroonian Adults," *Journal of Personality* 83, no. 2 (2015): 167–78.

16. M. Gagné and E. L. Deci, "Self-Determination Theory and Work Motivation," *Journal of Organizational Behavior* 26, no. 4 (2005): 331–62; and D. T. Kong and V. T. Ho, "A Self-Determination Perspective of Strengths Use at Work: Examining Its Determinant and Performance Implications," *Journal of Positive Psychology* 11, no. 1 (2016): 15–25.

17. C. P. Cerasoli, J. M. Nicklin, and M. T. Ford, "Intrinsic Motivation and Extrinsic Incentives Jointly Predict Performance: A 40-Year Meta-Analysis," *Psychological Bulletin* 140, no. 4 (2014): 980–1008.

18. J. E. Bono and T. A. Judge, "Self-Concordance at Work: Toward Understanding the Motivational Effects of Transformational Leaders," *Academy of Management Journal* 46, no. 5 (2003): 554–71.

19. K. M. Sheldon, A. J. Elliot, and R. M. Ryan, "Self-Concordance and Subjective Well-Being in Four Cultures," *Journal of Cross-Cultural Psychology* 35, no. 2 (2004): 209–23.

20. L. M. Graves, M. N. Ruderman, P. J. Ohlott, and J. Webber, "Driven to Work and Enjoyment of Work: Effects on Managers' Outcomes," *Journal of Management* 38, no. 5 (2012): 1655–80.

21. J. P. Meyer, T. E. Becker, and C. Vandenberghe, "Employee Commitment and Motivation: A Conceptual Analysis and Integrative Model," *Journal of Applied Psychology* 89, no. 6 (2004): 991–1007.

22. E. A. Locke and G. P. Latham, "New Directions in Goal-Setting Theory," *Current Directions in Psychological Science* 15, no. 5 (2006): 265–68.

23. Ibid.

24. C. Gabelica, P. Van den Bossche, M. Segers, and W. Gijselaers, "Feedback, a Powerful Lever in Teams: A Review," *Educational Research Review* 7, no. 2 (2012): 123–44.

25. J. Lee and F. Wei, "The Mediating Effect of Psychological Empowerment on the Relationship between Participative Goal Setting and Team Outcomes—A Study in China," *International Journal of Human Resource Management* 22, no. 2 (2011): 279–95.

26. S. W. Anderson, H. C. Dekker, and K. L. Sedatole, "An Empirical Examination of Goals and Performance-to-Goal Following the Introduction of an Incentive Bonus Plan with Participative Goal Setting," *Management Science* 56, no. 1 (2010): 90–109.

27. T. S. Bateman and B. Bruce, "Masters of the Long Haul: Pursuing Long-Term Work Goals," *Journal of Organizational Behavior* 33, no. 7 (2012): 984–1006.

28. Ibid.

29. J. E. Bono and A. E. Colbert, "Understanding Responses to Multi-Source Feedback: The Role of Core Self-Evaluations," *Personnel Psychology* 58, no. 1 (2005): 171–203; and S. A. Jeffrey, A. Schulz, and A. Webb, "The Performance Effects of an Ability-Based Approach to Goal Assignment," *Journal of Organizational Behavior Management* 32 (2012): 221–41.

30. T. Tammemagi, D. O'Hora, and K. A. Maglieri, "The Effects of a Goal Setting Intervention on Productivity and Persistence in an Analogue Work Task," *Journal of Organizational Behavior Management* 33, no. 1 (2013): 31–54.

31. D. F. Crown, "The Use of Group and Groupcentric Individual Goals for Culturally Heterogeneous and Homogeneous Task Groups: An Assessment of European Work Teams," *Small Group Research* 38, no. 4 (2007): 489–508.

32. K. Lanaj, C. D. Chang, and R. E. Johnson, "Regulatory Focus and Work-Related Outcomes: A Review and Meta-Analysis," *Psychological Bulletin* 138, no. 5 (2012): 998–1034.

33. D. L. Ferris, R. E. Johnson, C. C. Rosen, E. Djurdjevic, C.-H. Chang, and J. A. Tan, "When Is Success Not Satisfying? Integrating Regulatory Focus and Approach/Avoidance Motivation Theories to Explain the Relation between Core Self-Evaluation and Job Satisfaction," *Journal of Applied Psychology* 98, no. 2 (2013): 342–53.

34. M. Roskes, A. J. Elliot, and C. K. W. De Dreu, "Why Is Avoidance Motivation Problematic, and What Can Be Done about It?" *Current Directions in Psychological Science* 23, no. 2 (2014): 133–38.

35. "KEYGroup Survey Finds Nearly Half of All Employees Have No Set Performance Goals," *IPMA-HR Bulletin,* March 10, 2006, 1; S. Hamm, "SAP Dangles a Big, Fat Carrot," *BusinessWeek,* May 22, 2006, 67–68; and "A. G. Lafley (CEO of Proctor & Gamble), interview by E. Amendola, P&G CEO Wields High Expectations But No Whip," *USA Today,* February 19, 2007, 3B.

36. See, for example, E. Lindberg and T. L. Wilson, "Management by Objectives: The Swedish Experience in Upper Secondary Schools," *Journal of Educational Administration* 49, no. 1 (2011): 62–75; and A. C. Spaulding, L. D. Gamm, and J. M. Griffith, "Studer Unplugged: Identifying Underlying Managerial Concepts," *Hospital Topics* 88, no. 1 (2010): 1–9.

37. M. B. Kristiansen, "Management by Objectives and Results in the Nordic Countries: Continuity and Change, Differences and Similarities," *Public Performance and Management Review* 38, no. 3 (2015): 542–69.

38. See, for instance, M. Tanikawa, "Fujitsu Decides to Backtrack on Performance-Based Pay," *The New York Times,* March 22,

2001, W1; and W. F. Roth, "Is Management by Objectives Obsolete?" *Global Business and Organizational Excellence* 28, no. 4 (2009): 36–43.

39. F. Gino and C. Mogilner, "Time, Money, and Morality," *Psychological Science* 25, no. 2 (2014): 414–21.

40. V. Lopez-Kidwell, T. J. Grosser, B. R. Dineen, and S. P. Borgatti, "What Matters When: A Multistage Model and Empirical Examination of Job Search Effort," *Academy of Management Journal* 56, no. 6 (2012): 1655–78.

41. J. W. Beck and A. M. Schmidt, "State-Level Goal Orientations as Mediators of the Relationship between Time Pressure and Performance: A Longitudinal Study," *Journal of Applied Psychology* 98, no. 2 (2013): 354–63.

42. J. R. Themanson and P. J. Rosen, "Examining the Relationships between Self-Efficacy, Task-Relevant Attentional Control, and Task Performance: Evidence from Event-Related Brain Potentials," *British Journal of Psychology* 106, no. 2 (2015): 253–71.

43. A. Bandura, "Cultivate Self-Efficacy for Personal and Organizational Effectiveness," in *Handbook of Principles of Organizational Behavior*, ed. E. Locke (Malden, MA: Blackwell, 2004), 120–36; and M. Ventura, M. Salanova, and S. Llorens, "Professional Self-Efficacy as a Predictor of Burnout and Engagement: The Role of Challenge and Hindrance Demands," *Journal of Psychology* 149, no. 3 (2015): 277–302.

44. M. Salanova, S. Llorens, and W. B. Schaufeli, "Yes I Can, I Feel Good, and I Just Do It! On Gain Cycles and Spirals of Efficacy Beliefs, Affect, and Engagement," *Applied Psychology* 60, no. 2 (2011): 255–85.

45. J. R. Themanson and P. J. Rosen, "Examining the Relationships between Self-Efficacy, Task-Relevant Attentional Control, and Task Performance: Evidence from Event-Related Brain Potentials."

46. M. Ben-Ami, J. Hornik, D. Eden, and O. Kaplan, "Boosting Consumers' Self-Efficacy by Repositioning the Self," *European Journal of Marketing* 48, no. 11/12 (2014): 1914–38; L. De Grez and D. Van Lindt, "Students' Gains in Entrepreneurial Self-Efficacy: A Comparison of 'Learning-by-Doing' versus Lecture-Based Courses," *Proceedings of the 8th European Conference on Innovation and Entrepreneurship* (2013): 198–203; and K. S. Hendricks, "Changes in Self-Efficacy Beliefs over Time: Contextual Influences of Gender, Rank-Based Placement, and Social Support in a Competitive Orchestra Environment," *Psychology of Music* 42, no. 3 (2014): 347–65.

47. T. A. Judge, C. L. Jackson, J. C. Shaw, B. Scott, and B. L. Rich, "Self-Efficacy and Work-Related Performance: The Integral Role of Individual Differences," *Journal of Applied Psychology* 92, no. 1 (2007): 107–27.

48. Ibid.

49. A. M. Paul, "How to Use the 'Pygmalion' Effect," *Time*, April 1, 2013, http://ideas.time.com/2013/04/01/how-to-use-the-pygmalion-effect/.

50. A. Friedrich, B. Flunger, B. Nagengast, K. Jonkmann, and U. Trautwein, "Pygmalion Effects in the Classroom: Teacher Expectancy Effects on Students' Math Achievement," *Contemporary Educational Psychology* 41 (2015): 1–12.

51. L. Karakowsky, N. DeGama, and K. McBey, "Facilitating the Pygmalion Effect: The Overlooked Role of Subordinate Perceptions of the Leader," *Journal of Occupational and Organizational Psychology* 85, no. 4 (2012): 579–99; and P. Whiteley, T. Sy, and S. K. Johnson, "Leaders' Conceptions of Followers: Implications for Naturally Occurring Pygmalion Effects," *Leadership Quarterly* 23, no. 5 (2012): 822–34.

52. A. Gegenfurtner, C. Quesada-Pallares, and M. Knogler, "Digital Simulation-Based Training: A Meta-Analysis," *British Journal of Educational Technology* 45, no. 6 (2014): 1097–114.

53. E. C. Dierdorff, E. A. Surface, and K. G. Brown, "Frame-of-Reference Training Effectiveness: Effects of Goal Orientation and Self-Efficacy on Affective, Cognitive, Skill-Based, and Transfer Outcomes," *Journal of Applied Psychology* 95, no. 6 (2010): 1181–91; and R. Grossman and E. Salas, "The Transfer of Training: What Really Matters," *International Journal of Training and Development* 15, no. 2 (2011): 103–20.

54. K. M. Eddington, C. Majestic, and P. J. Silvia, "Contrasting Regulatory Focus and Reinforcement Sensitivity: A Daily Diary Study of Goal Pursuit and Emotion," *Personality and Individual Differences* 53, no. 3 (2012): 335–40.

55. B. F. Skinner, "'Superstition' in the Pigeon". *Journal of Experimental Psychology* 38, no. 2 (1948).

56. M. J. Goddard, "Critical Psychiatry, Critical Psychology, and the Behaviorism of B. F. Skinner," *Review of General Psychology* 18, no. 3 (2014): 208–15.

57. J. R. Brauer and C. R. Tittle, "Social Learning Theory and Human Reinforcement," *Sociological Spectrum* 32, no. 2 (2012): 157–77.

58. C. Buzea, "Equity Theory Constructs in a Romanian Cultural Context," *Human Resource Development Quarterly* 25, no. 4 (2014): 421–39; A. W. Cappelen, K. Eichele, K. Hugdahl, K. Specht, and B. Tungodden, "Equity Theory and Fair Inequality: A Neuroeconomic Study," *Proceedings of the National Academy of Sciences in the United States of America* 111, no. 43 (2014): 15368–72; C. Maslach and M. P. Leiter, "Early Predictors of Job Burnout and Engagement", *Journal of Applied Psychology* 93, no. 3 (2008): 498–512; and Q. Xiaoqing, K. Zhang, and Y. Xu, "Applicable Scope of Equity Theory and Reaction on Productivity under the Influence of Traditional Culture," 2014 2nd International Conference on Social Science and Health, Pt. 3 in *Advances in Education Research* 57 (2014): 365–69.

59. J. Bai, "Analysis of Equity Theory in the Modern Enterprise Staff Motivation," *Proceedings of the 2012 International Conference on Management Innovation and Public Policy* (2012): 165–67; C. Buzea, "Equity Theory Constructs in a Romanian Cultural Context," *Human Resource Development Quarterly* 25, no. 4 (2014): 421–39; and L. K. Scheer, N. Kumar, and J.-B. E. M. Steenkamp, "Reactions to Perceived Inequity in U.S. and Dutch Interorganizational Relationships," *Academy of Management* 46, no. 3 (2003): 303–16.

60. See, for instance, T. Simons and Q. Roberson, "Why Managers Should Care about Fairness: The Effects of Aggregate Justice Perceptions on Organizational Outcomes," *Journal of Applied Psychology* 88, no. 3 (2003): 432–43; and B. C. Holtz and C. M. Harold, "Fair Today, Fair Tomorrow? A Longitudinal Investigation of Overall Justice Perceptions," *Journal of Applied Psychology* 94, no. 5 (2009): 1185–99.

61. C. O. Trevor, G. Reilly, and B. Gerhart, "Reconsidering Pay Dispersion's Effect on the Performance of Interdependent Work: Reconciling Sorting and Pay Inequality," *Academy of Management Journal* 55, no. 3 (2012): 585–610.

62. A. Caza, M. W. McCarter, and G. B. Northcraft, "Performance Benefits of Reward Choice: A Procedural Justice Perspective," *Human Resource Management Journal* 25, no. 2

(2015): 184–99; R. E. Johnson, K. Lanaj, and C. M. Barnes, "The Good and Bad of Being Fair: Effects of Procedural and Interpersonal Justice Behaviors on Regulatory Resources," *Journal of Applied Psychology* 99, no. 4 (2014): 635–50; and D. Liu, M. Hernandez, and L. Wang, "The Role of Leadership and Trust in Creating Structural Patterns of Team Procedural Justice: A Social Network Investigation," *Personnel Psychology* 67, no. 4 (2014): 801–45.

63. H. He, W. Zhu, and X. Zheng, "Procedural Justice and Employee Engagement: Roles of Organizational Identification and Moral Identity Centrality," *Journal of Business Ethics* 122, no. 4 (2014): 681–95.

64. J. C. Shaw, E. Wild, and J. A. Colquitt, "To Justify or Excuse? A Meta-Analytic Review of the Effects of Explanations," *Journal of Applied Psychology* 88, no. 3 (2003): 444–58.

65. R. J. Bies, "Are Procedural and Interactional Justice Conceptually Distinct?" in *Handbook of Organizational Justice*, eds. J. Greenberg and J. A. Colquitt (Mahwah, NJ: Erlbaum, 2005), 85–112; and B. A. Scott, J. A. Colquitt, and E. L. Paddock, "An Actor-Focused Model of Justice Rule Adherence and Violation: The Role of Managerial Motives and Discretion," *Journal of Applied Psychology* 94, no. 3 (2009): 756–69.

66. G. A. Van Kleef, A. C. Homan, B. Beersma, D. V. Knippenberg, B. V. Knippenberg, and F. Damen, "Searing Sentiment or Cold Calculation? The Effects of Leader Emotional Displays on Team Performance Depend on Follower Epistemic Motivation," *Academy of Management Journal* 52, no. 3 (2009): 562–80.

67. "Rutgers Fires Mike Rice," *ESPN*, April 3, 2013, http://espn.go.com/sportsnation/post/_/id/9129245/rutgers-fires-mike-rice.

68. J. M. Robbins, M. T. Ford, and L. E. Tetrick, "Perceived Unfairness and Employee Health: A Meta-Analytic Integration," *Journal of Applied Psychology* 97, no. 2 (2012): 235–72.

69. K. Leung, K. Tong, and S. S. Ho, "Effects of Interactional Justice on Egocentric Bias in Resource Allocation Decisions," *Journal of Applied Psychology* 89, no. 3 (2004): 405–15; and L. Francis-Gladney, N. R. Manger, and R. B. Welker, "Does Outcome Favorability Affect Procedural Fairness as a Result of Self-Serving Attributions," *Journal of Applied Social Psychology* 40, no. 1 (2010): 182–94.

70. L. J. Barlcay and D. P. Skarlicki, "Healing the Wounds of Organizational Injustice: Examining the Benefits of Expressive Writing," *Journal of Applied Psychology* 94, no. 2 (2009): 511–23.

71. This section is based on B. A. Scott, A. S. Garza, D. E. Conlon, and Y. J. Kim, "Why Do Managers Act Fairly in the First Place? A Daily Investigation of 'Hot' and 'Cold' Motives and Discretion," *Academy of Management Journal* 57, no. 6 (2014): 1571–91.

72. F. F. T. Chiang and T. Birtch, "The Transferability of Management Practices: Examining Cross-National Differences in Reward Preferences," *Human Relations* 60, no. 9 (2007): 1293–330; and M. J. Gelfand, M. Erez, and Z. Aycan, "Cross-Cultural Organizational Behavior," *Annual Review of Psychology* 58 (2007): 479–514.

73. M. C. Bolino and W. H. Turnley, "Old Faces, New Places: Equity Theory in Cross-Cultural Contexts," *Journal of Organizational Behavior* 29, no. 1 (2008): 29–50.

74. R. Shao, D. E. Rupp, D. P. Skarlicki, and K. S. Jones, "Employee Justice across Cultures: A Meta-Analytic Review," *Journal of Management* 39, no. 1 (2013): 263–301.

75. R. L. Purvis, T. J. Zagenczyck, and G. E. McCray, "What's in It for Me? Using Expectancy Theory and Climate to Explain Stakeholder Participation, Its Direction and Intensity," *International Journal of Project Management* 33, no. 1 (2015): 3–14.

76. Y. Hao and G. Jianping, "Expectancy Theory and Nascent Entrepreneurship," *Small Business Economics* 39, no. 3 (2012), 667–84; and G. Yu and J. Guo, "Research on Employee Motivation Mechanism in Modern Enterprises Based on Victor H. Vroom's Expectancy Theory," in *Proceedings of the 9th International Conference on Innovation and Management*, eds. G. Duysters, A. DeHoyos, and K. Kaminishi (2012): 988–91.

77. Vroom refers to these three variables as expectancy, instrumentality, and valence, respectively.

78. J. Nocera, "The Anguish of Being an Analyst," *The New York Times,* March 4, 2006, B1, B12.

79. Y. Hao and G. Jianping, "Research on Employee Motivation Mechanism in Modern Enterprises Based on Victor H. Vroom's Expectancy Theory." (2012): 988–91.

80. H.-T. Chang, H.-M. Hsu, J.-W. Liou, and C.-T. Tsai, "Psychological Contracts and Innovative Behavior: A Moderated Path Analysis of Work Engagement and Job Resources," *Journal of Applied Social Psychology* 43, no. 10 (2013): 2021–135.

81. See topics of employee engagement from Gallup, "Employee Engagement", *Gallup*, accessed May 28, 2015, http://www.gallup.com/topic/employee_engagement.aspx.

82. M. S. Christian, A. S. Garza, and J. E. Slaughter, "Work Engagement: A Quantitative Review and Test of Its Relations with Task and Contextual Performance," *Personnel Psychology* 64, no. 1 (2011): 89–136.

83. W. B. Schaufeli, A. B. Bakker, and W. van Rhenen, "How Changes in Job Demands and Resources Predict Burnout, Work Engagement, and Sickness Absenteeism," *Journal of Organizational Behavior* 30, no. 7 (2009): 893–917; E. R. Crawford, J. A. LePine, and B. L. Rich, "Linking Job Demands and Resources to Employee Engagement and Burnout: A Theoretical Extension and Meta-Analytic Test," *Journal of Applied Psychology* 95, no. 5 (2010): 834–48; and D. Xanthopoulou, A. B. Bakker, E. Demerouti, and W. B. Schaufeli, "Reciprocal Relationships between Job Resources, Personal Resources, and Work Engagement," *Journal of Vocational Behavior* 74, no. 3 (2009): 235–44.

84. B. L. Rich, J. A. LePine, and E. R. Crawford, "Job Engagement: Antecedents and Effects on Job Performance," *Academy of Management Journal* 53, no. 3 (2010): 617–35.

85. M. Tims, A. B. Bakker, and D. Xanthopoulou, "Do Transformational Leaders Enhance Their Followers' Daily Work Engagement?" *Leadership Quarterly* 22, no. 1 (2011): 121–31; and F. O. Walumbwa, P. Wang, H. Wang, J. Schaubroeck, and B. J. Avolio, "Psychological Processes Linking Authentic Leadership to Follower Behaviors," *Leadership Quarterly* 21, no. 5 (2010): 901–14.

CHAPTER 8

1. C. B. Gibson, J. L. Gibbs, T. L. Stanko, P. Tesluk, and S. G. Cohen, "Including the 'I' in Virtuality and Modern Job Design: Extending the Job Characteristics Model to Include the Moderating Effect of Individual Experiences of Electronic Dependence and Copresence," *Organization Science* 22, no. 6 (2011): 1481–99.

2. S. E. Humphrey, J. D. Nahrgang, and F. P. Morgeson, "Integrating Motivational, Social, and Contextual Work Design Features: A Meta-Analytic Summary and Theoretical Extension of the Work Design Literature," *Journal of Applied Psychology* 92, no. 5 (2007): 1332–56.

3. B. M. Meglino and A. M. Korsgaard, "The Role of Other Orientation in Reactions to Job Characteristics," *Journal of Management* 33, no. 1 (2007): 57–83.

4. J. L. Pierce, I. Jussila, and A. Cummings, "Psychological Ownership within the Job Design Context: Revision of the Job Characteristics Model," *Journal of Organizational Behavior* 30, no. 4 (2009): 477–96.

5. C. B. Gibson, J. L. Gibbs, T. L. Stanko, P. Tesluk, and S. G. Cohen, "Including the 'I' in Virtuality and Modern Job Design: Extending the Job Characteristics Model to Include the Moderating Effect of Individual Experiences of Electronic Dependence and Copresence."

6. B. M. Naba and L. Fan, "Employee Motivation and Satisfaction in Niger: An Application of the Job Characteristics Model." In *Proceedings of the 10th International Conference on Innovation and Management*, eds. A. de Hoyos, K. Kaminishi, and G. Duysters (2013), 523–27.

7. M. F. Peterson and S. A. Ruiz-Quintanilla, "Cultural Socialization as a Source of Intrinsic Work Motivation," *Group & Organization Management* 28, no. 2 (2003): 188–216.

8. T. Silver, "Rotate Your Way to Higher Value," *Baseline,* March/April 2010, 12; and J. J. Salopek, "Coca-Cola Division Refreshes Its Talent with Diversity Push on Campus," *Workforce Management Online,* March 21, 2011, http://www.workforce.com/2011/03/21/coca-cola-division-refreshes-its-talent-with-diversity-push-on-campus/

9. Review of Singapore Airlines, *Skytrax,* accessed May 31, 2013, www.airlinequality.com/Airlines/SQ.htm

10. S.-Y. Chen, W.-C. Wu, C.-S. Chang, and C.-T. Lin, "Job Rotation and Internal Marketing for Increased Job Satisfaction and Organisational Commitment in Hospital Nursing Staff," *Journal of Nursing Management* 23, no. 3 (2015): 297–306.

11. A. Christini and D. Pozzoli, "Workplace Practices and Firm Performance in Manufacturing: A Comparative Study of Italy and Britain," *International Journal of Manpower* 31, no. 7 (2010): 818–42; and K. Kaymaz, "The Effects of Job Rotation Practices on Motivation: A Research on Managers in the Automotive Organizations," *Business and Economics Research Journal* 1, no. 3 (2010): 69–86.

12. S.-H. Huang and Y.-C. Pan, "Ergonomic Job Rotation Strategy Based on an Automated RGB-D Anthropometric Measuring System," *Journal of Manufacturing Systems* 33, no. 4 (2014): 699–710; and P. C. Leider, J. S. Boschman, M. H. W. Frings-Dresen, and H. F. van der Molen, "Effects of Job Rotation on Musculoskeletal Complaints and Related Work Exposures: A Systematic Literature Review," *Ergonomics* 58, no. 1 (2015): 18–32.

13. A. M. Grant, "Leading with Meaning: Beneficiary Contact, Prosocial Impact, and the Performance Effects of Transformational Leadership," *Academy of Management Journal* 55, no. 2 (2012): 458–76; and A. M. Grant and S. K. Parker, "Redesigning Work Design Theories: The Rise of Relational and Proactive Perspectives," *Annals of the Academy of Management* 3, no. 1 (2009): 317–75.

14. J. Devaro, "A Theoretical Analysis of Relational Job Design and Compensation," *Journal of Organizational Behavior* 31, no. 2–3 (2010): 279–301.

15. K. Pajo and L. Lee, "Corporate-Sponsored Volunteering: A Work Design Perspective," *Journal of Business Ethics* 99, no. 3 (2011): 467–82.

16. K. Bal, "Does Flextime Penalize Night Owls?" *Human Resource Executive,* June 23, 2014, http://www.hreonline.com/HRE/view/story.jhtml?id=534357257.

17. T. Kato, "Work and Family Practices in Japanese Firms: Their Scope, Nature, and Impact on Employee Turnover," *International Journal of Human Resource Management* 20, no. 2 (2009): 439–56; and P. Mourdoukoutas, "Why Do Women Fare Better in the German World of Work Than in the US?" *Forbes,* March 25, 2013, www.forbes.com/sites/panosmourdoukoutas/2013/03/25/why-do-women-fare-better-in-the-german-world-of-work-than-in-the-us/.

18. R. Waring, "Sunday Dialogue: Flexible Work Hours," *The New York Times,* January 19, 2013, www.nytimes.com.

19. B. Y. Lee and S. E. DeVoe, "Flextime and Profitability," *Industrial Relations* 51, no. 2 (2012): 298–316.

20. See, for example, K. M. Shockley and T. D. Allen, "When Flexibility Helps: Another Look at the Availability of Flexible Work Arrangements and Work–Family Conflict," *Journal of Vocational Behavior* 71, no. 3 (2007): 479–93; J. G. Grzywacz, D. S. Carlson, and S. Shulkin, "Schedule Flexibility and Stress: Linking Formal Flexible Arrangements and Perceived Flexibility to Employee Health," *Community, Work, and Family* 11, no. 2 (2008): 199–214; and L. A. McNall, A. D. Masuda, and J. M. Nicklin "Flexible Work Arrangements, Job Satisfaction, and Turnover Intentions: The Mediating Role of Work-to-Family Enrichment," 144, no. 1 (2010): 61–81.

21. K. M. Shockley and T. D. Allen, "Investigating the Missing Link in Flexible Work Arrangement Utilization: An Individual Difference Perspective," *Journal of Vocational Behavior* 76, no. 1 (2010): 131–42.

22. D. Eldridge and T. M. Nisar, "Employee and Organizational Impacts of Flextime Work Arrangements," *Industrial Relations* 66, no. 2 (2011): 213–34.

23. J. LaReau, "Ford's 2 Julies Share Devotion—And Job," *Automotive News,* October 25, 2010, 4.

24. S. Adams, "Workers Have More Flextime, Less Real Flexibility, Study Shows," *Forbes,* May 2, 2014, http://www.forbes.com/sites/susanadams/2014/05/02/workers-have-more-flextime-less-real-flexibility-study-shows/.

25. C. B. Mulligan, "What Job Sharing Brings," *Forbes,* May 8, 2013, http://economix.blogs.nytimes.com/2013/05/08/what-job-sharing-brings/; and "ObamaCare Employer Mandate," *ObamacareFacts.com,*" http://obamacarefacts.com/obamacare-employer-mandate/.

26. L. Woellert, "U.S. Work Share Program Helps Employers Avoid Layoffs," *Bloomberg Businessweek,* January 24, 2013, www.businessweek.com/articles/2013-01-24/u-dot-s-dot-work-share-program-helps-employers-avoid-layoffs.

27. P. R. Gregory, "Why Obama Cannot Match Germany's Jobs Miracle," *Forbes,* May 5, 2013, www.forbes.com/sites/paulroderickgregory/2013/05/05/why-obama-cannot-match-germanys-jobs-miracle/.

28. See, for example, E. J. Hill, M. Ferris, and V. Martinson, "Does It Matter Where You Work? A Comparison of How Three Work Venues (Traditional Office, Virtual Office, and Home Office) Influence Aspects of Work and Personal/Family Life," *Journal of Vocational Behavior* 63, no. 2 (2003): 220–41; B. Williamson, "Managing Virtual Workers," *Bloomberg Businessweek,* July 16, 2009, http://www.bloomberg.com/news/articles/2009-07-15/managing-virtual-workers; and B. A. Lautsch and E. E. Kossek, "Managing a Blended Workforce: Telecommuters and Non-Telecommuters," *Organizational Dynamics* 40, no. 1 (2010): 10–17.

29. S. Raghuram and D. Fang, "Telecommuting and the Role of Supervisory Power in China," *Asia Pacific Journal of Management* 31, no. 2 (2014): 523–47.

30. D. Wilkie, "Has the Telecommuting Bubble Burst?" *HR Magazine,* June 1, 2015, https://www.shrm.org/hr-today/news/hr-magazine/pages/june-2015.aspx.

31. B. W. Reynolds, "100 Top Companies with Remote Jobs in 2015," *Flexjobs,* January 20, 2015, http://www.flexjobs.com/blog/post/100-top-companies-with-remote-jobs-in-2015.

32. S. Florentine, "10 Most Telecommuting-Friendly Tech Companies," *CIO,* January 15, 2014, http://www.cio.com/article/2369810/telecommuting/136064-10-Most-Telecommuting-Friendly-Tech-Companies.html#slide11.

33. See, for instance, M. Conlin, "The Easiest Commute of All," *BusinessWeek,* December 12, 2005: 78; and E. O'Keefe, "Teleworking Grows But Still a Rarity," *The Washington Post,* February 22, 2011, B3.

34. See, for example, P. Brotherton, "For Teleworkers, Less Is Definitely More," *TD* 65, March, 19, 2011: 29; and M. Virick, N. DaSilva, and K. Arrington, "Moderators of the Curvilinear Relation between Extent of Telecommuting and Job and Life Satisfaction: The Role of Performance Outcome Orientation and Worker Type," *Human Relations* 63, no. 1 (2010): 137–54.

35. M. C. Noonan and J. L. Glass, "The Hard Truth about Telecommuting," *Monthly Labor Review* 135, no. 6 (2012): 38–45.

36. J. Welch and S. Welch, "The Importance of Being There," *BusinessWeek,* April 16, 2007, 92; and Z. I. Barsness, K. A. Diekmann, and M. L. Seidel, "Motivation and Opportunity: The Role of Remote Work, Demographic Dissimilarity, and Social Network Centrality in Impression Management," *Academy of Management Journal* 48, no. 3 (2005): 401–19.

37. P. Zhu and S. G. Mason, "The Impact of Telecommuting on Personal Vehicle Usage and Environmental Sustainability," *International Journal of Environmental Science and Technology* 11, no. 8 (2014): 2185–200.

38. M. Marchington, "Analysing the Forces Shaping Employee Involvement and Participation (EIP) at Organisation Level in Liberal Market Economies (LMEs)," *Human Resource Management Journal* 25, no. 1 (2015): 1–18.

39. See, for example, the literature on empowerment, such as S. E. Seibert, S. R. Silver, and W. A. Randolph, "Taking Empowerment to the Next Level: A Multiple-Level Model of Empowerment, Performance, and Satisfaction," *Academy of Management Journal* 47, no. 3 (2004): 332–49; M. M. Butts, R. J. Vandenberg, D. M. DeJoy, B. S. Schaffer, and M. G. Wilson, "Individual Reactions to High Involvement Work Processes: Investigating the Role of Empowerment and Perceived Organizational Support," *Journal of Occupational Health Psychology* 14, no. 2 (2009): 122–36; R. Park, E. Applebaum, and D. Kruse, "Employee Involvement and Group Incentives in Manufacturing Companies: A Multi-Level Analysis," *Human Resource Management Journal* 20, no. 3 (2010): 227–43; D. C. Jones, P. Kalmi, and A. Kauhanen, "How Does Employee Involvement Stack Up? The Effects of Human Resource Management Policies in a Retail Firm," *Industrial Relations* 49, no. 1 (2010): 1–21; and M. T. Maynard, L. L. Gilson, and J. E. Mathieu, "Empowerment—Fad or Fab? A Multilevel Review of the Past Two Decades of Research," *Journal of Management* 38, no. 4 (2012): 1231–81.

40. See, for instance, A. Sagie and Z. Aycan, "A Cross-Cultural Analysis of Participative Decision-Making in Organizations,"

Human Relations 56, no. 4 (2003): 453–73; and J. Brockner, "Unpacking Country Effects: On the Need to Operationalize the Psychological Determinants of Cross-National Differences," in *Research in Organizational Behavior, vol. 25,* eds. R. M. Kramer and B. M. Staw (Oxford, UK: Elsevier, 2003), 336–40.

41. Z. X. Chen and S. Aryee, "Delegation and Employee Work Outcomes: An Examination of the Cultural Context of Mediating Processes in China," *Academy of Management Journal* 50, no. 1 (2007): 226–38.

42. G. Huang, X. Niu, C. Lee, and S. J. Ashford, "Differentiating Cognitive and Affective Job Insecurity: Antecedents and Outcomes," *Journal of Organizational Behavior* 33, no. 6 (2012): 752–69.

43. Z. Cheng, "The Effects of Employee Involvement and Participation on Subjective Wellbeing: Evidence from Urban China," *Social Indicators Research* 118, no. 2 (2014): 457–83.

44. M. Marchington, "Analysing the Forces Shaping Employee Involvement and Participation (EIP) at Organisation Level in Liberal Market Economies (LMEs)."

45. J. J. Caughron and M. D. Mumford, "Embedded Leadership: How Do a Leader's Superiors Impact Middle-Management Performance?" *Leadership Quarterly* 23, no. 3 June 2012: 342–53.

46. See, for instance, A. Pendleton and A. Robinson, "Employee Stock Ownership, Involvement, and Productivity: An Interaction-Based Approach," *Industrial and Labor Relations Review* 64, no. 1 (2010): 3–29.

47. D. K. Datta, J. P. Guthrie, and P. M. Wright, "Human Resource Management and Labor Productivity: Does Industry Matter?" *Academy of Management Journal* 48, no. 1 (2005): 135–45; C. M. Riordan, R. J. Vandenberg, and H. A. Richardson, "Employee Involvement Climate and Organizational Effectiveness." *Human Resource Management* 44, no. 4 (2005): 471–88; and J. Kim, J. P. MacDuffie, and F. K. Pil, "Employee Voice and Organizational Performance: Team versus Representative Influence," *Human Relations* 63, no. 3 (2010): 371–94.

48. M. Marchington, "Analysing the Forces Shaping Employee Involvement and Participation (EIP) at Organisation Level in Liberal Market Economies (LMEs)."

49. E. White, "Opportunity Knocks, and It Pays a Lot Better," *The Wall Street Journal,* November 13, 2006, B3.

50. M. Sabramony, N. Krause, J. Norton, and G. N. Burns "The Relationship between Human Resource Investments and Organizational Performance: A Firm-Level Examination of Equilibrium Theory," *Journal of Applied Psychology* 93, no. 4 (2008): 778–88.

51. C. Isidore, "Walmart Ups Pay Well above Minimum Wage," CNN Money, February 19, 2015, http://money.cnn.com/2015/02/19/news/companies/walmart-wages/.

52. See, for example, M. Damiani and A. Ricci, "Managers' Education and the Choice of Different Variable Pay Schemes: Evidence from Italian Firms," *European Management Journal* 32, no. 6 (2014): 891–902; and J. S. Heywood and U. Jirjahn, "Variable Pay, Industrial Relations and Foreign Ownership: Evidence from Germany," *British Journal of Industrial Relations* 52, no. 3 (2014): 521–52.

53. S. Miller, "Variable Pay Spending Spikes to Record High," *Society for Human Resource Management: Compensation Topics & Strategy,* September 2, 2014, http://www.shrm.org/hrdisciplines/compensation/articles/pages/variable-pay-high.aspx.

54. S. Miller, "Companies Worldwide Rewarding Performance with Variable Pay," *Society for Human Resource Management: Compensation Topics & Strategy,* March 1, 2010, https://www.shrm.org/resourcesandtools/hr-topics/compensation/pages/variableworld.aspx.

55. S. Miller, "Asian Firms Offer More Variable Pay Than Western Firms," *Society for Human Resource Management: Compensation Topics & Strategy,* March 28, 2012, https://www.shrm.org/resourcesandtools/hr-topics/compensation/pages/asianvariablepay.aspx.

56. H. Kim, K. L. Sutton, and Y. Gong, "Group-Based Pay-for-Performance Plans and Firm Performance: The Moderating Role of Empowerment Practices," *Asia Pacific Journal of Management* 30, no. 1 2013: 31–52.

57. J. Cloutier, D. Morin, and S. Renaud, "How Does Variable Pay Relate to Pay Satisfaction among Canadian Workers?" *International Journal of Manpower* 34, no. 5 (2013): 465–85.

58. E. Belogolovsky and P. A. Bamberger, "Signaling in Secret: Pay for Performance and the Incentive and Sorting Effects of Pay Secrecy," *Academy of Management Journal* 57, no. 6 (2014): 1706–33.

59. Ibid.

60. C. B. Cadsby, F. Song, and F. Tapon, "Sorting and Incentive Effects of Pay for Performance: An Experimental Investigation," *Academy of Management Journal* 50, no. 2 (2007): 387–405.

61. J. H. Han, K. M. Barol, and S. Kim, "Tightening Up the Performance-Pay Linkage: Roles of Contingent Reward Leadership and Profit-Sharing in the Cross-Level Influence of Individual Pay-for-Performance," *Journal of Applied Psychology* 100, no. 2 (2015): 417–30.

62. K. A. Bender, C. P. Green, and J. S. Heywood, "Piece Rates and Workplace Injury: Does Survey Evidence Support Adam Smith?" *Journal of Population Economics* 25, no. 2 (2012): 569–90.

63. J. S. Heywood, X. Wei, and G. Ye, "Piece Rates for Professors," *Economics Letters* 113, no. 3 (2011): 285–87.

64. A. Baker and V. Mertins, "Risk-Sorting and Preference for Team Piece Rates," *Journal of Economic Psychology* 34 (2013): 285–300.

65. A. Clemens, "Pace of Work and Piece Rates," *Economics Letters* 115, no. 3 (2012): 477–79.

66. K. A. Bender, C. P. Green, and J. S. Heywood, "Piece Rates and Workplace Injury: Does Survey Evidence Support Adam Smith?"

67. S. L. Rynes, B. Gerhart, and L. Parks, "Personnel Psychology: Performance Evaluation and Pay for Performance," *Annual Review of Psychology* 56, no. 1 (2005): 571–600.

68. "Paying Doctors for Performance," *The New York Times,* January 27, 2013, A16.

69. S. Halzack, "Companies Look to Bonuses Instead of Salary Increases in an Uncertain Economy," *The Washington Post,* November 6, 2012, https://www.washingtonpost.com/business/economy/companies-look-to-bonuses-instead-of-salary-increases-in-an-uncertain-economy/2012/11/06/52a7ec12-2751-11e2-9972-71bf64ea091c_story.html.

70. E. J. Castillo, "Gender, Race, and the New (Merit-Based) Employment Relationship," *Industrial Relations* 51, no. S1 (2012): 528–62.

71. P. Furman, "Ouch! Top Honchos on Wall Street See Biggest Cuts to Bonuses," *New York Daily News,* February 18, 2013, http://www.nydailynews.com/new-york/ouch-top-honchos-wall-street-biggest-cuts-bonues-article-1.1267228.

72. N. Chun and S. Lee, "Bonus Compensation and Productivity: Evidence from Indian Manufacturing Plant-Level Data," *Journal of Productivity Analysis* 43, no. 1 (2015): 47–58.

73. E. White, "Employers Increasingly Favor Bonuses to Raises," *The Wall Street Journal,* August 28, 2006, B3.

74. B. Goyette "Mark Zuckerberg Reaped $2.3 Billion on Facebook Stock Options," *The Huffington Post,* April 26, 2013, http://www.huffingtonpost.com/2013/04/26/zuckerberg-stock-options_n_3166661.html?utm_hp_ref=business.

75. D. D'Art and T. Turner, "Profit Sharing, Firm Performance, and Union Influence in Selected European Countries," *Personnel Review* 33, no. 3 (2004): 335–50; and D. Kruse, R. Freeman, and J. Blasi, *Shared Capitalism at Work: Employee Ownership, Profit and Gain Sharing, and Broad-Based Stock Options* (Chicago: University of Chicago Press, 2010).

76. A. Bayo-Moriones and M. Larraza-Kintana, "Profit-Sharing Plans and Affective Commitment: Does the Context Matter?" *Human Resource Management* 48, no. 2 (2009): 207–26.

77. N. Chi and T. Han, "Exploring the Linkages between Formal Ownership and Psychological Ownership for the Organization: The Mediating Role of Organizational Justice," *Journal of Occupational and Organizational Psychology* 81, no. 4 (2008): 691–711.

78. J. H. Han, K. M. Barol, and S. Kim, "Tightening Up the Performance-Pay Linkage: Roles of Contingent Reward Leadership and Profit-Sharing in the Cross-Level Influence of Individual Pay-for-Performance."

79. R. P. Garrett, "Does Employee Ownership Increase Innovation?" *New England Journal of Entrepreneurship* 13, no. 2, (2010): 37–46.

80. D. McCarthy, E. Reeves, and T. Turner, "Can Employee Share-Ownership Improve Employee Attitudes and Behaviour?" *Employee Relations* 32, no. 4 (2010): 382–95.

81. A. Pendleton, "Shared Capitalism at Work: Employee Ownership, Profit and Gain Sharing, and Broad-Based Stock Options," *Industrial and Labor Relations Review* 64, no. 3 (2011): 621–22.

82. A. Pendleton and A. Robinson, "Employee Stock Ownership, Involvement, and Productivity: An Interaction-Based Approach," *Industrial and Labor Relations Review* 64, no. 1 (2010): 3–29.

83. X. Zhang, K. M. Bartol, K. G. Smith, M. D. Pfarrer, and D. M. Khanin, "CEOs on the Edge: Earnings Manipulation and Stock-Based Incentive Misalignment," *Academy of Management Journal* 51, no. 2 (2008): 241–58.

84. Z. Lin, J. Kelly, and L. Trenberth, "Antecedents and Consequences of the Introduction of Flexible Benefit Plans in China," *International Journal of Human Resource Management* vol. 22, no. 5 (2011): 1128–45.

85. Ibid.

86. R. C. Koo, "Global Added Value of Flexible Benefits," *Benefits Quarterly* 27, no. 4 (2011): 17–20.

87. P. Stephens, "Flex Plans Gain in Popularity," *CA Magazine,* January/February 2010, 10.

88. D. Lovewell, "Flexible Benefits: Benefits on Offer," *Employee Benefits,* March 2010, S15.

89. S. J. Peterson and F. Luthans, "The Impact of Financial and Nonfinancial Incentives on Business Unit Outcomes over Time," *Journal of Applied Psychology* 91, no. 1 (2006): 156–65.

90. C. Xu and C. Liang, "The Mechanisms Underlying an Employee Recognition Program," in *Proceedings of the International Conference on Public Human Resource Management and Innovation*, eds. L. Hale and J. Zhang (2013), 28–35.

91. See F. Luthans and A. D. Stajkovic, "Provide Recognition for Performance Improvement," in *Handbook of Principles of Organizational Behavior*, ed. E. A. Locke (Malden, MA: Blackwell, 2004): 166–80.

CHAPTER 9

1. E. J. Boothby, M. S. Clark, and J. A. Bargh, "Shared Experiences Are Amplified," *Psychological Science* 25, no. 12 (2014): 2209–16.

2. B. Bastien, J. Jetten, and L. J. Ferris, "Pain as Social Glue: Shared Pain Increases Cooperation," *Psychological Science* 25, no. 11 (2014): 2079–85.

3. O. Yakushko, M. M. Davidson, and E. N. Williams, "Identity Salience Model: A Paradigm for Integrating Multiple Identities in Clinical Practice," *Psychotherapy* 46, no. 2 (2009): 180–92; and S. M. Toh and A. S. Denisi, "Host Country Nationals as Socializing Agents: A Social Identity Approach," *Journal of Organizational Behavior* 28, no. 3 (2007): 281–301.

4. N. Karelaia and L. Guillén, "Me, a Woman and a Leader: Positive Social Identity and Identity Conflict," *Organizational Behavior and Human Decision Processes* 125, no. 2 (2014): 204–19.

5. S. Zhang, G. Chen, X.-P. Chen, D. Liu, and M. D. Johnson, "Relational versus Collective Identification within Workgroups: Conceptualization, Measurement Development, and Nomological Network Building," *Journal of Management* 40, no. 6 (2014): 1700–31.

6. G. J. Lewis and T. C. Bates, "Common Heritable Effects Underpin Concerns over Norm Maintenance and In-Group Favoritism: Evidence from Genetic Analyses of Right-Wing Authoritarianism and Traditionalism," *Journal of Personality* 82, no. 4 (2014): 297–309.

7. S. L. Neuberg et al., "Religion and Intergroup Conflict: Findings from the Global Group Relations Project," *Psychological Science* 25, no. 1 (2014): 198–206.

8. W. M. L. Finlay, "Denunciation and the construction of Norms in Group Conflict: Examples from an Al-Qaeda-Supporting Group," *British Journal of Social Psychology* 53, no. 4 (2014): 691–710.

9. M. J. Garfield and A. R. Denis, "Toward an Integrated Model of Group Development: Disruption of Routines by Technology-Induced Change," *Journal of Management Information Systems* 29, no. 3 (2012): 43–86; and A. Chang, P. Bordia, and J. Duck, "Punctuated Equilibrium and Linear Progression: Toward a New Understanding of Group Development," *Academy of Management Journal* 46, no. 1 (2003): 106–17.

10. M. M. Kazmer, "Disengaging from a Distributed Research Project: Refining a Model of Group Departures," *Journal of the American Society for Information Science and Technology* 61, no. 4 (2010): 758–71.

11. William Shakespeare. As You Like It. First Folio 1623

12. K. Giese and A. Theil, "The Psychological Contract in Chinese–African Informal Labor Relations," *International Journal of Human Resource Management* 26, no. 14 (2015): 1807–26; L. Sels, M. Janssens, and I. Van den Brande, "Assessing the Nature of Psychological Contracts: A Validation of Six Dimensions," *Journal of Organizational Behavior* 25, no. 4 (2004): 461–88; and C. Gui, C. Lee, and D. M. Rousseau, "Psychological Contract and Organizational Generalizability and Instrumentality," *Journal of Applied Psychology* 89, no. 2 (2004): 311–21.

13. M. D. Collins, "The Effect of Psychological Contract Fulfillment on Manager Turnover Intentions and Its Role as a Mediator in a Casual, Limited-Service Restaurant Environment," *International Journal of Hospitality Management* 29, no. 4 (2010): 736–42; J. M. Jensen, R. A. Opland, and A. M. Ryan, "Psychological Contracts and Counterproductive Work Behaviors: Employee Responses to Transactional and Relational Breach," *Journal of Business and Psychology* 25, no. 4 (2010): 555–68.

14. K. S. Wilson and H. M. Baumann, "Capturing a More Complete View of Employees' Lives outside of Work: The Introduction and Development of New Interrole Conflict Constructs," *Personnel Psychology* 68, no. 2 (2015): 235–82.

15. Ibid

16. See, for example, F. T. Amstad, L. L. Meier, U. Fasel, A. Elfering, and N. K. Semmer, "A Meta-Analysis of Work-Family Conflict and Various Outcomes with a Special Emphasis on Cross-Domain versus Matching-Domain Relations," *Journal of Occupational Health Psychology* 16, no. 2 (2011): 151–69.

17. Y. Huang, K. M. Kendrick, and R. Yu, "Conformity to the Opinions of Other People Lasts for No More Than 3 Days," *Psychological Science* 25, no. 7 (2014): 1388–93.

18. M. S. Hagger, P. Rentzelas, and N. K. D. Chatzisrantis, "Effects of Individualist and Collectivist Group Norms and Choice on Intrinsic Motivation," *Motivation and Emotion* 38, no. 2 (2014): 215–23; and M. G. Ehrhart and S. E. Naumann, "Organizational Citizenship Behavior in Work Groups: A Group Norms Approach," *Journal of Applied Psychology* 89, no. 6 (2004): 960–74.

19. E. Delvaux, N. Vanbeselaere, and B. Mesquita, "Dynamic Interplay between Norms and Experiences of Anger and Gratitude in Groups," *Small Group Research* 46, no. 3 (2015): 300–23.

20. R. B. Cialdini and N. J. Goldstein, "Social Influence: Compliance and Conformity," *Annual Review of Psychology* 55 (2004): 591–621.

21. P. Kundu and D. D. Cummins, "Morality and Conformity: The Asch Paradigm Applied to Moral Decisions," *Social Influence* 8, no. 4 (2013): 268–79.

22. S. Sansfacon and C. E. Amiot, "The Impact of Group Norms and Behavioral Congruence on the Internalization of an Illegal Downloading Behavior," *Group Dynamics: Theory Research and Practice* 18, no. 2 (2014): 174–88; and L. Rosh, L. R. Offermann, and R. Van Diest, "Too Close for Comfort? Distinguishing between Team Intimacy and Team Cohesion," *Human Resource Management Review* 22, no. 2 (2012): 116–27.

23. J. S. Hassard, "Rethinking the Hawthorne Studies: The Western Electric Research in Its Social, Political, and Historical Context," *Human Relations* 65, no. 11 (2012): 1431–61.

24. J. A. Goncalo, J. A. Chatman, M. M. Duguid, and J. A. Kennedy, "Creativity from Constraint? How the Political Correctness Norm Influences Creativity in Mixed-Sex Work Groups," *Administrative Science Quarterly* 60, no. 1 (2015): 1–30.

25. E. Gonzalez-Mule, D. S. DeGeest, B. W. McCormick, J. Y. Seong, and K. G. Brown, "Can We Get Some Cooperation around Here? The Mediating Role of Group Norms on the Relationship between Team Personality and Individual Helping

Behaviors," *Journal of Applied Psychology* 99, no. 5 (2014): 988–99.

26. T. Masson and I. Fritsche, "Adherence to Climate Change-Related Ingroup Norms: Do Dimensions of Group Identification Matter?" *European Journal of Social Psychology* 44, no. 5 (2014): 455–65.

27. See R. J. Bennett and S. L. Robinson, "The Past, Present, and Future of Workplace Deviance," in *Organizational Behavior: The State of the Science*, 2nd ed., ed. J. Greenberg (Mahwah, NJ: Erlbaum, 2003), 237–71; and C. M. Berry, D. S. Ones, and P. R. Sackett, "Interpersonal Deviance, Organizational Deviance, and Their Common Correlates: A Review and Meta-Analysis," *Journal of Applied Psychology* 92, no. 2 (2007): 410–24.

28. M. A. Baysinger, K. T. Scherer, and J. M. LeBreton, "Exploring the Disruptive Effects of Psychopathy and Aggression on Group Processes and Group Effectiveness," *Journal of Applied Psychology* 99, no. 1 (2014): 48–65.

29. T. C. Reich and M. S. Hershcovis, "Observing Workplace Incivility," *Journal of Applied Psychology* 100, no. 1 (2015): 203–15; and Z. E. Zhou, Y. Yan, X. X. Che, and L. L. Meier, "Effect of Workplace Incivility on End-of-Work Negative Affect: Examining Individual and Organizational Moderators in a Daily Diary Study," *Journal of Occupational Health Psychology* 20, no. 1 (2015): 117–30.

30. See C. Pearson, L. M. Andersson, and C. L. Porath, "Workplace Incivility," in *Counterproductive Work Behavior: Investigations of Actors and Targets*, eds. S. Fox and P. E. Spector (Washington, DC: American Psychological Association, 2005), 177–200.

31. S. Lim, L. M. Cortina, and V. J. Magley, "Personal and Workgroup Incivility: Impact on Work and Health Outcomes," *Journal of Applied Psychology* 93, no. 1 (2008): 95–107.

32. M. S. Christian and A. P. J. Ellis, "Examining the Effects of Sleep Deprivation on Workplace Deviance: A Self-Regulatory Perspective," *Academy of Management Journal* 54, no. 5 (2011): 913–34.

33. M. S. Hagger, P. Rentzelas, and N. K. D. Chatzisrantis, "Effects of Individualist and Collectivist Group Norms and Choice on Intrinsic Motivation."

34. J. Dippong and W. Kalkhoff, "Predicting Performance Expectations from Affective Impressions: Linking Affect Control Theory and Status Characteristics Theory," *Social Science Research* 50 (2015): 1–14; and A. E. Randel, L. Chay-Hoon, and P. C. Earley, "It's Not Just about Differences: An Integration of Role Identity Theory and Status Characteristics Theory," in *Research on Managing Groups and Teams*, ed. M. C. T. Hunt (2005), 23–42.

35. A. E. Randel, L. Chay-Hoon, and P. C. Earley, "It's Not Just about Differences: An Integration of Role Identity Theory and Status Characteristics Theory."

36. P. F. Hewlin, "Wearing the Cloak: Antecedents and Consequences of Creating Facades of Conformity," *Journal of Applied Psychology* 94, no. 3 (2009): 727–41.

37. B. Groysberg, J. T. Polzer, and H. A. Elfenbein, "Too Many Cooks Spoil the Broth: How High-Status Individuals Decrease Group Effectiveness."

38. C. Bendersky and N. P. Shah, "The Cost of Status Enhancement: Performance Effects of Individuals' Status Mobility in Task Groups," *Organization Science* 23, no. 2 (2012): 308–22.

39. B. Groysberg, J. T. Polzer, and H. A. Elfenbein, "Too Many Cooks Spoil the Broth: How High-Status Individuals Decrease Group Effectiveness.

40. A. M. Christie and J. Barling, "Beyond Status: Relating Status Inequality to Performance and Health in Teams," *Journal of Applied Psychology* 95, no. 5 (2010): 920–34; and L. H. Nishii and D. M. Mayer, "Do Inclusive Leaders Help to Reduce Turnover in Diverse Groups? The Moderating Role of Leader–Member Exchange in the Diversity to Turnover Relationship," *Journal of Applied Psychology* 94, no. 6 (2009): 1412–26.

41. M. Cikara and J. J. Van Bavel, "The Neuroscience of Intergroup Relations: An Integrative Review," *Perspectives on Psychological Science* 9, no. 3 (2014): 245–74.

42. M. Rubin, C. Badea, and J. Jetten, "Low Status Groups Show In-Group Favoritism to Compensate for Their Low Status and Compete for Higher Status," *Group Processes & Intergroup Relations* 17, no. 5 (2014): 563–76.

43. C. L. Wilkins, J. D. Wellman, L. G. Babbitt, N. R. Toosi, and K. D. Schad, "You Can Win But I Can't Lose: Bias against High-Status Groups Increases Their Zero-Sum Beliefs about Discrimination," *Journal of Experimental Social Psychology* 57 (2014): 1–14.

44. R. B. Lount Jr. and S. L. Wilk, "Working Harder or Hardly Working? Posting Performance Eliminates Social Loafing and Promotes Social Laboring in Workgroups," *Management Science* 60, no. 5 (2014): 1098–106; S. M. Murphy, S. J. Wayne, R. C. Liden, and B. Erdogan, "Understanding Social Loafing: The Role of Justice Perceptions and Exchange Relationships," *Human Relations* 56, no. 1 (2003): 61–84; and R. C. Liden, S. J. Wayne, R. A. Jaworski, and N. Bennett, "Social Loafing: A Field Investigation," *Journal of Management* 30, no. 2 (2004): 285–304.

45. C. Rubino, D. R. Avery, S. D. Volpone, and L. Ford, "Does Teaming Obscure Low Performance? Exploring the Temporal Effects of Team Performance Diversity," *Human Performance* 27, no. 5 (2014): 416–34.

46. D. L. Smrt and S. J. Karau, "Protestant Work Ethic Moderates Social Loafing," *Group Dynamics: Theory Research and Practice* 15, no. 3 (2011): 267–74.

47. M. C. Schippers, "Social Loafing Tendencies and Team Performance: The Compensating Effect of Agreeableness and Conscientiousness," *Academy of Management Learning & Education* 13, no. 1 (2014): 62–81.

48. A. Gunnthorsdottir and A. Rapoport, "Embedding Social Dilemmas in Intergroup Competition Reduces Free-Riding," *Organizational Behavior and Human Decision Processes* 101, no. 2 (2006): 184–99; and E. M. Stark, J. D. Shaw, and M. K. Duffy, "Preference for Group Work, Winning Orientation, and Social Loafing Behavior in Groups," *Group & Organization Management* 32, no. 6 (2007): 699–723.

49. R. B. Lount Jr. and S. L. Wilk, "Working Harder or Hardly Working? Posting Performance Eliminates Social Loafing and Promotes Social Laboring in Workgroups."

50. A. Gunnthorsdottir and A. Rapoport, "Embedding Social Dilemmas in Intergroup Competition Reduces Free-Riding;" and E. M. Stark, J. D. Shaw, and M. K. Duffy, "Preference for Group Work, Winning Orientation, and Social Loafing Behavior in Groups."

51. L. L. Greer, "Group Cohesion: Then and Now," *Small Group Research* 43, no. 6 (2012): 655–61.

52. D. S. Staples and L. Zhao, "The Effects of Cultural Diversity in Virtual Teams Versus Face-to-Face Teams," *Group Decision and Negotiation* 15, no. 4 (2006): 389–406.

53. K. J. Klein, A. P. Knight, J. C. Ziegert, B. C. Lim, and J. L. Saltz, "When Team Members' Values Differ: The

Moderating Role of Team Leadership," *Organizational Behavior and Human Decision Processes* 114, no. 1 (2011): 25–36; and G. Park and R. P. DeShon, "A Multilevel Model of Minority Opinion Expression and Team Decision-Making Effectiveness," *Journal of Applied Psychology* 95, no. 5 (2010): 824–33.

54. J. S. Chun and J. N. Choi, "Members' Needs, Intragroup Conflict, and Group Performance," *Journal of Applied Psychology* 99, no. 3 (2014): 437–50.

55. M. Rigoglioso, "Diverse Backgrounds and Personalities Can Strengthen Groups," Stanford Knowledgebase, August 15, 2006, https://www.gsb.stanford.edu/insights/diverse-backgrounds-personalities-can-strengthen-groups.

56. K. W. Phillips and D. L. Loyd, "When Surface and Deep-Level Diversity Collide: The Effects on Dissenting Group Members," *Organizational Behavior and Human Decision Processes* 99, no. 2 (2006): 143–60; and S. R. Sommers, "On Racial Diversity and Group Decision Making: Identifying Multiple Effects of Racial Composition on Jury Deliberations," *Journal of Personality and Social Psychology* 99, no. 4 (April 2006): 597–612.

57. J. S. Chun and J. N. Choi, "Members' Needs, Intragroup Conflict, and Group Performance."

58. E. Mannix and M. A. Neale, "What Differences Make a Difference? The Promise and Reality of Diverse Teams in Organizations," *Psychological Science in the Public Interest*, 6, no. 2 (2005): 31–55.

59. E. P. Apfelbaum, K. W. Phillips, and J. A. Richeson, "Rethinking the Baseline in Diversity Research: Should We Be Explaining the Effects of Homogeneity?" *Perspectives on Psychological Science* 9, no. 3 (2014): 235–44.

60. See M. B. Thatcher and P. C. Patel, "Group Faultlines: A Review, Integration, and Guide to Future Research," *Journal of Management* 38, no. 4 (2012): 969–1009.

61. K. Bezrukova, S. M. B. Thatcher, K. A. Jehn, and C. S. Spell, "The Effects of Alignments: Examining Group Faultlines, Organizational Cultures, and Performance," *Journal of Applied Psychology* 97, no. 1 (2012): 77–92.

62. R. Rico, M. Sanchez-Manzanares, M. Antino, and D. Lau, "Bridging Team Faultlines by Combining Task Role Assignment and Goal Structure Strategies," *Journal of Applied Psychology* 97, no. 2 (2012): 407–20.

63. J. S. Chun and J. N. Choi, "Members' Needs, Intragroup Conflict, and Group Performance."

64. B. L. Bonner, S. D. Sillito, and M. R. Baumann, "Collective Estimation: Accuracy, Expertise, and Extroversion as Sources of Intra-Group Influence," *Organizational Behavior and Human Decision Processes* 103, no. 1 (2007): 121–33.

65. J. E. Kammer, W. Gaissmaier, T. Reimer, and C. C. Schermuly, "The Adaptive Use of Recognition in Group Decision Making," *Cognitive Science* 38, no. 5 (2014): 911–42.

66. G. Park and R. P. DeShon, "A Multilevel Model of Minority Opinion Expression and Team Decision-Making Effectiveness," *Journal of Applied Psychology* 95, no. 5 (2010): 824–33.

67. R. Benabou, "Groupthink: Collective Delusions in Organizations and Markets," *Review of Economic Studies* 80 (2013): 429–62.

68. See S. Schultz-Hardt, F. C. Brodbeck, A. Mojzisch, R. Kerschreiter, and D. Frey, "Group Decision Making in Hidden Profile Situations: Dissent as a Facilitator for Decision Quality," *Journal of Personality and Social Psychology* 91, no. 6 (2006): 1080–93.

69. See I. Yaniv, "Group Diversity and Decision Quality: Amplification and Attenuation of the Framing Effect," *International Journal of Forecasting* 27, no. 1 (2011): 41–49.

70. M. P. Brady and S. Y. Wu, "The Aggregation of Preferences in Groups: Identity, Responsibility, and Polarization," *Journal of Economic Psychology* 31, no. 6 (2010): 950–63.

71. Z. Krizan and R. S. Baron, "Group Polarization and Choice-Dilemmas: How Important Is Self-Categorization?" *European Journal of Social Psychology* 37, no. 1 (2007): 191–201.

72. See R. P. McGlynn, D. McGurk, V. S. Effland, N. L. Johll, and D. J. Harding, "Brainstorming and Task Performance in Groups Constrained by Evidence," *Organizational Behavior and Human Decision Processes* 93, no. 1 (2004): 75–87; and R. C. Litchfield, "Brainstorming Reconsidered: A Goal-Based View," *Academy of Management Review* 33, no. 3 (2008): 649–68.

73. N. L. Kerr and R. S. Tindale, "Group Performance and Decision-Making," *Annual Review of Psychology* 55 (2004): 623–55.

74. C. Faure, "Beyond Brainstorming: Effects of Different Group Procedures on Selection of Ideas and Satisfaction with the Process," *Journal of Creative Behavior* 38, no. 1 (2004): 13–34.

75. P. L. Perrewé, K. L. Zellars, G. R. Ferris, A. M. Rossi, C. J. Kacmar, and D. A. Ralston, "Neutralizing Job Stressors: Political Skill as an Antidote to the Dysfunctional Consequences of Role Conflict," *Academy of Management Journal* 47, no. 1 (2004): 141–52.

CHAPTER 10

1. R. Karlgaard, "Think (Really!) Small," *Forbes,* April 13, 2015, 32.

2. J. C. Gorman, "Team Coordination and Dynamics: Two Central Issues," *Current Directions in Psychological Science* 23, no. 5 (2014): 355–60.

3. Ibid.

4. J. Mathieu, M. T. Maynard, T. Rapp, and L. Gilson, "Team Effectiveness 1997–2007: A Review of Recent Advancements and a Glimpse into the Future," *Journal of Management* 34, no. 3 (2008): 410–76.

5. See, for example, S.-B. Yang and M. E. Guy, "The Effectiveness of Self-Managed Work Teams in Government Organizations," *Journal of Business and Psychology* 26, no. 4 (2011): 531–41; and G. S. Van der Vegt, S. Bunderson, and B. Kuipers, "Why Turnover Matters in Self-Managing Work Teams: Learning, Social Integration, and Task Flexibility," *Journal of Management* 36, no. 5 (2010): 1168–91.

6. G. L. Stewart, S. H. Courtright, and M. R. Barrick, "Peer-Based Control in Self-Managing Teams: Linking Rational and Normative Influence with Individual and Group Performance," *Journal of Applied Psychology* 97, no. 2 (2012): 435–47.

7. C. W. Langfred, "The Downside of Self-Management: A Longitudinal Study of the Effects of Conflict on Trust, Autonomy, and Task Interdependence in Self-Managing Teams," *Academy of Management Journal* 50, no. 4 (2007): 885–900.

8. B. H. Bradley, B. E. Postlethwaite, A. C. Klotz, M. R. Hamdani, and K. G. Brown, "Reaping the Benefits of Task Conflict in Teams: The Critical Role of Team Psychological Safety Climate," *Journal of Applied Psychology,* 97, no. 1 (2012): 151–58.

9. J. Devaro, "The Effects of Self-Managed and Closely Managed Teams on Labor Productivity and Product Quality: An

Empirical Analysis of a Cross-Section of Establishments," *Industrial Relations* 47, no. 4 (2008): 659–98.

10. A. Shah, "Starbucks Strives for Instant Gratification with Via Launch," *PRWeek*, December 1, 2009, 15.

11. F. Aime, S. Humphrey, D. S. DeRue, and J. B. Paul, "The Riddle of Heterarchy: Power Transitions in Cross-Functional Teams," *Academy of Management Journal* 57, no. 2 (2014): 327–52.

12. See, for example, L. L. Martins, L. L. Gilson, and M. T. Maynard, "Virtual Teams: What Do We Know and Where Do We Go from Here?" *Journal of Management* 30, no. 6 (2004): 805–35; and B. Leonard, "Managing Virtual Teams," *HR Magazine,* June 2011, 39–42.

13. J. E. Hoch and S. W. J. Kozlowski, "Leading Virtual Teams: Hierarchical Leadership, Structural Supports, and Shared Team Leadership," *Journal of Applied Psychology* 99, no. 3 (2014): 390–403.

14. A. Malhotra, A. Majchrzak, and B. Rosen, "Leading Virtual Teams," *Academy of Management Perspectives* 21, no. 1 (2007): 60–70; and J. M. Wilson, S. S. Straus, and B. McEvily, "All in Due Time: The Development of Trust in Computer-Mediated and Face-to-Face Teams," *Organizational Behavior and Human Decision Processes* 19, no. 1 (2006): 16–33.

15. P. Balkundi and D. A. Harrison, "Ties, Leaders, and Time in Teams: Strong Inference about Network Structure's Effects on Team Viability and Performance," *Academy of Management Journal* 49, no. 1 (2006): 49–68; G. Chen, B. L. Kirkman, R. Kanfer, D. Allen, and B. Rosen, "A Multilevel Study of Leadership, Empowerment, and Performance in Teams," *Journal of Applied Psychology* 92, no. 2 (2007): 331–46; L. A. DeChurch and M. A. Marks, "Leadership in Multiteam Systems," *Journal of Applied Psychology* 91, no. 2 (2006): 311–29; A. Srivastava, K. M. Bartol, and E. A. Locke, "Empowering Leadership in Management Teams: Effects on Knowledge Sharing, Efficacy, and Performance," *Academy of Management Journal* 49, no. 6 (2006): 1239–51; and J. E. Mathieu, K. K. Gilson, and T. M. Ruddy, "Empowerment and Team Effectiveness: An Empirical Test of an Integrated Model," *Journal of Applied Psychology* 91, no. 1 (2006): 97–108.

16. R. B. Davison, J. R. Hollenbeck, C. M. Barnes, D. J. Sleesman, and D. R. Ilgen, "Coordinated Action in Multiteam Systems," *Journal of Applied Psychology* 97, no. 4 (2012): 808–24.

17. M. M. Luciano, J. E. Mathieu, and T. M. Ruddy, "Leading Multiple Teams: Average and Relative External Leadership Influences on Team Empowerment and Effectiveness," *Journal of Applied Psychology* 99, no. 2 (2014): 322–31.

18. R. Greenwald, "Freelancing Alone—But Together," *The Wall Street Journal,* February 3, 2014, R5.

19. V. Gonzalez-Roma and A. Hernandez, "Climate Uniformity: Its Influence on Team Communication Quality, Task Conflict, and Team Performance," *Journal of Applied Psychology* 99, no. 6 (2014): 1042–58; and C. F. Peralta, P. N. Lopes, L. L. Gilson, P. R. Lourenco, and L. Pais, "Innovation Processes and Team Effectiveness: The Role of Goal Clarity and Commitment, and Team Affective Tone," *Journal of Occupational and Organizational Psychology* 88, no. 1 (2015): 80–107.

20. P. Balkundi and D. A. Harrison, "Ties, Leaders, and Time in Teams: Strong Inference about Network Structure's Effects on Team Viability and Performance," *Academy of Management Journal* 49, no. 1 (2006): 49–68; G. Chen, B. L. Kirkman,

R. Kanfer, D. Allen, and B. Rosen, "A Multilevel Study of Leadership, Empowerment, and Performance in Teams," *Journal of Applied Psychology* 92, no. 2 (2007): 331–46; L. A. DeChurch and M. A. Marks, "Leadership in Multiteam Systems," *Journal of Applied Psychology* 91, no. 2 (2006): 311–29; A. Srivastava, K. M. Bartol, and E. A. Locke, "Empowering Leadership in Management Teams: Effects on Knowledge Sharing, Efficacy, and Performance," *Academy of Management Journal* 49, no. 6 (2006): 1239–51; and J. E. Mathieu, K. K. Gilson, and T. M. Ruddy, "Empowerment and Team Effectiveness: An Empirical Test of an Integrated Model," *Journal of Applied Psychology* 91, no. 1 (2006): 97–108.

21. J. Schaubroeck, S. S. K. Lam, and A. C. Peng, "Cognition-Based and Affect-Based Trust as Mediators of Leader Behavior Influences on Team Performance," *Journal of Applied Psychology* 96, no. 4, (2011).

22. B. A. De Jong and K. T. Dirks, "Beyond Shared Perceptions of Trust and Monitoring in Teams: Implications of Asymmetry and Dissensus," *Journal of Applied Psychology* 97, no. 2 (2012): 391–406.

23. G. Brown, C. Crossley, and S. L. Robinson, "Psychological Ownership, Territorial Behavior, and Being Perceived as a Team Contributor: The Critical Role of Trust in the Work Environment," *Personnel Psychology* 67, no. 2 (2014): 463–85.

24. See F. Aime, C. J. Meyer, and S. E. Humphrey, "Legitimacy of Team Rewards: Analyzing Legitimacy as a Condition for the Effectiveness of Team Incentive Designs," *Journal of Business Research* 63, no. 1 (2010): 60–66; P. A. Bamberger and R. Levi, "Team-Based Reward Allocation Structures and the Helping Behaviors of Outcome-Interdependent Team Members," *Journal of Managerial Psychology* 24, no. 4 (2009): 300–27; and M. J. Pearsall, M. S. Christian, and A. P. J. Ellis, "Motivating Interdependent Teams: Individual Rewards, Shared Rewards, or Something in Between?" *Journal of Applied Psychology* 95, no. 1 (2010): 183–91.

25. A. Bryant, "Taking Your Skills with You," *The New York Times,* May 31, 2015.

26. R. R. Hirschfeld, M. H. Jordan, H. S. Feild, W. F. Giles, and A. A. Armenakis, "Becoming Team Players: Team Members' Mastery of Teamwork Knowledge as a Predictor of Team Task Proficiency and Observed Teamwork Effectiveness," *Journal of Applied Psychology* 91, no. 2 (2006): 467–74; and K. R. Randall, C. J. Resick, and L. A. DeChurch, "Building Team Adaptive Capacity: The Roles of Sensegiving and Team Composition," *Journal of Applied Psychology* 96, no. 3 (2011): 525–40.

27. H. Moon, J. R. Hollenbeck, and S. E. Humphrey, "Asymmetric Adaptability: Dynamic Team Structures as One-Way Streets," *Academy of Management Journal* 47, no. 5 (2004): 681–95; A. P. J. Ellis, J. R. Hollenbeck, and D. R. Ilgen, "Team Learning: Collectively Connecting the Dots," *Journal of Applied Psychology* 88, no. 5 (2003): 821–35; C. L. Jackson and J. A. LePine, "Peer Responses to a Team's Weakest Link: A Test and Extension of LePine and Van Dyne's Model," *Journal of Applied Psychology* 88, no. 3 (2003): 459–75; and J. A. LePine, "Team Adaptation and Postchange Performance: Effects of Team Composition in Terms of Members' Cognitive Ability and Personality," *Journal of Applied Psychology* 88, no. 1 (2003): 27–39.

28. C. C. Cogliser, W. L. Gardner, M. B. Gavin, and J. C. Broberg, "Big Five Personality Factors and Leader Emergence in Virtual Teams: Relationships with Team Trustworthiness,

Member Performance Contributions, and Team Performance," *Group & Organization Management* 37, no. 6 (2012): 752–84; and "Deep-Level Composition Variables as Predictors of Team Performance: A Meta-Analysis," *Journal of Applied Psychology* 92, no. 3 (2007): 595–615.

29. T. A. O'Neill and N. J. Allen, "Personality and the Prediction of Team Performance," *European Journal of Personality* 25, no. 1 (2011): 31–42.

30. S. E. Humphrey, J. R. Hollenbeck, C. J. Meyer, and D. R. Ilgen, "Personality Configurations in Self-Managed Teams: A Natural Experiment on the Effects of Maximizing and Minimizing Variance in Traits," *Journal of Applied Psychology* 41, no. 7 (2011): 1701–32.

31. A. P. J. Ellis, J. R. Hollenbeck, and D. R. Ilgen, "Team Learning: Collectively Connecting the Dots." C. O. L. H. Porter, J. R. Hollenbeck, and D. R. Ilgen, "Backing up Behaviors in Teams: The Role of Personality and Legitimacy of Need," *Journal of Applied Psychology* 88, no. 3 (2003): 391–403; and M. C. Schilpzand, D. M. Herold, and C. E. Shalley, "Members' Openness to Experience and Teams' Creative Performance," *Small Group Research* 42, no. 1 (2011): 55–76.

32. B. H. Bradley, B. E. Postlewaite, and K. G. Brown, "Ready to Rumble: How Team Personality Composition and Task Conflict Interact to Improve Performance," *Journal of Applied Psychology* 98, no. 2 (2013): 385–92.

33. E. Gonzalez-Mule, D. S. DeGeest, B. W. McCormick, J. Y. Seong, and K. G. Brown, "Can We Get Some Cooperation around Here? The Mediating Role of Group Norms on the Relationship between Team Personality and Individual Helping Behaviors," *Journal of Applied Psychology* 99, no. 5 (2014): 988–99.

34. S. E. Humphrey, F. P. Morgeson, and M. J. Mannor, "Developing a Theory of the Strategic Core of Teams: A Role Composition Model of Team Performance," *Journal of Applied Psychology* 94, no. 1 (2009): 48–61.

35. Ibid.

36. A. Joshi, "The Influence of Organizational Demography on the External Networking Behavior of Teams," *Academy of Management Review* 31, no. 3 (2006): 583–95.

37. A. Joshi and H. Roh, "The Role of Context in Work Team Diversity Research: A Meta-Analytic Review," *Academy of Management Journal* 52, no. 3 (2009): 599–627; S. K. Horwitz and I. B. Horwitz, "The Effects of Team Diversity on Team Outcomes: A Meta-Analytic Review of Team Demography," *Journal of Management* 33, no. 6 (2007): 987–1015; and S. T. Bell, A. J. Villado, M. A. Lukasik, L. Belau, and A. L. Briggs, "Getting Specific about Demographic Diversity Variable and Team Performance Relationships: A Meta-Analysis," *Journal of Management* 37, no. 3 (2011): 709–43.

38. S. Mohammed and L. C. Angell, "Surface- and Deep-Level Diversity in Workgroups: Examining the Moderating Effects of Team Orientation and Team Process on Relationship Conflict," *Journal of Organizational Behavior* 25, no. 8 (2004): 1015–39.

39. Y. F. Guillaume, D. van Knippenberg, and F. C. Brodebeck, "Nothing Succeeds Like Moderation: A Social Self-Regulation Perspective on Cultural Dissimilarity and Performance," *Academy of Management Journal* 57, no. 5 (2014): 1284–308.

40. D. Coutu, "Why Teams Don't Work," *Harvard Business Review*, May 2009, 99–105. The evidence in this section is described in L. L. Thompson, *Making the Team*, 5th ed. (New York, NY: Pearson, 2013), 65–67. See also R. C. Liden, S. J. Wayne, and R. A. Jaworski, "Social Loafing: A Field Investigation," *Journal of Management* 30, no. 2 (2004): 285–304.

41. R. Karlgaard, "Think (Really!) Small," Forbes, April 13, 2015, 32.

42. Ibid.

43. Ibid.

44. "Is Your Team Too Big? Too Small? What's the Right Number?" *Knowledge@Wharton*, June 14, 2006, http://knowledge .wharton.upenn.edu/article/is-your-team-too-big-too-small-whats-the-right-number-2/; see also A. M. Carton and J. N. Cummings, "A Theory of Subgroups in Work Teams," *Academy of Management Review* 37, no. 3 (2012): 441–70.

45. S. A. Kiffin-Peterson and J. L. Cordery, "Trust, Individualism, and Job Characteristics of Employee Preference for Teamwork," *International Journal of Human Resource Management* 14, no. 1 (2003): 93–116.

46. J. A. LePine, R. F. Piccolo, C. L. Jackson, J. E. Mathieu, and J. R. Saul, "A Meta-Analysis of Teamwork Processes: Tests of a Multidimensional Model and Relationships with Team Effectiveness Criteria," *Personnel Psychology* 61, no. 2 (2008): 273–307.

47. J. F. Dovidio, "Bridging Intragroup Processes and Intergroup Relations: Needing the Twain to Meet," *British Journal of Social Psychology* 52, no. 1 (2013): 1–24; and J. Zhou, J. Dovidio, and E. Wang, "How Affectively-Based and Cognitively-Based Attitudes Drive Intergroup Behaviours: The Moderating Role of Affective-Cognitive Consistency," *Plos One* 8, no. 11 (2013): article e82150.

48. J. A. LePine, R. F. Piccolo, C. L. Jackson, J. E. Mathieu, and J. R. Saul, "A Meta-Analysis of Teamwork Processes: Tests of a Multidimensional Model and Relationships with Team Effectiveness Criteria;" and J. E. Mathieu and T. L. Rapp, "Laying the Foundation for Successful Team Performance Trajectories: The Roles of Team Charters and Performance Strategies," *Journal of Applied Psychology* 94, no. 1 (2009): 90–103.

49. A. Gurtner, F. Tschan, N. K. Semmer, and C. Nagele, "Getting Groups to Develop Good Strategies: Effects of Reflexivity Interventions on Team Process, Team Performance, and Shared Mental Models," *Organizational Behavior and Human Decision Processes* 102, no. 2 (2007): 127–42; M. C. Schippers, D. N. Den Hartog, and P. L. Koopman, "Reflexivity in Teams: A Measure and Correlates," *Applied Psychology: An International Review* 56, no. 2 (2007): 189–211; and C. S. Burke, K. C. Stagl, E. Salas, L. Pierce, and D. Kendall, "Understanding Team Adaptation: A Conceptual Analysis and Model," *Journal of Applied Psychology* 91, no. 6 (2006): 1189–207.

50. A. N. Pieterse, D. van Knippenberg, and W. P. van Ginkel, "Diversity in Goal Orientation, Team Reflexivity, and Team Performance," *Organizational Behavior and Human Decision Processes* 114, no. 2 (2011): 153–64.

51. See R. P. DeShon, S. W. J. Kozlowski, A. M. Schmidt, K. R. Milner, and D. Wiechmann, "A Multiple-Goal, Multilevel Model of Feedback Effects on the Regulation of Individual and Team Performance," *Journal of Applied Psychology* 89, no. 6 (2004): 1035–56.

52. K. Tasa, S. Taggar, and G. H. Seijts, "The Development of Collective Efficacy in Teams: A Multilevel and Longitudinal Perspective," *Journal of Applied Psychology* 92, no. 1 (2007): 17–27; D. I. Jung and J. J. Sosik, "Group Potency and Collective Efficacy: Examining Their Predictive Validity, Level

of Analysis, and Effects of Performance Feedback on Future Group Performance," *Group & Organization Management* 28, no. 3 (2003): 366–91; and R. R. Hirschfeld and J. B. Bernerth, "Mental Efficacy and Physical Efficacy at the Team Level: Inputs and Outcomes among Newly Formed Action Teams," *Journal of Applied Psychology* 93, no. 6 (2008): 1429–37.

53. A. W. Richter, G. Hirst, D. van Knippenberg, and M. Baer, "Creative Self-Efficacy and Individual Creativity in Team Contexts: Cross-Level Interactions with Team Informational Resources," *Journal of Applied Psychology* 97, no. 6 (2012): 1282–90.

54. N. Ellemers, E. Sleebos, D. Stam, and D. de Gilder, "Feeling Included and Valued: How Perceived Respect Affects Positive Team Identity and Willingness to Invest in the Team," *British Journal of Management* 24, no. 1 (2013): 21–37.

55. T. A. De Vries, F. Walter, G. S. Van derr Vegt, and P. J. M. D. Essens, "Antecedents of Individuals' Interteam Coordination: Broad Functional Experiences as a Mixed Blessing," *Academy of Management Journal* 57, no. 5 (2014): 1334–59.

56. S. Chang, L. Jia, R. Takeuchi, and Y. Cai, "Do High-Commitment Work Systems Affect Creativity? A Multilevel Combinational Approach to Employee Creativity," *Journal of Applied Psychology* 99, no. 4 (2014): 665–80.

57. S. Mohammed, L. Ferzandi, and K. Hamilton, "Metaphor No More: A 15-Year Review of the Team Mental Model Construct," *Journal of Management* 36, no. 4 (2010): 876–910.

58. A. P. J. Ellis, "System Breakdown: The Role of Mental Models and Transactive Memory on the Relationships between Acute Stress and Team Performance," *Academy of Management Journal* 49, no. 3 (2006): 576–89.

59. L. A. DeChurch and J. R. Mesmer-Magnus, "The Cognitive Underpinnings of Effective Teamwork: A Meta-Analysis," *Journal of Applied Psychology* 95, no. 1 (2010): 32–53.

60. S. W. J. Kozlowski and D. R. Ilgen, "Enhancing the Effectiveness of Work Groups and Teams," *Psychological Science in the Public Interest* 7, no. 3 (2006): 77–124; and B. D. Edwards, E. A. Day, W. Arthur Jr., and S. T. Bell, "Relationships among Team Ability Composition, Team Mental Models, and Team Performance," *Journal of Applied Psychology* 91, no. 3 (2006): 727–36.

61. M. Kolbe, G. Grote, M. J. Waller, J. Wacker, B. Grande, and D. R. Spahn, "Monitoring and Talking to the Room: Autochthonous Coordination Patterns in Team Interaction and Performance," *Journal of Applied Psychology* 99, no. 6 (2014): 1254–67.

62. J. Farh, C. Lee, and C. I. C. Farh, "Task Conflict and Team Creativity: A Question of How Much and When," *Journal of Applied Psychology* 95, no. 6 (2010): 1173–80.

63. K. H. Price, D. A. Harrison, and J. H. Gavin, "Withholding Inputs in Team Contexts: Member Composition, Interaction Processes, Evaluation Structure, and Social Loafing," *Journal of Applied Psychology* 91, no. 6 (2006): 1375–84.

64. G. Hertel, U. Konradt, and K. Voss, "Competencies for Virtual Teamwork: Development and Validation of a Web-Based Selection Tool for Members of Distributed Teams," *European Journal of Work and Organizational Psychology* 15, no. 4 (2006): 477–504.

65. T. V. Riper, "The NBA's Most Overpaid Players," *Forbes,* April 5, 2013, http://www.forbes.com/sites/tomvanriper/2013/04/05/the-nbas-most-overpaid-players/.

66. E. Kearney, D. Gebert, and S. C. Voelpel, "When and How Diversity Benefits Teams: The Importance of Team Members'

Need for Cognition," *Academy of Management Journal* 52, no. 3 (2009): 581–98.

67. H. M. Guttman, "The New High-Performance Player," *The Hollywood Reporter,* October 27, 2008, www.hollywoodreporter.com.

68. C.-H. Chuang, S. Chen, and C.-W. Chuang, "Human Resource Management Practices and Organizational Social Capital: The Role of Industrial Characteristics," *Journal of Business Research* 66, no. 5 (2013): 678–87.

69. T. Erickson and L. Gratton, "What It Means to Work Here," *BusinessWeek,* January 10, 2008, www.businessweek.com.

70. M. D. Johnson, J. R. Hollenbeck, S. E. Humphrey, D. R. Ilgen, D. Jundt, and C. J. Meyer, "Cutthroat Cooperation: Asymmetrical Adaptation to Changes in Team Reward Structures," *Academy of Management Journal* 49, no. 1 (2006): 103–19.

71. C. E. Naquin and R. O. Tynan, "The Team Halo Effect: Why Teams Are Not Blamed for Their Failures," *Journal of Applied Psychology* 88, no. 2 (2003): 332–40.

72. E. R. Crawford and J. A. Lepine, "A Configural Theory of Team Processes: Accounting for the Structure of Taskwork and Teamwork," *Academy of Management Review* 38, no. 1 (2013): 32–48.

CHAPTER 11

1. R. Wijn and K. Van den Bos, "On the Social-Communicative Function of Justice: The Influence of Communication Goals and Personal Involvement on the Use of Justice Assertions," *Personality and Social Psychology Bulletin* 36, no. 2 (2010): 161–72.

2. R. Swarns, "After Uneasy First Tries, Coworkers Find a Way to Talk about Race," *The New York Times,* March 23, 2015, A15.

3. D. C. Barnlund, "A Transactional Model of Communication," in *Communication Theory,* ed. C. D. Mortenson (New Brunswick, NJ: Transaction, 2008), 47–57; and see K. Byron, "Carrying Too Heavy a Load? The Communication and Miscommunication of Emotion by E-mail," *Academy of Management Review* 33, no. 2 (2008): 309–27.

4. A. Tenhiaelae and F. Salvador, "Looking inside Glitch Mitigation Capability: The Effect of Intraorganizational Communication Channels," *Decision Sciences* 45, no. 3 (2014): 437–66.

5. S. Jhun, Z.-T. Bae, and S.-Y. Rhee, "Performance Change of Managers in Two Different Uses of Upward Feedback: A Longitudinal Study in Korea," *International Journal of Human Resource Management* 23, no. 20 (2012): 4246–64; B. Oc, M. R. Bashshur, and C. Moore, "Speaking Truth to Power: The Effect of Candid Feedback on How Individuals with Power Allocate Resources," *Journal of Applied Psychology* 100, no. 2 (2015): 450–63; and J. W. Smither and A. G. Walker, "Are the Characteristics of Narrative Comments Related to Improvement in Multirater Feedback Ratings over Time?" *Journal of Applied Psychology* 89, no. 3 (2004): 575–81.

6. J. S. Lublin, "Managers Need to Make Time for Face Time," *The Wall Street Journal,* March 18, 2015, B6.

7. E. Nichols, "Hyper-Speed Managers," *HR Magazine,* April 2007, 107–10.

8. R. Walker, "Declining an Assignment, with Finesse," *The New York Times,* August 24, 2014, 8.

9. See, for example, G. Michelson, A. van Iterson, and K. Waddington, "Gossip in Organizations: Contexts, Consequences,

and Controversies," *Group & Organization Management* 35, no. 4 (2010): 371–90.

10. G. Van Hoye and F. Lievens, "Tapping the Grapevine: A Closer Look at Word-of-Mouth as a Recruitment Source," *Journal of Applied Psychology* 94, no. 2 (2009): 341–52.

11. J. K. Bosson, A. B. Johnson, K. Niederhoffer, and W. B. Swann Jr., "Interpersonal Chemistry through Negativity: Bonding by Sharing Negative Attitudes about Others," *Personal Relationships* 13, no. 2 (2006): 135–50.

12. T. J. Grosser, V. Lopez-Kidwell, and G. Labianca, "A Social Network Analysis of Positive and Negative Gossip in Organizational Life," *Group & Organization Management* 35, no. 2 (2010): 177–212.

13. R. Feintzeig, "The Boss's Next Demand: Make Lots of Friends," *The Wall Street Journal,* February 12, 2014, B1, B6.

14. R. E. Silverman, "A Victory for Small Office Talkers," *The Wall Street Journal,* October 28, 2014, D2.

15. L. Dulye, "Get Out of Your Office," *HR Magazine,* July 2006, 99–101.

16. E. Bernstein, "How Well Are You Listening?" *The Wall Street Journal,* January 13, 2015, D1.

17. E. Bernstein, "How 'Active Listening' Makes Both Participants in a Conversation Feel Better," *The Wall Street Journal,* January 12, 2015, http://www.wsj.com/articles/how-active-listening-makes-both-sides-of-a-conversation-feel-better-1421082684.

18. S. Shellenbarger, "Work & Family Mailbox," *The Wall Street Journal,* July 30, 2014, D2.

19. E. C. Ravlin, A.-K. Ward, and D. C. Thomas, "Exchanging Social Information across Cultural Boundaries," *Journal of Management* 40, no. 5 (2014): 1437–65.

20. V. N. Giri, "Nonverbal Communication Theories," in *Encyclopedia of Communication Theory,* eds. S. W. Littlejohn and K. A. Foss (Washington, DC: Sage, 2009).

21. C. K. Goman, "5 Body Language Tips to Increase Your Curb Appeal," *Forbes,* March 4, 2013, www.forbes.com/sites/carolkinseygoman/2013/03/14/5-body-language-tips-to-increase-your-curb-appeal/.

22. See N. Kock, "The Psychobiological Model: Towards a New Theory of Computer-Mediated Communication Based on Darwinian Evolution," *Organization Science* 15, no. 3 (2004): 327–48; and C. E. Timmerman and S. N. Madhavapeddi, "Perceptions of Organizational Media Richness: Channel Expansion Effects for Electronic and Traditional Media across Richness Dimensions," *IEEE Transactions on Professional Communication* 51, no. 1 (2008): 18–32.

23. R. L. Daft and R. A. Noe, *Organizational Behavior* (Fort Worth, TX: Harcourt, 2001), 311.

24. S. Shellenbarger, "Is This How You Really Talk?" *The Wall Street Journal,* April 24, 2013, D1, D3.

25. B. Giamanco and K. Gregoire, "Tweet Me, Friend Me, Make Me Buy," *Harvard Business Review,* July–August 2012, 88–93.

26. "At Many Companies, Hunt for Leakers Expands Arsenal of Monitoring Tactics," *The Wall Street Journal,* September 11, 2006, B1, B3; and B. J. Alge, G. A. Ballinger, S. Tangirala, and J. L. Oakley, "Information Privacy in Organizations: Empowering Creative and Extrarole Performance," *Journal of Applied Psychology* 91, no. 1 (2006): 221–32.

27. R. E. Petty and P. Briñol, "Persuasion: From Single to Multiple to Metacognitive Processes," *Perspectives on Psychological Science* 3, no. 2 (2008): 137–47; F. A. White, M. A. Charles, and J. K. Nelson, "The Role of Persuasive Arguments in Changing Affirmative Action Attitudes and Expressed

28. K. L. Blankenship and D. T. Wegener, "Opening the Mind to Close It: Considering a Message in Light of Important Values Increases Message Processing and Later Resistance to Change," *Journal of Personality and Social Psychology* 94, no. 2 (2008): 196–213.

29. See, for example, Y. H. M. See, R. E. Petty, and L. R. Fabrigar, "Affective and Cognitive Meta-Bases of Attitudes: Unique Effects of Information Interest and Persuasion," *Journal of Personality and Social Psychology* 94, no. 6 (2008): 938–55; M. S. Key, J. E. Edlund, B. J. Sagarin, and G. Y. Bizer, "Individual Differences in Susceptibility to Mindlessness," *Personality and Individual Differences* 46, no. 3 (2009): 261–64; and M. Reinhard and M. Messner, "The Effects of Source Likeability and Need for Cognition on Advertising Effectiveness under Explicit Persuasion," *Journal of Consumer Behavior* 8, no. 4 (2009): 179–91.

30. M. Richtel, "Lost in E-Mail, Tech Firms Face Self-Made Beast," *The New York Times,* June 14, 2008, http://www.nytimes.com/2008/06/14/technology/14email.html.

31. S. Norton, "A Post-PC CEO: No Desk, No Desktop," *The Wall Street Journal,* November 20, 2014, B5.

32. P. Briñol, R. E. Petty, and J. Barden, "Happiness versus Sadness as a Determinant of Thought Confidence in Persuasion: A Self-Validation Analysis," *Journal of Personality and Social Psychology* 93, no. 5 (2007): 711–27.

33. R. C. Sinclair, S. E. Moore, M. M. Mark, A. S. Soldat, and C. A. Lavis, "Incidental Moods, Source Likeability, and Persuasion: Liking Motivates Message Elaboration in Happy People," *Cognition and Emotion* 24, no. 6 (2010): 940–61; and V. Griskevicius, M. N. Shiota, and S. L. Neufeld, "Influence of Different Positive Emotions on Persuasion Processing: A Functional Evolutionary Approach," *Emotion* 10, no. 2 (2010): 190–206.

34. J. Sandberg, "The Jargon Jumble: Kids Have 'Skeds,' Colleagues, 'Needs,'" *The Wall Street Journal,* October 24, 2006, http://online.wsj.com/article/SB116165746415401680.html.

35. Ibid.

36. B. E. Ashforth and V. Anand, "The Normalization of Corruption in Organizations," *Research in Organizational Behavior* 25 (2003): 1–52; and E. Liu and M. E. Roloff, "Exhausting Silence: Emotional Costs of Withholding Complaints," *Negotiation and Conflict Management Research* 8, no. 1 (2015): 25–40.

37. F. J. Milliken, E. W. Morrison, and P. F. Hewlin, "An Exploratory Study of Employee Silence: Issues That Employees Don't Communicate Upward and Why," *Journal of Management Studies* 40, no. 6 (2003): 1453–76.

38. L. A. Withers and L. L. Vernon, "To Err Is Human: Embarrassment, Attachment, and Communication Apprehension," *Personality and Individual Differences* 40, no. 1 (2006): 99–110.

39. See, for instance, B. D. Blume, T. T. Baldwin, and K. C. Ryan, "Communication Apprehension: A Barrier to Students' Leadership, Adaptability, and Multicultural Appreciation," *Academy of Management Learning & Education* 12, no. 2 (2013): 158–72; B. D. Blume, G. F. Dreher, and T. T. Baldwin, "Examining the Effects of Communication Apprehension within Assessment Centres," *Journal of Occupational and Organizational Psychology* 83, no. 3 (2010): 663–71; and X. Shi, T. M. Brinthaupt, and M. McCree, "The Relationship of Self-Talk Frequency to Communication Apprehension and Public

Behavior in Higher Education," *Journal of Applied Psychology* 93, no. 6 (2008): 1271–86.

Speaking Anxiety," *Personality and Individual Differences* 75 (2015): 125–9.

40. See, for example, T. L. Rodebaugh, "I Might Look OK, But I'm Still Doubtful, Anxious, and Avoidant: The Mixed Effects of Enhanced Video Feedback on Social Anxiety Symptoms," *Behaviour Research and Therapy* 42, no. 12 (2004): 1435–51.

41. K. B. Serota, T. R. Levine, and F. J. Boster, "The Prevalence of Lying in America: Three Studies of Self-Reported Lies," *Human Communication Research* 36, no. 1 (2010): 2–25.

42. C. E. Naguin, T. R. Kurtzberg, and L. Y. Belkin, "The Finer Points of Lying Online: E-Mail versus Pen and Paper," *Journal of Applied Psychology* 95, no. 2 (2010): 387–94.

43. See W. L. Adair, "Integrative Sequences and Negotiation Outcome in Same- and Mixed-Culture Negotiations," *International Journal of Conflict Management* 14, nos. 3–4 (2003): 1359–92; W. L. Adair and J. M. Brett, "The Negotiation Dance: Time, Culture, and Behavioral Sequences in Negotiation," *Organization Science* 16, no. 1 (2005): 33–51; E. Giebels and P. J. Taylor, "Interaction Patterns in Crisis Negotiations: Persuasive Arguments and Cultural Differences," *Journal of Applied Psychology* 94, no. 1 (2009): 5–19; and M. G. Kittler, D. Rygl, and A. Mackinnon, "Beyond Culture or Beyond Control? Reviewing the Use of Hall's High-/Low-Context Concept," *International Journal of Cross-Cultural Management* 11, no. 1 (2011): 63–82.

44. M. C. Hopson, T. Hart, and G. C. Bell, "Meeting in the Middle: Fred L. Casmir's Contributions to the Field of Intercultural Communication," *International Journal of Intercultural Relations* 36, no. 6 (2012): 789–97.

CHAPTER 12

1. N. Ensari, R. E. Riggio, J. Christian, and G. Carslaw, "Who Emerges as a Leader? Meta-Analyses of Individual Differences as Predictors of Leadership Emergence," *Personality and Individual Differences* 51, no. 4 (2011): 532–36.

2. See M. H. Do and A. Minbashian, "A Meta-Analytic Examination of the Agentic and Affiliative Aspects of Extraversion on Leadership Outcomes," *Leadership Quarterly* 25, no. 5 (2014): 1040–53.

3. D. R. Ames and F. J. Flynn, "What Breaks a Leader: The Curvilinear Relation between Assertiveness and Leadership," *Journal of Personality and Social Psychology* 92, no. 2 (2007): 307–24.

4. A. E. Colbert, M. R. Barrick, and B. H. Bradley, "Personality and Leadership Composition in Top Management Teams: Implications for Organizational Effectiveness," *Personnel Psychology* 67, no. 2 (2014): 351–87.

5. K.-Y. Ng, S. Ang, and K. Chan, "Personality and Leader Effectiveness: A Moderated Mediation Model of Leadership Self-Efficacy, Job Demands, and Job Autonomy," *Journal of Applied Psychology* 93, no. 4 (2008): 733–43.

6. R. B. Kaiser, J. M. LeBreton, and J. Hogan, "The Dark Side of Personality and Extreme Leader Behavior," *Applied Psychology: An International Review* 64, no. 1 (2015): 55–92.

7. B. H. Gaddis and J. L. Foster, "Meta-Analysis of Dark Side Personality Characteristics and Critical Work Behaviors among Leaders across the Globe: Findings and Implications for Leadership Development and Executive Coaching," *Applied Psychology: An International Review* 64, no. 1 (2015): 25–54.

8. R. H. Humphrey, J. M. Pollack, and T. H. Hawver, "Leading with Emotional Labor," *Journal of Managerial Psychology* 23, no. 2 (2008): 151–68.

9. F. Walter, M. S. Cole, and R. H. Humphrey, "Emotional Intelligence: Sine Qua Non of Leadership or Folderol?" *Academy of Management Perspectives* 25, no. 1 (2011): 45–59.

10. S. Côté, P. N. Lopes, P. Salovey, and C. T. H. Miners, "Emotional Intelligence and Leadership Emergence in Small Groups," *Leadership Quarterly* 21, no. 3 (2010): 496–508.

11. This research is updated in T. A. Judge, R. F. Piccolo, and R. Ilies, "The Forgotten Ones? The Validity of Consideration and Initiating Structure in Leadership Research," *Journal of Applied Psychology,* 89 no. 1 (2004): 36–51.

12. D. Akst, "The Rewards of Recognizing a Job Well Done," *The Wall Street Journal,* January 31, 2007, D9.

13. M. Javidan, P. W. Dorfman, M. S. de Luque, and R. J. House, "In the Eye of the Beholder: Cross Cultural Lessons in Leadership from Project GLOBE," *Academy of Management Perspectives* 20, no. 1 (2006): 67–90.

14. For a more current discussion on the model, see S. Altmaee, K. Tuerk, and O.-S. Toomet, "Thomas-Kilmann's Conflict Management Modes and Their Relationship to Fiedler's Leadership Styles (Basing on Estonian Organizations)," *Baltic Journal of Management* 8, no. 1 (2013): 45–65.

15. See, for instance, G. Thompson and R. P. Vecchio, "Situational Leadership Theory: A Test of Three Versions," *Leadership Quarterly* 20, no. 5 (2009): 837–48; and R. P. Vecchio, C. R. Bullis, and D. M. Brazil, "The Utility of Situational Leadership Theory—A Replication in a Military Setting," *Small Group Research* 37, no. 5 (2006): 407–24.

16. R. Fehr, K. C. Yam, and C. Dang, "Moralized Leadership: The Construction and Consequences of Ethical Leader Perceptions," *Academy of Management Review* 40, no. 2 (2015): 182–209; and M. Hernandez, C. P. Long, and S. B. Sitkin, "Cultivating Follower Trust: Are All Leader Behaviors Equally Influential?" *Organization Studies* 35, no. 12 (2014): 1867–92.

17. S. J. Perry, L. A. Witt, L. M. Penney, and L. Atwater, "The Downside of Goal-Focused Leadership: The Role of Personality in Subordinate Exhaustion," *Journal of Applied Psychology* 95, no. 6 (2010): 1145–53.

18. R. R. Vecchio, J. E. Justin, and C. L. Pearce, "The Utility of Transactional and Transformational Leadership for Predicting Performance and Satisfaction within a Path-Goal Theory Framework," *Journal of Occupational and Organizational Psychology* 81 (2008): 71–82.

19. V. H. Vroom and A. G. Jago, "The Role of the Situation in Leadership," *American Psychologist* 62, no. 1 (2007): 17–24.

20. W. Bennis, "The Challenges of Leadership in the Modern World," *American Psychologist* 62, no. 1 (2007): 2–5.

21. X. Zhou and C. A. Schriesheim, "Supervisor–Subordinate Convergence in Descriptions of Leader–Member Exchange (LMX) Quality: Review and Testable Propositions," *Leadership Quarterly* 20, no. 6 (2009): 920–32.

22. B. Erdogan and T. N. Bauer, "Differentiated Leader–Member Exchanges: The Buffering Role of Justice Climate," *Journal of Applied Psychology* 95, no. 6 (2010): 1104–20; and X. Zhou and C. A. Schrisheim, "Quantitative and Qualitative Examination of Propositions Concerning Supervisor–Subordinate Convergence in Descriptions of Leader–Member Exchange (LMX) Quality," *Leadership Quarterly* 21, no. 5 (2010): 826–43.

23. M. Uhl-Bien, "Relationship Development as a Key Ingredient for Leadership Development," in *Future of Leadership*

Development, eds. S. E. Murphy and R. E. Riggio (Mahwah, NJ: Lawrence Erlbaum, 2003), 129–47.

24. R. Vecchio and D. M. Brazil, "Leadership and Sex-Similarity: A Comparison in a Military Setting," *Personnel Psychology* 60, no. 2 (2007): 303–35.

25. See, for instance, R. Ilies, J. D. Nahrgang, and F. P. Morgeson, "Leader–Member Exchange and Citizenship Behaviors: A Meta-Analysis," *Journal of Applied Psychology* 92, no. 1 (2007): 269–77; and Z. Chen, W. Lam, and J. A. Zhong, "Leader–Member Exchange and Member Performance: A New Look at Individual-Level Negative Feedback-Seeking Behavior and Team-Level Empowerment Culture," *Journal of Applied Psychology* 92, no. 1 (2007): 202–12.

26. R. Eisenberger et al. "Leader-Member Exchange and Affective Organizational Commitment: The Contribution of Supervisor's Organizational Embodiment," *Journal of Applied Psychology* 95, no. 6 (2010): 1085–103.

27. J. Bagger and A. Li, "How Does Supervisory Family Support Influence Employees' Attitudes and Behaviors? A Social Exchange Perspective," *Journal of Management* 40, no. 4 (2014): 1123–50.

28. B. Erdogan and T. N. Bauer, "Differentiated Leader–Member Exchanges: The Buffering Role of Justice Climate," *Journal of Applied Psychology* 95, no. 6 (2010): 1104–20.

29. D. Liu, M. Hernandez, and L. Wang, "The Role of Leadership and Trust in Creating Structural Patterns of Team Procedural Justice: A Social Network Investigation," *Personnel Psychology* 67, no. 4 (2014): 801–45.

30. A. N. Li and H. Liao, "How Do Leader–Member Exchange Quality and Differentiation Affect Performance in Teams? An Integrated Multilevel Dual Process Model," *Journal of Applied Psychology* 99, no. 5 (2014): 847–66.

31. J. Hu and R. C. Liden, "Relative Leader-Member Exchange within Team Contexts: How and When Social Comparison Impacts Individual Effectiveness," *Personnel Psychology* 66, no. 1 (2013): 127–72.

32. M. Weber, *The Theory of Social and Economic Organization*, trans A. M. Henderson and T. Parsons (Eastford, CT: Martino Fine Books, 2012).

33. V. Seyranian and M. C. Bligh, "Presidential Charismatic Leadership: Exploring the Rhetoric of Social Change," *Leadership Quarterly* 19, no. 1 (2008): 54–76.

34. Ibid.

35. A. Xenikou, "The Cognitive and Affective Components of Organisational Identification: The Role of Perceived Support Values and Charismatic Leadership," *Applied Psychology: An International Review* 63, no. 4 (2014): 567–88.

36. P. A. Vlachos, N. G. Panagopoulos, and A. A. Rapp, "Feeling Good by Doing Good: Employee CSR-Induced Attributions, Job Satisfaction, and the Role of Charismatic Leadership," *Journal of Business Ethics* 118, no. 3 (2013): 577–88.

37. A. Deinert, A. C. Homan, D. Boer, S. C. Voelpel, and D. Gutermann, "Transformational Leadership Sub-Dimensions and Their Link to Leaders' Personality and Performance," *Leadership Quarterly* 26, no. 6 (2015): 1095–1120; and R. E. de Vries, "Personality Predictors of Leadership Styles and the Self-Other Agreement Problem," *Leadership Quarterly* 23, no. 5 (2012): 809–21.

38. P. Balkundi, M. Kilduff, and D. A. Harrison, "Centrality and Charisma: Comparing How Leader Networks and Attributions Affect Team Performance," *Journal of Applied Psychology* 96, no. 6 (2012): 1209–22.

39. A. Erez, V. F. Misangyi, D. E. Johnson, M. A. LePine, and K. C. Halverson, "Stirring the Hearts of Followers: Charismatic Leadership as the Transferal of Affect," *Journal of Applied Psychology* 93, no. 3 (2008): 602–15. On the role of vision in leadership, see M. Hauser and R. J. House, "Lead through Vision and Values," in *Handbook of Principles of Organizational Behavior*, ed. E. A. Locke (Malden, MA: Blackwell, 2004), 257–73.

40. D. N. Den Hartog, A. H. B. De Hoogh, and A. E. Keegan, "The Interactive Effects of Belongingness and Charisma on Helping and Compliance," *Journal of Applied Psychology* 92, no. 4 (2007): 1131–39.

41. J. C. Pastor, M. Mayo, and B. Shamir, "Adding Fuel to Fire: The Impact of Followers' Arousal on Ratings of Charisma," *Journal of Applied Psychology* 92, no. 6 (2007): 1584–96.

42. F. Cohen, S. Solomon, M. Maxfield, T. Pyszczynski, and J. Greenberg, "Fatal Attraction: The Effects of Mortality Salience on Evaluations of Charismatic, Task-Oriented, and Relationship-Oriented Leaders," *Psychological Science* 15, no. 12 (2004), 846–51; and J. Griffith, S. Connelly, C. Thiel, and G. Johnson, "How Outstanding Leaders Lead with Affect: An Examination of Charismatic, Ideological, and Pragmatic Leaders," *Leadership Quarterly* 26, no. 4 (2015): 502–17.

43. See, for instance, J. A. Raelin, "The Myth of Charismatic Leaders," *Training and Development Journal,* March 2003, 47–54; and P. A. Vlachos, N. G. Panagopoulos, and A. A. Rapp, "Feeling Good by Doing Good: Employee CSR-Induced Attributions, Job Satisfaction, and the Role of Charismatic Leadership," *Journal of Business Ethics* 118, no. 3 (2013): 577–88.

44. B. M. Galvin, D. A. Waldman, and P. Balthazard, "Visionary Communication Qualities as Mediators of the Relationship between Narcissism and Attributions of Leader Charisma," *Personnel Psychology* 63, no. 3 (2010): 509–37.

45. See, for instance, D. Deichmann and D. Stam, "Leveraging Transformational and Transactional Leadership to Cultivate the Generation of Organization-Focused Ideas," *Leadership Quarterly* 26, no. 2 (2015): 204–19; H.-J. Wolfram and L. Gratton, "Gender Role Self-Concept, Categorical Gender, and Transactional-Transformational Leadership: Implications for Perceived Workgroup Performance," *Journal of Leadership & Organizational Studies* 21, no. 4 (2014): 338–53; and T. A. Judge and R. F. Piccolo, "Transformational and Transactional Leadership: A Meta-Analytic Test of Their Relative Validity," *Journal of Applied Psychology* 89, no. 5 (2004): 755–68.

46. A. E. Colbert, M. R. Barrick, and B. H. Bradley, "Personality and Leadership Composition in Top Management Teams: Implications for Organizational Effectiveness," *Personnel Psychology* 67, no. 2 (2014): 351–87.

47. A. M. Grant, "Leading with Meaning: Beneficiary Contact, Prosocial Impact, and the Performance Effects of Transformational Leadership," *Academy of Management Journal* 55, no. 2 (2012): 458–76.

48. D. Deichmann and D. Stam, "Leveraging Transformational and Transactional Leadership to Cultivate the Generation of Organization-Focused Ideas;" and H.-J. Wolfram and L. Gratton, "Gender Role Self-Concept, Categorical Gender, and Transactional-Transformational Leadership: Implications for Perceived Workgroup Performance."

49. T. R. Hinkin and C. A. Schriesheim, "An Examination of 'Nonleadership': From Laissez-Faire Leadership to Leader Reward Omission and Punishment Omission," *Journal of Applied Psychology* 93, no. 6 (2008): 1234–48.

50. Y. Ling, Z. Simsek, M. H. Lubatkin, and J. F. Veiga, "Transformational Leadership's Role in Promoting Corporate Entrepreneurship: Examining the CEO-TMT Interface," *Academy of Management Journal* 51, no. 3 (2008): 557–76.

51. X. Zhang and K. M. Bartol, "Linking Empowering Leadership and Employee Creativity: The Influence of Psychological Empowerment, Intrinsic Motivation, and Creative Process Engagement," *Academy of Management Journal* 53, no. 1 (2010): 107–28.

52. S. A. Eisenbeib and S. Boerner, "A Double-Edged Sword: Transformational Leadership and Individual Creativity," *British Journal of Management* 24, no. 1 (2013): 54–68.

53. A. E. Colbert, A. E. Kristof-Brown, B. H. Bradley, and M. R. Barrick, "CEO Transformational Leadership: The Role of Goal Importance Congruence in Top Management Teams," *Academy of Management Journal* 51, no. 1 (2008): 81–96.

54. D. Zohar and O. Tenne-Gazit, "Transformational Leadership and Group Interaction as Climate Antecedents: A Social Network Analysis," *Journal of Applied Psychology* 93, no. 4 (2008): 744–57.

55. R. T. Keller, "Transformational Leadership, Initiating Structure, and Substitutes for Leadership: A Longitudinal Study of Research and Development Project Team Performance," *Journal of Applied Psychology* 91, no. 1 (2006): 202–10.

56. G. Wang, I. Oh, S. H. Courtright, and A. E. Colbert, "Transformational Leadership and Performance across Criteria and Levels: A Meta-Analytic Review of 25 Years of Research," *Group & Organization Management* 36, no. 2 (2011): 223–70.

57. Y. Ling, Z. Simsek, M. H. Lubatkin, and J. F. Veiga, "The Impact of Transformational CEOs on the Performance of Small- to Medium-Sized Firms: Does Organizational Context Matter?" *Journal of Applied Psychology* 93, no. 4 (2008): 923–34.

58. X. Wang and J. M. Howell, "Exploring the Dual-Level Effects of Transformational Leadership on Followers," *Journal of Applied Psychology* 95, no. 6 (2010): 1134–44.

59. N. Li, D. S. Chiaburu, B. L. Kirkman, and Z. Xie, "Spotlight on the Followers: An Examination of Moderators of Relationships between Transformational Leadership and Subordinates' Citizenship and Taking Charge," *Personnel Psychology* 66, no. 1 (2013): 225–60.

60. M. Birasnav, "Knowledge Management and Organizational Performance in the Service Industry: The Role of Transformational Leadership beyond the Effects of Transactional Leadership," *Journal of Business Research* 67, no. 8 (2014): 1622–29; H. Hetland, G. M. Sandal, and T. B. Johnsen, "Burnout in the Information Technology Sector: Does Leadership Matter?" *European Journal of Work and Organizational Psychology* 16, no. 1 (2007): 58–75; and A. K. Tyssen, A. Wald, and S. Heidenreich, "Leadership in the Context of Temporary Organizations: A Study on the Effects of Transactional and Transformational Leadership on Followers' Commitment in Projects," *Journal of Leadership & Organizational Studies* 21, no. 4 (2014): 376–93.

61. B. P. Owens and D. R. Hekman, "Modeling How to Grow: An Inductive Examination of Humble Leader Behaviors, Contingencies, and Outcomes," *Academy of Management Journal* 55, no. 4 (2012): 787–818.

62. K. M. Hmieleski, M. S. Cole, and R. A. Baron, "Shared Authentic Leadership and New Venture Performance," *Journal of Management* 38, no. 5 (2012), 1476–99.

63. R. Ilies, F. P. Morgeson, and J. D. Nahrgang, "Authentic Leadership and Eudaemonic Well-Being: Understanding Leader-Follower Outcomes," *Leadership Quarterly* 16, no. 3 (2005): 373–94; B. Levin, "Raj Rajaratnam Did Not Appreciate Rajat Gupta's Attempt to Leave the Goldman Board, Join 'The Billionaire Circle,'" *NetNet with John Carney,* March 14, 2011, accessed July 26, 2011, from www.cnbc.com/.

64. J. Stouten, M. van Dijke, and D. De Cremer, "Ethical Leadership: An Overview and Future Perspectives," *Journal of Personnel Psychology* 11, no. 1 (2012): 1–6.

65. J. M. Schaubroeck et al. "Embedding Ethical Leadership within and across Organization Levels," *Academy of Management Journal* 55, no. 5 (2012): 1053–78.

66. K. M. Kacmar, D. G. Bachrach, K. J. Harris, and S. Zivnuska, "Fostering Good Citizenship through Ethical Leadership: Exploring the Moderating Role of Gender and Organizational Politics," *Journal of Applied Psychology,* 96, no. 3 (2011): 633–42; and F. O. Walumbwa and J. Schaubroeck, "Leader Personality Traits and Employee Voice Behavior: Mediating Roles of Ethical Leadership and Work Group Psychological Safety," *Journal of Applied Psychology* 94, no. 5 (2009): 1275–86.

67. D. M. Mayer, K. Aquino, R. L. Greenbaum, and M. Kuenzi, "Who Displays Ethical Leadership, and Why Does It Matter? An Examination of Antecedents and Consequences of Ethical Leadership," *Academy of Management Journal* 55, no. 1 (2012): 151–71.

68. D. van Knippenberg, D. De Cremer, and B. van Knippenberg, "Leadership and Fairness: The State of the Art," *European Journal of Work and Organizational Psychology* 16, no. 2 (2007): 113–40.

69. M. E. Brown and L. K. Treviño, "Socialized Charismatic Leadership, Values Congruence, and Deviance in Work Groups," *Journal of Applied Psychology* 91, no. 4 (2006): 954–62.

70. M. E. Brown and L. K. Treviño, "Leader-Follower Values Congruence: Are Socialized Charismatic Leaders Better Able to Achieve It?" *Journal of Applied Psychology* 94, no. 2 (2009): 478–90.

71. S. A. Eisenbeiß and S. R. Giessner, "The Emergence and Maintenance of Ethical Leadership in Organizations," *Journal of Personnel Psychology* 11, no. 1 (2012): 7–19.

72. D. van Dierendonck, "Servant Leadership: A Review and Synthesis," *Journal of Management* 37, no. 4 (2011): 1228–61.

73. S. J. Peterson, F. M. Galvin, and D. Lange, "CEO Servant Leadership: Exploring Executive Characteristics and Firm Performance," *Personnel Psychology* 65, no. 3 (2012): 565–96.

74. F. Walumbwa, C. A. Hartnell, and A. Oke, "Servant Leadership, Procedural Justice Climate, Service Climate, Employee Attitudes, and Organizational Citizenship Behavior: A Cross-Level Investigation," *Journal of Applied Psychology* 95, no. 3 (2010): 517–29.

75. D. De Cremer, D. M. Mayer, M. van Dijke, B. C. Schouten, and M. Bardes, "When Does Self-Sacrificial Leadership Motivate Prosocial Behavior? It Depends on Followers' Prevention Focus," *Journal of Applied Psychology* 94, no. 4 (2009): 887–99.

76. J. Hu and R. C. Liden, "Antecedents of Team Potency and Team Effectiveness: An Examination of Goal and Process Clarity and Servant Leadership," *Journal of Applied Psychology,* 96, no. 4 (2011): 851–62.

77. M. J. Neubert, K. M. Kacmar, D. S. Carlson, L. B. Chonko, and J. A. Roberts, "Regulatory Focus as a Mediator of the Influence of Initiating Structure and Servant Leadership on Employee Behavior," *Journal of Applied Psychology* 93, no. 6 (2008): 1220–33.

78. R. C. Liden, S. J. Wayne, C. Liao, and J. D. Meuser, "Servant Leadership and Serving Culture: Influence on Individual and Unit Performance," *Academy of Management Journal* 57, no. 5 (2014): 1434–52.

79. T. Menon, J. Sim, J. Ho-Ying Fu, C. Chiu, and Y. Hong, "Blazing the Trail versus Trailing the Group: Culture and Perceptions of the Leader's Position," *Organizational Behavior and Human Decision Processes* 113, no. 1 (2010): 51–61.

80. J. A. Simpson, "Psychological Foundations of Trust," *Current Directions in Psychological Science* 16, no. 5 (2007): 264–68.

81. F. D. Schoorman, R. C. Mayer, and J. H. Davis, "An Integrative Model of Organizational Trust: Past, Present, and Future," *Academy of Management Review* 32, no. 2 (2007): 344–54.

82. J. Schaubroeck, S. S. K. Lam, and A. C. Peng, "Cognition-Based and Affect-Based Trust as Mediators of Leader Behavior Influences on Team Performance," *Journal of Applied Psychology,* 96, no. 4 (July 2011): 863–71.

83. See, for instance, K. Boies, J. Fiset, and H. Gill, "Communication and Trust Are Key: Unlocking the Relationship Between Leadership and Team Performance and Creativity," *Leadership Quarterly* 26, no. 6 (2015): 1080–94; D. I. Jung and B. J. Avolio, "Opening the Black Box: An Experimental Investigation of the Mediating Effects of Trust and Value Congruence on Transformational and Transactional Leadership," *Journal of Organizational Behavior* 21, no. 8 (2000), 949–64; and A. Zacharatos, J. Barling, and R. D. Iverson, "High-Performance Work Systems and Occupational Safety," *Journal of Applied Psychology* 90, no. 1 (2005), 77–93.

84. J. R. Detert and E. R. Burris, "Leadership Behavior and Employee Voice: Is the Door Really Open?" *Academy of Management Journal* 50, no. 4 (2007): 869–84.

85. J. A. Colquitt, B. A. Scott, and J. A. LePine, "Trust, Trustworthiness, and Trust Propensity: A Meta-Analytic Test of Their Unique Relationships with Risk Taking and Job Performance," *Journal of Applied Psychology* 92, no. 4 (2007): 909–27.

86. J. A. Colquitt, B. A. Scott, and J. A. LePine, "Trust, Trustworthiness, and Trust Propensity: A Meta-Analytic Test of Their Unique Relationships with Risk Taking and Job Performance;" and F. D. Schoorman, R. C. Mayer, and J. H. Davis, "An Integrative Model of Organizational Trust: Past, Present, and Future."

87. Cited in D. Jones, "Do You Trust Your CEO?" *USA Today,* February 12, 2003, 7B.

88. M. J. Ashleigh, M. Higgs, and V. Dulewicz, "A New Propensity to Trust Scale and Its Relationship with Individual Well-Being: Implications for HRM Policies and Practices," *Human Resource Management Journal* 22, no. 4 2012, 360–76; R. C. Mayer and M. B. Gavin, "Trust in Management and Performance: Who Minds the Shop While the Employees Watch the Boss?" *Academy of Management Journal* 48, no. 5 (2005): 874–88; and C. F. Peralta and M. F. Saldanha, "Knowledge-Centered Culture and Knowledge Sharing: The Moderator Role of Trust Propensity," *Journal of Knowledge Management* 18, no. 3 (2014): 538–50.

89. J. A. Simpson, "Foundations of Interpersonal Trust," in *Social Psychology: Handbook of Basic Principles*, 2nd ed., eds. A. W. Kruglanski and E. T. Higgins (New York: Guilford, 2007), 587–607.

90. X.-P. Chen, M. B. Eberly, T.-J. Chiang, J.-L. Farh, and B.-Shiuan Cheng, "Affective Trust in Chinese Leaders: Linking Paternalistic Leadership to Employee Performance," *Journal of Management* 40, no. 3 (2014): 796–819.

91. J. A. Simpson, "Foundations of Interpersonal Trust."

92. B. Groysberg and M. Slind, "Leadership Is a Conversation," *Harvard Business Review,* June 2012, 76–84.

93. H. Zhao, S. J. Wayne, B. C. Glibkowski, and J. Bravo, "The Impact of Psychological Contract Breach on Work-Related Outcomes: A Meta-Analysis," *Personnel Psychology* 60, no. 3 (2007): 647–80.

94. D. L. Shapiro, A. D. Boss, S. Salas, S. Tangirala, and M. A. Von Glinow, "When Are Transgressing *Leaders* Punitively Judged? An Empirical Test," *Journal of Applied Psychology* 96, no. 2 (2011): 412–22.

95. D. L. Ferrin, P. H. Kim, C. D. Cooper, and K. T. Dirks, "Silence Speaks Volumes: The Effectiveness of Reticence in Comparison to Apology and Denial for Responding to Integrity- and Competence-Based Trust Violations," *Journal of Applied Psychology* 92, no. 4 (2007): 893–908.

96. M. E. Schweitzer, J. C. Hershey, and E. T. Bradlow, "Promises and Lies: Restoring Violated Trust," *Organizational Behavior and Human Decision Processes* 101, no. 1 (2006): 1–19.

97. See, for example, L. Eby, M. Buits, and A. Lockwood, "Protégés' Negative Mentoring Experiences: Construct Development and Nomological Validation," *Personnel Psychology* 57, no. 2 (2004): 411–47.

98. J. U. Chun, J. J. Sosik, and N. Y. Yun, "A Longitudinal Study of Mentor and Protégé Outcomes in Formal Mentoring Relationships," *Journal of Organizational Behavior* 33, no. 8 (2012): 35–49.

99. See, for instance, B. Schyns, J. Felfe, and H. Blank, "Is Charisma Hyper-Romanticism? Empirical Evidence from New Data and a Meta-Analysis," *Applied Psychology: An International Review* 56, no. 4 (2007): 505–27.

100. M. J. Martinko, P. Harvey, D. Sikora, and S. C. Douglas, "Perceptions of Abusive Supervision: The Role of Subordinates' Attribution Styles," *Leadership Quarterly* 22, no. 4 (2011): 751–64.

101. M. C. Bligh, J. C. Kohles, C. L. Pearce, J. E. Justin, and J. F. Stovall, "When the Romance Is Over: Follower Perspectives of Aversive Leadership," *Applied Psychology: An International Review* 56, no. 4 (2007): 528–57.

102. B. R. Agle, N. J. Nagarajan, J. A. Sonnenfeld, and D. Srinivasan, "Does CEO Charisma Matter?" *Academy of Management Journal* 49, no. 1 (2006): 161–74.

103. M. C. Bligh, J. C. Kohles, C. L. Pearce, J. E. Justin, and J. F. Stovall, "When the Romance Is Over."

104. B. Schyns, J. Felfe, and H. Blank, "Is Charisma Hyper-Romanticism?"

105. M. Van Vugt and B. R. Spisak, "Sex Differences in the Emergence of Leadership during Competitions within and between Groups," *Psychological Science* 19, no. 9 (2008): 854–8.

106. R. E. Silverman, "Who's the Boss? There Isn't One," *The Wall Street Journal,* June 20, 2012, B1, B8.

107. See, for instance, L. Pedraja-Rejas, "The Importance of Leadership in the Knowledge Economy," *Interciencia* 40, no. 10 (2015): 654.

108. L. A. Hambley, T. A. O'Neill, and T. J. B. Kline, "Virtual Team Leadership: The Effects of Leadership Style and Communication Medium on Team Interaction Styles and Outcomes," *Organizational Behavior and Human Decision Processes* 103, no. 1 (2007): 1–20; and B. J. Avolio and S. S. Kahai, "Adding the 'E' to E-Leadership: How It May Impact Your Leadership," *Organizational Dynamics* 31, no. 4 (2003): 325–38.

109. S. J. Zaccaro and P. Bader, "E-Leadership and the Challenges of Leading E-Teams: Minimizing the Bad and Maximizing the Good," *Organizational Dynamics* 31, no. 4 (2003): 381–85.

110. C. E. Naquin and G. D. Paulson, "Online Bargaining and Interpersonal Trust," *Journal of Applied Psychology* 88, no. 1 (2003), 113–20.

CHAPTER 13

1. B. Oc, M. R. Bashshur, and C. Moore, "Speaking Truth to Power: The Effect of Candid Feedback on How Individuals with Power Allocate Resources," *Journal of Applied Psychology* 100, no. 2 (2015): 450–63.

2. E. Landells and S. L. Albrecht, "Organizational Political Climate: Shared Perceptions about the Building and Use of Power Bases," *Human Resource Management Review* 23, no. 4 (2013): 357–65; P. Rylander, "Coaches' Bases of Power: Developing Some Initial Knowledge of Athletes' Compliance with Coaches in Team Sports," *Journal of Applied Sport Psychology* 27, no. 1 (2015): 110–21; and G. Yukl, "Use Power Effectively," in *Handbook of Principles of Organizational Behavior*, ed. E. A. Locke (Malden, MA: Blackwell, 2004), 242–47.

3. See, for example, O. Baumann and N. Stieglitz, "Rewarding Value-Creating Ideas in Organizations: The Power of Low-Powered Incentives," *Strategic Management Journal* 35, no. 3 (2014): 358–75.

4. S. R. Giessner and T. W. Schubert, "High in the Hierarchy: How Vertical Location and Judgments of Leaders' Power Are Interrelated," *Organizational Behavior and Human Decision Processes* 104, no. 1 (2007): 30–44.

5. S. Perman, "Translation Advertising: Where Shop Meets Hip Hop," *Time,* August 30, 2010, http://content.time.com/time/magazine/article/0,9171,2011574,00.html.

6. R. E. Sturm and J. Antonakis, "Interpersonal Power: A Review, Critique, and Research Agenda," *Journal of Management* 41, no. 1 (2015): 136–63.

7. M. C. J. Caniels and A. Roeleveld, "Power and Dependence Perspectives on Outsourcing Decisions," *European Management Journal* 27, no. 6 (2009): 402–17; and R.-J. B. Jean, D. Kim, and R. S. Sinkovics, "Drivers and Performance Outcomes of Supplier Innovation Generation in Customer-Supplier Relationships: The Role of Power-Dependence," *Decision Sciences* 43, no. 6 (2012): 1003–38.

8. R.S. Burt, M. Kilduff, and S. Tasselli, "Social Network Analysis: Foundations and Frontiers on Advantage," *Annual Review of Psychology* 64 (2013): 527–47; M. A. Carpenter, M. Li, and H. Jiang, "Social Network Research in Organizational Contexts: A Systematic Review of Methodological Issues and Choices," *Journal of Management* 38, no. 4 (2012): 1328–61; and M. Kilduff and D. J. Brass, "Organizational Social Network Research: Core Ideas and Key Debates," *Academy of Management Annals* 4 (2010): 317–57.

9. J. Gehman, L. K. Treviño, and R. Garud, "Values Work: A Process Study of the Emergence and Performance of Organizational Values Practices," *Academy of Management Journal* 56, no. 1 (2013): 84–112.

10. J. Battilana and T. Casciaro, "Change Agents, Networks, and Institutions: A Contingency Theory of Organizational Change," *Academy of Management Journal* 55, no. 2 (2012): 381–98.

11. S. M. Soltis, F. Agneessens, Z. Sasovova, and G. Labianca, "A Social Network Perspective on Turnover Intentions: The Role of Distributive Justice and Social Support," *Human Resource Management* 52, no. 4 (2013): 561–84.

12. R. Kaše, Z. King, and D. Minbaeva, "Using Social Network Research in HRM: Scratching the Surface of a Fundamental Basis of HRM," *Human Resource Management* 52, no. 4 (2013): 473–83; R. Cross and L. Prusak, "The People Who Make Organizations Go—Or Stop," *Harvard Business Review,* June 2002, https://hbr.org/2002/06/the-people-who-make-organizations-go-or-stop.

13. See, for example, D. M. Cable and T. A. Judge, "Managers' Upward Influence Tactic Strategies: The Roll of Manager Personality and Supervisor Leadership Style," *Journal of Organizational Behavior* 24, no. 2 (2003): 197–214; M. P. M. Chong, "Influence Behaviors and Organizational Commitment: A Comparative Study," *Leadership and Organization Development Journal* 35, no. 1 (2014): 54–78; and M. Lewis-Duarte and M. C. Bligh, "Agents of 'Influence': Exploring the Usage, Timing, and Outcomes of Executive Coaching Tactics," *Leadership & Organization Development Journal* 33, nos. 3–4 (2012): 255–81.

14. G. R. Ferris, W. A. Hochwarter, C. Douglas, F. R. Blass, R. W. Kolodinsky, and D. C. Treadway, "Social Influence Processes in Organizations and Human Resource Systems," in *Research in Personnel and Human Resources Management*, vol. 21, eds. G. R. Ferris and J. J. Martocchio (Oxford, UK: JAI Press/Elsevier, 2003), 65–127; C. A. Higgins, T. A. Judge, and G. R. Ferris, "Influence Tactics and Work Outcomes: A Meta-Analysis," *Journal of Organizational Behavior* 24, no. 1 (2003): 89–106; and M. Uhl-Bien, R. E. Riggio, K. B. Lowe, and M. K. Carsten, "Followership Theory: A Review and Research Agenda," *Leadership Quarterly* 25, no. 1 (2004): 83–104.

15. M. P. M. Chong, "Influence Behaviors and Organizational Commitment: A Comparative Study."

16. R. E. Petty and P. Briñol, "Persuasion: From Single to Multiple to Metacognitive Processes," *Perspectives on Psychological Science* 3, no. 2 (2008): 137–47.

17. J. Badal, "Getting a Raise from the Boss," *The Wall Street Journal,* July 8, 2006, B1, B5.

18. M. P. M. Chong, "Influence Behaviors and Organizational Commitment: A Comparative Study."

19. Ibid.

20. O. Epitropaki and R. Martin, "Transformational-Transactional Leadership and Upward Influence: The Role of Relative Leader–Member Exchanges (RLMX) and Perceived Organizational Support (POS), *Leadership Quarterly* 24, no. 2 (2013): 299–315.

21. A. W. Kruglanski, A. Pierro, and E. T. Higgins, "Regulatory Mode and Preferred Leadership Styles: How Fit Increases Job Satisfaction," *Basic and Applied Social Psychology* 29, no. 2 (2007): 137–49; and A. Pierro, L. Cicero, and B. H. Raven, "Motivated Compliance with Bases of Social Power," *Journal of Applied Social Psychology* 38, no. 7 (2008): 1921–44.

22. G. Yukl, P. P. Fu, and R. McDonald, "Cross-Cultural Differences in Perceived Effectiveness of Influence Tactics for Initiating or Resisting Change," *Applied Psychology: An International Review* 52, no. 1 (2003): 66–82; and P. P. Fu, T. K. Peng, J. C. Kennedy, and G. Yukl, "Examining the Preferences of Influence Tactics in Chinese Societies: A Comparison of Chinese Managers in Hong Kong, Taiwan, and Mainland China," *Organizational Dynamics* 33, no. 1 (2004): 32–46.

23. C. J. Torelli and S. Shavitt, "Culture and Concepts of Power," *Journal of Personality and Social Psychology* 99, no. 4 (2010): 703–23.

24. P. P. Fu, T. K. Peng, J. C. Kennedy, and G. Yukl, "Examining the Preferences of Influence Tactics in Chinese Societies: A Comparison of Chinese Managers in Hong Kong, Taiwan, and Mainland China."

25. G. R. Ferris, D. C. Treadway, P. L. Perrewé, R. L. Brouer, C. Douglas, and S. Lux, "Political Skill in Organizations," *Journal of Management* 33, no. 3 (2007): 290–320; K. J. Harris, K. M. Kacmar, S. Zivnuska, and J. D. Shaw, "The Impact of Political Skill on Impression Management Effectiveness," *Journal of Applied Psychology* 92, no. 1 (2007): 278–85; W. A. Hochwarter, G. R. Ferris, M. B. Gavin, P. L. Perrewé, A. T. Hall, and D. D. Frink, "Political Skill as Neutralizer of Felt Accountability–Job Tension Effects on Job Performance Ratings: A Longitudinal Investigation," *Organizational Behavior and Human Decision Processes* 102, no. 2 (2007): 226–39; and D. C. Treadway, G. R. Ferris, A. B. Duke, G. L. Adams, and J. B. Tatcher, "The Moderating Role of Subordinate Political Skill on Supervisors' Impressions of Subordinate Ingratiation and Ratings of Subordinate Interpersonal Facilitation," *Journal of Applied Psychology* 92, no. 3 (2007): 848–55.

26. M. C. Andrews, K. M. Kacmar, and K. J. Harris, "Got Political Skill? The Impact of Justice on the Importance of Political Skills for Job Performance," *Journal of Applied Psychology* 94, no. 6 (2009): 1427–37.

27. C. Anderson, S. E. Spataro, and F. J. Flynn, "Personality and Organizational Culture as Determinants of Influence," *Journal of Applied Psychology* 93, no. 3 (2008): 702–10.

28. Y. Cho and N. J. Fast, "Power, Defensive Denigration, and the Assuaging Effect of Gratitude Expression," *Journal of Experimental Social Psychology* 48, no. 3 (2012): 778–82.

29. M. Pitesa and S. Thau, "Masters of the Universe: How Power and Accountability Influence Self-Serving Decisions under Moral Hazard," *Journal of Applied Psychology* 98, no. 3 (2013): 550–58; N. J. Fast, N. Sivanathan, D. D. Mayer, and A. D. Galinsky, "Power and Overconfident Decision-Making," *Organizational Behavior and Human Decision Processes* 117, no. 2 (2012): 249–60; and M. J. Williams, "Serving the Self from the Seat of Power: Goals and Threats Predict Leaders' Self-Interested Behavior," *Journal of Management* 40, no. 5 (2014): 1365–95.

30. J. K. Maner, M. T. Gaillot, A. J. Menzel, and J. W. Kunstman, "Dispositional Anxiety Blocks the Psychological Effects of Power," *Personality and Social Psychology Bulletin* 38, no. 11 (2012): 1383–95.

31. N. J. Fast, N. Halevy, and A. D. Galinsky, "The Destructive Nature of Power without Status," *Journal of Experimental Social Psychology* 48, no. 1 (2012): 391–94.

32. T. Seppälä, J. Lipponen, A. Bardi, and A. Pirttilä-Backman, "Change-Oriented Organizational Citizenship Behaviour: An Interactive Product of Openness to Change Values, Work Unit Identification, and Sense of Power," *Journal of Occupational and Organizational Psychology* 85, no. 1 (2012): 136–55.

33. K. A. DeCelles, D. S. DeRue, J. D. Margolis, and T. L. Ceranic, "Does Power Corrupt or Enable? When and Why Power Facilitates Self-Interested Behavior," *Journal of Applied Psychology* 97, no. 3 (2012): 681–89.

34. "Facts about Sexual Harassment," The U.S. Equal Employment Opportunity Commission, accessed June 19, 2015 www.eeoc.gov/facts/fs-sex.html.

35. F. Ali and R. Kramar, "An Exploratory Study of Sexual Harassment in Pakistani Organizations," *Asia Pacific Journal of Management* 32, no. 1 (2014): 229–49.

36. Ibid.

37. "Workplace Sexual Harassment Statistics", Association of Women for Action and Research, 2015, http://www.aware.org.sg/ati/wsh-site/14.

38. R. Ilies, N. Hauserman, S. Schwochau, and J. Stibal, "Reported Incidence Rates of Work-Related Sexual Harassment in the United States: Using Meta-Analysis to Explain Reported Rate Disparities," *Personnel Psychology* 56, no. 3 (2003): 607–31; and G. Langer, "One in Four U.S. Women Reports Workplace Harassment," *ABC News,* November 16, 2011, http://abcnews.go.com/blogs/politics/2011/11/one-in-four-u-s-women-reports-workplace-harassment/.

39. "Sexual Harassment Charges," Equal Employment Opportunity Commission, accessed August 20, 2015, www.eeoc.gov/eeoc/statistics/.

40. B. Popken, "Report: 80% of Waitresses Report Being Sexually Harassed," *USA Today,* October 7, 2014, http://www.today.com/money/report-80-waitresses-report-being-sexually-harassed-2D80199724.

41. G. R. Ferris, D. C. Treadway, R. W. Kolokinsky, W. A. Hochwarter, C. J. Kacmar, and D. D. Frink, "Development and Validation of the Political Skill Inventory," *Journal of Management* 31, no. 1 (2005): 126–52.

42. A. Pullen and C. Rhodes, "Corporeal Ethics and the Politics of Resistance in Organizations," *Organization* 21, no. 6 (2014): 782–96.

43. G. R. Ferris and W. A. Hochwarter, "Organizational Politics," in *APA Handbook of Industrial and Organizational Psychology*, vol. 3, ed. S. Zedeck (Washington, DC: American Psychological Association, 2011), 435–59.

44. D. A. Buchanan, "You Stab My Back, I'll Stab Yours: Management Experience and Perceptions of Organization Political Behavior," *British Journal of Management* 19, no. 1 (2008): 49–64.

45. M. A. Finkelstein and L. A. Penner, "Predicting Organizational Citizenship Behavior: Integrating the Functional and Role Identity Approaches," *Social Behavior and Personality* 32, no. 4 (2004): 383–98; and J. Schwarzwald, M. Koslowsky, and M. Allouf, "Group Membership, Status, and Social Power Preference," *Journal of Applied Social Psychology* 35, no. 3 (2005): 644–65.

46. See, for example, J. Walter, F. W. Kellermans, and C. Lechner, "Decision Making within and between Organizations: Rationality, Politics, and Alliance Performance," *Journal of Management* 38, no. 5 (2012): 1582–610.

47. G. R. Ferris, D. C. Treadway, P. L. Perrewé, R. L. Grouer, C. Douglas, and S. Lux, "Political Skill in Organizations."

48. J. Shi, R. E. Johnson, Y. Liu, and M. Wang, "Linking Subordinate Political Skill to Supervisor Dependence and Reward Recommendations: A Moderated Mediation Model," *Journal of Applied Psychology* 98, no. 2 (2013): 374–84.

49. W. A. Gentry, D. C. Gimore, M. L. Shuffler, and J. B. Leslie, "Political Skill as an Indicator of Promotability among Multiple Rater Sources," *Journal of Organizational Behavior* 33, no. 1 (2012): 89–104; and I. Kapoutsis, A. Paplexandris, A. Nikolopoulous, W. A. Hochwarter, and G. R. Ferris, "Politics Perceptions as a Moderator of the Political Skill–Job Performance Relationship: A Two-Study, Cross-National, Constructive Replication," *Journal of Vocational Behavior* 78, no. 1 (2011): 123–35.

50. M. Abbas, U. Raja, W. Darr, and D. Bouckenooghe, "Combined Effects of Perceived Politics and Psychological Capital on Job Satisfaction, Turnover Intentions, and Performance," *Journal of Management* 40, no. 7 (2014): 1813–30; and C. C. Rosen, D. L. Ferris, D. J. Brown, and W.-W. Yen, "Relationships among Perceptions of Organizational Politics (POPs), Work Motivation, and Salesperson Performance," *Journal of Management and Organization* 21, no. 2 (2015): 203–16.

51. See, for example, M. D. Laird, P. Harvey, and J. Lancaster, "Accountability, Entitlement, Tenure, and Satisfaction in Generation Y," *Journal of Managerial Psychology* 30, no. 1 (2015): 87–100; J. M. L. Poon, "Situational Antecedents and Outcomes of Organizational Politics Perceptions," *Journal of Managerial Psychology* 18, no. 2 (2003): 138–55; and K. L. Zellars, W. A. Hochwarter, S. E. Lanivich, P. L. Perrewe, and G. R. Ferris, "Accountability for Others, Perceived Resources, and Well Being: Convergent Restricted Non-Linear Results in Two Samples," *Journal of Occupational and Organizational Psychology* 84, no. 1 (2011): 95–115.

52. J. Walter, F. W. Kellermanns, and C. Lechner, "Decision Making within and between Organizations: Rationality, Politics, and Alliance Performance," *Journal of Management* 38, no. 5 (2012): 1582–610.

53. W. A. Hochwarter, C. Kiewitz, S. L. Castro, P. L. Perrewé, and G. R. Ferris, "Positive Affectivity and Collective Efficacy as Moderators of the Relationship between Perceived Politics and Job Satisfaction," *Journal of Applied Social Psychology* 33, no. 5 (2003): 1009–35; and C. C. Rosen, P. E. Levy, and R. J. Hall, "Placing Perceptions of Politics in the Context of Feedback Environment, Employee Attitudes, and Job Performance," *Journal of Applied Psychology* 91, no. 1 (2006): 211–30.

54. S. Aryee, Z. Chen, and P. S. Budhwar, "Exchange Fairness and Employee Performance: An Examination of the Relationship between Organizational Politics and Procedural Justice," *Organizational Behavior and Human Decision Processes* 94, no. 1 (2004): 1–14.

55. M. C. Andrews, L. A. Witt, and K. M. Kacmar, "The Interactive Effects of Organizational Politics and Exchange Ideology on Manager Ratings of Retention," *Journal of Vocational Behavior* 62, no. 2 (2003): 357–69.

56. O. J. Labedo, "Perceptions of Organisational Politics: Examination of the Situational Antecedent and Consequences among Nigeria's Extension Personnel," *Applied Psychology: An International Review* 55, no. 2 (2006): 255–81.

57. K. M. Kacmar, M. C. Andrews, K. J. Harris, and B. Tepper, "Ethical Leadership and Subordinate Outcomes: The Mediating Role of Organizational Politics and the Moderating Role of Political Skill," *Journal of Business Ethics* 115, no. 1 (2013): 33–44.

58. Ibid.

59. K. M. Kacmar, D. G. Bachrach, K. J. Harris, and S. Zivnuska, "Fostering Good Citizenship through Ethical Leadership: Exploring the Moderating Role of Gender and Organizational Politics," *Journal of Applied Psychology* 96, no. 3 (2011): 633–42.

60. C. Homburg and A. Fuerst, "See No Evil, Hear No Evil, Speak No Evil: A Study of Defensive Organizational Behavior towards Customer Complaints," *Journal of the Academy of Marketing Science* 35, no. 4 (2007): 523–36.

61. See, for instance, M. C. Bolino and W. H. Turnley, "More Than One Way to Make an Impression: Exploring Profiles of Impression Management," *Journal of Management* 29, no. 2 (2003): 141–60; S. Zivnuska, K. M. Kacmar, L. A. Witt, D. S. Carlson, and V. K. Bratton, "Interactive Effects of Impression Management and Organizational Politics on Job Performance," *Journal of Organizational Behavior* 25, no. 5 (2004): 627–40; and M. C. Bolino, K. M. Kacmar, W. H. Turnley, and J. B. Gilstrap, "A Multi-Level Review of Impression Management Motives and Behaviors," *Journal of Management* 34, no. 6 (2008): 1080–109.

62. L. A. McFarland, A. M. Ryan, and S. D. Kriska, "Impression Management Use and Effectiveness across Assessment Methods," *Journal of Management* 29, no. 5 (2003): 641–61; C. A. Higgins and T. A. Judge, "The Effect of Applicant Influence Tactics on Recruiter Perceptions of Fit and Hiring Recommendations: A Field Study," *Journal of Applied Psychology* 89, no. 4 (2004): 622–32; and W. C. Tsai, C.-C. Chen, and S. F. Chiu, "Exploring Boundaries of the Effects of Applicant Impression Management Tactics in Job Interviews," *Journal of Management* 31, no. 1 (2005): 108–25.

63. M. R. Barrick, J. A. Shaffer, and S. W. DeGrassi. "What You See May Not Be What You Get: Relationships among Self-Presentation Tactics and Ratings of Interview and Job Performance," *Journal of Applied Psychology,* 94, no. 6 (2009): 1394–411.

64. E. Molleman, B. Emans, and N. Turusbekova, "How to Control Self-Promotion among Performance-Oriented Employees: The Roles of Task Clarity and Personalized Responsibility," *Personnel Review* 41, no. 1 (2012): 88–105.

65. K. J. Harris, K. M. Kacmar, S. Zivnuska, and J. D. Shaw, "The Impact of Political Skill on Impression Management Effectiveness," *Journal of Applied Psychology* 92, no. 1 (2007): 278–85; and D. C. Treadway, G. R. Ferris, A. B. Duke, G. L. Adams, and J. B. Thatcher, "The Moderating Role of Subordinate Political Skill on Supervisors' Impressions of Subordinate Ingratiation and Ratings of Subordinate Interpersonal Facilitation," *Journal of Applied Psychology* 92, no. 3 (2007): 848–55.

66. J. D. Westphal and I. Stern, "Flattery Will Get You Everywhere (Especially If You Are a Male Caucasian): How Ingratiation, Boardroom Behavior, and Demographic Minority Status Affect Additional Board Appointments of U.S. Companies," *Academy of Management Journal* 50, no. 2 (2007): 267–88.

67. Y. Liu, G. R. Ferris, J. Xu, B. A. Weitz, and P. L. Perrewé, "When Ingratiation Backfires: The Role of Political Skill in the Ingratiation-Internship Performance Relationship," *Academy of Management Learning & Education* 13, no. 4 (2014): 569–86.

68. E. Vigoda, "Reactions to Organizational Politics: A Cross-Cultural Examination in Israel and Britain," *Human Relations* 54, no. 11 (2001), 1483–1518; and Y. Zhu and D. Li, "Negative Spillover Impact of Perceptions of Organizational Politics on Work-Family Conflict in China," *Social Behavior and Personality* 43, no. 5 (2015): 705–14.

69. J. L. T. Leong, M. H. Bond, and P. P. Fu, "Perceived Effectiveness of Influence Strategies in the United States and Three Chinese Societies," *International Journal of Cross Cultural Management* 6, no. 1 (2006): 101–20.

70. Y. Miyamoto and B. Wilken, "Culturally Contingent Situated Cognition: Influencing Other People Fosters Analytic Perception in the United States But Not in Japan," *Psychological Science* 21, no. 11 (2010): 1616–22.

71. D. Clark, "A Campaign Strategy for Your Career," *Harvard Business Review,* November 2012, 131–34.

CHAPTER 14

1. See, for instance, D. Tjosvold, A. S. H. Wong, and N. Y. F. Chen, "Constructively Managing Conflicts in Organizations," *Annual Review of Organizational Psychology and Organizational Behavior* 1 (2014): 545–68; and M. A. Korsgaard, S. S. Jeong, D. M. Mahony, and A. H. Pitariu, "A Multilevel View of Intragroup Conflict," *Journal of Management* 34, no. 6 (2008): 1222–52.

2. J. Farh, C. Lee, and C. I. C. Farh, "Task Conflict and Team Creativity: A Question of How Much and When," *Journal of Applied Psychology* 95, no. 6 (2010): 1173–80.

3. B. H. Bradley, B. F. Postlethwaite, A. C. Klotz, M. R. Hamdani, and K. G. Brown, "Reaping the Benefits of Task Conflict in Teams: The Critical Role of Team Psychological Safety Climate," *Journal of Applied Psychology* 97, no. 1 (2012), 151–58.

4. S. Benard, "Cohesion from Conflict: Does Intergroup Conflict Motivate Intragroup Norm Enforcement and Support for Centralized Leadership?" *Social Psychology Quarterly* 75, no. 2 (2012): 107–30.

5. G. A. Van Kleef, W. Steinel, and A. C. Homan, "On Being Peripheral and Paying Attention: Prototypicality and Information Processing in Intergroup Conflict," *Journal of Applied Psychology* 98, no. 1 (2013): 63–79.

6. R. S. Peterson and K. J. Behfar, "The Dynamic Relationship between Performance Feedback, Trust, and Conflict in Groups: A Longitudinal Study," *Organizational Behavior and Human Decision Processes* 92, nos. 1–2 (2003): 102–12.

7. T. M. Glomb and H. Liao, "Interpersonal Aggression in Work Groups: Social Influence, Reciprocal, and Individual Effects," *Academy of Management Journal* 46, no. 4 (2003): 486–96; and V. Venkataramani and R. S. Dalal, "Who Helps and Harms Whom? Relational Aspects of Interpersonal Helping and Harming in Organizations," *Journal of Applied Psychology* 92, no. 4 (2007): 952–66.

8. R. Friedman, C. Anderson, J. Brett, M. Olekalns, N. Goates, and C. C. Lisco, "The Positive and Negative Effects of Anger on Dispute Resolution: Evidence from Electronically Mediated Disputes," *Journal of Applied Psychology* 89, no. 2 (2004): 369–76.

9. J. S. Chun and J. N. Choi, "Members' Needs, Intragroup Conflict, and Group Performance," *Journal of Applied Psychology* 99, no. 3 (2014): 437–50.

10. See, for instance, J. R. Curhan, "What Do People Value When They Negotiate? Mapping the Domain of Subjective Value in Negotiation," *Journal of Personality and Social Psychology* 91, no. 3 (2006): 117–26; and N. Halevy, E. Chou, and J. K. Murnighan, "Mind Games: The Mental Representation of Conflict," *Journal of Personality and Social Psychology* 102, no. 1 (2012): 132–48.

11. A. M. Isen, A. A. Labroo, and P. Durlach, "An Influence of Product and Brand Name on Positive Affect: Implicit and Explicit Measures," *Motivation and Emotion* 28, no. 1 (2004): 43–63.

12. Ibid.

13. C. Montes, D. Rodriguez, and G. Serrano, "Affective Choice of Conflict Management Styles," *International Journal of Conflict Management* 23, no. 1 (2012): 6–18.

14. See, for example, R. Troetschel and P. M. Gollwitzer, "Implementation Intentions and the Willful Pursuit of Prosocial Goals in Negotiations," *Journal of Experimental Social Psychology* 43, no. 4 (2007): 579–98.

15. See P. Badke-Schaub, G. Goldschmidt, and M. Meijer, "How Does Cognitive Conflict in Design Teams Support the Development of Creative Ideas?" *Creativity and Innovation Management* 19, no. 2 (2010): 119–33; and Z. Ma, A. Erkus, and A. Tabak, "Explore the Impact of Collectivism on Conflict Management Styles: A Turkish Study," *International Journal of Conflict Management* 21, no. 2 (2010): 169–85.

16. L. A. DeChurch, J. R. Mesmer-Magnus, and D. Doty, "Moving beyond Relationship and Task Conflict: Toward a Process-State Perspective," *Journal of Applied Psychology* 98, no. 4 (2013): 559–78.

17. G. Todorova, J. B. Bear, and L. R. Weingart, "Can Conflict Be Energizing? A Study of Task Conflict, Positive Emotions, and Job Satisfaction," *Journal of Applied Psychology* 99, no. 3 (2014): 451–67.

18. B. A. Nijstad and S. C. Kaps, "Taking the Easy Way Out: Preference Diversity, Decision Strategies, and Decision Refusal in Groups," *Journal of Personality and Social Psychology* 94, no. 5 (2008), pp. 860–870.

19. M. E. Zellmer-Bruhn, M. M. Maloney, A. D. Bhappu, and R. Salvador, "When and How Do Differences Matter? An Exploration of Perceived Similarity in Teams," *Organizational Behavior and Human Decision Processes* 107, no. 1 (2008): 41–59.

20. P. J. Hinds and D. E. Bailey, "Out of Sight, Out of Sync: Understanding Conflict in Distributed Teams," *Organization Science* 14, no. 6 (2003): 615–32.

21. K. A. Jehn, L. Greer, S. Levine, and G. Szulanski, "The Effects of Conflict Types, Dimensions, and Emergent States on Group Outcomes," *Group Decision and Negotiation* 17, no. 6 (2005): 777–96.

22. M. E. Zellmer-Bruhn, M. M. Maloney, A. D. Bhappu, and R. Salvador, "When and How Do Differences Matter?"

23. J. Fried, "I Know You Are, But What Am I?" *Inc.,* July/August 2010, 39–40.

24. K. J. Behfar, R. S. Peterson, E. A. Mannix, and W. M. K. Trochim, "The Critical Role of Conflict Resolution in Teams: A Close Look at the Links between Conflict Type, Conflict Management Strategies, and Team Outcomes," *Journal of Applied Psychology* 93, no. 1 (2008): 170–88; and A. G. Tekleab, N. R. Quigley, and P. E. Tesluk, "A Longitudinal Study of Team Conflict, Conflict Management, Cohesion, and Team Effectiveness," *Group & Organization Management* 34, no. 2 (2009): 170–205.

25. A. Somech, H. S. Desivilya, and H. Lidogoster, "Team Conflict Management and Team Effectiveness: The Effects of Task Interdependence and Team Identification," *Journal of Organizational Behavior* 30, no. 3 (2009): 359–78.

26. W. Liu, R. Friedman, and Y. Hong, "Culture and Accountability in Negotiation: Recognizing the Importance of In-Group Relations," *Organizational Behavior and Human Decision Processes* 117, no. 1 (2012): 221–34; and B. C. Gunia, J. M. Brett, A. K. Nandkeolyar, and D. Kamdar, "Paying a Price: Culture, Trust, and Negotiation Consequences," *Journal of Applied Psychology* 96, no. 4 (2010): 774–89.

27. See, for instance, D. Druckman and L. M. Wagner, "Justice and Negotiation," *Annual Review of Psychology,* 67 (2016): 387–413.

28. See, for example, D. R. Ames, "Assertiveness Expectancies: How Hard People Push Depends on the Consequences They Predict," *Journal of Personality and Social Psychology* 95, no. 6 (2008): 1541–57; and J. R. Curhan, H. A. Elfenbein, and H. Xu, "What Do People Value When They Negotiate? Mapping the Domain of Subjective Value in Negotiation," *Journal of Personality and Social Psychology* 91, no. 3 (2006): 493–512.

29. R. Lewicki, D. Saunders, and B. Barry, *Negotiation,* 6th ed. (New York: McGraw-Hill/Irwin, 2009).

30. J. C. Magee, A. D. Galinsky, and D. H. Gruenfeld, "Power, Propensity to Negotiate, and Moving First in Competitive Interactions," *Personality and Social Psychology Bulletin* 33, no. 2 (2007): 200–12.

31. E. Wilson, "The Trouble with Jake," *The New York Times,* July 15, 2009, www.nytimes.com.

32. This model is based on R. J. Lewicki, D. Saunders, and B. Barry, *Negotiation,* 7th ed. (New York: McGraw-Hill, 2014).

33. R. P. Larrick and G. Wu, "Claiming a Large Slice of a Small Pie: Asymmetric Disconfirmation in Negotiation," *Journal of Personality and Social Psychology* 93, no. 2 (2007): 212–33.

34. L. L. Thompson, J. Wang, and B. C. Gunia, "Negotiation," *Annual Review of Psychology* 61, (2010): 491–515.

35. M. Schaerer, R. I. Swaab, and A. D. Galinsky "Anchors Weigh More Than Power: Why Absolute Powerlessness Liberates Negotiators to Achieve Better Outcomes," *Psychological Science* 26, no. 2 (2014): 170–81:10.1177/0956797614558718.

36. J. R. Curhan, H. A. Elfenbein, and G. J. Kilduff, "Getting off on the Right Foot: Subjective Value versus Economic Value in Predicting Longitudinal Job Outcomes from Job Offer Negotiations," *Journal of Applied Psychology* 94, no. 2 (2009): 524–34.

37. H. A. Elfenbein, "Individual Difference in Negotiation: A Nearly Abandoned Pursuit Revived," *Current Directions in Psychological Science* 24, no. 2 (2015): 131–36.

38. S. Sharma, W. Bottom, and H. A. Elfenbein, "On the Role of Personality, Cognitive Ability, and Emotional Intelligence in Predicting Negotiation Outcomes: A Meta-Analysis," *Organizational Psychology Review* 3, no. 4 (2013): 293–336.

39. G. Lelieveld, E. Van Dijk, I. Van Beest, and G. A. Van Kleef, "Why Anger and Disappointment Affect Other's Bargaining Behavior Differently: The Moderating Role of Power and the Mediating Role of Reciprocal Complementary Emotions," *Personality and Social Psychology Bulletin* 38, no. 9 (2012): 1209–21.

40. S. Côté, I. Hideg, and G. A. Van Kleef, "The Consequences of Faking Anger in Negotiations," *Journal of Experimental Social Psychology* 49, no. 3 (2013): 453–63.

41. G. A. Van Kleef and C. K. W. De Dreu, "Longer-Term Consequences of Anger Expression in Negotiation: Retaliation or Spillover?" *Journal of Experimental Social Psychology* 46, no. 5 (2010): 753–60.

42. H. Adam and A. Shirako, "Not All Anger Is Created Equal: The Impact of the Expresser's Culture on the Social Effects of Anger in Negotiations," *Journal of Applied Psychology* 98, no. 5 (2013): 785–98.

43. M. Olekalns and P. L Smith, "Mutually Dependent: Power, Trust, Affect, and the Use of Deception in Negotiation," *Journal of Business Ethics* 85, no. 3 (2009): 347–65.

44. A. W. Brooks and M. E. Schweitzer, "Can Nervous Nellie Negotiate? How Anxiety Causes Negotiators to Make Low First Offers, Exit Early, and Earn Less Profit," *Organizational Behavior and Human Decision Processes* 115, no. 1 (2011): 43–54.

45. M. Sinaceur, H. Adam, G. A. Van Kleef, and A. D. Galinsky, "The Advantages of Being Unpredictable: How Emotional Inconsistency Extracts Concessions in Negotiation," *Journal of Experimental Social Psychology* 49, no. 3 (2013): 498–508.

46. K. Leary, J. Pillemer, and M. Wheeler, "Negotiating with Emotion," *Harvard Business Review,* January–February 2013, 96–103.

47. L. A. Liu, R. Friedman, B. Barry, M. J. Gelfand, and Z. Zhang, "The Dynamics of Consensus Building in Intracultural and Intercultural Negotiations," *Administrative Science Quarterly* 57, no. 2 (2012): 269–304.

48. M. Liu, "The Intrapersonal and Interpersonal Effects of Anger on Negotiation Strategies: A Cross-Cultural Investigation," *Human Communication Research* 35, no. 1 (2009): 148–69; and H. Adam, A. Shirako, and W. W. Maddux, "Cultural Variance in the Interpersonal Effects of Anger in Negotiations," *Psychological Science* 21, no. 6 (2010): 882–89.

49. P. D. Trapnell and D. L. Paulhus, "Agentic and Communal Values: Their Scope and Measurement," *Journal of Personality Assessment* 94, no. 1 (2012): 39–52.

50. C. T. Kulik and M. Olekalns, "Negotiating the Gender Divide: Lessons from the Negotiation and Organizational Behavior Literatures," *Journal of Management* 38, no. 4 (2012): 1387–415.

51. C. Suddath, "The Art of Haggling," *Bloomberg Businessweek,* November 26, 2012, 98.

52. J. Mazei, J. Hüffmeier, P. A. Freund, A. F. Stuhlmacher, L. Bilke, and G. Hertel, "A Meta-Analysis on Gender Differences in Negotiation Outcomes and Their Moderators," *Psychological Bulletin* 141, no. 1 (2015): 85–104.

53. D. T. Kong, K. T. Dirks, and D. L. Ferrin, "Interpersonal Trust within Negotiations: Meta-Analytic Evidence, Critical Contingencies, and Directions for Future Research," *Academy of Management Journal* 57, no. 5 (2014): 1235–55.

54. G. R. Ferris, J. N. Harris, Z. A. Russell, B. P. Ellen, A. D. Martinez, and F. R. Blass, "The Role of Reputation in the Organizational Sciences: A Multilevel Review, Construct Assessment, and Research Directions," *Research in Personnel and Human Resources Management* 32 (2014): 241–303.

55. R. Zinko, G. R. Ferris, S. E. Humphrey, C. J. Meyer, and F. Aime, "Personal Reputation in Organizations: Two-Study Constructive Replication and Extension of Antecedents and Consequences," *Journal of Occupational and Organizational Psychology* 85, no. 1 (2012): 156–80.

56. A. Hinshaw, P. Reilly, and A. Kupfer Schneider, "Attorneys and Negotiation Ethics: A Material Misunderstanding?" *Negotiation Journal* 29, no. 3 (2013): 265–87; and N. A. Welsh, "The Reputational Advantages of Demonstrating Trustworthiness: Using the Reputation Index with Law Students," *Negotiation Journal* 28, no. 1 (2012): 117–45.

57. J. R. Curhan, H. A. Elfenbein, and X. Heng, "What Do People Value When They Negotiate? Mapping the Domain of Subjective Value in Negotiation," *Journal of Personality and Social Psychology* 91, no. 3 (2006): 493–512.

58. W. E. Baker and N. Bulkley, "Paying It Forward vs. Rewarding Reputation: Mechanisms of Generalized Reciprocity," *Organization Science* 25, no. 5 (2014): 1493–510.

59. G. A. Van Kleef, C. K. W. De Dreu, and A. S. R. Manstead, "An Interpersonal Approach to Emotion in Social Decision Making: The Emotions as Social Information Model" in *Advances in Experimental Social Psychology* vol. 42, ed. M. P. Zanna, (2010), 45–96.

60. F. Lumineau and J. E. Henderson, "The Influence of Relational Experience and Contractual Governance on the Negotiation Strategy in Buyer–Supplier Disputes," *Journal of Operations Management* 30, no. 5 (2012): 382–95.

61. U.S. Equal Employment Opportunity Commission, Questions and Answers About Mediation, accessed June 9, 2015, http://www.eeoc.gov/eeoc/mediation/qanda.cfm.

CHAPTER 15

1. See, for instance, R. L. Daft, *Organization Theory and Design,* 10th ed. (Cincinnati, OH: South-Western Publishing, 2010).
2. J. G. Miller, "The Real Women's Issue: Time," *The Wall Street Journal,* March 9–10, 2013, C3.
3. T. W. Malone, R. J. Laubacher, and T. Johns, "The Age of Hyperspecialization," *Harvard Business Review,* July–August 2011, 56–65.
4. C. Woodyard, "Toyota Brass Shakeup Aims to Give Regions More Control," *USA Today,* March 6, 2013, www.usatoday.com/story/money/cars/2013/03/06/toyota-shakeup/1966489/.
5. S. Ballmer, "One Microsoft: Company Realigns to Enable Innovation at Greater Speed, Efficiency," Microsoft, July 11, 2013, http://blogs.microsoft.com/firehose/2013/07/11/one-microsoft-company-realigns-to-enable-innovation-at-greater-speed-efficiency/.
6. Ibid.
7. A. Wilhelm, "Microsoft Shakes Up Its Leadership and Internal Structure as its Fiscal Year Comes to a Close," *TechCrunch,* June 17, 2015, http://techcrunch.com/2015/06/17/microsoft-shakes-up-its-leadership-and-internal-structure-as-its-fiscal-year-comes-to-a-close/#.mcn-4eo:OnA3.
8. See, for instance, "How Hierarchy Can Hurt Strategy Execution," *Harvard Business Review,* July–August 2010, 74–75.
9. F. A. Csascar, "Organizational Structure as a Determinant of Performance: Evidence from Mutual Funds," *Strategic Management Journal* 33, no. 6 (2013): 611–32.
10. B. Brown and S. D. Anthony, "How P&G Tripled Its Innovation Success Rate," *Harvard Business Review,* June 2011, 64–72.
11. A. Leiponen and C. E. Helfat, "Location, Decentralization, and Knowledge Sources for Innovation," *Organization Science* 22, no. 3 (2011): 641–58.
12. K. Parks, "HSBC Unit Charged in Argentine Tax Case," *The Wall Street Journal,* March 19, 2013, C2.
13. P. Hempel, Z.-X. Zhang, and Y. Han, "Team Empowerment and the Organizational Context: Decentralization and the Contrasting Effects of Formalization," *Journal of Management* 38, no. 2 (2012): 475–501.
14. J. E. Perry-Smith and C. E. Shalley, "A Social Composition View of Team Creativity: The Role of Member Nationality-Heterogeneous Ties Outside of the Team," *Organization Science* 25, no. 5 (2014): 1434–52; J. Han, J. Han, and D. J. Brass, "Human Capital Diversity in the Creation of Social Capital for Team Creativity," *Journal of Organizational Behavior* 35, no. 1 (2014): 54–71; N. Sivasubramaniam, S. J. Liebowitz, and C. L. Lackman, "Determinants of New Product Development Team Performance: A Meta Analytic Review," *Journal of Product Innovation Management* 29, no. 5 (2012): 803–20.
15. T. A de Vries, F. Walter, G. S. Van der Vegt, and P. J. M. D. Essens, "Antecedents of Individuals' Interteam Coordination: Broad Functional Experiences as a Mixed Blessing," *Academy of Management Journal* 57, no. 5 (2014): 1334–59.
16. N. J. Foss, K. Laursen, and T. Pedersen, "Linking Customer Interaction and Innovation: The Mediating Role of New Organizational Practices," *Organization Science* 22, no. 4 (2011): 980–99; N. J. Foss, J. Lyngsie, and S. A. Zahra, "The Role of External Knowledge Sources and Organizational Design in the Process of Opportunity Exploitation," *Strategic Management Journal* 34, no. 12 (2013): 1453–71; and A. Salter, P. Crisuolo, and A. L. J. Ter Wal, "Coping with Open Innovation: Responding to the Challenges of External Engagement in R&D," *California Management Review* 56, no. 2 (2014): 77–94.
17. A. Murray, "Built Not to Last," *The Wall Street Journal,* March 18, 2013, A11.
18. For a quick overview, see J. Davoren, "Functional Structure Organization Strength and Weakness," *Small Business Chronicle,* accessed June 25, 2015, http://smallbusiness.chron.com/functional-structure-organization-strength-weakness-60111.html.
19. See, for instance, A. Writing, "Different Types of Organizational Structure," *Small Business Chronicle,* accessed June 25, 2015, http://smallbusiness.chron.com/different-types-organizational-structure-723.html.
20. For a quick overview, see "Types of Business Organizational Structures," *Pingboard,* July 24, 2013, accessed June 25, 2015 https://pingboard.com/blog/types-business-organizational-structures/.
21. J. R. Galbraith, *Designing Matrix Organizations That Actually Work: How IBM, Procter & Gamble, and Others Design for Success* (San Francisco: Jossey-Bass, 2009); and E. Krell, "Managing the Matrix," *HR Magazine,* April 2011, 69–71.
22. See, for instance, M. Bidwell, "Politics and Firm Boundaries: How Organizational Structure, Group Interests, and Resources Affect Outsourcing," *Organization Science* 23, no. 6 (2012): 1622–42.
23. See, for instance, T. Sy and L. S. D'Annunzio, "Challenges and Strategies of Matrix Organizations: Top-Level and Mid-Level Managers' Perspectives," *Human Resource Planning* 28, no. 1 (2005): 39–48; and T. Sy and S. Coté, "Emotional Intelligence: A Key Ability to Succeed in the Matrix Organization," *Journal of Management Development* 23, no. 5 (2004): 437–55.
24. N. Anand and R. L. Daft, "What Is the Right Organization Design?" *Organizational Dynamics* 36, no. 4 (2007): 329–44.
25. See, for instance, N. S. Contractor, S. Wasserman, and K. Faust, "Testing Multitheoretical, Multilevel Hypotheses about Organizational Networks: An Analytic Framework and Empirical Example," *Academy of Management Review* 31, no. 3 (2006): 681–703; and Y. Shin, "A Person-Environment Fit Model for Virtual Organizations," *Journal of Management* 30, no. 5 (2004): 725–43.
26. J. Schramm, "At Work in a Virtual World," *HR Magazine,* June 2010, 152.
27. C. B. Gibson and J. L. Gibbs, "Unpacking the Concept of Virtuality: The Effects of Geographic Dispersion, Electronic Dependence, Dynamic Structure, and National Diversity on Team Innovation," *Administrative Science Quarterly* 51, no. 3 (2006): 451–95; H. M. Latapie and V. N. Tran, "Subculture Formation, Evolution, and Conflict between Regional Teams in Virtual Organizations," *The Business Review,* Summer 2007, 189–93; and S. Davenport and U. Daellenbach, "'Belonging' to a Virtual Research Center: Exploring the Influence of Social Capital Formation Processes on Member Identification in a Virtual Organization," *British Journal of Management* 22, no. 1 (2011): 54–76.
28. See, for instance, E. Devaney, "The Pros & Cons of 7 Popular Organizational Structures," *Hubspot,* December 23, 2014, 6:00AM, accessed June 25, 2015, http://blog.hubspot.com/marketing/team-structure-diagrams/.
29. J. Scheck, L. Moloney, and A. Flynn, "Eni, CNPC Link Up in Mozambique," *The Wall Street Journal,* March 15, 2013, B3.

30. E. Devaney, "The Pros & Cons of 7 Popular Organizational Structures."

31. L. Gensler, "American Express to Slash 4,000 Jobs on Heels of Strong Quarter," *Forbes,* January 21, 2015, http://www.forbes.com/sites/laurengensler/2015/01/21/american-express-earnings-rise-11-on-increased-cardholder-spending/.

32. L. I Alpert, "Can Imported CEO Fix Russian Cars?" *The Wall Street Journal,* March 20, 2013, http://www.wsj.com/articles/SB10001424127887323396045783701213942 14736.

33. K. Walker, N. Ni, and B. Dyck, "Recipes for Successful Sustainability: Empirical Organizational Configurations for Strong Corporate Environmental Performance," *Business Strategy and the Environment* 24, no. 1 (2015): 40–57.

34. See, for instance, J. R. Hollenbeck et al., "Structural Contingency Theory and Individual Differences: Examination of External and Internal Person-Team Fit," *Journal of Applied Psychology* 87, no. 3 (2002): 599–606; and A. Drach-Zahavy and A. Freund, "Team Effectiveness under Stress: A Structural Contingency Approach," *Journal of Organizational Behavior* 28, no. 4 (2007): 423–50.

35. K. Walker, N. Ni, and B. Dyck, "Recipes for Successful Sustainability: Empirical Organizational Configurations for Strong Corporate Environmental Performance."

36. See, for instance, S. M. Toh, F. P. Morgeson, and M. A. Campion, "Human Resource Configurations: Investigating Fit with the Organizational Context," *Journal of Applied Psychology* 93, no. 4 (2008): 864–82.

37. M. Mesco, "Moleskine Tests Appetite for IPOs," *The Wall Street Journal,* March 19, 2013, B8.

38. J. Backaler, "Haier: A Chinese Company That Innovates," *Forbes,* June 17, 2010, http://www.forbes.com/sites/china/2010/06/17/haier-a-chinese-company-that-innovates/.

39. See, for instance, J. A. Cogin and I. O. Williamson, "Standardize or Customize: The Interactive Effects of HRM and Environment Uncertainty on MNC Subsidiary Performance," *Human Resource Management* 53, no. 5 (2014): 701–21; G. Kim and M.-G. Huh, "Exploration and Organizational Longevity: The Moderating Role of Strategy and Environment," *Asia Pacific Journal of Management* 32, no. 2 (2015): 389–414.

40. R. Greenwood, C. R. Hinings, and D. Whetten, "Rethinking Institutions and Organizations," *Journal of Management Studies,* 51, no. 7 (2014): 1206–20; and D. Chandler and H. Hwang, "Learning from Learning Theory: A Model of Organizational Adoption Strategies at the Microfoundations of Institutional Theory," *Journal of Management* 41, no. 5 (2015): 1446–76.

41. C. S. Spell and T. J. Arnold, "A Multi-Level Analysis of Organizational Justice and Climate, Structure, and Employee Mental Health," *Journal of Management* 33, no. 5 (2007): 724–51; and M. L. Ambrose and M. Schminke, "Organization Structure as a Moderator of the Relationship between Procedural Justice, Interactional Justice, Perceived Organizational Support, and Supervisory Trust," *Journal of Applied Psychology* 88, no. 2 (2003): 295–305.

42. See, for instance, C. S. Spell and T. J. Arnold, "A Multi-Level Analysis of Organizational Justice and Climate, Structure, and Employee Mental Health;" J. D. Shaw and N. Gupta, "Job Complexity, Performance, and Well-Being: When Does Supplies-Value Fit Matter?" *Personnel Psychology* 57, no. 4 (2004); and C. Anderson and C. E. Brown, "The Functions and Dysfunctions of Hierarchy," *Research in Organizational Behavior* 30 (2010): 55–89.

43. T. Martin, "Pharmacies Feel More Heat," *The Wall Street Journal,* March 16–17, 2013, A3.

44. See, for instance, R. E. Ployhart, J. A. Weekley, and K. Baughman, "The Structure and Function of Human Capital Emergence: A Multilevel Examination of the Attraction-Selection-Attrition Model," *Academy of Management Journal* 49, no. 4 (2006): 661–77.

45. J. B. Stewart, "A Place to Play for Google Staff," *The New York Times,* March 16, 2013, B1.

46. See, for instance, B. K. Park, J. A. Choi, M. Koo, S. Sul, and I. Choi, "Culture, Self, and Preference Structure: Transitivity and Context Independence Are Violated More by Interdependent People," *Social Cognition* 31, no. 1 (2013): 106–18.

47. J. Hassard, J. Morris, and L. McCann, "'My Brilliant Career?' New Organizational Forms and Changing Managerial Careers in Japan, the UK, and USA," *Journal of Management Studies* 49, no. 3 (2012): 571–99.

CHAPTER 16

1. See, for example, B. Schneider, M. G. Ehrhart, and W. H. Macey, "Organizational Climate and Culture," *Annual Review of Psychology* 64 (2013): 361–88.

2. I. Borg, J. F. Groenen, K. A. Jehn, W. Bilsky, and S. H. Schwartz, "Embedding the Organizational Culture Profile into Schwartz's Theory of Universals in Values," *Journal of Personnel Psychology* 10, no. 1 (2011): 1–12.

3. See, for example, C. Ostroff, A. J. Kinicki, and M. M. Tamkins, "Organizational Culture and Climate," in *Handbook of Psychology: Industrial and Organizational Psychology,* eds. W. C. Borman, D. R. Ilgen, and R. J. Klimoski (Hoboken, NJ: Wiley, 2003), 565–93.

4. D. A. Hoffman and L. M. Jones, "Leadership, Collective Personality, and Performance," *Journal of Applied Psychology* 90, no. 3 (2005), 509–22.

5. T. Hsieh, "How I did it: Zappos's CEO on Going to Extremes for Customers" *Harvard Business Review,* July–August 2010, 41–45.

6. P. Lok, R. Westwood, and J. Crawford, "Perceptions of Organisational Subculture and Their Significance for Organisational Commitment," *Applied Psychology: An International Review* 54, no. 4 (2005): 490–514; and B. E. Ashforth, K. M. Rogers, and K. G. Corley, "Identity in Organizations: Exploring Cross-Level Dynamics," *Organization Science* 22, no. 5 (2011): 1144–56.

7. For discussion of how culture can be evaluated as a shared perception, see D. Chan, "Multilevel and Aggregation Issues in Climate and Culture Research," in *The Oxford Handbook of Organizational Climate and Culture,* eds. B. Schneider and K. M. Barbera (New York, NY: Oxford University Press, 2014), 484–495.

8. L. M. Kotrba, M. A. Gillespie, A. M. Schmidt, R. E. Smerek, S. A. Ritchie, and D. R. Denison, "Do Consistent Corporate Cultures Have Better Business Performance: Exploring the Interaction Effects," *Human Relations* 65, no. 2 (2012): 241–262; and M. W. Dickson, C. J. Resick, and P. J. Hanges, "When Organizational Climate Is Unambiguous, It Is Also Strong," *Journal of Applied Psychology* 91, no. 2 (2006): 351–364.

9. M. Schulte, C. Ostroff, S. Shmulyian, and A. Kinicki, "Organizational Climate Configurations: Relationships to Collective Attitudes, Customer Satisfaction, and Financial Performance," *Journal of Applied Psychology* 94, no. 3 (2009): 618–634.

10. S. Maitlis and M. Christianson, "Sensemaking in Organizations: Taking Stock and Moving Forward," *The Academy of Management Annals* 8, (2014): 57–125; and K. Weber and M. T. Dacin, "The Cultural Construction of Organizational Life," *Organization Science* 22, no. 2 (2011): 287–298.

11. Y. Ling, Z. Simsek, M. H. Lubatkin, and J. F. Veiga, "Transformational Leadership's Role in Promoting Corporate Entrepreneurship: Examining the CEO-TMT Interface," *Academy of Management Journal* 51, no. 3 (2008): 557–76; and A. Malhotra, A. Majchrzak, and B. Rosen, "Leading Virtual Teams," *Academy of Management Perspectives* 21, no. 1 (2007): 60–70.

12. L. R. James et al., "Organizational and Psychological Climate: A Review of Theory and Research," *European Journal of Work and Organizational Psychology* 17, no. 1 (2008): 5–32; and B. Schneider and K. M. Barbera, "Introduction and Overview," in *The Oxford Handbook of Organizational Climate and Culture*, eds. B. Schneider and K. M. Barbera (New York, NY: Oxford University Press, 2014), 3–22.

13. J. Z. Carr, A. M. Schmidt, J. K. Ford, and R. P. DeShon, "Climate Perceptions Matter: A Meta-Analytic Path Analysis Relating Molar Climate, Cognitive and Affective States, and Individual Level Work Outcomes," *Journal of Applied Psychology* 88, no. 4 (2003): 605–619.

14. M. Schulte, C. Ostroff, S. Shmulyian, and A. Kinicki, "Organizational Climate Configurations: Relationships to Collective Attitudes, Customer Satisfaction, and Financial Performance."

15. S. D. Pugh, J. Dietz, A. P. Brief, and J. W. Wiley, "Looking Inside and Out: The Impact of Employee and Community Demographic Composition on Organizational Diversity Climate," *Journal of Applied Psychology* 93, no. 6 (2008): 1422–1428; K. H. Ehrhart, L. A. Witt, B. Schneider, and S. J. Perry, "Service Employees Give as They Get: Internal Service as a Moderator of the Service Climate-Service Outcomes Link," *Journal of Applied Psychology* 96, no. 2 (2011): 423–31; and A. Simha and J. B. Cullen, "Ethical Climates and Their Effects on Organizational Outcomes: Implications from the Past and Prophecies for the Future," *Academy of Management Perspectives* 26, no. 4 (2011): 20–34.

16. J. C. Wallace, D. Johnson, K. Mathe, and J. Paul, "Structural and Psychological Empowerment Climates, Performance, and the Moderating Role of Shared Felt Accountability: A Managerial Perspective," *Journal of Applied Psychology* 96, no. 3 (2011): 840–850.

17. J. M. Beus, S. C. Payne, M. E. Bergman, and W. Arthur, "Safety Climate and Injuries: An Examination of Theoretical and Empirical Relationships," *Journal of Applied Psychology* 95, no. 4 (2010): 713–727.

18. A. Simha and J. B. Cullen, "Ethical Climates and Their Effects on Organizational Outcomes: Implications from the Past and Prophecies for the Future," *Academy of Management Perspectives* 26, no. 4 (2011): 20–34.

19. Ibid.

20. J. Howard-Greenville, S. Bertels, and B. Lahneman, "Sustainability: How It Shapes Organizational Culture and Climate," in *The Oxford Handbook of Organizational Climate and Culture*, eds. B. Schneider and K. M. Barbera (New York, NY: Oxford University Press, 2014), 257–275.

21. P. Lacy, T. Cooper, R. Hayward, and L. Neuberger, "A New Era of Sustainability: UN Global Compact-Accenture CEO Study 2010," Joint Report from Accenture and the United Nations: The Global Compact, June 2010, https://www .unglobalcompact.org/docs/news_events/8.1/UNGC_Accenture_CEO_Study_2010.pdf.

22. B. Fitzgerald, "Sustainable Farming Will Be Next, 'Revolution in Agriculture,'" *Australian Broadcasting Company: Rural,* May 28, 2015, 10:12PM, http://www.abc.net.au/news/2015-05-29/state-of-tomorrow-sustainable-farming/6504842.

23. A. A. Marcus and A. R. Fremeth, "Green Management Matters Regardless," *Academy of Management Perspectives* 23, no. 3 (2009): 17–26.

24. P. Bansal, "From Issues to Actions: The Importance of Individual Concerns and Organizational Values in Responding to Natural Environmental Issues," *Organization Science* 14, no. 5 (2003): 510–527; P. Bansal, "Evolving Sustainably: A Longitudinal Study of Corporate Sustainable Development," *Strategic Management Journal* 26, no. 3 (2005): 197–218; and J. Howard-Grenville and A. J. Hoffman, "The Importance of Cultural Framing to the Success of Social Initiatives in Business," *Academy of Management Executive* 17, no. 2 (2003): 70–84.

25. A. R. Carrico and M. Riemer, "Motivating Energy Conservation in the Workplace: An Evaluation of the Use of Group-Level Feedback and Peer Education," *Journal of Environmental Psychology* 31, no. 1 (2011): 1–13.

26. J. P. Kotter, "Change Management: Accelerate!" *Harvard Business Review,* November 2012: 44–58.

27. R. Walker, "Behind the Music," *Fortune,* October 29, 2012, 57–58.

28. J. P. Titlow, "How Spotify's Music-Obsessed Culture Keeps Employees Hooked," *Fast Company,* August 20, 2014, http://www.fastcompany.com/3034617/how-spotifys-music-obsessed-culture-makes-the-company-rock.

29. E. Ries, *The Lean Startup* (New York: Crown Publishing, 2011).

30. M. Herper, "Niche Pharma," *Forbes,* September 24, 2012, 80–89.

31. J. Bandler and D. Burke, "How HP Lost Its Way," *Fortune,* May 21, 2012, 147–164.

32. G. F. Lanzara and G. Patriotta, "The Institutionalization of Knowledge in an Automotive Factory: Templates, Inscriptions, and the Problems of Durability," *Organization Studies* 28, no. 5 (2007): 635–660; and T. B. Lawrence, M. K. Mauws, B. Dyck, and R. F. Kleysen, "The Politics of Organizational Learning: Integrating Power into the 4I Framework," *Academy of Management Review* 30, no. 1 (2005): 180–191.

33. L. G. Flores, W. Zheng, D. Rau, and C. H. Thomas, "Organizational Learning: Subprocess Identification, Construct Validation, and an Empirical Test of Cultural Antecedents," *Journal of Management* 38, no. 2 (2012): 640–667; and W. S. Shim and R. M. Steers, "Symmetric and Asymmetric Leadership Cultures: A Comparative Study of Leadership and Organizational Culture at Hyundai and Toyota," *Journal of World Business* 47, no. 4 (2012): 581–591.

34. See D. L. Stone, E. F. Stone-Romero, and K. M. Lukaszewski, "The Impact of Cultural Values on the Acceptance and Effectiveness of Human Resource Management Policies and Practices," *Human Resource Management Review* 17, no. 2 (2007): 152–165; D. R. Avery, "Support for Diversity in Organizations: A Theoretical Exploration of Its Origins and Offshoots," *Organizational Psychology Review* 1, no. 3 (2011): 239–256; and A. Groggins and A. M. Ryan, "Embracing Uniqueness: The Underpinnings of a Positive Climate for Diversity," *Journal of Occupational and Organizational Psychology* 86, no. 2 (2013): 264–282.

35. D. Liu, T. R. Mitchell, T. W. Lee, B. C. Holtom, and T. R. Hinkin, "When Employees Are out of Step with Coworkers: How Job Satisfaction Trajectory and Dispersion Influence Individual and Unit-Level Voluntary Turnover," *Academy of Management Journal* 55, no. 6 (2012): 360–1380.

36. R. A. Weber and C. F. Camerer, "Cultural Conflict and Merger Failure: An Experimental Approach," *Management Science* 49, no. 4 (2003): 400–412; I. H. Gleibs, A. Mummendey, and P. Noack, "Predictors of Change in Postmerger Identification during a Merger Process: A Longitudinal Study," *Journal of Personality and Social Psychology* 95, no. 5 (2008): 1095–1112; and F. Bauer and K. Matzler, "Antecedents of M&A Success: The Role of Strategic Complementarity, Cultural Fit, and Degree and Speed of Integration," *Strategic Management Journal* 35, no. 2 (2014): 269–291.

37. K. Voigt, "Mergers Fail More Often Than Marriages," *CNN,* May 22, 2009, http://edition.cnn.com/2009/BUSINESS/05/21/merger.marriage/.

38. Y. L. Zhao, O. H. Erekson, T. Wang, and M. Song, "Pioneering Advantages and Entrepreneurs' First-Mover Decisions: An Empirical Investigation for the United States and China," *Journal of Product Innovation Management* 29, no. S1 (2012): 190–210.

39. E. H. Schein, *Organizational Culture and Leadership*, Vol. 2. (New York, NY: John Wiley & Sons, 2010).

40. See, for example, D. E. Bowen and C. Ostroff, "The 'Strength' of the HRM System, Organizational Climate Formation, and Firm Performance," *Academy of Management Review* 29, no. 2 (2004): 203–221.

41. W. Li, Y. Wang, P. Taylor, K. Shi, and D. He, "The Influence of Organizational Culture on Work-Related Personality Requirement Ratings: A Multilevel Analysis," *International Journal of Selection and Assessment* 16, no. 4 (2008): 366–384; I. Oh, K. S. Kim, and C. H. Van Iddekinge, "Taking It to another Level: Do Personality-Based Human Capital Resources Matter to Firm Performance?" *Journal of Applied Psychology* 100, no. 3 (2015): 935–947; and A. Bardi, K. E. Buchanan, R. Goodwin, L. Slabu, and M. Robinson, "Value Stability and Change during Self-Chosen Life Transitions: Self-Selection versus Socialization Effects," *Journal of Personality and Social Psychology* 106, no. 1 (2014): 131–147.

42. D. C. Hambrick, "Upper Echelons Theory: An Update," *Academy of Management Review* 32, no. 2 (2007): 334–343; M. A. Carpenter, M. A. Geletkanycz, and W. G. Sanders, "Upper Echelons Research Revisited: Antecedents, Elements, and Consequences of Top Management Team Composition," *Journal of Management* 30, no. 6 (2004): 749–778; and H. Wang, A. S. Tsui, and K. R. Xin, "CEO Leadership Behaviors, Organizational Performance, and Employees' Attitudes," *Leadership Quarterly* 22, no. 1 (2011): 92–105.

43. V. Tabvuma, Y. Georgellis, and T. Lange, "Orientation Training and Job Satisfaction: A Sector and Gender Analysis," *Human Resource Management* 54, no. 2 (2015): 303–321; and T. N. Bauer, T. Bodner, B. Erdogan, D. M. Truxillo, and J. S. Tucker, "Newcomer Adjustment during Organizational Socialization: A Meta-Analytic Review of Antecedents, Outcomes, and Methods," *Journal of Applied Psychology* 92, no. 3 (2007): 707–721.

44. R. E. Silverman, "Companies Try to Make the First Day for New Hires More Fun," *The Wall Street Journal,* May 28, 2013, http://online.wsj.com/article/SB10001424127887323336104578501631475934850.html.

45. D. M. Cable, F. Gino, and B. R. Staats, "Breaking Them in or Eliciting Their Best? Reframing Socialization around Newcomers' Authentic Self-Expression," *Administrative Science Quarterly* 58, no. 1 (2013): 1–36; and M. Wang, J. Kammeyer-Mueller, and Y. Liu, "Context, Socialization, and Newcomer Learning," *Organizational Psychology Review* 5, no. 1 (2015): 3–25.

46. C. J. Collins, "The Interactive Effects of Recruitment Practices and Product Awareness on Job Seekers' Employer Knowledge and Application Behaviors," *Journal of Applied Psychology* 92, no. 1 (2007): 180–190.

47. J. D. Kammeyer-Mueller and C. R. Wanberg, "Unwrapping the Organizational Entry Process: Disentangling Multiple Antecedents and Their Pathways to Adjustment," *Journal of Applied Psychology* 88, no. 5 (2003): 779–794; E. W. Morrison, "Longitudinal Study of the Effects of Information Seeking on Newcomer Socialization," *Journal of Applied Psychology* 78, no. 2 (2003): 173–183; and M. Wang, Y. Zhan, E. McCune, and D. Truxillo, "Understanding Newcomers' Adaptability and Work-Related Outcomes: Testing the Mediating Roles of Perceived P-E Fit Variables," *Personnel Psychology* 64, no. 1 (2011): 163–189.

48. A. M. Ellis, T. N. Bauer, L. R. Mansfield, B. Erdogan, D. M. Truxillo, and L. S. Simon, "Navigating Uncharted Waters: Newcomer Socialization through the Lens of Stress Theory," *Journal of Management* 41, no. 1 (2015): 203–235; and E. Lapointe, C. Vandenberghe, and J.-S. Boudrias, "Organizational Socialization Tactics and Newcomer Adjustment: The Mediating Role of Role Clarity and Affect-Based Trust Relationships," *Journal of Occupational and Organizational Psychology* 87, no. 3 (2014): 599–624.

49. T. N. Bauer, T. Bodner, B. Erdogan, D. M. Truxillo, and J. S. Tucker, "Newcomer Adjustment during Organizational Socialization: A Meta-Analytic Review of Antecedents, Outcomes, and Methods," *Journal of Applied Psychology* 92, no. 3 (2007): 707–721.

50. W. R. Boswell, A. J. Shipp, S. C. Payne, and S. S. Culbertson, "Changes in Newcomer Job Satisfaction over Time: Examining the Pattern of Honeymoons and Hangovers," *Journal of Applied Psychology* 94, no. 4 (2009): 844–858; and W. R. Boswell, J. W. Boudreau, and J. Tichy, "The Relationship between Employee Job Change and Job Satisfaction: The Honeymoon-Hangover Effect," *Journal of Applied Psychology* 90, no. 5 (2005): 882–892.

51. J. D. Kammeyer-Mueller, C. R. Wanberg, A. L. Rubenstein, and Z. Song, "Support, Undermining, and Newcomer Socialization: Fitting in during the First 90 Days," *Academy of Management Journal* 56, no. 4 (2013): 1104–1124; and M. Jokisaari and J. Nurmi, "Change in Newcomers' Supervisor Support and Socialization Outcomes after Organizational Entry," *Academy of Management Journal* 52, no. 3 (2009): 527–544.

52. C. Vandenberghe, A. Panaccio, K. Bentein, K. Mignonac, and P. Roussel, "Assessing Longitudinal Change of and Dynamic Relationships among Role Stressors, Job Attitudes, Turnover Intention, and Well-Being in Neophyte Newcomers," *Journal of Organizational Behavior* 32, no. 4 (2011): 652–671.

53. E. Ransdell, "The Nike Story? Just Tell It!" *Fast Company,* January–February 2000, 44–46; and A. Muccino, "Exclusive Interview with Chuck Eichten," *Liquid Brand Summit* (blog), February 4, 2011, http://blog.liquidbrandsummit.com/once-there-was-a-brand-qa-with-nike-design-director-chuck-eichten/.

54. S. L. Dailey and L. Browning, "Retelling Stories in Organizations: Understanding the Functions of Narrative Repetition," *Academy of Management Review* 39, no. 1 (2014): 22–43.

55. A. J. Shipp and K. J. Jansen, "Reinterpreting Time in Fit Theory: Crafting and Recrafting Narratives of Fit in Medias Res," *Academy of Management Review* 36, no. 1 (2011): 76–101.

56. See G. Islam and M. J. Zyphur, "Rituals in Organizations: A Review and Expansion of Current Theory," *Group & Organization Management* 34, no. 1 (2009): 114–39.

57. M. Moskowitz and F. Levering, "The 100 Best Companies to Work For," *Fortune,* February 6, 2012, 120.

58. A. Bryant, "Take the Bus, and Watch the Ideas Flow," *The New York Times,* September 16, 2012, 2.

59. M. G. Pratt and A. Rafaeli "Artifacts and Organizations: Understanding Our Objective Reality," in *Artifacts and Organizations: Beyond Mere Symbolism*, eds. A. Rafaeli and M. G. Pratt (Mahwah, NJ: Lawrence Erlbaum, 2006), 279–288.

60. B. Gruley, "Relaxed Fit," *Bloomberg Businessweek,* September 17–23, 2012, 98–99.

61. M. Moskowitz and R. Levering, "The 100 Best Companies to Work For," *Fortune,* February 6, 2012, 117–124.

62. A. Ardichvilli, J. A. Mitchell, and D. Jondle, "Characteristics of Ethical Business Cultures," *Journal of Business Ethics* 85, no. 4 (2009): 445–451; D. M. Mayer, "A Review of the Literature on Ethical Climate and Culture," in *The Oxford Handbook of Organizational Climate and Culture*, eds. B. Schneider and K. M. Barbera (New York, NY: Oxford University Press, 2014), 415–440.

63. J. P. Mulki, J. F. Jaramillo, and W. B. Locander, "Critical Role of Leadership on Ethical Climate and Salesperson Behaviors," *Journal of Business Ethics* 86, no. 2 (2009): 125–141; M. Schminke, M. L. Ambrose, and D. O. Neubaum, "The Effect of Leader Moral Development on Ethical Climate and Employee Attitudes," *Organizational Behavior and Human Decision Processes* 97, no. 2 (2005): 135–151; and M. E. Brown, L. K. Treviño, and D. A. Harrison, "Ethical Leadership: A Social Learning Perspective for Construct Development and Testing," *Organizational Behavior and Human Decision Processes* 97, no. 2 (2005): 117–134.

64. D. M. Mayer, M. Kuenzi, R. Greenbaum, M. Bardes, and S. Salvador, "How Low Does Ethical Leadership Flow? Test of a Trickle-Down Model," *Organizational Behavior and Human Decision Processes* 108, no. 1 (2009): 1–13; and L. J. Christensen, A. Mackey, and D. Whetten, "Taking Responsibility for Corporate Social Responsibility: The Role of Leaders in Creating, Implementing, Sustaining, or Avoiding Socially Responsible Firm Behaviors," *Academy of Management Perspectives* 28, no. 2 (2014): 164–178.

65. B. Sweeney, D. Arnold, and B. Pierce, "The Impact of Perceived Ethical Culture of the Firm and Demographic Variables on Auditors' Ethical Evaluation and Intention to Act Decisions," *Journal of Business Ethics* 93, no. 4 (2010): 531–551.

66. M. L. Gruys, S. M. Stewart, J. Goodstein, M. N. Bing, and A. C. Wicks, "Values Enactment in Organizations: A Multi-Level Examination," *Journal of Management* 34, no. 4 (2008): 806–843.

67. D. L. Nelson and C. L. Cooper eds., *Positive Organizational Behavior* (London, UK: Sage, 2007); K. S. Cameron, J. E. Dutton, and R. E. Quinn, eds., *Positive Organizational Scholarship: Foundations of a New Discipline* (San Francisco, CA: Berrett-Koehler, 2003); and F. Luthans and C. M. Youssef, "Emerging Positive Organizational Behavior," *Journal of Management* 33, no. 3 (2007): 321–349.

68. S. Fineman, "On Being Positive: Concerns and Counterpoints," *Academy of Management Review* 31, no. 2 (2006): 270–291.

69. E. Poole, "Organisational Spirituality: A Literature Review," *Journal of Business Ethics* 84, no. 4 (2009): 577–588.

70. L. W. Fry and J. W. Slocum, "Managing the Triple Bottom Line through Spiritual Leadership," *Organizational Dynamics* 37, no. 1 (2008): 86–96.

71. See, for example, C. L. Jurkiewicz and R. A. Giacalone, "A Values Framework for Measuring the Impact of Workplace Spirituality on Organizational Performance," *Journal of Business Ethics* 49, no. 2 (2004): 129–142.

72. See, for example, B. S. Pawar, "Workplace Spirituality Facilitation: A Comprehensive Model," *Journal of Business Ethics* 90, no. 3 (2009): 375–386; and L. Lambert, *Spirituality Inc.: Religion in the American Workplace* (New York: University Press, 2009).

73. M. Oppenheimer, "The Rise of the Corporate Chaplain," *Bloomberg Businessweek,* August 23, 2012, 58–61.

74. M. Lips-Miersma, K. L. Dean, and C. J. Fornaciari, "Theorizing the Dark Side of the Workplace Spirituality Movement," *Journal of Management Inquiry* 18, no. 4 (2009): 288–300.

75. J.-C. Garcia-Zamor, "Workplace Spirituality and Organizational Performance," *Public Administration Review* 63, no. 3 (2003): 355–363; and L. W. Fry, S. T. Hannah, M. Noel, and F. O. Walumbwa, "Impact of Spiritual Leadership on Unit Performance," *Leadership Quarterly* 22, no. 2 (2011): 259–270.

76. A. Rego and M. Pina e Cunha, "Workplace Spirituality and Organizational Commitment: An Empirical Study," *Journal of Organizational Change Management* 21, no. 1 (2008): 53–75; R. W. Kolodinsky, R. A. Giacalone, and C. L. Jurkiewicz, "Workplace Values and Outcomes: Exploring Personal, Organizational, and Interactive Workplace Spirituality," *Journal of Business Ethics* 81, no. 2 (2008): 465–480; and M. Gupta, V. Kumar, and M. Singh, "Creating Satisfied Employees through Workplace Spirituality: A Study of the Private Insurance Sector in Punjab, India," *Journal of Business Ethics* 122, no. 1 (2014): 79–88.

77. D. J. McCarthy and S. M. Puffer, "Interpreting the Ethicality of Corporate Governance Decision in Russia: Utilizing Integrative Social Contracts Theory to Evaluate the Relevance of Agency Theory Norms," *Academy of Management Review* 33, no. 1 (2008): 11–31.

CHAPTER 17

1. See, for instance, J. Birkinshaw, G. Hamel, and M. J. Mol, "Management Innovation," *Academy of Management Review* 33, no. 4 (2008): 825–845; and J. Welch and S. Welch, "What Change Agents Are Made Of," *BusinessWeek*, October 20, 2008, 96.

2. P. G. Audia and S. Brion, "Reluctant to Change: Self-Enhancing Responses to Diverging Performance Measures," *Organizational Behavior and Human Decision Processes* 102, no. 2 (2007): 255–269.

3. M. Fugate, A. J. Kinicki, and G. E. Prussia, "Employee Coping with Organizational Change: An Examination of Alternative Theoretical Perspectives and Models," *Personnel Psychology* 61, no. 1 (2008): 1–36.

4. R. B. L. Sijbom, O. Janssen, and N. W. Van Yperen, "How to Get Radical Creative Ideas into a Leader's Mind? Leader's

Achievement Goals and Subordinates' Voice of Creative Ideas," *European Journal of Work and Organizational Psychology* 24, no. 2 (2015): 279–296.

5. J. D. Ford, L. W. Ford, and A. D'Amelio, "Resistance to Change: The Rest of the Story," *Academy of Management Review* 33, no. 2 (2008): 362–377.

6. R. K. Smollan, "The Multi-Dimensional Nature of Resistance to Change," *Journal of Management & Organization* 17, no. 6 (2011): 828–849.

7. P. C. Fiss and E. J. Zajac, "The Symbolic Management of Strategic Change: Sensegiving via Framing and Decoupling," *Academy of Management Journal* 49, no. 6 (2006): 1173–1193.

8. A. E. Rafferty and S. L. D. Restubog, "The Impact of Change Process and Context on Change Reactions and Turnover during a Merger," *Journal of Management* 36, no. 5 (2010): 1309–1338.

9. D. M. Herold, D. B. Fedor, and S. D. Caldwell, "Beyond Change Management: A Multilevel Investigation of Contextual and Personal Influences on Employees' Commitment to Change," *Journal of Applied Psychology* 92, no. 4 (2007): 942–951; and G. B. Cunningham, "The Relationships among Commitment to Change, Coping with Change, and Turnover Intentions," *European Journal of Work and Organizational Psychology* 15, no. 1 (2006): 29–45.

10. R. Peccei, A. Giangreco, and A. Sebastiano, "The Role of Organizational Commitment in the Analysis of Resistance to Change: Co-predictor and Moderator Effects," *Personnel Review* 40, no. 2 (2011): 185–204.

11. J. P. Kotter, "Leading Change: Why Transformational Efforts Fail," *Harvard Business Review,* January 2007, 96–103.

12. K. van Dam, S. Oreg, and B. Schyns, "Daily Work Contexts and Resistance to Organisational Change: The Role of Leader–Member Exchange, Development Climate, and Change Process Characteristics," *Applied Psychology: An International Review* 57, no. 2 (2008): 313–334.

13. A. H. Y. Hon, M. Bloom, and J. M. Crant, "Overcoming Resistance to Change and Enhancing Creative Performance," *Journal of Management* 40, no. 3 (2014): 919–941.

14. S. Oreg and N. Sverdlik, "Ambivalence toward Imposed Change: The Conflict between Dispositional Resistance to Change and the Orientation toward the Change Agent," *Journal of Applied Psychology* 96, no. 2 (2011): 337–349.

15. D. B. Fedor, S. Caldwell, and D. M. Herold, "The Effects of Organizational Changes on Employee Commitment: A Multilevel Investigation," *Personnel Psychology* 59, no. 1 (2006): 1–29; and R. D. Foster, "Resistance, Justice, and Commitment to Change," *Human Resource Development Quarterly* 21, no. 1 (2010): 3–39.

16. S. Oreg, "Personality, Context, and Resistance to Organizational Change," *European Journal of Work and Organizational Psychology* 15, no. 1 (2006): 73–101.

17. S. M. Elias, "Employee Commitment in Times of Change: Assessing the Importance of Attitudes toward Organizational Change," *Journal of Management* 35, no. 1 (2009): 37–55.

18. J. W. B. Lang and P. D. Bliese, "General Mental Ability and Two Types of Adaptation to Unforeseen Change: Applying Discontinuous Growth Models to the Task-Change Paradigm," *Journal of Applied Psychology* 94, no. 2 (2009): 411–428.

19. See, for instance, A. Karaevli, "Performance Consequences for New CEO 'Outsiderness': Moderating Effects of Pre- and Post-Succession Contexts," *Strategic Management Journal* 28, no. 7 (2007): 681–706.

20. See, for instance, J. Manchester et al., "Facilitating Lewin's Change Model with Collaborative Evaluation in Promoting Evidence Based Practices of Health Professionals," *Evaluation and Program Planning* 47 (2014): 82–90.

21. P. G. Audia, E. A. Locke, and K. G. Smith, "The Paradox of Success: An Archival and a Laboratory Study of Strategic Persistence Following Radical Environmental Change," *Academy of Management Journal* 43, no. 5 (2000): 837–853; and P. G. Audia and S. Brion, "Reluctant to Change: Self-Enhancing Responses to Diverging Performance Measures," *Organizational Behavior and Human Decision Processes* 102, no. 2 (2007): 255–269.

22. See, for instance, J. Kim, "Use of Kotter's Leading Change Model to Develop and Implement a Heart Failure Education Program for Certified Nursing Assistants in a Long-Term Care Facility," *Nursing Research* 64, no. 2 (2015): E35; and J. Pollack and R. Pollack, "Using Kotter's Eight Stage Process to Manage an Organisational Change Program: Presentation and Practice," *Systemic Practice and Action Research* 28, no. 1 (2015): 41–66.

23. See, for example, L. S. Lüscher and M. W. Lewis, "Organizational Change and Managerial Sensemaking: Working through Paradox," *Academy of Management Journal* 51, no. 2 (2008): 221–240.

24. For example, see R. J. Marshak and D. Grant, "Organizational Discourse and New Organization Development Practices," *British Journal of Management* 19, no. 1 (2008): S7–S19.

25. See, for instance, R. Lines, "Influence of Participation in Strategic Change: Resistance, Organizational Commitment and Change Goal Achievement," *Journal of Change Management* 4, no. 3 (2004): 193–215.

26. M. J. Mol and J. Birkinshaw, "The Role of External Involvement in the Creation of Management Innovations," *Organization Studies* 35, no. 9 (2014): 1287–1312; and R. Slater and A. Coyle, "The Governing of the Self/the Self-Governing Self: Multi-Rater Feedback and Practices 1940–2011," *Theory & Psychology* 24, no. 2 (2014): 233–255.

27. T. Fauth, K. Hattrub, K. Mueller, and B. Roberts, "Nonresponse in Employee Attitude Surveys: A Group-Level Analysis," *Journal of Business and Psychology* 28, no. 1 (2013): 1–16.

28. F. J. Lambrechts, R. Bouwen, S. Grieten, J. P. Huybrechts, and E. H. Schein, "Learning to Help through Humble Inquiry and Implications for Management Research, Practice, and Education: An Interview with Edgar H. Schein," *Academy of Management Learning & Education* 10, no. 1 (2011): 131–148.

29. W. W. G. Dyer, W. G. Dyer, and J. H. Dyer, *Team Building: Proven Strategies for Improving Team Performance* (Hoboken, NJ: Jossey-Bass, 2007).

30. U. Wagner, L. Tropp, G. Finchilescu, and C. Tredoux, eds., *Improving Intergroup Relations* (New York, NY: Wiley-Blackwell, 2008).

31. See, for example, B. Verleysen, F. Lambrechts, and F. Van Acker, "Building Psychological Capital with Appreciative Inquiry: Investigating the Mediating Role of Basic Psychological Need Satisfaction," *Journal of Applied Behavioral Science* 51, no. 1 (2015): 10–35.

32. P. Jarzabkowski, J. Lê, and A. Van de Ven, "Responding to Competing Strategic Demands: How Organizing, Belonging, and Performing Paradoxes Coevolve," *Strategic Organization* 11, no. 3 (2013): 245–280; and W. K. Smith, "Dynamic

Decision Making: A Model of Senior Leaders Managing Strategic Paradoxes," *Academy of Management Journal* 57, no. 6 (2014): 1592–1623.

33. J. Jay, "Navigating Paradox as a Mechanism of Change and Innovation in Hybrid Organizations," *Academy of Management Journal* 56, no. 1 (2013): 137–159.

34. Y. Zhang, D. A. Waldman, Y. Han, and X. Li, "Paradoxical Leader Behaviors in People Management: Antecedents and Consequences," *Academy of Management Journal* 58, no. 2 (2015): 538–566.

35. See, for instance, G. P. Pisano, "You Need an Innovation Strategy," *Harvard Business Review,* June 2015, 44–54.

36. H. W. Volberda, F. A. J. Van den Bosch, and C. V. Heij, "Management Innovation: Management as Fertile Ground for Innovation," *European Management Review* 10, no. 1 (2013): 1–15.

37. F. Damanpour, "Organizational Innovation: A Meta-Analysis of Effects of Determinants and Moderators," *Academy of Management Journal* 34, no. 3 (1991): 555–590; and G. Westerman, F. W. McFarlan, and M. Iansiti, "Organization Design and Effectiveness over the Innovation Life Cycle," *Organization Science* 17, no. 2 (2006): 230–238.

38. See P. Schepers and P. T. Van den Berg, "Social Factors of Work-Environment Creativity," *Journal of Business and Psychology* 21, no. 3 (2007): 407–428.

39. S. Chang, L. Jia, R. Takeuchi, and Y. Cai, "Do High-Commitment Work Systems Affect Creativity? A Multilevel Combinational Approach to Employee Creativity," *Journal of Applied Psychology* 99, no. 4 (2014): 665–680.

40. M. E. Mullins, S. W. J. Kozlowski, N. Schmitt, and A. W. Howell, "The Role of the Idea Champion in Innovation: The Case of the Internet in the Mid-1990s," *Computers in Human Behavior* 24, no. 2 (2008): 451–467.

41. C. Y. Murnieks, E. Mosakowski, and M. S. Cardon, "Pathways of Passion: Identity Centrality, Passion, and Behavior among Entrepreneurs," *Journal of Management* 40, no. 6 (2014): 1583–1606.

42. S. C. Parker, "Intrapreneurship or Entrepreneurship?" *Journal of Business Venturing* 26, no. 1 (2011): 19–34.

43. M. Č, M. Jaklič, and M. Škerlavaj, "Decoupling Management and Technological Innovations: Resolving the Individualism-Collectivism Controversy," *Journal of International Management* 19, no. 2 (2013): 103–117.

44. See, for example, T. B. Lawrence, M. K. Mauws, B. Dyck, and R. F. Kleysen, "The Politics of Organizational Learning: Integrating Power into the 4I Framework," *Academy of Management Review* 30, no. 1 (2005): 180–191.

45. J. Kim, T. Egan, and H. Tolson, "Examining the Dimensions of the Learning Organization Questionnaire: A Review and Critique of Research Utilizing the DLOQ," *Human Resource Development Review* 14, no. 1 (2015): 91–112.

46. L. Berghman, P. Matthyssens, S. Streukens, and K. Vandenbempt, "Deliberate Learning Mechanisms for Stimulating Strategic Innovation Capacity," *Long Range Planning* 46, nos. 1–2 (2013): 39–71.

47. M.-G. Seo, M. S. Taylor, N. S. Hill, X. Zhang, P. E. Tesluk, and N. M. Lorinkova, "The Role of Affect and Leadership during Organizational Change," *Personnel Psychology* 65, no. 1 (2012): 121–165.

48. M. Fugate, G. E. Prussia, and A. J. Kinicki, "Managing Employee Withdrawal during Organizational Change: The Role of Threat Appraisal," *Journal of Management* 38, no. 3 (2012): 890–914.

49. J. Shin, M. S. Taylor, and M.-G. Seo, "Resources for Change: The Relationships of Organizational Inducements and Psychological Resilience to Employees' Attitudes and Behaviors toward Organizational Change," *Academy of Management Journal* 55, no. 3 (2012): 727–748.

50. B. Mirza, "Workplace Stress Hits Three-Year High," *HR Magazine,* April 2012, 15.

51. "What Is Stress?" from The American Institute of Stress website, accessed February 24, 2016, http://www.stress.org/what-is-stress.

52. Ibid.

53. N. P. Podsakoff, J. A. LePine, and M. A. LePine, "Differential Challenge-Hindrance Stressor Relationships with Job Attitudes, Turnover Intentions, Turnover, and Withdrawal Behavior: A Meta-Analysis," *Journal of Applied Psychology* 92, no. 2 (2007): 438–54; and J. A. LePine, M. A. LePine, and C. L. Jackson, "Challenge and Hindrance Stress: Relationships with Exhaustion, Motivation to Learn, and Learning Performance," *Journal of Applied Psychology* 89, no. 5 (2004): 883–891.

54. J. C. Wallace, B. D. Edwards, T. Arnold, M. L. Frazier, and D. M. Finch, "Work Stressors, Role-Based Performance, and the Moderating Influence of Organizational Support," *Journal of Applied Psychology* 94, no. 1 (2009): 254–262.

55. IBID

56. A. B. Bakker, E. Demerouti, and A. I. Sanz-Vergel, "Burnout and Work Engagement: The JD-R Approach," *Annual Review of Organizational Psychology and Organizational Behavior* 1 (2014): 389–411.

57. "Stress in America: Paying with Our Health," *American Psychological Association press release,* February 4, 2015, from the APA website, https://www.apa.org/news/press/releases/stress/2014/stress-report.pdf.

58. J. de Jonge and C. Dormann, "Stressors, Resources, and Strain at Work: A Longitudinal Test of the Triple-Match Principle," *Journal of Applied Psychology* 91, no. 5 (2006): 1359–1374.

59. D. C. Ganster and C. C. Rosen, "Work Stress and Employee Health: A Multidisciplinary Review," *Journal of Management* 39, no. 5 (2013): 1085–1122.

60. P. Sterling, "Allostasis: A Model of Predictive Regulation," *Physiology & Behavior* 106, no. 1 (2012): 5–15.

61. S. Gilboa, A. Shirom, Y. Fried, and C. L. Cooper, "A Meta-Analysis of Work Demand Stressors and Job Performance: Examining Main and Moderating Effects," *Personnel Psychology* 61, no. 2 (2008): 227–271.

62. A. E. Rafferty and M. A. Griffin, "Perceptions of Organizational Change: A Stress and Coping Perspective," *Journal of Applied Psychology* 71, no. 5 (2007): 1154–1162.

63. R. Ilies, N. Dimotakis, and I. E. De Pater, "Psychological and Physiological Reactions to High Workloads: Implications for Well-Being," *Personnel Psychology* 63, no. 2 (2010): 407–436; and A. B. Bakker, E. Demerouti, and A. I. Sanz-Vergel, "Burnout and Work Engagement: The JD–R Approach," *Annual Review of Organizational Psychology and Organizational Behavior* 1 (2014): 389–411.

64. T. L. Smith-Jackson and K. W. Klein, "Open-Plan Offices: Task Performance and Mental Workload," *Journal of Environmental Psychology* 29, no. 2 (2009): 279–289.

65. C. Fritz and S. Sonnentag, "Antecedents of Day-Level Proactive Behavior: A Look at Job Stressors and Positive Affect during the Workday," *Journal of Management* 35, no. 1 (2009): 94–111.

66. S. Lim, L. M. Cortina, and V. J. Magley, "Personal and Work-group Incivility: Impact on Work and Health Outcomes," *Journal of Applied Psychology* 93, no. 1 (2008): 95–107; N. T. Buchanan and L. F. Fitzgerald, "Effects of Racial and Sexual Harassment on Work and the Psychological Well-Being of African American Women," *Journal of Occupational Health Psychology* 13, no. 2 (2008): 137–151; C. R. Willness, P. Steel, and K. Lee, "A Meta-Analysis of the Antecedents and Consequences of Workplace Sexual Harassment," *Personnel Psychology* 60, no. 1 (2007): 127–162; and B. Moreno-Jiménez, A. Rodríguez-Muñoz, J. C. Pastor, A. I. Sanz-Vergel, and E. Garrosa, "The Moderating Effects of Psychological Detachment and Thoughts of Revenge in Workplace Bullying," *Personality and Individual Differences* 46, no. 3 (2009): 359–364.

67. L. Yang, J. Bauer, R. E. Johnson, M. W. Groer, and K. Salomon, "Physiological Mechanisms That Underlie the Effects of Interactional Unfairness on Deviant Behavior: The Role of Cortisol Activity," *Journal of Applied Psychology* 99, no. 2 (2014): 310–321.

68. M. T. Schmitt, N. R. Branscombe, T. Postmes, and A. Garcia, "The Consequences of Perceived Discrimination for Psychological Well-Being: A Meta-Analytic Review," *Psychological Bulletin* 140, no. 4 (2014): 921–948.

69. "Stress in America: Paying with Our Health," *American Psychological Association,* February 4, 2015, http://www.apa.org/news/press/releases/stress/2014/stress-report.pdf.

70. Q. Hu, W. B. Schaufeli, and T. W. Taris, "The Job Demands–Resources Model: An Analysis of Additive and Joint Effects of Demands and Resources," *Journal of Vocational Behavior* 79, no. 1 (2011): 181–190.

71. E. R. Crawford, J. A. LePine, and B. L. Rich, "Linking Job Demands and Resources to Employee Engagement and Burnout: A Theoretical Extension and Meta-Analytic Test," *Journal of Applied Psychology* 95, no. 5 (2010): 834–848.

72. See J. B. Halbesleben, "Sources of Social Support and Burnout: A Meta-Analytic Test of the Conservation of Resources Model," *Journal of Applied Psychology* 91, no. 5 (2006): 1134–1145; N. Bolger and D. Amarel, "Effects of Social Support Visibility on Adjustment to Stress: Experimental Evidence," *Journal of Applied Psychology* 92, no. 3 (2007): 458–475; and C. Fernet, M. Gagné, and S. Austin, "When Does Quality of Relationships with Coworkers Predict Burnout over Time? The Moderating Role of Work Motivation," *Journal of Organizational Behavior* 31, no. 8 (2010): 1163–1180.

73. J. B. Avey, F. Luthans, and S. M. Jensen, "Psychological Capital: A Positive Resource for Combating Employee Stress and Turnover," *Human Resource Management* 48, no. 5 (2009): 677–693.

74. See, for example, C. M. Middeldorp, D. C. Cath, A. L. Beem, G. Willemsen, and D. I. Boomsma, "Life Events, Anxious Depression, and Personality: A Prospective and Genetic Study," *Psychological Medicine* 38, no. 11 (2008): 1557–1565; A. A. Uliaszek et al. "The Role of Neuroticism and Extraversion in the Stress-Anxiety and Stress-Depression Relationships," *Anxiety, Stress, and Coping* 23, no. 4 (2010): 363–381.

75. J. D. Kammeyer-Mueller, T. A. Judge, and B. A. Scott, "The Role of Core Self-Evaluations in the Coping Process," *Journal of Applied Psychology* 94, no. 1 (2009): 177–195.

76. J. Chen, C. Silverthorne, and J. Hung, "Organization Communication, Job Stress, Organizational Commitment, and Job Performance of Accounting Professionals in Taiwan and America," *Leadership & Organization Development Journal* 27, no. 4 (2006): 242–249; and C. Liu, P. E. Spector, and L. Shi, "Cross-National Job Stress: A Quantitative and Qualitative Study," *Journal of Organizational Behavior* 28, no. 2 (2007): 209–239.

77. P. E. Spector et al., "Cross National Differences in Relationships of Work Demands, Job Satisfaction, and Turnover Intention with Work-Family Conflict," *Personnel Psychology* 60, no. 4 (2007): 805–835.

78. H. M. Addae and X. Wang, "Stress at Work: Linear and Curvilinear Effects of Psychological-, Job-, and Organization-Related Factors: An Exploratory Study of Trinidad and Tobago," *International Journal of Stress Management* 13, no. 4 (2006): 476–493.

79. M. Kivimäki, J. Head, J. E. Ferrie, E. Brunner, M. G. Marmot, J. Vahtera, and M. J. Shipley, "Why Is Evidence on Job Strain and Coronary Heart Disease Mixed? An Illustration of Measurement Challenges in the Whitehall II Study," *Psychosomatic Medicine* 68, no. 3 (2006): 398–401.

80. M. Borritz et al., "Impact on Burnout and Psychosocial Work Characteristics on Future Long-Term Sickness Absence, Prospective Results of the Danish PUMA Study among Human Service Workers," *Journal of Occupational and Environmental Medicine* 52, no. 10 (2010): 964–970.

81. R. Ilies, N. Dimotakis, and I. E. DePater, "Psychological and Physiological Reactions to High Workloads: Implications for Well-Being," *Personnel Psychology* 63, no. 2 (2010): 407–463.

82. D. Örtqvist and J. Wincent, "Prominent Consequences of Role Stress: A Meta-Analytic Review," *International Journal of Stress Management* 13, no. 4 (2006): 399–422.

83. J. J. Hakanen, A. B. Bakker, and M. Jokisaari, "A 35-Year Follow-Up Study on Burnout among Finnish Employees," *Journal of Occupational Health Psychology* 16 no. 3 (2011): 345–360; E. R. Crawford, J. A. LePine, and B. L. Rich, "Linking Job Demands and Resources to Employee Engagement and Burnout: A Theoretical Extension and Meta-Analytic Test," *Journal of Applied Psychology* 95, no. 5 (2010): 834–848; and G. A. Chung-Yan, "The Nonlinear Effects of Job Complexity and Autonomy on Job Satisfaction, Turnover, and Psychological Well-Being," *Journal of Occupational Health Psychology* 15, no. 3 (2010): 237–251.

84. L. L. Meier, N. K. Semmer, A. Elfering, and N. Jacobshagen, "The Double Meaning of Control: Three-Way Interactions between Internal Resources, Job Control, and Stressors at Work," *Journal of Occupational Health Psychology* 13, no. 3 (2008): 244–258.

85. E. M. de Croon, J. K. Sluiter, R. W. B. Blonk, J. P. J. Broersen, and M. H. W. Frings-Dresen, "Stressful Work, Psychological Job Strain, and Turnover: A 2-Year Prospective Cohort Study of Truck Drivers," *Journal of Applied Psychology* 89, no. 3 (2004): 442–454; R. Cropanzano, D. E. Rupp, and Z. S. Byrne, "The Relationship of Emotional Exhaustion to Work Attitudes, Job Performance, and Organizational Citizenship Behaviors," *Journal of Applied Psychology* 88, no. 1 (2003): 160–169; and S. Diestel and K. Schmidt, "Costs of Simultaneous Coping with Emotional Dissonance and Self-Control Demands at Work: Results from Two German Samples," *Journal of Applied Psychology* 96, no. 3 (2011): 643–653.

86. Y.-C. Wu, "Job Stress and Job Performance among Employees on the Taiwanese Finance Sector: The Role of Emotional Intelligence," *Social Behavior and Personality* 39, no. 1 (2011): 21–31. This study was replicated with similar results in U.

Yozgat, S. Yurtkoru, and E. Bilginoglu, "Job Stress and Job Performance among Employees in Public Sector in Istanbul: Examining the Moderating Role of Emotional Intelligence," in *Procedia—Social and Behavioral Sciences* vol. 75, ed. E. Eren (2013), 518–524.

87. K. M. Richardson and H. R. Rothstein, "Effects of Occupational Stress Management Intervention Programs: A Meta-Analysis," *Journal of Occupational Health Psychology* 13, no. 1 (2008): 69–93.

88. R. W. Renn, D. G. Allen, and T. M. Huning, "Empirical Examination of Individual-Level Personality-Based Theory of Self-Management Failure," *Journal of Organizational Behavior* 32, no. 1 (2011): 25–43; and P. Gröpel and P. Steel, "A Mega-Trial Investigation of Goal Setting, Interest Enhancement, and Energy on Procrastination," *Personality and Individual Differences* 45, no. 5 (2008): 406–411.

89. S. Klaperski, B. von Dawans, M. Heinrichs, and R. Fuchs, "Does the Level of Physical Exercise Affect Physiological and Psychological Responses to Psychosocial Stress in Women?" *Psychology of Sport and Exercise* 14, no. 2 (2013): 266–274.

90. K. M. Richardson and H. R. Rothstein, "Effects of Occupational Stress Management Intervention Programs: A Meta-Analysis," *Journal of Occupational Health Psychology* 13, no. 1 (2008): 69–93.

91. V. C. Hahn, C. Binnewies, S. Sonnentag, and E. J. Mojza, "Learning How to Recover from Job Stress: Effects of a Recovery Training Program on Recovery, Recovery-Related Self-Efficacy, and Well-Being," *Journal of Occupational Health Psychology* 16, no. 2 (2011): 202–216; and C. Binnewies, S. Sonnentag, and E. J. Mojza, "Recovery during the Weekend and Fluctuations in Weekly Job Performance: A Week-Level Study Examining Intra-Individual Relationships," *Journal of Occupational and Organizational Psychology* 83, no. 2 (2010): 419–41.

92. E. R. Greenglass and L. Fiksenbaum, "Proactive Coping, Positive Affect, and Well-Being: Testing for Mediation Using Path Analysis," *European Psychologist* 14, no. 1 (2009): 29–39; and P. Miquelon and R. J. Vallerand, "Goal Motives, Well-Being, and Physical Health: Happiness and Self-Realization as Psychological Resources under Challenge," *Motivation and Emotion* 30, no. 4 (2006): 259–272.

93. M. M. Butts, R. J. Vandenberg, D. M. DeJoy, B. S. Schaffer, and M. G. Wilson, "Individual Reactions to High Involvement Work Processes: Investigating the Role of Empowerment and Perceived Organizational Support," *Journal of Occupational Health Psychology* 14, no. 2 (2009): 122–136.

94. "100 Best Companies to Work For," *Fortune*, August 17, 2011, http://money.cnn.com/magazines/fortune.

95. L. Blue, "Making Good Health Easy," *Time*, February 12, 2009, http://content.time.com/time/magazine/article/0,9171,1879199,00.html; and M. Andrews, "America's Best Health Plans," *US News and World Report*, November 5, 2007, 54–60.

96. K. M. Richardson and H. R. Rothstein, "Effects of Occupational Stress Management Intervention Programs: A Meta-Analysis."

97. L. L. Berry, A. M. Mirabito, and W. B. Baun, "What's the Hard Return on Employee Wellness Programs?" *Harvard Business Review*, December 2010, https://hbr.org/2010/12/whats-the-hard-return-on-employee-wellness-programs.

98. S. Mattke, et al. *Workplace Wellness Programs Study* (Santa Monica, CA: RAND, 2013).

GLOSSARY

ability An individual's capacity to perform the various tasks in a job.

accommodating The willingness of one party in a conflict to place the opponent's interests above his or her own.

action research A change process based on the systematic collection of data and the selection of a change action based on what the analyzed data indicate.

affect A broad range of feelings that people experience.

affect intensity Individual differences in the strength with which individuals experience their emotions.

affective component The emotional or feeling segment of an attitude.

affective events theory (AET) A model that suggests that workplace events cause emotional reactions on the part of employees, which then influence workplace attitudes and behaviors.

agreeableness A personality dimension that describes someone who is good natured, cooperative, and trusting.

allostasis Working to change behavior and attitudes to find stability.

anchoring bias A tendency to fixate on initial information, from which one then fails to adequately adjust for subsequent information.

anthropology The study of societies to learn about human beings and their activities.

appreciative inquiry (AI) An approach that seeks to identify the unique qualities and special strengths of an organization, which can then be built on to improve performance.

arbitrator A third party to a negotiation who has the authority to dictate an agreement.

attitudes Evaluative statements or judgments concerning objects, people, or events.

attribution theory An attempt to determine whether an individual's behavior is internally or externally caused.

attribution theory of leadership A leadership theory that says that leadership is merely an attribution that people make about other individuals.

authority The rights inherent in a managerial position to give orders and to expect the orders to be obeyed.

automatic processing A relatively superficial consideration of evidence and information making use of heuristics.

autonomy The degree to which a job provides substantial freedom and discretion to the individual in scheduling the work and in determining the procedures to be used in carrying it out.

availability bias The tendency for people to base their judgments on information that is readily available to them.

avoiding The desire to withdraw from or suppress a conflict.

BATNA The best alternative to a negotiated agreement; the least the individual should accept.

behavioral component An intention to behave in a certain way toward someone or something.

behavioral ethics Analyzing how people actually behave when confronted with ethical dilemmas.

behavioral theories of leadership Theories proposing that specific behaviors differentiate leaders from nonleaders.

behaviorism A theory that behavior follows stimuli in a relatively unthinking manner.

big five model A personality assessment model that taps five basic dimensions.

biographical characteristics Personal characteristics—such as age, gender, race, and length of tenure—that are objective and easily obtained from personnel records. These characteristics are representative of surface-level diversity.

bonus A pay plan that rewards employees for recent performance rather than historical performance.

boundary spanning When individuals form relationships outside their formally assigned groups.

bounded rationality A process of making decisions by constructing simplified models that extract the essential features from problems without capturing all their complexity.

brainstorming An idea-generation process that specifically encourages any and all alternatives while withholding any criticism of those alternatives.

bureaucracy An organization structure with highly routine operating tasks achieved through specialization, very formalized rules and regulations, tasks that are grouped into functional departments, centralized authority, narrow spans of control, and decision making that follows the chain of command.

centralization The degree to which decision making is concentrated at a single point in an organization.

chain of command The unbroken line of authority that extends from the top of the organization to the lowest echelon and clarifies who reports to whom.

challenge stressors Stressors associated with workload, pressure to complete tasks, and time urgency.

change Making things different.

change agents People who act as catalysts and assume the responsibility for managing change activities.

channel richness The amount of information that can be transmitted during a communication episode.

charismatic leadership theory A leadership theory that states that followers make attributions of heroic or extraordinary leadership abilities when they observe certain behaviors.

circular structure An organization structure in which executives are at the center, spreading their vision outward in rings grouped by function (managers, then specialists, then workers).

coercive power A power base that is dependent on fear of the negative results from failing to comply.

cognitive component The opinion or belief segment of an attitude.

cognitive dissonance Any incompatibility between two or more attitudes or between behavior and attitudes.

cognitive evaluation theory A version of self-determination theory in which allocating extrinsic rewards for behavior that had been previously intrinsically rewarding tends to decrease the overall level of motivation if the rewards are seen as controlling.

cohesiveness The degree to which group members are attracted to each other and are motivated to stay in the group.

collaborating A situation in which the parties to a conflict each desire to satisfy fully the concerns of all parties.

collectivism A national culture attribute that describes a tight social framework in which people expect others in groups of which they are a part to look after them and protect them. Collectivistic countries/cultures in which people see themselves as interdependent and seek community and group goals. Collectivistic values are found in Asia, Africa, and South America, for example.

communication The transfer and the understanding of meaning.

communication apprehension Undue tension and anxiety about oral communication, written communication, or both.

communication process The steps between a source and a receiver that result in the transfer and understanding of meaning.

competing A desire to satisfy one's interests, regardless of the impact on the other party to the conflict.

compromising A situation in which each party to a conflict is willing to give up something.

conciliator A trusted third party who provides an informal communication link between the negotiator and the opponent.

confirmation bias The tendency to seek out information that reaffirms past choices and to discount information that contradicts past judgments.

conflict A process that begins when one party perceives that another party has negatively affected, or is about to negatively affect, something that the first party cares about.

conflict management The use of resolution and stimulation techniques to achieve the desired level of conflict.

conflict process A process that has five stages: potential opposition or incompatibility, cognition and personalization, intentions, behavior, and outcomes.

conformity The adjustment of one's behavior to align with the norms of the group.

conscientiousness A personality dimension that describes someone who is responsible, dependable, persistent, and organized.

consideration The extent to which a leader is likely to have job relationships characterized by mutual trust, respect for subordinates' ideas, and regard for their feelings.

contingency variables Situational factors or variables that moderate the relationship between two or more variables.

contrast effect Evaluation of a person's characteristics that is affected by comparisons with other people recently encountered who rank higher or lower on the same characteristics.

controlled processing A detailed consideration of evidence and information relying on facts, figures, and logic.

core self-evaluation (CSE) Believing in one's inner worth and basic competence.

core values The primary or dominant values that are accepted throughout the organization.

corporate social responsibility (CSR) An organization's self-regulated actions to benefit society or the environment beyond what is required by law.

cost-minimization strategy A strategy that emphasizes tight cost controls, avoidance of unnecessary innovation or marketing expenses, and price cutting.

counterproductive work behavior (CWB) Intentional employee behavior that is contrary to the interests of the organization.

creativity The ability to produce novel and useful ideas.

cross-functional teams Employees from about the same hierarchical level, but from different work areas, who come together to accomplish a task.

dark triad A constellation of negative personality traits consisting of Machiavellianism, narcissism, and psychopathy.

decentralized decision making The degree to which decision making is pushed down to the managers closest to the action or to workgroups.

decisions Choices made from among two or more alternatives.

deep acting Trying to modify one's true inner feelings based on display rules.

deep-level diversity Differences in values, personality, and work preferences that become progressively more important for determining similarity as people get to know one another better.

defensive behaviors Reactive and protective behaviors to avoid action, blame, or change.

demands Responsibilities, pressures, obligations, and even uncertainties that individuals face in the workplace.

departmentalization The basis by which jobs in an organization are grouped together.

dependence *B*'s relationship to *A* when *A* possesses something that *B* requires.

deviant workplace behavior Voluntary behavior that violates significant organizational norms and, in so doing, threatens the well-being of the organization or its members. Also called antisocial behavior or workplace incivility.

discrimination Noting of a difference between things; often we refer to unfair discrimination, which means making judgments about individuals based on stereotypes regarding their demographic group.

displayed emotions Emotions that are organizationally required and considered appropriate in a given job.

distributive bargaining Negotiation that seeks to divide up a fixed amount of resources; a win–lose situation.

distributive justice Perceived fairness of the amount and allocation of rewards among individuals.

diversity The extent to which members of a group are similar to, or different from, one another.

diversity management The process and programs by which managers make everyone more aware of and sensitive to the needs and differences of others.

divisional structure An organization structure that groups employees into units by product, service, customer, or geographical market area.

dominant culture A culture that expresses the core values that are shared by a majority of the organization's members.

driving forces Forces that direct behavior away from the status quo (Lewin).

dyadic conflict Conflict that occurs between two people.

dysfunctional conflict Conflict that hinders group performance.

effectiveness The degree to which an organization meets the needs of its clientele or customers.

efficiency The degree to which an organization can achieve its ends at a low cost.

emotion regulation The process of identifying and modifying felt emotions.

emotional contagion The process by which people's emotions are caused by the emotions of others.

emotional dissonance Inconsistencies between the emotions people feel and the emotions they project.

emotional intelligence (EI) The ability to detect and to manage emotional cues and information.

emotional labor A situation in which an employee expresses organizationally desired emotions during interpersonal transactions at work.

emotional stability A personality dimension that characterizes someone as calm, self-confident, and secure (positive) versus nervous, depressed, and insecure (negative).

emotions Intense feelings that are directed at someone or something.

employee engagement An individual's involvement with, satisfaction with, and enthusiasm for the work he or she does.

employee involvement and participation (EIP) A participative process that uses the input of employees to increase employee commitment to organizational success.

employee recognition program A plan to encourage specific employee behaviors by formally appreciating specific employee contributions.

employee stock ownership plan (ESOP) A company-established benefits plan in which employees acquire stock, often at below-market prices, as part of their benefits.

encounter stage The stage in the socialization process in which a new employee sees what the organization is really like and confronts the possibility that expectations and reality may diverge.

environment Forces outside an organization that potentially affect the organization's structure.

equity theory A theory that individuals compare their job inputs and outcomes with those of others and then respond to eliminate any inequities.

escalation of commitment An increased commitment to a previous decision in spite of negative information.

ethical dilemmas and ethical choices Situations in which individuals are required to define right and wrong conduct.

ethical work climate (EWC) The shared concept of right and wrong behavior in the workplace that reflects the true values of the organization and shapes the ethical decision making of its members.

evidence-based management (EBM) The basing of managerial decisions on the best available scientific evidence.

exit Dissatisfaction expressed through behavior directed toward leaving the organization.

expectancy theory A theory that the strength of a tendency to act in a certain way depends on the strength of an expectation that the act will be followed by a given outcome and on the attractiveness of that outcome to the individual.

expert power Influence based on special skills or knowledge.

extraversion A personality dimension describing someone who is sociable, gregarious, and assertive.

faultlines The perceived divisions that split groups into two or more subgroups based on individual differences such as sex, race, age, work experience, and education.

feedback The degree to which carrying out the work activities required by a job results in the individual obtaining direct and clear information about the effectiveness of his or her performance.

felt conflict Emotional involvement in a conflict that creates anxiety, tenseness, frustration, or hostility.

felt emotions An individual's actual emotions.

femininity A national culture attribute that indicates little differentiation between male and female roles; a high rating indicates that women are treated as the equals of men in all aspects of the society.

Fiedler contingency model The theory that effective groups depend on a proper match between a leader's style of interacting with subordinates and the degree to which the situation gives control and influence to the leader.

filtering A sender's manipulation of information so that it will be seen more favorably by the receiver.

fixed pie The belief that there is only a set amount of goods or services to be divvied up between the parties.

flexible benefits A benefits plan that allows each employee to put together a benefits package individually tailored to his or her own needs and situation.

flextime Flexible work hours.

formal channels Communication channels established by an organization to transmit messages related to the professional activities of members.

formal group A designated workgroup defined by an organization's structure.

formalization The degree to which jobs within an organization are standardized.

full range of leadership model A model that depicts seven management styles on a continuum: laissez-faire, management by exception, contingent reward leadership, individualized consideration, intellectual stimulation, inspirational motivation, and idealized influence.

functional conflict Conflict that supports the goals of the group and improves its performance.

functional structure An organization structure that groups employees by their similar specialties, roles, or tasks.

fundamental attribution error The tendency to underestimate the influence of external factors and overestimate the influence of internal factors when making judgments about the behavior of others.

general mental ability (GMA) An overall factor of intelligence, as suggested by the positive correlations among specific intellectual ability dimensions.

goal-setting theory A theory that specific and difficult goals, with feedback, lead to higher performance.

grapevine An organization's informal communication network.

group Two or more individuals, interacting and interdependent, who have come together to achieve particular objectives.

group cohesion The extent to which members of a group support and validate one another while at work.

group functioning The quantity and quality of a group's work output.

groupshift A change between a group's decision and an individual decision that a member within the group would make; the shift can be toward either conservatism or greater risk but it generally is toward a more extreme version of the group's original position.

groupthink A phenomenon in which the norm for consensus overrides the realistic appraisal of alternative courses of action.

halo effect The tendency to draw a general impression about an individual on the basis of a single characteristic.

heredity Factors determined at conception; one's biological, physiological, and inherent psychological makeup.

hierarchy of needs Abraham Maslow's hierarchy of five needs—physiological, safety, social, esteem, and self-actualization—in which, as each need is substantially satisfied, the next need becomes dominant.

high-context cultures Cultures that rely heavily on nonverbal and subtle situational cues in communication.

hindrance stressors Stressors that keep you from reaching your goals (for example, red tape, office politics, confusion over job responsibilities).

hindsight bias The tendency to believe falsely, after an outcome of an event is actually known, that one would have accurately predicted that outcome.

idea champions Individuals who take an innovation and actively and enthusiastically promote the idea, build support, overcome resistance, and ensure that the idea is implemented.

idea evaluation The process of creative behavior involving the evaluation of potential solutions to problems to identify the best one.

idea generation The process of creative behavior that involves developing possible solutions to a problem from relevant information and knowledge.

identification-based trust Trust based on a mutual understanding of each other's intentions and appreciation of each other's wants and desires.

illusory correlation The tendency of people to associate two events when in reality there is no connection.

imitation strategy A strategy that seeks to move into new products or new markets only after their viability has already been proven.

impression management (IM) The process by which individuals attempt to control the impression others form of them.

individualism A national culture attribute that describes the degree to which people prefer to act as individuals rather than as members of groups. In individualistic countries/cultures, people see themselves as independent and desire personal goals and personal control. Individualistic values are present in North America and Western Europe, for example.

informal channels Communication channels that are created spontaneously and that emerge as responses to individual choices.

informal group A group that is neither formally structured nor organizationally determined; such a group appears in response to the need for social contact.

information gathering The stage of creative behavior when possible solutions to a problem incubate in an individual's mind.

information overload A condition in which information inflow exceeds an individual's processing capacity.

informational justice The degree to which employees are provided truthful explanations for decisions.

ingroup favoritism Perspective in which we see members of our ingroup as better than other people, and people not in our group as all the same.

initiating structure The extent to which a leader is likely to define and structure his or her role and those of subordinates in the search for goal attainment.

innovation A new idea applied to initiating or improving a product, process, or service.

innovation strategy A strategy that emphasizes the introduction of major new products and services.

inputs Variables like personality, group structure, and organizational culture that lead to processes.

institutionalization A condition that occurs when an organization takes on a life of its own, apart from any of its members, and acquires immortality.

institutions Cultural factors that lead many organizations to have similar structures, especially those factors that might not lead to adaptive consequences.

instrumental values Preferable modes of behavior or means of achieving one's terminal values.

integrative bargaining Negotiation that seeks one or more settlements that can create a win–win solution.

intellectual abilities The capacity to do mental activities—thinking, reasoning, and problem solving.

intentions Decisions to act in a given way.

interacting groups Typical groups in which members interact with each other face to face.

intergroup conflict Conflict between different groups or teams.

intergroup development Organizational development (OD) efforts to change the attitudes, stereotypes, and perceptions that groups have of each other.

interpersonal justice The degree to which employees are treated with dignity and respect.

interrole conflict A situation in which the expectations of an individual's different, separate groups are in opposition.

intragroup conflict Conflict that occurs within a group or team.

intuition An instinctive feeling not necessarily supported by research.

intuitive decision making An unconscious process created out of distilled experience.

job characteristics model (JCM) A model that proposes any job can be described in terms of five core job dimensions: skill variety, task identity, task significance, autonomy, and feedback.

job design The way the elements in a job are organized.

job embeddedness The extent to which an employee's connections to the job and community result in an increased commitment to the organization.

job engagement The investment of an employee's physical, cognitive, and emotional energies into job performance.

job involvement The degree to which a person identifies with a job, actively participates in it, and considers performance important to their self-worth.

job rotation The periodic shifting of an employee from one task to another.

job satisfaction A positive feeling about one's job resulting from an evaluation of its characteristics.

job sharing   An arrangement that allows two or more individuals to split a traditional full-time job.

leader–member exchange (LMX) theory   A theory that supports leaders' creation of ingroups and outgroups; subordinates with ingroup status will likely have higher performance ratings, less turnover, and greater job satisfaction.

leader–member relations   The degree of confidence, trust, and respect subordinates have in their leader.

leader-participation model   A leadership theory that provides a set of rules to determine the form and amount of participative decision making in different situations.

leadership   The ability to influence a group toward the achievement of a vision or set of goals.

learning organization   An organization that has developed the continuous capacity to adapt and change.

least preferred coworker (LPC) questionnaire   An instrument that measures whether a person is task- or relationship-oriented.

legitimate power   The power a person receives as a result of his or her position in the formal hierarchy of an organization.

long-term orientation   A national culture attribute that emphasizes the future, thrift, and persistence.

low-context cultures   Cultures that rely heavily on words to convey meaning in communication.

loyalty   Dissatisfaction expressed by passively waiting for conditions to improve.

Machiavellianism   The degree to which an individual is pragmatic, maintains emotional distance, and believes that ends can justify means.

management by objectives (MBO)   A program that encompasses specific goals, participatively set, for an explicit time period and including feedback on goal progress.

masculinity   A national culture attribute that describes the extent to which the culture favors traditional masculine work roles of achievement, power, and control. Societal values are characterized by assertiveness and materialism.

material symbols   What conveys to employees who is important, the degree of egalitarianism top management desires, and the kinds of behavior that are appropriate.

matrix structure   An organization structure that creates dual lines of authority and combines functional and product departmentalization.

McClelland's theory of needs   A theory that achievement, power, and affiliation are three important needs that help explain motivation.

mechanistic model   A structure characterized by extensive departmentalization, high formalization, a limited information network, and centralization.

mediator   A neutral third party who facilitates a negotiated solution by using reasoning, persuasion, and suggestions for alternatives.

mental models   Team members' knowledge and beliefs about how the work gets done by the team.

mentor   A senior employee who sponsors and supports a less-experienced employee, called a protégé.

merit-based pay plan   A pay plan based on performance appraisal ratings.

metamorphosis stage   The stage in the socialization process in which a new employee changes and adjusts to the job, workgroup, and organization.

mindfulness   Objectively and deliberately evaluating the emotional situation in the moment.

model   An abstraction of reality, a simplified representation of some real-world phenomenon.

moods   Feelings that tend to be less intense than emotions and that lack a contextual stimulus.

moral emotions   Emotions that have moral implications because of our instant judgment of the situation that evokes them.

motivating potential score (MPS)   A predictive index that suggests the motivating potential in a job.

motivation   The processes that account for an individual's intensity, direction, and persistence of effort toward attaining a goal.

multiteam system   A collection of two or more interdependent teams that share a superordinate goal; a team of teams.

Myers-Briggs Type Indicator (MBTI)   A personality test that taps four characteristics and classifies people into 1 of 16 personality types.

narcissism   The tendency to be arrogant, have a grandiose sense of self-importance, require excessive admiration, and have a sense of entitlement.

need for achievement (nAch)   The drive to excel, to achieve in relationship to a set of standards, and to strive to succeed.

need for affiliation (nAff)   The desire for friendly and close interpersonal relationships.

need for cognition   A personality trait of individuals depicting the ongoing desire to think and learn.

need for power (nPow)   The need to make others behave in a way in which they would not have behaved otherwise.

negative affect   A mood dimension that consists of emotions such as nervousness, stress, and anxiety at the high end and relaxation, tranquility, and poise at the low end.

neglect   Dissatisfaction expressed through allowing conditions to worsen.

negotiation   A process in which two or more parties exchange goods or services and attempt to agree on the exchange rate for them.

neutralizers   Attributes that make it impossible for leader behavior to make any difference to follower outcomes.

nominal group technique   A group decision-making method in which individual members meet face to face to pool their judgments in a systematic but independent fashion.

norms   Acceptable standards of behavior within a group that are shared by the group's members.

openness to experience   A personality dimension that characterizes someone in terms of imagination, sensitivity, and curiosity.

organic model   A structure that is flat, uses cross-hierarchical and cross-functional teams, has low formalization, possesses a comprehensive information network, and relies on participative decision making.

organizational behavior   A field of study that investigates the impact individuals, groups, and structure have on behavior within organizations, for the purpose of applying such knowledge toward improving an organization's effectiveness.

organizational citizenship behavior (OCB)   Discretionary behavior that contributes to the psychological and social environment of the workplace.

organizational climate   The shared perceptions organizational members have about their organization and work environment.

organizational commitment The degree to which an employee identifies with a particular organization and its goals and wishes to maintain membership in the organization.

organizational culture A system of shared meaning held by members that distinguishes the organization from other organizations.

organizational demography The degree to which members of a work unit share a common demographic attribute, such as age, sex, race, educational level, or length of service in an organization, and the impact of this attribute on turnover.

organizational development (OD) A collection of planned change interventions, built on humanistic–democratic values, that seeks to improve organizational effectiveness and employee well-being.

organizational justice An overall perception of what is fair in the workplace, composed of distributive, procedural, informational, and interpersonal justice.

organizational structure The way in which job tasks are formally divided, grouped, and coordinated.

organizational survival The degree to which an organization is able to exist and grow over the long term.

outcomes Key factors that are affected by some other variables.

outgroup The inverse of an ingroup; an outgoup can mean anyone outside the group, but more usually an identified other group.

paradox theory The theory that the key paradox in management is that there is no final optimal status for an organization.

participative management A process in which subordinates share a significant degree of decision-making power with their immediate superiors.

path–goal theory A theory that states that it is the leader's job to assist followers in attaining their goals and to provide the necessary direction and/or support to ensure that their goals are compatible with the overall objectives of the group or organization.

perceived conflict Awareness by one or more parties of the existence of conditions that create opportunities for conflict to arise.

perceived organizational support (POS) The degree to which employees believe an organization values their contribution and cares about their well-being.

perception A process by which individuals organize and interpret their sensory impressions in order to give meaning to their environment.

personality The sum total of ways in which an individual reacts to and interacts with others.

personality traits Enduring characteristics that describe an individual's behavior.

personality–job fit theory A theory that identifies six personality types and proposes that the fit between personality type and occupational environment determines satisfaction and turnover.

person–organization fit A theory that people are attracted to and selected by organizations that match their values, and leave when there is not compatibility.

physical abilities The capacity to do tasks that demand stamina, dexterity, strength, and similar characteristics.

piece-rate pay plan A pay plan in which workers are paid a fixed sum for each unit of production completed.

planned change Change activities that are intentional and goal oriented.

political behavior Activities that are not required as part of a person's formal role in the organization but that influence, or attempt to influence, the distribution of advantages and disadvantages within the organization.

political skill The ability to influence others in such a way as to enhance one's objectives.

position power Influence derived from one's formal structural position in the organization; includes power to hire, fire, discipline, promote, and give salary increases.

positive affect A mood dimension that consists of specific positive emotions such as excitement, self-assurance, and cheerfulness at the high end and boredom, sluggishness, and tiredness at the low end.

positive diversity climate In an organization, an environment of inclusiveness and an acceptance of diversity.

positive organizational culture A culture that emphasizes building on employee strengths, rewards more than it punishes, and encourages and growth.

positive organizational scholarship An area of OB research that concerns how organizations develop human strengths, foster vitality and resilience, and unlock potential.

positivity offset The tendency of most individuals to experience a mildly positive mood at zero input (when nothing in particular is going on).

power A capacity that A has to influence the behavior of B so that B acts in accordance with A's wishes.

power distance A national culture attribute that describes the extent to which a society accepts that power in institutions and organizations is distributed unequally.

power tactics Ways in which individuals translate power bases into specific actions.

prearrival stage The period of learning in the socialization process that occurs before a new employee joins the organization.

prevention focus A self-regulation strategy that involves striving for goals by fulfilling duties and obligations.

proactive personality People who identify opportunities, show initiative, take action, and persevere until meaningful change occurs.

problem A discrepancy between the current state of affairs and some desired state.

problem formulation The stage of creative behavior that involves identifying a problem or opportunity requiring a solution that is as yet unknown.

problem-solving teams Groups of 5 to 12 employees from the same department who meet for a few hours each week to discuss ways of improving quality, efficiency, and the work environment.

procedural justice The perceived fairness of the process used to determine the distribution of rewards.

process conflict Conflict over how work gets done.

process consultation (PC) A meeting in which a consultant assists a client in understanding process events with which he or she must deal and identifying processes that need improvement.

processes Actions that individuals, groups, and organizations engage in as a result of inputs and that lead to certain outcomes.

productivity The combination of the effectiveness and efficiency of an organization.

profit-sharing plan An organization-wide program that distributes compensation based on some established formula designed around a company's profitability.

promotion focus A self-regulation strategy that involves striving for goals through advancement and accomplishment.

psychological contract An unwritten agreement that sets out what management expects from an employee and vice versa.

psychological empowerment Employees' belief in the degree to which they affect their work environment, their competence, the meaningfulness of their job, and their perceived autonomy in their work.

psychology The science that seeks to measure, explain, and sometimes change the behavior of humans and other animals.

psychopathy The tendency for a lack of concern for others and a lack of guilt or remorse when actions cause harm.

punctuated-equilibrium model A set of phases that temporary groups go through that involves transitions between inertia and activity.

randomness error The tendency of individuals to believe that they can predict the outcome of random events.

rational Characterized by making consistent, value-maximizing choices within specified constraints.

rational decision-making model A decision-making model that describes how individuals should behave in order to maximize some outcome.

reference groups Important groups to which individuals belong or hope to belong and with whose norms individuals are likely to conform.

referent power Influence based on identification with a person who has desirable resources or personal traits.

reflexivity A team characteristic of reflecting on and adjusting the master plan when necessary.

reinforcement theory A theory that behavior is a function of its consequences.

relational job design Constructing jobs so employees see the positive difference they can make in the lives of others directly through their work.

relationship conflict Conflict based on interpersonal relationships.

representative participation A system in which workers participate in organizational decision making through a small group of representative employees.

resources Things within an individual's control that can be used to resolve demands.

restraining forces Forces that hinder movement from the existing equilibrium (Lewin).

reward power Compliance achieved based on the ability to distribute rewards that others view as valuable.

risk aversion The tendency to prefer a sure gain of a moderate amount over a riskier outcome, even if the riskier outcome might have a higher expected payoff.

rituals Repetitive sequences of activities that express and reinforce the key values of the organization, which goals are most important, which people are important, and which are expendable.

role A set of expected behavior patterns attributed to someone occupying a given position in a social unit.

role conflict A situation in which an individual is confronted by divergent role expectations.

role expectations How others believe a person should act in a given situation.

role perception An individual's view of how he or she is supposed to act in a given situation.

selective perception The tendency to selectively interpret what one sees on the basis of one's interests, background, experience, and attitudes.

self-concordance The degree to which people's reasons for pursuing goals are consistent with their interests and core values.

self-determination theory A theory of motivation that is concerned with the beneficial effects of intrinsic motivation and the harmful effects of extrinsic motivation.

self-efficacy theory An individual's belief that he or she is capable of performing a task.

self-managed work teams Groups of 10 to 15 people who take on responsibilities of their former supervisors.

self-monitoring A personality trait that measures an individual's ability to adjust his or her behavior to external, situational factors.

self-serving bias The tendency for individuals to attribute their own successes to internal factors and put the blame for failures on external factors.

sensitivity training Training groups that seek to change behavior through unstructured group interaction.

servant leadership A leadership style marked by going beyond the leader's own self-interest and instead focusing on opportunities to help followers grow and develop.

sexual harassment Any unwanted activity of a sexual nature that affects an individual's employment and creates a hostile work environment.

short-term orientation A national culture attribute that emphasizes the present and accepts change.

simple structure An organization structure characterized by a low degree of departmentalization, wide spans of control, authority centralized in a single person, and little formalization.

situation strength theory A theory indicating that the way personality translates into behavior depends on the strength of the situation.

situational leadership theory (SLT) A contingency theory that focuses on followers' readiness.

skill variety The degree to which a job requires a variety of different activities.

social identity theory A perspective that considers when and why individuals consider themselves members of groups.

social loafing The tendency for individuals to expend less effort when working collectively than when working individually.

social psychology An area of psychology that blends concepts from psychology and sociology to focus on the influence of people on one another.

socialization A process that adapts employees to the organization's culture.

socialized charismatic leadership A leadership concept that states that leaders convey values that are other-centered versus self-centered and who role-model ethical conduct.

social-learning theory The view that we can learn through both observation and direct experience.

sociology The study of people in relation to their social environment or culture.

span of control The number of subordinates a manager can efficiently and effectively direct.

status A socially defined position or rank given to groups or group members by others.

status characteristics theory A theory that states that differences in status characteristics create status hierarchies within groups.

stereotype threat The degree to which we internally agree with the generally negative stereotyped perceptions of our groups.

stereotyping Judging someone on the basis of one's perception of the group to which that person belongs.

stress An unpleasant psychological condition that occurs in response to environmental pressures.

strong culture A culture in which the core values are intensely held and widely shared.

subcultures Minicultures within an organization, typically defined by department designations and geographical separation.

substitutes Attributes, such as experience and training, that can replace the need for a leader's support or ability to create structure.

surface acting Hiding one's inner feelings and forgoing emotional expressions in response to display rules.

surface-level diversity Differences in easily perceived characteristics such as gender, race, ethnicity, age, or disability, that do not necessarily reflect the ways people think or feel but that may activate certain stereotypes.

survey feedback The use of questionnaires to identify discrepancies among member perceptions; discussion follows and remedies are suggested.

sustainability Organization practices that can be sustained over a long period of time because the tools or structures that support them are not damaged by the processes.

systematic study Looking at relationships, attempting to attribute causes and effects, and drawing conclusions based on scientific evidence.

task conflict Conflict over content and goals of the work.

task identity The degree to which a job requires completion of a whole and identifiable piece of work.

task performance The combination of effectiveness and efficiency at doing core job tasks.

task significance The degree to which a job has a substantial impact on the lives or work of other people.

task structure The degree to which job assignments are procedurized.

team building High interaction among team members to increase trust and openness.

team cohesion A situation when team members are emotionally attached to one another and motivated toward the team because of their attachment.

team efficacy A team's collective belief among team members that they can succeed at their tasks.

team identity A team member's affinity for and sense of belongingness to his or her team.

team structure An organization structure that replaces departments with empowered teams, and which eliminates horizontal boundaries and external barriers between customers and suppliers.

technology The way in which an organization transfers its inputs into outputs.

telecommuting Working from home at least two days a week on a computer that is linked to the employer's office.

terminal values Desirable end-states of existence; the goals a person would like to achieve during his or her lifetime.

three-stage model of creativity The proposition that creativity involves three stages: causes (creative potential and creative environment), creative behavior, and creative outcomes (innovation).

trait activation theory (TAT) A theory that predicts that some situations, events, or interventions "activate" a trait more than others.

trait theories of leadership Theories that consider personal qualities and characteristics that differentiate leaders from nonleaders.

transactional leaders Leaders who guide or motivate their followers in the direction of established goals by clarifying role and task requirements.

transformational leaders Leaders who inspire followers to transcend their own self-interests and who are capable of having a profound and extraordinary effect on followers.

trust A positive expectation that another person will not act opportunistically.

trust propensity How likely an employee is to trust a leader.

two-factor theory A theory that relates intrinsic factors to job satisfaction and associates extrinsic factors with dissatisfaction. Also called motivation-hygiene theory.

uncertainty avoidance A national culture attribute that describes the extent to which a society feels threatened by uncertain and ambiguous situations and tries to avoid them.

unity of command The idea that a subordinate should have only one superior to whom he or she is directly responsible.

utilitarianism A system in which decisions are made to provide the greatest good for the greatest number.

value system A hierarchy based on a ranking of an individual's values in terms of their intensity.

values Basic convictions that a specific mode of conduct or end-state of existence is personally or socially preferable to an opposite or converse mode of conduct or end-state of existence.

variable-pay program A pay plan that bases a portion of an employee's pay on some individual and/or organizational measure of performance.

virtual structure A small, core organization that outsources major business functions.

virtual teams Teams that use computer technology to tie together physically dispersed members in order to achieve a common goal.

vision A long-term strategy for attaining a goal or goals.

vision statement A formal articulation of an organization's vision or mission.

voice Dissatisfaction expressed through active and constructive attempts to improve conditions.

wellness programs Organizationally supported programs that focus on the employee's total physical and mental condition.

whistle-blowers Individuals who report unethical practices by their employer to outsiders.

withdrawal behavior The set of actions employees take to separate themselves from the organization.

work specialization The degree to which tasks in an organization are subdivided into separate jobs.

work team A group whose individual efforts result in performance that is greater than the sum of the individual inputs.

workforce diversity The concept that organizations are becoming more heterogeneous in terms of gender, age, race, ethnicity, sexual orientation, and other characteristics.

workgroup A group that interacts primarily to share information and make decisions to help each group member perform within his or her area of responsibility.

workplace spirituality The recognition that people have an inner life that nourishes and is nourished by meaningful work that takes place in the context of community.

zero-sum approach A negotiation approach that treats the reward "pie" as fixed, so any gain one person or group achieves comes at the expense of another person or group.

INDEX

Page references with "e" indicate exhibits

A

Ability
  intellectual, 27–29, 28e
  physical, 29, 30e
  of team members, 161
Absenteeism, 44
Accommodation, 232
Acquisitions, mergers, 273
Acting, 55
Action research, 291
Affect, 47–49, 48e
  intensity, 52
Affective circumplex, 50e
Affective component of attitudes, 35
Affective events theory (AET), 56
Affirmative action programs (AAP), 32
Age, 21–22, 54
Agreeableness, 67, 68e, 69
Allostasis, 298
Anchoring bias, 89–90
Anthropology, 7
Appeals, 212
Appreciative inquiry (AI), 293
Arbitrator, 242
Arousal, 108
Attitudes, 14
  behavior and, 36
  components of, 35, 35e
  definition of, 34
  development and perception of, 3
  toward job, 37–38, 61
  summary of, 46
Attribution theory, 84, 85e
  of leadership, 203–204
Authentic leadership, 199
Automatic processing, 178–179
Autonomy, 121
  predictability vs., 263
Availability bias, 90
Avoidance, 71, 232

B

Bargaining
  distributive, 236, 236e
  integrative, 236–237
  method selection, 237
  negotiation and, 235–237, 235e, 236e
  problem solving and, 238–239
  strategies of, 235–237, 235e, 236e

Behavior, 146–149
  See also Group, behavior;
    Organizational behavior (OB);
    Political behavior
  attitudes and, 36
  defense, 220
  deviant, 61–62
  ethical, 12, 95
  managing, 171
  norms and, 142
  stress and, 302
  withdrawal, 14
Behavioral component of attitudes, 35
Behavioral ethics, 12, 95
Behavioral theories of leadership,
    188–189
Behaviorism, 110
Benevolence, 281
Big data
  current usage of, 5
  limitations of, 5–6
  new trends in, 5
Big Five Model, 67–69, 68e, 187–188
Biographical characteristics
  age, 21–22
  cultural identity, 27
  disabilities, 23–25
  race and ethnicity, 23
  religion, 25
  sex, 22–23
  sexual orientation and gender identity,
    25–26
Bonuses, 131–132
Borderline personality, 71
Boundary spanning, 251–252
Bounded rationality, 88
Brainstorming, 151
Bureaucracy, 253–254

C

Capacity, of organization's environment, 260
Casmir, Fred, 183
Causation, internal and external, 84
Centralization, 250–251, 263
Chain of command, 248–249
Challenge stressors, 297
Change
  See also Organizational change
  agents of, 286

  barriers to, 272
  planned, 286
  processes, 3
Channel richness, 177–178
Charismatic leadership theory
  born vs. learned qualities, 194–195
  dark side of, 195–196
  influencing followers, 195
  situational contingencies, 195
  transformational leadership vs., 199
Circular structure, 257
Clarity, Element of Situational Strength, 73
Coalitions, 212
Coercion, 289
Coercive power, 208–209
Cognition, need for, 179
Cognitive component of attitudes, 35
Cognitive dissonance, 36
Cognitive evaluation theory, 104–105
Cohesiveness, 146–147
Collaboration, 231
Collectivism, 49, 78
Communication, 230
  apprehension, 182–183
  barriers to, 180–182
  channels for, 172
    choosing, 176–178, 177–178
  cultural barriers and, 182–183
  cultural context and, 183, 183e
  cultural factors and, 182–184, 183e
  cultural guide for, 183–184
  direction of, 172–175, 174e
  downward, 173
  emotions and, 181
  functions of, 171–172
  information security and, 178
  interpersonal, 3
  interunit, 294
  language and, 181
  lateral, 173
  lying and, 182
  modes of, 175–176
  nonverbal, 176
  oral, 175–176
  organizational, 304
  persuasive, 178–180
  process of, 172, 172e
  silence and, 181
  summary of, 185–186
  tailoring messages, 179–180